Photogravure

Survey of India Offices, Calcutta, 1915

SIR DENZIL CHARLES JELF IBBETSON, K.C.S.I.

PANJAB CASTES

PANJAB CASTES

Being A Reprint Of The Chapter On "The Races, Castes And Tribes Of The People"

By

Denzil Ibbetson

GYAN

Published by

Gyan Publishing House
5, Ansari Road
Daryaganj, New Delhi-110002
Phone: 011-47034999, 9811692060
E-mail: books@gyanbooks.com

Distribution Network
gyanbooks.com
India, USA, Canada, UK, Australia, France

ISBN : 978-81-212-6276-7 (PB)
First Published, 1916

2nd Impression 2022

Printed at: Gyan Press, Delhi.

PANJAB CASTES
Author: Denzil Ibbetson

PANJAB CASTES.

Being a reprint of the chapter on "The Races, Castes and Tribes of the People" in the Report on the Census of the Panjab published in 1883 by the late Sir Denzil Ibbetson, K.C.S.I.

1916.

CONTENTS.

INTRODUCTORY NOTE.

THE Census of the Panjáb Province was carried out in 1881 by Mr. (afterwards Sir Denzil) Ibbetson of the Indian Civil Service and his Report on the Census was published in 1883. The Report has always been recognised as one of the most remarkable official publications in India, and a work of the greatest value both from the administrative and from the literary and scientific point of view. It at once attracted widespread attention, more especially in view of the copious information which it provided regarding the people of the Province, and a separate volume was issued in 1883, under the title of "Panjáb Ethnography" which contained a reprint of those portions of the Report which dealt with the Religions, the Languages, and the Races, Castes and Tribes of the people. The number of copies published, however, both of the Report and of the Ethnography, was comparatively small and they are now difficult to procure outside Indian official circles. There are at the same time indications of a continuing demand for the Report, and more especially for the ethnological portion of it, and to meet this demand the Punjab Government has determined to undertake the issue of the present volume.

This volume reproduces a portion only,—but that is the most important portion,—of the original Report, namely the chapter on the Races, Castes and Tribes of the Panjáb. The chapters on Religion and Language, which formed part of the "Ethnography" published in 1883, though valuable and interesting, have necessarily lost something of their original importance owing to the progress made in scientific enquiry during the last thirty years, but the chapter on the Races, Castes and Tribes still contains much valuable information that cannot be obtained elsewhere, and this chapter must always command attention and respect for its vigorous and comprehensive treatment of the subject. The figures are, of course, out of date and the territorial boundaries of the Province and districts with which the chapter deals are now considerably altered. There are also, no doubt, points on which later investigation suggests modification of the facts and opinions originally given, but it has been thought best to reproduce the chapter as it stands, without any attempt to annotate it or bring it up to date. It is believed that in this way the wishes of most readers will best be met, and it is felt that by this course the volume will best fulfil the further object which the Government of the Panjáb has in view, namely, the perpetuation of the memory of the original writer.

There are so many still alive to whom Sir Denzil Ibbetson was personally known that anything like a complete description of his career in this introduction is unnecessary, but it may not be out of place to mention a few of its outstanding features. He was born on August 30th, 1847, and after being educated at St. Peter's College, Adelaide, and St. John's College, Cambridge, entered the Indian Civil Service in 1870. He was early in his service selected for the special posts of Settlement Officer of the Karnál District and Superintendent of Census Operations in the Panjáb. He subsequently filled from time to time the appointments of Director of Public Instruction and Financial Commissioner in the Panjáb, Secretary to the Government of India in the Revenue and Agricultural Department, Chief Commissioner of the Central Provinces, and Member of the Viceroy's Council. In 1907 he became Lieutenant-Governor of the Panjáb, but held that important post for all too short a time, succumbing to a fatal malady on the 21st of February 1908.

No one to whom Sir Denzil Ibbetson was known can ever forget his personality: his tall and commanding presence, his vivacious and original conversation, his constant sense of humour, his quick indignation and his equally quick sympathy. For the thoroughness of his erudition in many directions he was unsurpassed in India and as an administrator there are not a few who hold him to have been the greatest Indian Civil Servant of our time. His character and career are admirably summed up in an inscription placed by the Viceroy on whose Council he served on the walls of the Simla Church which runs as follows :—

UNTIRING IN ADMINISTRATION,
FEARLESS IN DOING RIGHT,
A SCHOLAR AND A MAN OF AFFAIRS,
LOYAL IN CO-OPERATION, DEVOTED IN FRIENDSHIP,
HE GAVE TO INDIA HIS LOVE
AND HIS LIFE.

ORIGINAL PREFACE

TO THE REPORT ON THE CENSUS OF 1881.

IN writing the accompanying report on the Panjáb Census of 1881, I have steadily kept two main objects before me. *Firstly,* I have attempted to produce a work which shall be useful to District officers as a handbook of reference on all the subjects dealt with in the Census Schedules, and which shall stand with regard to such subjects in a position somewhat similar to that occupied by the modern Settlement Report in respect of revenue matters. *Secondly,* I have endeavoured to record in some detail the experience gained at this Census, for guidance on the occasion of future enumerations. My pursuance of each of these objects has helped to swell the size of the report.

It would have been easy to write a short notice of some of the more obvious conclusions to be drawn from the Census totals of the Province as a whole; and such a notice would doubtless have technically sufficed as a report to Government upon the operations which I had superintended. But it would have been of small use for future reference, and would have served no purpose beyond that of furnishing the text for a Government resolution. A Census report is not meant merely for the information of the Secretariat; it is intended to be constantly referred to in every office of the Province. The mere results would ill serve this end in the absence of an interpreter. It is of but small advantage to cast voluminous tables of naked figures at the heads of District officers, without at the same time explaining what they represent, which can be done by no one but him who compiled them, and drawing from them the more important conclusions to which they lead, which few will draw but he whose special business it is to do so.[1]

In the ordinary routine of district work, information is constantly needed regarding some feature or other of the society which we govern. That information often exists in print; but in India libraries are few and books scarce; while where the latter are available, they are often too detailed or too learned for the practical purposes of the District officer. It has been my endeavour to furnish such a sketch of the salient features of native society in the Panjáb as will often supply the immediate need, and at the same time to indicate where, if anywhere, further details may be found. A Census report is not

[1] Much of the length of the report is due to the exceptionally large number of the administrative units for which the separate figures had to be discussed. (See section 929, page 468.) The Native States took great pains with the Census; and, apart from the intrinsic value of the results, it would have been ungracious to discuss their figures less fully than our own.

light reading; and men take it up, not to read it through, but to obtain from it information on some definite point. It is therefore more important that it should be complete than that it should be brief; and so long as its arrangement directs the student at once to the place where he will find what he wants, without compelling him to wade through irrelevant matter, the fuller the information which he there finds on the subject, the more valuable will the report be to him. I have therefore omitted nothing relevant that seemed to me to be interesting or useful, simply because it occupied space.

The difficulty of an Indian Census springs mainly from two sources; the infinite diversity of the material to be dealt with, and our own infinite ignorance of that material. The present Census was, as regards the Panjáb and in respect of its minuteness and accuracy of detail, practically a first experiment; and one of its most valuable results has been to show us where our chief difficulties lie, and how and why we have on this occasion frequently failed to overcome them. If the present Census had been one for all time, nothing more would have been needed than such a brief account of the operations as would have explained to the student of the results how those results had been obtained. If, on the other hand, a Census were of annual recurrence, an "office," with its permanent staff and traditions, would have taken the place of the record of the experience which I have attempted to frame. But the operations will be repeated after intervals of ten years. It has therefore been my endeavour to record the experience now gained in such detail as may enable us to avoid past errors on a future occasion, to point out every defect that the test of actual practice disclosed in the scheme, and to put forth every suggestion that my experience led me to think could be of use to my successor in 1891.

Till now nothing of the sort has been attempted in the Panjáb. The meagre report on the Census of 1868 affords no record of the experience of the past or suggestions for guidance in the future; while though Settlement reports and similar publications contain a vast mass of invaluable information regarding the people, it is scattered and fragmentary, and needed to be collected, compared, and consolidated. A Census recurs only after considerable intervals, and it will not be necessary on each subsequent occasion to rewrite the whole of the present report. Much will be added; more will be corrected; the new figures will be examined and compared with the present ones; the old conclusions will be modified, and new ones drawn. But the main groundwork of the report will stand unaltered.

I have not absolutely confined myself in the following pages to facts and figures which will be immediately useful for the actual purposes of administration. I have not hesitated to enter occasionally into general discussions on certain subjects, such as religion and caste, and to express my own views on the matter. I venture to think that these digressions are not the least interesting portions of the volume; and in a report which must of necessity consist for the most part of a dry discussion of figures, any passage of general interest is welcome, if only as a relief. But my chief object in entering upon these discussions has been, to draw the attention of my readers to the extraordinary interest of the material which lies in such abundance ready to the hand of all Indian officials, and which would, if collected and recorded, be of such immense value to students of sociology. Our ignorance of the customs and beliefs of the people among whom we dwell is surely in some respects a reproach to us; for not only does that ignorance deprive European science of material which it greatly needs, but it also involves a distinct loss of administrative power to ourselves. And if aught that I have written in this report should incline any from among my readers to a study of the social and religious phænomena by which they are surrounded, I at any rate shall be amply repaid for my labour.

Moreover, Indian official literature is gradually gaining for itself students from beyond the limits of India, and European scholars are turning to it for the facts of which they find themselves in need. In his *Village Communities* (pages 34-5) Sir Henry Maine writes of Indian Settlement reports: "They "constitute a whole literature of very great extent and variety, and of the "utmost value and instructiveness. I am afraid I must add that the English "reader, whose attention is not called to it by official duty, not unusually finds "it very unattractive or even repulsive. But the reason I believe to be, that "the elementary knowledge which is the key to it has for the most part never "been reduced to writing at all." I see no reason why an Indian report should of necessity be repulsive or unintelligible; and I have ventured, here and there, to add at the expense of brevity matter which would perhaps be superfluous if addressed exclusively to Indian officials.

The more we learn of the people and their ways, the more profoundly must we become impressed with the vastness of the field and with the immense diversity which it presents. Not only is our knowledge of the facts as nothing compared with our ignorance; but the facts themselves vary so greatly from one part of the Panjáb to another, that it is almost impossible to make any general statement whatever concerning them which shall be true for the whole Province. I have not always stopped to say so; and I have not unfrequently made assertions, as it were *ex cathedrâ infallibili*. But I would always be understood to mean, in writing of the people, that while I have taken pains to obtain the best and most trustworthy information available, I only present it for what it is worth, and that it will almost certainly be inapplicable to some parts at least of the Panjáb. Yet I do not think that the uncertain value which attaches to the information that I have recorded renders that information less worthy of record. In matters such as are discussed in this report, the next best thing to having them put rightly is to have them put wrongly, if only the wrongness be an intelligent wrongness ; for so we stimulate inquiry and provoke criticism ; and it is only by patient and widespread inquiry and incessant and minute criticism, that we can hope to arrive on these subjects at accurate information and sound generalisations. Nothing would be so welcome to me as to find the officers of the Province setting to work to correct and supplement the information given in my report ; for the more holes they will pick and the more publicly they will pick them, the faster shall we extend and improve our knowledge of the matters discussed.[1]

I need not apologise for the many and palpable defects of the report, so far as they are due to the haste with which all official publications have to be prepared. Pages which have been written against time in the first instance, which have been sent to press often without even the most cursory revision, and which, when once in type, the writer has not felt at liberty to improve save by the most trifling corrections, must not be judged by any literary standard. But I must, in justice to myself, be allowed to make one explanation which will account for much hurried and slovenly work that is only too apparent in the following pages. On the 13th of January 1883, I received orders from the Panjáb Government to the effect that the report must be finished without fail by the end of the following February. When these orders reached me, I had completed only Chapters I, II, and IV, and the first two Parts of Chapter III ; while Part II of Chapter VI which deals with Patháns and Biloches, and the greater portion of Chapters XI and XII and of the first two Parts of Chapter XIII, were written in the rough, though exceedingly incomplete. Thus I had six weeks allowed me within which to fill in the *lacunæ* in these last sections, to discuss increase and decrease of population, language, caste with the exception of Patháns and Biloches, age, sex, and civil condition, occupations, education, and infirmities, and to summarise the results of our Census experience. The portion of the report which was wholly written within these six weeks comprises some 260 pages of print. It is hardly to be wondered that my treatment of these subjects is hasty and imperfect. My own feeling on looking back, is one of surprise that I accomplished the task after any fashion whatever. But on the 26th of February the MS. of my report was completely ready for press, and has not been touched since then. The press has been kept fully supplied with copy from the end of October 1882 ; and the subsequent delay is wholly due to the difficulty experienced in getting the report printed and published.

[1] I would suggest the pages of *Panjáb Notes and Queries*, a small periodical just started under the Editorship of Captain Temple of Ambála, as a convenient medium for discussion.

I need hardly say how largely I am indebted to others for both facts and ideas. The greater part of the information contained in the report has been either taken from scattered publications and from district Settlement or Census reports, or furnished me by correspondents. I owe much to Mr. Wilson's Code of Tribal Custom in Sirsa and to Mr. Barkley's notes on the Jálandhar district, both of which the writers placed in my hands in MS., and to Mr. Tupper's work on Panjáb Customary Law; while every chapter of the report attests my obligations to Mr. Alex. Anderson for the prompt and complete manner in which he answered my numerous inquiries about the peculiar and interesting tract of which he was in charge. In one respect I was singularly ill-fitted for the task entrusted to me; for practically speaking my whole Indian service had been confined to a single district (Karnál), which does not even lie in the Panjáb proper. Thus I have been throughout in the greatest danger of wrongly extending to the Province, as a whole, knowledge acquired in a small and very special portion of it. I can hardly hope that I have altogether escaped this pitfall; but that I have not fallen into it more frequently, is wholly due to the invaluable assistance rendered me by Messrs. Alex. Anderson, Coldstream, Douie, O'Brien, Steedman, Thomson, and Wilson. These gentlemen have carefully read the proofs of the report as they issued from the press; and their criticisms have enabled me to correct many faults and errors, and to add much that is valuable. I cannot express too strongly my obligation to them for undertaking and carrying through in their hardly-earned leisure so tedious and uninteresting a task. My warmest thanks are also due to Messrs. Cunningham, Douie, and Merk for valuable help unsparingly given on all points relating to the frontier tribes; to Major Plowden for his careful examination of the sections on the Patháns and their language; to Mr. Christie for his copious and suggestive annotation of my discussion of the vagrant and criminal classes; to Mr. Tupper for much valuable help given in the earlier stages of the operations; and to Dr. Dickson and the Rev. Mr. Wherry for the personal attention they most kindly bestowed on the Census printing, without which I should scarcely have succeeded in getting the work done. But these are only a few among the many who have helped me. I applied for assistance to many officers of many Departments, and to none in vain; and it is to the help thus received by me, that whatever value my report may be found to possess is mainly due.

My warmest acknowledgments are due to Mr. W. C. Plowden, Commissioner of Census, for his ever ready help and counsel, for the patient consideration with which he listened to my difficulties and suggestions, and for the kind anxiety which he evinced from first to last to do anything and everything that might make matters easier for me, so far as the unity of the Imperial scheme permitted.

Finally, I would express my grateful sense of the courtesy and consideration which I experienced at the hands of District officers throughout the operations. My position as Superintendent of the Census was one of some delicacy; for it obliged me to inspect, criticise, and report on the work of officers much senior to myself. That my relations with those officers were throughout of the most pleasant and cordial nature, is due to a good feeling on their part for which I am indebted to them.

SIMLA:
The 30th August 1883.

DENZIL IBBETSON.

PANJAB CASTES.

(BEING A REPRINT OF THE CHAPTER ON 'THE RACES, CASTES AND TRIBES OF THE PEOPLE' IN THE REPORT ON THE PANJAB CENSUS OF 1881.)

(The bracketed figures in the margin refer to the pages of the original edition and those without brackets to the pages of this reprint.)

PART I.—CASTE IN THE PANJAB.

[P. 172] 333. **The popular conception of caste.**—An old agnostic is said to have summed up his philosophy in the following words :—" The only thing I know "is that I know nothing; and I am not quite sure that I know that." His words express very exactly my own feelings regarding caste in the Panjáb. My experience is that it is almost impossible to make any statement whatever regarding any one of the castes we have to deal with, absolutely true as it may be as regards one part of the Province, which shall not presently be contradicted with equal truth as regards the same people in some other district. Yet I shall attempt to set forth briefly what seem to me the fundamental ideas upon which caste is based; and in doing so I shall attempt partly to explain why it is that the institution is so extraordinarily unstable, and its phænomena so diverse in different localities. What I propound in the following paragraphs is simply my working hypothesis as it at present stands ; but I shall not stop to say so as I write, though almost every proposition made must be taken subject to limitations, often sufficiently obvious, and not unfrequently involved in some other proposition made in the very next paragraph. My views are of little weight so long as they are not illustrated and supported by instances drawn from actually existing fact. Such instances I have in great abundance, and they will be found in part in the detailed description of castes which follow this discussion. But I have leisure neither to record all my evidence, nor to marshal what I have recorded; and I give my conception of caste with a crudeness of exposition which lack of time forbids me to modify, not because I think that it is anything even distantly approaching to the whole truth, but because I believe that it is nearer to that truth than is the generally received theory of caste as I understand it.[1]

The popular and currently received theory of caste I take to consist of three main articles :—

(1) that caste is an institution of the Hindu religion, and wholly peculiar to that religion alone :

(2) that it consists primarily of a fourfold classification of people in general under the heads of Bráhman, Kshatriya, Vaisya, and Súdra :

[1] Owing to the limitation of the time allowed me to complete the report, the whole of this chapter except Part II was written in less than three weeks. It would have taken me as many months to have digested and put into shape the whole of my material.

(3) that caste is perpetual and immutable, and has been transmitted from generation to generation throughout the ages of Hindu history and myth without the possibility of change.

Now I should doubtless be exaggerating in the opposite direction, but I think that I should still be far nearer to the truth if, in opposition to the popular conception thus defined, I were to say—

(1) that caste is a social far more than a religious institution; that it has no necessary connection whatever with the Hindu religion, further than that under that religion certain ideas and customs common to all primitive nations have been developed and perpetuated in an unusual degree; and that conversion from Hinduism to Islám has not necessarily the slightest effect upon caste:

(2) that there are Bráhmans who are looked upon as outcasts by those who under the fourfold classification would be classed as Súdras; that there is no such thing as a Vaisya now existing; that it is very doubtful indeed whether there is such a thing as a Kshatriya, and if there is, no two people are agreed as to where we shall look for him; and that Súdra has no present significance save as a convenient term of abuse to apply to somebody else whom you consider lower than yourself; while the number of castes which can be classed under any one or under no one of the four heads, according as private opinion may vary, is almost innumerable:

(3) that nothing can be more variable and more difficult to define than caste; and that the fact that a generation is descended from ancestors of any given caste creates a presumption, and nothing more, that that generation also is of the same caste, a presumption liable to be defeated by an infinite variety of circumstances.

334. The hereditary nature of occupations.—Among all primitive peoples we find the race split up into a number of tribal communities held together by the tie of common descent, each tribe being self-contained and self-sufficing, and bound by strict rules of marriage and inheritance, the common object of which is to increase the strength and preserve the unity of the tribe. There is as yet no diversity of occupation. Among more advanced societies, where occupations have become differentiated, the tribes have almost altogether disappeared; and we find in their place corporate communities or guilds held together by the tie of common occupation rather than of common blood, each guild being self-contained and self-governed, and bound by strict rules, the common object of which is to strengthen the guild and to confine to it the secrets of the craft which it practises. Such were the trades-guilds of the middle ages as we first meet with them in European history. But all modern [P. 173]
inquiry into their origin and earlier constitution tends to the conclusion—and modern authorities on the development of primitive institutions are rapidly accepting that conclusion—that the guild in its first form was, no less than the tribe, based upon common descent; and that the fundamental idea which lay at the root of the institution in its inception was the hereditary nature of occupation. Now here we have two principles, community of blood and community of occupation. So long as the hereditary nature of occupation was in-

violable, so long as the blacksmith's son must be and nobody else could be a blacksmith, the two principles were identical. But the struggle for existence is too severe, the conditions of existence too varied, and the character and capacity of individuals too diverse to permit of this inviolability being long maintained; and in any but the most rudimentary form of society it must, like the socialist's dream of equal division of wealth, cease to exist from the very instant of its birth. And from the moment when the hereditary nature of occupation ceases to be invariable and inviolable, the two principles of community of blood and community of occupation become antagonistic. The antagonism still continues. In every community which the world has ever seen there have been grades of position and distinctions of rank; and in all societies these grades and distinctions are governed by two considerations, descent and calling. As civilisation advances and the ideas of the community expand in more liberal growth, the latter is ever gaining in importance at the expense of the former; the question what a man is, is ever more and more taking precedence of the question what his father was. But in no society that the world has yet seen has either of these two considerations ever wholly ceased to operate; in no community has the son of the coal-heaver been born the equal of the son of the nobleman, or the man who dies a trader been held in the same consideration as he who dies a statesman; while in all the son has begun where the father left off. The communities of India in whose midst the Hindu religion has been developed are no exceptions to this rule; but in their case special circumstances have combined to preserve in greater integrity and to perpetuate under a more advanced state of society than elsewhere the hereditary nature of occupation, and thus in a higher degree than in other modern nations to render identical the two principles of community of blood and community of occupation. And it is this difference, a difference of degree rather than of kind, a survival to a later age of an institution which has died out elsewhere rather than a new growth peculiar to the Hindu nation, which makes us give a new name to the old thing and call caste in India what we call position or rank in England.

335. Occupation the primary basis of caste.—The whole basis of diversity of caste is diversity of occupation. The old division into Bráhman, Kshatriya, Vaisya, Súdra, and the Mlechchha or outcast who is below the Súdra, is but a division into the priest, the warrior, the husbandman, the artisan, and the menial; and the more modern development which substituted trader for husbandman as the meaning of Vaisya or "the people" did not alter the nature of the classification. William Priest, John King, Edward Farmer, and James Smith are but the survivals in England of the four *varnas* of Manu. But in India which, as I have already explained in chapter IV, sections 211-12, to which I would here refer the reader, was priest-ridden to an extent unknown to the experience of Europe even in the middle ages, the dominance of one special occupation gave abnormal importance to all distinctions of occupation. The Bráhman, who could at first claim no separate descent by which he should be singled out from among the Aryan community, sought to exalt his office and to propitiate his political rulers, who were the only rivals he had to fear, by degrading all other occupations and conditions of life. Further, as explained in the sections just referred to, the principle of hereditary occupation was to him as a class one of the most vital importance. As the Bráhmans increased in number, those numbers necessarily exceeded the possible requirements of the laity so far as the mere performance of priestly functions was concerned, while it became impossible for them to keep up as a whole even the semblance of sacred learning. Thus they ceased to be wholly priests and a large proportion of them became mere Levites. The only means of preserving its overwhelming influence to the body at large was to substitute Levitical descent for priestly functions as the basis of that influence, or rather perhaps to check the natural course of social evolution which would have substituted the latter for the former; and this they did by giving the whole sanction of religion to the principle of the hereditary nature of occupation. Hence sprang that tangled web of caste restrictions and distinctions, of ceremonial obligations, and of artificial purity and impurity, which has rendered the separation of occupation from descent so slow and so difficult in Hindu society, and which collectively constitutes what we know as caste. I do not mean that the Bráhmans invented the principle which they thus turned to their own purpose; on the contrary, I have said that it is found in all primitive societies that have outgrown the most rudimentary stage. Nor do I suppose that they deliberately set to work to produce any craftily designed effect upon the growth of social institutions. But circumstances had raised them to a position of extraordinary power; and naturally, and probably almost unconsciously, their teaching took the form which tended most effectually to preserve that power unimpaired.

Indeed in its earlier form, neither caste nor occupation was even supposed in India to be necessarily or invariably hereditary. It is often forgotten that there are two very distinct epochs in the post-Vedic history of the Hindu nations, which made respectively contributions of very different nature to that body of Hindu scriptures which we are too apt to confuse under the generic name of the Shástras, and which affected in very different manners the form of the Hindu religion. The earlier is the epoch of the Bráhmanas and the Upanishads, while Hinduism was a single and comparatively simple creed, or at most a philosophical abstraction; and the later is the epoch of the Puránas and Tantras, with their crowded Pantheon, their foul imaginings, their degraded idolatry, and their innumerable sects. The former may be said to end with the rise and the latter to begin with the growing degeneracy of Buddhism. In the earlier Hinduism we find that, while caste distinctions were primarily based upon occupation, considerable license in this respect was permitted to the several castes, while the possibility of the individual rising from one caste to another was distinctly recognised. This was the case even as late as the age of Manu, by which time the caste system had assumed great strictness, and the cardinal importance of occupation had become a prominent part of the Brahminical teaching, though its hereditary nature had not yet been so emphatically insisted on.[1] It was in the dark ages of Hindu history, about [P. 174]
the beginning of an æra during which Brahminism was substituted for Hinduism and the religion became a chaos of impure and degraded doctrine and sectarian teaching, that the theory of the necessarily hereditary nature of occupation seems to have taken its present form. In the earlier epoch the priest was always a Bráhman; in the later the Bráhman was always a priest.

336. But if occupation was not necessarily transmitted by descent and if caste varied with change of occupation in the earlier æra of Hinduism, it is no

---

[1] For instances of the possibility of change of caste it will be sufficient to refer the reader to Cunningham's History of the Sikhs, Appendix IV, to Muir's *Sanskrit Texts*, Vol. I, Chap. IV, and still more to a Buddhist pamphlet called Vajra Shúchi which is translated at Vol. I, pages 296 *ff* of Wilson's *Indian Caste*, and which for direct vigorous reasoning and scathing humour would not disgrace the best days of English party polemics.

less true that this is the case in the present day; though under caste restrictions as they now stand the change, in an upward direction at least, is infinitely slower and more difficult than then, and is painfully effected by the family or tribe in the course of generations instead of by the individual in the course of years. The following pages will contain numerous instances of the truth of this assertion, and the whole body of tribal and caste tradition in the Panjáb supports it. I have not always thought it necessary to state their traditions in discussing the various castes; and I have seldom stopped to comment on the facts. But the evidence, imperfect as it is, will be found to possess no inconsiderable weight; while the very fact of the general currency of a set of traditions, groundless as they may be in individual instances, shows that the theory of society upon which they are based is at least not repugnant to the ideas and feelings and even practice of the people who believe them. Indeed, for the purposes of the present enquiry it would almost be allowable to accept traditional origin; for though the tradition may not be true, it might have been, or it would never have arisen. Instances of fall in the social scale are naturally more often met with than instances of rise, for he who has sunk recalls with pride his ancestral origin, while he who has risen hastens to forget it.

337. The political and artificial basis of caste.—But before proceeding to give specific instances of recent change of caste, I must adopt a somewhat extended definition of occupation, and must take a somewhat wider basis than that afforded by mere occupation, even so defined, as the foundation of caste.

In India the occupation of the great mass of what may be called the upper or yeoman classes is the same. Setting aside the priests and traders on the one hand and the artisans and menials on the other, we have left the great body of agriculturists who constitute by far the larger portion of the population. This great body of people subsists by husbandry and cattle-farming, and so far their occupation is one and the same. But they are also the owners and occupiers of the land, the holders of more or less compact tribal territories; they are overlords as well as villains; and hence springs the cardinal distinction between the occupation of ruling and the occupation of being ruled. Where the actual calling of every-day life is the same, social standing, which is all that caste means, depends very largely upon political importance, whether present or belonging to the recent past. There is the widest distinction between the dominant and the subject tribes; and a tribe which has acquired political independence in one part of the country, will there enjoy a position in the ranks of caste which is denied it in tracts where it occupies a subordinate position.

Again, the features of the caste system which are peculiar to Brahminical Hinduism, and which has already been alluded to, have operated to create a curiously artificial standard of social rank. There are certain rules which must be observed by all at the risk of sinking in the scale. They are, broadly speaking, that widow marriage shall not be practised; that marriages shall be contracted only with those of equal or nearly equal standing; that certain occupations shall be abstained from which are arbitrarily declared to be impure, such as growing or selling vegetables, handicrafts in general, and especially working or trading in leather and weaving; that impure food shall be avoided; and that no communion shall be held with outcasts, such as scavengers, eaters of carrion or vermin, and the like. There are other and similarly artificial considerations which affect social standing, such as the practice of secluding the women of the family, the custom of giving daughters in marriage only to classes higher than their own, and the like; but these are of less general application than those first mentioned. Many of these restrictions are exceedingly irksome. It is expensive to keep the women secluded, for others have to be paid to do their work; it is still more expensive to purchase husbands for them from a higher grade of society, and so forth; and so there is a constant temptation to disregard these rules, even at the cost of some loss of social position.

Thus we have, as the extended basis of caste, first occupation, and within a common occupation political prominence and social standing, the latter being partly regulated by a set of very arbitrary rules which are peculiar to Indian caste, and which are almost the only part of the system which is peculiar to it. It is neither tautology nor false logic to say that social standing is dependent upon caste and caste upon social standing, for the two depend each upon the other in different senses. The rise in the social scale which accompanies increased political importance will presently be followed by a rise in caste; while the fall in the grades of caste which a disregard of the arbitrary rules of the institution entails, will surely be accompanied by loss of social standing.

338. **Instances of the mutability of caste.**—The Bráhmans are generally husbandmen as well as Levites, for their numbers are so great that they are obliged to supplement the income derived from their priestly office. But when a Bráhman drops his sacerdotal character, ceases to receive food or alms as offerings acceptable to the gods, and becomes a cultivator pure and simple, he also ceases to be a Bráhman, and has to employ other Bráhmans as priests. Witness the Taga Bráhmans of the Dehli division, who are Tagas, not Bráhmans, because they have "abandoned" (*tág dena*) their priestly character. Indeed in the hills the very practice of agriculture as a calling or at least the actual following of the plough is in itself sufficient to deprive a Bráhman of all but the name of his caste; for Mr. Lyall points out that in the following quotation from Mr. Barnes "ploughing" should be read for "agriculture" or "husbandry," there being very few, even of the highest Bráhman families, who abstain from other sorts of field work.

"It will afford a tolerable idea of the endless ramification of caste to follow out the details of "even the Sarsut tribe as established in these hills. The reader acquainted with the country will "know that Brahmins, though classed under a common appellation, are not all equal. There are "primarily two great distinctions in every tribe claiming to be of such exalted origin as the "Brahmins,—*viz.*, those who follow and those who abstain from agriculture. This is the great "touchstone of their creed. Those who have never defiled their hands with the plough, but have "restricted themselves to the legitimate pursuits of the caste, are held to be pure Brahmins; "while those who have once descended to the occupation of husbandry retain indeed the name, "but are no longer acknowledged by their brethren, nor held in the same reverence by the people "at large." [P. 175]

So again if a Bráhman takes to handicrafts he is no longer a Bráhman, as in the case of the Thávis of the hills, some of whom were Bráhmans in the last generation. The Dharúkras of Dehli are admittedly Bráhmans who have within the last few generations taken to widow marriage; and the Chamarwa Sádhs and the whole class of the so-called Bráhmans who minister to the outcast classes, are no longer Bráhmans in any respect beyond the mere retention of the name. The Mahá Bráhman, so impure that in many villages he is not allowed to enter the gates, the Dákaut and Gújráti, so unfortunate that other Bráhmans will not accept offerings at their hands, are all Bráhmans, but are practically differentiated as distinct castes by their special occupations. Turning to the second of Manu's four great classes, we find the Mahájan a Mahájan in the hills so long as he is a merchant, but a Káyath as soon as he becomes a clerk; while the Dasa Banya of the plains who has taken to the practice of widow marriage is a Banya only by name and occupation, not being admitted to communion or intermarriage by the more orthodox classes who bear the same title. The impossibility of fixing any line between Rájpúts on the one hand, and Jats, Gújars, and castes of similar standing on the other, is fully discussed in the subsequent parts of this chapter, in the paragraphs on the Jat in general, on the Rájpúts of the eastern hills, and on the Thakar and Ráthi. I there point out that the only possible definition of a Rájpút, in the Panjáb at least, is he who, being the descendant of a family that has enjoyed political importance, has preserved his ancestral status by strict observance of the caste rules enumerated above. The extract there quoted from Mr. Lyall's report sums up so admirably the state of caste distinctions in the hills that I make no apology for repeating it. He says:—

"Till lately the limits of caste do not seem to have been so immutably fixed in the hills as "in the plains. The Raja was the fountain of honour, and could do much as he liked. I have "heard old men quote instances within their memory in which a Raja promoted a Girth to be a "Rathi, and a Thakur to be a Rájput, for service done or money given; and at the present day "the power of admitting back into caste fellowship persons put under a ban for some grave act of "defilement is a source of income to the Jagirdar Rajas.

"I believe that Mr. Campbell, the present Lieutenant-Governor of Bengal, has asserted that "there is no such thing as a distinct Rájput stock; that in former times, before caste distinctions "had become crystallized, any tribe or family whose ancestor or head rose to royal rank became in "time Rájput.

"This is certainly the conclusion to which many facts point with regard to the Rájputs of "these hills. Two of the old royal and now essentially Rájput families of this district, *viz.*, "Kotlehr and Bangahal, are said to be Bráhmin by original stock. Mr. Barnes says that in "Kángra the son of a Rájput by a low-caste woman takes place as a Ráthi: in Seoraj and other "places in the interior of the hills I have met families calling themselves Rájputs, and growing "into general acceptance as Rájputs, in their own country at least, whose only claim to the title "was that their father or grandfather was the offspring of a Kanetni by a foreign Bráhmin. On "the border line in the Himalayas, between Thibet and India proper, any one can observe caste "growing before his eyes; the noble is changing into a Rájput, the priest into a Bráhmin, "the peasant into a Jat; and so on down to the bottom of the scale. The same process was, "I believe, more or less in force in Kángra proper down to a period not very remote from "to-day."

And Kángra is of all parts of the Panjáb the place in which the proudest and most ancient Rájpút blood is to be found. As Captain Cunningham says in his *History of the Sikhs:* "It may be assumed as certain that, had "the conquering Mughals and Patháns been without a vivid belief and an "organised priesthood, they would have adopted Vedism and become enrolled "among the Kshatriya or Rájpút races." In Sirsa we have instances of clans who were a few generations ago accounted Jat being now generally classed as Rájpúts, having meanwhile practised greater exclusiveness in matrimonial matters, and having abandoned widow marriage; while the reverse process is no less common. So the Chauháns of Dehli are no longer recognized as Rájpúts since they have begun to marry their widows. Finally, we have the whole traditions of the Panjáb tribes of the Jat and Gújar status to the effect that they are descended from Rájpúts who married below them, ceased to seclude their women, or began to practise widow marriage; and the fact that one and the same tribe is often known as Rájpút where it has, and as Jat where it has not risen to political importance.

339. But it is possible for Rájpúts and Jats to fall still lower. The Sahnsars of Hushyárpur were admittedly Rájpúts till only a few generations ago, when they took to growing vegetables, and now rank with Aráins. Some of the Tarkháns, Lohárs, and Náis of Sirsa are known to have been Jats or Rájpúts who within quite recent times have taken to the hereditary occupations of these castes; and some of the Chauháns of Karnál, whose fathers were born Rájpúts, have taken to weaving and become Shekhs. So too the landowning castes can rise. A branch of the Wattu Rájpúts of the Satluj, by an affectation of peculiar sanctity, have in the course of a few generations become Bodlas, and now deny their Rájpút and claim Qureshi's origin; and already the claim is commonly admitted. A clan of Ahírs in Rewári has begun to seclude their women and abandon widow marriage; they no longer intermarry with the other Ahírs, and will presently be reckoned a separate caste; and there is a Kharral family lately settled in Baháwalpur who have begun to affect peculiar holiness and to marry only with each other, and their next step will certainly be to claim Arab descent. The process is going on daily around us, and it is certain that what is now taking place is only what has always taken place during the long ages of Indian history. The ease with which Saiyads are manufactured is proverbial, and some of our highest Rájpút tribes are beginning in the Salt-range to claim Mughal or Arab origin. On the frontier the dependence upon occupation of what there most nearly corresponds with caste, as distinct from tribe, is notorious. A Máchhi is a Máchhi so long as he catches fish, and a Jat directly he lays hold of a plough. There are no Rájpúts because there are no Rájás; and those who are notoriously of pure Rájpút descent are Jats because they till the land.

Among the artisan and menial tribes the process is still more common, and the chapter on this section of the community abounds with instances. One Chamár takes to weaving instead of leather-working and becomes a Chamar-Juláha; presently he will be a Juláha pure and simple: another does the same and becomes a Rangreta or a Búnia: a Chúhra refuses to touch night-soil and becomes a Musalli or a Kutána. Within the castes the same process is observable. The Chándar Chamár will not eat or marry with the Jatia Chamár because the latter works in the hides of impure animals; one [P. 176] section of the Kumhárs will hold no communion with another because the latter burn sweepings as fuel; a third section has taken to agriculture and looks down upon both. In all these and a thousand similar instances the sections are for all practical purposes distinct castes, though the caste name, being based upon and expressive of the hereditary occupation, is generally retained where the main occupation is not changed. Indeed I have my doubts whether, setting aside the absolutely degrading occupations such as scavengering, the caste does not follow the occupation in the case of even each individual among these artisan and menial castes much more generally than we suppose. We know next to nothing about their organisation, and I do not pretend to make anything more than a suggestion. But it is certain that these lower castes have retained the organisation of the guild in extraordinary completeness long after the organisation of the tribe or caste has almost completely died out among the landowning classes whom they serve. And it may be, especially in towns and cities, that this organisation is meant to protect the craft in the absence of the bond of common descent, and that men belonging by birth to other castes and occupations may on adopting a new occupation be admitted to the fraternity which follows it.

340. The nature and evolution of the institution of caste.—Thus we see that in India, as in all countries, society is arranged in strata which are based upon differences of social or political importance, or of occupation. But here the classification is hereditary rather than individual to the persons included under it, and an artificial standard is added which is peculiar to caste and which must be conformed with on pain of loss of position, while the rules which forbid social intercourse between castes of different rank render it infinitely difficult to rise in the scale. So too, the classification being hereditary, it is next to impossible for the individual himself to rise; it is the tribe or section of the tribe that alone can improve its position; and this it can do only after the lapse of several generations, during which time it must abandon a lower for a higher occupation, conform more strictly with the arbitrary rules, affect social exclusiveness or special sanctity, or separate itself after some similar fashion from the body of the caste to which it belongs. The whole theory of society is that occupation and caste are hereditary; and the presumption that caste passes unchanged to the descendants is exceedingly strong. But the presumption is one which can be defeated, and has already been and is now in process of being defeated in numberless instances. As in all other countries and among all other nations, the graduations of the social scale are fixed; but society is not solid but liquid, and portions of it are continually rising and sinking and changing their position as measured by that scale; and the only real difference between Indian society and that of other countries in this respect is, that the liquid is much more viscous, the friction and inertia to be overcome infinitely greater, and the movement therefore far slower and more difficult in the former than in the latter. This friction and inertia are largely due to a set of artificial rules which have been grafted on to the social prejudices common to all communities by the peculiar form which caste has taken in the Brahminical teachings. But there is every sign that these rules are gradually relaxing. Sikhism did much to weaken them in the centre of the Panjáb, while they can now hardly be said to exist on the purely Mahomedan frontier; and I think that we shall see a still more rapid change under the influences which our rule has brought to bear upon the society of the Province. Our disregard for inherited distinctions have already done something, and the introduction of railways much more, to loosen the bonds of caste. It is extraordinary how incessantly, in reporting customs, my correspondents note that the custom or restriction is fast dying out. The liberty enjoyed by the people of the Western Panjáb is extending to their neighbours in the east, and especially the old tribal customs are gradually fading away. There cannot be the slighest doubt that in a few generations the materials for a study of caste as an institution will be infinitely less complete than they are even now.

341. Thus, if my theory be correct, we have the following steps in the process by which caste has been evolved in the Panjáb—(1) the tribal divisions common to all primitive societies; (2) the guilds based upon hereditary occupation common to the middle life of all communities; (3) the exaltation of the priestly office to a degree unexampled in other countries; (4) the exaltation of the Levitical blood by a special insistence upon the necessarily hereditary nature of occupation; (5) the preservation and support of this principle by the elaboration from the theories of the Hindu creed or cosmogony of a purely artificial set of rules, regulating marriage and intermarriage, declaring certain occupations and foods to be impure and polluting, and prescribing the conditions and degree of social intercourse permitted between the several castes. Add to these the pride of social rank and the pride of blood which are natural to man, and which alone could reconcile a nation to restrictions at once irksome from a domestic and burdensome from a material point of view; and it is hardly to be wondered at that caste should have assumed the rigidity which distinguishes it in India.

342. The tribal type of caste.—Thus caste in the Panjáb is based primarily upon occupation, and given that the occupation is that most respectable of all occupations, the owning and cultivation of land, upon political position. But there are other forms which are assumed by caste, or at least by what most nearly corresponds with it in some parts of the Province, which may in general be referred to two main types. The first type is based upon community of blood; the second is a trades-guild pure and simple. Both are strictly analogous to caste proper; but the existence of both in their present forms appears to be due to the example of those Musalmán nations who have exerted such immense influence in the Panjáb, and both differ from caste proper in the absence of those artificial restrictions which are the peculiar product of Brahminism. The purest types of the ethnic or national caste are the Patháns and Biloches, both untainted by any admixture of Hindu feeling or custom. Here the fiction which unites the caste, race, nation, or whatever you may choose to call it, is that of common descent from a traditional ancestor. In the main it is something more than a fiction, for if the common ancestor be mythical, as he probably is, there is still a very real bond of common origin, common habitat, common customs and modes of thought, and tribal association continued through several centuries, which holds these people together. But even here the stock is not even professedly pure. It will be seen from my description of the two great frontier races whom I have quoted as types, that each of them includes in its tribal organisation affiliated tribes of foreign origin, who sometimes but by no means always preserve the tradition of their separate descent, but are recognised [P. 177]
to the full as being, and for all practical purposes actually *are* Biloch or Pathán as truly as are the tribes who have certainly sprung from the parent stock. Still more is this the case with the Mughal, Shekh, and Saiyad, who are only strangers in the land. "Last year I was a weaver, this "year I am a Shekh; next year if prices rise I shall be a Saiyad." The process of manufacture in these cases is too notorious for it to be necessary for me to insist upon it; and so long as the social position of the new claimant is worthy of the descent he claims, the true Mughals, Shekhs, and Saiyads, after waiting for a generation or so till the absurdity of the story is not too obvious, accept the fiction and admit the brand new brother into their fraternity.

Throughout the Western Plains, and in a somewhat lower degree throughout the cis-Indus Salt-range Tract, where Islám has largely superseded Brahminism and where the prohibition against marriage with another caste is almost universally neglected, we find the distribution of the landowning classes based upon tribe rather than upon caste. The necessity for community of present caste as a condition of intermarriage having disappeared, the more comprehensive classification of caste has become a mere tradition of ancestral status, and the immediate question is, not is a man a Rájpút or a Jat, but is he a Siál or a Chhádhar, a Janjúa or a Manhás. The restrictions upon intermarriage are in actual practice almost as strict as ever; but they are based upon present social rank, without reference to the question whether that rank has yet received the impress or sanction of admission into the caste with which it would correspond. In fact the present tendency even in the case of Rájpúts, and still more in that of lower castes of Indian origin, is markedly to reject their original Hindu caste, and to claim connection with the Mughal conquerors of their country or the Arab founders of their faith. Thus we have no broad classification of the people under a few great castes with their internal division into tribes, such as we find in the Hindu portion of the Panjáb; or rather this classification is of far less importance, being little more than a memory of origin, or a token of a social rank which is more precisely expressed by the tribal name.

343. **The effect of occupation upon the tribal form of caste.**—So too, the lines which separate occupations one from another are relaxed. In the case of the impure occupations which render those who follow them outcasts, this is not indeed the case. The Pathán who should become a scavenger would no longer be recognised as a Pathán, though he might still claim the name; indeed, as already pointed out in the Chapter on Religion, the prejudice is carried into the very mosque, and the outcast who has adopted Islám is not recognised as a Musalmán unless at the same time he abandon his degrading occupation. But the taint is not so markedly hereditary, nor is the prejudice against menial occupations or handicrafts generally so strong. A Pathán who became a weaver would still remain a Pathán, and would not be thought to be polluted; though, as in all countries, he would be held to have fallen in the social scale, and the better class of Pathán would not give him his daughter to wife. In fact the difference between the condition of a Pathán who took to weaving on the frontier and the Rájpút who took to weaving in the Dehli Territory, would be precisely that between caste in India and social standing in Europe. The degradation would not in the case of the former be ceremonial or religious, nor would it be hereditary save in the sense that the children would be born in a lower condition of life; but the immediate and individual loss of position would be as real as among the strictest castes of the Hindus. Thus we find on the frontier men of all castes engaging from poverty or other necessity in all occupations save those of an actually degrading nature. Between these two extremes of the purely Mahomedan customs of the Indus and the purely Hindu customs of the Jamna we meet with a very considerable variety of intermediate conditions. Yet the change is far less gradual than might have been supposed probable, the break from Islám to Brahminism, from tribal position and freedom of occupation to the more rigid restraints of caste, taking place with some suddenness about the meridian of Lahore, where the great rivers enter the fertile zone and the arid grazing grounds of the West give place to the arable plains of the East. The submontane zone retains its social as well as its physical characteristics much further west than do the plains which lie below it, and here the artificial restrictions of caste can hardly be said to cease till the Salt-range is crossed.

Closely allied with these tribal or ethnic communities based upon identity of recent descent, is the association which binds together small colonies of foreign immigrants under names denoting little more than their origin. Such are the Púrbi, the Kashmíri, the Bangáli. These people have their own distinctions of caste and tribe in the countries whence they came. But isolation from their fellows in a land of strangers binds them together in closer union. The Púrbi is a Púrbi to the people of the Panjáb, and nothing more; and in many cases this looseness of classification spreads to the people themselves, and they begin to class themselves as Púrbi and forget their original divisions. Examples may be found even nearer home. The Hindu is a small class on the frontier, and he is generically classed as Kirár without regard to his caste. The men of the Bágar are strangers in the Panjáb, and they are commonly known as Bágri irrespective of whether they are Jats or Rájpúts. Many more instances of similar confusion might be given. Even community of creed, where the numbers concerned are small, constitutes a bond which cannot be distinguished from that of caste. The resident Sikhs on the Peshâwar frontier are a caste for all practical purposes; while the case of the Bishnois of Hariána who are chiefly recruited from two very different castes is still more striking.

344. **The trades-guild type of caste.**—The second type which I have included together with castes proper and the western tribes in my caste tables, is almost precisely the trades-guild of Europe in the middle ages. And it again owes its existence very largely to the prevalence of Mahomedan ideas. It is found chiefly in the larger cities, and is almost always known by a Persian or Arabic name. The class of Darzis or tailors is a good example of what I mean. Here the caste organisation, the regulations of the fraternity, and the government by common council or *pancháyat* are as complete as among the true castes. But there is no longer even the fiction of common origin, and the only bond which unites the members of the guild is that of common occupation—a bond which is severed when the occupation is abandoned and renewed when it is resumed. I have already said that I am not at all sure whether this is not the case with the artisan castes in general in a far greater degree than is commonly supposed. It appears to me that in the case of the menial and artisan classes the real caste is what I have already noticed, and shall presently describe more particularly, under the name of the *section*; [P. 178]
and that the caste name is often merely a generic term used to include all who follow the same occupation. If the numerous agricultural tribes of the Indus who are included under the generic term Jat observed caste distinctions and refused to eat together and intermarry, we should have a state of things corresponding exactly with what we find throughout the Province among the industrial classes, where each so-called caste comprises under a common occupational term a number of sections of different geographical origin and of different habits, who refuse to hold communion with one another, and are for all practical purposes separate castes. But even here the distinction is often based upon minor differences in the occupation or in the mode of following it; and community of origin in the remote past is often, though by no means always, admitted. And even if my suggestion be well-founded, there is still this cardinal distinction, that in the case of the caste or section of the caste the basis of the organisation is hereditary, and the stranger is admitted voluntarily and deliberately; whereas in the case of the guild there is no pretence to community of blood, and anybody following the craft is admitted almost as a matter of right. To this class probably belong the Malláh, the Qassáb, the Sabzi-farosh, the Máshqi when not a Jhínwar, the Núngar, and many of those quasi-castes of whom I have to say that I cannot tell whether the name signifies anything more than the occupation of the people included under it. Somewhat similar to these are the followers of divers occupations which are

almost if not altogether confined, in the east of the Province at least, to the members of a single caste, of which the chapter on artisan and menial castes furnishes so many examples. The Bharbhúnja is *almost* always, I believe, a Jhínwar; the Jarráh is *almost* always a Nái; but it would not have been safe to class them as Jhínwar and Nái respectively, and so I have shown them separately in my tables. Yet another form of quasi-caste is afforded by the religious and ascetic orders of *fakírs* which, in the absence of all pretence of community of blood and the purely voluntary nature of their association, are somewhat analogous to the trades-guild. These men abandon caste properly so called on entering the order to which they belong; but it would have been absurd to omit them altogether or to show them under "Miscellaneous," and I have therefore ranked them in my tables as castes. Many of them are subject to some form of authority which is exercised by the order in its corporate capacity; but many of them are absolutely free from restrictions of any kind, and the word caste is not really applicable to these classes.

345. Different types included in the caste-tables.—Thus the figures of my tables of tribes and castes include groups formed upon several very distinct types. There is the true caste in the Brahminical sense of the term, the Bráhman, Rájpút, Banya, and so forth; the tribe or race based upon common blood, such as the Pathán, Biloch, Káthia; there is the colony of foreigners like the Púrbi and Kashmírí, or of believers in a strange creed like the Bishnoi; there is the true occupational caste such as the Nái, the Chamár, and the Chúhra; there is the common trades-guild like the Darzi and the Qassáb; there is the occupation pure and simple as the Jarráh and Gharámi; there is the ascetic order as the Gosáin and Nirmala; and besides these there are all possible intermediate stages. Moreover, the name which is applied to a true caste or race in one part of the Panjáb, in another merely signifies an occupation; of which fact Aráin and Biloch are two notable examples, the first meaning nothing more than a market-gardener in the Salt-range Tract, the latter little more than a camelman in the centre of the Province, and each in either case including an indefinite number of castes or tribes with nothing but community of occupation to connect them.

346. Effect of conversion upon caste.—At the beginning of this chapter I stated, admittedly as an exaggeration of the truth, that caste has little necessary connection with the Hindu religion, and that conversion from Hinduism to Islám has not necessarily the slightest effect upon it. I shall now consider how far that statement has to be modified. I have attempted to show in the preceding paragraphs that pride of blood, especially in the upper, and shame of occupation, especially in the lower classes, are in all societies the principal factors which regulate social rank; and that when Brahminism developed caste, all that it did was to bind the two together, or at least to prevent the dissolution of the tie which bound them and which would have broken down in the ordinary course of social evolution, and while thus perpetuating the principle of the hereditary nature of occupation and social status, to hedge it round and strengthen it by a network of artificial rules and restrictions which constitute the only characteristic peculiar to the institution of caste. This I take to constitute the only connection between Hinduism and caste; and it is obvious, that these restrictions and prejudices once engrafted on the social system, mere change of creed has no necessary effect whatever upon their nature or their operation. As a fact in the east of the Panjáb conversion has absolutely *no* effect upon the caste of the convert. The Musalmán

Rájpút, Gújar, or Jat is for all social, tribal, political, and administrative purposes exactly as much a Rájpút, Gújar or Jat as his Hindu brother. His social customs are unaltered, his tribal restrictions are unrelaxed, his rules of marriage and inheritance unchanged; and almost the only difference is that he shaves his scalplock and the upper edge of his moustache, repeats the Mahomedan creed in a mosque, and adds the Musalmán to the Hindu wedding ceremony. As I have already shown in the chapter on Religion, he even worships the same idols as before, or has only lately ceased to do so.[1]

347. The fact is that the people are bound by social and tribal custom far more than by any rules of religion. Where the whole tone and feeling of the country-side is Indian, as it is in the Eastern Panjáb, the Musalmán is simply the Hindu with a difference. Where that tone and feeling is that of the country beyond the Indus, as it is on the Panjáb frontier, the Hindu even is almost as the Musalmán. The difference is national rather than religious. The laxity allowed by Mahomet in the matter of intermarriage has no effect upon the Musalmán Jat of the Dehli division, for he has already refused to avail himself even of the smaller license allowed by the Hindu priests and scriptures, and bound himself by tribal rules far stricter than those of either religion. But the example of the Pathán and the Biloch has had a very great effect upon the Jat of the Multán division; and he recognises, not indeed the prohibitions of Mahomet,—or rather not only them, for they represent the [P. 179] irreducible minimum,—but the tribal rules of his frontier neighbours, more strict than those of his religion but less strict than those of his nation. I believe that the laxity of the rules and restrictions imposed by the customs of castes and tribes which is observable in the Western Panjáb, and among the Hindus no less than among the Musalmáns, is due far more to the example of the neighbouring frontier tribes than to the mere change of faith. The social and tribal customs of the eastern peasant, whether Hindu or Musalmán, are those of India; while in the west the people, whether Hindu or Musalmán, have adopted in great measure, though by no means altogether, the social and tribal customs of Afghánistán and Bilochistán. In both cases those rules and customs are tribal or national, rather than religious.

At the same time there can be no doubt that both the artificial rules of Hindu caste, and the tribal customs which bind both Hindu and Musalmán, have lately begun to relax, and with far greater rapidity among the Musalmáns than among the Hindus. And this difference is no doubt really due to the difference in religion. There has been within the last 30 years a great Musalmán revival in the Panjáb; education has spread, and with it a more accurate knowledge of the rules of the faith; and there is now a tendency, which is day by day growing stronger, to substitute the law of Islám for tribal custom in all matters, whether of intermarriage, inheritance, or social intercourse. The movement has as yet materially affected only the higher and more educated classes; but there can be little doubt that it is slowly working down through the lower grades of society. The effect of conversion to Sikhism has already been noticed in the chapter on Religion, as has the effect of change of creed upon the menial classes; and this latter will be dealt with more at length in that part of the present chapter which treats of those castes.

[1] This is much less true of the middle classes of the towns and cities. They have no reason to be particularly proud of their caste; while the superior education and the more varied constitution of the urban population weaken the power of tribal custom. In such cases the convert not unfrequently takes the title of Shekh: though even here a change of caste name on conversion is probably the exception.

348. Effect of Islam in strengthening the bonds of caste.—But if the adoption of Islám does not absolve the individual from the obligations common to his tribe or caste, still less does its presence as such tend to weaken those obligations. Indeed it seems to me exceedingly probable that where the Musalmán invasion has not, as in the Western Panjáb, been so wholesale or the country of the invaders so near as to change bodily by force of example the whole tribal customs of the inhabitants, the Mahomedan conquest of Northern India has tightened and strengthened rather than relaxed the bonds of caste; and that it has done this by depriving the Hindu population of their natural leaders the Rájpúts, and throwing them wholly into the hands of the Bráhmans. The full discussion of this question would require a far wider knowledge of Indian comparative sociology than I possess. But I will briefly indicate some considerations which appear to me to point to the probable truth of my suggestion. I have said that caste appears to have been far more loose and less binding in its earlier form than as it appeared in the later developments of Brahminism; and we know that, at least in the earlier and middle stages of Hinduism, the contest between the Bráhman and the Rájpút for the social leadership of the people was prolonged and severe (see Muir's Sanskrit Texts, Vol. I). The Mahomedan invaders found in the Rájpút Princes political enemies whom it was their business to subdue and to divest of authority; but the power of the Bráhmans threatened no danger to their rule, and that they left unimpaired. The Brahminic influence was probably never so strong in the Panjáb as in many other parts of India; but it is markedly strongest in the Dehli Territory, or in that portion of the Province in which, lying under the very shadow of the Mughal court, Rájpút power was most impossible. Moreover, it is curious that we find the institutions and restrictions of caste as such most lax, and a state of society most nearly approaching that which existed in the earlier epoch of Hinduism, in two very dissimilar parts of the Panjáb. One is the Indus frontier, where Mahomedanism reigns supreme; the other is the Kángra hills, the most exclusively Hindu portion of the Province. On the Indus we have the Saiyad and the Pír, the class of Ulama or divines who take the place of the Bráhman; the Pathán or Biloch as the case may be, who correspond with the Kshatriya; the so-called Jat, who is emphatically the "people" or Vaisya in the old sense of the word, and includes all the great mass of husbandmen of whatever caste they may be, Awáns, Jats, Rájpúts and the like, who cannot pretend to Kshatriya rank; the Kirár or trader of whatever caste, Banya, Khatri, or Arora, corresponding with the later use of Vaisya; the artisan or Súdra; and the outcast or Mlechchha. The two last classes have no generic names; but the three first correspond almost exactly with the Bráhman, the Kshatriya, and the Vaisya of the middle Hindu scriptures, nor are the boundaries of these divisions more rigorously fixed than we find them in those scriptures. The other portion of the Province in which caste restrictions are most loose and caste divisions most general and indefinite is the Kángra hills; or precisely the only part of the Panjáb into which Mahomedanism has found no entrance, in which Mahomedan ideas have had no influence, in which Hinduism has remained absolutely sheltered from attack from without, and in which the oldest Rájpút dynasties in India have preserved their supremacy unbroken up to within the last eighty years. On the Indus we appear to have caste as it is under the Mahomedan, on the Jamna as it is under the Bráhman, and in the Himálayas of Kángra as it is under the Rájpút. The state of caste relations in the Kángra hills is fully described under the heads of Jats in general, Rájpúts of the Eastern Hills, Thakars and Ráthís, Kanets, and Hill Menials. The whole matter is summed up in the quotation from Mr. Lyall given on page 175. Here the Rájpút is the fountain of honour, and the very Bráhman is content to accept rank at his hands. Mr. Barnes writes of the Kángra Bráhmans :—

"The hills, as I have already stated, were the seats of petty independent princes, and in every "principality the Bráhmans are arranged into classes of different degrees of purity. The Raja was "always considered the fountain of all honour, and his classification, made probably at the counsel "of his religious advisers, was held binding upon the brotherhood. In these graduated lists no "account was ever taken of the zamindar Bráhmins, as they were contemptuously styled;—they "were left to themselves in ignoble obscurity. Thus, in the days of Raja Dharm Chand, the two "great tribes of Kángra Bráhmins,—the 'Nagarkotias' (from Nagarkot, the ancient name of "Kángra) and the 'Batehrus,'—were formally sub-divided into clans. Of the Nagarkotias "Dharm Chand established 13 different families, of which, at the risk of being considered tedious, "I subjoin a catalogue."

So we find the Rája of Kángra bribed to elevate a caste in the social scale; and the Rája of Alwar making a new caste of a section of the Mínas, and prescribing limits to their intermarriage with those who had till then been considered their brothers.

Under Mahomedan rule the Rájpút disappeared, and for the Hindu population the Bráhman took his place. Hence the wide differences between caste in Kángra and caste in the Dehli Territory. In the Hills, the very [P. 180] stronghold at once of Rájpút power and of Hindusim in its most primitive form, we have the Bráhman, but with a wide difference between the Bráhman who prays and the Bráhman who ploughs; we have the Rájpút, a name strictly confined to the royal families and their immediate connections, and refused to such even of those as soil their hands with the plough; we have the great cultivating class, including the Thakars and Ráthís of acknowledged and immediate Rájpút descent who furnish wives even to the Rájpúts themselves, and the Ráwats, Kanets, and Ghiraths of somewhat lower status; we have the Kirár or Mahájan, including not only traders, but all the Káyaths and the clerkly class, and even Bráhmans who take to these pursuits; we have the respectable artisan class, the carpenter, mason and water-carrier; and finally we have the Koli or Dági, the outcast or Mlechchha of the hills. And from top to bottom of this social scale, no single definite line can be drawn which shall precisely mark off any one caste or grade from the one below it. Each one takes its wives from and eats with the one immediately below it, and the members of each can, and they occasionally do, rise to the one immediately above it.

349. Tribal divisions among the landowning castes.—Within the caste the first great division of the landowning classes is into tribes; and the tribe appears to me to be far more permanent and indestructible than the caste. I have already shown how in the west of the Panjáb the broader distinctions of caste have become little more than a tradition or a convenient symbol for social standing, while the tribal groups are the practical units of which the community is composed. There is, I fancy, little doubt that when a family or section of a caste rises or sinks in the social scale, while it changes the name of its caste, it often retains its tribal designation; indeed it is probable that that designation not unseldom becomes the name of a new caste by which it is to be known in future. Thus the widow-marrying Chauhán Rájpúts of Dehli are now known as Chauháns, and not as Rájpúts; while their brethren of the next district, Karnál, who have not infringed the caste rule, are known as Rájpúts, and only secondarily as Chauhán Rájpúts. This theory is in accordance with the tradition by which the constant recurrence of tribal names in different castes is accounted for by the people themselves. The Chauhán Gújars, for instance, will tell you that their ancestor was a Chauhán Rájpút who married a Gújar woman; and that his descendants retained the tribal name, while sinking to the rank of Gújars owing to his infringement of caste regulations.[1] Indeed this is simply the process which we see in actual operation before our very eyes. As I have already remarked, the same tribe is known as Rájpút in a tract where it has, and as Jat in a tract where it has not risen to political importance; but the tribal name, indicating a far stronger and more enduring bond than that of common caste, still remains to both. Sir Henry Maine has pointed out how two considerations gradually tend to be substituted for or added to the tie of common descent as the basis of tribal unity, common occupation of land, and common subjection to tribal authority. He writes :—

"From the moment when a tribal community settles down finally upon a definite space of "land, the land begins to be the basis of society instead of the kinship. The change is exceed- "ingly gradual, and in some particulars it has not even now been fully accomplished; but it has "been going on through the whole course of history. The constitution of the family through "actual blood relationship is of course an observable fact; but for all groups of men larger than "the family, the land on which they live tends to become the bond of union between them, at "the expense of kinship ever more and more vaguely conceived." And again—"Kinship as the "tie binding communities together tends to be regarded as the same thing with subjection to com- "mon authority. The notions of Power and Consanguinity blend, but they in nowise supersede "one another."

The institution of *hamsáyah* among the Biloches and Patháns, by which refugees from one tribe who claim the protection of the chief of another tribe are affiliated to, and their descendants become an integral part of the latter, is an admirable example of the second of these two processes; and in the substitution of land for blood as the basis of tribal unity, we very probably find the explanation of that standing puzzle of Indian tribal tradition, how the common ancestor managed to conquer the tribal territory single-handed, or how, if he had followers, it happens that all the living members of the tribe trace their descent from him, while the lineage of those followers is nowhere discoverable.

350. Within the tribe the same basis of sub-division is often found to exist, the clans being apparently territorial, while the smaller septs are probably founded upon real descent. In fact it is exceedingly difficult to draw the line between tribe and clan, except where the two are connected by the present occupation of common territory and subjection to a common tribal authority. When a section of a great tribe such as the Punwár Rájpúts separates from the parent tribe and acquires for itself a new territory as did the Siáls, the section becomes for all practical purposes a new and independent tribe, and the memory of the old tribe is to the new one what caste is to tribes in the west, a mere tradition of origin. So when a member of a tribe rises to such importance as to become independent of tribal authority, he practically founds a new tribe, even though he may still occupy the territory formerly held as part of the old tribal domain; as, for instance, appears to have been the case with the Barár section of the Sidhu Jats. Perhaps the most striking instance of the degree in which tribal divisions depend upon political and territorial independence, is afforded by the Biloch

[1] There is another possible explanation of the tradition, and that is that the caste was inherited in the female line. There is no inconsiderable weight of evidence to show that this was the custom, at any rate among certain classes, within comparatively recent times. But the matter, like all other similar matters, needs further examination.

tribes, who were orginally five. Of these two, the Rind and Lashári, rose to prominence and divided the nation into two corresponding sections. As time went on the nation broke up into a number of independent tribes, each with a separate territory and organisation of its own; and now, though every Biloch refers himself to either Rind or Lashári stock, the names are but a tradition of origin, and in the Panjáb at least no Rind or Lashári tribe can be said to exist as such. The groups of tribes found in different parts of the Province who claim common descent from some one of the great Rájpút races, the Bhatti, Chauhán, Punwár, and the like, are instances of the same process. The local tribes are now independent units, and can hardly be included under the original tribal name save as a symbol of origin. Thus the line of demarcation between tribe and clan is no better defined than is that between caste and tribe. As soon as a section of a caste abandons the customs of the parent stock, whether as regards hereditary occupation or social habits, it tends to become a new caste. As soon as a clan separates itself from the territory and organisation of the parent tribe, it tends to become a new tribe. Where the Indian tribal and caste restrictions upon intermarriage are still observed, the best definition would probably be obtained by taking endogamy and [P. 181] exogamy as the differentiæ of the caste and tribe respectively; a caste being the smallest group outside which, and a tribe the largest group within which marriage is forbidden. But in a great part of the Panjáb this test does not apply.

351. Tribal divisions among the priestly and mercantile castes.—In the case of the castes or classes who, not being essentially landowners, possess no political or territorial organisation, the basis of tribal division is very different. Here we have no compact tribes based upon real or fictitious community of blood and occupying tribal territories. The Bráhman has almost invariably accompanied his clients in their migrations; and indeed it will sometimes be found that the Bráhmans of a tribe or of a group of village communities, being too small in number to be independent, have kept up the connection with their place of origin long after it has fallen into neglect or even oblivion among the landowning communities with whom they dwell. Thus we find Bráhmans of different *gotras* or clans scattered haphazard over the country without any sort of tribal localization, and the same is true of the mercantile classes also. In both cases the divisions are wholly based upon real or imaginary common descent. The *gotras* of the Bráhmans, the clans of the Khatris and Aroras are innumerable; but they are not localised, and are therefore probably more permanent than are the territorial tribes of the landowners. This absence of tribal organisation is perhaps one of the reasons why, of all classes of the community, the Bráhmans and traders observe most strictly the artificial rules which preserve the integrity of caste organisation. How far the Brahminical *gotra* is really tribal is a distinct question to which I shall presently return.

But in the case of both the priestly and the mercantile classes, we find that their castes are broken up into sections, too large and too devoid of cohesion to be called tribes, and approaching much more nearly to separate castes, both in the actual effect of the divisions upon social intercourse and intermarriage, and probably also in their origin. These divisions are generally known by geographical designations, such as the Gaur Bráhmans of the ancient Gaur and the Sársút Bráhmans of the Saruswati and the Panjáb, the Uttarádhi Aroras of the north and the Dakhani Aroras of the south, the

Agarwál Banyas of Agroha and the Oswál Banyas of Osia. But the present distinction between these sections is as a rule based upon difference of social and religious customs. It is not unnatural that, in the course of ages, the strictness with which the artificial restrictions which regulate social and caste matters are observed should vary in different parts of the country; and it is no less natural that, where the two standards come into contact, those whose standard is the stricter should look down upon those whose practice is more lax. The Gaur Bráhman sees with horror his Sársút brother eat bread from the hands of other than Bráhmans, and do a thousand things which to him would be pollution. The result is that the Gaur refuses to eat or intermarry with the Sársút, and that for all practical purposes the sections are not one but two castes; far more so indeed than, for instance, the Jat and the Gújar. Nor does it seem to me impossible that these sections may in some cases represent real diversity of race or origin; that the Gaurs may have been the Bráhmans of Gaur and the Sársúts the Bráhmans of the Panjáb, both called Bráhmans because they were priests, but having nothing else in common. Again, among some of the Panjáb trading castes great sections have been fixed within recent times, which are based not upon geographical distribution, but upon voluntary divergence of social custom. Such are the great Dhaighar, Chárzáti and other sections of the Khatrís described under that caste heading. Throughout all these great sections, whether geographical or social, the same tribal divisions are commonly found unchanged. The tribes or clans of the Gaur and Sársút Bráhmans, of the Uttarádhi and Dakhani Aroras, of the Agarwál and Oswál Banya are in great part identical. Now where these divisions are really tribal, and based upon common descent, this must mean that the tribal divisions preceded the divergence of custom which resulted in the formation of what I have here called sections, and that the original stock was one and the same. But where, as is often the case, they are mere Bráhmnical *gotras*, I do not think that this necessarily follows.[1]

352. Tribal divisions among artisan and menial castes.—Among the artisan and menial castes we find precisely the same great sections, based either upon differences of custom which in turn depend upon geographical distribution or, I believe in very many cases indeed, upon difference of origin, one section of an industrial caste being descended from Jats who have sunk in the social scale, another perhaps from Ahírs, while a third is the original stock to which the industry has been hereditary beyond the memory of the tribe. The Chamár of the middle Satluj will not intermarry with the Jatia Chamár of the Dehli Territory because the latter works in the skins of impure animals; the Suthár carpenter from Sindh looks down upon and abstains from marriage with the Kháti of the Málwa; and so forth throughout the list. Among the menial castes moreover, as among the priestly and mercantile, we have a double classification: and by the side of the great sections we find what correspond with tribal divisions. But among the menial castes, or at least among those who occupy the position of hereditary village servants, I believe that these divisions often have their origin rather in allegiance to the tribal master than in any theory of common descent. It has often been noticed that the menial castes denote their tribal sub-divisions by names famous in political history, such as Bhatti, Khokhar or Chauhán; and our present papers furnish abundant instances. Now on the frontier a Lohár who is attached to the village of the Muhammadzai tribe will call himself Lohár Muhammadzai, while one

[1] See further section 353 on the next page.

who lives in the service of the Daulatkhel will call himself Lohár Daulatkhel. There can be no doubt that the connection between the village menials and the agricultural communities whom they serve was in old times hereditary and not voluntary, and that the former were in every sense of the word *adscripti glebæ*. In fact, as I shall presently explain in greater detail, we still find the tribal organisation of the territorial owners of a tract perpetuated in great integrity by the territorial organisation of the village menials, where all but its memory has died out among their masters. It seems to me more than probable that in old days, when menials were bound more closely to the tribes they served, the names of those tribes were used to distinguish the several groups of menials; and that for instance Chamárs serving Bhattis would be called Chamár tribe Bhatti, and those serving Khokhars called Chamár tribe Khokhar. When the bonds grew less rigid and a change of masters became possible, the old name would be retained though the reason for it had ceased to exist, and thus we should find Bhatti and Khokhar [P. 18 Chamárs scattered throughout the Province. In fact the process would be simply another instance of that substitution of the idea of subjection to a common authority for that of common blood as the basis of tribal division, regarding which I have already quoted Sir H. Maine's language in section 349.

353. The Brahminical gotras.—I have said that among the priestly and mercantile castes we find a set of divisions corresponding with the true tribal divisions of the landowning classes, which runs through the great geographical or social sections which I have described above. These divisions are, among the Khatris and Aroras, in all probability real tribes denoting common descent, or at any rate special association of some sort, at an earlier stage in the history of the caste, of the ancestors of all those who now bear the same tribal name. Among the Bráhmans and Banyas these divisions are known as *gotras*, and it is not so certain that their origin, among the Banyas at least, is tribal. The word *gotra*, more commonly known under the corrupted form of *got*, means a family or lineage, the descendants from a common ancestor, and it also means a flock, those who shelter within a common fold. The Bráhmans say that their *gotras* are named after the great Hindu Rishis, though it does not clearly appear whether the members of each *gotra* claim descent from the Rishi whose name it bears as from a carnal or as from a spiritual father. It is curious that the names of many of the founders of these *gotras* occur among the ancient genealogies of the prehistoric Rájpút dynasties, the Rájas in question being not merely namesakes of, but distinctly stated to be the actual founders of the *gotra*; and it would be strange if inquiry were to show that the priestly classes, like the menials just discussed, own their tribal divisions to the great families to whom their ancestors were attached.[1] At any rate, whatever their origin, the Brahminical *gotras* have among the Bráhmans become absolutely hereditary; and every Bráhman, whether Gaur, Sársút, Dákaut, or otherwise belongs to some one or other of these *gotras*. Thus, taking these great sections as tribes, the *gotra* is wider than the tribe; and while new tribes and clans can be and are constantly being formed, no new *go'ra* is possible.[2]

---

[1] For a curious instance of classification of Bráhmans into tribes by the command of a Rajput ruler, see the quotation from Mr. Barnes given on page 179. [Census Report.]

[2] Is it possible that the *gotra* is a relic of descent through the female line, like the corresponding phænomenon among the Australian and North American Indians? [Census Report.]

But the Brahminical *gotra* extends far beyond the body of Bráhmans; for the theory of the Hindu religion is that every Hindu, whatever be his caste, belongs to some one or other of them. The *gotra* thus defined is used only at marriage, on the occasion of *sankalpa*, and in similar formal ceremonies; and the great majority of the Hindu peasantry do not so much as know that they have a *gotra* at all, much less what it is. But all the stricter Hindu castes, such as the Banyas and Khatris and Aroras, know and recognize their *gotra*. Indeed the Banyas have, so far as I know, no tribal divisions within the great sections of Agarwál, Oswál and the like, except these Brahminical *gotras*. Thus the question suggests itself whether the universal currency of the same set of *gotras* throughout the whole Bráhman caste, and their adoption by the Banyas, is not due to a wish to conform with the rule of Hinduism just enunciated, rather than to any real community of descent denoted by a common *gotra*. In any case these *gotras* are of singularly little importance. Except to the priests and merchants and to some of the stricter and more educated classes they mean little or nothing; while although to those priests and merchants they do stand in some degree in the place of tribal divisions, yet as they are in no way localised their significance is almost wholly religious, and the divisions which are really important among these castes are what I have called the great sections. It matters little or nothing whether a Bráhman, a Banya, or an Arora is of the Gautama or of the Bháradwáj *gotra*; what we really want to know is whether he is Gaur or Sársút, Agarwál or Oswál, Uttarádhi or Dakhani. The horrible trouble and confusion which resulted in the Census from the fact that the peasantry of the eastern Panjáb call their tribes by the same word *got* as is commonly used for the Brahminical *gotra*, will be noticed presently.

354. Tribal divisions of women.—A curious question arose in the record of tribes in the Census schedules; namely, whether a woman changed her father's tribal name for that of her husband on marriage. There is no doubt whatever that the Brahminical *gotra* follows that of the husband; and the more educated enumerators, knowing this, often objected to record the *got* or tribe of the wife as different from that of the husband. I asked some of my friends to make enquiries as to the custom in various parts of the Province, but in many cases the *got* and *gotra* have evidently been confused in their investigations and replies. But on the whole the result seems to be as follows. With Bráhmans, Banyas, Khatris, Káyaths, and Aroras the woman's *got* follows that of her husband. But this is almost certainly the Brahminical *gotra*. In some of the cases it must be so, as the sections do not intermarry, and there is nothing else to change. Among the Khatrís it would be interesting to know whether a Kapúr woman marrying a Mahra man would be considered a Kapúr or a Mahra. Throughout the Western Plains Hindus change the clan; but here again they almost all belong to the castes mentioned above. In the hills and the sub-montane tracts the tribe is certainly changed; for in the lower hills there is a formal ceremony called *got kunála* or "the tribal trencher," at which the women of the tribe eat with the bride and thus admit her to the community. In the eastern districts the tribe is as certainly *not* changed at marriage, nor does a boy change it on adoption. It is born and dies unaltered with both man and woman. In Sirsa it does not change, for a man always speaks of his wife by her tribal and not by her personal name; and the same custom obtains among the Dehli Gújars. On the other hand in Fírozpur, which adjoins Sirsa, the custom of *got kunála* is said to obtain. Among the Musalmáns of the west the tribe does not appear to change by marriage; but if the wife is of standing which is nearly but not quite equal to that of her husband, she is often addressed by courtesy as belonging to the tribe of the latter. The point is practically important in this way. The diversity of custom which prevails, added to the interference of the educated enumerator, makes the record of tribal divisions for women of exceedingly uncertain value; and it would have been better to tabulate the males only for the several tribes and clans. At a future Census the enumerator should be directed to record the clan or tribe of a married woman as stated by her husband, whether the same as his own or different.

355. The tribal organisation of the people.—An extensive collection of facts bearing upon the tribal organisation of the people, together with a most valuable dissertation on the general subject, will be found in Vol. II of Mr. Tupper's treatise on *Panjáb Customary Law*. The Panjáb affords a peculiarly complete series of stages between the purely tribal organisation of the Pathán or Biloch of the frontier hills and the village communities of the Jamna districts. The territorial distribution of the frontier tribes in the fastnesses of their native mountains is strictly tribal. Each clan of each tribe has a tract allotted to it; and within that tract the families or small groups of nearly related families either lead a semi-nomad life, or inhabit rude villages round which lie the fields which they cultivate and the rough irrigation works which they have constructed. In these they have property, but beyond them there are no boundaries in the common pasture lands of the clan. Where the tribe or clan has occupied a tract within our border in sufficient numbers to undertake its cultivation, the distribution differs little from that obtaining beyond the border. We have indeed laid down boundaries which mark off areas held by groups of families; but these boundaries are often purely artificial, and include hamlets which are united by no common tie and separated from their neighbours by no line of demarcation save one based upon administrative convenience. When however the tribe conquered rather than occupied the tract, and its cultivation is still in the hands of the people whom they subjugated, we find that they did almost exactly what we have done in the case last described. They drew arbitrary boundaries which divided out the land into great blocks or village areas, and each clan or section of a clan took one of these blocks as its share, left the cultivating population scattered in small hamlets over the fields, and themselves occupied central villages of some strength and size. These two types are found more or less prevailing throughout the Western Plains and Salt-range Tract. But in the great grazing grounds we find, perhaps even more commonly than either of these, a third type which is not based upon any sort of tribal organisation. A miscellaneous collection of cultivators have broken up the land and so acquired rights in it, or have been settled by capitalists who acquired grants of land on condition of bringing it under cultivation. This form of settlement was especially encouraged under Sikh rule; when the cardinal principle of administration was to crush the gentry, to encourage cultivation, and to take so much from the actual cultivator as to leave nothing for the landlord. [P. 183]

356. In the east of the Province we find the village community about which so much has been written; and nowhere perhaps in more vigorous perfection than in the south-eastern districts. But it is a great mistake to suppose that the village community wholly supersedes tribal organisation. The tribal maps of the Panjáb when published will show how very generally tribes hold compact territories, even where the village communities are strongest. Where this is the case the villages of the tribe constitute one or more *thapas,* or tribal groups of village communities held together by feudal ties and by the fact or fiction of common ancestry. Under the Mughals the revenue administration used to be based upon these *thapas,* the revenue being assessed upon the group of villages as a whole, and being distributed among them by the headmen of the collective villages under the presidency of the headman of the parent village. So too, till our time the definite boundaries which now separate each village from its neighbours were very indefinitely marked even in the cultivated tracts, as is proved by the manner in which they zig-zag in and out among the fields; while in the common pastures they were probably almost unknown, as to this day the cattle of neighbouring villages belonging to the same tribe graze in common without reference to boundaries. The following description of the *thapa* organisation is taken from my settlement report of Karnál. The vigorous organisation of the priestly and menial castes, based upon the tribal organisation of their clients and masters, is especially interesting with reference to the remarks made in sections 351-52. It would be interesting to know whether the same holds good with the mercantile castes.

"A tribal community having obtained possession of a tract, in course of time it would be "inconvenient for them all to live together, and a part of the community would found a new "village, always on the edge of a drainage line from which their tanks would be filled. This pro- "cess would be repeated till the tract became dotted over with villages, all springing originally "from one parent village. The people describe the facts by saying that of several brothers one "settled in one village and one in another; but this no doubt means that the parts of the com- "munity that migrated consisted of integral families or groups of families descended in one "common branch from the ancestor. In this way were divided the many villages known by the "same name, with the addition of the words *kalán* and *khurd* (big and little). This by no means "implies that kalán is *larger* than khurd, but only that the elder branch settled in kalán.

"The group of villages so bound together by common descent form a *thapa,* and are con- "nected by sub-feudal ties which are still recognized, the village occupied by the descendants of "the common ancestor in the eldest line being, however small or reduced in circumstances, still "acknowledged as the head. To this day when a headman dies, the other villages of the *thapa* "assemble to instal his heir, and the turban of the parent village is first tied on his head. When "Bráhmans and the brotherhood are fed on the occasion of deaths, &c., it is from the *thapa* "villages that they are collected; and the Bráhmans of the head village are fed first, and receive "double fees. So among the menial castes, who still retain an internal organization of far greater "vitality than the higher castes now possess, the representative of the head village is always the "foreman of the caste jury which is assembled from the *thapa* villages to hear and decide disputes. "In old days the subordinate villages used to pay some small feudal fees to the head village on "the day of the great Diwáli. The head village is still called 'the great village,' the 'turban "'village,' 'the village of origin,' or 'the *tika* village,' *tika* being the sign of authority formally "impressed in old days on the forehead of the heir of a deceased leader in the presence of the "assembled *thapa.* In one case a village told me that it had changed its *thapa* because there "were so many Bráhmans in its original *thapa* that it found it expensive to feed them. I spoke "to the original *tika* village about it, and they said that no village *could* change its *thapa,* and "quoted the proverb[1] 'A son may forget his sonship; but not a mother her motherhood.'"

It is curious to note how the fiction of common descent is preserved when strangers are admitted into these tribal groups or village communities. The stranger who receives by gift a share of another's land is called a *bhúmbhái* or "earth brother;" and if a landowner of a tribe other than that of the original owners is asked how he acquired property in the village, his invariable answer is "they settled me as a brother."

357. Marriage and intermarriage between tribes.—The restrictions upon intermarriage will be given in some detail in Part II of Chapter VII in

[1] Mr. Douie notes that the members of all the villages included in the *thapa* make offerings once a year at the *Satti* of the *tika* village. (See paragraph 220 *supra.*)

treating of civil condition; and it is unnecessary to repeat the information here. The custom as to intermarriage in the hills will be found described in the sections on Rájpúts of the eastern hills, Ráthis and Ráwats, and Kolis and [P. 184]
Dágis; while the curious rule against taking a bride from a village marching with one's own has already been discussed in section 136. The marriage customs of the people of Karnál will be found minutely described at pages 127 to 134 of my settlement report on that district. A brief notice of some curious customs will be found in the present chapter under the head of Jats of the western sub-montane. The subject is one of great interest and value, and sadly needs more detailed inquiry. Customs of this sort are of all others the most persistent, and often throw most valuable light upon the origin and affinities of the tribes. The reason why I allude to the subject in this place is, because I wish to point out how obviously the rules and customs regulating marriage point to the former existence of marriage by capture and, perhaps less obviously, of an intermediate stage when the capture had become fictitious, but the fiction was enacted with greater veri-similitude than now-a-days. Some of the suggestions I am about to make may very probably be fanciful; but the general tendency of the facts is beyond the possibility of a doubt. The strict rule of tribal exogamy which still binds all classes both Hindu and Musalmán throughout the Eastern Plains, excepting however the priests and traders who observe only the prohibitions of the Sanskrit scriptures; especially the rule against marrying from a neighbouring village; the formal nature of the wedding procession, which must be as far as possible mounted on horses, and in which only males may take part; the preparatory oiling of the bridegroom, the similar treatment of the bride being perhaps a later institution; all point to marriage by capture. So does the use of the mark of the bloody hand at both villages. The marking all the turnings from the village gate to the bride's house may be a survival of a very common intermediate stage, where the bridegroom visits the bride by stealth. The rule that the procession must reach the girl's village after midday, and must not enter the village, but remain outside in a place allotted to them; the fight between the girl's and boy's parties at the door of the bride's house; the rule that the girl shall wear nothing belonging to herself; the hiding of the girl from the boy's people at the wedding ceremony; all point to marriage by capture. So do the rule by which the boy's party must not accept food at the hands of the girl's people after the wedding, and must pay them for what they eat on the succeeding night, and the fiction by which the girl's father is compelled to ignore all payment of money by the bridegroom's friends. The bloody hand stamped on the shoulder of the boy's father by the girl's mother as he departs, and the custom which directs the girl to go off bewailing some one of her male relatives who has lately died, saying "Oh my father is dead," or "Oh my brother is dead," are very marked; as is the fight with sticks between the bride and bridegroom. Finally we have the rule that after the ceremonial goings and comings are over, the wife must never visit her father's house without his special leave; and the fact that—

"the village into which his daughter is married is utterly tabooed for her father, her elder brother, "and all near elder relatives. They may not go into it or even drink water from a well in that "village, for it is shameful to take anything from one's daughter or her belongings. Even her "more distant elder relations will not eat or drink from the house into which the girl is married, "though they do not taboo the whole village. The boy's father can go to the girl's village by leave "of her father, but not without."

Similarly, all words denoting male relations by marriage are commonly used as terms of abuse; as, for instance, *súsra, sála, baknoi, jawái,* or father-in-law, wife's brother, sister's husband, and daughter's husband. Of these the first two are considered so offensive, that they are seldom used in their ordinary sense.[1]

358. Social intercourse between castes.—The rules regulating social intercourse between different castes as they exist in the Jamna districts are given in the following quotation from the Karnál Settlement Report.

"Broadly speaking, no superior tribe will eat or drink from the hands or vessels of an inferior "one, or smoke its pipes. But the reputed purifying influences of fire especially as exercised upon "*ghi* and sugar, and the superior cleanliness of metal over earthen vessels, are the foundation of a "broad distinction. All food is divided into *pakki roti*, or fried dry with *ghi*, and *kachchi roti*, or "not so treated. Thus, among the Hindus a Gújráti Bráhman will eat *pakki*, but not *kachchi* "*roti*, from a Gaur, a Gaur from a Taga, any Bráhman or Taga from a Rájpút, any Bráhman, "Taga or Rájpút from a Ját, Gújar, or Ror. Excepting Bráhmans and Tagas, each caste will "drink water from a metal vessel if previously scoured with earth (*mánjna*), and will smoke from a "pipe with a brass bowl, taking out the stem and using the hand with the fingers closed instead, "from the same people with whom they will eat *pakki* bread; but they will not drink or smoke "from earthen vessels, or use the same pipe-stem, except with those whose *kachchi* bread they can "eat. Játs, Gújars, Rors, Rahbáris and Ahírs eat and drink in common without any scruples. "These again will eat a goldsmith's *pakki* bread, but not in his house; and they used to smoke "with carpenters, but are ceasing to do so. Musalmáns have lately become much less strict about "these rules as governing their intercourse among themselves, and many of them now eat from "any respectable Musalmán's hand, especially in the cities. And, subject strictly to the above "rules, any Musalmán will eat and drink without scruple from a Hindu; but no Hindu will touch "either *pakki* or *kachchi* from any Musalmán, and will often throw it away if only a Musalmán's "shadow falls upon it, partly perhaps because Musalmáns eat from earthen vessels, which no "Hindu can do unless the vessel has never been used before. This affords an easy mode of telling "whether a deserted site has been held by Musalmáns or Hindus. If the latter, there will be "numbers of little earthen saucers (*rikábis*) found on the spot. Bráhmans and Rájpúts will not "eat from any one below a Ját, Gújar, or Ror, while these three tribes themselves do not as a "rule eat or drink with any of the menial castes; and the following castes are absolutely impure "owing to their occupation and habits, and their mere touch defiles food; leather-maker, washer-"man, barber, blacksmith, dyer (*chhímpi*), sweeper, *dúm*, and *dhának*. The potter is also looked "upon as of doubtful purity. The pipes of a village, being often left about in the common rooms "and fields, are generally distinguished by a piece of something tied round the stem—blue rag for "a Musalmán, red for a Hindu, leather for a *Chamár*, string for a sweeper, and so forth; so that "a friend wishing for a smoke may not defile himself by mistake.

"*Gur* and most sweetmeats can be eaten from almost anybody's hand, even from that of a "leather-worker or sweeper; but in this case they must be whole, not broken."

The extraordinary state of matters in the hills is described under the heads Hill Menials, and Kolis and Dágis. In the west of the Province, where all caste restrictions are so lax, any Musalmán will eat from the hands of any respectable member of the same faith, while even Hindus are much less strict than in the east. So in the Sikh tract also; but here the rule against a Hindu eating from the hand of a Musalmán seems to be even more strict than in the east. In all parts of the Province and among all classes any sort of intercourse with the impure castes, whether polluted by their occupation or by the nature of their food, is scrupulously avoided.

Community of food is formally used as an outward and visible token of
[P. 185] community of blood; and any ceremony in which the tribe, clan, or other agnatic group takes a part as such, generally includes some sort of formal

[1] Mr. Wilson writes: "There is a very general rule against speaking of one's wife's father as "'father-in-law' (*súsra*). The Musalmáns of Sirsa call him 'uncle' (*táya* or *chácha*); the "Bráhmans of Gurgáon, 'Pandit Ji' or 'Misr Ji;' the Káyaths, 'Rai Sáhib;' the Banyas, 'Lála "Sáhib' or 'Sáh Ji;' the Meos, 'Chaudhri' or 'Muqaddam' or—a specially Meo usage—*dokra* "or 'old man' (see Fallon); insomuch that if you call a Meo woman *dokri*, she will fly at you "with 'Do you call me your mother-in-law!'; while if you address her as *burhya*, which really "means exactly the same thing, she will reply 'Very well, my son! Very well!'"

eating together or *confarreatio*, more especially when the object of the ceremony is to admit a new member into the group, as at adoption or marriage.[1]

359 General distribution of agricultural castes.—Abstract No. 64 on the next page* shows the general distribution of castes throughout the Province, the figures representing the proportion borne by each group of castes to every thousand of total population. *P. 28-9.

The distribution of each caste will be discussed more fully when the caste itself comes under consideration. It will of course be understood that the castes are grouped very roughly. Indeed it will be apparent from the following pages that any but the roughest classification is impossible, for not only is the class within which any given caste should fall incapable of exact definition, but it varies in different parts of the Province. Still some sort of classification was necessary on which to arrange the chapter, and I have therefore divided the various castes and tribes into three great groups. The first or landowning and agricultural group comprises half of the total population of the Panjáb, and is even more important socially, administratively, and politically than it is numerically. It is divided into six sections. The first includes the two great frontier races, the Biloches and Patháns; and with the latter I have taken the Tanáoli, Tájik and Hazára, as closely allied to them if not really entitled to be ranked with them. Next follows the great Jat race, and after that the Rájpúts, with the Thákars and Ráthis whom it is so impossible to separate from them, and one or two minor castes which are perhaps rather Rájpút tribes than separate castes. The next class, the minor dominant tribes, includes all those castes which, while hardly less important in their particular territories, are less numerous and less widely distributed than the four great races already specified. Such are the Gakkhars and Awáns of the Salt-range Tract, the Kharrals and Dáúdpotras of the Western Plains, the Dogars and Rors of the Eastern Plains, the Meos of Gurgáon, and the Gújars of the hills. Next follow the minor agricultural tribes, the Sainis, Aráíns, Kanets, Ghiraths, Ahírs, Mahtams and the like, who, while forming a very important factor in the agricultural community of the Panjáb, occupy a social and political position of far less importance than that of the dominant tribes. The last class is headed Foreign Races, and includes Shekhs, Mughals, Túrks, and the like, most of whom perhaps have no real title to the name under which they have returned themselves, while many of them own no land and are mere artisans, though these cannot be separated from the still greater number who are landowners.

360. The distribution of these classes is very marked. The Biloches and Patháns are of course chiefly to be found in the trans-Indus districts; but while the latter form the great bulk of the group in the districts where they prevail, the former, who have settled in the Province at a far more recent date, are accompanied by a very large class of inferior cultivating classes of all castes who are, in accordance with the custom of the lower Indus, grouped under the comprehensive name of Jat, a term whose significance is in these parts occupational as much as ethnic. Setting these districts aside, the Jats are to be found in greatest predominance in the great Sikh States and districts, and in the south-east of the Province in Rohtak and Hissár. In the sub-montane districts, the Salt-range Tract, and Kángra,

[1] For instance, the ceremony of *got kunála* described in section 354. The eating together very commonly takes the form of a distribution of *gur* or sweatmeats.

and throughout the cis-Indus districts of the Western Plains, excepting Muzaffargarh which goes with the trans-Indus group, the Rájpút to a great extent takes the place of the Jat. In the Hill States, with the exception of Chamba, Rájpúts are few, and are important by their social and political position rather than by their numbers. But the figures are of no very certain significance, since the line of demarcation between Thakar and Ráthi who have been classed with Rájpúts, and Kanets and Giraths who have been classed as minor agricultural tribes, is exceedingly difficult to draw, and the abnormal figures for Chamba are due to this cause. The proportion of minor dominant tribes naturally varies from district to district, and their distribution is discussed in the section devoted to their consideration. The same may be said of the minor agricultural castes, the group being too miscellaneous in its composition for its distribution to present very general features. But it is noticeable that where the Jat, who prefers to do his own cultivation is numerous, these castes are fonnd only in small numbers, while they bear the highest proportion to total population in those tracts where the Hill Rájpút, who looks upon agriculture as degrading, is most largely represented. Taking the landowning and agricultural castes as a whole, they form the largest proportion of the population in the trans-Indus districts; and this is due to the freedom from occupational restraints which I have already noticed as prevailing on the frontier, a very large proportion of the industrial and menial work being done on the frontier by members of the dominant and agricultural tribes, and not, as in the rest of the Province, by separate castes. They are least numerous in the sub-montane tract and in the Eastern Plains, where they are assisted in the cultivation by a numerous class of village menials, and where, the Hindu religion being most prevalent and commerce most important, the religious and mercantile elements of societies are most numerous.

361. General distribution of professional castes.—The next great group consists of the priestly, ascetic, professional, and mercantile castes, and includes people of very different social positions, from the priestly Bráhman to the wandering pedlar. As a whole they occupy a position superior to that of the landowning classes if measured by a religious standard, for the great mercantile castes come next after the Bráhmans in strictness of religious observance; but indefinitely inferior if the comparison be made from a social or political standpoint. The Bráhmans are naturally most numerous in the Hindu and the Saiyads in the Musalmán portions of the Province, the former being extraordinarily numerous in the hills where Hinduism is stronger than in any other part of the Panjáb. The ascetic orders are chiefly to be found in the eastern and central districts, partly perhaps because they are more common among Hindus than among Mahomedans, but still more I suspect because it is in these districts that the wealth of the Province is concentrated, and in them that there is most hope for an idle man who wishes to live at the expense of his fellows. The minor professional group consists of Náís, [P. 187] Mírásis, Jogis, and the like, and its numbers are tolerably constant throughout the cis-Indus Panjáb, while beyond the Indus it is hardly represented. Taking the professional group as a whole, and especially the religious element, its numbers decrease steadily from east to west; chiefly because the Bráhmans, who form an integral portion of the stock from which the Hindu population has chiefly sprung, are naturally far more numerous than the Saiyads, who are but foreign immigrants in the Panjáb. The mercantile castes are found in

Abstract No. 64, showing the General Distribution of Castes for Districts and States.

	Landowning and Agricultural.							Professional and Mercantile Caste.							Vagrants. Menials and Artisans.											
	1	2	3	4	5	6	1 to 6.	7	8	9	10	7 to 10	11	12	13	14	15	16	17	18	19	20	21	22	23	13 to 23.
	Biloch and Pathán, &c.	Jat	Rájpút, &c.	Minor Dominant Tribes.	Minor Agricultural Tribes.	Foreign Races.	Total Landowning and Agricultural Castes.	Bráhmans, &c.	Saiyid, &c.	Faqirs.	Minor Professional Castes.	Total Professional Castes.	Mercantile Castes.	Miscellaneous Castes.	Vagrant Castes.	Scavengers.	Leather-workers.	Weavers.	Watermen and Cooks.	Blacksmiths and Carpenters.	Potters.	Washermen and Dyers.	Oilmen, &c.	Other Artisans.	Hill Menials.	Total Vagrant Menial and Artisan Castes.
Dehli ...	27	166	53	71	60	87	464	95	14	19	30	158	79	7	1	54	98	14	26	26	21	12	17	8	7	284
Gurgáon ...	11	100	41	200	116	18	486	82	7	27	31	147	63	1	9	39	111	11	22	25	22	11	30	9	9	298
Karnál ...	10	153	87	101	52	23	426	89	7	24	39	159	72	1	4	57	87	21	55	38	24	17	25	9	...	337
Hissar ...	6	268	121	27	40	9	471	63	4	15	29	111	93	17	17	53	99	3	9	37	39	19	41	8	1	326
Rohtak ...	13	330	54	5	44	16	462	105	2	21	32	160	79	1	4	72	90	2	21	35	22	18	22	8	...	292
Sirsa ...	11	253	185	5	34	14	502	22	3	11	32	68	66	3	33	73	83	11	15	35	64	15	21	10	...	360
Ambála ...	10	160	90	53	106	28	447	61	8	19	30	118	54	6	3	40	132	29	47	40	15	12	30	17	2	367
Lúdhiána ...	7	360	53	59	46	11	536	41	6	31	29	107	49	4	5	30	109	24	27	44	13	15	24	10	...	301
Simla ...	33	5	43	4	228	90	403	65	7	4	9	85	44	9	3	43	83	22	9	41	4	23	5	31	106	370
Jálandhar ...	6	208	59	40	187	14	514	39	9	24	30	102	41	2	7	41	121	20	34	51	16	18	18	10	2	338
Hushyárpur ...	8	162	113	92	143	10	528	86	4	18	23	131	32	...	...	20	127	23	28	49	12	12	17	8	11	307
Kángra ...	1	15	222	12	242	2	494	151	...	9	22	182	28	6	1	1	71	38	18	46	14	10	11	5	74	289
Amritsar ...	6	230	31	12	68	12	359	39	7	22	34	102	74	37	8	120	28	47	54	61	33	21	27	10	15	424
Gurdáspur ...	12	157	95	54	93	16	427	58	7	14	36	115	48	8	8	69	44	49	46	57	21	16	23	7	55	395
Siálkot ...	4	264	57	32	66	16	439	36	15	12	39	102	65	19	12	78	26	27	37	60	29	20	17	9	58	373
Lahore ...	14	171	59	18	133	23	418	23	9	8	30	70	100	15	15	107	25	39	53	50	34	19	29	11	5	387
Gújránwala ...	6	282	59	5	36	15	403	29	17	8	46	100	92	11	9	94	36	43	37	65	44	20	20	12	8	338
Fírozpur ..	8	287	61	41	97	12	506	19	7	11	26	63	58	5	20	107	40	31	39	44	23	19	21	9	...	362

Ráwalpindi ...	45	58	177	197	52	62	591	23	25	2	27	77	73	29	3	27	28	45	12	42	18	16	16	16	...	219
Jahlam ...	13	150	98	210	54	33	558	17	25	3	33	78	90	16	...	42	37	49	16	42	17	17	19	13	...	252
Gujrat ...	4	263	32	156	33	19	507	13	27	2	32	74	80	48	3	56	48	35	30	51	24	16	15	9	3	289
Shahpur ...	28	82	196	141	22	24	493	13	22	5	39	79	126	...	3	67	36	53	29	36	28	14	17	9	...	292
Multán ...	50	187	108	26	56	32	459	8	21	7	28	64	175	2	11	53	34	43	33	28	25	24	13	10	...	274
Jhang ...	42	122	227	34	15	22	462	13	18	9	37	77	164	1	1	53	36	61	32	29	39	14	14	5	...	284
Montgomery ...	37	100	132	47	119	15	450	7	14	9	39	69	142	1	12	68	34	48	52	31	42	18	17	11	...	333
Muzaffargrh ...	184	323	23	5	21	18	574	5	24	6	24	59	115	1	12	33	33	41	41	31	20	19	10	6	...	246
D. I. Khan ...	259	465	4	2	2	15	747	8	20	3	12	43	113	...	1	20	11	13	16	12	6	6	4	2	...	91
D. G. Khan ...	346	442	7	1	2	14	812	6	24	2	5	37	112	...	4	13	3	2	5	3	...	2	1	1	...	34
Bannú ...	431	162	10	63	12	36	714	6	37	2	23	68	87	...	...	18	12	11	15	31	13	7	9	11	...	127
Pesháwar ...	474	8	5	188	37	32	744	6	12	1	17	36	37	22	1	13	13	26	3	32	13	11	15	8	...	135
Hazára ...	257	1	61	349	25	33	726	11	38	1	15	65	38	36	...	6	16	29	4	34	9	10	7	3	...	118
Kohát ...	643	8	11	90	6	25	783	5	44	1	21	71	46	1	...	7	11	10	6	33	7	7	9	5	...	95
British Territory	**62**	**189**	**82**	**74**	**75**	**22**	**504**	**43**	**13**	**12**	**29**	**97**	**74**	**11**	**5**	**54**	**59**	**30**	**30**	**41**	**22**	**15**	**20**	**9**	**11**	**296**
Patiála ...	6	308	46	30	84	11	485	64	5	24	30	123	70	1	8	50	100	15	25	41	19	12	23	11	8	312
Nábha ...	8	326	50	23	83	9	499	69	4	25	32	130	72	...	4	46	98	18	22	46	19	14	17	9	...	293
Kapúrthala ...	4	155	80	40	224	12	515	32	11	29	29	101	41	1	5	65	65	29	49	48	19	17	26	9	2	334
Jind	6	350	41	12	44	17	470	110	1	24	37	172	71	1	12	58	90	5	20	38	21	18	21	8	...	291
Faridkot ...	6	369	44	21	27	9	476	21	1	17	28	67	58	1	42	138	46	27	25	53	17	17	27	5	...	397
Maler Kotla ..	16	328	48	34	88	15	529	36	12	24	32	104	65	3	4	22	105	24	23	48	16	12	24	8	...	286
Kalsia ...	10	167	51	71	100	10	409	52	3	23	32	110	61	3	5	46	142	55	48	45	15	13	33	8	...	410
Total East. Plains	*7*	*296*	*50*	*28*	*94*	*12*	*487*	*64*	*5*	*24*	*31*	*124*	*68*	*1*	*8*	*54*	*94*	*17*	*27*	*43*	*19*	*14*	*23*	*10*	*4*	*313*
Baháwalpur ...	103	208	159	30	54	29	583	6	16	3	25	50	109	...	13	32	31	30	64	22	19	18	9	6	10	254
Mandi ...	2	2	47	9	478	1	539	109	...	5	6	120	30	...	3	...	56	24	2	17	10	4	5	3	182	306
Chamba ...	3	3	376	8	97	20	507	133	.	6	17	156	17	...	...	1	42	20	5	30	13	3	2	2	194	312
Náhan ...	2	2	28	22	345	4	403	49	1	4	120	174	27	1	7	6	40	6	16	27	2	2	4	12	275	397
Bilászpur ...	1	17	93	36	240	1	388	286	...	6	8	300	25	2	3	1	96	55	21	26	10	9	5	5	53	284
Bashahr ...	...	...	33	...	606	1	640	78	...	2	2	82	5	...	9	...	1	...	1	32	1	...	...	2	222	268
Nalagarh ...	5	15	18	168	307	9	522	107	1	11	16	135	22	...	4	12	108	12	8	26	8	8	11	7	105	309
Suket ...	1	0	34	2	426	...	469	127	...	5	8	140	21	...	6	1	48	17	3	39	6	1	2	2	240	365
Total Hill States	*2*	*5*	*92*	*23*	*342*	*6*	*470*	*134*	*1*	*5*	*39*	*179*	*21*	...	*5*	*2*	*54*	*17*	*7*	*26*	*8*	*3*	*3*	*6*	*190*	*321*
British Territory	**62**	**189**	**82**	**74**	**75**	**22**	**504**	**43**	**13**	**12**	**29**	**97**	**74**	**11**	**5**	**54**	**59**	**30**	**30**	**41**	**22**	**15**	**20**	**9**	**11**	**296**
Native States ...	**20**	**225**	**75**	**27**	**142**	**14**	**503**	**70**	**6**	**17**	**29**	**122**	**64**	...	**10**	**41**	**77**	**19**	**28**	**36**	**17**	**13**	**18**	**8**	**40**	**307**
Province ...	**56**	**195**	**81**	**67**	**89**	**21**	**509**	**48**	**12**	**13**	**29**	**102**	**71**	**9**	**6**	**52**	**62**	**29**	**31**	**40**	**21**	**15**	**19**	**8**	**15**	**298**

greatest abundance in the south-western districts; not because commerce is there peculiarly extensive, but because the Aroras, the principal mercantile castes of these parts, are not mere traders, but largely follow all sorts of occupations both industrial and agricultural. Setting these districts aside the trading-castes are least numerous in the hills, where commerce is very much in the hands of the Bráhmans. The miscellaneous class is largely composed of Kashmíris, who are chiefly to be found in the districts on the Kashmír border, and in the great Kashmíri colonies of Amritsar and Lúdhiána.

362. **General distribution of menial castes.**—The last of the three groups comprises all the lower strata of society, the vagrant, criminal, and gipsy tribes, the village menials, and the industrial classes. I shall show when I come to discuss these castes in greater detail, how wholly impossible it is to class them by occupation with even approximate accuracy. Thus the classes into which I have divided them in the abstract have no very definite significance. Still certain broad facts are brought out by the figures. The vagrant tribes are chiefly to be found in two parts of the Province, on the Rájpútána border and under the central and western hills. Among the village menial castes who perform so large a part of the agricultural labour in the Panjáb, namely the leather-workers, scavengers and watermen, the leather-workers prevail throughout the eastern districts, the hills and the great Sikh states. In the centre of the Panjáb, and to a less degree in the Western Plains, their place is taken by the scavengers, and partly by the watermen. The menial and industrial class as a whole is most numerous in the hills where they have much of the cultivation in their hands, and in the sub-montane and central districts where wealth is greatest and the standard of cultivation highest. It is curiously scanty in the west, and particularly on the Indus frontier; and this partly because, as I have already pointed out, the hereditary restrictions upon occupation are more lax, and the poor Pathán thinks it no shame to earn his bread by callings which would involve social degradation where caste-feeling is stronger; but also very largely because on the lower Indus the menial who cultivates becomes a Jat by mere virtue of the fact, and is classed as such, whereas in the rest of the Panjáb he would have retained his menial caste unaltered. In Sirsa, and to a less degree in Hissár, the exact opposite is the case. There the menial classes are more numerous than in the neighbouring districts because the tract is to a great extent newly settled, and land is so plentiful and the demand for agricultural labour so great that the lower classes have flocked into these districts, and though retaining at present their caste unaltered, have risen in the social scale by the acquisition of land or at least by the substitution of husbandry for menial callings.

363. **Arrangement and contents of the caste-chapter.**—The rough classification adopted in Abstract No. 64 on the opposite page* will serve as a clue to the arrangement of the detailed description of the various castes. A complete index of castes and tribes will be found at the end of the volume. I shall close this part of the chapter by discussing the system adopted for the record of castes and tribes and their sub-division at the present Census, and the nature of the results obtained. The matter is one of considerable moment, and the system followed has been the subject of adverse criticism both within and without the Province. The tribal constitution of the population possesses much more political and administrative importance in the

*P. 28-

Panjáb than in most other parts of Northern India, and indeed it may be said that the statistics which display it are almost the most valuable results of a Panjáb Census. The remaining parts of the chapter will be devoted to an examination of the figures for each caste, and a description of the caste so far as my knowledge enables me to describe it. The crudeness and imperfection of this portion of the work are to me a source of great regret. It is not only that our knowledge is as nothing compared with our ignorance of the subject; that is unavoidable. But I have to feel that of the information that I have collected only a portion has been utilised, while even that portion has been hastily put on record without any attempt to arrange or digest the material. I had intended to make some attempt at classification of the various castes based in some measure upon what appeared to be their ethnic affinities, and to examine carefully the question of the probable origin of each with the help of the whole of my material; and indeed I have carried out this intention to some extent with regard to the Biloch and Pathán tribes, the sections on which were written before orders regarding the early completion of the report were received. But as regards the remaining castes and tribes the time allowed me was too short to permit of any such treatment of the subject; and I was compelled to arrange the castes roughly in classes, and to content myself with stating the leading facts regarding each. The chapter has been written backwards, beginning from the end, and I have not been able even to read over again what I had written before sending it to press. As I proceeded with the work faults in the classification became only too apparent, new lights were thrown upon what had gone before, and new facts were brought to light. There was no time to re-write what had once been written, and all that I could do was to add the new to the old. Thus I shall often be found to repeat myself, the sequence of ideas will often appear to be broken and irregular, and even conflicting statements may have escaped my notice. But the present chapter must be taken as only a rough preliminary outline of the subject. Detailed tables of tribes and clans are now in course of preparation which will embody all the sub-divisions of castes entered in the schedules of the present Census. Maps showing the distribution of the landowning castes and tribes have been prepared for each district and state and though it would have been impossible without great delay and expense to reproduce them with the present Report, I hope that the material thus collected will be more fully utilised on some future occasion. One apparent omission in my treatment of the subject calls for a word of explanation. I had prepared tables comparing the caste figures of the present with those of the last Census. But I found that the classification followed in 1868 had so evidently varied from district to district that the figures were devoid of any determinate meaning, and it would have been sheer waste of time to attempt any such comparison. To take one instance only, I find that in the Census of 1868, of 205,000 Musalmán Jats returned for the Multán division,
[P. 188] 159,000 are in Muzaffargarh, 29,000 in Montgomery, 17,000 in Jhang, and only 63 in Multán. In Dera Ismáíl Khán and Sháhpur this column is actually blank.

364. Scheme adopted for the record of castes and tribes.—Unless I have utterly failed to express the facts, a perusal of the foregoing paragraphs will have made it clear that we have three main units of social and ethnic classification to deal with in the Panjáb; the caste or race, the tribe proper, and what I have for want of a better word called the section of the caste. Now these three units are of very different value in different parts of the Province and among various classes of the community. In the east caste is of primary importance; among the landowning communities of the west it is little more than a tradition of ancient origin. Among the agricultural

classes the tribe is most important, and in the west it is the one great fact to be ascertained; among the priestly and mercantile classes it is almost meaningless, and what we want is the section of the caste. What we did was to attempt to record all three facts, where they existed, intending afterwards to select our figures. If we had asked for two only we should have run the risk of getting one we did not want and missing one that we did want. Of two Khatri brothers one would have returned himself as Khatri Kapúr and the other as Khatri Chárzáti; of two Bráhman brothers one would have appeared as Bráhman Sársút and the other as Bráhman Gautama; of two Biloch brothers one would have been recorded as Biloch Rind and the other as Biloch Laghári; tabulation would have given us wholly meaningless and imperfect figures. We therefore divided our caste column into three sub-columns headed "original caste or tribe," "clan," and "*got* or sept." Now the first difficulty we encountered was the translation of these headings. In the east *qaum* is used for religion and *zát* for caste; in the west *qaum* for caste, *zát* for tribe or clan. In the east *got* is the universal word for tribe among the peasantry, insomuch that the Rájpúts call their royal races not *kuls* but *gots*; everywhere it is used by Bráhmans, Banyas and the like for the Brahminical *gotra*; in the west it is unknown save in the latter sense. As for the local term for smaller tribes or clans they vary almost from district to district and from caste to caste. After consulting Commissioners we translated our headings '*asl qaum*,' '*zát ya firqah*,' '*got ya shákh*.' The instructions issued for filling up these columns will be found in general letter C., Appendix D., section 5, at section 13 of the enclosed instructions to enumerators and at section 25 of the enclosed instructions to supervisors. Their general tenour was that the caste or race such as Rájpút or Pathán was to be shown in the first, its principal section such as Rind, Gaur, Agarwál in the second, and its secondary sub-section such as Chauhán, Ghatwál, Bháradwáj in the third column; that the *got* if there was any was always to go into the third column; and that where there was only one division the second column was to be left empty. The staff was warned against the loose use of the terms Jat and Gújar as names of occupations, and it was explained that the 'original caste' column was intended to contain, not the caste of traditional origin, but the actual caste to which the people were recognized as now belonging. To these instructions was appended a sample schedule filled up by way of example.

365. Errors in the record of castes and tribes.—I should explain that when I drafted these instructions I knew nothing of any portion of the Panjáb except the Jamna districts, and had no conception how utterly different the divisions of the population and the relations between tribe and caste were in the west of the Province. For my sample schedule I procured specimens filled up by District and Settlement Officers from all parts of the Province, and consulted many natives of different castes, yet there were several mistakes in the schedule; in fact I believe it would be impossible to frame a set of entries which should not contain errors if judged by the varying standards current in different parts of the Panjáb. More than this, there were errors in the very examples given in the instructions; for I had not properly apprehended the nature of what I have called "sections," and I did not rightly estimate the relation between the Rájpút tribes of the Panjáb and the great *kuls* or royal races. But the worst mistake of all was the use of the word *asl* or "original" with caste, and the use of the word "*got*." The addition of *asl* induced many of the tribes of the western districts and Salt-range Tract to return, not their caste, or tribe as it now stands, but the Mughal, Kureshi, or other stock from which they are so fond of claiming descent; and it doubtless tempted many undoubted Jats to record their Rájpút origin. And the use of the word *got* set people to find out what was the Brahminical *gotra* of the person under enumeration. In the eastern districts the word was perfectly understood. But in the hills and in the Western Plains it is only used in the sense of *gotra*. It did not matter that I had asked for *got* or *shákh*. The latter word is not commonly used in connection with family or tribe; the former is; and every enumerator insisted upon each person having a *got*. In Plách Mr. Anderson found a village all entered as of one *gotra*, and that an uncommon one. "On "inquiry from the people themselves they said they really did not know what was their *got*, but "that some one in the village had consulted the Bráhmans at Nirmand, who told him he was of "the Pethinesi *got*, and the whole village followed him. The headman of the village when asked "of what *got* he was, could not even pronounce the word. The better and more intelligent "classes know their *gots*, and others did not wish to be behind them." Now all this trouble was obviously caused by asking for the *gotra*. What I wanted, and what I said I wanted plainly enough in the instructions, was the tribe or sub-division of the caste; and that the people could probably have given readily enough. What was needed was to substitute the local term, whatever it might have been, for *got* or *shákh*; but the people knew what a *got* was, even if they did not know what was their *got*, and hence the confusion. Another great cause of error was the insistence with which the Census Staff demanded that all three columns should be filled up for each person. I had said that I only wanted two entries where there was no second sub-division, as is the case in a very large number of cases, but that did not matter; the columns were there with separate headings, and one after another the District Officers in their reports point out the difficulty of getting entries for all three, the reason being that in many cases there were only facts enough for two. The result is that many of the Jats entered as the third heading the name of the Rájpút tribe from which they claim to have sprung. And another most fertile cause of error must have been the efforts that were made to attain uniformity. In many districts committees were held and a scheme of entries decided upon and prescribed for the guidance of all enumerators. I have discussed the danger of all such attempts in my section on Difficulties and Suggestions in Chapter XIII under the head 'Discretion to be allowed in enumeration.' Educated natives are almost more apt than we ourselves to go wrong in such matters, for we at least are free from prejudice and are ready to admit our ignorance; and a committee composed of the Tahsildárs and Extra Assistants of a district with power to decide upon the entries of castes and tribes, would ensure with absolute certainty the ruin of a caste Census as an independent means of acquiring information.

366. Inherent difficulties of a record of caste. - But even supposing that I had not made any mistakes in my instructions and examples, and supposing that they had been rigidly followed according to their intention, the difficulties inherent in the case are still so enormous that a really accurate record which should be correct in all its details would have been quite beyond hope of attainment. I have attempted to show in the preceding pages that it is almost impossible to define a caste and difficult to define a tribe, and that it is often impossible to draw a clearly marked line between two castes of similar standing. In fact the tribe proper is a far more definite and permanent unit than the caste. Mr. Steedman, who has criticised the scheme more severely and at greater length than any other officer, sets forth the difficulties so ably and completely that I quote the passage in full :—

"With the exception of the three columns relating to caste no difficulty was found in filling "the schedules up. It will be understood that my remarks regarding these three columns are "solely applicable to the Western Panjáb. I have had no experience in the Panjáb east of the "Rávi. Having spent three years in Gujrát, 3½ in Jhang, and 2 in Dera Ismail Khán, I think "that my remarks will apply to the Mahomedan population of most districts west of the "Chenáb.

"These three columns assume, as Mr. Finlay very truly wrote, that the zemindars know far "more about their ancestry and tribal divisions that they actually do. I do not deny that the "three columns could be filled up correctly for each caste by an intelligent enumerator who "understood exactly what was wanted, and who was acquainted with the tribes whose members "he had to enumerate; but the Census economy prohibited the employment of men of this stamp. "There are a considerable number of Mahomedan Rájpúts in the Western Panjáb, known as Syáls "or Chaddhars in Jhang, Janjúhas, Bhakhráls, Budhals, Satis, Dhunds, Alpiáls, Jodras, &c., &c., "in the Ráwalpindi Division. Now any member of these tribes if asked what his 'kaum' was, "would reply Bhakhrál or Sati, &c., as the case might be. Or he might very probably give the "sub-division to which he belonged. A Syál would be sure to answer thus. You would in nine "cases out of ten have to put some distinctly leading question before you ascertained whether he "claimed to be a Rájpút or not. The result is that sometimes Rájpút the 'asl kaum,' some- "times 'Syal' the clan, and sometimes Chachkana the sept or family, is entered in the first of the "three sub-divisions of column 7: I noticed many entries of this description. In fact most of "the Rájpúts of this district would give Rájpút as their '*got*,' placing their tribe as the 'asl "kaum.' Entries of this description naturally depreciate the tabulation results considerably.

"Similar errors crept into the entries of the village artisans. A man may ply the trade of a "weaver, oil-presser, or shoe-maker without being a weaver, oil-presser, or shoe-maker, by caste. [P. 189] "In Jhang weaving had been taken to as a livelihood by many persons who were not "of the weaver tribe. Yet many of these I have no doubt will be put down as weavers "in the 'asl kaum' column. Again men of these low castes are very fond of claiming "relationship with the higher tribes, especially those of Rajput origin. I saw many entries "such as these—'asl kaum' Mochi 'zát' Janjuha, Bhatti, Awan, &c. Now Janjuhas and "Bhattis are Rajputs. If the Mochi was a Janjuha originally his 'asl kaum' is Rajput, "his zát Janjuha, and shoe-making is his trade. If he is a Janjuha by fiction then "Janjuha must be put down as he states. Shekhs, *i.e.* converted Hindus, or men of low caste "who have risen in the world, also advance most ungrounded claims in the way of descent. "Apparently there is no escape from these difficulties in the case of village artisans, Shekhs, and "other similar tribes; but in the case of agriculturists I think more definite instructions would "have left the tabulation entries much more trustworthy.

"I now venture to criticise some of the specimen entries attached to the enumerator's in- "structions. The entries opposite the name of Mahomed Ibrahim are 1, Rajput; 2, Syál; "3, Panwár.[1] I can confidently assert that not one man in a hundred of the Syáls is aware that "he is a Panwar Rajput. I wonder if there are ten men who have heard they are descended from "this *got* of the Rajput tribe. I know exactly what answers an enumerator would get from a "representative Syal zamindar. *Question.*—What is your tribe (*kaum*)? *Answer.*—Bharwana: "*Question.*—What is your clan (*zát*)? *Answer.*—Syál. *Question.*—What is your family (*got* or "*shákh*)? *Answer.*—God only knows. He will inevitably give his sub-division as his *asl kaum*

[1] This is one of the mistakes I have already referred to. The entry should have been "*Rájpút—Punwár—Siál.*"

"and his clan as his *zát*. Nothing less than a direct question as to whether he is a Rájpút or a "Ját will elicit from him the fact that he is a Rájpút. As for '*got*' he probably has never heard "the word. The truth is that the present Mahomedan tribes of the Western Panjáb, though "immigrants from Hindustan, have forgotten their '*gots*' entirely and very often their '*asl* "'*kaum*.' In some few instances only is the name of the '*got*' preserved, and then the tribesmen "are quite unaware that their tribal name is that of their old '*got*.'

"The next question is, What are the *asl kaums* in each district? I notice that in one of the "specimen entries Gújar is so entered. There are various theories as to whether the Gujar is a "separate tribe of Tartar or Hindu origin, or whether it is an offshoot of the great Jat tribe. In "Jhang and Dera Ismail Khan and Shahpur the Mahomedan agriculturists are usually divided "into Rájpúts and Jats in local parlance. I mean that if a Rájpút is asked whether he is a Jat "he will at once deny it, while a Jat admits that he is a member of the tribe. I do not mean to "assert that, excluding Rájpúts and other tribes who have migrated from the other side of the "Indus, all other agriculturists must be Jats; but if they are not I ask who are the numerous "tribes who reside in the Chach and Sind Sagar Doabs and along the left bank of the Chanab? "What is their *asl kaum*? Their Hindu origin is undoubted. They are not Rájpúts. If they "were they would claim their relationship. I have not room here to go fully into this question. I "have noticed it in the Final Report of the Jhang Settlement. But my object is I think attained, "and that is to indicate how very necessary it is that instructions should be given separately for "each district as to what tribes are to be considered 'Asl kaum.' Take the Khokhars. They are "an influential tribe in Jhelam, Shahpur, and Gujrát. Are they converted Rájpúts as many "claim, or descendants of the son-in-law of the prophet as the Shahpur Khokhars state, or mere "Jats as their enemies allege. In the second case only can they be an asl kaum. If in the "tabulation of different districts the tribe is sometimes entered as an 'asl kaum' and at others as "a branch of the Rájpút and Jat tribes, the results are likely to be misleading. Then again there "are tribes who are admittedly of ancient standing and yet have no traditions. Who are these? "It is not unlikely that they were the original inhabitants before the immigration of the Hindu "settlers. As far as my limited experience goes I think it would be an easy matter to settle this "point beforehand for all the main tribes of each district, and also to give a few general instructions "as to how doubtful tribes were to be treated. The question Are you a Rajput or a Jat? would "clear up most cases of doubt where the tribe was originally Hindu, the enumerator being warned "of the custom of calling all agriculturists Jats. Then all tribes who came from the other side of "the Indus would also be 'asl kaum,' the Patháns, Biloches, Mughals, &c. The village Kamins "would also be included in the same list. Here the enumerators would be warned to ask the "individual whether he was a Kamin by trade only or both by trade and tribe.[1] I would "arbitrarily class all agriculturists who admitted that they were not Rájpúts and who were of "undoubted Hindu origin, as Jats. This classification is perhaps not ethnologically accurate, but "every Patwari and most zamindars would understand what is meant. I think too for the "Mahomedan population two columns would have been enough. It seems unnecessary to ascer-"tain the numbers of each sub-division. We want to know the total Syál, Ghakkar, and Awan "population. I do not think much is gained by working out returns showing the total population "of the Bharwána, Chuchkana, Admál, Firozál, and Bugdial families. There are no restrictions on "intermarriage between members of the different families."

I have already explained the reason why three columns were taken instead of two. We wanted two facts only; but we wanted to make sure of getting them in the many cases where three facts were available and one was not wanted, by recording all three and rejecting for ourselves the useless one; otherwise if we had had two columns only, one of them might have been wasted on the useless fact. As it was, one of our three columns was commonly occupied by the name of some wholly unimportant sept or family. And I do not agree with Mr. Steedman in his proposal to issue detailed instructions concerning the agricultural tribes of each district. Who is to issue them; and how is it to be ensured that the same tribe is classed similarly in two different districts?

367. Reasons why the scheme did not work.—I think that on the whole the scheme was the best that could have been adopted; and if it had been possible to carry it out to the end as it had been intended to do when the instructions were framed, I believe that results of very considerable accuracy would have been obtained. What was intended was this—to record everything, to tabulate all the entries, and *then* to classify them throughout and produce the results as the final caste table. Thus, supposing one man had entered himself as Jat Bhatti and another as Rájpút Bhatti, or one man as Qureshi Khattar, another as Awán Khattar, and a third as Qutbshahi Khattar, we should have tabulated them all separately, and then classed them as might be decided upon after consideration and inquiry. It was not expected that the material would be properly arranged in the schedules; but we hoped that it would all be recorded

---

[1] Would not this suggest to the artisan the setting up for himself of a mythical origin from some caste of glorious renown?

there, to be arranged afterwards. But when we came to examine the schedules we found that the separate entries in the caste column alone were numbered by thousands, while the sub-divisions were numbered by tens of thousands. I certainly had not, and I do not believe that any body else concerned had, the very faintest conception of how numerous the entries would be. At any rate it was obviously quite out of the question to tabulate and examine them all before compilation; and what was done was to deal with the entries in the first or caste column only, so far as the compilation of the final Census Table VIII was concerned. Even those entries I was compelled, for reasons given in the Chapter on Tabulation, to allow the Divisional Officers to classify for themselves where there appeared to be no reasonable doubt as to the classification. With the headings for which they returned separate figures I dealt as is described in the Chapter on Compilation. The figures for the sub-divisional entries were tabulated in detail; but only certain selected entries were taken out to be used in the Census Report, the principles on which the selection was made being explained in the Chapter on Compilation.

368. Nature and degree of error in the final figures.—Thus the figures as now given in the abstracts and appendices of this report are liable to error in several ways. In the first place many members of a caste or tribe entered as their caste some race to which they are pleased to refer their origin in remote antiquity. For instance, some Gakkhars returned themselves as Gakkhar and others as Mughal, and are shown under those headings respectively in the final tables, which therefore do not give the total number of Gakkhars in the Panjáb. So some low caste men returned their caste as Rájpút or Mughal or Quresh 'out of joke' as several Deputy Commissioners note. On the other hand some men of good caste, such as Siál, Khokhar, or Mughal, who were following the trade of weaver or carpenter, returned their *caste* as Páoli or Tarkhán, though the adoption of that hereditary occupation had been in many cases too recent to have brought about a change of caste. This last error was for the most part confined to the Western Plains. Again, persons who belonged to the same tribe and returned that tribe as their caste will have been differently classed in different divisional offices, or classed under one heading in one division and returned separately and then classed by myself under another heading in another division. Thus the Bhattis will have been classed as Jats by the Deraját and as Rájpúts by the Ráwalpindi office. So the Langáhs were classed as Jats in Multán, while the Deraját returned them separately and I classed them as Patháns. These errors however affect only those cases where the tribe was returned and not the caste. Where a man returned himself as Jat, Rájpút, Pathán and so forth,
[P. 190] he was treated as such although the tribe he gave might raise suspicion as to the correctness of the returns. Moreover the errors, if they must be so called, do represent actual facts. The Bhatti is a Rájpút in Ráwalpindi because there Rájpúts are recognised. In the Deraját he is a Jat, because there no distinction is drawn between Jat and Rájpút. And it must be remembered that though the cases in which the errors detailed above occurred are numerous, the total figures affected are seldom large. There were certainly hundreds, I believe there were thousands of so-called castes returned in the Multán division which only included ten or fifteen people in the whole division. The great mass of each caste returned themselves rightly and are shown correctly in our tables: the items that are wrongly classed are wholly insignificant in their total amount as compared with the items that are rightly classed. But there are exceptions to this statement. The distinction between Jat and Rájpút is so indefinite and so variable that it can hardly be called a mistake to class a tribe as Jat in one place and Rájpút in another. This however has been done. But I have picked out the figures in each case and put them side by side in the abstracts contained in the section on these two castes, and I think the error which has not been corrected may be taken as exceedingly small. It is now in each man's power to transfer the figures for any tribe from Jat to Rájpút or *vice versá*, according to individual taste. The other chief exceptions are in the case of Mughals and Shekhs. For Shekhs I was prepared. I knew that all sorts of low caste men, recent converts to Islám, would return themselves as Shekh; and I had the figures examined with a view to separate these, and the details will be found in the text of this chapter. But I did not know that in some parts of the western Panjáb Mughal was as favourite a supposititious origin as Shekh is in other parts of the Province, and I have not had the details worked out so carefully. Still almost all the large numbers have been separated from these two entries. So with Pathans. Many people, such as Dilazák, have returned themselves as Patháns who do not really belong to the race; but their claim to the name is often admitted, and they have become in a way affiliated to the nation. Thus the considerable errors in the caste tables, as corrected in this chapter, amount to this; that there is a confusion between Jat and Rájpút and between Pathán and certain allied races, which exists in actual fact fully as much as in the figures; that some tribes or castes have been wrongly shown as Mughal and Shekh; and that some of the artisan castes have been shown as belonging to the higher castes, while some of the higher castes have been included in the artisan castes merely because they followed their occupation. Taking the Province as a whole the errors are probably insignificant, and hardly affect the general distribution of the population by caste. They are probably greatest in the cis-Indus Salt-range tract, where the tendency to claim Mughal origin in strongest.

369. Error in the figures for tribes and sub-divisions.—The figures for tribes and sub-divisions given in this chapter are professedly only rough approximations. The manner in which they were tabulated and the final figures compiled will be explained in Book II under the heads Tabulation and Compilation. The whole process was intended to be merely a rough one. The detailed tabulation is now in progress, and I hope within the next few years to bring out detailed tables of tribes and clans for the whole Panjáb. But besides inaccuracies that will have crept into the work of tabulation, there are several causes of error inherent in the material. In the first place the spelling of local names of tribes, as rendered by the enumerating staff, varied extraordinarily. Some were evidently mere variations, as Dháríwál, Dhálíwál and Dhánìwál; some I knew to represent separate tribes, as Sidhu and Sindhu, Chhína and Chíma; some I am still in doubt about, as Búta and Bhútta, Sará and Sarai. In working with a staff not always acquainted with the names of the clans, figures referring to two different tribes must often have been joined together, and other figures wrongly omitted because of some variation in the spelling. Another source of error doubtless was the uncertainty regarding the woman's clans discussed in section 354. On a future occasion I would tabulate sub-divisions of castes for males only. Again many of the people are presented twice over in two columns. Thus the Siál are Punwár Rájpúts by origin. Suppose that 1,000 Siáls returned themselves as Rájpút Punwár Siál, another thousand as Siál Punwár, another 1,000 as Rájpút Siál, and a fourth 1,000 as Rájpút Punwár. All the 4,000 people would be shown in Table VIII as Rájpút; but in the details of tribes we should have 3,000 Siál and 3,000 Punwár or 6,000 in all. This was quite unavoidable so long as only one tribal division was tabulated; but as a fact the cases in which this happened were few, or at least the numbers affected small. I had all cases in which the same people were entered twice over shown in a separate memorandum attached to the tribes table, and wherever the numbers were at all considerable I have mentioned the fact of their double inclusion in the text. This double entry occurred most often with the Jat tribes, who, in order to fill up their three columns, entered the Rájpút tribe from which they claimed origin as well as their own Jat tribe, so that we had people returning themselves as Jat Sidhu Bhatti, and such people appear among the Jat tribes both as Sidhu and as Bhatti.

370. Proposals for next Census.—What then is best to be done at next Census? It will be seen that many of the difficulties are due to the intrinsic difficulty of the question and to the varying nature of caste in the Panjáb. So far as this is the case no scheme will help us. In one respect, however, I hope that the task will be made much easier by next Census. I hope by then to have brought out classified lists of all the tribes and clans returned in the present Census. The way in which they will facilitate the treatment of the subject is explained in the section on Tabulation. If I had had such a classified list my task on this occasion would have been easy enough; and it is I think one of the most valuable results of the present Census that it has given us materials for the preparation of such a list. With such a list the three columns of the schedule of 1881 are almost perfect in theory. But I do not think they worked as well in practice. I believe that the three columns which they erroneously thought they were bound to fill up, puzzled both people and staff, and caused a good many of our difficulties. Thus in future I would have but two columns, and would head them *Quam* and *Shákh*. I would not care whether caste or tribe was entered in the first column, as the classified list would show the tabulator how to class the tribe; and I would hope that the second column at any rate would generally give tribe. In very many cases it would not. There would be entries like Biloch Rind instead of Biloch Laghári, Bráhman Bashisht instead of Bráhman Sársút, Banya Kásib instead of Banya Agarwál, and so forth. But on the whole I think it would be better to accept the fact that the entries must be incomplete, whatever scheme be adopted; and would prefer the certainty of error of the two columns, rather than the confusion and perplexity which the three columns cause to those concerned in the enumeration. Above all things I would avoid the words *asl* and *got*. I would let the patwaris, who should make the preliminary record, exercise their discretion about entering high castes for menials or artisans, directing them to show the caste by which the people were commonly known in the village. I would tabulate both males and females for tribes and clans, and arrange them in order of numbers; and I would have the Deputy Superintendent personally examine the tribal tables for all above say 500, before compiling his final caste tables. Such an examination would do an immense deal towards increasing the accuracy of the caste figures; but it was impossible in the present Census owing to the double sub-division. I would show in my tribal tables the figures for males only, though those for females must be tabulated in the first instance in order to allow of transfer of entries from one caste heading to another.

371. Bibliography.—The most detailed and accurate information available in print regarding certain, and those the most important from an administrative point of view, of the Panjáb castes is to be found in the numerous Settlement Reports, and more especially in those of recent years. Unfortunately they deal almost exclusively with the landowning and cultivating castes. Sir H. Elliott's *Races of the N. W. P.*, edited by Mr Beames, is, so far as it goes, a mine of information regarding the castes of the eastern districts. Sherring's *Hindu Castes* contains much information of a sort, the first volume being really valuable, but the second and third being infinitely less so; while the whole is rendered much less useful than it might be by the absence of any index save one that maddens the anxious inquirer. On the ancient form of the institution of Caste, Wilson's treatise on *Indian Caste*, and Vol. I of Muir's *Sanskrit Texts* are the authorities. The second volume of General Cunningham's *Archæological Reports* has a dissertation on Panjáb Ethnology by way of introduction, and there are many small pamphlets which contain useful information. But on the whole it is wonderful how little has been published regarding the specially Panjáb castes, or indeed regarding any of the menial and outcast classes. Sir Geo. Campbell's *Indian Ethnology* I have not seen; but it should be instructive. At the head of the section on Patháns and Biloches I have noticed the books which may be most usefully consulted. In the case of the other castes I know of no works that deal with any one particular, or indeed with our Panjáb castes in general save those specified above.

PART II.—THE BILOCH, PATHAN, AND ALLIED RACES.

372. Introductory and General.—Of the Panjáb castes and tribes I shall [P. 191]
first discuss the Biloch and Patháu who hold all our trans-Indus frontier, and with them two or three races found in the Province only in small numbers which, though not Patháu by origin or indeed in name, have by long association with the Patháns become so closely assimilated to them that it is best to take them here. The figures will be found in Abstract No. 65 below :—

Abstract No. 65, showing Biloches, Pathans, and Allied Races for Districts and States.

		Figures.					Proportion per 1,000 of Total Population.						
		18	6	54	145	183	18	6	54	145	183		
		Biloch.	Pathán.	Tanáoli.	Tájik.	Hazára.	Biloch.	Pathán.	Tanáoli.	Tájik.	Hazára.	Total.	Grand Total.
Delhi	...	1,318	15,969	...	1	...	2	25		...	...	25	27
Gurgaon	..	2,166	4,945	...	...	...	3	8	...	...	...	8	11
Karnal	...	440	5,898	...	...	...	1	9	...	...	...	9	10
Hissár	...	554	2,416	...	...	...	1	5	...	...	...	5	6
Rohtak	...	1,986	5,155	...	...	...	4	9	...	...	...	9	13
Sirsa	...	1,380	1,554	...	...	...	5	6	...	...	...	6	11
Ambala	...	1,070	9,845	...	...	...	1	9	...	...	...	9	10
Lúdhiána	...	425	3,629	...	...	...	1	6	...	...	...	6	7
Simla	...	...	1,420	...	...	...	...	33	...	...	...	33	33
Jalandhar	...	379	4,808	...	...	...	...	6		...	...	6	6
Hushyarpur	...	94	7,514	...	...	..	...	8	...	...	...	8	8
Kángra	..	40	1,095	...	...	...	...	1	...	...	...	1	1
Amritsar	...	548	4,349	...	...	...	1	5	...	...	...	5	6
Gurdaspur	...	124	9,784	...	...	...		12		.	...	12	12
Sialkot	...	339	4,118	...	...	...		4		...	...	4	4
Lahore	...	5,247	6,976	...	...	1	6	8	...	...	...	8	14
Gujranwala	...	2,800	912		...	...	5	1	...	...	...	1	6
Firozpur	...	1,766	3,122	...	...	...	3	5	...	...	...	5	8
Ráwalpindi	...	906	36,465	3	11	...	1	44	...	...		44	45
Jehlam	...	2,840	4,618	1	...	...	5	8	...	...	...	8	13
Gujrat	...	886	2,033	...	...	...	1	3	...	...		3	4
Shahpur	..	8,865	3,076	...	...	...	21	7	...	...	...	7	28

Abstract No. 65, showing Biloches, Pathans, and Allied Races for Districts and States—*concluded.*

	Figures.					Proportion per 1,000 of Total Population.						
	18	6	54	145	183	18	6	54	145	183		
	Biloch.	Pathán.	Tanáoli.	Tájik.	Hazára	Biloch.	Pathán.	Tanáoli.	Tájik.	Hazára.	Total.	Grand Total.
Multán ...	18,547	9,067	...	...	...	34	16	...	...	...	16	50
Jhang ...	15,093	1,710	...	...	...	38	4	...	...	...	4	42
Montgomery ...	13,513	1,987	...	...	..	32	5	...	...	...	5	37
Muzaffargarh ...	58,356	3,959	...	...	...	172	12	...	...		12	184
Derah Ismail Khán.	41,356	73,022		...	...	94	165	...		...	165	259
Derah Ghazi Khán.	115,749	9,871	...	...	...	319	27	...	..	...	27	346
Bannu ...	2,189	141,022	...	...	...	7	424	...		...	424	431
Peshávar ...	449	276,656	1,866	1,889	358	1	467	2	3	1	473	474
Hazara ...	33	64,695	39,981	147	...	...	159	98	...	...	257	257
Kohat ...	504	116,431	37	...	...	3	640		...	...	640	643
British Territory	299,962	838,233	41,388	2,048	359	16	44	2	...		46	62
Patiala ...	1,184	6,647	...	...	...	1	5	...	...	...	5	6
Nabha ...	295	1,691	...	...	...	1	7	...	...	...	7	8
Kapurthala ...	80	1,125	...	...	...	...	4	...	..	...	4	4
Jind ...	193	1,126	...	...	...	1	5	...	...	...	5	6
Maler Kotla ...	...	1,165	...	...	...	...	16		...	...	16	16
Total East. Plains	2,099	14,196	...	...	...	1	6	...	...	...	6	7
Bahawalpur ...	53,175	5,567	...	...	...	98	10	.	...	...	10	103
Total Hill States	2	1,586	...	...	...	...	2	...	...	...	2	2
British Territory	299,962	838,233	41,388	2,048	359	16	44	2	...	...	46	62
Native States	55,276	21,349	...	...	...	14	6	...	...	...	6	20
Province	355,238	859,582	1,388	2,048	359	16	38	2	...	...	40	56

These two great nations, the Pathán and Biloch, hold the whole country to the west of the Panjáb, the latter lying to the south and the former to the north of a line drawn from the western face of the Sulemáns opposite Derah Ghází Khán almost due west to Quetta. But in the trans-Indus valley and on the Panjáb face of the Sulemán Range the Biloches have pushed much further north than this, and the southern border of the Derah Ismáíl Khán tahsíl roughly marks the common boundary, while on this side the river the Biloches again stretch somewhat further to the north than on the other. On either bank their common frontier is held by a tribe of mixed affinities, the Khetrán being Biloch in Derah Ghází, Pathán
[P. 192] in Derah Ismáíl, and probably of Jat origin in both; while in the *thal* the southernmost Pathán tribe is the Balúch, which is probably of Biloch descent.

These two great races present many features of unusual interest. Among both the tribal organisation still survives, in parts at least, in the most complete integrity, and affords us examples of one extreme of that series which terminates at the other in the compact village communities of our eastern districts. Moreover the intense tribal feeling of the Biloch and Pathán and the care with which they keep up their genealogies, enable us to point to both nations for undoubted examples of the process by which a race possessed of pride of blood in an extreme degree affiliates to itself sections of other races, gives them a place in its tribal organisation on condition only of subjection to the supreme authority, and after a time invents a fiction of common descent by which to account for their presence. There can be little doubt that the process which we know has taken place among the Pathán and Biloch has not been without examples among the other races of the Panjáb, and that aboriginal, Mongol, and other elements have in a similar manner been absorbed into the tribal or caste organisation of the Aryan stock.

373. The Patháns and the Biloches are both foreigners in the Panjáb proper, and have entered its political boundaries within the last few hundred years, though it is not impossible that in doing so the Patháns only re-entered a country which their ancestors had left more than a thousand years ago. Yet their freedom from the irksome and artificial restrictions of caste, and the comparative license which their tribal customs permit them in the matter of intermarriage, have caused their example to produce a wonderful effect upon the neighbouring Indian races; and it is the proximity of these races, and the force of that example daily set before them by nations living next door, to which, far more than to the mere political supremacy of a Mahomedan dynasty or adoption of the Mahomedan creed, I attribute the laxity of caste rules and observances which characterises the people of our Western Plains. The point has already been noticed in section 347. Some of the social and tribal customs of these people are exceedingly curious. Unfortunately we know but little of them, and what little information I have been able to collect I have not had leisure to record in the following pages. I may however mention two of their most striking customs. One is the prevalence of the *vesh* or periodical distribution of land among the component households of a clan, which we found to be the practice on some parts of the frontier when we annexed the Panjáb, while it still exists in full force among both the Biloches and the Patháns of Independent Territory. The second custom is also one common to both nations, though not I believe to all their tribes. It is the existence of a Levitical clan, often called Mírkhel among the Patháns, who have the exclusive privilege of performing certain priestly functions connected, not with the Mahomedan religion but with tribal ceremonies, such for instance as the dedication by passing under spears of the fighting men of the tribe when about to go to war.

374. Tabulation of tribal statistics.—Political considerations rendered it far more important to obtain for administrative purposes fairly correct statistics of the Biloch and Pathán tribes than of the more settled tribes of the cis-Indus Panjáb. But when I took up the question I found the difficulties so great, and my own ignorance of the subject so complete, that I obtained the sanction of Government to have these figures compiled by the Deputy Commissioners of the frontier districts. The difficulties mainly arose from three causes. In the first place the same word is, especially among the Patháns, constantly recurring among the various tribes as the name of clans who are wholly distinct from one another. Secondly, the same clan, especially among the Biloches, is affiliated to a larger tribe in one district while in another it forms a distinct tribe of itself. Thirdly, many of the entries did not show full details of the tribe and clan, often only giving the names of the sept or family; and the only hope of classing such entries rightly lay in having the classification made on the spot. The system adopted was as follows. Each Deputy Commissioner drew up a list of the tribes and clans for which he wished to obtain separate figures for his own district. Of this list he sent copies to all the other districts concerned. A joint list was then drawn up including all tribes or clans mentioned in any one of these district lists, and the figures were tabulated in accordance with that joint list. The Biloch tribal figures were then compiled on the spot in the two Derahs and Muzaffargarh, and those for Patháns in the Peshâwar Division, Derah Ismáíl Khán, and Bannu. For other districts and for Native States the figures were compiled to the best of our ability in the Central Office in accordance with the joint list already mentioned.

THE BILOCH (CASTE No. 18).

375. Meaning of Biloch—Bibliography.[1]—The word Biloch is variously used in the Panjáb to denote the following people:—

(1) The Biloch proper, a nation which traces its origin from the direction of Makrán, and now holds the lower Sulemáns;

(2) A criminal tribe settled in the great jungles below Thánesar;

(3) Any Musalmán camelman except in the extreme east and the extreme west of the Panjáb;

(4) A small Pathán tribe of Derah Ismáíl Khán, more properly called Balúch.

The criminal tribe will be described under vagrant and gispy tribes. It is almost certainly of true Biloch stock. The Pathán tribe will be noticed under the Patháns of Derah Ismáíl. It also is in all probability a small body of true Biloches who have become affiliated to the Patháns. Our figures for the most part refer to the true Biloch of the lower frontier and to their representatives who are scattered throughout the Panjáb. But in the upper grazing grounds of the Western Plains the Biloch settlers have taken to the grazing and breeding of camels rather than to husbandry; and thus the word Biloch has become associated with the care of camels, insomuch that throughout the Peshâwar, Ráwalpindi, Lahore, Amritsar, and Jálandhar divisions, the word Biloch is used for any Musalmán camelman whatever be his caste, every Biloch being supposed to be a camelman and every Mahomedan camelman to be a Biloch. In Sirsa we have Punwár Rájpúts from Multán who are known as Biloch because they keep camels, and several Deputy Commissioners recommended that Untwál, Sárbán, and Biloch should be taken together as one caste. The headmen of these people are called *Malik*, and I have classed some five hundred Musalmáns who returned themselves under this name, chiefly in the Lahore division, as Biloch. It is impossible to say how many of the men returned as Biloch because they keep camels are of true Biloch origin. Settlements of Biloches proper are, excluding the Multán and Deraját divisions, and Sháhpur, reported in Dehli, Gurgáon, Karnál, Hissár, Rohtak, Lúdhiána, Amritsar, Gújránwála, Fírozpur, and Ráwalpindi; but in all these districts except the first five the word is used for camelmen also, and the figures cannot be separated.

Bibliography.—The following books will be found to contain information regarding the Biloch nation: Hughes' *Bilochistán*, a useful compilation of perhaps somewhat doubtful authority; Bruce's *Memorandum on the Derah Ghâzi District* (*Panjáb Selections, IX, 1871*) chiefly statistical, and by no means free from error; Douie's *Bilochi Námah* translated; and Dames' *Biloch Vocabulary* (*J. A. S. B., 1880*), both including collections of Bilochi folklore; Pottinger's
[P. 193] *Travels in Bilochistán and Sindh* and Massons' Travels in the same countries. Fryers' *Settlement Report of Derah Ghâzi Khân* and Macgregor's *Gazetteer of the N. W. Frontier* give most valuable accounts of the Biloch tribes; while the Settlement Reports of those other districts in which Biloches are found in any numbers contain much useful information.

376. Description of the Biloch.—The Biloch presents in many respects a very strong contrast with his neighbour the Pathán. The political organisation of each is tribal; but while the one yields a very large measure of obedience to a chief who is a sort of limited monarch, the other recognises no authority save that of a council of the tribe. Both have most of the virtues and many of the vices peculiar to a wild and semi-civilised life. To both hospitality

[1] I had, with the valuable assistance of Mr. Douie, written a far more complete account of the Biloch than that given in the following pages. But after Mr. Douie had left India and many of my notes had been destroyed, a great part of the MS. was lost in the office; and I had to rewrite it as best I could with very incomplete materials, and a very short time in which to complete it.

is a sacred duty and the safety of the guest inviolable; both look upon the exaction of "blood for blood" as the first duty of man; both follow strictly a code of honour of their own, though one very different from that of modern Europe; both believe in one God whose name is Alláh, and whose prophet is Mahomet. But the one attacks his enemy from in front, the other from behind; the one is bound by his promises,[1] the other by his interests; in short, the Biloch is less turbulent, less treacherous, less bloodthirsty, and less fanatical than the Pathán: he has less of God in his creed and less of the devil in his nature.

His frame is shorter and more spare and wiry than that of his neighbour to the north; though generations of independence have given to him too a bold and manly bearing. Frank and open in his manners and without servility, fairly truthful when not corrupted by our Courts, faithful to his word, temperate and enduring, and looking upon courage as the highest virtue, the true Biloch of the Deraját frontier is one of the pleasantest men we have to deal with in the Panjáb. As a revenue payer he is not so satisfactory, his want of industry, and the pride which looks upon manual labour as degrading, making him but a poor husbandman. He is an expert rider, horse-racing is his national amusement, and the Biloch breed of horses is celebrated throughout Northern India. Till quite lately he killed his colts as soon as they were born; and his preference for mares is expressed in the proverb—"A man with his saddle on a mare has his saddle on a horse; a "man with his saddle on a horse has his saddle on his head." If he cannot afford a whole mare he will own as many legs of one as he can manage; and, the Biloch mare having four legs, will keep her a quarter of each year for each leg of which he is master, after which she passes on to the owner of the remaining legs. He is a thief by tradition and descent, for he says, "God "will not favour a Biloch who does not steal and rob" and "the Biloch who "steals secures heaven to seven generations of his ancestors." But he has become much more honest under the civilising influences of our rule.

His face is long and oval, his features finely cut, and his nose aquiline; he wears his hair long and usually in oily curls and lets his beard and whiskers grow, and he is very filthy in person, considering cleanliness as a mark of effeminacy. He usually carries a sword, knife and shield; he wears a smock frock reaching to his heels and pleated about the waist, loose drawers and a long cotton scarf; and all these must be white or as near it as dirt will allow of, insomuch that he will not enter our army because he would there be obliged to wear a coloured uniform. His wife wears a sheet over her head, a long sort of nightgown reaching to her ankles, and wide drawers; her clothes may be red or white; and she plaits her hair in a long queue.

377. As the true Biloch is nomad in his habits he does not seclude his women; but he is extremely jealous of female honour. In cases of detected adultery the man is killed, and the woman hangs herself by order. Even when on the war-trail, the women and children of his enemy are safe from him. The Biloch of the hills lives in huts or temporary camps, and wanders with his herds from place to place. In the plains he has settled in small villages; but the houses are of the poorest possible description. When a male child is born to him, ass's dung in water, symbolical of pertinacity, is dropped into his mouth from the point of a sword before he is given the breast. A

[1] There is, in the hills above Harand, a "stone or cairn of cursing," erected as a perpetual memorial of the treachery of one who betrayed his fellow.

tally of lives due is kept between the various tribes or families; but when the account grows complicated it can be settled by betrothals, or even by payment of cattle. The rules of inheritance do not follow the Islamic law, but tend to keep property in the family by confining succession to agnates; though some of the leading and more educated men are said to be trying to introduce the *shara* into their tribes.

The Biloches are nominally Musalmáns, but singularly ignorant of their religion and neglectful of its rites and observances; and though they once called themselves and were called by old historians "friends of Ali," and though, if their account of their ejection from Arabia be true, they must have originally been Shíah, they now belong almost without exception to the Sunni sect. Like many other Musalmán races of the frontier they claim to be Qureshi Arabs by origin, while some hold them to be of Túrkomán stock; their customs are said to support the latter theory: their features certainly favour the former. The question is discussed at pages 19*ff* of Mr. Fryer's Settlement Report of Derah Ghází. Their language is a branch of the old Persian, and apparently contains many archaic forms which throw light upon other modern developments from the same source. It is described in the Chapter on Languages. It is now hardly spoken, so far as the Panjáb is concerned, beyond the tribal organisation of the Derah Ghází Biloches; and even among them it is being gradually superseded by Multáni or Jatki, the language of the plains, and a Biloch Chief has been known to learn the language in order to talk it to English officials. They have no written character, and no literature; but they are passionately fond of poetry, chiefly consisting of ballads describing the events of national or tribal history, and of love-songs; and local poets are still common among them.

378. Early history of the Biloch.—Their account of their origin is that they are descended from Mír Hamzah, a Qureshi Arab and an uncle of the Prophet, and were settled at Halab or Aleppo, till, siding with Husen, they were expelled by Yazíz, the second of the Umeyid Caliphs. This would be about 680 A. D. They fled to the hill country of Kirmán in Persia, where they lived quietly for some time, and so increased in numbers that the King became desirous of binding them to himself by ties of marriage. He accordingly demanded a wife from each of the forty-four *bolaks* or tribes into which
[P. 194] they are said to have then been divided, though all traces of them have long since been lost. But their fathers had never given their daughters in wedlock to a stranger, and they therefore sent forty-four boys dressed up in girls' clothes, and fled before the deception could be discovered. They moved south-eastwards into Kech Makrán or the tract between Afghánistán and the coast of the Arabian Sea, then but partially inhabited, and there finally settled in the country which is now known as Bilochistán.[1]

From Jalál Khán, the Chief under whose leadership they made their last migration, sprang four sons, Rind, Hot, Lashári and Korai, and a daughter Jato. Five of their tribes still bear these names, but the Rind and Lashári appear to have been pre-eminent; and the Biloches, or at least that portion of the nation which later on moved northwards to our border, were divided into two great sections under those names, and I believe that all Biloch tribes still consider themselves as belonging to one or other of these sections. Thus

[1] Mr. Fryer quotes authorities for the occupation of the Makrán Mountains by Biloches at least as early as (1) the beginning of the fifth century; (2) the middle of the seventh century. (Derah Ghází Settlement Report, p. 19.)

the Mazári and Drishak, who trace their descent from Hot, claim to belong to the Rind section. Some five hundred years after their settlement in Kech Makrán, the Rind, Lashári, and Jatoi moved northwards into the country about Kelát, to the west of the lower Sulemáns, "the Rind settling in Shorán, "the Lashári in Gandáva, and the Jatoi in Sevi and Dhádon, while the Khosa "remained in Kech and the Hot in Makrán."[1] They are said to have dispossessed and driven into Sindh a Jat people, ruled over by a Hindu prince with the Sindhi title of Jám and the name of Nindáva, whose capital was at Kelát. After a time the charms of a woman led to jealousy between the nephews of Mír Chákar and Mír Gwáhrám Khán, the Chiefs of the Rind and Lashári sections. Their claims were to be decided by a horse-race held in Rind Territory, in which the hosts loosened the girth of their rival's saddle. A fight resulted, and the Rind, who were at first worsted, called to their aid Sultán Husen,[2] King of Khorásán, and drove the Lashári out into Haidarábád and Tatta in Sindh, where they no longer exist as an individual tribe. From this event the Biloches date the growth of their present tribal organisation; and as there is now no localised tribe bearing the name of Rind, and as almost all the great tribes of our frontier claim to be of Rind extraction, it is probable that the Rind, left sole possessors of the hill country of Kelát (for the Jatoi also consider themselves as belonging to the Rind section of the nation), gradually split up into the tribes which we now find on the Derah Gházi border. Several of these tribes have taken their names from the localities which they now hold, which shows that their names are not older than their occupation of their present territories.[3]

379. Advance of the Biloches into the Panjab.—The Biloches had thus spread as far north as the Bolán; but apparently they had not yet encroached upon the Sulemán range which lay to the east of them, and which was held by Patháns, while a Jat population occupied the valley of the Indus and the country between the Sulemáns and the river. But about the middle of the 15th century, the Túrks or Mughals under their Arghún leader invaded Kachhi and Sindh, and twice took Sibi, in 1479 and in 1511 A.D. About the same time the Brahoi, a tribe believed to be of Dravidian origin,[4] and who appear to have followed in their tracks, drove the the Biloch out of the fertile valley of Kelát and established a supremacy over their northern tribes. Yielding to the pressure thus put upon them, the Kelát tribes moved eastwards into the lower Sulemáns[5] driving the Patháns before them along the

[1] Shorán is probably another reading of Sarávan, the country between Quetta and Kelát; Gandáva is on the northern frontier of Sindh, south-east of Saráwan; Sevi and Dhádon are doubtless other forms of Sibi and Dádar, north of Gandáva and south-east of Quetta.

[2] This name should fix the date of the contest; but I have been unable to identify the sovereign in question, who is also described as Sultán Sháh Husen, King of Persia. Mír Chákar lived in the time of Humáyún, about the middle of the 16th century; but it is probable that these events took place at least two centuries earlier. Mír Chákar and Mír Gwáhrám are renowned in Biloch story as the national heroes, and it is not unnatural that any great event should be referred to them.

[3] When the name applies to a tract, the tract may have been called after the tribe; but where the name belongs to a mountain, river, or other natural feature, the converse seems more probable.

[4] It is thought probable by some that the Brahoi language will be found, when we learn more about it, to be Iranian and not Dravidian.

[5] One account postpones the occupation of the lower Sulemáns by Biloches to the expedition with Humáyún to be mentioned presently. It is true that about the time of Humáyún's conquest of India the Patháns of the Derah Ismáíl frontier were at their weakest, as will be explained when those tribes come under discussion. But it is also true that there is a tendency to refer all past events to the time of any famous incident, such as the march to Dehli with Humáyún.

range, while the Biloches from Sindh began to spread up the Indus. Many of these latter took service with the Langáh rulers of Multán and were granted lands along the river; and about 1480 A. D. Ismáíl Khán and Fatah Khán, the two sons of Malik Sohráb Khán, and Gházi Khán, son of Háji Khán, all Dodai Biloches and of Rind extraction, founded the three Derahs which still bear their names, overcame the Lodis of Sítpur, and established themselves as independent rulers of the lower Deraját and Muzaffargarh, which position they and their descendants maintained for nearly 300 years.[1] Thus the Southern Biloches gradually spread up the valleys of the Indus, Chanáb, and Satluj; while the Derah Gházi tribes came down from their hills into the *pachhád* or sub-montane tract, displacing a Jat population and driving them down to the river, where they still form an important element of the population even in tracts owned by Biloches. In 1555 a large body of Biloches accompanied Humáyún, whom they had previously harassed in his retreat, in his victorious re-entry into India, under the leadership of Mír Chákar, the great Rind hero of Biloch story. They are said to have consisted chiefly of Lagháři, Drishak, Gopáng, and Jatoi. Mír Chákar eventually settled in Montgomery, where a considerable tract, still partly held by Biloches, was granted to him by the grateful sovereign, and died and was buried at Satgarh in that district. It is probable that many of the Biloch settlements in the eastern districts of the Province sprang from Humáyún's attendants.

The tribal organisation of the Biloches now covers the whole of our southern frontier as far north as the boundary between the two Derahs, being confined for the most part to the hills and the land immediately under them, but stretching east to the Indus in the neighbourhood of Rájanpur. There is also a large Biloch element throughout the river lands of the Indus in both the Derahs, more especially in the southern and northern portion of Derah Gházi and just above the Derah Ismáíl border; while in Baháwalpur and Muzaffargarh they form a large proportion of the whole population, and they hold considerable areas on the Satluj in Multán, to the north of the Ravi in Montgomery, on the right bank
[P. 195] of the Chanáb and along the Jahlam in Jhang, and on the latter river in Sháhpur. But outside the Derah Gházi Khán district, and indeed along the greater part of the river border of that district, the Biloch settlers own no allegiance to any tribal Chief, are altogether external to the political organisation of the nation, and do not hold that dominant position among their neighbours which is enjoyed by the organised tribes of Derah Gházi. Many of them have been settled in their present holdings within comparatively recent times or, to use the words of Mr. Tucker, have acquired them "as cultivating proprietors, rather than as a military caste which ruled the country but left the occupation of the land to the Jats." Figures showing the dis-
* P. 38-9 tribution of the Biloches will be found in Abstract No. 65, page 191.*

380. Tribal organisation of the Biloches.—Sohráb Khán, the chief of the Dumki, a Rind tribe, is the nominal head of the Biloches, or at any rate of those on our frontier; while all the northern tribes beyond our border acknowledge the supremacy of the Brahoi Khán of Kelát, a supremacy the reality of which has always varied with the personal character of the Khán, and which it is probable that our own frontier policy has lately saved from total extinction. But for all practical purposes the frontier tribes are

[1] The subsequent history of these tribes is related in section 385.

independent both of foreigners and of one another, and are held together by a common nationality against outsiders only. The tribe, at least in its present form, is a political and not an ethnic unit, and consists of a conglomeration of clans bound together by allegiance to a common Chief. Probably every tribe contains a nucleus of two, three, or more clans descended from a single ancestor. But round these have collected a number of affiliated sections; for the cohesion between the various parts of a tribe or clan is not always of the strongest, and it is not very uncommon for a clan or a portion of a clan to quarrel with its brethren, and leaving its tribe to claim the protection of a neighbouring Chief. They then become his *hamsáyahs* or dwellers beneath the same shade, and he is bound to protect them and they to obey him. In this manner a small section formerly belonging to the Lagh´ri tribe, and still bearing its name, has attached itself to the Qasráni; while there is a Jiskáni section in both the Drishak and the Gurcháni tribes. Thus too, Rind tribes are sometimes found to include Lasbári clans. So when Násir Khán, the great Khán of Kelát who assisted Ahmad Sháh in his invasion of Dehli, reduced the Hasanni tribe and drove them from their territory, they took refuge with the Khetrán, of which tribe they now form a clan. Even strangers are often affiliated in this manner. Thus the Lagbári tribe includes a section of Náhar Patháns (the family from which sprung the Lodi dynasty of Dehli), who are not Biloch but who are Khetrán. And the Gurcháni tribe includes sections which, though bearing a Biloch name and talking the Bilochi language, are not allowed to be of Biloch race and are almost certainly Jat.

The tribe (*tuman*[1]) under its chief or *tumandár* is sub-divided into a small number of clans (*pára*) with their *muqaddams* or headmen, and each clan into more numerous septs (*phalli*). Below the *phalli* come the families, of which it will sometimes contain as few as a dozen. The clans are based upon common descent; and identity of clan name, even in two different tribes, almost certainly indicates a common ancestor. The sept is of course only an extended family. The tribal names are often patronymics ending in the Bilochi termination *áni*, such as Gurcháni, Bálacháni; or in some few cases in the Pashto *zai*. An individual is commonly known by the name of his clan, the sept being comparatively unimportant. Marriage within the sept is forbidden,[2] and this appears to be the only restriction. The Biloches freely marry Jat women, though the first wife of a Chief will always be a Bilochni. They say that they never give their daughters to Jats; but this assertion, though probably true on the frontier, is most certainly not so beyond the tribal limits.

The tract occupied by each division of a Biloch tribe is sufficiently well defined; but within this area the people are either wholly nomad or, as is the case within our frontier, live in small hamlets, each inhabited by only a few families, having property in their cultivated lands and irrigation works, but without any actual demarcation of the surrounding pasture lands. Thus the large and compact village community of the Eastern Panjáb is unknown, and our village or *mauzah* is in these parts merely a collection of hamlets included within a common boundary for administrative purposes.

---

[1] A Persian (? Túrkomán) word meaning 10,000; a body of 10,000 troops; a district or *tribe* furnishing a body of 10,000 troops.

[2] But Mr. Fryer says that cousins commonly intermarry.

*P. 48-9. †P. 50-51 ‡P. 52. **381. Tribal statistics.**—Abstract No. 66 on the next page* shows the figures for the main Biloch tribes, Abstract No. 67† gives those for minor tribes for certain districts only, while Abstract No. 68‡ shows the principal clans.

The percentage of the Biloch population not included in these details is small in the districts where the Biloch element has any importance, being only 9 per cent. in Derah Ghâzi Khán, 13 per cent. in Derah Ismáíl Khán, 15 per cent. in Muzaffargarh, and 19 per cent. in Multán. In other districts it is much larger. As has already been explained, sections of the same name occur in different tribes; while a clan of one tribe will bear the tribal name of another tribe. Thus, where the columns for sub-divisions of caste have not been filled up with sufficient care, errors in tabulation are almost unavoidable. For this reason the tribal and clan figures were tabulated in the district offices. Unfortunately, the Deputy Commissioner of Derah Ghâzi, from whom I had hoped for great assistance, was so busy that he was unable to pay any attention to the matter; and one or two of the results which the Derah Ghâzi figures give are patently absurd. It is to be regretted that the opportunity which a Census affords only at long intervals of obtaining an accurate detail of the Ghâzi tribes, should not have been made the most of. The points in which the figures are untrustworthy are indicated below.

382. The organised Biloch tribes of the Derajat.—It is only in Derah Ghâzi Khán and on its frontier that we have to do with Biloch tribes having a distinct tribal and political organisation. Elsewhere in the Panjáb the tribal tie is merely that of common descent, and the tribe possesses no corporate coherence. The Derah Ghâzi tribes are in the main of Rind origin. They are, beginning from the south, Mazári, Bugti, Marri, Drishak, Gurcháni, Tibbi Lund, Laghári, Khetrán, Khosa, Sori Lund, Bozdár, Qasráni, and Nutkáni; and of these the Marri, Bugti and Khetrán are wholly, and the Gurcháni and the Legbári partly independent, while the Nutkáni has recently lost its individuality as a tribe. The figures for both the Lunds are certainly, and those for the Gurcháni possibly wrong, as is noted under the respective tribes.

[P. 197] **The Mazari (No. 11)** are practically found only in Derah Ghâzi Khán, of which they occupy the southernmost portion, their western boundary being the hills and their eastern the river. Their country extends over the Sindh frontier into Jacobábád, and stretches northwards as far as Umrkot and the Pitok pass. Rojhán is their headquarters. They say that about the middle of the 17th century they quarrelled with the Chándia of Sindh, and moved into the Siáháf valley and Maráo plain, and the hill country to the west now occupied by the Bugti; but obtaining grants of land in the lowlands gradually shifted eastwards towards the river. Mr. Fryer puts their fighting strength at 4,000, but our returns show only 9,000 souls in the Province and there are very few beyond our border, the Shambáni territory lying just behind it. The tribe traces its descent from Hot, son of Jalál, and is divided into four clans, Rustamáni, Masidáni, Bálacháni, and Sargáni; of which the first two are the more numerous, though the chief is a Bálacháni.

The Marri, and the Bugti or Zarkanni (No. 38) hold the country beyond our southern border; and are wholly independent, or rather nominally subject to the Khán of Kelát, not being found within the Panjáb. They are both of Rind origin. The Marri, who hold a large area bounded by the Khetrán on the east, the Bugti on the south, Kachhi of Kelát on the west, and Afghánistán on the north, are the most powerful and consequently the most troublesome of all the Biloch tribes. They have four clans, the Ghazani, Loharáni, Mazaráni and Bijaráni, of which the Mazaráni live beyond Sibi and the Bolán and are almost independent of the tribe. The tribe is wholly nomad and prædatory. The Bugti, who occupy the angle between the frontiers of the Panjáb and Upper Sindh, are also called Zarkanni[1] and their clans are the Raheja, Nutháni, Musúri, Kalpúr, Phong, and Shambáni or Kíazai. The last, which is an almost independent section, separates the main tribe from our border; while the Marri lie still further west. Both these tribes are pure Rind.

[1] A sept of their Raheja clan is also called Zarkanni.

Abstract No. 66, showing the principal [P. 196]

	1	2	3	4	5	6	7	8	9
	Rind.	Laghári.	Jatoi.	Gurcháni.	Lasbári.	Khosa.	Korái.	Tibbi-Lund.	Chándia.
Lahore	351	...	1,045	...	86	...	56	...	...
Gujranwala ..	...	...	147	...	78	...	...	...	...
Firozpur	36	...	595	...	80	...	30	...	...
Rawalpindi ...	49	...	...	...	16	...	102	...	...
Jhelam	87	...	400	...	148	...	916	...	49
Gujrat	...	...	13	...	14	...	71	...	...
Shahpur	1,350	...	2,229	...	1,053	...	402	...	35
Multan	6,008	35	506	...	1,865	...	2,695	...	872
Jhang	5,223	167	1,849	...	696	...	197	...	187
Montgomery ...	1,460	...	4,106	...	754	...	805	...	4
Muzaffargarh ...	4,536	1,159	4,574	...	2,629	106	3,385	...	7,290
Derah Ismail Khan ...	2,233	2,195	1,232	42	4,270	33	1,231	...	1,812
Derah Ghazi Khan ...	6,136	22,980	2,829	17,099	1,354	11,308	727	10,888	412
Bannu	237	75	1	...	325	...	70	...	124
Dehli Division ...	158	...	...	...	...	...	15	...	...
Hissar Division ...	108	...	504	...	467	...	69	...	...
Ambala Division ...	...	...	65	...	18	...	23	...	...
Jalandhar Division...	1	...	48	...	...	...	...	...	...
Amritsar Division ...	...	...	9	...	46	...	29	...	..
Peshawar Division ...	16	25	7	...	3	...	179	...	...
British Territory	27,988	26,636	20,159	17,141	13,902	11,446	10,995	10,888	10,785
Nabha and Faridkot	68	...	163	...	98	...	30	...	...
Bahawalpur ...	8,287	97	4,272	...	3,295	1,011	4,435	...	1,263
Total Province...	36,343	26,733	24,598	17,141	17,295	12,457	15,461	10,888	12,048

Biloch Tribes for Districts and States.

10 Gopang.	11 Mazari.	12 Hot.	13 Nutkani.	14 Gurmani.	15 Kulachi.	16 Qasrani.	17 Jiskani.	18 Drishak.	
...	...	78	...	..	...	...	...	...	Lahore.
...	...	148	...	...	...	...	...	...	Gujranwala.
...		56	...	...	...	...	...	...	Firozpur.
...	...	21	...	...	...	...	13	...	Rawalpindi.
...	...	121	...	...	...	...	...	...	Jhelam.
...	...	1	...	...	...	...	...	...	Gujrat.
...	...	176	...	...	...	...	...	...	Shahpur.
992	2	842	...	62	457	4	78	...	Multan.
17	...	774	21	...	53	59	270	...	Jhang.
1	...	654	...	...	41	...	...	...	Montgomery.
8,160	7	1,106	257	2,522	977	...	317	374	Muzaffargarh.
24	5	1,072	597	1,076	3,724	1,675	3,705	...	Derah Ismail Khan
1,230	8,649	282	4,671	1,666	...	2,615	13	3,796	Derah Ghazi Khan.
...	...	66	...	1	14	...	2	...	Bannu.
...	...	11	...	...	2	7	...	...	Dehli Division.
14	...	317	...	...	...	58	...	...	Hissar Division.
...	...	7	...	...	...	...	...	...	Ambala Division.
...	...	4	...	...	...	...	...	...	Jalandhar Division.
...	...	10	...	...	...	...	...	...	Amritsar Division.
...	.	36	..	...	...	...	...	...	Peshawar Division.
10,788	8,668	5,783	5,546	5,327	5,268	4,418	4,398	4,170	**British Territory.**
...	...	14	...	...	...	...	...	...	Nabha and Faridkot.
5,437	548	3,341	..	...	371	...	333	74	Bahawalpur.
16,175	9,311	9,138	5,546	5,327	5,639	4,418	4,731	4,244	**Total Province.**

Abstract No. 67, showing [P. 196]

Districts and States, &c.	19 Petáfi.	20 Gashkori.	21 Mihráni.	22 Bozdár.	23 Mastoi.	24 Mashori.	25 Dasti.	26 Hajáni.
Derah Ismail Khan ...	1,344	1,752	2,188	285	28	140	813	...
Derah Ghazi Khan ...	133	92	91	1,715	1,300	53	610	1,017
Muzaffargarh	1,441	893	...	107	685	1,743	406	655
Other districts	16	118	...	4	77	151	255	...
Total British Territory ...	2,934	2,855	2,279	2,111	2,090	2,087	2,083	1,672
Bahawalpur	810	62	...	73	686	...	1,808	...
Total Province ...	3,744	2,917	2,279	2,184	2,776	2,087	3,891	1,672

Districts and States, &c.	36 Kashák.	37 Khetrán.	38 Bugti.	39 Bujráni.	40 Badáṅ.	41 Pachár.	42 Tanwári.
Derah Ismail Khan ...	...	340	234	504	...	28	13
Derah Ghazi Khan ...	...	246	295	...	...	...	...
Muzaffargarh ...	580	...	...	...	291	309	151
Other districts ...	106	...	...	...	...	...	...
Total British Territory	686	586	529	504	291	397	164
Bahawalpur ...	...	19	...	...	...	...	...
Total Province ...	686	605	529	504	291	397	164

minor Biloch Tribes.

27	28	29	30	31	32	33	34	35	
Sahráni.	Sanjráni.	Laskáni.	Magassi.	Ahmadáni.	Gabol.	Qandráni.	Kupcháni.	Aliáni.	DISTRICTS AND STATES, &C.
...	10	271	748	...	...	...	795	612	Derah Ismail Khan.
...	1,094	528	33	1,132	...	...	...	...	Derah Ghazi Khan.
1,629	293	505	303	...	960	842	...	...	Muzaffargarh.
...	...	40	175	...	2	...	...	135	Other districts.
1,629	1,397	1,344	1,259	1,132	962	842	795	747	Total British Territory.
...	...	...	42	...	42	6	...	...	Bahawalpur.
1,629	1,397	1,344	1,301	1,132	1,004	848	795	747	Total Province.

43	44	45	46	47	48	49	50	51	
Jáfar.	Hijbáni.	Sargáni.	Shekháni.	Sháháni.	Lund.	Mariáni.	Sakháni.	Mazkáni.	DISTRICTS AND STATES, &C.
24	363	...	12	...	84	15	99	2	Derah Ismail Khan.
22	64	21	...	23	...	...	...	...	Derah Ghazi Khan.
...	45	57	...	...	98	...	...	...	Muzaffargarh.
...	...	...	...	...	...	...	...	...	Other districts.
46	472	78	12	23	182	15	99	284	Total British Territory.
...	...	...	...	...	...	...	...	...	Bahawalpur.
46	472	78	12	23	182	15	99	284	Total Province.

Abstract No. 68, showing the principal Biloch Clans. [P. 196.]

District.	2. Laghari. Aliáni.	Haddiáni.	Bughláni.	Haibatáni.	Other Lagháris.	Total.	3. Jatoi. Bhund.	Zaugeja.	Vadáli.	Other Jatoi.	Total.
Derah Ghazi Khan	3,031	54	1,753	1,031	17,111	22,980	...	...	...	...	...
Derah Ismail Khan	...	567	...	...	1,628	2,195	272	891	24	45	1,232
Muzaffargarh ...	89	...	...	...	1,070	1,159	...		...	...	...
Total ...	3,120	621	1,753	1,031	19,809	26,234	272	891	24	45	1,232

District.	4. Gurchani. Shaháni.	Lashári	Petáfi.	Durkáni.	Other Gurcháni.	Total.	6. Khosa. Babeláni.	Isáni.	Other Khosa.	Total.
Derah Ghazi Khan	659	9,525	1,798	51	5,066	17,099	1,797	2,619	6,892	11,308
Derah Ismail Khan	...	...	...	42	...	42	...	...	32	32
Muzaffargarh ...		...	...	...	...	...	...	...	106	106
Total ...	659	9,525	1,798	93	5,066	17,141	1,797	2,619	7,030	11,446

District.	8. Tibbi Lund. Lund.	Other Tibbi Lund.	Total.	11. Mazari. Bálacháni.	Rustamáni.	Masidáni.	Sargáni.	Other Mazári.	Total.
Derah Ghazi Khan	7,188	3,700	10,888	1,179	2,772	2,760	1,257	681	8,649
Derah Ismail Khan	...	...	...	...	...	...	...	5	5
Muzaffargarh ...	...	...	...	...	...	...	...	7	7
Total ...	7,188	3,700	10,888	1,179	2,772	2,760	1,257	693	8,661

District.	17. Jiskani. Sargáni.	Shábáni.	Lashkaráni	Mamdáni.	Other Jiskáni.	Total	18. Drishak. Kirmáni	Gulfáz.	Other Drishak.	Total.	38. Bugti. Shambáni.	Other Bugti.	Total.
Derah Ghazi Khan	...	...	...	...	...	...	210	724	2,862	3,796	160	135	295
Derah Ismail Khan	1,020	506	910	813	456	3,705	...	...	...	...	...	234	234
Muzaffargarh ...	...	...	...	...	...	...	...	52	322	374	...	...	...
Total ...	1,020	506	910	813	456	3,705	210	776	3,184	4,170	160	369	529

The Drishak (No. 18) are the most scattered of all the Derah Ghází tribes, many of their villages lying among a Jat population on the bank of the Indus; and this fact renders the tribe less powerful than it should be from its numbers. They hold no portion of the hills, and are practically confined to the Ghází district, lying scattered about between the Pitok pass on the north and the Sori pass on the south. The tribe belongs to the Rind section; but claims descent from Hot, son of Jalál Khán. Its sections are the Kirmáni, Mingwáni, Gulfáz, Sargáni, Arbáni and Jiskáni, the chief belonging to the first of these. Their headquarters are at Asni close to Rájanpur. They are said to have descended into the plains after the Mazári, or towards the end of the 17th century.

The Gurchani (No. 4) own the Mári and Drágal hills, and their boundary extends further into the mountains than that of any other of the tribes subject to us; while their territory does not extend much to the east of the Sulemáns. They are divided into eleven clans, of which the chief are the Durkáni, Shekháni, Lashári, Petáfi, Jiskáni, and Sabzáni. The last four are true Biloches and the last three Rinds; the remainder of the tribe being said to have descended from Gorish, a grandson of Rája Bhímsen of Haidarábád, who was adopted by the Biloches and married among them. He is said to have accompanied Humáyún to Dehli, and on his return to have collected a Biloch following and ejected the Pathán holders from the present Gurchání holdings. It is not impossible that a considerable number of the Lashári clan, who are not too proud of their affiliation to the Gurcháni, may have returned themselves as Lashári simply, and so have been included in the Lashári tribe. The whole of the Durkáni and about half of the Lashári live beyond our border, and are not subject to us save through their connection with the tribe. The latter is the most turbulent of all the clans, and they and the Petáfi used to rival the Khosa tribe in lawlessness of conduct. They have lately been given fresh lands and are gradually settling down. The Gurcháni tribe is said to possess 2,600 fighting men. They are not found in any other part of the Panjáb than Derah Ghází.

The Tibbi Lund (No. 8) are also wholly confined to the Ghází district, where they occupy a small area in the midst of the Gurcháni country. They are composed of Lunds, Rinds and Khosas, all of true Rind origin, the Lund clan comprising some two-thirds of their whole numbers. These three sections were only quite recently united under the authority of the Tibbi Lund *tumandár*. Unfortunately, the figures given for this tribe evidently include those of the Sori Lund mentioned below.

The Laghari (No. 22) occupy the country from the Kúra pass, which is the Gurcháni northern border, to the Sakhi Sarwar pass a little to the north of Derah, which divides them from the Khosa. They are of pure Rind origin and are divided into four sections, the Haddiáni, Aliáni, Bughláni, and Haibatáni, of which the first inhabit the hills beyond our border and are not subject to our rule, and are, or were in 1830, nomadic and inveterate thieves. The chief belongs to the Aliáni clan. Their head-quarters are at Chhoti Zerín, where they are said to have settled after their return from accompanying Humáyún, expelling the Ahmadánis who then held the present Laghári country. The tribe numbers some 5,000 fighting men. They are also found in considerable numbers in Derah Ismáíl and Muzaffargarh; but these outlying settlements own no allegiance to the tribe. The Tálpúr dynasty of Sindh belonged to this tribe,[1] and there is still a considerable Laghári colony in that Province. It appears probable that the representatives of several of the Northern Biloch tribes which are now found in Sindh, are descended from people who went there during the Tálpúr rule.

383. **The Khetran (No. 37)** are an independent tribe living beyond our border at the back of the Laghári, Khosa, and Lund country. Their original settlement was at Vahoa in the country of the Qasráni of Derah Ismáíl Khán, where many of them still live and hold land between the Qasráni and the river. But the Emperor Akbar drove out the main body of the tribe, and they took refuge in the Bárkhán valley of the Laghári hills, and still hold the surrounding tract and look to the Laghári chief as their protector. They are certainly not pure Biloch, and are held by
P. 66-71 many to be Patháns, descended from Miána (No. 87 in the Pathán table of tribes, page 205), brother of Tarín, the ancestor of the Abdáli; and they do not in some cases intermarry with Patháns But they confessedly resemble Biloches in features, habits, and general appearance, the names of their septs end in the Biloch patronymic termination *áni*, and they are now for all practical purposes a Biloch tribe. It is probable that they are in reality a remnant of the original Jat population; they speak a dialect of their own called Khetránki which is an Indian dialect closely allied with Sindhi, and in fact probably a form of the Jatki speech of the lower Indus. They are the least warlike of all the Biloch tribes, capital cultivators, and in consequence exceedingly wealthy. In this Census they returned themselves as follows within British Territory:—

	Patháns.	*Biloches.*	*Total.*
Derah Ismáíl Khán	1,324	340	1,664
Derah Ghází Khán	32	246	278
Total Province	1,558	605	2,163

[1] See Macgregor's *Gazetteer of the North-West Frontier*, Vol. II, page 259, for an account of its origin.

The tribe as it now stands is composed of four clans, of which the Ganjúra represents the original Khetrán nucleus, while to them are affiliated the Dháriwál[1] or Chácha who say that they are Dodai Biloches, the Hasanni, once an important Biloch tribe which was crushed by Násir Khán, the great Khán of Kelát, and took refuge with the Khetrán of whom they are now almost independent, and the Náhar or Bábar, who are by origin Lodi Patháns.

The Khosa (No. 6) occupy the country between the Laghári and the Qasráni, their territory being divided into a northern and a southern portion by the territory of the Lunds, and stretching from the foot of the hills nearly across to the river. They are said to have settled originally in Kech; but with the exception of a certain number in Baháwalpur, they are, so far as the Panjáb is concerned, only found in Derah Gházi. They hold, however, extensive lands in Sindh, which were granted them by Humáyún in return for military service. They are one of the most powerful tribes on the border, and very independent of their Chief and are "admitted to be among the bravest of the Biloches." They are true Rinds and are divided into six clans, of which the Babeláni and Isáni are the most important, the latter being an offshoot of the Khetrán affiliated to the Khosa. The other four are Jaggel, Jandáni, Jarwár, and Mahrwáni. The Chief belongs to the Bátel clan. The Khosa is the most industrious of the organised tribes; and at the same time the one which next to the Gurcháni bears the worst character for lawlessness. In 1859 Major Pollock wrote: "It is rare to find a Khosa who has not been in prison for cattle-stealing, or deserved to "be; and a Khosa who has not committed a murder or debauched his neighbour's wife or destroyed "his neighbour's landmark is a decidedly creditable specimen." And even now the description is not very much exaggerated.

The Lund (No. 49) or Sori Lund, as they are called to distinguish them from the Tibbi Lund, are a small tribe which has only lately risen to importance. Their territory divides that of the Khosa into two parts, and extends to the bank of the Indus. They are not pure Biloches, and are divided into six clans, the Haidaráni, Bakráni, Zariáni, Garzwáni, Nuháni, and Gurcháni, none of which are important. The figures given for this tribe are obviously absurd, and they have apparently been included with the Tibbi Lund (No. 8). [P. 198]

The Bozdar (No. 22) are an independent tribe situated beyond our frontier at the back of the Qasráni Territory. They hold from the Sanghar Pass on the north to the Khosa and Khetrán country on the south; and they have the Lúni and Músa Khel Patháns on their western border. Abstract No. 67 shows over 2,000 men as having been within the Panjáb at the time of the Census, almost all of them in the Ghází district. These live in scattered villages about Rájanpur and among the Laghári tribe, and have no connection with the parent tribe. The Bozdár are of Rind extraction, and are divided into the Duláni, Ladwáni, Ghulámáni, Chakráni, Siháni, Sháhwáni, Jaláláni, Jáfiráni, and Rustamáni clans. They are more civilized than most of the transfrontier tribes and are of all the Biloches the strictest Musalmáns. Unlike all other Biloches they fight with the matchlock rather than with the sword. They are great graziers, and their name is said to be derived from the Persian *buz*, a "goat."

The Qasrani (No. 16) are the northernmost of the tribes which retain their political organisation, their territory lying on either side of the boundary between the two Derahs, and being confined to the hills both within and beyond our frontier and the sub-montane strip. Their name is written Qaizaráni or Imperial. The tribe is a poor one, and is divided into seven clans, the Lashkaráni, Khúbdín, Budáni, Vaswáni, Laghári, Jarwár, and Rustamáni, none of which are important. They are of Rind origin, and are not found in the Panjáb in any number beyond the Derah district.

The Nutkani (No. 13) are a tribe peculiar to Derah Ghází Khán, which holds a compact territory stretching eastward to the Indus and between the Northern Khosa and the Qasráni. The tribe once enjoyed considerable influence and importance, holding rights of superior ownership over the whole of the Sanghar country. But it no longer possesses a political organization, having been crushed out of tribal existence in the early days of Ranjít Singh's rule. But the event is so recent that it still retains much of its tribal coherence and of the characteristics of its race.

384. The broken Biloch tribes of Derah Ghazi.—The tribes above enumerated are the only ones to be found within or immediately upon our border which have a regular tribal organisation. But there are many other Biloch tribes, and among them some of those most numerously represented in the Panjáb, which occupy large areas in the south-western districts of the Province. They no longer hold compact territories exclusively as their own, while to great extent in the Derаját itself, and still more outside it, they have lost their peculiar language and habits, and can hardly be distinguished from the Jat population with whom they are more or less intermixed, and from whom

[1] Dháriwál is the name of an important Jat tribe.

they differ in little but race. The history of the Biloches of the Derah Ghází lowlands is briefly sketched in the next paragraph. Their most important tribes are the Rind,[1] the Jatoi, who still hold as a tribe, though without political organisation, a compact tract in Sindh between Shikárpur and the Indus, the Lashári,[1] Gopáng, Gurmáni, Mastoi, Hajáni, Sanjráni, and Ahmadáni. These all lie scattered along the edge of the Indus, intermingled with the Jats of the Kachi or low riverain tract.

385. **Biloch tribes of Derah Ismail.**—I have already stated that the three sons of Malik Sohráb Khán and Ghází Khán, Dodais, founded Derah Ghází, Derah Ismáíl, and Derah Fatah Khán. The tribal name of Dodai seems to have been soon dropped, or perhaps the leaders were of a different tribe from their followers; for the representatives and tribesmen of Ghází Khán are locally known as Mihráni, those of Ismáíl Khán as Hot, and those of Fatah Khán as Kuláchi. The party of Fatah Khán never seems to have attained to any importance, and was almost from the beginning subject to the Hot. With Ghází Khán came the Jiskáni, who occupied the cis-Indus tract above Bhakkar, while with the Hots came the Korái whose name is associated with them in an old Biloch verse. "The Hots and Korái are joined together; "they are equal with the Rind." The Korái do not appear to have exercised independent rule. At the zenith of their power the Hot, Mihráni, and Jiskáni held sway over almost the whole of the Indus valley and of the *thal* between the Indus and the Chanáb, from the centre of the Muzaffargarh district to the Salt-range Tract, the northern boundary of Sanghar and Leiah being the northern boundary of the Mihráni, while the Indus separated the Hot from Jiskáni. During the latter half of the 16th century Dáúd Khán, a Jiskani and the descendant of one of Ghází Khán's followers, moved southwards and subjugated to himself the greater part of the Leiah country. Akbar dispersed his tribe, but early in the 17th century the independence of the Jiskáni under Biloch Khán was recognised, and it is from Biloch Khán that the Jiskáni, Mandráni, Mamdáni, Sargáni, Qandráni, and Maliáni, who still occupy the Bhakkar and Leiah tahsíls, trace their descent. In about 1750—1770 A. D. the Mihráni, who sided with the Kalhoras or Saráis of Sindh in their struggle with Ahmad Sháh Durráni, were driven out of Derah Ghází by the Jiskáni and fled to Leiah, where many of them are still to be found; and a few years later the Kalhoras, expelled from Sindh, joined with the always turbulent Sargáni to crush the Jiskáni rule. About the same time the Hot were overthrown after a desperate struggle by the Gandápur Patháns.

The Biloches of Dera Ismáíl are now confined to the low lands, with the exception of the Qasráni and Khetrán of the southern border who have already been noticed in section 383. The upper hills are held by Patháns. The principal tribes are the Lashári,[2] the Kuláchi and the Jiskáni. After them come the Rind, the Laghári, the Jatoi, the Korái, the Chándia, the Hot, the Gurmáni, the Petáfi, the Gashkori, and the Mihráni. Of the four last all but the Petáfi seem almost confined to Derah Ismáíl.

386. **The Biloch tribes of Muzaffargarh.**—In Muzaffargarh more perhaps than in any other district the Biloch is intermingled with the Jat population, and the tribal name merely denotes common descent, its common owners

[1] It is possible that some Biloches may have returned themselves as Rind or Lashári with reference to their original stock rather than to their present tribe; and that some of the Lashári clans of the Gurcháni tribe may have been included in the Lashári tribe.

[2] See note to the preceding paragraph.

possess no sort of tribal coherence. The reason doubtless is that since the Biloch immigration the district has formed the borderland between the Lodi of Sítpur, the Dáúdpotra of Baháwalpur, the Mihráni of Derah Gházi, and the Langáh of Multán. The Gopáng, the Chándia, the Rind, the Jatoi, and the Korái are the tribes most numerously represented. Then came the Laghári, the Lashári, the Hot, the Gurmáni, the Petáfi, the Mashori, and the Sahráni, of which the last two are hardly found elsewhere.

387. **The Biloch tribes of the Lower Indus and Satluj.**—A very considerable number of Biloches are scattered along the lower Indus and Satluj in Baháwalpur and Multán, and especially in the former. The most important are the Rind,[1] the Korái, the Gopáng, the Jatoi, the Lashári,[1] and the Hot, while less numerous but still important are the Chándia, the Khosa, and the Dasti. [P 199]

388. **The Biloch tribes of the Ravi, upper Jahlam, and Chanab.**—The Biloches of the Rávi are chiefly found in the *bár* of the Montgomery and Jhang districts, where they occupy themselves in camel-breeding, holding but little land as cultivators. They consist almost wholly of Jatoi and Rind, which latter tribe has penetrated in some numbers as high up as Lahore. They are probably descendants of the men who under Mír Chákar accompanied Humáyún and received a grant of land in Montgomery in return for their services. In the Jhang and Shahpur districts, on the Jahlam and the right bank of the Chanáb, the principal tribes to be found are the Rind, the Jatoi, the Lashári, and the Korái.

389. **Course of migration of the Biloch tribes.**—Of the original location of the tribes I know next to nothing, and what information I have been able to collect is given in section 378. But the above sketch of their existing distribution enables us to follow with some certainty the later routes by which they arrived at their present settlements. The organised tribes of Derah Ghází, including the Nutkáni, would appear to have descended from the hills eastwards towards the river; and the four most insignificant of the broken tribes, the Mastoi, the Hajáni, the Sanjráni, and the Ahmadáni, seem to have followed the same course. A few Laghári are found in Derah Ismáíl and Muzaffargarh, and a few Khosa in Baháwalpur; but with these exceptions not one of the above tribes is represented in the Panjáb outside the Ghází district, except the Qasráni whose hill territory extends into Derah Ismáíl. On the other hand all the larger broken tribes of Derah Ghází, with the single exception of the Nutkáni which was till lately organised, and all the remaining tribes which possess any numerical importance in the Panjáb except four Derah Ismáíl tribes to be mentioned presently, seem to have spread up the Indus from below, as they are without exception strongly represented on the lower course of the river, and not at all in the hill country. The Rind and the Jatoi seem to have come up the Indus in very great numbers, and to have spread high up that river, the Chanáb, the Jahlam, the Rávi, and the Satluj. The Lashári and the Korái followed in their track in slightly smaller numbers, but avoided to a great extent the Rávi valley. The Chándia, the Gopáng, the Hot, and the Gurmáni seem to have confined themselves chiefly to the valley of the Indus, the Chándia having perhaps passed up the left bank, as they are found in Derah Ismáíl but not in Derah Ghází. So indeed are the Hot,

[1] See note to section 384.

but that is accounted for by their seat of Government having been Derah Ismáíl. Four tribes, the Kuláchi, the Jiskáni, the Gashkori, and the Mihráni, the two last of which are comparatively insignificant, are found in Derah Ismáíl and nowhere else save in Muzaffargarh, where the first three occur in small numbers. As already stated in section 385, the Jiskáni and Kuláchi apparently had their origin as tribes in Leiah and Derah Fatah Khán, while the Mihráni were driven there from Derah Ghází. It would seem probable that the Gashkori either came across the hills in the south of the district, or are a local sub-division of some larger tribe which followed the usual track along the river. The Korái are Rind; the Gopáng and the Dasti are not pure Biloch, but are said to have accompanied the Rind in their wanderings.

THE PATHAN (CASTE No. 6).

390. Figures and Bibliography for Pathans.—The figures given in Table VIII A., under the head Pathán, almost certainly include many persons whose Pathán origin is to say the least doubtful; while the figures to be discussed in the following pages show that such tribes as Tanáoli, Jadún, Dilazák, Tájik, Khetrán, and even Mughals have returned themselves as Patháns. Major Wace writes: "The tribes in the west and north-west of the Panjáb, who during the "last three centuries were frequently raided upon by Afgháns, got into the habit of inventing "histories of Afghán origin as a protection against ill-treatment:" and even where this motive was absent, the general tendency to claim kinship with the dominant race would produce the same effect. Moreover the origin of some of the tribes on the Peshάwar frontier is doubtful, and their affiliation with the Patháns incomplete, and thus they would set up a claim to be Pathán which the true Pathán would indignantly repudiate. Mr. Thorburn notices the many and bitter disputes caused by the preparation of the genealogical trees during the Bannu Settlement, and the attempts made by Jat clans to be recorded as Patháns. He writes: "A "low-caste man born and brought up in a Pathán country, if serving away from his home, "invariably affixes Khán to his name and dubs himself Pathán. It goes down if he can talk "Pashto, and his honour proportionally goes up." Still the great mass of those returned as Patháns are probably really so, and the figures represent very fairly the general distribution of the race.

In the second place, it must be remembered that of those who are really Pathán and returned as such, many are not British subjects at all. Such tribes as the Bar Mohmand of the Peshάwar frontier, who, while essentially independent tribes, hold land within our border, come down in considerable numbers in the winter to cultivate their fields; while in the summer they retreat to their cool valleys in independent territory. So too the very numerous *Pawindahs* of Derah Ismáíl only winter in the Panjáb, and the number thus temporarily added to our Pathán population is exceedingly large (section 398). Again, almost the whole of the local trade across the border is in the hands of independent tribes whose members come into our districts in considerable numbers with merchandize of sorts; while the seasons of drought and distress which preceded the Census drove many of the frontier hill-men into our districts in search of employment, and especially on the Bannu border, and on the Thal road in Kohát and the Swát canal in Peshάwar.

As for the figures for the separate tribes, they were classified, not by my central office, but by the Deputy Commissioners of the several frontier districts, at least so far as regards the figures of those districts. Thus far greater accuracy will have been secured than would otherwise have been possible. But the lists of tribes received from some of the districts, on which the selection of tribes for tabulation was based (see Chapter on Tabulation, Book II), were in some instances very imperfect and the classification exceedingly faulty; tribes of considerable numerical importance in British Territory being omitted, frontier tribes represented in the Panjáb by only a few score of persons being included, and tribes, clans, and septs being mixed up in a perfect chaos of cross-classification. So too the constant recurrence of the same clan name among the various tribes was a certain source of error. Such names as Daulat Khel, Fíroz Khel, Usmánzai, and Mahammadzai recur in many separate tribes; and where the schedule entry of sub-divisions did not specify the tribe, no certain classification could be made.

The best authorities on the subject of the Pathán nation as a whole are Dorn's translation of Niámat Ullah's *History of the Afgháns* (*Oriental Translation Committee, London, 1829*), Priestly's translation of the Haiyát-i-Afgháni called *Afghánistán and its Inhabitants* (*Lahore, 1874*), Elphinstone's *Kábul*, and Bellew's *Races of Afghánistán*. Bellew's *Yúsufzai*, Plowden's translation of the *Kalíd-i-Afgháni*, and the Settlement Reports of the districts of the northern frontier contain full information concerning the Pathâns of the Panjáb border, as do Macgregor's *Gazetteer of the N.-W. Frontier*, and Paget's *Expeditions against the N.-W. Frontier Tribes.*

391. Description of the Pathans.—The true Pathán is perhaps the most barbaric of all the races with which we are brought into contact in the Panjáb. His life is not so primitive as that of the gipsy tribes. But he is bloodthirsty, cruel, and vindictive in the highest degree: he does not know what truth or faith is, insomuch that the saying *Afghán be imán* has passed into a proverb among his neighbours; and though he is not without courage of a sort and is often curiously reckless of his life, he would scorn to face an enemy whom he could stab from behind, or to meet him on equal terms if it were possible to take advantage of him, however meanly. It is easy to convict him out of his own mouth; here are some of his proverbs: "A Pathán's enmity smoulders like a dung-fire."—"A cousin's tooth breaks upon a cousin."—"Keep a cousin poor, but "use him."—"When he is little play with him: when he is grown up he "is a cousin; fight him."—"Speak good words to an enemy very softly: "gradually destroy him root and branch.[1]" At the same time he has his code of honour which he observes strictly, and which he quotes with pride under the name of Pakhtúnwáli. It imposes upon him three chief obligations, *Nanawátai* or the right of asylum, which compels him to shelter and protect even an enemy who comes as a suppliant; *Badal* or the necessity to revenge by retaliation; and *Melmastia* or open-handed hospitality to all who may demand it. And of these three perhaps the last is greatest. And there is a sort of charm about him, especially about the leading men, which almost makes one forget his treacherous nature. As the proverb says—"The Pathán is one moment a saint, and the next a devil." For centuries he has been, on our frontier at least, subject to no man. He leads a wild, free, active life in the rugged fastnesses of his mountains; and there is an air of masculine independence about him which is refreshing in a country like India. He is a bigot of the most fanatical type, exceedingly proud, and extraordinarily superstitious. He is of stalwart make, and his features are often of a markedly Semitic type. His hair, plentifully oiled, hangs long and straight to his shoulder;[2] he wears a loose tunic, baggy drawers, a sheet or blanket, sandals, and a sheepskin coat with its wool inside; his favourite colour is dark-blue,[3] and his national arms the long heavy Afghán knife and the matchlock or *jazail*. His women wear a loose shift, wide wrinkled drawers down to their ankles, and a wrap over the head; and are as a rule jealously secluded. Both sexes are filthy in their persons. [P. 200]

Such is the Pathán in his home among the fastnesses of the frontier ranges. But the Patháns of our territory have been much softened by our rule and by the agricultural life of the plains, so that they look down upon the Patháns of the hills, and their proverbs have it —"A hill man is no man," and again, "Don't class burrs as grass or a hill man as a human being." The nearer he is to the frontier the more closely the Pathán assimilates to the original type; while on this side of the Indus, even in the riverain itself, there is little or nothing, not even language, to distinguish him

[1] The Pashto word *tarbúr* is used indifferently for "cousin" or for "enemy;" and tarbúrwáli either for "cousinhood" or for "enmity."

[2] This is not true of the northern Patháns, who shave their heads, and often their beards also.

[3] The colour and cut of the clothes vary greatly with the tribe.

from his neighbours of the same religion as himself. The Patháns are extraordinarily jealous of female honour, and most of the blood feuds for which they are so famous originate in quarrels about women. As a race they strictly seclude their females, but the poorer tribes and the poorer members of all tribes are prevented from doing so by their poverty. Among the tribes of our territory a woman's nose is cut off if she be detected in adultery; and it is a favourite joke to induce a Pathán woman to unveil by saying to her suddenly "You have no nose!" The Pathán pretends to be purely endogamous and beyond the border he probably is so; while even in British Territory the first wife will generally be a Pathán, except among the poorest classes. At the same time Pathán women are beyond the Indus seldom if ever married to any but Patháns. They intermarry very closely, avoiding only the prohibited degrees of Islám. Their rules of inheritance are tribal and not Mahomedan, and tend to keep property within the agnatic society, though some few of the more educated families have lately begun to follow the Musalmán law. Their social customs differ much from tribe to tribe, or rather perhaps from the wilder to the more civilised sections of the nation. The Patháns beyond and upon our frontier live in fortified villages, to which are attached stone towers in commanding positions which serve as watch-towers and places of refuge for the inhabitants. Small raids from the hills into the plains below are still common; and beyond the Indus the people, even in British Territory, seldom sleep far from the walls of the village.

The figures showing the distribution of Patháns are given in Abstract
P.38-9. No. 65 on page 191. They are the dominant race throughout the whole tract west of the Indus as far south as the southern border of the tahsíl of Derah Ismáíl Khán, which roughly divides the Pathán from the Biloch. On this side of the Indus they hold much of the Chach country of Hazára and Ráwalpindi, they have considerable colonies along the left bank of the Indus till it finally leaves the Salt-range, and they hold the northern portion of the Bhakkar *thal*. Besides those tracts which are territorially held by Patháns, there are numerous Pathán colonies scattered about the Province, most of them descendants of men who rose to power during the Pathán dynasties of Dehli, and received grants of land-revenue which their children often increased at the expense of their neighbours during the turmoil of the 18th century.

392. Origin of the Pathan.—The Afgháns proper claim descent from Saul, the first Jewish King, and there is a formidable array of weighty authority in favour of their Semitic origin. The question of their descent is discussed and authorities quoted in Chapter VI of the Pesháwar Settlement Report, and in Dr. Bellew's *Races of Afghánistán*.[1] Mr. Thorburn quotes in support of their Jewish extraction, "some peculiar customs obtaining "among the tribes of purest blood, for instance the Passover-like practice "of sacrificing an animal and smearing the doorway with its blood in order "to avert calamity, the offering up of sacrifices, the stoning to death of "blasphemers, the periodical distribution of land, and so forth;" and he

[1] Dr. Bellew suggests that the original Afgháns were the Solymi of Herodotus, and were Qureshi Arabs who lived in Syria and there became intermingled with the Jews, or who migrated to Ghor where the fugitive Jews took refuge with them. This supposition would explain the name Sulemáni which is often applied to the Afgháns, and their own assertion that Khalíd ibn Wálid the Qureshi was of the same stock with themselves.

points out that most of the learned men who reject the tradition of Jewish descent have no personal acquaintance with the Afghán people. The Afghán proper is said still to call himself indifferently Ban-i-Afghán or Ban-i-Isráíl to distinguish himself from the Pathán proper who is of Indian, and the Ghilzai who is probably of mixed Turkish and Persian extraction. Pashto, the common language of all three, is distinctly Aryan, being a branch of the old Persian stock. It is described in Chapter V, sections 322-3 of this Report.

There is great conflict of opinion concerning both the origin and constitution of the Pathán nation. Not a few deny that there is any distinction whatever between the original Afghán and Pathán stocks, though these are for the most part officers of our frontier who are not brought into contact with the original Afgháns. I have however been obliged to adopt some one theory of the constitution of the nation as a basis for my classification of tribes; and I have therefore adopted that of Dr. Bellew, who probably has a greater knowledge of the Afgháns of Afghánistán as distinct from the Panjáb frontier, and especially of the old histories of the nation, than any other of the authorities who have treated of the matter. The constitution and early history of the nation according to Dr. Bellew's account are discussed in the paragraphs presently following. But whatever the origin of Afgháns and Patháns proper may be, the nation to which the two names are now applied indifferently in Persian and Pashto respectively, occupying as it does the mountain country lying between the Persian empire on the west, the Indian on the east, the Mongol on the north, and the Biloch on the south, includes as at present constituted many tribes of very diverse origin. They are without exception Mussalmáns, and for the most part bigoted followers of the Sunni sect, hating and persecuting Shíahs, or as they call them Ráfazis.[1] [P. 201]

393. Tribal organisation of the Pathans.—The tribe is probably far more homogeneous in its constitution among the Patháns than among the Biloches. Saiyad, Túrk, and other clans have occasionally been affiliated to it; but as a rule people of foreign descent preserve their tribal individuality, becoming merely associated, and not intermingled, with the tribes among whom they have settled. Even then they generally claim Pathán origin on the female side, and the tribe is usually descended in theory at least from a common ancestor. The *hamsáyah* custom described in section 380, by which strangers are protected by the tribe with which they dwell, is in full force among the Patháns as among the Biloches. But with the former though it does protect in many cases families of one tribe who have settled with another, it seldom accounts for any considerable portion of the tribe; and its action is chiefly confined to traders, menials, and other dependents of foreign extraction, who are protected by but not received into the tribe. Thus a blacksmith living in an Utmánzai village will give his clan an Utmánzai; but his caste will of course remain Lohár. The nation is divided genealogically into a few great sections which have no corporate existence, and the tribe is now the practical unit, though the common name and tradition of common descent are still carefully preserved in the memory of the people. Each section of a tribe,

[1] The 52 Hindus shown in the tables are probably traders living under Pathán protection, or due to errors in enumeration. There are several Shíah clans among the Orakzai of Tiráh on the Kohát border. The people of the Sámilzai *tapah* of the Kohát district, which is conterminous with the territory of these clans, are also Shíahs. All own allegiance to the Shíah Saiyads of the Orakzai Tiráh; while everywhere many of the tribes which claim Saiyad origin are Shíahs.

however small, has its leading man who is known as Malik, a specially Pathán title. In many, but by no means in all tribes, there is a Khán Khel or Chief House, usually the eldest branch of the tribe, whose Malik is known as Khán, and acts as chief of the whole tribe. But he is seldom more than their leader in war and their agent in dealings with others; he possesses influence rather than power; and the real authority rests with the *jirgah*, a democratic council composed of all the Maliks. The tribe is split up into numerous clans, and these again into septs. The tribe, clan, and sept are alike distinguished by patronymics formed from the name of the common ancestor by the addition of the word *Zai* or *Khel*, *Zai* being the corruption of the Pashto *zoe* meaning "son," while *Khel* is an Arabic word meaning an association or company. Both terms are used indifferently for both the larger and smaller divisions.[1] The stock of names being limited, the nomenclature is exceedingly puzzling, certain names recurring in very different tribes in the most maddening manner. Moreover the title which genealogical accuracy would allot to a tribe or clan is often very different from that by which it is known for practical purposes, the people having preferred to be called by the name of a junior ancestor who had acquired local renown. The frontier tribe whether within or beyond our border has almost without exception a very distinct corporate existence, each tribe and within the tribe each clan occupying a clearly defined tract or country, though they are in the Indus Valley often the owners merely rather than the occupiers of the country, the land and smaller villages being largely in the hands of a mixed population of Hindu origin who cultivate subject to the superior rights of the Patháns. These people are included by the Patháns under the generic and semi-contemptuous name of Hindki; a term very analogous to the Jat of the Biloch frontier, and which includes all Mahomedans who, being of Hindu origin, have been converted to Islám in comparatively recent times.[2]

394. Constitution of the Pathan nation.—The words Pathán and Afghán are used indifferently by the natives of India to designate the nation under discussion.[3] But the two words are not used as synonyms by the people themselves. The original Afgháns are a race of probably Jewish or Arab extraction; and they, together with a tribe of Indian origin with which they have long been blended, still distinguish themselves as the true Afgháns, or since the rise of Ahmad Sháh Durráni as Durránis,[4] and class all non-Durráni Pashto-speakers as Opra. But they have lately given their name to Afghánistán, the country formerly known as Khorásán, over which they have now held sway for more than a century, and which is bounded on the north by the Oxus, on the south by Bilochistán, on the east by the middle course of the Indus, and on the west by the Persian desert; and, just as the English and Scotch who early in the 17th century settled among and intermarried with the Irish are now called Irish, though still a very distinct section of the population, so all inhabitants of Afghánistán are now in common parlance known as

---

[1] When our ill-fated Resident Major Cavagnari was lately living at Kábul under the Amír Yákúb Khán, those who favoured the British were known as Cavagnarizai, and the national party as Yákúbzai. The ending *zai* is never used by the Afrídi.

[2] The Dilazák are often called Hindkis by the true Patháns, as having come from India and not from Afghánistán.

[3] In Hindustán they are often called Rohillahs, or Highlanders, from Rohi the mountain country of the Patháns (*Roh*=*Koh*, a mountain.)

[4] Either from *Durr-i-Daurán* "pearl of the age" or from *Durr-i-Durrán* "pearl of pearls." The title was adopted by Ahmad Sháh Abdáli when he ascended the throne, in allusion to the Abdáli custom of wearing a pearl stud in the right ear.

Afghán, the races thus included being the Afghán proper, the Pathán proper, the Gilzai, the Tájik, and the Hazára, besides tribes of less importance living on the confines of the country.

The true Patháns are apparently of Indian origin. Their language is called Pashto or Pakhto and they call themselves Pukhtána[1] or Pakhto-speakers; and it is this word of which Pathán is the Indian corruption. They held in the early centuries of our æra the whole of the Safed Koh and Northern Sulemán systems, from the Indus to the Helmand and from the sources of the [P. 202] Swát river and Jalálábád to Peshín and Quetta. The Afgháns and Gilzais spread into their country and adopted their language and customs; and just as Irish, Scotch, and Welsh speaking the English language are commonly called Englishmen, so all who speak the Pakhto tongue came to be included under the name Pathán. Thus the Afgháns and Gilzais are Patháns by virtue of their language, though not of Pathán origin; the Tájiks and Hazáras, who have retained their Persian speech, are not Patháns; while all five are Afgháns by virtue of location, though only one of them is of Afghán race.

395. **Early history of the Afghans.**—The origin and early history of the various tribes which compose the Afghán nation are much disputed by authorities of weight who hold very different views. I have in the following sketch followed the account given by Dr. Bellew, as it affords a convenient framework on which to base a description of those tribes. But it is said to be doubtful whether the distinction which he so strongly insists upon between Pathán proper and Afghán proper really exists or is recognised by the people; while the Jewish origin of any portion of the nation is most uncertain. But the division of the nation into tribes, the internal affinities of those tribes, and the general account of their wanderings are all beyond question; and the theories which account for them are only accepted by me to serve as connecting links which shall bind them into a consecutive story. The traditions of the true Afgháns who trace their name and descent from Afghána, the son of Jeremiah, the son of Saul, and Solomon's commander-in-chief and the builder of his temple, say that they were carried away from Syria by Nebuchadnezzar and planted as colonists in Media and Persia. Thence they emigrated eastwards into the mountains of Ghor and the modern Hazára country. The Afgháns early embraced the creed of Islám, to which they were converted by a small body of their tribe on their return from Arabia, where they had fought for Mahomet under their leader Kais. It is from this Kais or Kish, namesake of Saul's father, who married a daughter of Khalíd-ibn-Wálid a Qureshi Arab and Mahomet's first apostle to the Afgháns, that the modern genealogists trace the descent alike of Patháns, Afgháns, and Gilzai, or at any rate of such tribes of these races as we have here to deal with; and to him they say that the Prophet, pleased with his eminent services, gave the title of *Pathán*, the Syrian word for rudder, and bade him direct his people in the true path. Meanwhile, about the 5th and 6th century of our æra, an irruption of Scythic tribes from beyond the Hindu Kush into the Indus Valley drove a colony of the Buddhist Gandhári, the Gandarii of Herodotus and one of the four great divisions of that Pactyan nation which is now represented by the Patháns proper, from their homes in the Pesháwar valley north of the Kábul river and in the hills circling it to the north; and

[1] Dr. Bellew and Major James identify them with the Pactiyans of Herodotus, and seem half inclined to connect them with the Picts of Britain, as also the Scyths with the Scots, and certain Pathán and Brahoi tribes with Cambrians and Ligurians!

they emigrated *en masse* to a kindred people on the banks of the Helmand, where they established themselves and founded the city which they named Gandhár after their native capital, and which is now called Kandahár.

It is not certain when the Afgháns of Ghor moved down into the Kandahár country where the Gandhári colony was settled; but they probably came as conquerors with the Arab invaders of the 1st century of the Mahomedan æra. They soon settled as the dominant race in their new homes, intermarried with and converted the Gandhári, and adopted their language; and in course of time the two races became fused together into one nation under the name of Afgháns, as distinguished from the neighbouring Patháns of whom I shall presently speak, though the original stock of Ghor still called themselves Ban-i-Isráíl to mark the fact that their origin was distinct from that of their Gandhári kinsmen. It is probable that this tradition of Jewish origin was little more distinct than is the similar tradition of Norman descent which some of our English families still preserve. Thus the Afghán proper includes, firstly the original Afgháns of Jewish race whose principal tribes are the Tarín, Abdáli or Durráni and Shiráni, and secondly the descendants of the fugitive Gandhári, who include the Yúsufzai, Mohmand, and other tribes of Pesháwar. These latter returned about the first half of the 15th century of our æra to their original seat in the Pesháwar valley which they had left nearly ten centuries before; while the original Afgháns remained in Kandahár, where in the middle of the 18th century they made themselves rulers of the country since known as Afghánistán, and shortly afterwards moved their capital to Kábul. The tribes that returned to the Pesháwar country were given by Ahmad Sháh the title of Bar or "upper" Durráni, to distinguish them from the Abdáli Durráni who remained at Kandahár.

396. I have said that the Gandhári were one of the four great divisions of the Pactiyæ of Herodotus. The other three nations included under that name were the Aparytæ or Afrídi[1], the Satragyddæ or Khatak, and the Dadicæ or Dádi, all alike of Indian origin. At the beginning of the Mahomedan æra the Afrídi held all the country of the Safed Koh, the Satragyddæ held the Sulemán range and the northern part of the plains between it and the Indus, while the Dádi held modern Sewestán and the country between the Kandahár Province and the Sulemáns. These three nations constitute the nucleus of the Patháns proper. But around this nucleus have collected many tribes of foreign origin, such as the Scythic Kákar, the Rájpút Wazíri, and the many tribes of Túrk extraction included in the Karlánri section who came in with Sabuktagin and Taimur;[2] and these foreigners have so encroached upon the original territories of the Pactyan nation that the Khatak and Afrídi now hold but a small portion of the countries which they once occupied, while the Dádi have been practically absorbed by their Kákar invaders. The whole have now become blended into one nation by long association and intermarriage, the invaders have adopted the Pakhto language, and all alike have accepted Islám and have invented traditions of common descent which express their present state of association. The Afrídi were nominally converted to Islám by Mahmúd of Ghazni; but the real conversion of the Pathán tribes dates from the time of Shaháb-ul-dín Ghori, when Arab apostles with the title

---

[1] The Afrídi still call themselves Aparídc. There is no *f* in Pashto proper.

[2] The various accounts given of Karlán's origin all recognise the fact that he was not a Pathán by birth; and even the affiliation of the Karlánri is doubtful, some classing them as Sarbani and not Ghurghushti.

of Saiyad and Indian converts who were called Shekh spread through the country, and settled among, married with, and converted the Pathâns. The descendants of these holy men still preserve distinct tribal identity, and as a rule claim Saiyad origin.

The Gilzai are a race probably of Turkish origin, their name being another form of Khilchi, the Turkish word for "swordsman," who early settled, perhaps as mercenaries rather than as a corporate tribe, in the Siáh-band range of the Ghor mountains where they received a large admixture of Persian blood. The official spelling of the name is still Ghaleji at Kábul and Kandahár. They first rose into notice in the time of Mahmúd Ghaznavi, whom they accompanied in his invasions of India. Not long afterwards they conquered the tract between Jalálábád and Kelát-i-Ghilzai, and spread east and [P. 203]
west over the country they now hold. In the beginning of the 18th century they revolted against their Persian rulers, established themselves under Mír Wais as independent rulers at Kandahár, and overran Persia. But a quarter of a century later they were reduced by Nádir Sháh, and their rule disappeared, to be succeeded not long after by that of the Durráni.

With the remaining races of the Tájik and Hazára which form part of the Pathán nation in its widest sense, we have little concern in the Panjáb. The former are the remnants of the old Persian inhabitants of Afghánistán, and the word is now loosely used to express all Patháns who speak Persian and are neither true Afgháns, Saiyads, nor Hazáras. They are scattered through Afghánistán, Persia, and Túrkistán, in which last they hold some hill fastnesses in independent sovereignty. The Hazáras are Tartar by origin, and are supposed to have accompanied Chengiz Khán in his invasion. They occupy all the mountain country formed by the western extensions of the Hindu Kush between Ghazni, Balkh, Hírát, and Kandahár. I have included in my account of the Patháns a few allied races, who though not usually acknowledged as Patháns, have by long association become closely assimilated with them in manners, customs, and character. They chiefly occupy Hazára, and are called Dilazák, Swáti, Jodún, Tanáoli, and Shilmáni.

397. Tribal affinities and statistics.—The Pathán genealogies, which were probably concocted not more than 400 years ago, teem with obvious absurdities. But they are based upon the existing affinities of the people whom they trace back to Kais; and they will therefore afford a useful basis for a discussion of the tribes with which we in the Panjáb are concerned. I give in Abstract No. 69 on pages 204 and 205* a table showing the traditional grouping of the *P.
divisions of the Pathán nation. This grouping corresponds fairly well with 66-71.
their present distribution by locality, and I shall therefore take the tribes in order as they lie along our border, beginning from the south where they march with the Biloches. Unfortunately the figured details for the various tribes which I give in Abstract No. 70, on page 206† are in many ways † P. 72-5
unsatisfactory. I have already explained that the Deputy Commissioners of the frontier districts were asked to prepare lists of the tribes for which figures should be separately tabulated for each district, and it is now apparent that these lists were drawn up far more with regard to the political needs of each district than with reference to any ethnic or tribal system of classification. The figures given, however, will probably satisfy all administrative requirements: though they are so full of double or incomplete classification that they are of little use to me in the description of the tribes, and I have hardly alluded to them in the following pages. I have, however, grouped the figures

on the basis of the tribal classification adopted in Abstract No. 69, and have added below each heading in Abstract No. 70 the serial numbers of the tribes shown in Abstract No. 69 which it may be considered to include, so that the information contained in the figures is connected as closely as possible with the grouping of the tribes which I have followed. The figures being tabulated on the spot by a local staff are probably as accurate as the material will permit of. But errors must have occurred, both from the constant recurrence of the same clan name in different tribes, and from the difficulty pointed out in the following quotation from Mr. Beckett's Peshávar Census Report :—

"Among Muhammadans, especially among Afghána, tribes or sections multiply with generations; for instance as the descendants increase their branches or sections increase with them, so the mistake which has occurred is that, of a few men whose origin was the same, some were placed under the name of the old ancestor of the family, some under the name of an intermediate ancestor, and others under the name of a more modern or lower generation. Similarly those who should have been entered under the original branch were shown under numerous branches."

398. Pathan tribes of Derah Ismail Khan.—The tribes of our lower frontier belong almost exclusively to the lineage of Shekh Baitan[1], third son of Kais. His descendants in the male line are known as Bitanni, and are comparatively unimportant. But while, in the early part of the 8th century, Baitan was living in his original home on the western slopes of the Siáh-band range of the Ghor mountains, a prince of Persian origin flying before the Arab invaders took refuge with him, and there seduced and married his daughter Bibi Matto. From him are descended the Matti section of the nation, which embraces the Ghilzai, Lodi, and Sárwáni Patháns. The Ghilzai were the most famous of all the Afghán tribes till the rise of the Durráni power, while the Lodi section gave to Dehli the Lodi and Súr dynasties. The Sarwáni never rose to prominence, and are now hardly known in Afghánistán. To the Ghilzai and Lodi, and especially to the former, belong almost all the tribes of warrior traders who are included under the term *Pawindah*, from *Parwindah*, the Persian word for a bale of goods or, perhaps more probably, from the same root as *powal*, a Pashto word for "to graze."[2] They are almost wholly engaged in the carrying trade between India and Afghánistán and the Northern States of Central Asia, a trade which is almost entirely in their hands. They assemble every autumn in the plains east of Ghazni, with their families, flocks, herds, and long strings of camels laden with the goods of Bukhára and Kandahár; and forming enormous caravans, numbering many thousands, march in military order through the Kákar and Wazíri country to the Gomal and Zhob passes through the Sulemáns. Entering the Derah Ismáíl Khán district, they leave their families, flocks, and some two-thirds of their fighting men in the great grazing grounds which lie on either side of the Indus, and while some wander off in search of employment, others pass on with their laden camels and merchandize to Multán, Rájpútána, Lahore, Amritsar, Dehli, Cawnpore, Benáres, and even Patna. In the spring they again assemble, and return by the same route to their homes in the hills about Ghazni and Kelát-i-Ghilzai. When the hot weather begins the men, leaving their belongings behind them, move off to Kandahár, Hírát and Bukhára with the Indian and European merchandize which they have brought from Hindústán. In October they return and prepare to start once more for India.

[1] Dr. Bellew points out that Baitan has an Indian sound; while Shekh is the title given, in contradistinction to Saiyad, to Indian converts in Afghánistán. Thus the Ghilzai (the Túrk term for swordsman) are probably of Túrk extraction, with Indian and Persian admixtures.

[2] The pronunciation is Powindah, rather than Pawindah.

Abstract No. 69, showing the [P. 204]

Serial No.	Origin and natural Divisions and Affinities.				Tribal Divisions.								Serial No.
1	A Túrk stock (Khilchi or Ghilzai) combined with Persian blood; the two fused together under a traditional descent from a Persian father and an Afghán mother.		GHILZAI NATION.	The Ghilzai proper, combined with tribes of Persian origin, in the male line at least, all claiming descent from the Pathán progenitor Kais.	Baitani Patháns, descended from Baitan, son of Kais.	Matti tribe, descended from Sháh Husen, a Persian prince.	By Mussammat Mahiya		Sarwáni.			Sarwáni ...	1
2		Doubtful.					By Bibi Matto, daughter of Baitan.		Khasor.			Khasor ...	2
3									Prángi.			Prángi ...	3
4								Lodi.	Siáni.	Ismaíl.	Súr.	Súr ...	4
5											Lohání.	Tátor	5
6		Doubtful.										Balúch ...	6
7												Daulat Khel ...	7
8												Mián Khel ..	8
9		Saiyad										Bakhtiár (*a*) ..	9
10												Marwat ..	10
11									Niázi			Niázi (proper) ...	11
12												Kundi ..	12
13									Dutanni ...			Dutanni .	13
14								Ghilzai (proper).	Turán ...			Hotak ..	14
15												Tokhi ...	15
16		Doubtful.										Násar ..	16
17												Kharoti ..	17
18									Ibráhímzai			Sulemán Khel ..	18
19												Ali Khel ...	19
20												Aka Khel ...	20
21												Isháq ..	21
22												Andar ...	22
23												Tarakki ...	23

Principal Divisions of the Pathan Nation.

Notes.	Present Holdings.	Country, district, or frontier to which each tribe appertains.	Sections of the report in which each tribe is described.	Serial No.
No longer found in Afghánistán. Maler Kotla family belongs to the Sarípál clan.	Scattered through Hindústán ...	Hindústán	398-9	1
A small tribe of doubtful origin ...	Trans-Indus Salt Range of Derah Ismáíl Khán.	D. I. Khán	390-402	2
Gave Lodi dynasty to Dehli } Migrated to Hindústán.	Scattered through Hindústán ...	Hindústán	399	3
Gave Súr dynasty to Dehli } Migrated to Hindústán.			398-9	4
Insignificant, since crushed by Nádir Sháh	Tánk in Derah Ismáíl Khán ...	Derah Ismáíl Khán District.	401	5
Small and of uncertain origin. Affiliated to No. 7.	Dera Ismáíl Khán Salt Range and cis-Indus plain.		390-402	6
A sept of the Mámú Khel, to the whole of which it has given its name. Rulers of Tánk are of the Katti Khel sept.	Part of Tánk in Derah Ismáíl Khán		401	7
Often held to include Bakhtiár, No. 9... ...	The central part of trans-Indus Derah Ismáíl Khán.		401-2	8
A Saiyad tribe from Persia, affiliated to No. 8. See also No. 29.			401	9
Known as Spín Lohání. Nos. 5 to 9 being called Túr Lohání.	South-west portion of Bannu District.	Bannu.	404	10
Chief clans, Isákhel, Sarhang, Musháni ...	Both banks of Indus in north of Bannu.		403	11
The Niázi descent not always admitted ...	Part of Tánk in Derah Ismáíl Khán	Derah Ismáíl Khán District.	402	12
Unimportant	*Pawindah* tribes with homes in the Ghilzai country, between Jalálábád and Kelát-Ghilzai. Their families spend the winter there, and the summer in the Derah Ismáíl Khán plains. For a description of the *Pawindah* traffic, see Section 398.		402	13
Gave the Ghilzai kings to Kandahár. Crushed by Nádir Sháh			402	14
Once the principal Ghilzai tribe ...			402	15
Their Ghilzai origin is doubtful ...			402	16
Their Ghilzai origin is doubtful ...			402	17
Now the principal Ghilzai tribe ...			402	18
Unimportant				19
Unimportant				20
Chief clan is Yúsuf Khel				21
The Músa Khel Kákar are affiliated to this tribe.			402	22
			402	23

Abstract No. 69, showing the

Serial No.	Origin and natural Divisions and Affinities.				Tribal Divisions.						Serial No.
24			PATHANS PROPER.		Baitani Patháns	Bitanní.				Bitanni ...	24
25	An ancient Indian stock, including the Afrídi (Aparytæ), Khatak (Satragydæ) and Dádi (Dadicæ), three of the four Pactyan nations of Herodotus; but with a very large admixture of Túrk (Karlánri) and Scythic (Kákar) blood; probably introduced, the latter by irruptions of Jats and Scyths in 5th and 6th centuries, the former by Sabuktagin and Changiz in end of 10th and beginning of 13th centuries.	Sarbanni Afghán, affiliated with the Patháns.		The Kakar, a Scythic stock, with affiliated tribes of Indian origin.	Ghurghushti Patháns, descended from Ghurghusht, son of Kais.	Kákar and affiliated tribes.	Shiráni and affiliated tribes.	Shiráni ...		Shiráni (proper) ...	25
26										Haripál ...	26
27										Jalwáni ...	27
28										Bábar ...	28
29		Saiyad origin.						Saiyad tribes affiliated to Shiráni.	Bakhtiár.	Bakhtiár (b) ..	29
30									Ushtaráni.	Ushtaráni (proper)	30
31										Gandápur ...	31
32		Probably Scythic.					Kákar			Kákar proper ...	32
33										Bábe Khel ...	33
34										Mandu Khel ...	34
35		? Rájpút old Indian.								Panni ...	35
36										Nághar ...	36
37										Dádi or Khundi ...	37
38				The Karlanri, Indian in the mass (Afrídi, Khatak, Wazíri, &c.,) but with a large admixture of Túrk tribes.		Karlánri.	Kakái.	Wazíri ...		Lálai	38
39										Mahsúd ...	39
40										Gurbuz ...	40
41										Dervesh Khel ...	41
42								Shitak married Musammát Bannu.		Bannúchi ...	42
43										Daur	43
44		Doubtful.						Khugiáni ...		Tano ...	44
45		Túrk tribes.								Jáji	45
46										Túri	46
47										Khostwál ...	47
48										Darman ...	48
49										Parba ...	49
50										Khugiáni (proper)	50
51								Burhán ...		Khatak ...	51
52										Afrídi ...	52
53										Utmán Khel ...	53
54		? Túrk.								Jadrán ...	54
55		? Túrk.					Kodai.	Kodai ...		Mangal ...	55
56		Saiyad.								Wardag ...	56
57										Hanni ...	57
58		Rájpút or Scythic.								Dilazák ...	58
59		? Scythic.								Orakzai ...	59
60		Arab or Scythic.				Bangash.				Bangash ...	60

[P. 205]

Principal Divisions of the Pathan Nation—continued.

Notes.	Present Holdings.	Country, district, or frontier to which each tribe appertains.	Sections of the report in which each tribe is described.	Serial No.
Clans Warshpún and Kajin (septs Dhanne and Tatte).	North-West of Derah Ismáíl Khán	Derah Ismáíl Khan District.	401	24
Descended from Sharkabún by a Kákar mother. Shiráni quarrelled with his brothers, and allied himself to the Kákar branch of the Ghurghusht section, with which his descendants are still associated. See No. 86.	Country round and west of the Takht-i-Sulemán on the Derah Ismáíl Khán border.		402	25
			402	26
			402	27
	South of Derah Ismáíl Khán, and adjoining parts of Sulemán mountains.		401	28
Saiyad tribes affiliated to the Shiráni. No. 31 includes several clans of true Pathán origin.	*Pawindah* tribe in the Ghilzai country.		401	29
	South-west of Derah Ismáíl Khán		401	30
	North-west of Derah Ismáíl Khán		401	31
Bellew allies the Kákar to the Gakkhars. They include several clans of distinct origin, all called Kákar after the chief tribe.	Kákaristán in south-east of Afghánistán, between the Ghilzai, Spín, Tarín, and Biloch territories and the Sulemán mountains.	Afghánistán.	396	32
				33
				34
Of Rájpút origin. The larger portion of them is still settled in Shekháwatti and Haidarábád.			412	35
				36
The representatives of the ancient Dadicæ.			396	37
Ancestor separated from his brother through a feud.	Northern slopes of Western Safed Koh.		405	38
Chief clans Alízai and Bahlolzai ...	Hills on north-west frontier of Derah Ismáíl Khán.	Bannu and Dera Ismáíl Khán Border.	405	39
Unimportant. Practically a separate tribe.			405	40
Chief clan Utmánzai and Ahmadzai ...	Hills on the Bannu border ...		405	41
Hybrid tribe, with many clans of mixed origin.	North-west of Bannu district ...	Bannu.	404	42
Unimportant	Both banks of River Tochi on Bannu border.		403	43
[P. 205] Pathán origin doubtful	South-west corner of Khost ...			44
Claim descent from Khugiáni; but of doubtful Pathán origin, and now separate tribes. Very probably Túrks who came in with Changiz and Taimur.	Head of Kurram valley ...	Afghánistán.	406	45
	Kurram valley		406	46
	Khost			47
				48
				49
Should perhaps be classed as Durráni (Nos. 82, 83).	North-west slopes of Safed Koh, west of Shinwári.	Kohát and Peshawar.	406	50
Chief clans Buláqi, Tari Tarkai. Two territorial sections, Akora or Eastern and Teri or Western.	South, centre, and east of Kohát; south-east of Peshawar, and west of Baizai valley; north-east of Bannu.		407	51
Chief clans Adam Khel, Aka Khel, and Khaibar Afrídi (Kúki Khel, Malikdín Khel, Qambar Khel, Kamar Khel, Zakha Khel, Sepáh).	Khaibar range, hills on south-west border of Peshawar south of Kábul river, and north-east border of Kohát.	Peshawar border.	411	52
Accompanied Yúsufzai to Peshawar ...	Banks of Swát river to Arang Barang and in Baizai valley.	Afghánistán.	411	53
Perhaps of Túrk origin	Hills between Khost and Zurmat...			54
Formerly closely associated with No. 56 ...	Mountains west of Khost and Kurram.		403	55
This and No. 57 affiliated to Karlánri ...	Between Hazára and North Ghilzai countries.			56
No longer a separate tribe	Scattered	Scattered.	403	57
Ditto ditto Probably of Scythic origin.	Scattered through India ...		406-9	58
Includes clans of distinct origin. Begam of Bhopál belongs to this tribe.	Mountains of Tíráh west of Adam Khel.	Kohát.	407	59
Chief clans Gár (clans Baizai and Míránzai) and Sámil. Nawábs of Furrukhábád are Bangash.	Míránzai and Kohát valleys in north-west of Kohát district, and in Kurram.		407	60

Abstract No. 69, showing the

Serial No.	Origin and natural Divisions and Affinities.				Tribal Divisions.							Serial No.
61	Sprung from the fusion of a Jewish or Arab stock (original Afghán) with a colony of Gandhári, an ancient Indian race, into one nation. The descent in the male lines has probably been kept distinct, as shown below.		AFGHANS PROPER.	Representatives of the ancient Gandhari emigrants from Peshâwar to Kandahár. Blended with the original Afgháns of Ghor.	Sarbani Patháns, descended from Sarban, son of Kais.	Descended from Kharshabún.	Zamand				Khweshgi	61
62											Muhammadzai	62
63		? Persian.					Kánsi				Shinwári	63
64							Descended from Kand.	Khakhai Khel.	Yúsufzai (from Mand).	Mandanr.	Usmánzai	64
65											Utmánzai	65
66											Saddozai	66
67											Razar	67
68										Yúsufzai (proper).	Bádi Khel	68
69											Isázai	69
70											Iliászai	70
71											Malízai	71
72											Akozai	72
73									Tarklánri		Gugiáni	73
74									Surgiáni		Tarklánri	74
75		Doubtful.						Ghoria Khel.			Mullágori	75
76											Bar Mohmand	76
77											Plain Mohmand	77
78											Dáúdzai	78
79											Khalíl	79
80		? Persian.									Chamkanni	80
81											Ziráni	81
82				Original Afghans from Ghor; of Jewish or Arab descent, or both.		Descended from Sharkabún.	Abdáli or Durráni				Zirak	82
83											Panjpai	83
84							Tarín				Túr Tarín	84
85											Spín Tarín	85
86							Shirani				Shiráni	86
87							Miána				Miána	87
88							Baraich				Baraich	88
89							Urmar				Urmar	89

Principal Divisions of the Pathan Nation—concluded.

Notes.	Present Holdings.	Country, district, or frontier to which each tribe appertains.	Sections of the report in which each tribe is described.	Serial No.
Scattered. Some in Multán	Some in Ghorband Mountains ...	Afghánistán	413	61
Accompanied Yúsufzai to Peshawar ...	Hashtnaghar, in Peshawar ...	Peshawar District and border.	408-10	62
Probably accompanied Yúsufzai to Peshawar. Connected with Ghilzai.	Northern slopes of Safed Koh, east of Khugiani.	Peshawar District and border.	411	63
Clans Kamálzai and Amázai	Yúsufzai plains in Peshawar, the Chamlah valley, and the left bank of Indus in Hazára.	Peshawar District and border.	409-10	64
Both Usmánzai by descent, though now separate.	Yúsufzai plains in Peshawar, the Chamlah valley, and the left bank of Indus in Hazára.	Peshawar District and border.	409-12	65
Both Usmánzai by descent, though now separate.	Yúsufzai plains in Peshawar, the Chamlah valley, and the left bank of Indus in Hazára.	Peshawar District and border.	409-10	66
Brother of Mandan, but now included in Mandanr.	Yúsufzai plains in Peshawar, the Chamlah valley, and the left bank of Indus in Hazára.	Peshawar District and border.	409-10	67
Almost extinct	Swát, Buner, and the hills north of Peshawar, and a part of the Lundkhwár valley in Peshawar.	Peshawar District and border.	411	68
Clans Hasanzai, Akázai, Maddo Khel ...	Swát, Buner, and the hills north of Peshawar, and a part of the Lundkhwár valley in Peshawar.	Peshawar District and border.	411	69
	Swát, Buner, and the hills north of Peshawar, and a part of the Lundkhwár valley in Peshawar.	Peshawar District and border.	411	70
Clans Daulatzai, Chagharzai, Núrazai ...	Swát, Buner, and the hills north of Peshawar, and a part of the Lundkhwár valley in Peshawar.	Peshawar District and border.	411	71
Clans Ránízai, Khwájazai, Baizai ...	Swát, Buner, and the hills north of Peshawar, and a part of the Lundkhwár valley in Peshawar.	Peshawar District and border.	410	72
Descended from Mak, a brother of Mand ...	Doába of Peshawar, between Swát and Kábul rivers.	Peshawar District and border.	408-10	73
Descended from Mak, a brother of Mand ...	Bajaur, north-west of Peshawar ...	Peshawar District and border.	408-9	74
Pathán origin doubtful. Vassals of No. 76	Hills west of Peshawar border along both banks of Kábul river.	Peshawar District and border.	411	75
Of common descent, but now separate tribes.	Hills west of Peshawar border along both banks of Kábul river.	Peshawar District and border.	409-11	76
Of common descent, but now separate tribes.	South-west plain of Peshawar, south of Kábul river.	Peshawar District and border.	409-10	77
	South-west plain of Peshawar, south of Kábul river.	Peshawar District and border.	409-10	78
	South-west plain of Peshawar, south of Kábul river.	Peshawar District and border.	409-10	79
Early separated from kinsmen. Perhaps Persians.	South-eastern Safed Koh, north of Kurram.	Afghánistán.	406	80
Insignificant, often confounded with Tájik	Scattered through Afghánistán ...	Afghánistán.	400	81
Clans Popalzai (sept Saddozai), Bárakzai, Alikozai. Saddozai gave Sháhs to Kandahár; and Bárakzai, Amírs to Kábul.	All the Kandahár country in south of Afghánistán. The Multáni Patháns are Abdáli.	Afghánistán.	395	82
Clans Isháqzai, Núrzai, Khakwáni, Máhu...	All the Kandahár country in south of Afghánistán. The Multáni Patháns are Abdáli.	Afghánistán.	395	83
	Peshín, south of Abdáli country ...	Afghánistán.	408-11	84
The Zaimusht clan is in Kurram on Kohát border.	Sewestan, in south-east of Afghánistán.	Afghánistán.	408-11	85
Classed with Ghurghushti Patháns, Nos. 25-28.	Takht-i-Suleman. See Nos. 25-28	D. I. Khán.	402	86
Only the Khetrán of the Derájat exists as a tribe.	Scattered through Afghánistán ...	Afghánistán.	383	87
Insignificant tribe	Lóhra river between Abdáli and Biloch territory.	Afghánistán.		88
Speak Hindki. Probably of Hindu origin...	Scattered through Afghánistán ...	Afghánistán.		89

Abstract No. 70, showing the distribution of the principal [P. 206]

Serial No.	1	2	3	4	5	6	7	8	9	10
	GHILZAI									
	LODI SECTION.									GHILZAI
TRIBAL DIVISIONS.			*Lohani.*				*Niázi*			
	Lodi.	Khasor.	Balúch.	Daulat Khel.	Mián Khel.	Marwat.	Niázi.	Kundi.	Dutanni.	Ghilzai.
Nos. of Abstract No. 69, pages 66-71.	2 to 13	2	6	7	8	10	11	12	13	14 to 23
Dehli ...	536	...	...	2	...	...	...	...	...	38
Gurgaon ...	81	...	...	...	...	...	...	...	...	16
Karnál ...	456	...	...	...	...	...	...	...	...	...
Rohtak ...	32	...	...	...	...	...	...	...	...	...
Ambála ...	1,910	...	...	...	...	...	117	...	...	25
Jálandhar ...	1,147	...	...	...	...	...	65	...	...	21
Hushyárpur ...	884	...	...	...	...	...	12	...	...	298
Lahore ...	536	...	...	33	...	...	30	...	...	23
Ráwalpindi ...	1,035	...	...	9	...	1	71	...	...	1,768
Derah Ismáíl Khán.	192	2,092	3,203	888	3,646	6,771	2,377	3,590	1,328	2,453
Derah Ghází Khán.	67	...	2	6	140	1	201	5	...	100
Bannu ...	15	6	544	193	10	40,765	30,199	21	35	3,280
Peshávar ...	294	...	...	97	1,085	...	1	...	...	2,643
Hazára ...	279	...	...	...	...	1	...	.	...	...
Kohát ...	...	...	...	...	...	...	2,677	...	...	2,962
British Territory.	11,793	2,099	3,749	1,386	5,498	47,546	36,314	3,667	1,363	14,011
Native States	1,368	...	...	1	63	...	57	...	...	155
Province ...	13,161	2,099	3,749	1,387	5,561	47,546	36,371	3,667	1,363	14,166

Pathan Tribes for Districts and States.

11	12	13	14	15	16	17	18	19	20	21	22	23
NATION.			PATHAN NATION.									
SECTION.				KAKAR SECTION.								
				Shírání.					*Kákar.*			
Sulemán Khel.	Násar.	Kharote.	Bitanni.	Shiráni.	Miáni.	Bábar.	Ushtaráni	Gandápur.	Kákar.	Músa Khel.	Ghorezai.	Panni.
18	16	17	24	25		28	30	31	32			
...	...	...	...	...	...	...	...	...	...	...	...	...
...	...	...	...	...		1	...	...	...	12	...	...
...	...	..	...	...	...	...	...	...	...	...	...	...
...	...	...	...	...	6	...	...	...	...	...	...	...
...	...	...	...	...	12	...	...	...	117	...	7	...
...	...	...	...	...	106	14	...	...	2	...	324	...
...	...	...	24	...	...	...	...	...	11	11	...	...
...	...	...	...	...	...	...	...	...	211	4	138	...
...	...	...	...	...	5	...	...	...	406	201	1	...
2,861	8,419	5,136	2,671	1,252	1,716	1,223	1,517	7,875	666	683	470	...
...	...	...	10	21	89	36	87	75	732	979	11	...
1,970	570	2,003	806	7	16	21	16	44	113	...	17	...
374	16	5	14	...	...	465	...	...	716	2	84	...
...	...	...	...	...	...	...	...	...	256	...	...	1,241
...	...	...	...	...	...	...	...	...	...	...	...	...
5,205	9,005	7,144	3,574	1,310	2,202	2,222	1,42	8,082	4,748	1,998	1,256	1,241
...	...	5	...	...	9	209	4	13	11	...	553	...
5,205	9,005	7,149	3,574	1,310	2,211	2,431	1,646	8,095	4,759	1,998	1,809	1,241

Abstract No. 70, showing the distribution of the principal

Serial No.	24	25	26	27	28	29	30	31
	PATHAN NATION.							AFGHAN
	KARLANRI SECTION.							ORIGINAL
TRIBAL DIVISIONS.	Wazíri.	Bannúchi.	Khatak.	Afrídi.	Utmán Khel.	Orakzai.	Bangash.	Muhammadzai.
Nos. of Abstract No. 69, pages 66-71.	38 to 41	42	51	52	53	59	60	62
Dehli	100	...	4	785	...	...	291	111
Gurgaon ...	...	...	983	10	...	...	19	31
Karnál	...	...	11	236	...	...	...	79
Rohtak	...	...	...	4	...	...	...	27
Ambála	...	...	1	20	...	...	91	60
Jálandhar ...	...	...	14	...	...	...	1	94
Hushyárpur ...	...	...	9	...	...	...	...	13
Lahore	...	...	13	117	...	3	37	38
Ráwalpindi ...	...	...	347	52	148	14	360	212
Derah Ismáíl Khán ...	454	123	144	64	...	4	3	6
Derah Gházi Khán ...	7	2	41	52	...	...	54	15
Bannu	19,262	20,182	13,265	151	...	1	101	8
Pesháwar ...	...	...	36,447	6,590	6,768	874	...	18,035
Hazára	...	...	333	46	...	...	5	12
Kohát	909	...	66,278	8,715	...	6,245	16,437	...
British Territory ...	20,741	20,307	118,048	17,323	6,923	7,157	17,565	19,426
Native States ...	2	...	2	103	1	...	...	178
Province ...	20,743	20,307	118,050	17,426	6,924	7,157	17,565	19,604

*NOTE.—I am informed that Sargáni is the same as Sarwáni, tribe No. 1

Pathan Tribes for Districts and States—concluded.

32	33	34	35	36	37	38	39	40	41	42	43
NATION.											
INDIAN SECTION.						ORIGINAL AFGHAN SECTION.					
Yúsufzai.							*Tarín.*				
Yúsufzai.	Utmánzai.	Mullágori.	Mohmand.	Dáúdzai.	Khalíl.	Abdáli.	Tarín.	Zaimusht.	Khetrán.	Urmar.	Sargári.
64 to 72	65	75	76 to 77	78	79	82 and 83	84 and 85	85	87	89	*
3,901	...	...	...	...	...	...	6	...	...	...	1
1,083	...	...	...	...	...	...	...	...	...	...	...
1,890	...	...	...	6	...	4	36	...	...	...	429
1,854	...	...	...	...	...	4	7	...	...	...	140
4,641	...	...	1	...	3	12	205	...	...	...	153
478	...	30	1	...	...	...	36	...	...	...	9
921	...	26	...	10	5	...	114	...	...	...	...
1,466	...	11	215	24	44	78	60	...	...	...	1
1,550	296	27	400	1	107	60	608	...	...	...	674
204	41	...	96	...	...	1,029	90	...	1,324	34	16
595	27	...	12	3	22	21	192	...	32	...	...
992	1	...	33	...	...	476	20	...	..	340	...
70,235	...	652	40,080	4,949	13,268	7,231	660	...	...	3,187	795
929	5,156	...	41	5	5	272	1,355	...	...	...	...
637	...	...	2,414	..	...	264	...	1,835	...	176	...
95,426	5,547	1,249	43,960	5,890	13,595	9,738	4,902	1,335	1,558	3,737	3,159
3,551	...	...	49	8	...	...	910	...	...	...	781
98,977	5,547	1,249	44,009	5,898	13,595	9,738	5,812	1,335	1,558	3,737	3,940

of Abstract No. 69; if so they should have come first in this table.

In 1877 the number of these traders which passed into the district of Derah Ismáíl Khán was 76,400, of which nearly half were grown men. In the year of the Census, the number was 49,392. These Pawindah tribes speak the soft or western Pashto, and have little connection with the settled tribes of the same stock.[1]

399. It is not to be wondered at that these warlike tribes cast covetous [P. 207] eyes on the rich plains of the Indus, held as they were by a peaceful Jat population. Early in the 13th century, about the time of Shaháb-ud-dín Ghori, the Prángi and Súr tribes of the Lodi branch with their kinsmen the Sarwáni, settled in the northern part of the district immediately under the Sulemáns, the Prángi and Súr holding Tánk and Rori, while the Sarwáni settled south of the Lúni in Drában and Chandhwán. With them came the Balúch, Khasor, and other tribes who occupied the branch of the Salt-range which runs along the right bank of the river, and still hold their original location. In the early part of the 15th century the Niázi, another Lodi tribe, followed their kinsmen from Ghazni into Tánk, where they lived quietly as *Pawindahs* for nearly a century, when they crossed the trans-Indus Salt-range and settled in the country now held by the Marwat in the south of the Bannu district, then almost uninhabited save by sprinkling of pastoral Jats, where Bábar mentions them as cultivators in 1505.

During the reign of the Lodi and Súr Sultáns of Dehli (1450 to 1555 A.D.), the Prángi and Súr tribes from which these dynasties sprang, and their neighbours the Niázi, seem to have migrated almost bodily from Afghánistán into Hindústán, where the Niázi rose to great power, one of their tribe being Súbahdár of Lahore. These last waxed insolent and revolted in alliance with the Gakkhars, and in 1547 Sultán Salím Sháh Súri crushed the rebellion, and with it the tribe. At any rate, when in the early days of Akbar's reign the Loháni, another Lodi tribe, who had been expelled by the Sulemán Khel Ghilzai from their homes in Katawáz in the Ghazni mountains, crossed the Sulemáns, the Lodi tribes were too weak to resist them; and they expelled the remaining Prángi and Súr from Tánk, killing many, while the remainder fled into Hindústán. The Loháni are divided into four great tribes, the Marwát, Daulat Khel,[2] Mián Khel, and Tátor.[3] About the beginning of the 17th century the Daulat Khel quarrelled with the Marwats and Mián Khel and drove them out of Tánk. The Marwats moved northwards across the Salt-range and drove the Niázi eastwards across the Kurram and Salt-range into Isa Khel on the banks of the Indus, where they found a mixed Awán and Jat population, expelled the former, and reduced the latter to servitude. The Mián Khel passed southward across the Lúni river and, with the assistance of the Bakhtiár, a small Persian tribe of Ispahán origin who had become associated with them in their nomad life,[4] drove the Sarwáni, already

---

[1] The *Pawindahs* are well described at pages 103*ff* of Dr. Bellow's *Races of Afghánistán*, and at pages 18*ff* of Priestley's translation of the *Haiyát-i-Afgháni*, while Mr. Tucker gives much detailed information concerning them at pages 184*ff* of his Settlement Report of Derah Ismáíl Khán.

[2] The Daulat Khel is really only a clan of the Mámu Khel tribe; but it has become so prominent as practically to absorb the other clans, and to give its name to the whole tribe.

[3] Wrongly spelt Játor throughout Mr. Tucker's settlement report.

[4] They are a section of the Bakhtiári of Persia. They first settled with the Shiráni Afgháns and a section now lives at Marghu in the Ghilzai country, and is engaged in the *pawindah* trade but has little or no connection with the Bakhtiár of Derah Ismáíl.

weakened by feuds with the Súr, out of their country into Hindústán. In this quarrel the Daulat Khel were assisted by the Gandápur, a Saiyad tribe of Ushtaráni stock (see next paragraph); and the latter were settled by them at Rori and gradually spread over their present country.

400. The Shiráni Afgháns had been settled from of old in the mountains about the Takht-i-Sulemán. They are by descent Sarbani Afgháns; but their ancestor, having quarrelled with his brothers, left them and joined the Kákar from whom his mother had come; and his descendants are now classed as Ghurghushti and not as Sarbani. About the time that the Loháni came into the district, the Bábar, a Shiráni tribe, descended from the hills into the plains below and subjugated the Jat and Biloch population. Finally, about a century ago, the Ushtaráni proper, a Saiyad tribe affiliated to the Shiráni Afgháns, having quarrelled with the Músa Khel, acquired a good deal of the plain country below the hills at the foot of which they still live, subjugating the Biloch inhabitants and encroaching northwards upon the Bábar. These are the most recently located of the trans-Indus tribes of Derah Ismáíl Khán. Thus the Patháns hold a broad strip of the trans-Indus portion of the district running northwards from the border of the Khetrán and Qasráni Biloches (see section 383) along the foot of the hills and including the western half of the plain country between them and the Indus, and turning eastwards below the Salt-range to the river. They also hold the trans-Indus Salt-range, and the Sulemáns as far south as the Biloch border. But while in the extreme northern portion of the tract the population is almost exclusively Pathán, the proportion lessens southwards, the Patháns holding only the superior property in the land, which is cultivated by a subject population of Jat and Biloch. Beyond the Indus the Balúch who hold the north of the Bhakkar *thal* are the only Pathán tribe of importance. Their head-quarters are at Paniála in the trans-Indus Salt-range, and they seem to have spread across the river below Miánwáli, and then to have turned southwards down the left bank. Although living at a distance from the frontier, they still talk Pashto and are fairly pure Patháns. The other Patháns of the Khasor hills, though trans-Indus, are, like all the cis-Indus Patháns, so much intermixed with Jats as to have forgotten their native tongue. The Mián Khel and Gandápur were deprived of many of their eastern villages in the beginning of this century by Nawáb Muhammad Khán Saddozai, Governor of Leiah.

401. The Pathan tribes of Derah Ismail Khan continued.—I now proceed to give a brief description of the various tribes beginning from the south:—

The Ushtarani.—The Ushtaráni proper are the descendants of Hannar, one of the sons of Ustaryáni, a Saiyad who settled among and married into the Shiráni section of Afgháns, and whose progeny are shewn in the margin. They were settled with the Shiránis to the south of the Takht-i-Sulemán, and till about a century ago they were wholly pastoral and *pawindah*. But a quarrel with their neighbours the Músa Khel put a stop to their annual westward migration, and they were forced to take to agriculture. Their descent into the plains has been described in section 400. They still own a large tract of hill country, in which indeed most of them live, cultivating land immediately under the hills and pasturing their flocks beyond the border. Their territory only includes the eastern slopes of the Sulemáns, the crest of the range being held by the Músa Khel and Zmari. They are divided into two main clans, the Ahmadzai or Amazai and the Gagalzai, and these again into numerous septs. They are a fine manly race, many of them are in our army and police, and they are quiet and well behaved, cultivating largely with their own hands. A few of them are still *pawindahs*. They are much harassed by the independent Bozdár (Biloch). They

		Sons		Tribe
Ustaryáni	...	Hannar	...	Ushtaráni.
		Amarkhel	...	Gandápur.
		Gandápur	...	
		Marere	...	
		Shekhi	...	

are all Sunnis. The boundary between the Ushtaráni and Bábar was originally the Ramak stream. But in a war between them the former drove the latter back beyond the Shiran stream which now forms their common boundary.

The Babar are a tribe of the Shiráni stock whose affinities have been described in section 400, though they are now quite separate from the Shiráni proper. They are divided into two sections, [P 208] one living wholly within our border, while the other holds the hill country opposite, but on the other side of the Sulemáns The two have now little connection with each other. The Bábar of the plains hold some 180 square miles between the Ushtaráni and Míán Khel, Chandwán being their chief town; and include the Mahsúd and Ghora Khel clans of the tribe. The result of their quarrels with the Ushtaráni has just been mentioned, while their advent in the plains has been described in section 400. They are a civilised tribe, most of them being able to read and write, and are much addicted to commerce, being the richest, quietest, and most honest tribe of the sub-Sulemán plains. Sir Herbert Edwardes considered them "the most superior race in the whole of "the trans-Indus districts," and their intelligence has given rise to the saying "A Bábar fool is a "Gandápur sage." They are extremely democratic, and have never had any recognized Chief. Indeed the tribe is a scattered one, many of them still residing in Kandahár and other parts of Khorásán. Some of them are still engaged in the *pawindah* traffic. They cultivate but little themselves.

The Mian Khel are a Loháni tribe whose coming to the district and subsequent movements have already been described in section 339. They hold some 260 square miles of plain country between the Gandápur and the Bábar. With them are associated the Bakhtiár (see section 339) who, though of Persian origin, now form one of their principal sections. The greater number of them still engage in the trans-Indus trade; and they are the richest of all the *pawindah* tribes, dealing in the more costly descriptions of merchandize. They are divided by locality into the Drában and Músa Khel sections, the latter of which hold the south-west quarter of their tract. They are a peaceable people with pleasant faces, and more civilised than most of the *pawindah* tribes. They seldom take military service, and cultivate but little themselves, leaving the business of agriculture to their Jat tenants. They have a hereditary Khán who has never possessed much power.

The Gandapur.—The origin of the Gandápur has been described in section 399. Besides the original stock, they include by affiliation some off-shoots of the Shiráni, the Múshezai section of the Ghurghushti Patháns, and the Ráuízai section of the Yúsafzai tribe. The manner in which they obtained their present country is described in section 339. They hold the whole of the north-western part of trans-Indus Derah Ismáíl east of Tánk and south of the Nila Koh ridge of the Salt-range, comprising an area of 460 square miles abutting on the Sulemáns to the west; and the town of Kuláchi is their head-quarters. They were originally a poor *pawindah* and pastoral tribe, but they now cultivate more largely than any other Derah Ismáíl Patháns. They reached the height of their prosperity about the middle of the 18th century, but lost their eastern possessions some 70 years later, they being confiscated by the Saddozai Governor of Leiah. They still engage in the *pawindah* traffic. They are lawless, brutal and uncivilised; and their hereditary Khán has but little power.

The Bitanni include all the descendants in the male line of Baitan, the third son of Kais. They originally occupied the western slopes of the northern Sulemáns; but, being hard pressed by the Ghilzai, moved, in the time of Bahlol Lodi, through the Gomal Pass and occupied the eastern side of the north of the range, as far north on its junction with the Salt-range and as far west as Kánígurum. Some time after the Wazíri drove them back to beyond Garangi, while the Gurbuz contested with them the possession of the Ghabbar mountain. They now hold the hills on the west border of Tánk and Bannu, from the Ghabbar on the north to the Gomal valley on the south. In their disputes many of the tribe left for Hindústán where their Lodi kinsmen occupied the throne of Dehli, and the tribe has thus been much weakened. Sheikh Baitan had four sons, Tajín, Kajín, Ismáíl, and Warshpún. The tribe consists chiefly of the descendants of Kajín, with a few of those of Warshpún. Ismáíl was adopted by Sarban, and his descendants still live with the Sarbani Afgháns. The Tajín branch is chiefly represented by the clans Dhanne and Tatte, said to be descended from slaves of Tajín. A small Saiyad clan called Koti is affiliated to the Bitanni. Till some 50 years ago they lived wholly beyond our border; but of late they have spread into the Tánk plains where they now form a large proportion of the Pathán population, occupying some 550 square miles, chiefly south of the Takwára. They also hold some land in the Bannu district at the mouth of the passes which lead up into their hills. They are a rude people just emerging from barbarism, but keen-witted. They are of medium weight, wiry, and active, and inveterate thieves and abettors of thieves; and they have been called the jackals of the Wazíri. They have no common Chief. The proverbial wit of the countryside thus expresses their stupidity and thriftlessness.—"The drum was beating in the plains and the Bitanni were dancing on the hills;" and "A hundred Bitanni eat a hundred sheep."

The Daulat Khel.—The coming of this tribe to the district has been described in section 399. Their principal clan was the Katti Khel; and under their Chief Katál Khan the Daulat Khel ruled Tánk and were numerous and powerful about the middle of the 18th century. They accompanied the Durráni into Hindústán, and brought back much wealth But since that time the Bitanni and other tribes have encroached, and they are now small and feeble. The Nawáb of Tánk, the principal jágírdár of the district, is a Katti Khel.

The Tator have been mentioned in section 399. They were very roughly treated by Nádir Sháh, and the Daulat Khel completed their ruin. They are now almost extinct. Their two clans, the Bára Khel and Dari Khel, hold a small area on the Tánk and Kuláchi frontier.

402. Pawindah, Border, and other tribes.—The tribes not possessing sufficient importance to merit detailed description are—

The Zarkani, a small colony of Shekhs who settled some 500 years ago in a corner between the Gandápur and Mián Khel country, under the foot of the Sulemáns.

The Baluch, a small tribe of uncertain origin affiliated to the Lodi tribes.[1] They seem to have come in with the earliest Pathán invaders. They hold the country round Paniála, at the foot of the Salt-range where it leaves the Indus to turn northwards, and are the dominant race in the north of the cis-Indus portion of the district.

The Khasor, with the **Nur Khel** and **Malli Khel**, form a small tribe which claims kinship with the Lodi, who repudiate the claim. They hold the Khasor range, or the ridge, of the lower Salt-range which runs down the right bank of the Indus.

The Ghorezai, a petty clan of the Tabarak Káka, and the **Miani**, an insignificant *pawindah* clan of the Shiráni tribe, hold lands in the Gomal valley, the former lying south and the latter north of the Lúni river. They graze their flocks during summer on the western slopes of the Sulemáns. A portion of the Miáni are independent *pawindahs*, but closely allied to those of our plains.

The Kundi are a small *pawindah* clan who claim descent from the ancestor of the Niázi. They settled in Tánk with the Daulat Khel Loháni, and originally held the tract along the Suheli stream in the North-east corner of Tánk. But within the last 50 years Marwat immigrants have encroached largely on their eastern lands. They are a lawless set and great robbers, and the proverb runs—"A dead Kundi is better than a live one."[2]

The Pawindah Tribes.—These tribes, which have been described generally in section 398, although not holding lands in the district, are of considerable administrative interest, as enormous numbers of them spend the cold weather in the pastures on either side of the Indus. The principal tribes are noticed below:—

The Nasar claim descent from Hotak, a grandson of Ghilzai; but the Hotak say that they are a Biloch clan, and merely dependent on them.[3] They speak Pashto, but differ from the Ghilzai in physique. They are the least settled of all the *pawindahs*, and winter in the Deraját and summer in the Ghilzai country, having no home of their own. Their chief wealth is in flocks and herds, and they act as carriers rather than as traders. They are a rough sturdy lot, but fairly well behaved.

The Kharoti say they are an offshoot of Tokhi, mother of Hotak mentioned above. But the Tokhi say they are descended from a foundling whom the tribe adopted. They hold the country about the sources of the Gomal river in Warghún south by east of Ghazni, and they winter in the Tánk tahsíl. They are a poor tribe, and many of them work as labourers or carriers. Dr. Bellew identifies them with the Arachoti of Alexander's historians, and points out that they still live in the ancient Arachosia. He considers them and the Násar to be of different origin from the mass of the Ghilzai.

The Suleman Khel are the most numerous, powerful, and warlike of all the Ghilzai
[P. 202] tribes, and hold a large tract stretching nearly the whole length of the Ghilzai country. Those who trade with India come chiefly from the hills east of Ghazni and winter in the northern trans-Indus tract. They bring but little merchandize with them, but go down-country in great numbers, where they act as brokers or *dalláls* between the merchants and other *pawindahs*. They are fine strong men and fairly well behaved, though not bearing the best of characters.

The Mian Khels have already been described in section 401. The trading and landowning sections are still closely connected, and in fact to some extent indistinguishable.

The Dutanni inhabit the Warrak valley and the country between the Wazíri hills and Gomal. They are a small, but well-to-do tribe, and trade with Bukhára.

---

[1] It is not perhaps impossible that these may be of Biloch origin. The Khetrán, perhaps of Pathán origin, have become the nucleus of a Biloch tribe; while 351 men of Derah Ismáíl returned themselves in this Census as caste Biloch, tribe Andar, which latter is one of the *Pawindah* tribes of Patháns.

[2] Macgregor says they are quiet and inoffensive.

[3] One story makes them the descendants of a gang of blacksmiths who in the 14th century accompanied the Mián Khel on one of their return journeys to Khorásán and settled there.

The Tokhi were the most prominent of all the Ghilzai tribes till the Hotak gave rulers to Kandahár about 1700 A.D. They hold the valley of the Tarnak and the north valley of the Argandáb, with Kelát-i-Ghilzai as their principal centre.

The Andar occupy nearly the whole of the extensive district of Shálgar south of Ghazni. With them are associated the Músa Khel Kákar, who are descended from an Andar woman, and live south and west of Shálgar.[1]

The Tarakki winter about Kandahár. They are largely nomad.

The Border tribes.—The most important tribes on the Derah Ismáíl border are, beginning from the south, the Qasráni Biloch and the Ushtaráni, already described in sections 383 and 401, the Shiráni, and the Mahsúd Wazíri. The Wazíri will be described when I come to the border tribes of Bannu (section 404).

The Shirani have already been mentioned and their origin described in section 400. They occupy the country round the Takht-i-Sulemán, bounded to the north by the Zarkanni stream and to the south by the Ushtaráni border, their principal habitat being the low valleys to the east of the Takht. They are divided into the Shiráni proper who hold the greater part of the tract, the Bábar of our plains described in section 401, and the small tribes of Haripál and Jalwáni lying to the south of the Shiráni proper. They are of medium height, wiry, and active, and wild and manly in their appearance. Their dress consists of a couple of coarse blankets, and their principal occupation is agriculture.

403. The Pathan tribes of Bannu.—On the southern border of the Bannu district, marching with Derah Ismáíl, we find the Marwat and the Niázi, the northernmost of the Indian descendants of Baitan, while further north lie the Wazíri and Bannúchi of the great Karlánri section of Patháns. The migration of the Niázi from Tánk across the Salt-range, and how the Marwat followed them and drove them across the Kurram, have already been described in section 399. Their ancestor Niázai had three sons, Bahai, Jamál, and Khánku. The descendants of the first are no longer distinguishable; while the Isa Khel among the Jamál, and the Musháni and Sarhang clans among the Khánku, have overshadowed the other clans and given their names to the most important existing divisions of the tribe. The Isa Khel settled in the south and the Musháni in the north of the country between the Kohát Salt-range and the Indus, while the Sarhang crossed the river,[2] and after a struggle lasting nearly a century and a half with their quondam allies the Gakkhars and their Jat and Awán subjects, finally drove the Gakkhars, whose stronghold on the Indus was destroyed by Ahmad Sháh in 1748, eastwards across the Salt-range, and established themselves in Miánwáli.

Towards the close of the 13th century[3] the Mangal, a tribe of the Kodai Karlánri, and the Hanni, an affiliated tribe of Saiyad origin, left their Karlánri home in Birmil, crossed the Sulemáns into the Bannu district, and settled in the valleys of the Kurram and Gambíla rivers. About a century later the Bannúchi, the descendants of Shitak, a Kakai Karlánri by his wife Mussammát Bannu, who with their Daur kinsmen then held the hills lying east of the Khost range in the angle between the Kohát and Bannu districts, with their head-quarters at Shawál, were driven from their homes by the Wazíri, and, sweeping down the Kurram valley, drove the Mangal and Hanni back again into the mountains of Kohát and Kurram where they still dwell, and occupied the country between the Kurram and Tochi rivers which they now hold in the north-western corner of the district.

---

[1] The figures for Biloch include 351 Andar in this district, who returned themselves as Biloch Andar.

[2] The *Kalíd-i-Afghání* says that they held Lakki and were driven out across the river by the Khatak. This seems improbable.

[3] The *Kalíd-i-Afghání* fixes this date at the middle of the 12th century, and that of the Bannúchi invasion at about 1,300 A.D.

At the same time the Daur, a tribe of evil repute in every sense of the word, occupied the banks of the Tochi beyond our border, which they still hold. Some 400 years ago the Bangi Khel Khatak, whose history will be sketched in sections 406-7, occupied the trans-Indus portion of the district above Kálábágh and the spur which the Salt-range throws out at that point. This they have since held without disturbance.

When the Darvesh Khel Wazíri (see above), moving from their ancestral homes in Birmil, drove the Bannúchi out of the Shawál hills, they occupied the country thus vacated, and for 350 years confined themselves to the hills beyond our border. But during the latter half of last century they began to encroach upon the plain country of the Marwat on the right bank of the Tochi, and of the Bannúchi on the left bank of the Kurram. At first their visits were confined to the cold season; but early in the present century, in the period of anarchy which accompanied the establishment of the Sikh rule in Bannu, they finally made good their footing in the lands which they had thus acquired and still hold.

The latest comers are the Bitanni (see section 401), who have within the last 60 years occupied a small tract on the north-eastern border of the Marwat at the foot of the hills. Thus Patháns hold all trans-Indus Bannu, and as much of the cis-Indus portion of the district as lies north of a line joining the junction of the Kurram and Indus with Sakesar, the peak at which the Salt-range enters the district and turns northwards. The trans-Indus Patháns, with the partial exception of the Niázi, speak Pashto of the soft and western dialect; the Niázi speak Hindko, especially east of the Indus.

404. I now proceed to a detailed description of the different tribes, beginning from the south :—

The Marwat hold almost the whole of the Lakki tahsil, that is to say the south-eastern half and the whole central portion of the country between the trans-Indus Salt-range and the Wazíri hills. Within the last fifty years they have begun to retrace their footsteps and have passed southwards over the Salt-range into Derah Ismáíl, where they occupy small tracts wrested from the Kundi in the northern corner of Tánk and along the foot of the hills and from the Balúch in the Paniála country. Their most important clans are the Músa Khel, Acha Khel, Khuda Khel, Bahrám, and Tapí. With them are associated a few of the Niázi, who remained behind when the main body of the tribe was expelled. The Marwat are as fine and law-abiding a body of men as are to be found on our border. They are a simple, manly, and slow-witted people, strongly attached to their homes, good cultivators, and of pleasing appearance. Their women are not secluded. Their history has been sketched in section 399. Their hereditary enemies the Khatak say of them: "Keep a Marwat to look after asses; "his stomach well filled and his feet well worn."

The Bannuchi hold the central portion of the Bannu tahsíl, between the Kurram and Tochi rivers. Their history is narrated in section 403. They are at present perhaps more hybrid than any other Pathán tribe. They have attracted to themselves Saiyads and other doctors of
[P. 210] Islám in great numbers, and have not hesitated to intermarry with these, with the scattered representatives of the former inhabitants of their tract who remained with them as *hamsáyah*, and with the families of the various adventurers who have at different times settled amongst them; insomuch that "Bannúchi in its broadest sense now means all Mahomedans, and by "a stretch, even Hindus long domiciled within the limits of the irrigated tract originally "occupied by the tribe." The descendants of Shitak, however, still preserve the memory of their separate origin and distinguish themselves as Bannúchi proper. They are of inferior physique, envious, secretive, cowardly, lying, great bigots, inoffensive, and capital cultivators. Sir Herbert Edwardes says of them: "The Bannúchis are bad specimens of Afghâns; can "worse be said of any race? They have all the vices of Patháns rankly luxuriant, their "virtues stunted." Their Isakhi clan, however, is famed for the beauty of its women. "Who "marries not an Isakhi woman deserves an ass for a bride."

The Niazi hold all the southern portion of Isa Khel and the country between Míánwáli and the hills; in other words so much of the Bannu district as is contained between the Salt-range on either side the Indus, and the Kurram and a line drawn from its mouth due east across the Indus. Their history and distribution have been related in sections 399 and 403. They are indifferent cultivators, and still retain much of the Pathán pride of race. The cis-Indus branch is the more orderly and skilful in agriculture. The Isa Khel is the predominant and most warlike section; but they all make good soldiers. A section of them is still independent and engaged in *pawindah* traffic, spending the summer about Kandahár and wintering in Derah Ismáfl. They are strict Sunnis. They seem to be a quarrelsome people, for the proverb says— "The Niázi like rows."

Minor tribes are the **Mughal Khel** clan of Yúsufzai who conquered a small tract round Gheriwál some seven centuries ago, and still show their origin in speech and physiognomy. The Khatak will be described when I discuss the Kohát tribes.

405. The Wazíri.—The whole of the Bannu portion beyond our border is occupied by the Darvesh Khel Wazíri, while south of them, along the Derah Ismáíl border, behind the Bitanni country, and as far south as the Gomal pass, lie the Mahsúd clan of the same tribe. The Wazíri are descended from Sulemán, son of Kakai, and are one of the Karlánri tribes.[1] The original seat of the tribe was in the Birmil hills, west of the Khost range which separates them from their kinsmen the Bannúchi descendants of Shitak. Sulemán had two sons, Lálai and Khizrai. Lálai had to fly by reason of a blood feud, and settled in Ningrahár on the northern slopes of the western Safed Koh, where his descendants the Lálai Wazíri are still settled. Khizrai had three sons, Músa, Mahsúd, and Gurbuz. From Mahsúd are descended the Mahsúd Wazíri, divided into the Alizai and Bahlolzai; while from Músa Darvesh are descended the Utmánzai and Ahmadzai clans, usually joined under the title of Darvesh Khel Wazíri.

About the close of the 14th century the Wazíri began to move eastwards. They first crossed the Khost range and drove the Bannúchi out of Shawál, and occupied the hills of the Bannu and Kohát border north of the Tochi. Then, crossing that river, they drove the Urmar Afghánś, descendants of Urmar, son of Sharkabún and near kinsmen of the Abdáli,[2] out of the hills south of the Tochi on the lower Bannu and Tánk borders to take refuge in the Loghar valley near Kábul, and dislodging the Bitanni from Káníguram, drove them back beyond Garangi to the low hills on our immediate frontier. They thus obtained possession of all that confused system of mountains which, starting from the Gomal pass which marks the northern extremity of the Sulemáns proper, runs northwards along our border to Thal and the Kurram river, where it joins the lower ranges of the Safed Koh. Their two main sections are the Mahsúd and Darvesh Khel, the former holding the hills to the south, and the latter those to the north of the Tochi river and the Khasor pass; while of the Darvesh Khel country, the Ahmadzai occupy the southern and the Utmánzai the northern parts. The Hasan Khel, an important Utmánzai sept, hold the extreme north-western portion of the tract. The two great sections are practically independent tribes, owning no common head, and with but little common feeling. They still nominally hold the Birmil country, though the Sulemán Khel and Kharoti Ghilzai winter there with their flocks, and during their stay the Wazíri are confined to their walled villages. They were till lately wholly nomad and pastoral; but they have of late years encroached upon the plain country of the Marwat, Bannúchi, and Khatak, and now hold cultivated lands in Bannu and Kohát.

The Gurbuz, an unimportant tribe, accompanied the Wazíri in their movements, and once occupied the hills between their Mahsúd and Darvesh Khel brethren, where, as already narrated, they disputed the possession of the Ghabbar peak with the Bitanni. They have now returned to their original seat west of the Khost range, and north of the Daur who hold the trans-border banks of the Tochi river.

The Wazíri are one of the most powerful and most troublesome tribes on our border, the Mahsúd being pre-eminent for turbulence and lawlessness. They are exceedingly democratic and have no recognised headmen, which increases the difficulty of dealing with them. They are tall, active, muscular, and courageous, and their customs differ in several respects from those of the Patháns in general. They are still in a state of semi-barbarism. They are well described in the *Haiyát-i-Afghání* (pages 227 *ff* of the translation). The large number of Wazíris shown in the Bannu district is partly due to the Census having been held on the night of the weekly fair. But Mr. Thorburn estimates the Wazíri population of the purely Wazíri border villages alone at 13,523, and there are always many members of the tribe scattered about the district 'in search of work or of opportunities for theft,' especially during the spring months. On the Bannu border distress owing to failure of rain had probably made the number of such persons unusually high at the time of the census.

---

[1] Dr. Bellew makes them the Wairsi sept of the Lodha tribe of Pramara Rájpúts; and says that they crossed from the Indus riverain across the Sham plain into the Birmil hills, then held by the Khatak whom they drove northwards, taking the whole of their country from the Sham plain to the Kohát valley. He gives no authority for these statements.

[2] This is according to the genealogies. But the Urmar are probably of Hindki origin, and speak a Panjábi dialect known as Urmari, of which a grammar has just been submitted to Government for approval.

406. The Pathan tribes of Kohat.[1]—The Patháns of Kohát belong almost entirely to two great tribes, the Khatak of the the Kakai section of the Karlánri, and the Bangash, a Qureshi tribe of Arab descent. The original home of the Khatak, in common with the other sections of the Karlánri, was the west face of the northern Sulemáns, where they held the valley of Shawál now occupied by the Wazíri.[2] Towards the close of the 13th century[3] they, with the Mangal and Hanni, two tribes of the Kodai section of the Karlánri, moved eastwards, the two last descending into the Bannu district and settling along the Kurram and Gambíla, while the Khatak held the hills to the west of our border. A century later the Bannúchi drove, as already related in section 403, the Mangal and Hanni out of Bannu; and not long after this the Khatak, quarrelling with the Bannúchi, moved to the north and east and occupied the hilly country, then uninhabited, which stretches across the centre of the Kohát district to the Indus, leaving behind them the Chamkanni, a tribe (perhaps of Persian origin) who had taken refuge with them, and the bulk of whom now occupy the north-east corner of the Kurram Valley, while another section still lives in a state of barbarism about Káníguram as the subjects of the Wazíri. At this time the Orakzai, another tribe of the Kodai Karlánri, held all the valley of Kohát in the north and north-east of the district from Resi on the Indus to Kohát; while the Bangash, already alluded to, lived in the country about Gardez in Zurmat. But in the latter part of the 14th century the Bangash,
[P. 211] increasing in number and being pressed upon by the Ghilzai, emigrated eastwards *en masse* and settled in Kurram. Being presently driven out by the Túri[4] and Jáji, tribes of doubtful origin who claim descent from Khugiáni, son of Kakai, but who are perhaps of Awán stock[5] though now Patháns for all practical purposes, and who still occupy the valley, they joined with the Khatak who had quarrelled with the Orakzai, and drove the latter out of Kohát. The struggle was prolonged for nearly a century; but by the close of the 15th century the Orakzai had been driven into the lower of the ranges which form the eastern extremity of the Safed Koh and lie along the north-western border of the Kohát District. The Khatak and Bangash then possessed themselves of all the northern and central portions of Kohát and divided the country between them, the former taking all the southern and central portions, while the latter took the northern and north-western tract consisting of the Kohát and Míránzai valleys up to the base of the Orakzai or Samána range; and the hills between Gada Khel and Láchi were then fixed and still remain as the boundary between the two tribes. In the time of Akbar, Malik Akor was the leader of the Khatak, and he was granted an extensive tract of land south of the Kábul river between Khairábád and Naushahra on condition of his

[1] Unfortunately the Settlement Officer of Kohát went on furlough without reporting his settlement. Consequently I have far less full information regarding this than regarding any other frontier district. I have, however, done my best to supply the defect from other sources.

[2] Dr. Bellew says that the Khatak held all the plain country of the Indus as far south as Derah Ismáíl Khán till driven out by the Wazíri, who being in their turn driven northwards by the pressure of Biloch tribes moving up the Indus valley, passed onwards into the hills then held by the Bannúchi. He gives no authority for this account, which does not agree with the traditions of the Khatak themselves as related in the *Kalíd-i-Afghání*.

[3] The *Kalíd-i-Afghání* places the migration in the middle of the 12th century, and the Bannúchi migration at about 1300 A.D.

[4] The Túri were originally *hamsáyahs* of the Bangash, but rose in rebellion against their masters.

[5] Mr. Merk, however, tells me that the Khugiáni claim Durráni origin; and that the claim is admitted by the Durráni, and supported by their genealogies.

guarding the high road between Attak and Peshâwar. This brought him into contact with the Mandanr of Yúsufzai who held the country opposite on the left bank of the Kábul river. Their quarrels were continual; and at length in the time of Sháh Jahán the Khatak crossed the river, possessed themselves of the strip of land along its north bank from the junction of the Swát river to the Indus and for a short distance along the right bank of the Indus, and also pushed across the plain and acquired a position about Jamálgarhi to the north of Mardán, in the very heart of the Mandanr country, which commands the approaches to Swát on the one hand and Buner on the other. They have also encroached on the Mohmand and Khalíl who lie to the west of their Peshâwar territory. Meanwhile they had gradually spread southwards to the trans-Indus Salt-range and the Bannu border, and across the Salt-range to the Indus at Kálábágh; and they now hold a broad strip running along its right bank from a little above the junction of the Kábul river to Kálábágh, all Kohát save the portion occupied by the Bangash in the north and north-west of the district, and the western half of the Lundkhwár valley in the north of Yúsufzai. They crossed the Indus and are said to have at one time conquered the Awán country as far east as the Jahlam. But about the middle of the 17th century they relinquished the greater part of this tract; and now only hold Makhad in the Ráwalpindi district, and the left bank of the river as far south as Mari in Bannu. There are other Khatak holdings scattered about the cis-Indus plains; but their owners have no connection with the tribe.

About the middle of the 18th century two parties grew up in the tribe. They temporarily combined to accompany and assist Ahmad Sháh Durráni in his invasion of Hindústán; but after his departure the division became permanent, the eastern or Akora faction holding the north-eastern portion of Kohát and all the Khatak country of Peshâwar, with their capital at Akora on the Kábul river, while the western or Teri division hold all the remainder of Kohát, including the south-eastern corner occupied by the Sághri clan, and the adjoining territory of the Bangi Khel Khatak of Bannu. The western section have their capital at Teri, south-west of Kohát, and in the centre of the hills they first occupied.

Thus with the exception of a few Awán villages in the Bangash country, and a Saiyad village here and there, the whole of Kohát is held by Patháns, and with the exception of a narrow strip of land stretching along the northern border of the Teri Khatak from Togh to Dhoda which is held by the Niázi (see section 400), the whole is in the hands of the Bangash and Khatak. The Nawáb of Khatak holds the Teri tract in jágír, possessing exclusive revenue jurisdiction, and large criminal and police powers.

407. The Khatak.—The history of the Khatak tribe has been sketched above. They are descended from Luqmán surnamed Khatak, son of Burhán, son of Kakai.[1] Luqmán had two sons Turman and Buláq. The descendants of the latter are still known as the Buláqi section; while Tarai, son of Turman, rose to such distinction that the whole section, including two main clans, the Tari proper and the Tarkai, is called by his name. They have absorbed several small tribes of doubtful origin, the Mugiaki and Samini[2] belonging to the Buláq, while the Jalozai, Dangarzai, and Uria Khel belong to the Tari section. The most important clans of the Tari section are the Anokhel to which the chief's family belongs, and which includes the septs of the upper and lower Mohmandi[3] who hold the right bank of the Indus below Attak, and the Mír

[1] Kakai was son of Karlán, founder of the Karlánri division of the Afgháns.
[2] Dr. Bellew interprets these names as meaning respectively Mongol and Chinese.
[3] The Mohmandi of the Khwarra valley of the Kohát District are quite distinct from the Mohmand of Peshâwar.

Khel who hold the Chauntra valley in the centre of the Teri tract. Among the Buláqi the most important clan is the Sághri, with its practically independent Bangi Khel sept. These hold the right bank of the Indus above Kálábágh, while the Sághri, with the Babar family of the Bangi Khel, also occupy the cis-Indus possessions of the tribe. Most of the Khatak in Yúsufzai are also Buláq. The Káka Khel section of the Khatak are descended from the famous saint Shekh Rahím Kár, and are consequently venerated by all northern Patháns. The Khatak are a fine manly race, and differ from all other Patháns in features, general appearance, and many of their customs. They are the northernmost of all the Patháns settled on our frontier who speak the soft or western dialect of Pashto. They are of a warlike nature and have been for centuries at feud with all their neighbours and with one another. They are active, industrious, and "a "most favourable specimen of Pathán," and are good cultivators, though their country is stony and unfertile. They are also great carriers and traders, and especially hold all the salt trade with Swát and Buner in their hands. They are all Sunnis. The Marwat, the hereditary enemy of the Khatak, says: "Friendship is good with any one but a Khatak: may the devil take a Khatak" and "A Khatak is a hen. If you seize him slowly he sits down; and if suddenly he clucks." Another proverb runs thus: "Though the Khatak is a good horseman, yet he is a man of but "one charge."

The Bangash.—The early history of the Bangash has been narrated above. Since they settled down in their Kohát possessions no event of importance has marked their history. They claim descent from Khalíd ibn Wálid, Mahomet's apostle to the Afgháns of Ghor,[1] and himself of the original stock from which they sprang; but they are Patháns "as regards character, cus- "toms, crimes, and vices." Their ancestor had two sons Gár and Sámil, who, on account of the bitter enmity that existed between them, were nicknamed Bunkash or root destroyers. These sons have given their names to the two great political factions into which not only the Bangash themselves, but their Afrídi, Orakzai, Khatak, Túri, Zaimusht, and other neighbours of the

[P. 212] Karlánri branch are divided, though the division has of late lost most of its importance.[2] The Gári are divided into Míránzai and Baizai clans. The Baizai hold the valley of Kohát proper; the Míránzai lie to the west of them in the valley to which they have given their name; while the Sámilzai occupy the northern portion of Kohát and hold Shalozán at the foot of the Orákzai hills, where they are independent, or live in Paiwár and Kurram under the protection of the Túri. The Bangash Nawábs of Furrukhábád belong to this tribe.

Border tribes.—The tribes on the Kohát border, beginning from the south, are the Darvesh Khel Wazíri, the Zaimusht, the Orakzai, and the Afrídi. The Wazíri have already been described in section 405. The Zaimusht are a tribe of Spín Tarín Afgháns who inhabit the hills between the Kurram and the Orakzai border on the north-west frontier of Kohát. They belong to the Sámil faction. The early history of the Orakzai has been given in section 406. With them are associated the Alíkhel, Míshti, the Shekhán, and some of the Malla Khel, all of whom are now classed as Orakzai of the Hamsáyah clan, though, as the name implies, distinct by descent. The Orakzai hold the lower south-eastern spurs of the Safed Koh and the greater part of Tíráh. They are divided into five great clans, the Allezai, Massozai, Daulatzai, Ismáílzai, and Lashkarzai, of which the Daulatzai and Massozai are the most numerous. The Muhammad Khel is the largest sept of the Daulatzai, and, alone of the Orakzai, belongs to the Shíah sect. They are a fine manly tribe, but exceedingly turbulent. They are divided between the Sámil and Gár factions. There are a considerable number of Orakzai tenants scattered about the Kohát District. The present rulers of Bhopál belong to this tribe. The Afrídi will be described among the border tribes of Peshbáwar.

408. The Pathan tribes of Peshawar.—The Patháns of Pesháwar belong, with the exception of the Khatak described above, almost wholly to the Afgháns proper, descendants of Sarban; and among them to the line of Karshabún or the representatives of the ancient Gandhári, as distinguished from the true Afgháns of Jewish origin who trace their descent from Sharkhabún. I have already told, in section 395, how during the 5th or 6th century a Gandhári colony emigrated to Kandahár, and there were joined and

---

[1] Dr. Bellew thinks that they and the Orakzai are perhaps both of Scythian origin, and belonged to the group of Túrk tribes, among whom he includes all the Karlánri, or, as he calls them, Túrklánri, who came in with the invasion of Sabuktagín in the 10th and Taimur in the 16th century of our æra.

[2] Dr. Bellew is of opinion that these names denote respectively the Magian and Buddhist religions of their ancestors. The present division of the tribes is given as follows by Major James: *Sámil.*—Half the Orakzai, half the Bangash, the Mohmand, and the Malikdín Khel, Sepáh, Kamr, Zakha Khel, Aka Khel, and Adam Khel clans of Afrídi. *Gár.*—Half the Orakzai, half the Bangash, the Khalíl, and the Kúki Khel and Qumbar Khel clans of Afrídi. The feud between the two factions is still very strong and bitter, and is supplemented by the sectarian animosity between Shíah and Sunni.

converted by the Afghán stock of Ghor who blended with them into a single nation. Their original emigration was due to the pressure of Jat and Scythic tribes who crossed the Hindu Kush and descended into the valley of the Kábul river. Among those tribes was probably the Dilazák,[1] who are now classed as one of the Kodai Karlánri, and who were converted by Mahmúd Ghaznavi in the opening of the 11th century. They extended their sway over the Ráwalpindi and Pesháwar districts and the valley of the Kábul as far west as Jalálábád, driving many of the original Hindki or Gandhári inhabitants into the valleys of Swát and Buner which lie in the hills to the north, and ravaging and laying waste the fertile plain country. Amalgamating with the remaining Hindkis they lost the purity of their faith, and were described as infidels by the Afgháns who subsequently drove them out.

The Kandahár colony of Gandhári was divided into two principal sections, the Khakhai and Ghoria Khel, besides whom it included the descendants of Zamand and Kánsi. I give below the principal tribes which trace their descent from Kharshabún for convenience of reference :—

Kand ...	Khakhai	Yúsufzai ...	Mandanr ...	Hold the Pesháwar plain north of the Kábul river, called British Yúsufzai, the Chamlah valley on the Pesháwar border, and part of the Haripur tract in Hazára.
			Yúsufzai proper.	Hold Swát, Buner, Panjkora, and Dír; the hills north of the Yúsufzai plain.
		Gugiáni	... ...	Hold Doába; the plains in the angle between the Kábul and Swát rivers.
		Tarklánri	... ...	Hold Bajaur tract west of Swát.
	Ghoria Khel.	Mohmand	Plains Mohmand.	Hold plains of Pesháwar on right bank of Bára river.
			Bar Mohmand.	Hold mountains north of Kábul river and west of the Swát-Kábul Doáb.
		Dáúdzai	... ...	Hold Pesháwar plain on right bank of Kábul river to a little below the junction of the Bára river.
	...	Khalíl	... ...	Hold the Pesháwar plains between the Dáúdzai and the Khaibar.
Zamand	...	Muhammadzai	...	Hold Hashtnaghar, the plains east of Swát river in Pesháwar.
		Others	... ...	Scattered.
Kánsi ...	...	Shinwári	... ...	Hold part of Khaibar mountains and the northern slopes of the Safed Koh.
		Others	... ...	Scattered.

About the middle of the 13th century they were settled about the head-waters of the Tarnak and Arghasán rivers, while the Tarín Afgháns held, as they still hold, the lower valleys of those streams. As they increased in numbers the weaker yielded to pressure, and the Khakhai Khel, accompanied by their first cousins the Muhammadzai descendants of Zamand, and by their Karlánri neighbours the Utmán Khel of the Gomal valley,[2] left their homes and migrated to Kábul. Thence they were expelled during the latter half of the 15th century by Ulugh Beg, a lineal descendant of Taimur and Bábar's uncle, and passed eastwards into Ningrahár on the northern slopes of the Safed Koh, and into the Jalálábád valley. Here the Gugiáni settled in eastern and the Muhammadzai in western Ningrahár, the Tarklánri occupied

[1] Dr. Bellew seems doubtful whether the Dilazák were of Jat or of Rájpút extraction. He says the name is of Buddhist origin.

[2] Another story makes the Utmán Khel descendants of one Utmán, a follower of Mahmúd Ghaznavi, who settled *circa* 1,000 A. D. in the country which they now hold.

Lughmán, while the Yúsufzai (I use the word throughout in its widest sense to include both the Mandanr and the Yúsufzai proper) and Utmán Khel moved still further east through the Khaibar pass to Peshávar. Here they settled peacefully for a while; but presently quarrelled with the Dilazák and expelled them from the Doába or plain country in the angle between the Swát and Kábul rivers, into which they moved. They then crossed the Swát river into Hashtnaghar and attacked the Eastern Shilmání, a tribe probably of Indian origin, who had only lately left their homes in Shilmán on the Kurram river for the Khaibar mountains and Hashtnaghar. These they dispossessed of Hashtnaghar and drove them northwards across the mountains into Swát, thus acquiring all the plain country north of the Kábul river and west of Hoti Mardán.

[P. 213] **409.** Meanwhile the Ghoria Khel whom they had left behind in the Kandahár country had been following in their track; and early in the 16th century they reached the western mouth of the Khaibar pass. Here they seem to have divided, a part of the Mohmand now known as the Bar Mohmand crossing the Kábul river at Dakka, while the remainder went on through the pass to the plain of Peshávar lately vacated by the Yúsufzai, where they defeated the Dilazák in a battle close to Peshávar, drove them across the Kábul river into what are now called the Yúsufzai plains, and occupied all the flat country south of the Kábul river and west of Jalozai. This they still hold, the Dáúdzai holding the right bank of the Kábul river, and the Khalíl the left bank of the Bára river and the border strip between the two streams facing the Khaibar pass, while the Mohmand took the country south of the Bára and along the right bank of the Kábul as far as Naushahra, though they have since lost the south-eastern portion of it to the Khatak. Meanwhile the Bar Mohmand made themselves masters of the hill country lying north of the Kábul river as far up as Lálpura and west of the Doába, and possessed themselves of their ancestral capital Gandhára, driving out into Káfiristán the inhabitants, who were probably their ancient kinsmen, the descendants of such Gandhári as had not accompanied them when, two centuries earlier, they had migrated to Kandahár. They then crossed the Kábul river, and possessed themselves of the country between its right bank and the crest of the Afrídi hills to the north of the Khaibar pass.

While these events were occurring, the Gugiáni, Tarklánri,[1] and Muhammadzai, who had been left behind in Ningrahár, moved eastwards, whether driven before them by the advancing Ghoria Khel, or called in as allies against the Dilazák by the Yúsufzai. At any rate they joined their friends in Doába and Hashtnaghar, and attacking the Dilazák, drove them out of Yúsufzai and across the Indus. They then divided their old and new possessions among the allies, the Gugiáni receiving Doába, the Muhammadzai Hashtnaghar, while the Yúsufzai, Utman Khel, and Tarklánri took the great Yúsufzai plain. During the next twenty years these three tribes made themselves masters of all the hill country along the Yúsufzai, Hashtnaghar, and Bar Mohmand border, from the Indus to the range separating the Kunar and Bajaur valleys, the inhabitants of which, again the ancient Gandhári who had already suffered at the hands of the Bar Mohmand, they drove east and west across the Indus into Hazára and across the Kurram into Káfiristán. This country also they divided, the Tarklánri taking Bajaur, and the Utmán Khel the valley of the Swát river up

[1] A section of the Tarklánri remained in Lughmán, where they still dwell.

to Arang Bárang and its junction with the Panjkora, while the Yúsufzai held all the hills to the east as far as the Indus and bordering upon their plain country, including lower Swát, Buner, and Chamlah. Some time later the Khatak obtained from Akbar, as has already been related in section 406, a grant of the plains in the south-east of the Pesháwar district. Thus the Khakhai and their allies held all the country north of the Kábul river from the Indus to Kunar, including the hills north of the Pesháwar border, but excluding those lying west of Doába which were occupied by the Bar Mohmand; while all the plain country south of the Kábul was held, in the east by the Khatak, and in the west by the Ghoria Khel. These last attempted to cross the river into Yúsufzai, but were signally defeated by the Yúsufzai, and have never extended their dominions. How the Khatak pushed across into the Yúsufzai plain has already been told (section 406). The Dilazák, thus expelled from their territory, made incessant efforts to recover it; until finally, as the cause of tumult and disorder, they were deported *en masse* by the Emperor Jahángír and scattered over the Indian peninsula. When the Yúsufzai settled in their possessions they divided the hill and plain country equally between their two great sections, the Mandanr and the Yúsufzai proper. But feuds sprang up amongst them which were fomented by the Mughal rulers; and early in the 17th century the Yúsufzai expelled the Mandanr from Swát and Buner, while the Mandanr in their turn expelled the Yúsufzai from the greater part of the Yúsufzai plain. Thus the Yúsufzai now hold Swát, Buner, and the Lundkhwár and Ránízai valleys in the north-west of Yúsufzai; while the Mandanr hold Chamlah and the remainder of the plain country.

410. The Pathan tribes of Peshawar continued.—The plain Mohmand.—I now proceed to describe the tribes in detail. Passing from Kohát into Pesháwar through the country of the Khatak, who have already been described in section 407, and turning west, we first come to the lower or Plain Mohmand, who occupy the south-west corner of the district, south of the Bára stream. They are divided into five main sections, the Mayárzai, Músazai, Dawezai, Matanni and Sarganni. Their headmen, in common with those of all the Ghoria Khel, are called *Arbáb*, a title meaning master, and conferred by the Mughal Emperors.[1] They are good and industrious cultivators, and peacefully disposed except on the Afrídi border. Their relation with the Bar Mohmand, from whom they are now quite separate, differing from them in both manners and customs, is described in section 409.

The Khalil occupy the left bank of the Bára, and the country along the front of the Khaibar pass. They have four main clans, Matúzai, Bározai, Isháqzai, and Tilarzai, of which the Bározai is the most powerful. They are not good cultivators. There are some of the tribe still to be found in Kandahár.

The Daudzai occupy the left bank of the Kábul river as far down as the junction of the Bára. The Mohmand and Dáúdzai are descended from a common ancestor Daulatyár, son of Ghorai the progenitor of the Ghoria Khel. Dáúd had three sons, Mandkai, Mámúr, and Yúsuf, from whom are descended the main sections of the tribe. Mandkai had three sons, Husen, Nekai, and Bálo, of whom only the first is represented in Pesháwar. Nekai fled into Hindústán, while Bálo's few descendants live in parts of Tíráh.

The Gugiani hold the Doába or plain country in the angle between the Kábul and Swát rivers. They are descended from Mak, the son of Khakhai, by a *hamsáyah* shepherd who married Mak's daughter Gugi, whence the name. They are divided into two great sections, Hotak and Zírak. Macgregor says that other Patháns do not recognise them as of pure Pathán blood.

The Muhammadzai[2] hold Hashtnaghar, a strip of territory some 13 miles broad running down the left bank of the Swát river from our border to Naushahra. They are descended from Muhammad, one of the sons of Zamand; and with them are settled a few descendants of his brothers, from one of whom, Kheshgi, one of their prinicipal villages is named. Their clans are Práng, Chársadda, Razar, Utmánzai, Turangzai, Umarzai, Sherpao, and Tangi with its two septs Barazai and Nasratzai.

The Baizai.—The Yúsufzai proper are divided into the Bádi Khel (now extinct), Isázai, Iliászai, Malízai, and Akozai. The Akozai are further divided into three clans, the Ránízai[3] who hold the

[1] Arbáb is the plural of the Arabic *Rab* or Lord; a term often applied to the Deity.
[2] The tribe is often called Mohmandzai or Mámanzai, and their ancestor, Mohmand or Máman.
[3] The *Haiyát-i-Afghání* calls the Ránízai a sept of the Baizai. This seems improbable, as they descend from different wives of Ako.

western portion of the hills between Yúsufzai and Swát, the Khwájazai who occupy the country between the Swát and Panjkora rivers, and the Baizai. The last originally held the Lundkhwár valley in the centre of the northernmost portion of the Peshawar district, and all the eastern hill country between that and the Swát river. The hills they still hold; but the Khatak have,[1] as already recounted
[P. 214] in section 406, obtained all the western portion of the valley, while the Utmán Khel Karlánri, whom the Baizai called in as allies in a feud with their neighbours and kinsmen the Ránízai, have obtained its north-east corner, and the Baizai now hold only a small tract to the south of these last. They are divided into six septs, Abha Khel, Azíz Khel, Bábozai, Matorezai, Músa Khel, and Zangi Khel. The last lies south of the Ilam range which divides Swát from Buner. The other five originally held the Baizai valley and the hills to the north; but since the irruption of the Khatak and Utmán Khel, only the first three hold land in our territory.

The Mandanr hold the remainder of the Peshawar district. They are divided into main clans as follows :—

- Mandanr ...
  - Usmánzai ...
    - Kamálzai ... Mishránzai. Kishránzai.
    - Amázai ... Daulatzai. Ismáílzai.
  - Utmánzai ... Alízai. Kanázai. Akázai.
  - Saddozai.
  - Razar ... Mánezai. Malakzai. Ako Khel. Khidrzai. Mámúzai.

The Saddozai are by origin a branch of the Utmánzai by a second wife of Utmán, but they are practically separated from them. The Usmánzai occupy all the northern and western portions of the Mandanr tract, the Kamálzai lying to the west immediately south of the Lundkhwár valley and stretching as far down as the border of the Buláq Khatak, while the Amázai lie to the east and south-east of the same valley. Of the septs, the Kishránzai, who hold Hoti and Mardán, and the Daulatzai lie to the north, and the Mishranzai and the Ismáílzai to the south of the respective tracts. South of the Amázai and between them and the Khatak territory come the Razar; while the Utmánzai and Saddozai hold the extreme east of the district on the right bank of the Indus, the Saddozai lying to the west and the Utmánzai to the east. These latter also hold a small area in the south of the independent Gadún valley, and early in the 18th century were called across the Indus by the Gújars of Hazára as allies against the Tarín Afgháns, and appropriated the Gandgarh tract from Torbela to the southern border of Hazára. In this tract all three of their main septs are represented, the Tarkheli section of the Alízai holding the southern half of the tract, and stretching across the border into Attak. The Khudu Khel, a Saddozai sept, occupy the valleys between Chamlah and the Gadún country. The valley of Chamlah on the Peshawar border and north of the Gadún country is occupied by a mixture of Mandanr clans, in which the Amázai, whose Ismáílzai sept hold the Mahában country, largely preponderate. The Mandanr, living almost wholly within our territory and long subject to the rulers of Peshawar, are perhaps more civilised and less impatient of control than any other Pathán tribe.

411. The Pathan tribes of the Peshawar border. The Afridi.—Dr. Bellew says that the Afrídi, whom he identifies with the Aparytæ of Herodotus, originally held the whole of the Safed Koh system between the Kábul and the Kurram river, from the Indus to the headwaters of the Kurram and the Pewár ridge. But since the great Scythic invasions of the 5th and succeeding centuries, they have been successively encroached upon by tribes of very diverse origin; first by the Orakzai and Bangash to the south, and later by the Wazíri and Túri to the south-west, the Khatak to the east, and the Ghilzai, Khugiáni and Shinwári to the west. They now hold only the central fastnesses of the eastern extremity of the Safed Koh; namely, the Khaibar mountains, the valley of the Bára and the range south of that valley which separates Kohát from Peshawar, and the northern parts of Tíráh, which they recovered from the Orakzai in the time of Jahángír. The Pathán historians trace their descent from Burhán, son of Kakai, grandson of Karlánri, by his son Usmán surnamed Afrídi, and say that in the 7th century the Khaibar tract was held by Rájpúts of the Bhatti tribe and Yadúbansi stock, subjects of the Rája of Lahore, who were constantly harassed by the Afgháns of Ghor and the Sulemáns; and that about the end of the century the Afrídi, then in alliance with the Gakkhars, obtained from the Lahore Government all the hill country west of the Indus and south of the Kábul river on condition of guarding the frontier against invasion. The Afrídi are divided into five clans, of which the Ula Khel and in it the Zakha Khel sept is the

[1] Some say that the Khatak, as well as the Utmán Khel, were called in as allies against the Ránízai.

largest, while the Míta Khel are no longer to be found in Afghánistán and the Míri Khel have been amalgamated with the Malikdín and Aka Khel. Some of the principal divisions are shown below :—

1. Míta Khel.
2. Míri Khel.
3. *Aka Khel* ... { Bassi Khel. / Madda Khel. / Sultán Khel. / Míro Khel. }
4. Ula Khel (Khaibar Afrídi). { Maimana Khel ... { Firoz Khel ... { *Kúki Khel.* / *Kamar Khel.* } / Mír Ahmad Khel { *Malikdín Khel.* / *Qambar Khel.* } / *Sepáh.* } / *Zakha Khel.* }
5. *Adam Khel* ... { Hasan Khel. / Jawáki. / Galli. / Ashu Khel. }

But for practical purposes they are divided at present into eight clans, *viz.*, Kúki Khel, Malikdín Khel, Qambar Khel, Kamar Khel, Zakha Khel, Aka Khel, Sepáh and Adam Khel, whose names are printed in italics in the above table.

The Adam Khel, who include the Hasan Khel and Jawáki septs so well known on our border, occupy the range between Kohát and Pesháwar, from Akor west of the Kohát pass to the Khatak boundary. The Hasan Khel hold the land along the southern border of the Pesháwar and the north-eastern border of the Kohát district. Next to them come the Aka Khel who hold the low range of hills from Akor to the Bára river, the Bassi Khel sept lying nearest to British territory. These two clans occupy the south-eastern corner of the Afrídi country, and lead a more settled life than their kinsmen, being largely engaged in the carriage of wood and salt between Independent Territory and British India. The other tribes are in some degree migratory, wintering in the lower hills and valleys, while in the hot weather they retire to the cool recesses of the upper mountains. But their general distribution is as follows: North of the Bára river is the Kajúri plain, which forms the winter quarters of the Malikdín Khel, Qambar Khel, Sepáh, and Kamar Khel. The Qambar Khel pass the summer in Tíráh. The Sepáh's summer quarters are in the Bára valley; while the Kamar Khel spend the hot months in the spurs of the Safed Koh between Maidán and Bára, and are better cultivators and graziers and less habitual robbers than their kinsmen. The Zakha Khel are the most wild and lawless of the Afrídi clans. Their upper settlements are in the Maidán and Bára districts, and their winter quarters lie in the Bazár valley north of Landi Kotal, and in the Khaibar from Ali Masjid to Landi Kotal. Their children are christened by being passed backwards and forwards through a hole made in a wall after the fashion of a burglar, while the parents repeat "Be a thief; be a thief," an exhortation which they comply with scrupulously when they arrive at years of discretion. They are notorious as liars and thieves, even among the lying and thieving Afrídi. The Kúki Khel hold the eastern mouth of the Khaibar, and the pass itself as far as Ali Masjid. In summer they retire to the glen of Rájgal, north of Maidán, in the Safed Koh. They trade in firewood, and offend rather by harbouring criminals than by overt acts of aggression. The Afrídi is the most barbarous of all the tribes of our border. All the Karlánri, with the single exception of the Khatak, are wild and uncontrollable; but most of all the Afrídi. "Ruthless "cowardly robbery and coldblooded treacherous murder are to an Afrídi the salt of life. Brought up "from earliest childhood amid scenes of appalling treachery and merciless revenge, nothing has yet "changed him: as he lives, a shameless cruel savage, so he dies. Yet he is reputed brave, and "that by men who have seen him fighting; and he is on the whole the finest of the Pathán races of [P. 215]
"our border. His physique is exceptionally fine, and he is really braver, more open and more "treacherous than other Patháns. This much is certain, that he has the power of prejudicing "Englishmen in his favour; and few are brought into contact with him who do not at least begin "with enthusiastic admiration for his manliness."[1] He is tall, spare, wiry, and athletic; hardy and active, but impatient of heat. His women are notoriously unchaste. He is only nominally a Musalmán, being wholly ignorant and intensely superstitious. The Zakha Khel removed the odium under which they suffered of possessing no shrine at which to worship, by inducing a sainted man of the Káka Khel to come and settle among them, and then murdering him in order to bury his corpse and thus acquire a holy place of their own. The Afrídi are intensely democratic, the nominal Chiefs having but little power.

The Mullagori.—North of the Afrídi come the Mullágori, a small and inoffensive tribe who are associated with the hill Mohmand, but whose Pathán origin is doubtful. They hold the Tartarah country north of the Khaibar range. They are noted thieves, but confine themselves to petty offences.

---

[1] Macgregor's *Gazetteer of the North-Western Frontier*, *verb.* Afrídi.

The Shinwari are the only branch of the descendants of Kánsi, third son of Karshabún,[1] who still retain a corporate existence as a tribe. They lie west of the Mullágori, hold the hills to the north of the western end of the Khaibar pass, and thence stretch along the northern slopes of the Safed Koh up to the Khugiáni territory. They are divided into four great clans, Sangu Khel, Ali Sher Khel, Sepáh, and Mandozai. The Khaibar Shinwári belong to the Ali Sher Khel, and live in the Loárgi valley at Landi Kotal. Their principal septs are Píro Khel, Mír Dád Khel, Khúga Khel, Shekh Mal Khel, and Sulemán Khel. They are largely engaged in the carrying trade beween Peshâwar and Kábul; and are stalwart, hardworking and inoffensive, though much addicted to petty thieving. They probably came up to this part of the country with the Ghoria Khel (see section 409).

The Bar Mohmand.—The history of the hill or Bar Mohmand has been related in section 409. They hold the hills to the west of the Doába between the Kábul river and Bajaur and the Utmán Khel country, the southern portion of Kunar, and some of the northern hills of the Khaibar. They have also spread across our border along the Kábul river, between the two branches of which the Halímzai clan hold a small area lying between the Dáúdzai and the Gugiáni. Their principal sections are Baizai, Khwáezai, Tawezai, Utmánzai, Kukozai, and Tarakzai, the last of which is divided into Halímzai, Isa Khel, Burhán Khel, and Tarakzai proper. The Halímzai and the Tarakzai proper hold land on our border, the others living further west. The Khán of Lálpura, Chief of the Mohmand, who belongs to the Tarakzai clan, probably enjoys more real power than any other tribal Chief among the Patháns of our immediate border. The Mohmand is almost as great a savage as the Afrídi, while his venality is even greater. "You have only "got to put a rupee in your eye, and you may look at any Mohmand, man or woman." They formerly gave much trouble on our border.

The Utman Khel.—The history of the Utmán Khel has already been sketched in sections 408-9. They occupy both banks of the Swát river beyond our border as far up as Arang Bárang, and have, as stated in section 410, obtained a portion of the Baizai valley of Lundkhwár. The two chief clans are Umar Khel and Asíl Khel, the former of which hold the hills on the Peshâwar frontier, while the latter who live on the Swát river are the more powerful. "They "are described as tall, stout, and fair, often going naked to the "waist. The women labour like the men, and everything shows "the absence of civilization. They are a sober people, with "none of the vices of the Yúsufzai."[2] They give us but little trouble.

Bádí Khel ...	(almost extinct).
Isázi ...	Hasanzai. Madákhel. Akázai.
Iliászai.	
Malízai ...	Daulatzai. Chagharzai. Núrazai.
Akozai ...	Ránízai. Khwájazai. Baizai.

The Yusufzai proper.—The history of the Yúsufzai has already been related in sections 408-9. Their main divisions are shown in the margin. The holdings of the Akozai clans have already been described in section 410. The Isázai hold the north-east slopes of Mahában, and the mountainous country on both sides of the Indus in Hazára and the Gadún valley. The Malízai hold eastern and the Iliászai western Buner. The Ránízai and Baizai septs of the Akozai hold all the hills beyond the northern border of Yúsufzai, the former to the west and the latter to the east. Beyond them in Buner lie the Salárzai sept of the Iliászai, and again between them and the Chamlah valley are the Núrazai of the Malízai clan, which include the Abazai section. The Yúsufzai are incredibly superstitious, proud, avaricious, turbulent, merciless, and revengeful. But they are of a lively, merry, sociable disposition, fond of music and poetry, and very jealous of the honour of their women. Their tribal constitution is distinctly democratic.

The Jadun Country.—South of the Yúsufzai territory come Chamlah and the Khudu Khel territory already noticed. The southern parts of the country between Peshâwar and Hazára constitute the Jadún or Gadún country. The holdings of other tribes in this valley have already been noticed. The Jadún themselves occupy all the eastern portions of the valley and the southern slopes of Mahában down to the Indus, as well as a considerable area in Hazára. They are described in section 417.

412. The Pathan Tribes of Hazara. The Hazára mountains on this side of the Indus were from a very early date inhabited by a mixed population of Indian origin, the Gakkhars occupying the portion to the south and having authority over the Rájpúts of the eastern hills, while a Gújar population held most of the northern and central parts of the district. In 1399 A.D. a family of Karlágh Túrks came into India with Taimur, settled in the Pakhli

[1] Dr. Bellews says they came from Persia in the time of Nádir Sháh, and settled among the Patháns.

[2] Macgregor's *Gazetteer, voce* Utmán Khel.

plain in the north and centre of the district, and established their rule over the whole of the district, then known as the kingdom of Pakhli.[1] I have already related how, about the middle of the 16th century, the Dilazák were driven out of Pesháwar across the Indus, and were presently followed by the representatives of the old Gandhári, the present inhabitants of Swát and Buner and the mountains north and east of Pesháwar. As the Afgháns who had possessed themselves of the trans-Indus tract opposite the Hazára District increased in numbers and extended their rule, successive bands of the old inhabitants crossed the river and settled in Hazára. About the end of the 17th century[2] a Saiyad named Jalál Bába, ancestor of the famous Saiyads of Kágán, came with a heterogeneous following from Swát, drove out the Karlágh, and appropriated the northern half of the district, including the valley of Kángár. About the same time the Tanáoli crossed the river and occupied the hill country between Abbottábád and the river, now known by their name as Tanáwal; while the Jadún came over from their original seat between Pesháwar and Hazára and possessed themselves of the tract south of Abbottábád, the Tarín drove out or subjected the Gújar families of the Hazára plain, and the Utmánzai, called across the Indus by the Gújars as allies, appropriated the Gandgarh tract along the bank of the river from Torbela to the boundary of the district. During the first 20 years of the 19th century the Durráni lost their hold on the district, something like anarchy prevailed, and the distribution of tribes gradually assumed its present form. This may be broadly described as follows. Afgháns hold the country between the Gandgarh range and the Indus, and the plains for some little distance south-east of the junction of the Siran and Dor. Tribes of Indian origin hold the whole south and south-east of the district and the eastern hills as high up as Garhi Habíbullah opposite Muzaffarábád, the Gakkhars holding the south of the tract along both banks of the Haro river, while above them the [P. 216] Dhúnds, Karráls, and Sarráras occupy the hills in the south-eastern corner of the district, and the adjoining Harípur plains are held by a mixed population of Awáns and Gújars. The remainder of the district, that is the northern and central portion, is held by tribes which, whatever their origin, have by long association become assimilated with the Patháns in language and customs, the Jadún holding the Dor valley from Bagra upwards to Mángal, the Tanáoli holding the Tanáwal tract in the west centre of the district between Abbottábád and the Indus, much of which belongs to the semi-independent Nawáb of Amb, while the Swátis hold the whole mountain country north of Mansahra and Garhi Habíbullah.

The Utmanzai have been already fully described in the discussion of the Pesháwar tribes. The **Tarkheli** is one of the principal Utmánzai clans in Hazára, and occupies the Gandgarh country. A few **Tarin** Afgháns, first cousins of the Abdáli, wrested a considerable portion of the Harípur plains from the Gújars early in the 18th century, and still live there, but are now few and unimportant. The **Mishwani** are descended from a Saiyad father by a Kákar woman, and are allied to the Kákar Patháns. A small number of them came across the Indus with the Utmánzai, to whom they were attached as retainers, and now occupy the north-eastern end of the Gandgarh range, about Sríkot. With the Utmánzai came also a few **Panni**, a Kákar sect, who are still settled among them.

413. Non-Frontier Pathans.—During the Lodi and Súr dynasties many Patháns migrated to India, especially during the reign of Bahlol Lodi

[1] Major Wace says they were a clan of the Hazára Túrks. But the Túrks who gave their name to the district are supposed to have come with Changiz Khán and not with Taimur. Perhaps they were the same men, and have confused the two invaders in their traditions.

[2] This is the date given approximately by Major Wace. It should perhaps be put a century earlier.

and Sher Sháh Súr. These naturally belonged to the Ghilzai section from which those kings sprang. But large numbers of Patháns also accompanied the armies of Mahmúd Ghaznavi, Shaháb-ul-dín, and Bábar, and many of them obtained grants of land in the Panjáb plains and founded Pathán colonies which still exist. Many more Patháns have been driven out of Afghánistán by internal feuds or by famine, and have taken refuge in the plains east of the Indus. The tribes most commonly to be found in Hindústán are the Yúsufzai including the Mandanr, the Lodi, Kákar, Sarwáni, Orakzai, the Karlánri tribes and the Zamand Patháns. Of these the most widely distributed are the Yúsufzai of whom a body of 1,200 accompanied Bábar in his final invasion of India, and settled in the plains of Hindústán and the Panjáb. But as a rule the Patháns who have settled away from the frontier have lost all memory of their tribal divisions, and indeed almost all their national characteristics.

The descendants of Zamand very early migrated in large numbers to Multán, to which Province they furnished rulers till the time of Aurangzeb; when a number of the Abdáli tribe under the leadership of Sháh Husen were driven from Kandahár by tribal feuds, took refuge in Multán, and being early supplemented by other of their kinsmen who were expelled by Mír Wais, the great Ghilzai Chief, conquered Multán and founded the tribe well known in the Panjáb as Multáni Patháns. Nawáb Muzaffar Khán of Multán was fourth in descent from Sháh Husen. When the Zamand section was broken up, the Khweshgi clan migrated to the Ghorband defile, and a large number marched thence with Bábar and found great favour at his hands and those of Humáyún. One section of them settled at Kasúr, and are now known as Kasúria Patháns. The Patháns of Guriáni and Gobána in Rohtak are Kákar. They are said to have settled in the time of Ibráhím Lodi. Those of Jhajjar in the same district are said to be Yúsufzai. In the time of Bahlol Lodi, Sarhind was ruled by members of the Prángi tribe from which he sprang, and many of this tribe are still to be found in Lúdhiánah, Rúpar, and the north of Ambála. The reigning family of Maler Kotla belong to the Sarípál clan of the Sarwáni Afgháns, who, as already related, were driven out of Afghánistán by the Mián Khel and Bakhtiár in the time of Humáyún, Jahángír, for what reason I do not know, deported the Míta Khel sept of the Afrídi to Hindústán; and some of the Afgháns of Pánípat and Lúdhiánah are said to be descended from this stock.

RACES ALLIED TO THE PATHAN.

414. The Tanaoli (Caste No. 54).—The Tanáoli are said to claim descent from Amír Khán, a Barlás Mughal, whose two sons Hind Khán and Pal Khán crossed the Indus some four centuries ago and settled in Tanáwal of Hazára; and they say that they are named after some other place of the same name in Afghánistán. But there can be little doubt that they are of Aryan and probably of Indian stock. We first find them in the trans-Indus basin of the Mahában, from which they were driven across the Indus by the Yúsufzai some two centuries ago. They now occupy Tanáwal or the extensive hill country between the river and the Urash plains. They are divided into two great tribes, the Hindwál and Pallál, of which the latter occupy the northern portion of Tanáwal, and their territory forms the *jágír* of the semi-independent Chief of Amb. Of the 40,000 Hazára Tanáolis, 8,737 have returned themselves as Pallál, 1,964 as Dafrál, a sept of the Pallál, and only 1,076 as Hindwál. It is probable that clans were not recorded in the Amb territory where the Hindwál, and indeed the great mass of the Tanáolis dwell. They are an industrious and peaceful race of cultivators; but their bad faith has given rise to the saying—*Tanáwali be-qauli*, "the Tanáoli's word "is naught."

415. The Dilazak and Tajik (Caste No. 145).—Acting upon the advice of an educated Extra Assistant Commissioner, a native of Peshâwar, I unfortunately took the figures for Tájik and Dilazák together under the head Tájik. In reality they are distinct. Of the 2,048 persons entered in my tables as Tájik, 1,519 are really Dilazák, and so returned themselves. Besides these there are 1,546 Dilazák who have returned themselves as Patháns, of whom 825 are in Ráwalpindi and 695 in Hazára. The origin and early history of the Dilazák have already been noticed in sections 408 and 409. They were the inhabitants of the Peshâwar valley before the Pathán invasion, and are apparently of Scythic origin and came into the Panjáb with the Jats and Katti in the 5th and 6th centuries. They soon became powerful and important and ruled the whole valley as far as the Indus and the foot of the northern hills. In the first half of the 13th century the Yúsufzai and Mohmand drove them across the Indus into Chach-Pakhli. But their efforts to regain their lost territories were such a perpetual source of disturbance, that at length Jahángír deported them *en masse* and distributed them over Hindústán and the Dakhan. Scattered families of them are still to be found along the left bank of the Indus in Hazára and Ráwalpindi.

The Tájik are apparently the original inhabitants of Persia; but now-a-days the word is used throughout Afghánistán to denote any Persian-speak- [P. 217] ing people who are not either Saiyad, Afghán, or Hazára; much as Jat or Hindki is used on the upper Indus to denote the speakers of Panjábi or its dialects. They are described by Dr. Bellew as peaceable, industrious, faithful, and intelligent. In the villages they cultivate, and in the towns they are artisans and traders; while almost all the clerkly classes of Afghánistán are Tájiks.

416. The Hazaras (Caste No. 183).—Besides the 38 Hazáras shown for the Peshâwar district in table VIII A., 44 others have returned themselves as Hazára Patháns, of whom 39 are in Kohát. But this certainly does not represent the whole number of Hazáras who were in the Panjáb at the time of the Census, and it is probable that most of them have returned themselves as Patháns simply, without specifying any tribe. The Hazáras of Kábul have already been noticed in section 396. They hold the Parapomisus of the ancients, extending from Kábul and Ghazni to Hírát, and from Kandahár to Balkh. They are almost certainly Mongol Tartars, and were settled in their present abodes by Changiz Khán. They have now almost wholly lost their Mongol speech, but retain the physical and physiognomic characters of the race, and are "as pure Mongols as when they settled 600 "years ago with their families, their flocks, and their worldly possessions." They intermarry only among themselves, and in the interior of their territory are almost wholly independent. They are described at length by Dr. Bellew in Chapter XIII of his *Races of Afghánistán*. General Cunningham says that in Bábar's time the Karlúki (? Karlághi) Hazáras held the country on both banks of the Sohán in Ráwalpindi; and he refers to them the well-known coins of Sri Hasan Karlúki of the bull and horseman type, which he ascribes to the beginning of the 13th century. But the descendants of these people are apparently returned as Túrks and not as Hazáras, and they will, be discussed later on under the former head. Their history in the Hazára district has been sketched in section 412. Dr. Bellew describes the Hazáras as a—

"very simple-minded people, and very much in the hands of their priests. They are for the "most part entirely illiterate, are governed by tribal and clan chiefs whose authority over their "people is absolute, and they are generally very poor and hardy. Many thousands of them come "down to the Panjáb every cold season in search of labour either on the roads, or as well-sinkers, "wall-builders, &c. In their own country they have the reputation of being a brave and hardy "race, and amongst the Afgháns they are considered a faithful, industrious and intelligent people "as servants. Many thousands of them find employment at Kábul and Ghazni and Kandahár "during the winter months as labourers—in the two former cities mainly in removing the snow from "the house-tops and streets. In consequence of their being heretics, the Sunni Afgháns hold them "in slavery, and in most of the larger towns the servant-maids are purchased slaves of this people."

They are all Shíahs.

417. The Jadun.—The Jadún or Gadún, as they are called indifferently,[1] have returned themselves as Patháns to the number of 17,256, of whom 16,962 are in Hazára and 279 in Ráwalpindi. They claim descent from Sarhang, a great-grandson of Ghurghusht, two of whose sons fled, they say, because of a blood feud to the mountains of Chach and Hazára. It is however almost certain that the Jadún are of Indian origin; and it has been suggested that in their name is preserved the name of Jádu or Yádu, the founder of the Rájpút Yádúbansi dynasty, many of whose descendants migrated from Gújarát some 1,100 years before Christ, and were afterwards found in the hills of Kábul and Kandahár. They occupy all the south-eastern portion of the territory between the Pesháwar and Hazára borders, and the southern slopes of Mahában; and when Jahángír finally crushed the Dilazák, they spread up the Dor valley as high as Abbottábád. Early in the 18th century, on the expulsion of the Karlágh Túrks by Saiyad Jalál Bába (section 412) they appropriated the country about Dhamtaur; and about a hundred years later they took the Bagra tract from the few remaining Dilazák who held it, while shortly before the Sikhs took the country their Hassazai clan deprived the Karrál of a portion of the Nilán valley. They are divided into three main clans, Sálár, Mansúr, and Hassazai, of which the last is not represented among the trans-Indus Jadún and has lost all connection with the parent tribe, having even forgotten its old Pashto language. Dr. Bellew makes them a Gakkhar clan, but this appears to be incorrect. The true Patháns of Hazára call them Mlátar or mercenaries, from the Pashto equivalent for *lakban* or "one who girds his loins." The Jadún clans returned in our tables are shown in the margin.

JADUN CLANS.	
Hassazai	... 6,421
Sálár	... 2,676
Mansúr	... 3,718

418. The Swati.—The Swátis have without exception returned themselves as Patháns. They number 28,906 souls, of whom 28,429 are in Hazára and 392 in Ráwalpindi. The original Swátis were a race of Hindu origin who once ruled the whole country from the Jahlam to Jalálábád. But as has already been recorded in sections 408-9, the Dilazák first drove them out of the plain country into the northern hills of Swát and Buner, and later on the Yúsufzai expelled them from those fastnesses and drove them east and west into Hazára and Káfiristán. As now existing they are probably a very mixed people, as the name is commonly applied to all descendants of the miscellaneous

[1] Trans-Indus they are always known as Gadún; Cis-Indus, as either Gadún or Jadún.

following of Saiyad Jalál mentioned in section 412.[1] They occupy the whole of the Mansahra *tahsil* of the Hazára district excepting the south-western corner which forms part of Tanáwal, and extend into the hills beyond its western border. The Pakhli tract is their chief seat. But the population of his tract is very mixed, Gújars forming by far the largest element, while Awáns and Saiyads are numerous. The Gújars are chiefly graziers in the frontier glens of the northern mountains, the Awáns lie chiefly to the south, while the Saiyads of Kágán are well known to fame. The Swátis are cowardly, deceptive, cruel, grasping, and lazy, and of miserable physique. Their bad faith is a proverb in the country; and they are credited with even attempting to cheat the devil by the old device, famous in European folklore, of dividing the crop above and below ground. They are all Musalmáns of the Sunni sect. They are divided into three great clans, Ghebari, Mamiáli, and Mitráwi, of which the first claims Tájik, the Mamiáli Yúsufzai, and the Mitráwi Durráni origin; but all three claims are almost certainly unfounded. At present the Mamiáli and Mitráwi, known as the sections of the Tarli or lower Pakhli, hold the southern and south-western portions of their tract, while the Ghebari, a section of the Utli or upper Pakhli, occupy Kágán and the [P. 218] north-eastern portion. The Swáti are often wrongly confused with the Degán, another branch of the original Hindu inhabitants of north-eastern Afghánistán, now only found in Kunar, Bajaur, Lughmán, and Ningrahár.

419. The Shilmani.—The Shilmáni are probably of Indian origin, and had their homes in Shilmán on the banks of the Kurram. From there they migrated to the Tátara mountains north of the Khaibar, whence a section of them moved on *viâ* Peshâwar to Hashtnaghar. About the end of the 15th century the Yúsufzai drove them out into Swát, where they found a refuge with Sultán Wais and presently became subjects of the advancing Yúsufzai. A few of them are scattered through the Hazára district, and they still hold a village in the Tátara range. But they are fast dying out of existence as a distinct people. They are often confounded with the Degán in the early Afghán histories. I am afraid that some who are not realy Shilmáni have been included in our figures. The tribe is sometimes called Sulemáni, a name also applied to Afgháns proper, while there is a separate tribe called Sulemán Khel; and it is not impossible that there has been some confusion. The Shilmáni have all returned themselves as Patháns, and their numbers are 1,557, of whom 969 are in Hazára, 174 in Ráwalpindi, and 200 in Delhi.

[1] At the Hazára settlement genealogical trees were prepared for the Swátis only for the last four or five generations; and this at their own request, as to have gone back further would have exposed in too public a manner their miscellaneous origin.

PART III.—THE JAT, RAJPUT, AND ALLIED CASTES.

[P. 219] **420. General and Indroductory.**—Abstract No. 71 below* shows the distribution of Jats, Rájpúts, and certain castes which I have taken with the
*P. 98-9 latter, as the line separating them is almost impossible of definition. The origin and distribution of these castes is fully discussed in the following pages, and there is no need here to anticipate my remarks. Indeed the distinction between Jat and Rájpút is in many parts of the Province so indefinite, that separate figures for these two castes can hardly be said to have any significance at all.

[P. 220] The two together constitute nearly 28 per cent. of the total population of the Panjáb, and include the great mass of the dominant land-owning tribes in the cis-Indus portion of the Province. Their political is even greater than their numerical importance; while they afford to the ethnologist infinite matter for inquiry and consideration. Their customs are in the main Hindu, though in the Western Plains and the Salt-range Tract the restrictions upon intermarriage have in many cases come to be based upon considerations of social standing only. But even here the marriage ceremony and other social customs retain the clear impress of Indian origin.

THE JAT (CASTE No. 1).

421. The origin of the Jat.—Perhaps no question connected with the ethnology of the Panjáb peoples has been so much discussed as the origin of the Jat race. It is not my intention here to reproduce any of the arguments adduced. They will be found in detail in the Archæological Survey Reports, Vol. II, pages 51 to 61; in Tod's *Rájasthán*, Vol. I, pages 52 to 75 and 96 to 101 (Madras Reprint, 1880); in Elphinstone's *History of India*, pages 250 to 253; and in Elliot's *Races of the N. W. P.*, Vol. I, pages 130 to 137. Suffice it to say that both General Cunningham and Major Tod agree in considering the Jats to be of Indo-Scythian stock. The former identifies them with the Zanthii of Strabo and the Jatü of Pliny and Ptolemy; and holds that they probably entered the Panjáb from their home on the Oxus very shortly after the Meds or Mands, who also were Indo-Scythians, and who moved into the Panjáb about a century before Christ. The Jats seem to have first occupied the Indus valley as far down as Sindh, whither the Meds followed them about the beginning of the present æra. But before the earliest Mahomedan invasion the Jats had spread into the Panjáb proper, where they were firmly established in the beginning of the 11th century. By the time of Bábar the Jats of the Salt-range Tract had been subdued by the Gakkhars, Awáns, and Janjúas, while as early as the 7th century the Jats and Meds of Sindh were ruled over by a Bráhman dynasty. Major Tod classes the Jats as one of the great Rájpút tribes, and extends his identification with the Getæ to both races; but here General Cunningham differs, holding the Rájpúts to belong to the original Aryan stock, and the Jats to belong to a later wave of immigrants from the North-west, probably of Scythian race.

Abstract No. 71, showing Jats, Rajputs, and Allied Castes for Districts and States.

	JATS AND RAJPUTS AND ALLIED RACES.															
	FIGURES.							PROPORTIONS PER 1,000 OF TOTAL POPULATION.								
	1	2	60	39	82	74	103	1	2	60	39	82	74	103		
	Jat.	Rájpút.	Thakar.	Ráthi.	Ráwat.	Dhúnd.	Kahút.	Jat.	Rájpút.	Thakar.	Ráthi.	Ráwat.	Dhúnd.	Kahút.	TOTAL.	GRAND TOTAL.
Dehli	107,075	33,823	...	...	...	...	2	166	53	...	...	...	...	...	53	219
Gurgaon	64,342	26,483	...	...	...	...	...	100	41	...	...	...	...	...	41	141
Karnal	95,108	53,260	...	...	1,025	...	3	153	85	...	...	2	...	...	87	240
Hissar	134,886	60,993	...	...	...	...	...	268	121	...	...	...	...	...	121	389
Rohtak	182,776	29,975	...	...	...	...	...	330	54	...	...	...	...	...	54	384
Sirsa	64,040	46,827	...	...	...	...	...	253	185	...	...	...	...	...	185	438
Ambala	171,257	92,033	12	...	4,402	...	...	160	86	...	...	4	...	...	90	250
Ludhiana	222,665	30,957	9	...	1,807	...	...	360	50	...	...	3	...	...	53	413
Simla	235	1,849	4	...	7	...	...	5	43	...	...	...	...	...	43	48
Jalandhar	163,757	43,789	20	304	2,438	...	...	208	56	...	...	3	...	...	59	267
Hushyarpur	145,743	101,384	480	200	275	...	...	162	112	1	...	...	...	...	113	275
Kangra	11,118	92,836	19,122	50,767	1	...	...	15	127	26	69	...	...	...	222	237
Amritsar	205,434	27,668	...	...	...	...	...	230	31	...	...	...	...	...	31	261
Gurdaspur	129,755	71,519	4,983	1,731	...	...	...	157	87	6	2	...	...	...	95	252
Sialkot	266,040	57,269	9	...	...	...	...	264	57	...	...	...	...	...	57	321
Lahore	157,670	54,577	...	...	5	...	2	171	59	...	...	...	...	...	59	230
Gujranwala	173,979	36,484	...	...	...	...	...	282	59	...	...	...	...	...	59	341
Firozpur	186,576	39,538	...	...	32	...	1	287	61	...	...	...	...	...	61	348
Rawalpindi	47,935	145,536	59	...	...	223	62	58	177	...	...	...	...	...	177	235
Jhelam	88,371	53,279	4	...	...	...	8,766	150	90	...	...	...	...	8	98	248
Gujrat	181,380	22,026	...	...	...	...	...	263	32	...	...	...	...	...	32	295
Shahpur	34,508	82,290	...	...	...	...	377	82	195	...	...	...	...	1	196	278

Multan	102,952	59,627	52	...	...	...	22	187	108	...	...	...	...	...	108	295
Jhang	48,242	89,641	...	...	...	...	25	122	227	...	...	...	...	...	227	349
Montgomery	42,707	56,575	5	...	...	...	...	100	132	...	...	...	...	...	132	232
Muzaffargarh ...	109,352	7,961	55	...	...	...	153	323	23	...	...	...	...	...	23	346
Derah Ismail Khan ...	205,360	1,750	1	...	...	...	...	465	4	...	...	...	...	...	4	469
Derah Ghazi Khan ...	160,405	2,667	45	...	...	1	1	442	7	...	...	...	...	...	7	449
Bannu	53,900	3,309	...	...	...	...	...	162	10	...	...	...	...	...	10	172
Peshawar	4,917	3,181	55	...	1	4	54	8	5	...	...	...	...	...	5	13
Hazara	515	4,777	1	...	1	20,085	...	1	12	...	...	...	49	...	61	62
Kohat	1,470	1,387	...	...	...	2	...	8	11	...	...	...	...	...	11	19
British Territory ...	3,564,519	1,436,058	24,984	53,002	9,994	20,315	9,468	189	76	1	3	1	1	...	82	271
Patiala	452,247	64,307	...	...	3,242	...	23	308	44	...	...	2	...	...	46	354
Nabha	85,414	12,733	...	...	266	...	10	326	49	...	...	1	...	...	50	376
Kapurthala	39,135	19,754	...	...	609	...	1	155	78	...	...	2	...	...	80	235
Jind	87,610	10,000	4	...	302	...	...	350	40	...	...	1	...	...	41	391
Faridkot	35,744	4,274	...	...	23	...	...	369	44	...	...	...	...	...	44	413
Maler Kotla	23,332	1,517	...	...	1,890	...	...	328	21	...	...	27	...	...	48	376
Kalsia	11,338	2,805	...	...	701	...	...	167	41	...	...	10	...	...	51	218
Total Eastern Plains ...	745,076	119,546	4	...	7,033	...	34	296	47	...	...	3	...	...	50	346
Bahawalpur	119,178	91,189	...	...	...	...	...	208	159	...	...	...	...	...	159	367
Mandi	353	6,981	...	...	...	...	...	2	47	...	...	...	...	...	47	49
Chamba	291	4,054	7,403	32,190	10	...	...	3	35	64	277	...	...	...	376	379
Nahan	266	3,079	...	...	155	...	...	2	27	...	...	1	...	...	28	30
Bilaspur	1,456	8,046	...	...	...	...	...	17	93	...	...	...	...	...	93	110
Bashahr	16	2,113	...	...	...	...	...	...	33	...	...	...	...	...	33	33
Nalagarh	824	980	...	...	...	...	...	15	18	...	...	...	...	...	18	33
Suket	320	1,425	375	...	...	...	...	6	27	7	...	...	...	...	34	40
Total Hill States ...	3,977	30,776	7,778	32,190	173	...	...	5	40	10	42	...	...	...	92	97
British Territory ...	3,564,519	1,436,058	24,984	53,002	9,994	20,315	9,468	189	76	1	3	1	1	...	82	271
Native States ...	868,231	241,511	7,782	32,190	7,206	...	34	225	63	2	8	2	...	...	75	300
Province	4,432,750	1,677,569	32,766	85,192	17,200	20,315	9,502	195	74	1	4	1	1	...	81	276

It may be that the original Rájpút and the original Jat entered India at different periods in its history, though to my mind the term Rájpút is an occupational rather than an ethnological expression. But if they do originally represent two separate waves of immigration, it is at least exceedingly probable, both from their almost identical physique and facial character and from the close communion which has always existed between them, that they belong to one and the same ethnic stock; while whether this be so or not, it is almost certain that they have been for many centuries and still are so intermingled and so blended into one people that it is practically impossible to distinguish them as separate wholes. It is indeed more than probable that the process of fusion has not ended here, and that the people who thus in the main resulted from the blending of the Jat and the Rájpút, if these two ever were distinct, is by no means free from foreign elements. We have seen how the Pathán people have assimilated Saiyads, Túrks, and Mughals, and how it was sufficient for a Jat tribe to retain its political independence and organisation in order to be admitted into the Biloch nation; we know how a character for sanctity and social exclusiveness combined will in a few generations make a Quresh or a Saiyad; and it is almost certain that the joint Jat-Rájpút stock contains not a few tribes of aboriginal descent, though it is probably in the main Aryo-Scythian, if Scythian be not Aryan. The Mán, Her, and Bhúlar Jats (section 435) are known as *asl* or original Jats because they claim no Rájpút ancestry, but are supposed to be descended from the hair (*jat*) of the aboriginal god Siva; the Jats of the south-eastern districts divide themselves into two sections, *Shivgotri* or of the family of Siva, and *Kasabgotri* who claim connection with the Rájpúts; and the names of the ancestor Bar of the Shivgotris and of his son Barbara are the very words which the ancient Bráhmans give us as the marks of the barbarian aborigines. Many of the Jat tribes of the Panjáb have customs which apparently point to non-Aryan origin, and a rich and almost virgin field for investigation is here open to the ethnologist.

422. **Are the Jats and Rajputs distinct?**—But whether Jats and Rájpúts were or were not originally distinct, and whatever aboriginal elements may have been affiliated to their society, I think that the two now form a common stock, the distinction between Jat and Rájpút being social rather than ethnic. I believe that those families of that common stock whom the tide of fortune has raised to political importance have become Rájpúts almost by mere virtue of their rise; and that their descendants have retained the title and its privileges on the condition, strictly enforced, of observing the rules by which the higher are distinguished from the lower castes in the Hindu scale of precedence; of preserving their purity of blood by refusing to marry with families of inferior social rank, of rigidly abstaining from widow marriage, and of refraining from degrading occupations. Those who transgressed these rules have fallen from their high position and ceased to be Rájpúts; while such families as, attaining a dominant position in their territory, began to affect social exclusiveness and to observe the rules, have become not only Rájas, but also Rájpúts or "sons of Rájas." For the last seven centuries the process of elevation at least has been almost at a stand-still. Under the Dehli Emperors king-making was practically impossible. Under the Sikhs the Rájpút was overshadowed by the Jat, who resented his assumption of superiority and his refusal to join him on equal terms in the ranks of the Khálsa, deliberately persecuted him wherever and whenever he had the power, and preferred his title of Jat Sikh to that of the proudest Rájpút. On the frontier the dominance of

Patháns and Biloches and the general prevalence of Mahomedan feelings and ideas placed recent Indian origin at a discount, and led the leading families who belonged to neither of these two races to claim connection, not with the Kshatriyas of the Sanskrit classics, but with the Mughal conquerors of India or the Qureshi cousins of the Prophet; insomuch that even admittedly Rájpút tribes of famous ancestry, such as the Khokhar, have begun to follow the example. But in the hills, where Rájpút dynasties with genealogies perhaps more ancient and unbroken than can be shown by any other royal families in
[P. 221] the world retained their independence till yesterday, and where many of them still enjoy as great social authority as ever, the twin processes of degradation from and elevation to Rájpút rank are still to be seen in operation. The Rája is there the fountain not only of honour but also of caste, which is the same thing in India. Mr. Lyall writes :—

"Till lately the limits of caste do not seem to have been so immutably fixed in the hills as in "the plains. The Raja was the fountain of honour, and could do much as he liked. I have heard "old men quote instances within their memory in which a Raja promoted a Girth to be a Ráthi, "and a Thakar to be a Rajput, for service done or money given; and at the present day the power "of admitting back into caste fellowship persons put under a ban for some grave act of defilement, "is a source of income to the Jagirdar Rajas.

"I believe that Mr. Campbell, the present Lieutenant-Governor of Bengal, has asserted that "there is no such thing as a distinct Rajput stock; that in former times before caste distinctions "had become crystallized, any tribe or family whose ancestor or head rose to royal rank became "in time Rajput. This is certainly the conclusion to which many facts point with regard to the "Rajputs of those hills. Two of the old royal and now essentially Rajput families of this district, "*viz.*, Kotlehr and Bangáhal, are said to be Brahmin by original stock. Mr. Barnes says that in "Kangra the son of a Rajput by a low-caste woman takes place as a Ráthi: in Seoráj and other "places in the interior of the hills I have met families calling themselves Rajputs, and growing "into general acceptance as Rajputs, in their own country at least, whose only claim to the title "was that their father or grandfather was the offspring of a Kanetni by a foreign Brahmin. On "the border line in the Himalayas, between Thibet and India proper, any one can observe caste "growing before his eyes; the noble is changing into a Rajput, the priest into a Brahmin, the "peasant into a Jat, and so on down to the bottom of the scale. The same process was, I believe, "more or less in force in Kangra proper down to a period not very remote from to-day."

423. The reverse process of degradation from Rájpút to lower rank is too common to require proof of its existence, which will be found if needed, together with further instances of elevation, in the section which treats of the Rájpúts and kindred castes. In the eastern districts, where Brahminism is stronger than in any other part of the Panjáb and Dehli too near to allow of families rising to political independence, it is probable that no elevation to the rank of Rájpút has taken place within recent times. But many Rájpút families have ceased to be Rájpúts. Setting aside the general tradition of the Panjáb Jats to the effect that their ancestors were Rájpúts who married Jats or began to practise widow-marriage, we have the Gaurwa Rájpúts of Gurgáon and Dehli, who have indeed retained the title of Rájpút because the caste feeling is too strong in those parts and the change in their customs too recent for it yet to have died out, but who have, for all purposes of equality, communion, or intermarriage, ceased to be Rájpúts since they took to the practice of *karewa*; we have the Sahnsars of Hushyárpur who were Rájpúts within the last two or three generations, but have ceased to be so because they grow vegetables like the Aráín; in Karnál we have Rájpúts who within the living generation have ceased to be Rájpúts and become Shekhs, because poverty and loss of land forced them to weaving as an occupation; while the Dehli Chauhán, within the shadow of the city where their ancestors once ruled and led the Indian armies in their last struggle with the Musalmán invaders, have lost their caste by yielding to the temptations of *karewa*. In the Sikh tract, as I have said, the Jat is content to be a Jat, and has never since the rise of Sikh power wished to be anything else. In the Western Plains the freedom of marriage allowed by Islám has superseded caste restrictions, and social rank is measured by the tribe rather than by the larger unit of caste. But even there, families who were a few generations ago reputed Jats have now risen by social exclusiveness to be recognised as Rájpúts, and families who were lately known as Rájpúts have sunk till they are now classed with Jats; while the great ruling tribes, the Siál, the Gondal, the Tiwána are commonly spoken of as Rájpúts, and their smaller brethren as Jats. The same tribe even is Rájpút in one district and Jat in another, according to its position among the local tribes. In the Salt-range Tract the dominant tribes, the Janjúa, Manhás and the like, are Rájpúts when they are not Mughals or Arabs: while all agricultural tribes of Indian origin who cannot establish their title to Rájpút rank are Jats. Finally, on the frontier the Pathán and Biloch have overshadowed Jat and Rájpút alike; and Bhatti, Punwár, Túnwar, all the proudest tribes of Rájpútána are included in the name and have sunk to the level of Jat, for there can be no Rájpúts where there are no Rájas or traditions of Rájas. I know that the views herein set forth will be held heretical and profane by many, and that they ought to be supported by a greater wealth of instance than I have produced in the following pages. But I have no time to marshal my facts; I have indeed no time to record more than a small proportion of them; and all I can now attempt is to state the conclusion to which my enquiries have led me, and to hope to deal with the subject in more detail on some future occasion.

424. **The position of the Jat in the Punjab.**—The Jat is in every respect the most important of the Panjáb peoples. In point of numbers he surpasses the Rájpút who comes next to him in the proportion of nearly three to one; while the two together constitute 27 per cent. of the whole population of the Province. Politically he ruled the Panjáb till the Khálsa yielded to our arms. Ethnologically he is the peculiar and most prominent product of the plains of the five rivers. And from an œconomical and administrative point of view he is the husbandman, the peasant, the revenue-payer *par excellence* of the Province. His manners do not bear the impress of generations of wild freedom which marks the races of our frontier mountains. But he is more honest, more industrious, more sturdy, and no less manly than they. Sturdy independence indeed and patient vigorous labour are his strongest characteristics. The Jat is of all Panjáb races the most impatient of tribal or communal control, and the one which asserts the freedom of the individual most strongly. In tracts where, as in Rohtak, the Jat tribes have the field to themselves, and are compelled, in default of rival castes as enemies, to fall back upon each other for somebody to quarrel with, the tribal ties are strong. But as a rule a Jat is a man who does what seems right in his own eyes and sometimes what seems wrong also, and will not be said nay by any man. I do not mean however that he is turbulent: as a rule he is very far from being so. He is independent and he is self-willed; but he is reasonable, peaceably inclined if left alone, and not difficult to manage. He is usually content to cultivate his fields and pay his revenue in peace and quietness if people will let him do so; though when he does go wrong he "takes to anything from gambling to "murder, with perhaps a preference for stealing other people's wives and cattle." As usual the proverbial wisdom of the villages describes him very fairly, though perhaps somewhat too severely: "The soil, fodder, clothes, hemp,

"grass fibre, and silk, these six are best beaten; and the seventh is the Jat." "A Jat, a Bhat, a caterpillar, and a widow woman; these four are best
[P. 222] "hungry. If they eat their fill they do harm." "The Jat, like a wound, is better "when bound." In agriculture the Jat is pre-eminent. The market-gardening castes, the Aráín, the Máli, the Saini, are perhaps more skilful cultivators on a small scale; but they cannot rival the Jat as landowners and yeoman cultivators. The Jat calls himself *zamíndár* or "husbandman" as often as Jat, and his women and children alike work with him in the fields: "The Jat's "baby has a plough handle for a plaything." "The Jat stood on his corn "heap and said to the king's elephant-drivers—'Will you sell those little "'donkeys?'" Socially, the Jat occupies a position which is shared by the Ror, the Gújar, and the Ahír, all four eating and smoking together. He is of course far below the Rájpút, from the simple fact that he practises widow-marriage. The Jat father is made to say, in the rhyming proverbs of the country side—"Come my daughter and be married; if this husband dies there "are plenty more." But among the widow-marrying castes he stands first. The Banya with his sacred thread, his strict Hinduism, and his twice-born standing, looks down on the Jat as a Súdra. But the Jat looks down upon the Banya as a cowardly spiritless money-grubber, and society in general agrees with the Jat. The Khatri, who is far superior to the Banya in manliness and vigour, probably takes precedence of the Jat. But among the races or tribes of purely Hindu origin, I think that the Jat stands next after the Bráhman, the Rájpút, and the Khatri.

There are, however, Jats and Jats. I shall briefly describe each class in the remarks prefixed to the various sections under which I discuss the Jat tribes; and I shall here do nothing more than briefly indicate the broad distinctions. The Jat of the Sikh tracts is of course the typical Jat of the Panjáb, and he it is whom I have described above. The Ját of the south-eastern districts differs little from him save in religion; though on the Bíkáner border the puny Bágri Ját, immigrant from his rainless prairies where he has been held in bondage for centuries, and ignorant of cultivation save in its rudest form, contrasts strongly with the stalwart and independent husbandman of the Málwa. On the Lower Indus the word Jat is applied generically to a congeries of tribes, Jats proper, Rájpúts, lower castes, and mongrels, who have no points in common save their Mahomedan religion, their agricultural occupation, and their subordinate position. In the great western grazing grounds it is, as I have said, impossible to draw any sure line between Jat and Rájpút, the latter term being commonly applied to those tribes who have attained political supremacy, while the people whom they have subdued or driven by dispossession of their territory to live a semi-nomad life in the central steppes are more often classed as Jats; and the state of things in the Salt-range Tract is very similar. Indeed the word Jat is the Panjábi term for a grazier or herdsman; though Mr. O'Brien says that in Jatki, Jat the cultivator is spelt with a hard, and Jat the herdsman or camel grazier with a soft *t*. Thus the word Jat in Rohtak or Amritsar means a great deal; in Muzaffargarh or Bannu it means nothing at all, or rather perhaps it means a great deal more than any single word can afford to mean if it is to be of any practical use; and the two classes respectively indicated by the term in these two parts of the Province must not be too readily confounded.

425. **The nature and meaning of the figures.**—Such being the state of things, it may be imagined that our figures do not always convey any very definite meaning. The 160,000 Jats of Derah Ghází Khán include 5,000 Mális, 2,000 Juláhas, 3,000 Tarkháns, 4,500 Kutánas, 4,400

Malláhs, 7,500 Mochis, 2,700 Máchhis, and so forth. In no other district does this confusion prevail to anything like so great an extent; but it does prevail in a smaller degree throughout the south-western districts; and till the detailed clan tables are complete it will be impossible to separate these incongruous items, or to find out with exactness what our figures do and what they do not include. The confusion is not wholly due to the entries in the schedules. On the Lower Indus and Chanáb the entries in the caste column were numbered by thousands, tribe being there the recognized unit rather than the more comprehensive caste; and it was absolutely necessary to allow the staff of the divisional offices, all picked men drawn from the very district with the figures of which they were dealing, some discretion in classifying these entries under larger heads. Thus in Jhang the Siál will have been rightly classed as Rájpúts, while in Derah Ghází they will, with equal correctness so far as local usage is concerned, have been very probably classed as Jats. Thus our figures are far from complete; but I have done my best to indicate in the following paragraphs the uncertainties and errors in classification as far as I could detect them. I had indeed hoped to treat the subject more fully, and especially more systematically than I have done. I had intended to attempt some sort of grouping of the great Jat tribes on the basis of their ethnic affinities, somewhat similar to that which I have attempted for the Patháns. But I was not allowed the time necessary for such an undertaking; and I have therefore roughly grouped the tribes by locality so far as my figures served to indicate it, and hurriedly stated the leading facts of which I was in possession regarding each, leaving any more elaborate treatment for a future occasion. The figures for tribes are, as already explained in section 369, necessarily imperfect, and must only be taken as approximations.

426. **Distribution of the Jats.**—Beyond the Panjáb, Jats are chiefly found in Sindh where they form the mass of the population, in Bíkáner, Jaisalmer, and Márwár, where they probably equal in numbers all the Rájpút races put together, and along the upper valleys of the Ganges and Jamna from Bareli, Farrukhábád, and Gwálior upwards. Within the Province their distribution is shown in Abstract No. 71 on page 219.* They are especially numerous in the central Sikh districts and States, in the south-eastern districts, and in the Deraját. Under and among the hills and in the Ráwalpindi division Rájpúts take their place, while on the frontier both upper and lower, they are almost wholly confined to the cis-Indus tracts and the immediate Indus riverain on both sides of the stream. The Jats of the Indus are probably still in the country which they have occupied ever since their first entry into India, though they have been driven back from the foot of the Sulemáns on to the river by the advance of the Pathán and the Biloch. The Jats of the Western Plains have almost without exception come up the river valleys from Sindh or Western Rájpútána. The Jats of the western and central sub-montane have also in part come by the same route; but some of them retain a traditional connection with Ghazni, which perhaps refers to the ancient Gajnípur, the site of the modern Ráwalpindi, while many of them trace their origin from the Jammu Hills.

*P. 98-9

The Jats of the Central and Eastern Panjáb have also in many cases come up the Satluj valley; but many of them have moved from Bíkáner straight into the Málwa, while the great central plains of the Málwa itself are probably the original home of many of the Jat tribes of the Sikh tract. The Jats of the south-eastern districts and the Jamna zone have for the most part worked up the Jamna valley from the direction of Bhartpur, with which some of them still retain a traditional connection; though some few have moved in eastwards from Bíkáner and the Málwa. The Bhartpur Jats are themselves said to be immigrants who left the banks of the Indus in the time of Aurangzeb. Whether the Jats of the great plains are really as late immigrants as they represent, or whether their story is merely founded upon a wish to show recent connection with the country of the Rájpúts, I cannot say. The [P. 223] whole question is one on which we are exceedingly ignorant, and which would richly repay detailed investigation.

427. Jats of the Western Plains.—First of all then let us purge our tables of that nondescript class known as Jats on the Indus, and, to a less extent, in the lower valleys of the Satluj, Chanáb, and Jahlam, and in the Salt-range Tract. Mr. O'Brien writes as follows of the Jats of Muzaffargarh :—

"In this district the word Jat includes that congeries of Muhammadan tribes which are "not Saiyads, Biloches, Patháns or Qureshis. According to this definition Jats would include "Rájpúts. This I believe is correct. The Jats have always been recruited from the Rájpúts. "There is not a Jat in the district who has any knowledge, real or fancied, of his ancestors that "would not say that he was once a Rájpút. Certain Jat tribes have names and traditions which "seem to connect them more closely with Hindustán. Some bear the Rájpút title of Rai, and "others, though Muhammadans, associate a Brahmin with the Mulla at marriage ceremonies, while "Púnwárs, Parihárs, Bhattis, Joyas, and others bear the names of well-known tribes of Rájpútána. "The fact is that it is impossible to define between Jats and Musalmán Rájpúts. And the "difficulty is rendered greater by the word Jat also meaning an agriculturist irrespective of his "race, and Jatáki agriculture. In conversation about agriculture I have been referred to a Saiyad "Zaildár with the remark—Ask Anwar Sháh ; he is a better Jat than we are.

"The Jat tribes are exceedingly numerous. There are 165 in the Sanánwán tahsil alone. "They have no large divisions embracing several small divisions. Nor do they trace their "origin to common stock. No tribe is pre-eminent in birth or caste. Generally Jats marry into "their own tribe, but they have no hesitation in marrying into other tribes. They give their "daughters freely to Biloches in marriage. But the Biloches say that they do not give their "daughters to Jats. This is, however, a Biloch story ; many instances of Jats married to Biloches "could be named."[1]

Besides this, the word Jat, spelt with a soft instead of a hard *t*, denotes a camel grazier or camel driver. "The camel cannot lift its load ; the camel-"man (Jat) bites its tail." The fact seems to be that the Biloches who came into the districts of the lower frontier as a dominant race, contemptuoulsy included all cultivating tribes who were not Biloch, or of some race such as Saiyad or Pathán whom they had been accustomed to look upon as their equals, under the generic name of Jat, until the people themselves have lost the very memory of their origin. It is possible that our own officers may have emphasized the confusion by adopting too readily the simple classification of the population as the Biloch or peculiar people on the one hand and the Jat or Gentile on the other, and that the so-called Jat is not so ignorant of his real origin as is commonly supposed. But the fact that in this part of the Panjáb tribe quite over-shadows and indeed almost supersedes caste, greatly increases the difficulty. As Mr. Roe remarks—"If you ask a Jat his caste "he will generally name some sub-division or clan quite unknown to fame." However caused, the result is that in the Deraját, Muzaffargarh, and much of Multán, if not indeed still further east and north, the word Jat means little more than the heading "others or unspecified" under which Census officers are so sorely tempted to class those about whom they know little or nothing. A curious instance of the manner in which the word is used in these parts is afforded by the result of some inquiries I made about the Máchhi or fisherman caste of Derah Ghází Khán. The reply sent me was that there were two castes, Máchhis or fishermen, and Jat Máchhis who had taken to agriculture. It is probable that not long hence these latter will drop the Máchhi, perhaps forget their Máchhi origin, and become Jats pure and simple ; though they may not improbably retain as their *clan* name the old Máchhi clan to which
P. 106-they belonged, or even the word Máchhi itself. I give on the next page a
107 list of castes which, on a rough examination of the clan tables of the Jats of the Multán and Deraját divisions and Baháwalpur, I detected among the

[1] Among the organised Biloch tribes of the frontier, however, Biloch girls are not given to Jats.

Abstract No. 72, showing other Castes [P. 224]

Caste.	Multan.	Jhang.	Montgomery.	Muzaffargarh.	Dera Ismail Khan.
Aráín, Maliár, Málí	255	389	2	3,125	2,755
Bhatyára ...	...	...	...	137	69
Bázígar ...	2	...	...	...	...
Biloch	92	96	31	145	...
Páolí, Juláha	112	529	41	89	1,252
Pungar	...	...	...	...	4
Pathán	102	65	226	90	...
Telí	5	14	...	6	181
Jogí	1	...	...	...	...
Charhoa	24	145	...	137	375
Chúhra	34	374	...	21	217
Khojah	7	38	...	440	453
Darzi	28	...	...	1	...
Dhobi	6	12	...	...	11
Tarkhán	37	257	11	190	2,935
Dúm	...	...	...	...	247
Rájpút	14	117	153	381	25
Zargar	6	2	...	...	...
Shekh	346	34	250	65	390
Siqlígar	...	...	...	...	49
Faqír	67	145	72	13	...
Qassáb	12	92	...	94	1,281
Qází	6	...	...	...	...
Quroshí	264	270	171	35	22
Kahár	...	...	...	...	...
Kutána	6	12	11	259	2,680
Kumhár	99	343	7	243	2,700
Kamángar	9	...	...	38	36
Kalál	14	...	14	5	9
Gújar	10	1	7	...	...
Labána	...	...	...	...	...
Lohár	18	117	...	46	1,304
Mujáwar	...	...	...	...	...
Mughal	17	15	8	...	...
Malláh	77	216	2	840	2,773
Mírásí	80	482	5	95	1,778
Mochí	58	415	17	178	3,916
Máchhí	104	332	11	1,013	3,465
Náí	65	208	...	95	1,462

returned as Jats in Multan and the Derajat.

Dera Ghazi Khan.	Bannu.	Total Multan and Derajat.	Bahawalpur.	GRAND TOTAL.	CASTE.
5,008	287	11,821	...	11,821	{ Aráín. Maliár. Málí.
679	...	885	...	885	Bhatyára.
...	...	2	...	2	Bázígar.
...	...	364	...	364	Biloch.
1,947	273	4,243	...	4,243	{ Páoli. Julába.
35	...	39	...	39	Pungar.
62	4	549	...	549	Pathán.
68	3	277	4	281	Telí.
...	...	1	85	86	Jogí.
1,484	111	2,276	...	2,276	Charhoa.
820	67	1,533	...	1,533	Chúhra.
1,755	34	2,727	...	2,727	Khojah.
...	...	29	...	29	Darzí.
95	...	124	...	124	Dhobi.
3,062	238	6,730	...	6,730	Tarkhán.
13	...	260	...	260	Dúm
...	...	690	...	690	Rájpút.
...	13	21	...	21	Zargar.
937	205	2,227	...	2,227	Shekh.
...	...	49	...	49	Siqlígar.
...	...	297	242	539	Faqír.
1,083	98	2,660	...	2,660	Qassáb.
...	...	6	...	6	Qází.
106	14	882	...	882	Qureshí.
...	...	...	3	3	Kahár.
4,539	119	7,626	...	7,626	Kutána.
1,837	125	5,354	...	5,354	Kumhár.
40	...	123	...	123	Kamángar.
13	...	55	...	55	Kalál.
...	...	18	...	18	Gújar.
...	...	...	4,317	4,317	Labána.
638	208	2,331	...	2,331	Lohár.
...	...	...	401	401	Mujáwar.
...	...	40	361	401	Mughal.
4,451	627	8,986	...	8,986	Malláh.
1,212	67	3,219	...	3,219	Mírásí.
7,389	320	12,293	865	13,158	Mochí.
2,733	180	7,838	241	8,079	Máchhí.
1,431	123	3,384	...	3,384	Náí.

sub-divisions of the Jats of those parts. Jat being essentially a word used for agriculturists only, it is more probable that a man who returns himself as Jat by caste and Bhatyára by tribe or clan should be a Bhatyára who has taken to agriculture, than that he should be a Jat who has taken to keeping a cook-shop; and the men shown below would probably have been more properly returned under the respective castes opposite which their numbers are given, than as Jats. A more careful examination of the figures would probably have increased the numbers; and the detailed clan tables will give us much information on the subject.

428. Further to the north and east, away from the Biloch territory, the difficulty is of a somewhat different nature. There, as already explained, the tribes are commonly known by their tribal names rather than by the name of the caste to which they belong or belonged; and the result is that claims to Rájpút, or now-a-days not unseldom to Arab or Mughal origin, are generally set up. The tribes who claim to be Arab or Mughal will be discussed either under their proper head or under Shekhs and Mughals. But the line between Jats and Rájpúts is a difficult one to draw, and I have been obliged to decide the question in a rough and arbitrary manner. Thus the Siál are admittedly of pure Rájpút origin, and I have classed them as Rájpúts as they are commonly recognized as such by their neighbours. The Súmra are probably of no less pure Rájpút extraction, but they are commonly known as Jats, and I have discussed them under that head. But in either case I shall show the Siál or Súmra who have returned themselves as Jats side by side with those who have returned themselves as Rájpúts, so that the figures may be as complete as possible. As a fact these people are generally known as Siál and Súmra rather than as Jats or Rájpúts; and the inclusion of them under either of the latter headings is a classification based upon generally reputed origin or standing, rather than upon any current and usual designation. Mr. Purser thus expresses the matter as he found it in Montgomery:—

> "There is a wonderful uniformity about the traditions of the different tribes. The ancestor of "each tribe was, as a rule, a Rájpút of the Solar or Lunar race, and resided at Hastinápur or Dárá-"nagar. He scornfully rejected the proposals of the Dehli Emperor for a matrimonial alliance "between the two families, and had then to fly to Sirsa or Bhatner, or some other place in that "neighbourhood. Next he came to the Rávi and was converted to Islám by Makhdúm Bahá-ul-"Haqq, or Bába Faríd. Then, being a stout-hearted man, he joined the Kharrals in their maraud-"ing expeditions, and so his descendants became Jats. In Kamar Singh's time they took to agricul-"ture and abandoned robbery a little; and now under the English Government they have quite given "up their evil ways, and are honest and well disposed."

Mr. Steedman writing from Jhang says:—

> "There are in this district a lot of tribes engaged in agriculture or cattle-grazing who have "no very clear idea of their origin but are certainly converted Hindus. Many are recognized "Jats, and more belong to an enormous variety of tribes, but are called by the one comprehensive "term Jat. Ethnologically I am not sure of my ground; but for practical convenience in this "part of the world, I would class as Jats all Muhammadans whose ancestors were converted from "Hinduism and who are now engaged in, or derive their maintenance from, the cultivation of land "or the pasturing of cattle."

The last words of this sentence convey an important distinction. The [P. 224]
Jat of the Indus and Lower Chanáb is essentially a husbandman. But in the great central grazing grounds of the Western Plains he is often pastoral rather than agricultural, looking upon cultivation as an inferior occupation which he leaves to Aráíns, Mahtams, and such like people.

On the Upper Indus the word Jat, or Hindki which is perhaps more often used, is applied in scarcely a less indefinite sense than in the Deraját;

while in the Salt-range Tract the meaning is but little more precise. Beyond the Indus, Jat or Hindki includes both Rájpúts and Awáns, and indeed all who talk Panjábi rather than Pashto. In the Salt-range Tract, however, the higher Rájpút tribes, such as Janjúa, are carefully excluded; and Jat means any Mahomedan cultivator of Hindu origin who is not an Awán, Gakkhar, Pathán, Saiyad, Qureshi, or Rájpút. Even there, however, most of the Jat clans are returned as Rájpúts also, and the figures for them will be found further on when I discuss the Jats of the sub-montane tracts. Major Wace writes :—

"The real Jat clans of the Ráwalpindi division have a prejudice against the name Jat, "because it is usually applied to camel-drivers, and to the graziers of the *bár* whom they look "down upon as low fellows. But there is, I think, no doubt that the principal agricultural "tribes whom we cannot class as Rájpúts are really of the same race as the Jats of the Lower "Panjáb."

The Jat in these parts of the country is naturally looked upon as of inferior race, and the position he occupies is very different from that which he holds in the centre and east of the Panjáb. Mr. O'Brien gives at page 78 of his *Multáni Glossary* a collection of the most pungent proverbs on the subject, of which I can only quote one or two :—"Though the Jat grows "refined, he will still use a mat for a pocket-handkerchief." "An ordinary "man's ribs would break at the laugh of a Jat." "When the Jat is pros- "perous he shuts up the path (by ploughing it up) : when the Kirár (money- "lender) is prosperous he shuts up the Jat." "A Jat like a wound is better "when bound." "Though a Jat be made of gold, still his hinder parts are of "brass." "The Jat is such a fool that only God can take care of him."

The Pathán proverbs are even less complimentary. "If a Hindki "cannot do you any harm, he will leave a bad smell as he passes you." "Get round a Pathán by coaxing; but heave a clod at a Hindki." "Though
[P. 225] "a Hindki be your right arm, cut it off." "Kill a black Jat rather than a black snake." The Jat of Derah Gházi is described as "lazy, dirty, and ignorant."

*P. 110-11 **429. Jat tribes of the Western Plains.**—Abstract No. 73 on the next page* gives the principal Jat tribes of the Western Plains; that is to say west of Lahore, excluding the trans-Salt-range and the sub-montane tracts. The tribes may be divided into three groups; the Tahím Bhutta, Langáh, Chhína, and Súmra lie chiefly westwards of the valley of the Jahlam-Chanáb; the Chhádhar and Sipra lie to the east of that line; while the Bhatti, Siál, Punwár, Joya, Dhúdhi, Khíchi, and Wattu are Rájpúts rather than Jats, and will be discussed when I come to the Rájpúts of the Western Plains. It must be remembered that these figures are very imperfect, as they merely give the numbers who have returned their tribe as one of those shown in the abstract, and do not include those who have returned only sub-sections of those tribes. The complete figures cannot be obtained till the detailed clan tables are ready. The double columns under Bhutta, Langáh, Súmra, Chhádhar and Dhúdhi show the numbers who have returned themselves as belonging to these tribes, but as being by caste Jat and Rájpút respectively.

The Tahím (No. 1).—The Tahím claim Arab origin, and to be descended from an Ansári Quresh called Tamím. They formerly held much property in the Chiniot *tahsíl* of Jhang, and there were Tahím Governors of those parts under the Dehli Emperors. It is said that the Awáns have a Tahím clan. The Tahím are not wholly agriculturists, and are said not unfrequently to work as butchers and cotton scutchers; or it may be merely that the butchers and cotton scutchers have a Tahím clan called after the tribe. They are, as far as our figures go, almost confined to Baháwalpur and the lower Indus and Chenáb in Multán, Muzaffargarh, and Derah Ghází Khán. The Multán Tahím say that their more immediate ancestor Sambhal Sháh came to that place some 700 years ago on a marauding expedition, and ruled at Multán for 40 years, after which he was killed and his followers scattered. In his invasion of India during the latter part of the 14th century, Taimur encountered his old foes "the Getæ (Jats), who inhabited the plains "of Tahím," and pursued them into the desert; and Tod mentions an extinct Rájpút tribe which he calls Dahíma.

Astract No. 73, showing the Jat [P. 226]

	JATS—WESTERN								
	1	2		3			4	5	
		Bhutta.		Langáh.				Súmra.	
	Tahím.	Jat.	Rájpút.	Jat.	Rájpút.	Pathán.	Chhína.	Jat.	Rájpút.
Ludhiana ...	8	36	7	...	...	...	...	847	...
Jalandhar ...	...	...	9	...	...	...	...	1,633	...
Hushyárpur ...	...	...	691	...	...	...	...	659	...
Amritsar ...	...	20	241	17	91	...	2,492	388	6
Gurdaspur ...	...	...	...	...	936	...	...	1,240	...
Sialkot ...	69	555	98	169	1	...	...	52	...
Lahore ...	98	73	150	...	196	...	...	205	16
Gujranwala ...	345	311	...	234	...	...	2,310	625	7
Firozpur ...	38	42	57	6	25	...	...	882	1
Rawalpindi ...	4	5	...	470	464	...	...	1	...
Jhelam ...	321	1,354	11	31	284	...	...	...	...
Gujrat ...	5	233	...	294	2	...	...	30	...
Shahpur ...	93	2,570	162	401	20	...	...	...	...
Multan ...	2,821	4,845	160	2,190	96	2,205	25	2,214	88
Jhang ...	640	1,612	3,231	341	41	83	...	...	1
Montgomery ...	304	102	20	177	174	56	...	...	5
Muzaffargarh ...	1,605	4,306	3	1,144	1	207	550	1,500	5
Derah Ismáíl Khan	765	1,014	...	778	4	...	4,411	951	2
Derah Ghazi Khan	2,220	3,162	...	2,305	...	...	408	887	...
Bannu ...	72	2	...	410	...	...	...	...	...
British Territory.	9,598	20,431	4,891	9,083	2,348	2,550	10,196	12,558	218
Patiala ...	...	663	104	...	...	...	...	...	1,604
Total East. Plains	...	757	104	50	1	...	...	...	2,101
Bahawalpur ...	13,862	1,351	...	...	...	...	...	...	...
British Territory.	9,598	20,431	4,891	9,083	2,348	2,550	10,196	12,558	218
Native States...	13,862	2,108	194	59	1	...	...	...	2,101
Province ...	23,460	22,539	5,085	9,142	2,349	2,550	10,196	12,558	2,319

Tribes of the Western Plains.

PLAINS.

6 Chhádhar. Jat.	6 Chhádhar. Rájpút.	7 Sipra.	8 Bhatti.	9 Siál.	10 Punwár.	11 Joya.	12 Dhúdhi.	13 Khíchi.	14 Wattu.	
...	...	...	1,004	5	10	...	8	...	...	Ludhiana.
489	...	346	367	31	87	...	348	...	...	Jalandhar.
...	...	106	43	333	...	...	...	...	...	Hushyárpur.
1,646	...	38	205	221	653	...	...	...	...	Amritsar.
232	...	...	5	137	2,387	...	...	...	...	Gurdaspur.
720	...	508	3,077	719	117	205	99	13	...	Sialkot.
2,600	4	14	10,287	1,243	311	390	710	518	739	Lahore.
5,537	333	1,119	7,722	433	538	995	561	432	312	Gujranwala.
347	...	131	590	285	716	782	264	36	704	Firozpur.
5	...	5	2,056	141	814	49	27	...	...	Rawalpindi.
1,805	131	156	6,241	256	524	...	733	74	7	Jhelam.
201	...	1,388	9,926	1,091	145	54	1,524	...	...	Gujrat.
1,672	1,877	1,794	396	71	71	516	426	57	43	Shahpur.
1,287	638	451	0,682	560	2,563	473	1,875	54	...	Multan.
3,272	13,390	5,185	2,874	437	284	1,533	1,578	483	107	Jhang.
3,076	61	747	3,528	1,202	726	2,165	1,349	373	454	Montgomery.
1,537	...	11	6,088	2,453	1,561	1,333	505	44	110	Muzaffargarh.
1,359	...	73	13,767	4,648	1,317	1,788	605	877	167	Derah Ismáil Khan.
388	...	171	12,971	2,536	1,919	1,421	66	355	13	Derah Ghazi Khan.
110	1	70	1,057	189	405	479	136	...	283	Bannu.
26,387	16,435	12,563	94,665	17,098	16,959	12,388	12,815	3,337	2,963	British Territory.
...	...	...	587	...	864	...	502	...	...	Patiala.
17	...	6	619	273	887	...	599	...	241	Total East.Plains.
...	1,311	...	569	...	...	...	470	254	3	Bahawalpur.
26,387	16,435	12,563	94,665	17,09 3	16,959	12,388	12,315	3,337	2,963	British Territory.
17	1,311	6	1,193	273	887	...	1,087	254	244	Native States.
26,404	17,746	12,569	95,858	17,366	17,846	12,388	13,402	3,591	3,207	Province.

The Bhutta (No. 2).—The Bhutta are said by Mr. O'Brien to have traditions connecting them with Hindústán, and they claim to be descended from Solar Rájpúts. But since the rise to opulence and importance of Pírzádah Murád Bakhsh Bhutta, of Multán, many of them have taken to calling themselves Pírzádahs. One account is that they are emigrants from Bhután—a story I fear too obviously suggested by the name. They also often practise other crafts, such as making pottery or weaving, instead of or in addition to agriculture. They are said to have held Uchh (in Baháwalpur) before the Saiyads came there. They are, according to our figures, chiefly found on the lower Indus, Chenáb and Jahlam, in Sháhpur, Jhang, Multán, Muzaffargarh, and Derah Ghází Khán. In Jhang most of them have returned themselves as Rájpúts. The Bhutta shown scattered over the Eastern Plains are perhaps members of the small Bhutna or Bhutra clan of Málwa Jats. (See also Buttar, section 436, and Búta, section 438).

The Langah (No. 3).—Mr. O'Brien thus describes the Langáh:—"A tribe of agriculturists "in the Multán and Muzaffargarh districts. They were originally an Afghán tribe who came to "Multán from Sivi and Dhádhar for purposes of trade, and eventually settled at Rapri and the "neighbourhood. In the confusion that followed the invasion of Tamerlane Multan became "independent of the throne of Dehli, and the inhabitants chose Sheikh Yusaf, Kureshi, head of "the shrine of Sheikh Bahauddin, as Governor. In 1445 A.D., Rai Sahra, Chief of the Langáhs, "whose daughter had been married to Sheikh Yusaf, introduced an armed band of his tribesmen "into the city by night, seized Sheikh Yusaf and sent him to Delhi, and proclaimed himself king "with the title Sultan Kutabuddin. The kings "of Multán belonging to the Langáh tribe are "shown in the margin.

Sultan Kutabaddin	1445 to 1460.
Sultan Hussain ...	1460 (extent of reign not known).
Sultan Firoz Sháh	Dates not known.
Sultán Mahmud	Dates not known.
Sultan Husain ...	1518 to 1526.

"The dynasty terminated with the capture "of Multán, after a siege of more than a year "by Sháh Hasan Arghun, Governor of Sindh, in "1526. For ten days the city was given up to "plunder and massacre, and most of the Langáhs were slain. Sultan Husain was made prisoner "and died shortly after. The Langáh dynasty ruled Multán for eighty years, during which time "Biloches succeeded in establishing themselves along the Indus from Sitpur to Kot Karor. The "Langáhs of Multán and Muzaffargarh are now very insignificant cultivators."

Farishtah is apparently the authority for their Afghán origin, which is doubtful to say the least. Pirzádah Murád Bakhsh Bhutta of Multán says that the Bhutta, Langáh, Kharral, Harral, and Lak are all Punwár Rájpúts by origin. But the Langáh are described by Tod as a clan of the Chalúk or Solánì tribe of Agnikula Rájpúts, who inhabited Multán and Jaisalmer and were driven out of the latter by the Bhatti at least 700 years ago. According to our figures the Panjáb Langáh are almost confined to the lower Indus and Chanáb. Unfortunately we classed 2,550 Langáh who had returned their *caste* as Langáh, under Patháns. I have added the figures in Abstract No. 73.

The Chhina (No. 4).—These I take to be distinct from the Chíma Jats of Siálkot and Gújránwála, though the two have certainly been confused in our tables. That there are Chhína in Siálkot appears from the fact that the town of Jámki in that district was founded by a Chhína Jat who came from Sindh and retained the title of Jám, the Sindhi equivalent for Chaudhri. Yet if the Chhína spread up the Chanáb into Siálkot and the neighbouring districts in such large numbers as are shown for Chíma in those districts, it is curious that they should not be found in the intermediate districts through which they must have passed. It is probable that the Chhína here shown for Gurdáspur, and perhaps those for Fírozpur also, should go with the Chíma who are described in section 432 among the Jat tribes of the sub-montane tract. These latter seem to trace their origin from Dehli. The Chhína of Derah Ismáíl Khán are chiefly found in the cis-Indus portion of the district.

430. Jat tribes of the Western Plains continued. The Sumra (No. 5.)—Mr. O'Brien describes the Súmra as originally Rájpúts:—"In A.D. 750 they expelled the first Arab invaders "from Sindh and Multán, and furnished the country with a dynasty which ruled in Multán from "1445 to 1526 A.D., when it was expelled by the Samma, another Rájpút tribe;" and Tod describes them as one of the two great clans Umra and Súmra of the Soda tribe of Punwár Rájpúts, who in remote times held all the Rájpútána deserts, and gave their names to Umrkot and Umra-sumra or the Bhakkar country on the Indus. He identifies the Soda with Alexander's Sogdi, the princes of Dhát. Here again the Súmra seem to have spread, according to our figures, far up the Satluj and Chanáb into the central districts of the Province. The figures for Derah Ismáíl Khán are probably understated, as there they hold a great portion of the Leiah *thal* between the Jhang border and the Indus. Some 2,000 of the Súmra have returned themselves as Rájpúts, chiefly in Patiála

The Chhadhar (No. 6).—The Chhádhar are found along the whole length of the Chanáb and Rávi valleys, but are far most numerous in Jhang, where they have for the most part returned themselves as Rájpúts. They claim to be descended from Rája Tur, Túnwar. They say that they left their home in Rájpútána in the time of Muhammad Ghori and settled in Baháwalpur, where they were converted by Sher Sháh of Uchh. Thence they came to Jhang, where they founded an important colony and spread in smaller numbers up the Chanáb and Rávi. Mr. Steedman describes them as good agriculturists, and less given to cattle-theft than their neighbours.

The Sipra (No. 7)—appear to be a sub-division of the Gil tribe of Jats, which gives its name to the famous battle-field of Sabráon. They too are found chiefly on the Jahlam and lower Chanáb and are most numerous in Jhang. They are not an important tribe.

The Bhatti, Sial, Punwar, Joya, Dhudhi, Khichi, and Wattu will be described under Rájpúts.

The Langrial are not separately shown in the abstract. They are however curious as being a nomad pastoral tribe who form almost the sole inhabitants of the Multán steppes. They appear to be found also in Ráwalpindi and Siálkot, and there to claim Solar Rájpút origin. But in Multán the Langrál say that their ancestor was a Bráhman Chāran from Bíkáner who was converted by Sultan Samráu. They originally settled in Ráwalpindi; thence they moved to Jhang, took some country from the Siál, and settled at Kot Kamália in Montgomery, whence they spread over the Multán *bár*. They derive their name from *langar* a "kitchen," because their ancestor used to keep open house to all the beggars and *faqírs* of the neighbourhood.

The Nol and Bhangu.—These appear to be among the earliest inhabitants of the Jhang district, and to be perhaps aboriginal. The Bhangu do not even claim Rájpút origin! The Nol held the country about Jhang and the Bhangu that about Shorkot when the Siál came to the district, but they eventually fell before the rising power of the new comers. The Siálkot Bhangu say they came from Nepal.

[P. 227] **The Kharral, Harral, and Marral.**—The Kharral will be discussed separately with the smaller agricultural tribes. The Harral claim to be descended from the same ancestor, Rai Bhúpa, as the Kharral, but by another son; and to be Punwár Rajpúts who came from Jaisalmer to Uchh, and thence to Kamália in the Montgomery district. Mr. Steedman says that in Jhang, where only they are found on the left bank of the Upper Chanáb, tradition makes them a branch of the Ahírs, and that they are almost the worst thieves in the district, owning large flocks and herds which they pasture in the central steppes, and being bad cultivators. The Marral seem to have been once of far greater importance than now in the Jhang district, which is their home. They claim to be Chauhán Rájpúts by origin, and to have come to the Upper Chanáb in the time of Akbar. They are a fine bold-looking set of men, but with a bad reputation for cattle-lifting, and are poor cultivators.

The Hans, Khagga, Jhandir, &c.—These tribes will be found described under Shekh, as they claim Qureshi origin, though often classed as Jats.

431. Jats of the western sub-montane.—The tribes which I shall next discuss are those of the foot of the hills west of Lahore, that is, of the Gújrát, Gújránwála and Siálkot districts. With them, however, I have included in the Abstract the so-called Jat tribes of the Salt-range Tract; for all the tribes of sufficient importance to be discussed separately that have returned themselves from this tract as Jats, are really Rájpúts rather than Jats, the greater number of their members have returned themselves as such, and they will be discussed under Rájpúts. Such are Dhaniál, Bhakrál, Janjúa, and Manhás. After these came the Mekan, Gondal, and Ránjha, who belong to the Salt-range sub-montane and will also be treated as Rájpúts. Then follow the true Jats, the Tárar, Varaich, Chíma, &c., whom I have endeavoured to arrange in order of locality from west to east. The Jats of the Salt-range and of the great plains below it I have already described sufficiently in the preceding sections 427-8. But directly we leave the Salt-range behind us and enter the Lahore and Amritsar divisions—directly, in fact, we come within the circle of Sikh influence as distinguished from mere political supremacy, we find the line between Jat and Rájpút sufficiently clearly marked. The Jat indeed, here as elsewhere, claims for himself Rájpút origin. But a Varaich does not say that he is now Rájpút. He is a Jat and content to be so. The fact is that within the pale of Sikhism Rájpúts were at a discount. The equality of all men preached by Guru Govind disgusted the haughty Rájpúts, and they refused to join his standard. They soon paid the penalty of their pride. The Jats who composed the great mass of the Khálsa rose to absolute power, and the Rájpút who had despised them was the peculiar object of their hatred. Their general policy led them to cut off such poppy heads as had not sprung from their own seed; and their personal feeling led them to treat the Rájpút, who as a native-born leader of the people should have joined them, and who would if he had done so have been a very important element of additional strength to the cause, with especial harshness. The old Settlement Reports are full of remarks upon the decadence if not the virtual disappearance of the Rájpút gentry in those districts where Sikh sway was most absolute. Thus the Jats we are considering are far more clearly marked off from the Rájpúts than are those of the Western Plains where everybody is a Jat, or of the Salt-range Tract where everybody who is not an Arab or a Mughal calls himself a Rájpút; indeed there is if anything a tendency here to call those Jats who are admitted to be Rájpúts further west. Only on the edge of the group, on the common border line of the Sikh tract, the Salt-range, and the great plains, do the Mekan, Gondal, Ránjha, and Tárar claim some to be Jats and some to be Rájpúts. The first two I have decided to describe under Rájpúts, the last under Jats; but this is more a matter of convenience than of ethnic classification. The Jat tribes now to be considered are, except perhaps on the confines of the Gújránwála *bár*, essentially agricultural, and occupy the same social position as do those of the Eastern Plains, whom indeed they resemble in all respects.

The most extraordinary thing about the group of Jat tribes found in Siálkot is the large number of customs still retained by them which are, so far as I know, not shared by any other people. They will be found described in Mr. Roe's translation of Amín Chand's *History of Siálkot*, and I shall notice one or two of them in the following paragraphs. Nothing could be more instructive than an examination of the origin, practice, and limits of this group of customs. They would seem to point to aboriginal descent. Another point worthy of remark is the frequent recurrence of an ancestor Mal, which may perhaps connect this group of tribes with the ancient Malli of Multán. Some of their traditions point to Sindh; while others are connected with the hills of Jammu. The whole group strikes me as being one of exceeding interest, and I much regret that I have no time to treat it more fully.

432. Jat tribes of the western sub-montane.—The figures for the tribe will be found in Abstract No. 74 on the next page.* I have already explained that the first seven tribes, which belong to the Salt-range and its vicinity, will be treated as and discussed with Rájpúts. *P. 116-17.

The Tarar (No. 8).—This is the only one of the tribes to be here discussed of which any considerable number of the members have returned themselves as Rájpúts, about half the Gújránwála and nearly all the Sháhpur Tárar having adopted this course. The Tárar claim Solar Rájpút origin, apparently from the Bhatti of Bhatner. They say that their ancestor Tárar took service with Mahmúd Ghaznavi and returned with him to Ghazni; but that his son Lohi, from whom they are descended, moved from Bhatner to Gújrát whence the tribe spread. Another story dates their settlement from the time of Humáyún. They intermarry with Gondal, Varaich, Gil, Virk, and other leading Jat tribes of the neighbourhood; and they have lately begun to intermarry within the tribe. Some of them are still Hindus. They hold land on both sides of the Upper Chanáb, about the junction and within the boundaries of the three districts of Gújrát, Gújránwála, and Sháhpur. They are described as "invariably lazy, idle and troublesome."

The Varaich (No. 9).—The Varaich is one of the largest Jat tribes in the Province. In Akbar's time they held two-thirds of the Gújrát district, though on less favourable terms than those allowed to the Gújars who held the remainder; and they still hold 170 villages in that district. They have also crossed the Chanáb into Gújránwála where they held a tract of 41 villages, and have spread along under the hills as far as Ludhiána and Maler Kotla. They do not always even pretend to be Rájpúts, but say that their ancestor Dhúdi, was a Jat who came into India with Mahmúd Ghaznavi and settled in Gújrát, where the tribe grew powerful and partly dispossessed the original Gújar lords of the soil. Another story is that their ancestor was a Súrajbansi Rájpút who came from Ghazni to Gújrát; while according to a third account their ancestor was a descendant of

Rája Karan who went from the city of Kisrah to Dehli and was settled by Jalál-ul-dín Fíroz Shah in Hissár, whence the tribe moved some five centuries ago to Gújránwála. But there is little doubt that Gújrát was their first home, and that their movement has been eastwards. The Wazírábád family of this tribe rose to importance under the Sikhs, and its history is narrated by Sir Lepel Griffin at pages 409 *ff* of his *Punjab Chiefs*. They are almost all Musalmáns, but retain all their tribal and many of their Hindu customs. They marry with the best local tribes. They appear to be known as Chúng or Varaich indifferently in the Lahore district.

The Sahi (No. 10).—The Sáhi also claim descent from a Solar Rájpút who went to Ghazni with Mahmúd, and returned to found the tribe, settling on the Rávi near Lahore. They are found in any numbers only in Gújrát and Siálkot. They have, in common with the Sindhu and Chíma of these parts, some peculiar marrriage cutsoms, such as cutting a goat's ear and marking their foreheads with the blood, making the bridegroom cut off a twig of the *Jhand* tree (*Prosopis spicigera*) and so forth; and they, like most of the tribes discussed in this section, worship the Jhand tree.

[P. 229] **The Hinjra (No. 11).**—The Hínjra of the Gújránwála *bár* are a pastoral tribe, perhaps of aboriginal extraction. They own 37 villages in Gújránwála which is their home, but have spread both east and west under the hills. They claim to be Saroha Rájpúts, and that their ancestor Hinjráno came from the neighbourhood of Hissár to Gújránwála and founded a city called Uskhab, the ruins of which still exist. Their immediate ancestors are Mal and Dhol, and they say that half their clans still live in the Hissár country. It would be interesting to know the names of these clans, and to examine the alleged connection between the two sections of the tribe. In the Hissár Settlement Report it is stated that "the Hinjráon Pachhádas trace "their origin to a Saroha Rájpút ancestor called Hinjráon. They are all Muhammadans in this "district, though in other places Hindu Hinjráon Pachhádas are to be found." Our figures show no Hínjra in Hissár, and only 30 in Sirsa; but they may have been returned as Hinjráon.

The Chima (No. 12).—The Chíma are one of the largest Jat tribes in the Punjáb. They say that some 25 generations back their ancestor Chíma, a Chauhán Rájpút, fled from Dehli after the defeat of Prithi Ráj by Shaháb-ul-dín Ghori, first to Kángra and then to Amritsar, where his son founded a village on the Beás in the time of Ala-ul-dín Ghori. His grandson was called Rána Kang, and Dhol (the same name as among the Hínjra) was the ancestor of their present clans. The Chíma have the peculiar marriage customs described under the Sáhi Jats, and they are said to be served by Jogis and not by Bráhmans, both which facts point strongly to aboriginal descent. They are a powerful and united tribe, but quarrelsome. They are said to marry within the tribe as well as with their neighbours. Many of them are Musalmáns, but retain their old customs. The Nagára is one of their principal clans. They are most numerous in Siálkot, but hold 42 villages in Gújránwála, and have spread both eastwards and westwards along the foot of the hills.

The Bajwa (No. 13).—The Bájwa or Bajju Jats and Rájpúts have given their names to the Bajwát or country at the foot of the Jammu hills in the Siálkot District. They say that they are Solar Rájpúts and that their ancestor Raja Shalíp was driven out of Multán in the time of Sikandar Lodi. His two sons Kals and Lís escaped in the disguise of falconers. Lís went to Jammu and there married a Rájpút bride, while Kals married a Jat girl in Pasrúr. The descendants of both live in the Bajwát, but are said to be distinguished as Bájwa Jats and Bajju Rájpúts. Another story has it that their ancestor Rai Jaisan was driven from Dehli by Rai Pitora and settled at Karbala in Siálkot. The Bajju Rájpúts admit their relationship with the Bájwa Jats. The Bajju Rájpúts are said to have had till quite lately a custom by which a Musalmán girl could be turned into a Hindu for purposes of marriage, by temporarily burying her in an underground chamber and ploughing the earth over her head. In the betrothals of this tribe dates are used, a custom perhaps brought with them from Multán; and they have several other singular customs resembling those of the Sáhi Jats already described. They are almost confined to Siálkot, though they have spread in small numbers eastwards as far as Patiála.

433. Jat tribes of the western sub-montane continued.—The Deo (No. 14).—The Deo are practically confined to the Siálkot District. They claim a very ancient origin but *not* Rájpút. Their ancestor's name is said to be Maháj, who came from "the Saki jungle" in Hindústán, and two of his sons were Aulakh and Deo who gave their names to two Jat tribes. But another story refers them to Rája Jagdeo, a Súrajbansi Rájpút. They have the same marriage ceremony as the Sáhi, and also use the goat's blood in a similar manner in honour of their ancestors, and have several very peculiar customs. They will not intermarry with the Mán Jats, with whom they have some ancestral connection.

The Ghumman (No. 15).—The Ghumman claim descent from Rája Malkír, a Lunar Rájpút and grandson of Rája Dalíp of Dehli, from whom are descended the Janjúa Rájpúts of the Salt-range Tract. One of his descendants Saupál married out of caste, and his son Ghumman, who came from Mukiála or Malhiána in the time of Fíroz Sháh and took service in Jammu, founded the present tribe. This tribe worships an idol made of grass and set within a square drawn in the corner

Abstract No. 74, showing Jat tribes [P. 228]

	JAT TRIBES OF THE								
	1	2	3	4	5	6	7	8	
								Tarar.	
	Dhaniál.	Janjúa.	Manhás.	Bhakrál.	Mekan.	Gondal.	Ránjha.	Jat.	Rájpút.
Ambala ...	...	...	2	...	...	8	...	...	...
Ludhiána ...	...	12	15	...	...	...	...	...	...
Jalandhar ...	...	...	144	...	...	24	...	...	...
Hushyárpur ...	...	60	90	...	...	203	...	...	...
Amritsar ...	...	11	524	...	...	65	...	1	...
Gurdáspur ...	...	610	67	...	...	443	230	76	...
Siálkot ...	...	1,110	1,156	21	67	1,791	...	900	...
Lahore ...	...	543	669	...	101	859	53	191	...
Gujránwála ...	...	1,048	1,724	...	12	3,953	1,160	2,373	2,822
Firozpur ...	...	44	158	...	52	161	14	...	...
Ráwalpindi ...	6,240	92	143	1,576	...	611	8	250	...
Jhelam ...	3,680	232	1,711	1,258	1,125	6,354	1,601	712	5
Gujrat ...	6	732	48	1,965	918	24,825	6,924	13,588	...
Shahpur ...	...	39	...	48	100	305	258	56	1,173
Multán ...	...	253	74	...	19	196	148	2	...
Jhang ...	...	306	...	...	220	649	102	210	70
Montgomery ...	...	57	...	...	...	122	1	203	168
Muzaffargarh ...	...	900	...	...	119	155	168	...	...
British Territory.	10,026	8,419	6,570	4,863	3,157	47,276	10,903	18,925	4,228
Patiála ...	...	...	15	13	...	...	10	...	...
Nábha ...	...	...	...	...	...	2	...	...	...
Kapurthala ...	...	...	...	...	...	...	17	...	...
Jind ...	...	...	...	...	...	...	...	...	...
Maler Kotla ...	...	...	...	...	...	...	...	...	...
Total East. Plains	...	...	15	13	...	86	40	19	...
British Territory.	10,026	8,419	6,570	4,863	3,157	47,276	10,903	18,925	4,228
Native States	...	15	15	13	...	325	53	19	...
Province ...	10,026	8,434	6,585	4,876	3,157	47,601	10,950	18,944	4,228

of the Western Sub-montane.

WESTERN SUB-MONTANE.

9	10	11	12	13	14	15	16	17	18	
Varaich.	Sáhi.	Hinjra.	Chíma.	Bájwa.	Deo.	Ghumman.	Káhlon.	Sarai.	Goráya.	
506	...	...	280	428	...	570	...	1,772	7	Ambala.
1,344	630	...	3,008	207	765	1,237	...	...	...	Ludhiána.
202	322	2,050	1,354	568	...	94	63	...	215	Jalandhar.
470	...	...	...	...	...	1,302	...	400	...	Hushyárpur.
2,205	154	2,227	1,119	1,177	615	1,022	1,155	1,043	...	Amritsar.
1,476	...	366	1,350	1,851	984	93	7,376	5,063	4,823	Gurdáspur.
5,780	5,784	2,515	35,722	25,303	4,873	14,228	13,756	4,660	6,385	Siálkot.
1,292	155	1,405	89	1,772	647	41	219	103	421	Lahore.
10,783	613	12,646	10,839	947	502	2,073	313	51	4,407	Gujránwála.
252	400	267	751	238	361	109	153	2,412	141	Firozpur.
362	3	122	502	47	...	...	10	144	91	Ráwalpindi.
504	578	20	219	52	...	37	...	...	42	Jhelam.
35,253	4,044	1,179	3,429	107	2	1,413	...	345	417	Gujrat.
443	140	820	125	...	...	...	...	...	156	Shahpur.
102	59	64	...	10	...	2	11	9	2	Multan.
59	110	482	2	...	...	78	...	225	5	Jhang.
202	160	600	40	30	...	...	...	50	64	Montgomery.
33	22	220	...	2	...	14	...	48	183	Muzaffargarh.
61,718	18,396	25,200	67,855	32,843	9,284	22,488	23,056	17,541	17,462	British Territory.
641	...	...	1,003	1,523	...	7,810	41	...	...	Patiála.
160	4	2	30	...	...	460	8	3	124	Nábha.
503	...	...	...	132	...	...	424	...	100	Kapurthala.
...	1	...	52	...	...	590	...	...	1	Jind.
1,151	...	8	600	...	...	...	...	...	...	Maler Kotla.
2,505	6	58	1,604	1,678	...	8,931	404	5	315	Total East. Plains
61,718	13,396	25,200	67,855	32,843	9,284	22,488	28,056	17,541	17,462	British Territory.
2,517		65	1,694	1,678	...	8,939	494	5	315	Native States.
64,235	13,402	25,265	69,549	34,521	9,284	31,427	23,550	17,546	17,777	Province.

of the house at weddings, and they cut the goat's ear and the Jhand twig like the Sáhi Jats. They also propitiate their ancestors by pouring water over a goat's head so that he shakes it off. They are chiefly found in Siálkot, though they have spread somewhat, especially eastwards.

The Kahlon (No. 16).—The Káhlon claim descent from Rája Vikramájít of the Lunar line through Rája Jagdeo of Dáránagar. Under his descendant Soli or Sodi they left Dáránagar and settled near Batála in Gurdáspur, whence they spread into Siálkot. Their marriage customs are very similar to those of the Sáhi Jats already described. They are almost confined to the southern portion of the districts of Gurdáspur and Siálkot. They intermarry with Jats, not with Rájpúts.

The Sarai (No. 17).—The Sarái Jats are, so far as our figures go, chiefly found in Gurdáspur and Siálkot, though there are a few on the upper and middle Satluj also. I cannot identify these people with certainty. There are said to be Sarái Rájpúts in Siálkot, who are Bhattis descended from an ancestor called Sarái who settled in the Háfizábád *tahsil*. There can hardly be any connection between them and the Saráis of the Kalhora family of Derah Gházi Khán, who are discussed under the head Shekh and who claim to be Qureshi. The Sarái are said to be a well-known Jat clan in Jálandhar and the neighbouring districts. Tod makes Sehrái the title of a race of Punwár Rájpúts who founded a dynasty at Aror in Sindh on the eastern bank of the Indus, and "gave their name Sehl or Sehr as a titular appellation to the country and its princes "and its inhabitants the Sehrais." (See further the Sara Jats of the central districts, section 436.) Of the Sarái of Gurdáspur 4,951 have entered themselves as tribe Sindhu, clan Sarái, and appear again in the Sindhu figures which will be discussed presently.

The Goraya (No. 18).—The Goráya are said by one account to be descended from the Saroha family of Lunar Rájpúts, and to have come to Gujránwála as a nomad and pastoral tribe from Sirsa. Another story is that they are descended from a Sombansi Rájpút called Guráya whose grandson Mal came from the Lakki *thal* some 15 generations ago. A third tradition is that Rána their founder came from the Jammu hills in the time of the Emperors. They are now found in Gújránwála, Siálkot, and Gurdáspur. They own 31 villages in Gújránwála and are excellent cultivators, being one of the most prosperous tribes in the district. They have the same peculiar marriage customs as the Sáhi Jats already described. The word *guraya* is said to be used for the *Nílgai* (*Porcax picta*) in Central India. They are sometimes said to be a clan of the Dhillon tribe.

The Dhotar and Lodike.—There are 1,454 Dhotar returned in our tables, of whom 1,428 are found in Gújránwála. They are mostly Hindus, and claim to be descended from a Solar Rájpút who emigrated from Hindústán or, according to another story, from Ghazni some 20 generations back. The Lodike are considered to be a clan of the Kharrals of the Montgomery district, who are described separately. In Gújránwála they are said to be of Solar Rájpút descent, and to have come from the Rávi, the Kharral head-quarters, to the Gújránwála *bár* some ten generations ago, and led a pastoral and marauding life till reverses at the hands of the Virk forced them to settle down and take to agriculture. They do not give their daughters to the local Jat tribes.

The Chatta—Appear to be confined to Gújránwála, in which district they hold 81 villages and number 2,271 souls. They claim to be descended from Chatta, a grandson of Prithi Rai, the Chauhán King of Dehli, and brother of the ancestor of the Chíma. In the 10th generation from Chatta or, as otherwise stated, some 500 years ago, was Dahru who came from Sambhal in Morádábád, where the bards of the Karnál Chauháns still live, to the banks of the Chanáb and married among the Jat tribes of the Gújránwála District. They were converted to Islám about 1,600 A.D. They rose to considerable political importance under the Sikhs; and the history of their leading family is told by Sir Lepel Griffin at pages 402 *ff* of his *Panjáb Chiefs*.

434. Jats of the Sikh tract.—The group of Jats we have now to consider are the typical Jats of the Panjáb, including all those great Sikh Jat tribes who have made the race so renowned in recent history. They occupy the central districts of the Panjáb, the upper Satluj, and the great Sikh States of the Eastern Plains. All that I have said in the preceding section (§ 431) regarding the absence of any wish on the part of the Jats of the Khálsa to be aught but Jats, applies here with still greater force. A Sidhu claims indeed Rájpút origin, and apparently with good reason. But he is now a Sidhu Jat, and holds that to be a prouder title than Bhatti Rájpút. The only tribe among this group of which any considerable numbers have returned themselves as Rájpúts are the Virk; and among them this has happened only in Gújránwála, on the extreme outskirts of the tract. These men are the backbone of the Panjáb by character and physique as well as by locality. They are stalwart, sturdy yeomen of great independence, industry, and agricultural skill, and collectively form perhaps the

finest peasantry in India. Unfortunately the Settlement Reports of this part of the country are often poor or even absent altogether, while much of
[P. 230] the tract consists of Native States. Thus except regarding such tribes as have risen to political importance, I can give but scanty information. The Jats of the Sikh tract are essentially husbandmen, and the standard of agricultural practice among those at any rate of the more fertile northern districts is as high as is reached in any portion of the Province. I would call special attention to the curious traditions of the Bhúlar, Mán, and Her tribes, an examination of which might produce interesting and valuable results.

* P. 120-21 Abstract No. 75 on the opposite page* gives the distribution of the tribes so far as it is shown by our figures. I have arranged them roughly in the order to which they appear to occur from west to east.

435. The Jat tribes of the Sikh tract. The Dhillon (No. 1).—The Dhillon is one of the largest and most widely distributed Jat tribes in the Province. Their head-quarters would appear from our figures to be Gújránwála and Amritsar; but they are found in large numbers along the whole course of the Satluj from Fírozpur upwards, and under the hills to the east of those two districts. The numbers returned for the Dehli District are curiously large, and I doubt somewhat whether they really refer to the same tribe. Like the Goráya they claim to be Saroha Rájpúts by origin, and to have come from Sirsa. If this be true they have probably moved up the Satluj, and then spread along westwards under the hills. But another story makes them descendants of a Súrajbansi Rájpút named Lu who lived at Khármor in the Málwa, and held some office at the Dehli court. They are said to be divided into three great sections, the Báj, Sáj, and Sánda.

The Virk (No. 2).—The head-quarters of the Virk appear to be the Gújránwála and Lahore Districts, especially the former in which they own 132 villages. They claim origin from a Manhás Rájpút called Virak, who left Jammu and settled at Ghuchli in Amritsar; and in Gújránwála nearly a third of them have returned themselves as Rájpúts, but they marry freely with the Jat tribes of the neighbourhood. They say that their ancestor Virak was descended from Malhan Nams (Mal again !) the founder of the Manhás tribe of Rájpúts, and was connected with the Rájas of Jammu. Leaving Parghowál in Jammu, he settled in Amritsar and married a Gil Jat girl. His descendants shortly afterwards moved westwards into Gújránwála. There are three main sections of the tribe, the Jopur, Vachra, and Jau. The tribe rose to some political importance about the end of last century, ruling a considerable tract in Gújránwála and Lahore till subdued by Ranjít Singh.

The Sindhu (No 3).—The Sindhu is, so far as our figures go, the second largest Jat tribe, being surpassed in numbers by the Sidhu only. Their head-quarters are the Amritsar and Lahore districts, but they are found all along the upper Satluj, and under the hills from Ambála in the east to Siálkot and Gújránwála in the west. They claim descent from the Raghobansi branch of the Solar Rájpúts through Rám Chandar of Ajudhia. They say that their ancestors were taken by or accompanied Mahmúd to Ghazni, and returned during the thirteenth century or in the reign of Fíroz Sháh from Afghánistán to India. Shortly afterwards they settled in the Mánjha near Lahore. Some of the Sindhu say that it was Ghazni in the Deccan, and not in Afghánistán, from which they came; while others have it that it was Ghadni in Bíkáner. The Jálandhar Sindhu say that they came from the south to the Mánjha some two or three centuries ago when the Patháns dispossessed the Manj Rájpúts, and shortly afterwards moved from Amritsar to Jálandhar at the invitation of the Gils to take the place of the ejected Manj. Sir Lepel Griffin is of opinion that the real origin of the tribe is from North-Western Rájpútána. The political history of the tribe, which was of capital importance under the Sikhs, is given is great detail at pages 225 *ff*, 360 *ff*, and 417 to 428 of the same writer's *Panjáb Chiefs*. The Sindhu have the same peculiar marriage customs already described as practised by the Sahi Jats. The Sindhu of Karnál worship Kála Mahar or Kála Pír, their ancestor, whose chief shrine is said to be at Thána Satra in Siálkot, their alleged place of origin.

The Bhular (No 4).—The Bhúlar, Her, and Mán tribes call themselves *asl* or "original" Jats, and are said to have sprung from the *Jat* or "Matted hair" of Mahádeo, whose title is Bhúla Mahádeo. They say that the Málwa was their original home, and are commonly reckoned as two and a half tribes, the Her only counting as a half. But the bards of the Mán, among which tribe several families have risen to political importance, say that the whole of the Mán and Bhúlar and half the Her tribe of Rájpúts were the earliest Kshatriya immigrants from Rájpútána to the Panjáb. The head-quarters of the Bhúlar appear to be Lahore and Fírozpur, and the confines of the Mánjha and Málwa; but they are returned in small numbers from every division in the Panjáb except Dehli, Ráwalpindi, and Peshawar, from almost every district, and from every Native State of the Eastern Plains except Dujána, Loháru, and Pataudi.

Abstract No. 75, showing the [P. 201]

	JATS OF THE									
	1	2		3	4	5	6	7	8	9
		Virk.								
	Dhillon.	Jat.	Rájpúts.	Sindhu.	Bhúlar.	Mán.	Her.	Buttar.	Odi.	Rai.
Dehli ...	6,852	116	...	27	...	1,902	185	16	...	...
Gurgaon ...	...	...	...	4	2	51	...	...	1	...
Karnál ...	44	...	...	1,488	2	1,135	23	...	6	31
Hissar ...	94	...	2	...	1,571	401	...	23	...	...
Rohtak ...	...	...	...	1	5	1,110	...	1	...	...
Sirsa ...	833	95	4	476	425	2,277	10	32	2	...
Ambala ...	2,822	438	...	6,340	343	3,217	2,744	72	...	433
Ludhiána ...	6,317	1,196	...	4,258	2,382	4,206	1,432	939	2	1,233
Jalandhar ...	2,219	1,125	...	7,930	676	3,741	2,004	453	...	421
Hushyárpur ...	2,334	680	...	5,314	551	4,531	4,048	...	...	120
Kángra ...	16	...	...	54	...	...	120	...	...	...
Amritsar ...	15,721	1,162	...	24,047	433	2,280	1,060	494	2	5,353
Gurdáspur ...	1,136	1,687	...	4,906	192	608	966	1,313	...	776
Siálkot ...	3,726	3,141	...	7,333	1,606	634	1,664	704	...	387
Lahore ...	3,626	6,164	2	42,208	9,711	899	391	3,240	...	144
Gujránwála ...	18,031	15,044	6,871	2,773	80	499	124	931	487	43
Fírozpur ...	5,602	1,380	2	8,979	3,007	3,477	1,058	1,191	8,722	233
Jhelum ...	...	99	...	362	...	1	313	58	...	...
Gujrát ...	7	852	...	622	5	20	1,588	58	390	8
Shahpur ...	...	346	66	19	...	...	248	...	...	1
Multan ...	...	220	28	326	103	85	676	...	...	...
Jhang ...	...	266	64	25	...	...	127	...	...	...
Montgomery ...	...	243	79	726	266	2	90	10	...	...
Muzaffargarh ...	...	135	...	2	256	...	234	...	...	...
Derah Ismail Khan	...	137	...	...	245	...	590	10	...	...
Derah Ghazi Khan	...	...	...	5	...	2	419	282	...	...
Bannu ...	3	13	...	2	...	...	948	...	...	...
British Territory.	**69,383**	**35,527**	**7,118**	**118,944**	**21,954**	**31,210**	**21,281**	**9,847**	**9,612**	**9,242**
Patiála ...	9,827	179	...	7,814	3,006	16,307	1,485	241	...	304
Nábha ...	3,717	...	...	1,701	1,634	2,985	147	531	824	5
Kapurthala ...	...	255	...	1,585	347	192	147	8	...	...
Jind ...	538	...	..	1,138	1,111	1,777	...	...	...	47
Faridkot ...	2,122	423	...	2,510	308	989	186	183	...	22
Maler Kotla ...	664	27	...	1,070	249	259	...	7	...	...
Kalsia ...	236	...	...	798	76	78	35	16	20	2
Total East. Plans ...	17,106	889	...	16,706	7,331	22,725	2,000	986	844	380
British Territory.	**69,383**	**35,527**	**7,118**	**118,944**	**21,054**	**31,210**	**21,281**	**9,847**	**9,612**	**9,243**
Native States...	**17,180**	**889**	**...**	**16,788**	**7,840**	**22,760**	**2,570**	**986**	**844**	**470**
Province ...	**85,563**	**36,416**	**7,118**	**135,732**	**29,294**	**53,970**	**23,851**	**10,833**	**10,456**	**9,721**

Jat Tribes of the Sikh Tract.

SIKH TRACT.

10	11	12	13	14	15	16	17	18	19	20	21
Pannún.	Mahal.	Aulak.	Gil.	Sidhu.	Barár.	Dhárfwál.	Sara.	Mángat.	Dhíndsa.	Gandhi.	Chahil.
...	8	2	124	54	...	34	...	...	...	...	148
...	...	...	...	...	1,037	523	...	...	...	...	...
...	43	56	65	...	105	220	...	...	16	...	1,629
...	...	25	14	916	...	234	...	...	9	...	1,377
...	...	...	2,378	23	1	58	...	...	...	...	1,881
...	83	513	728	8,037	296	731	1,131	36	12	...	712
138	...	236	3,475	3,207	245	2,915	...	603	1,770	726	3,471
480	110	804	11,809	13,104	32	12,145	2,062	3,724	1,044	4,064	5,452
...	2,406	63	5,188	3,210	7	3,562	...	561	1,833	...	2,001
...	200	158	2,124	388	33	1,110	...	...	...	...	1,664
...	...	...	960	3	...	62	...	...	...	...	1,163
5,298	2,381	8,053	30,737	5,424	702	1,968	...	200	...	...	4,558
1,864	318	1,535	3,503	2,881	...	2,250	...	...	255	...	3,627
...	...	927	4,005	...	...	1,854	1,465	100	849	52	1,031
247	75	1,573	7,740	10,459	101	1,955	921	146	...	...	699
54	276	1,300	2,150	1,022	104	633	1,982	883	...	...	1,056
806	...	1,122	26,192	40,104	32,256	15,658	814	103	...	...	1,711
...	46	12	80	...	...	11	...	52	...	...	20
...	566	20	801	1	129	287	...	1,108	105	..	23
...	...	3	40	214	...	13	...	136	...	...	...
...	...	31	115	...	171	12	1	3	...	...	114
...	...	4	208	184	...	...	...	20	...	...	1
2	...	20	148	474	13	121	...	40	...	...	69
63	10	97	15	2	54	35	...	...	...	...	...
...	26	167	167	3	...	1	...	5	...	...	...
22	50	13	185	1	8	...	...	8	...	...	...
2	...	18	4	1	...	...	...	...	...	...	...
9,097	6,598	16,866	103,684	99,053	36,283	46,437	8,889	7,936	5,901	5,742	32,490
802	621	3,626	10,877	41,990	...	19,556	9,719	3,583	7,710	5,405	21,674
20	229	1,100	4,483	12,115	4	6,628	1,404	70	804	365	1,830
...	...	62	670	1,231	...	1,904	...	...	...	...	1,459
...	137	556	928	604	2,180	352	718	1	313	68	2,175
...	26	504	2,375	...	14,921	1,326	1,220	22	1	...	712
...	...	1,040	387	...	...	1,071	116	42	152	...	2,631
...	...	28	760	303	47	196	260	7	...	805	118
822	1,020	6,816	20,480	56,252	17,061	31,123	13,437	3,725	8,980	6,733	30,590
9,097	6,598	16,866	103,664	99,053	36,283	46,437	8,889	7,936	5,901	5,742	32,400
822	1,032	6,823	20,508	56,279	17,061	31,223	13,437	3,725	8,980	6,733	30,666
9,919	7,630	23,689	124,172	155,332	53,344	77,660	21,826	11,661	14,881	12,475	63,156

The Man (No. 5).—The Mán, the second of the *asl* Jat tribes, do sometimes claim, as has just been stated, Rájpút ancestry; and it is said that Thákur Rájpúts of the Mán tribe are still to be found in Jaipur (see further Dalál in section 440). Several of the leading Sikh families belong to this tribe, and their history will be found at pages 177 to 183 and 307 to 314 of Sir Lepel Griffin's *Panjáb Chiefs*. That writer states that there is "a popular tradition in the Panjáb "which makes all of the Mán tribe brave and true." The home of the Mán is in the northern Málwa, to the east of that of the Bhúlar; but they too are widely distributed, being found in every district and state of the Panjáb east of Lahore, especially in the northern districts and along the Satluj. From the fact that the Mán both of Jálandhar and of Karnál trace their origin to the neighbourhood of Bhatinda, it would appear probable that there was the original home of the tribe.

The Her (No. 6).—The Her is the third of this group of tribes, and their home appears to lie north of the Satluj; indeed had not it been that I wished to keep the three together, I should have taken the Her with the Jats of the eastern sub-montane. They are found however in considerable numbers under the hills from Ambála in the east to Gújrát in the west, and throughout the whole upper valley of the Satluj. Of the number shown, 5,812 were entered in my tables as Aher, of whom 2,786 were in Hushyárpur, but I am informed that this is merely another way of spelling Her. Of course they returned themselves as Aher Jats, not as Aher or Ahír by caste. There is a very old village called Her in the Nakodar *tahsíl* of Jálandhar which is still held by Her Jats, who say that they have lived there for a thousand years, in other words for an indefinite period.

436. The Jat tribes of the Sikh tract continued. The Buttar (No. 7).—The Buttar are a small tribe found, so far as our figures go, chiefly on the Upper Satluj. I am not quite sure that they are distinct from the Bhutta Jats of the Western Plains, which have been already described in section 429, or from the Búta of Hushyárpur to be described in section 438. They are said to be descended from a Súrajbansi Rájpút who came from the Lakki jungle and settled first in Gújránwála.

The Odi (No. 8).—The Odi would appear from our figures to be confined to the Fírozpur District. They appear to be a clan of the Dháríwál tribe, as 8,715 of the 8,722 Odi in Fírozpur and 787 more in Nábha have returned themselves as Dháríwál Odi. They are shown in the Abstract under both headings. On the other hand the 390 Odi of Gújrát have returned themselves as Tárar Odi, as have 417 in Gújránwála.

The Bal (No. 9).—The Bal are another tribe of the Beás and Upper Satluj, and are said to be a clan of the Sekhu tribe with whom they do not intermarry. Their ancestor is also said to have been a Rájpút of royal race who came from Málwa. The name Bal, which is derived from a root meaning "strength," is a famous one in ancient Indian History, and recurs in all sorts of forms and places.

The Pannun (No. 10)—claim Solar Rájpút ancestry. They are chiefly found in Amritsar and Gurdáspur so far as our figures show; but they also own five villages in Siálkot. They say that their ancestors came from Ghazni; or according to another story, from Hindústán.

The Mahal (No. 11)—is a small tribe which appear to be chiefly found in Jálandhar and Amritsar. Their ancestor is said to have been a Rájpút from Modi in the Málwa.

The Aulak (No. 12).—The head-quarters of the Aulak Jats would appear to be in the Amritsar District; but they are found in the northern Málwa, as well as in the Mánjha and west of the Rávi. They are said to be of Solar descent, and their ancestor Aulak lived in the Mánjha. But another story makes their ancestor one Raja Lúi Lák, a Lunar Rájpút. They are related to the Sekhu and Deo tribes, with whom they will not intermarry.

The Gil (No. 13).—The Gil is one of the largest and most important of the Jat tribes. So far as our figures show, their head-quarters are the Lahore and Fírozpur Districts; but they are found all along the Beás and Upper Satluj, and under the hills as far west as Siálkot. Gil, their ancestor, and father of Shergil, the founder of another Jat tribe, was a Jat of Raghobansi Rájpút descent who lived in the Fírozpur District; he was a lineal descendant of Pirthi Pál, Rája of Garh Mithila and a Waria Rájpút, by a Bhúlar Jat wife. The tribe rose to some importance under the Sikhs, and the history of its principal family is told at pages 352 *ff* of Griffin's *Panjáb Chiefs*.

The Sidhu and Barar tribes (Nos. 14—15).—The Sidhu, with its branch the Barár or Sidhu-Barár, is the largest and most important of the Jat tribes of the Panjáb, for from it have [P. 232]
sprung the great Phúlkián families of Patiála, Nábha, and Jínd, and the Barár family of Farídkot. The Sidhu trace their origin to Jaisal, a Bhatti Rájpút and founder of Jaisalmer, who was driven from his kingdom by a successful rebellion and took refuge with Prithi Ráj, Chauhán, the last Hindu King of Dehli. His descendants overran Hissár and Sirsa and gave to the latter tract the name of Bhattiána. Among them was Khíwa, who married a Jat woman of the Ghaggar, and had by her Sidhu, the ancestor of the tribe. Sidhu had four sons, Devi, Búr, Súr, and Rúpach, and from Dhúl, the descendant of Búr, is sprung the Barár tribe. The pure Bhatti Rájpúts of Bhattiána still admit their relationship with the Sidhu and Barár. The early history of the tribes

is told in full detail at pages 1 to 10 and 546 to 518 of Griffin's *Panjáb Rájas*; indeed the whole book is a political history of the descendants of Sidhu; while the leading minor families are noticed at pages 429 to 436 of his *Panjáb Chiefs*. Some further details of their early ancestry will be found at page 8 of the Hisár Settlement Report. The original home of the tribe was the Málwa, and it is still there that they are found in larges t numbers. But they have also spread across the Satluj into Lahore, Amritsar, Jálandhar, and other districts. The Barár who are shown in the Abstract have returned themselves as Sidhu Barár in the Native States and, to the number of 4,220, in Fírozpur, and as Rai Barár in Gurgáon. The rest are returned as Barár simply. Sidhu Barár and Barár are synonymous; but whether I have done rightly in including the Gurgáon Rai Barár I cannot say. Moreover, 26,915 persons in Fírozpur and 2,358 in Nábha have returned their tribe as Sidhu and their clan as Barár, and are included in *both* columns, thus appearing twice over in the Abstract. Mr. Brandreth thus describes the Barár of Fírozpur :—

"The Barárs are said to have been Bhatti Rájpúts, of the same family as the Rájpúts "of Jaisalmer, where their original home was. The name of their ancestor was Sidhu, whose "grandson was named Barár, whence they are called indifferently both Sidhu and Barár. "Either Barár or some descendant of his migrated to Bhatinda, whence his offspring "spread over the neighbouring lands, and are now in possession of a very large tract of "country. They occupy almost the whole of ilaquas Mari, Múdki, Mokatsar, Bhúchon, Mehraj, "Sultan Khan, and Bhudaur in this district, the whole of Farídkot, a great part of Patiála, Nábha, "Jhúmbha and Mallaudh. The Chiefs of all these states belong to the same family. The Bhattis "of Sirsa who embraced Muhammadanism were also originally Bhatti Rájpúts, and related to the "Barárs, but their descent is traced to some common ancestor before the time of Sidhu.

"The Barárs are not equal to the other tribes of Jats as cultivators. They wear finer clothes "and consider themselves a more illustrious race. Many of them were desperate dacoits in former "years, and all the most notorious criminals of this description that have been apprehended and "brought to justice under our rule were Barárs. Female infanticide is said to have been practised "among them to a great extent in former times. I am told that a few years ago there was scarcely "a young girl to be found in any of the Barár villages. This crime is said to have originated in a "deceit that was once practised upon one of the chiefs of Nábha by which his daughter was "betrothed to a man of an inferior tribe; and though he considered himself bound to complete the "marriage, subsequently entered into an agreement with all his tribe to put to death all the "daughters that should be born to them hereafter, in order to prevent the possibility of such a "disgrace occurring again.

"From all accounts, however, this horrid practice has been almost entirely discontinued of late "years, and I can detect no difference now between the proportionate number of female children "in the Barár villages and in villages inhabited by other castes."

The Dhariwal (No. 16).—The Dháríwál, Dháníwál, or Dhálíwál for the name is spelt in all three ways, are also said to be Bhatti Rájpúts, and to take their name from their place of origin Dáránagar. They say that Akbar married the daughter of their Chief Mahr Mithra. They are found chiefly on the Upper Satluj and in the fertile district to the west, their head-quarters being the north-western corner of the Málwa, or Lúdhiána, Fírozpur, and the adjoining parts of Patiála. Mr. Brandreth describes them as splendid cultivators, and the most peaceful and contented portion of the population of the tract.

The Sara (No. 17).—The Sara Jats are, so far as our figures go, chiefly found in the Upper Málwa, in Lúdhiána, Farídkot, and the intervening country; but they also have crossed the Satluj into the fertile district to the north-west. They are said to be descended from a Bhatti Rájpút who 13 generations ago left the Málwa and settled in Gújránwála. But another tradition traces them to Rája Sálon (? Salváhan), a Lunar Rájpút who lived in Jammu, and whose two sons Sara and Basra were the eponymous ancestors of two Jat tribes. I presume that they are distinct from the Sarái noticed under Jats of the western sub-montane.

The Mangat (No. 18).—The Mángat would appear from our figures to be almost confined to Lúdhiána and the adjoining portion of Patiála. I have no information to give about them, unless indeed they are the same as the Mán, described under Jats of eastern sub-montane.

The Dhindsa (No. 19).—The Dhíndsa would appear to be confined to Ambála, Lúdhiána, and the adjoining portion of Patiála. They claim to be descended from Saroha Rájpúts.

The Gandhi (No. 20).—The Gandhi seem to be chiefly found in the same tract with the Mángat just mentioned. About them also I have no particulars to give.

The Chahil (No. 21).—The Cháhil appear to be one of the largest Jat tribes in the Province. They are found in greatest numbers in Patiála, but are very numerous in Ambála and Lúdhiána, Amritsar, and Gurdáspur, and extend all along under the hills as far west as Gújránwála and Siálkot. It is said that Raja Agarsen Súrajbansi had four sons Cháhil, Chhína, Chíma, and Sáhi, and that the four Jat tribes who bear these names are sprung from them. Their original home was Málwa, whence they migrated to the Panjáb. According to another story their ancestor was a Túnwar Rájpút called Rája Rikh, who came from the Deccan and settled at Kahlor. His son Bírsi married a Jat woman, settled at Matti in the Málwa about the time of Akbar, and founded the tribe.

437. Jats of the eastern sub-montane.—The small group of Jats which I shall next describe lie to the north of the Sikh Jats just discussed, all along under the foot of the hills from Ambála to Gurdáspur. There is no definite line of demarcation between them and the Sikh Jats to the south or the Jats of the western sub-montane to the west; and perhaps the only real distinction is that, speaking broadly, the first are Hindus, the second Sikhs, and the third Musalmáns, though of course followers of all three religions are to be found in almost every tribe. In character and position there is nothing to distinguish the tribes I am about to notice, save that they have never enjoyed the political importance which distinguished the Sikh Jats under the Khálsa. Abstract No. 76 on the opposite page gives the figures for these tribes roughly arranged in order from west to east. Here again there is no confusion between Jats and Rájpúts, though the reason of the precision with which they are distinguished is exactly the opposite of that already discussed in the case of the western sub-montane and Sikh Jats. In the Sikh tract the political position of the Jat was so high that he had no wish to be called Rájpút: under the hills the status of the Rájpút is so superior that the Jat has no hope of being called Rájpút. The only one of these tribes of which any considerable number have returned themselves as Jats as well as Rájpúts is the Manj, and that only in Gurdáspur on the extreme confines of the tract. Then I shall consider with the Rájpúts of the same name. In this tract the Settlement Reports are even more meagre than in the last; and my information is correspondingly imperfect.

438. The Jat tribes of the Eastern Sub-montane. The Randhawa (No. 2).—The Randháwa is a large and widely spread tribe whose head-quarters appear to be the Amritsar and Gurdáspur districts, but who are also found in considerable numbers in Lahore, Jálandhar, Hushyárpur, and Patiála. Their founder Randháwa, a Jádu or Bhatti Rájpút, lived in Bíkáner some seven centuries ago; and Kajjal, fifth in descent from him, migrated to Batála which had some time before been founded by Rám Deo another Bhatti. Here the tribe increased in numbers, possessed itself of a very considerable tract of country, and rose to some political importance. The history of the Randháwa family is fully detailed at pages 200 to 218 of the *Panjáb Chiefs*. A few Randháwa have shown themselves also as Bhatti in Gújránwála and as Virk in Fírozpur.

The Kang (No. 3).—This tribe is found chiefly in the angle between the Beás and Satluj, though they have crossed the latter river into Ambála and Fírozpur, and are apparently found in small numbers all along its banks and even on the Lower Indus. Their tradition is that they came from Garh Ghazni. They occupied a position of some considerable political importance in their own tract during the early days of Sikh rule. Mr. Barkley writes of the Jálandhar Kang:—"Most of the Sikh Sardárs of the Nakodar *tahsil* either belong to this tribe, or were connected "with it by marriage when they established their authority there. Tára Singh Gheba (*sic*), who "was their leader at the time of the conquest, was himself of this race and a native of Kang on "the Satluj, where it is said that eighteen Sardárs at one time resided; but on the village being "swept away by the river they dispersed themselves in their separate *jágirs* on both sides of the "river." The Kang are said to claim descent from the Solar Rájpúts of Ajudhia through their ancestor Jogra, father of Kang.

The Sohal (No. 4).—The Sohal are said to be of Chauhán Rájpút origin, their ancestor Sohal belonging to the family of Mahág. They appear to lie to the north of the Kang, close up under and even among the hills; but they are also found along the Satluj, though in smaller numbers.

The Bains (No. 5).—The head-quarters of the Bains appear to be in Hushyárpur and Jálandhar, though they have spread westwards even as far as Báwalpindi, and eastwards into Ambála and the adjoining Native States. They say that they are by origin Janjúa Rájpúts, and that their ancestor Bains came eastwards in the time of Fíroz Sháh. Bains is one of the 36 royal families of Rájpúts, but Tod believes that it is merely a sub-division of the Súryabansi section. They give their name to Baiswára, or the easternmost portion of the Ganges-Jamna *doáb*. The Sardárs of Aláwalpur in Jálandhar are Bains, whose ancestor came from Hushyárpur to Jalla near Sarhind in Nábha some twelve generations ago.

The Buta (No. 6).—The Búta are, as far as our figures go, confined to Hushyárpur. I have no information regarding them, and am not at all certain that they are distinct from the Bhutta of the Western Plains (section 429) and the Buttar of the Sikh tract (section 436).

Abstract No. 76, showing Jat Tribes of the Eastern Sub-montane.

	JATS OF THE EASTERN SUB-MONTANE.						
	1	2	3	4	5	6	7
	Manj.	Randháwa.	Kang.	Sohal.	Bains.	Búta.	Ithwál.
Dehli ...	...	...	...	3	8	...	6,619
Rohtak ...	...	...	786	5	1	...	17
Ambala ...	...	735	2,250	193	1,771	...	3,601
Ludhiana ...	...	1,683	331	1,255	554	13	1,872
Jalandhar ...	...	1,881	5,075	1,550	4,310	...	3,360
Hushyarpur ...	...	2,031	3,273	1,708	11,737	6,162	914
Kangra ...	...	...	...	69	311	...	23
Amritsar ...	58	20,103	3,531	2,932	19	...	445
Gurdaspur ...	1,599	13,030	424	796	3,330	...	1,188
Sialkot ...	81	3,494	689	401	960	...	244
Lahore ...	557	1,166	744	942	565	...	124
Gujranwala ...	38	258	397	114	...	...	36
Firozpur ...	43	973	2,168	123	34	...	129
Rawalpindi ...	...	4	40	...	1,022	...	2
Jhelam ...	7	4	...	...	630	...	...
Multan ...	25	7	917	10	14	...	435
Jhang ...	19	...	11	...	...	...	338
Montgomery ...	16	10	253	4	3	...	641
Muzaffargarh ...	...	...	1,120	...	13	...	55
Derah Ismail Khan ...	...	...	311	...	258	...	27
Derah Ghazi Khan ...	...	1	858	...	...	...	2
Hazara ...	...	...	621	...	...	...	...
British Territory	2,654	45,744	24,315	10,117	26,604	6,175	20,116
Patiala ...	...	4,047	...	1,611	814	...	2,508
Nabha ...	...	550	69	203	539	542	22
Kapurthala ...	...	755	22	280	391	...	123
Jind ...	...	251	...	...	382	...	7
Maler Kotla ...	...	335	...	20	43	...	1
Total Eastern Plains ...	1	6,101	178	2,213	2,170	542	2,668
Bahawalpur ...	...	...	288	...	...	...	307
British Territory	2,654	45,744	24,315	10,117	26,604	6,175	20,116
Native States ...		6,109	466	2,213	2,367	542	3,289
Province ...	2,655	51,853	24,781	12,330	28,971	6,717	23,405

The Ithwal (No. 7).—The Ithwál or Uthwál seem to be found chiefly in Ambála, Lúdhiánah, Jálandhar, and the adjoining territory of Patiála. But unless two distinct names have been confused, they have a curiously large colony in Dehli, which appears to be completely separated from that of Ambála. They are said to be descended from a Súrajbansi Rájpút called Mahárāj who received the nickname of Unthwál from his love for camel-riding!

439. **The Jats of the south-eastern districts.**—The last group of Jat tribes that I have to discuss is that which occupies the Jamna districts, Jínd, Rohtak, and Hissár. They call themselves Ját not Jat, and are the same people in every respect as the Ját of the Jamna-Ganges *doáb* and the lower Jamna valley, differing however in little save religion from the great Sikh Jat tribes of the Málwa; though perhaps the latter, inhabiting as they do the wide unirrigated plains of the central States, are of slightly finer physique than their neighbours of the damper riverain. The eastern Játs are almost without exception Hindu, the few among them who are Musalmán being known as Múla or "unfortunate," and dating their conversion almost without exception from an ancestor who was taken as a hostage to Dehli and there forcibly circumcised. Indeed these men were not unfrequently received back into caste on their return from captivity, and their descendants are in this case Hindus, though still known as Múla. Their traditions show them to have come up either from Bíkáner and Rájpútána, or northwards along the Jamna valley, and very few of them appear to have come from the Panjáb to the Jamna. The Játs of Gurgáon indeed still look upon the Rája of Bhartpur as their natural leader, and the fall of Bhartpur made such an impression on their minds that old men still refer to it as the æra from which they date events.

The Ját of these parts is, if anything, even a better cultivator than the Sikh Jat; and that, chiefly because his women assist him so largely in the field, performing all sorts of agricultural labour whether light or heavy, except ploughing for which they have not sufficient strength, and sowing which is under all circumstances a prerogative strictly confined to the made sex. Directly we leave the south-eastern districts and pass into the Sikh tract, women cease to perform the harder kinds of field-work, even among the Jats; while in the Musalmán districts they do not work at all in the fields. So essentially is the Ját a husbandman, and so especially is he *the* husbandman of these parts, that when asked his caste he will quite as often reply *zamíndár* [P. 234] as Ját, the two names being in that sense used as synonymous. The social standing of the Ját is that which the Gújar, Ahír, and Ror enjoy; in fact these four castes eat and smoke together. They stand at the head of the castes who practise *karewa* or widow-marriage, a good deal below the Rájpút, but far above the castes who grow vegetables, such as Aráín and Máli. If the social scale is regulated by the rules of the Hindu religion they come below Banyas, who are admittedly better Hindús. But the manly Ját despises the money-grubbing Banya, and all other castes and tribes agree with him.

In the extreme south-eastern corner of the Panjáb the Játs who have come in from the north and west, from Rájpútána and the Panjáb, are known as Dhe, to distinguish them from the original Ját tribes of the neighbourhood who are collectively called Hele, the two sections abstaining from intermarriage and having in some respects different customs. In Sirsa again, that meeting place of races, where the Bágri Ját from the Bíkáner prairies, the Sikh Jat from the Málwa, and the Musalmán Jat from the Satluj valley, meet the Ját of Hissár, the last are distinguished as Dese and the Musalmán Jats as Pachháde or western; but these terms appear to be unknown to the people in their respective homes. There the superiority of the Sikh and Dese Jats over the stunted Bágri and the indolent enervated Jat of the Satluj is most strikingly apparent.

There is an extraordinary division of the Játs of Dehli, Rohtak, and Karnál, and indeed of the other land-owning castes who have for the most part taken the one side or the other, into two factions known as Dehia and Haulánia. I quote the following passage from my Settlement Report of Karnál and Pánípat :—

"The Dehias are called after a Ját tribe of that name, with its head-quarters about Bhatgánw "in Sunpat, having originally come from Bawána near Dehli. The Haulánia faction is headed by "the Ghatwál or Malak Játs, whose head-quarters are Dher-ka-Ahulána in Gohána, and who were, "owing to their successful opposition to the Rájpúts, the accepted heads of the Játs in these parts. "Some one of the Emperors called them in to assist him in coercing the Mandahár Rájpúts, and "thus the old enmity was strengthened. The Dehia Játs, growing powerful, became jealous of the "supremacy of the Ghatwáls and joined the Mandahárs against them. Thus the country side was "divided into two factions; the Gújars and Tagas of the tract, the Jáglán Játs of *thapa* Naultha, "and the Látmár Játs of Rohtak joining the Dehias, and the Húda Játs of Rohtak, and most of "the Játs of the tract except the Jágláns, joining the Hauláinias. In the mutiny, disturbances "took place in the Rohtak district between these two factions, and the Mandahárs of the Nardak "ravaged the Haulánias in the south of the tract. And in framing my *sails* I had to alter my "proposed division so as to separate a Dehia village which I had included with Haulánias, and "which objected in consequence. The Dehia is also called the Ját, and occasionally the Mandahár "faction. Even Sir H. Elliott seems to have been unaware of the existence of these factions. The "Játs and Rájpúts seem, independently of these divisions, to consider each other, tribally speaking, "as natural enemies; and I have often been assured by Játs, though I do not believe it, that they "would not dare to go into a Rájpút village at night."

Mr. Maconachie quotes a Dehli tradition which makes two brothers from Rájpútána called Mom and Som the respective ancestors of the Haulánia Rájpúts of the *doáb* and the Haulánia Játs of Rohtak.

Here again, in the south-eastern districts, the distinction between Ját and Rájpút is definite and well-marked, the Ját always practising and the Rájpút always abstaining from *karewa*; though I do not think that here a family could raise itself from the former to the latter caste by discontinuing the custom, as would appear to be possible elsewhere. The figures for the tribes we are to consider are given in Abstract No. 77 on the opposite page,* the
*P. 128-29. tribes being roughly arranged from north to south down the Jamna valley, and then westwards along the southern border of the Province. The last five tribes will be considered under Rájpúts; and they are shown in this abstract, not because they are returned as Jats especially in this part of the Panjáb, but because the Rájpút tribes to which they belong will be discussed under the head of Rájpúts of the Eastern Plains. The tribes in this group are neither so large nor so important as those of the Sikh tracts, and in many cases I have little or no information to give concerning them. There seems a great tendency in these parts to split up into small clans, retaining the tradition of common tribal descent, but commonly using the name of the clan and not of the tribe.

440. The Jat tribes of the South-Eastern Districts. The Ghatwal (No. 1).—This is the only one of the tribes now under consideration who trace their origin from Ghar Ghazni; and even they place that city in the Deccan and not in Afghánistán. They claim descent from Saroha Rájpúts. Their head-quarters are at Ahulána in the Gohána *tahsil* of Rohtak, and they occupy the country between it and the Jamna, being numerous in the north of Dehli and the south of Karnál. I suspect that our figures for Rohtak are considerably under the truth. Ahulána is said to have been founded 22 generations ago, and gives its name to the Haulánia faction already mentioned. The Ghatwál are often called Malak, a title they are said to have obtained as follows:—

"In the old days of Rájpút ascendancy the Rájpúts would not allow Játs to cover their heads "with a turban, nor to wear any red clothes, nor to put a crown (*mor*) on the head of their "bridegroom, or a jewel (*nat*) in their women's noses. They also used to levy seignorial rights

Abstract No. 77, showing the Jat Tribes [P. 235]

	JATS OF THE									
	1	2	3	4	5	6	7	8	9	10
	Ghatwál.	Dágar.	Jákhar.	Sahráwat.	Dehia.	Golia.	Ráthi.	Khatri.	Dalál.	Ahláwat.
Dehli	4,434	8,558	122	4,292	14,334	...	1,476	11,008	1,860	1,746
Gurgaon	109	4,815	5,116	2,485	37	...	1,156	...	240	...
Karnal	261	40	3	740	...	3,070	718	...	22	2,763
Hissar	2,392	61	...	617	441	...	452	11	1,531	163
Rohtak	2,219	2,065	4,240	4,232	9,740	16,800	6,410	1,951	7,883	6,809
Sirsa	1	13	...	...	146	...	...	94	14	1
Ambala	46	...	...	34	...	53	359	...	...	41
Ludhiana	20	...	336	...	...	66	2,930	...	5	...
Jalandhar	550	...	2,769	...	...	...	...	...	...	...
Gurdaspur	29	...	...	...	...	...	...	...	...	...
Sialkot	238	...	...	...	...	...	...	...	583	...
Rawalpindi	138	...	...	...	...	138	2	...	443	...
British Territory ...	11,814	15,561	12,678	12,409	24,698	20,216	13,573	13,228	12,581	11,584
Patiala	77	162	168	1,204	80	...	150	1,939	313	...
Jind	164	60	...	635	8	93	...	20	1,342	765
Total Eastern Plains ...	315	287	230	1,958	127	108	440	1,959	1,794	801
Bahawalpur ...	797	...	...	...	...	...	...	...	45	...
Total Hill States ...	...	...	10	...	1	...	...	...	...	1
British Territory...	11,814	15,561	12,678	12,409	24,698	20,216	13,573	13,228	12,581	11,584
Native States ...	1,112	287	240	1,958	128	108	440	1,959	1,839	802
Province ...	12,926	15,848	12,918	14,367	24,826	20,324	14,013	15,187	14,420	12,386

of the South-Eastern Districts.

SOUTH-EASTERN DISTRICTS.

11	12	13	14	15	16	17	18	19	20	21	22
Deswál.	Dhankar.	Phoghát.	Sángwán.	Pawánia.	Bahniwál.	Nain.	Ráwat.	Bágri.	Chauhán.	Mandahár.	Túnwar.
720	...	196	288	...	...	928	2,669	...	257	...	141
1,408	772	1,222	33	157	...	...	2,214	...	1,580	...	5,933
2,045	39	5	508	...	...	351	45	...	635	...	39
52	...	372	2,263	7,278	3,726	1,074	51	872	677	...	219
4,099	4,039	2,386	4,604	2,163	1,739	111	44	2	121	...	205
...	...	21	45	1,583	1,846	201	...	32	241	...	53
356	9	...	16	3,083	1,160	233	23	262	275	1,570	...
...	...	...	...	...	146	...	...	125	616	158	[illegible]
...	...	...	...	...	...	...	...	...	292	...	176
375	...	...	...	...	...	...	...	...	254	...	50
...	...	...	...	...	637	...	...	930	1,524	89	1,324
...	...	...	...	...	...	...	...	45	1,037	...	92
9,055	4,898	4,202	7,757	14,812	9.411	3,074	5,046	3,519	27,109	1,827	12,63[illegible]
...	...	39	268	1,086	1,964	5,884	83	1,404	2,002	3,438	...
671	38	2,958	7,682	1,063	...	1	...	22	56	200	...
720	38	3,081	8,222	3,316	1,967	5,895	83	2,250	3,504	5,311	1
...	...	...	...	...	...	...	...	...	2	...	...
...	...	...	...	...	...	...	...	1	44	1	...
9,055	4,898	4,202	7,757	14,812	9,411	3,074	5,046	3,519	27,109	1,827	12,638
720	38	3,081	8,222	3,316	1,967	5,895	83	2,251	3,550	5,312	1
9,775	4,936	7,283	15,979	18,128	11,378	8,969	5,129	5,770	30,659	7,139	12,639

"from virgin brides. Even to this day Rájpúts will not allow inferior castes to wear red clothes or "ample loin clothes in their villages. The Ghatwáls obtained some successes over the Rájpúts, "especially over the Mandahárs of the *doáb* near Deoban and Manglaur, and over those of the Bágar "near Kálánaur and Dádri, and removed the obnoxious prohibitions. They thus acquired the title "of *Malak* (master) and a red turban as their distinguishing mark; and to this day a Ját with a "red pagri is most probably a Ghatwál."

Mr. Fanshawe says that the title is a mere nickname conferred by a Malik or chief called Rai Sál; yet in Rohtak they appear generally to be called Malak rather than Ghatwál, and perhaps this is the cause of the smallness of the Rohtak figures, though I ordered the two names to be taken together. Who the Ghatwál of Bahávalpur are, I cannot explain. I may notice that there are in several parts of India, and especially in Monghyr and its neighbourhood, tribes of low-class Rájpúts called Ghatwáls, who hold or held assignments of revenue on condition of defending the *ghá ts* or passes in the hills by which the hill tribes were wont to make prædatory incursions into the plains below.

The Dagar (No. 2).—The Dágar are numerous in Dehli and Gurgáon and there is a small colony in Rohtak. I have no information concerning them.

The Jakhar and Sangwan (Nos. 3 and 14).—These tribes are said to be descended from a Chauhán Rájpút only 20 generations back, who came from Bíkáner, and whose four sons founded the Jákhar, Sángwán, Piru, and Kádíán Játs, for the last two of which I do not show separate figures as they are of but little importance. The Sángwán are most numerous in Jínd and Hissár, though there is a small colony of them in Rohtak also; while the Jákhar are almost confined to Gurgáon and the adjoining Jhajjar *tahsíl* of Rohtak.

The Sahrawat (No. 4).—The Sahráwat claim to be descended from Sahra, a son or grandson of Rája Anangpál Túnwar. They are almost confined to Dehli, Gurgáon, Rohtak, and the adjoining Patiála territory. In Rohtak their settlement dates from some 25 generations back.

The Dehia (No. 5).—This is the tribe which has given its name to the Dehia faction mentioned in section 439. They are found on the north-eastern border of the Sámpla and the adjoining portion of the Sunpat *tahsíl* of Rohtak and Dehli. They claim to be descended from a Chauhán Rájpút named Mánik Rai by a Dhankar Ját woman. This is probably the Mánik Rai Chauhán who founded Hánsi. Another account makes their ancester Dhadhíj, son of Haria Harpál, son of Prithi Rája. The Dehia is one of the 36 royal tribes of Rájpúts, whose original home was about the confluence of the Satluj with the Indus. They are probably the Dahiæ of Alexander.

The Golia (No. 6).—The Golia or Gawália are a very curious tribe. They declare that they [P. 236]
were originally Bráhmans who lost caste by inadvertently drinking liquor placed outside a distiller's house in large vessels (*gol*). The Local Bráhmans apparently admit the truth of this story. They now intermarry with Játs, but not with the Dágar or Salanki; for while they were Bráhmans the latter were their clients, while when they first lost caste the former alone of all Ját tribes would give them their daughters to wife, and so have been adopted as *quási*-brethren. They came from Indor to Rohtak some 30 generations ago. They are only found in Rohtak and Karnál. The scattered entries probably refer to a few Gwálas or Ahírs who have been returned as Játs.

The Rathi (No. 7).—The word Ráth is used in Sirsa as synonymous with Pachháda, to denote Musalmán Jats or Rájpúts from the Satluj. It is said to mean "strong-handed" or *zabardast*. In Rohtak, however, there is a distinct Ráthi tribe of Játs who claim to be by origin Túnwar Rájpúts, and are among the oldest inhabitants of the tract. They are descended from a brother of the ancestor of the Rohal and Dhankar Játs, and the three tribes do not intermarry. They are found in Dehli and Gurgáon as well as in Rohtak, and apparently in Lúdhiána, though it is perhaps doubtful whether these last are the same tribe.

The Khatri (No. 8).—This tribe appears to be very numerous in Dehli, and to be found also in Rohtak and Patiála. I have no information regarding them.

The Dalal (No. 9).—This is another of the great Rohtak tribes, and is found also in the adjoining territory of Dehli, Hissár and Jínd. They claim to be descended from a Ráthor Rájpút who settled in Rohtak and married a Bargújar Ját woman some 30 generations back. By her he had four sons from whom the Dalál, Deswál, Mán, and Sewág (? Sewal) Játs have sprung, and these four tribes do not intermarry. But compare the account of the origin of the Mán given in section 435. The same four tribes have a tradition of common descent and a prohibition against inter-marriage in Karnál also.

The Ahlawat (No. 10).—The Ahláwat are said to be descended from a Chauhán Rájpút who came from Sámbhar in Jaipur some 30 generations ago. From him sprang the Ahláwat, Olián, Birma, Máre, and Jún Játs who do not intermarry. The tribe is found in Rohtak, Dehli and Karnál. Its members worship a common ancestor called Sadu Deb.

The Deswal (No. 11).—The Deswál or "men of the country" are, as already stated, sprung from the same stock as the Dalál. They are most numerous in Rohtak, Gurgáon, and Karnál. In Mewár and Ajmer, Musalmán Rájpúts are called Deswál, and are hardly recognised as Rájpúts.

The Dhankar (No. 12).—I have said that the Dhankar are of the same stock as the Ráthi. They are almost confined to Jhajjar in Rohtak, and are perhaps nothing more than a local clan of the Ráthi tribe.

The Phogat (No. 13).—This tribe possesses some importance in Jínd, and has spread into the neighbouring portions of Gurgáon and Rohtak. The only fact I have concerning them is that they will not intermarry with the Deswál; but the reason is not explained.

The Sangwan (No. 14).—The Sángwán are descended from the ancestor of the Jákhar already mentioned. Their head-quarters are in Jínd; but they are also found in Rohtak and Hissár.

The Pawania (No. 15).—The Pawánia are a Hissár tribe who are also found in Rohtak, Sirsa, Jínd, and the detached portion of Patiála and, curiously enough, in Ambála. I have no information to give regarding them.

The Bahniwal (No. 16).—The Bahníwál are found chiefly in the Hissár division and Patiála. They are also found on the Lower Satluj in Montgomery, where they have probably returned themselves as Bhatti Rájpúts, which they claim to be by descent. Mr. Purser says of them:—"In "numbers they are weak; but in love of robbery they yield to none of the tribes." They gave much trouble in 1857. In the 15th century the Bahníwál held one of the six cantons into which Bíkáner was then divided.

The Nain (No. 17).—The Nain are chiefly found in the detached portions of Patiála, but have spread into Hissár and Dehli. I have no information regarding them.

THE RÁJPÚT (CASTE No. 2).

441. The Rajputs of the Panjab.—The distribution of the Rájpúts
* P. 98-9. and allied races is shown in Abstract No. 71, page 219.* I do not propose to enter into any detailed description or discussion of the Rájpút. He is much the same all over Northern India, and more has been published about him than about any other Indian caste. The great authority is Tod's *Rájásthán*, while both Elliott and Sherring give much useful information. I have already expressed in sections 422-3 my views as to the identity of the Jat and Rájpút stock as it stands at present, and how the Rájpúts merely consist of the royal families of that stock. I might indeed have gone further, and have said that a tribe of any caste whatever which had in ancient times possessed supreme power throughout any fairly extensive tract of country, would be classed as Rájpút. It seems to me almost certain that some of the so-called Rájpút royal families were aboriginal; and notably the Chandel. How the aborigines of the Nepal Himálayas rose to be Kshatriya is well told by Hodgson in his Essay on the Military Tribes of Nepál. He points out that when the Bráhmans were driven up into the hills by the advancing tide of Mahomedan conquest, they wedded with the aboriginal women whom they found there. But to render this possible it was necessary to conciliate the people among whom they had come to dwell; and they called their first converts among them Kshatriya, while to their own offspring by the hill women they gave not only Kshatriya rank and privileges, but Brahminical patronymics.

"From these two roots mainly sprang the now numerous, predominant, and extensively "ramified tribe of Khas—originally the name of a small clan of creedless barbarians, but now the "proud title of the Kshatriya or military order of Nepal. Thus too the key to the anomalous "nomenclature of so many stirpes of these military tribes is to be sought in the nomenclature of the "sacred order." And even now in spite of the yearly increasing sway of Hinduism, and of the efforts of Bráhmans in high office to abolish the custom, the Khas still insist that "the fruits of "commerce (for marriage is now out of the question) between their females and males of the "sacred order shall be ranked as Kshatriya, wear the thread, and assume the patronymic title." So again, when the Rájpút immigrants from the plains took aboriginal women in concubinage (and concubinage among the hill people is for all purposes of legitimacy and inheritance the same as marriage), "they were permitted to give their children so begotten the patronymic title only, not "the rank of Kshatriya. But their children again, if they married for two generations with the "Khas, became pure Khas, or real Kshatriyas in point of privilege and rank though no longer so in "name. They were Khas, not Kshatriya, and yet they bore the proud title cognominal of the "martial order of the Hindus, and were in the land of their nativity entitled to every prerogative "which Kshatriya birth confers in Hindústán."

A reference to my description of the Kanets of our hills will show that something of the same sort has gone on in the Panjáb Himálayas, though necessarily in a much lower degree, since here the Aryan and not the aborigine was predominant; and the description of the Hill Rájpúts, and still more of the Thakars and Ráthis, which will be found in this section under their respective headings, will show how, if the Turanian is not as in Nepal admitted to Kshatriya rank, it is at any rate impossible to draw any line among the Aryan races, all above which shall be Rájpúts and all below it non-Rájpúts. As the Kángra proverb runs—"In the seventh generation the Ghirathni becomes a "queen."

The Rájpúts of the Panjáb are fine brave men, and retain the feudal instinct more strongly developed than perhaps any other non-menial caste, the tribal heads wielding extraordinary authority. They are very tenacious of the integrity of their communal property in the village lands, seldom admitting strangers to share it with them. Pride of blood is their strongest characteristic, for pride of blood is the very essence of their Rájpúthood. They are lazy and poor husbandmen and much prefer pastoral to agricultural pursuits, looking upon all manual labour as derogatory and upon the actual operation of ploughing as degrading; and it is only the poorest class of Rájpút who will himself follow the plough. They are, in most parts of the Panjáb plains, cattle-stealers by ancestral profession; but they exercise their calling in a gentlemanly way, and there is certainly honour among Rájpút thieves. [P. 237]

442. The Rajput tribes of the Panjab.—The Rájpúts of the Panjáb may be broadly divided into four groups, each of which I shall discuss separately in the following paragraphs. First come the Rájpúts of the Dehli Territory and Jamna valley, for the most part belonging to the two great tribes of Chaubán and Túnwar which gave Dehli its most famous dynasties. Next come the Rájpúts of the river valleys of the Western Plains, many of them hardly or not at all to be distinguished from Jats, and belonging for the most part to the Bhatti of Jaisalmer and Bíkáner, and their predecessors the Punwár. The third group is the Rájpúts of the western hills including the Salt-range Tract, comprising both dominant tribes of proud position such as the Janjuá and mongrel Rájpúts from the Jammu hills, and descendants either of the Yádúbansi (Bhatti) dynasty of Kashmír and the mythical Rája Rasálu of Siálkot so famous in Panjáb folklore, or of a group of tribes, apparently of Punwár origin, which now hold the hills on either bank of the Jahlam. Finally we have the Rájpúts of the Kángra hills of whom the Katoch may be taken as the type, so ancient that their very origin and advent to their present abodes are lost in the past; and the Rájpúts of the lower hills which fringe the Panjáb Himálayas. With the Rájpúts I take the Thakar and Ráthi who are lower grades of Rájpúts rather than separate castes, and the Ráwat whose position is still more difficult of definition. It will be noticed that I do not mention the Rájpúts of the Sikh tract, of the central districts, and of the Phúlkián States of the Eastern Plains. As a fact they are few, and the few there are are unimportant. Nor have I mentioned the Rájpúts of the frontier districts, for here again they are insignificant both in numbers and importance. The reason why the Rájpút disappears before the Sikh, the Pathán, and the Biloch I have already explained in section 422. Abstract No. 71, on page 219,* shows the distribution of Rájpúts and allied castes. The small number in the Hill States is curious. * P. 98-9.

There only the ruling families are Rájpút, the mass of the peasantry consisting of Kanets or Ghiraths, if indeed these last can be separated at all from Ráthis and Ráwats. In the Dehli division and Rohtak the Jat has largely taken the place of the Rájpút; but such Rájpúts as there are are Rájpúts in very deed. In the Multán division the number of Rájpúts returned is very large; but I have already shown how large a proportion of them should more properly be classed as Jats, if indeed any distinction can be drawn between the two.

443. **Tribal statistics for Rajputs.**—The figures for tribes will be given under the respective groups to which they belong. They are more than usually inaccurate, partly because a Rájpút is so difficult of definition, but still more because the Rájpúts are divided into a few great tribes or royal races as they are commonly called, the *kuls* of the Rájpút annals, and each of these tribes again into innumerable local clans or *sachi* or *gots*. Almost every Rájpút will refer himself rightly or wrongly to some one of the great *kuls*, as well as state the local clan to which he beyond all doubt belongs; and thus we have members of the same clan and descendants of the same ancestor returning themselves as belonging to different tribes, while multitudes of persons appear twice over in the Abstracts, first under their tribe or *kul*, and again under their clan or *got*.

It must be remembered that such of the figures as are shown for Rájpút tribes in the Abstracts of the following pages under the head Jat, refer to people who have returned themselves as Jat by *caste*, and Bhatti, Chauhán, and so forth by *tribe*. In the great majority of cases this latter entry represents mere traditional origin, rather than that the people in question actually claim that they are Bhatti or Chauhán at the present moment. In many cases they have returned their Jat tribe as well. Abstract No. 78 below gives the numbers entered for various tribes under Jat and Rájpút, respectively, and shows how extensively this sort of entry has been made.

Abstract No. 78, showing Tribes entered both as Jat and as Rajput.

JOINT LIST OF JAT AND RAJPUT CLANS.

Clans.	British Territory.		Native States.	
	Jats.	Rájpúts.	Jats.	Rájpúts.
Bágri	3,519	11,141	2,251	908
Bhakrál	4,863	5,144	13	3,378
Bahníwál	9,411	43	1,967	...
Bhatti	94,665	204,569	1,193	38,262
Bhutta	20,431	4,891	2,108	194
Chhádhár	26,387	16,435	17	1,311
Chauhán	27,109	145,195	3,550	18,831
Dhaniál	10,026	4,388	...	...
Dhudhi	12,315	7,649	1,087	113
Gondal	47,276	43,220	325	10
Janjuá	8,419	38,532	15	11
Joya	12,338	25,301	...	5,262
Kharral	18,582	14,242	237	2,042
Khíchi	3,337	12,721	254	608
Khokhar	42,110	45,731	221	9,649
Langáh	9,083	2,348	50	1
Mahal	6,598	118	1,032	721
Mandahár	1,827	14,693	15,312	2,637
Manhás	6,570	49,424	15	216
Manj	2,654	26,309	1	2,676
Mekan	3,157	5,968	...	...

Abstract No. 78, showing Tribes entered both as Jat and as Rajput— concluded.

JOINT LIST OF JAT AND RAJPUT CLANS.

Clans.	British Territory.		Native States.	
	Jats.	Rájpúts.	Jats.	Rájpúts.
Punwár	16,959	53,151	887	7,853
Ránjha	10,903	7,490	53	...
Ráthi	13,573	30	440	...
Ráwat	5,046	2,809	83	113
Siál	17,093	76,957	273	256
Súmra	12,558	218	...	2,101
Túnwar	12,638	35,919	1	3,200
Tárar	18,925	4,228	19	...
Virk	35,527	7,118	589	...
Wattu	2,963	17,484	244	3,704

444. Rajputs of the Eastern Plains.—The tribes which I shall first discuss [P. 238] are divided into two groups. All but the last four are almost confined to the Dehli territory, at least as Rájpúts proper, and are roughly arranged in order from north to south down the Jamna valley, and then westwards through Rohtak and Hissár. The last four tribes carry on the series through Patiála, Fírozpur, and Gújránwála, and connect the Rájpúts of the Eastern with those of the Western Plains. The first group belongs chiefly to the great royal families of the Rájpúts who, occupying the Dehli territory, have not as a rule superseded their old tribal designation by a local name, as has been so often the case in the west of the Panjáb. The great majority of them are descendants of the Túnwar and Chauhán dynasties of Dehli. Their local distribution is fairly well marked, the Túnwar lying to the north-west of the first group, and shutting off the Jat Tribes of the Central Plains from the Rájpúts of the Dehli territory, their line being broken only, I believe, by the Chauhán colony on the Ghaggar of the Hissár border. Next to them come the Chauhán, Mandahár, and Pundír of the Kurukshetr, and the Ráwat, Gaurwa, Bargújar, and Jádu of Dehli and Gurgáon, followed by the Játu, themselves Túnwar, and the Bágri of Hissár. The Punwár colony of Rohtak will be discussed with the Rájpúts of the Western Plains. The Jats who are shown in the Abstract on the next page* are very largely if not wholly true Jats, who have returned a real Jat tribe and have been shown under that tribe among Jats, but have also entered the Rájpút tribe from which they claim to be descended, and are thus entered under that head also. The Rájpút of these parts is a true Rájpút. Living in the shadow of Dehli, the capital of his ancestral dynasties, he clings to the traditions of his caste. He cultivates largely, for little other occupation is left him ; but he cultivates badly, for his women are more or less strictly secluded and never work in the fields, while he considers it degrading to actually follow the plough, and will always employ hired ploughmen if he can possibly afford it. He is a great cattle-grazier and as great a cattle-thief. His tribal feeling is strong, and the heads of the village or local group of villages have great influence. He is proud, lazy, sometimes

* P. 136-37.

turbulent, but generally with something more of the gentleman about him than we find in the more rustic Jat. Abstract No. 79 on the opposite page* gives the distribution of these tribes.

* p. 136-37.

445. The Rajput tribes of the Eastern Plains. The Tunwar (No. 1).—The Túnwar, although a sub-division of the Jádúbansi, is generally reckoned as one of the 36 royal tribes of Rájpúts. It furnished India with the dynasty of Vikramáditya, the beacon of later Hindu chronology, and Dehli with its last Indian rulers, Anangpál, the last Túnwar Rája, abdicating in favour of his Chauhán grandchild Pirthi Ráj, in whose time the Musalmáns conquered North-Western India. An early Anangpál Túnwar founded in 792 A.D. the city of Dehli on the ruins of the ancient Indrapat, and his dynasty ruled there for three and a half centuries. It is therefore natural that the Túnwar should be found chiefly in the eastern districts of the Province. In Dehli itself, indeed, they are less numerous than might have been expected. But they are exceedingly numerous in Ambála, Hissár, and Sirsa. The name being a famous one, many Rájpúts of various tribes which have no real connection with the Túnwar have returned it. Thus 1,200 men in Kárnal are returned as Chauhán Túnwar, who are probably Chauháns. So in Ráwalpindi 1,939 men are shown as Bhatti Túnwar, though here the confusion is more excusable, being justified by origin though not by modern usage. The figures are of course shown twice over in each case. The figures for Túnwar Jats probably represent nothing more than traditional origin. Half the number are in Gurgáon, where there is a considerable settlement of Túnwar Rájpúts.

The Túnwar are the westernmost of the great Rájpút tribes of the Eastern Panjáb. When ejected from Dehli they are said to have settled at Púndri in Karnál, on the Ambála border and once the seat of the Pundír, and thence to have spread both north and south. They now occupy Hariána or the greater part of the Hissár district, and stretch across Karnál and the south of Patiála into the west of the Ambála district, separating the Chauhán and other Rájpúts who hold the Jamna districts to the east of them from the great Jat tribes of the Málwa which lie to their west. There is, however, a Chauhán colony to the north-west of them on the Lower Ghaggar in the Hissár district and Patiála. The Játu of Hariána are a Túnwar clan.

The Chauhan (No. 2).—The Chauhán is one of the Agnikula tribes and also one of the 36 royal families. Tod calls them the most valiant of the whole Rájpút race, and to them belonged the last Hindu ruler of Hindústán. Before the seat of their power was moved to Dehli, Ajmer and Sámbhar in Jaipur seem to have been their home. After their ejectment from Dehli they are said to have crossed the Jamna to Sambhal in Murádábád, and there still dwell the genealogists and bards of the Chauhán of the Nardak of Karnál and Ambála. This tract, the ancient Kurukshetr or battle-field of the Kauravas and Pándavas, is still occupied very largely by Rájpúts; in the west by the Túnwar, themselves descendants of the Pándavas, but for the most part by the Chauhán whose central village is Júndla in Karnál, and who occupy all the country lying immediately to the east of the Túnwar tract in Ambála and Karnál and the adjoining parts of Patiála, Nábha, and Jínd. All this country was held by the Pundír Rájpúts till the Chauhán came over from Sambhal under Rána Har Rai some 20 generations ago, probably in the time of Bahlol Lodi, and drove the Pundír across the Jamna. The Chauhán appear from our figures to be numerous throughout the remaining districts of the Dehli and Hissár divisions and in Gújránwála, Fírozpur, Ráwalpindi, and Sháhpur. But Chauhán being perhaps the most famous name in the Rájpút annals, many people who have no title to it have shown themselves as Chauhán. In Karnál 1,520 Pundír, 850 Punwár, 1,200 Túnwar, 6,300 Mandahár, and some 900 of other tribes have shown themselves as Chauhán also. In Sháhpur 6,700 persons are returned as Gondal Chauhán, and this accounts for the so-called Chauháns of this district. The Jat Chauháns, too, are probably for the most part Jat tribes of alleged Chauhán origin. Thus among the Jats, in Gújránwála 2,200 Chíma and nearly 1,000 persons of other Jat tribes, in Fírozpur 600 Joya and 200 Sidhu, and in Jahlam 2,000, and in Gújrát 650 Gondal, have returned themselves as Chauhán also, and so in many minor instances. All these figures are shown twice over. The Khíchi and Varaich are also Chauhán clans numerous in the Panjáb, and have perhaps sometimes returned themselves as Chauhán only. The Chauhán of the Dehli district have taken to widow-marriage, and are no longer recognised by their fellow Rájpúts. The Chauhán of Gurgáon have, however, retained their pre-eminent position, and are connected with the Chauhán family of Nímrána, a small State now subject to Alwar.

The Mandahar (No. 3).—The Mandahár are almost confined to the Nardak of Karnál, Ambála and the neighbouring portion of Patiála. They are said to have come from Ajudhia to Jínd, driving the Chandel and Brá Rájpúts who occupied the tract into the Siwáliks and across the Ghaggar respectively. They then fixed their capital at Kaláyit in Patiála, with minor centres at Safídon in Jínd and Asandh in Karnál. They lie more or less between the Túnwar and Chauhán of the tract. But they have in more recent times spread down below the Chauhán into the Jamna riverain of the Karnál district, with Gharaunda as a local centre. They were settled in those parts before the advent of the Chauhán, and were chastised at Samána in Patiála by Fíroz Sháh. The Mandahár, Kandahár, Bargújar, Sankarwál, and Panihár Rájpúts are said to be descended from Láwa, a son of Rám Chandra, and therefore to be Solar Rájpúts; and in Karnál at

Abstract No. 79, showing the Rajput [P. 239]

	RAJPUTS OF THE									
	1		2		3		4	5		
	Tunwar.		Chauhan.		Mandahar.			Rawat.		
	Rájpút.	Jat.	Rájpút.	Jat.	Rájpút.	Jat.	Pundir.	Rájpút.	Jat.	Ráwat (Caste No. 32).
Dehli	1,038	141	3,656	257	38	...	10	1,323	2,069	...
Gurgaon	1,754	5,933	9,287	1,580	138	...	25	15	2,214	...
Karnál	3,076	30	31,642	635	10,743	...	1,753	8	45	1,025
Hissar	6,102	219	6,010	677	243	...	1	10	51	...
Rohtak	1,644	205	5,884	121	253	...	50	...	44	...
Sirsa	4,042	53	4,120	241	19	...	10	13	...	...
Ambala	9,867	...	43,555	275	2,270	1,570	2,106	...	23	4,403
Ludhiána	527	56	1,835	616	101	159	3	...	...	1,807
Jalandhar	928	176	1,515	282	...	...	...	...	...	2,438
Hushyárpur	170	...	2,402	75	...	...	53	405	...	275
Kángra	338	...	1,136	12	...	...	173	667	...	1
Amritsar	426	30	670	768	...	...	...	...	...	...
Gurdáspur	477	50	1,632	254	116	...	...	...	...	...
Sialkot	217	1,324	470	1,524	...	89	...	...	...	...
Lahore	707	201	2,230	946	...	...	...	...	...	
Gujránwála	140	724	4,834	7,604	...	...	...	...	...	...
Firozpur	1,223	2,763	4,785	1,405	457	10	...	274	...	32
Ráwalpindi	2,167	62	3,620	1,037	60	...	...	...	...	...
Jhelum	240	246	1,594	1,989	220	...	...	...	...	...
Gujrát	56	203	88	1,866	10	...	...	...	...	...
Shahpur	98	51	8,042	172	16	...	...	...	...	...
Multán	31	3	2,134	505	...	...	8	1	...	...
Jhang	157	27	226	165	...	...	...	...	...	...
Montgomery	439	41	1,355	1,702	...	...	...	2	...	...
Muzaffargarh	1	27	222	1,103	...	...	...	...	...	...
British Territory ...	**85,919**	**12,638**	**145,195**	**27,109**	**14,693**	**1,827**	**4,296**	**2,809**	**5,046**	**9,994**
Patiála	1,221	...	5,975	2,902	2,053	3,438	42	...	83	3,243
Nábha	821	...	2,083	480	68	218	5	41	...	266
Kapurthala	23	...	487	5	...	162	...	24	...	600
Jind	356	...	1,248	56	469	200	...	2	...	302
Faridkot	105	...	308	25	3	45	...	...	...	23
Maler Kotla	208	...	570	8	6	1,180	5	...	...	1,800
Kalsia	49	...	906	20	36	50	84	...	...	701
Total East. Plains ...	2,907	1	14,843	3,504	2,635	5,311	136	67	83	7,033
Baháwalpur	...	...	2,430	2	...	...	...	...	...	...
Total Hill States ...	392	...	1,549	41	2	1	469	46	...	173
British Territory ...	**35,919**	**12,638**	**145,195**	**27,109**	**14,693**	**1,827**	**4,298**	**2,809**	**5,046**	**9,994**
Native States ...	**3,299**	**1**	**18,831**	**3,550**	**2,637**	**5,312**	**605**	**113**	**83**	**7,206**
Province ...	**39,218**	**12,639**	**164,026**	**30,659**	**17,330**	**7,139**	**4,901**	**2,922**	**5,129**	**17,200**

Tribes of the Eastern Plains.

EASTERN PLAINS.										
6	7	8	9	10		11	12	13	14	
				BAGRI.						
Gaurwa.	Bargújar.	Jálu.	Játu.	Rájpút.	Jat.	Baria.	Atirás.	Naipál.	Ráthor.	
4,012	176	1,505	175	32	...	4	...	...	83	Delhi.
...	1,261	18	612	1,020	...	2	...	...	81	Gurgaon.
...	102	25	1,428	24	...	612	...	...	76	Karnál.
19	317	...	4,074	5,647	872	403	...	1	406	Hissar.
...	350	75	2,280	520	2	271	...	...	136	Rohtak.
4	57	2	73	6	32	824	...	38	374	Sirsa.
2	222	36	205	...	262	1,121	...	...	93	Ambala.
48	...	97	5	11	125	91	...	...	122	Ludhiána.
5	...	141	...	...	...	979	...	11	440	Jalandhar.
...	...	223	...	...	63	1,247	15	...	...	Hoshyárpur.
236	...	...	...	...	...	106	1	...	...	Kángra.
68	...	...	...	...	150	...	...	...	...	Amritsar.
...	...	...	...	3,712	...	25	...	...	...	Gurdáspur.
50	...	...	...	...	936	...	...	...	157	Sialkot.
6	...	...	4	9	15	...	...	261	1,580	Lahore.
150	...	1	...	3	...	...	...	6	88	Gujránwála.
40	13	...	...	147	345	42	...	1,354	810	Firozpur.
97	...	3	...	...	45	26	...	118	10	Ráwalpindi.
5	2	...	...	5	...	...	...	...	835	Jhelum.
51	...	...	...	...	246	...	...	...	1	Gujrát.
36	...	...	...	4	...	...	...	...	2	Shahpur.
162	...	5	2	1	10	57	...	...	37	Multán.
20	...	...	...	...	...	...	...	...	57	Jhang.
4	...	...	...	...	386	...	...	68	705	Montgomery.
2	...	1	...	...	25	...	...	...	132	Muzaffargarh.
5,983	2,515	2,138	8,857	11,141	3,519	5,916	16	1,858	6,355	**British Territory.**
204	18	2,206	100	32	1,404	7,818	6,550	...	212	Patiála.
49	46	24	551	6	113	4,144	...	...	31	Nábha.
3	...	...	2	...	...	...	...	...	...	Kapurthala.
...	20	1	956	707	22	131	...	...	175	Jind.
...	...	1	2	...	8	...	...	12	40	Faridkot.
...	...	...	7	...	572	466	...	...	3	Maler Kotla.
25	3	...	8	...	31	106	...	...	...	Kalsia.
281	198	2,345	1,946	908	2,250	12,665	6,550	12	476	Total East. Plains.
...	...	...	...	...	...	...	...	...	120	Baháwalpur.
2	...	97	...	...	1	80	...	...	66	Total Hill States.
5,983	2,515	2,138	8,957	11,141	3,519	5,916	16	1,858	6,355	**British Territory**
283	198	2,442	1,946	908	2,251	12,745	6,550	12	671	**Native States.**
6,266	2,713	4,580	10,903	12,049	5,770	18,661	6,566	1,870	7,026	**Province.**

least they do not intermarry. A few Mandahár are found east of the Jamna in Saháranpur, but the tribe appears to be very local.

The Pundir (No. 4).—The Pundír would appear to belong to the Dahíma royal race of which Tod says:—"Seven centuries have swept away all recollection of a tribe who once afforded one of the proudest themes for the song of the bard." They were the most powerful vassals of the Chauhán of Dehli, and Pundír commanded the Lahore frontier under Pirthi Ráj. The original seat of the Panjáb Pundír was Thánesar and the Kurukshetr of Karnál and Ambála, with local capitals at Púndri, Ramba, Hábri, and Púndrak; but they were dispossessed by the Chauhán under Rána Har Rai, and for the most part fled beyond the Jamna. They are, however, still found in the Indri pargannah of Karnál and the adjoining portion of Ambála.

The Rawat (No. 5).—The Ráwat has been returned as a Jat tribe, as a Rájpút tribe, and as a separate caste. I have shown the three sets of figures side by side in Abstract No. 79. The Ráwat is found in the sub-montane districts, and down the whole length of the Jamna valley. It is very difficult to separate these people from the Ráthis of the Kángra hills; indeed they would appear to occupy much the same position in the submontane as the Ráthis or even the Kanets do in the higher ranges. They are admittedly a clan of Chandel Rájpúts; but they are the lowest clan who are recognised as of Rájpút stock, and barely if at all admitted to communion with the other Rájpúts, while under no circumstances would even a Ráthi marry a Ráwat woman. They practise widow-marriage as a matter of course. There can, I think, be little doubt that the Chandel are of aboriginal stock, and probably the same as the Chandál of the hills of whom we hear so much; and it is not impossible that these men became Chandáls where they were conquered and despised outcasts, and Rájpúts where they enjoyed political power. The Ráwat is probably akin to the Ráo sub-division of the Kanets, whom again it is most difficult to separate from the Ráthis; and the Chandel Rájpúts also have a Ráo section. In Dehli 1,075 persons have shown themselves as Ráwat Gaure, and are included also under Gaurwa, the next heading. [P.240]

446. The Rajput tribes of the Eastern Plains continued. The Gaurwa (No. 6) and Gaur.—I am not at all sure that these figures do not include some Gaur as well as Gaurwa Rájpúts (see the last sentence *supra*) for the name was often spelt Gaura in the papers. The Gaur are that one of the 36 royal families to which belonged the Rájpút Kings of Bengal. They are found in the central Jamna-Ganges *doáb*, and are fully described by Elliott and Sherring. In our tables we have 1,790 Rájpúts returned as Gaur, mostly in Dehli and Gurgáon, and they are not shown in the Abstract. Gaurwa would seem to be applied generally to any Rájpúts who have lost rank by the practice of *karewa*. In Dehli however they form a distinct clan, both they and the Chauhán practising widow-marriage, but the two being looked upon as separate tribes. They are described by Mr. Maconachie as "especially noisy and quarrelsome, but sturdy in build, and "clannish in disposition," while the Dehli Chauhán are said to be "the best Rájpút cultivators in "the district, and otherwise decent and orderly."

The Bargujar (No. 7).—The Bargújar are one of the 36 royal families, and the only one except the Gahlot which claims descent from Láwa son of Rám Chandra. The connection between the Mandahár and Bargújar has already been noticed under the head Mandahár. They are of course of Solar race. Their old capital was Rájor, the ruins of which are still to be seen in the south of Alwar, and they held much of Alwar and the neighbouring parts of Jaipur till dispossessed by the Kachwáha. Their head-quarters are now at Anúpshahr on the Ganges, but there is still a colony of them in Gurgáon on the Alwar border. Curiously enough, the Gurgáon Bargújar say that they came from Jálandhar about the middle of the 15th century; and it is certain that they are not very old holders of their present capital of Sohna, as the buildings of the Kambohs who held it before them are still to be seen there and are of comparatively recent date. Our figures for Gurgáon are certainly very far below the truth.

The Jadu (No. 8).—The Jádu or Jádúbansi are of Lunar race, and are called by Tod "the "most illustrious of all the tribes of Ind." But the name has been almost overshadowed by Bhatti, the title of their dominant branch in modern times. Only 4,580 persons have returned themselves as Jádu, and those chiefly in Dehli and the south of Patiála.

The Jatu (No. 9).—The Játu are said to be a Túnwar clan who once held almost the whole of Hissár, and are still most numerous in that district and the neighbouring portions of Rohtak and Jínd. In fact the Túnwar of Hariána are said to have been divided into three clans named after and descended from three brothers, Játu, Raghu and Satraula, of which clans Játu was by far the largest and most important, and once ruled from Bhiwáni to Agroha. They are the hereditary enemies of the Punwár of Rohtak, and at length the sandhills of Mahm were fixed upon as the boundary between them, and are still known as *Játu Punwár ka daula* or the Játu-Punwár boundary. Of the Karnál Játu 500 have returned themselves as Chauhán also, and are included under both heads.

The Bagri (No. 10).—The word Bágri is applied to any Hindu Rájpút or Jat from the Bágar or prairies of Bíkáner, which lie to the south and west of Sirsa and Hissár. They are most numerous in the latter district, but are found also in some numbers under the heading of Jat in Siálkot and Patiála. The Gurdáspur Bágri are Salahria who have shown themselves also as Bágar or Bhágar by clan, and probably have no connection with the Bágri of Hissár and its neighbourhood. Or it may be that the word is a misreading for Nágri, who claim to be Chauhán Rajpúts who migrated from Dehli in the time of Ala-ud-din Ghori, and who hold 17 villages in the Siálkot district. These last are certainly Jats, not Rájpúts. The Bágri Rájpúts are probably Bhatti, or possibly Rahtor. The Godára and Púniya are probably the Ját tribes that are most numerous in the Bágar.

The Rangar.—Rángar is a term, somewhat contemptuous, applied in the eastern and south-eastern districts to *any* Musalmán Rájpút; and I only notice it here because the Rángar are often, though wrongly, held to be a Rájpút tribe. I am told, however, that in Fírozpur and Gurdáspur there are small Rájpút colonies known only by this name; and if so it is probable that they have migrated from the Dehli territory. If a Hindu Chauhán Rájpút became Musalmán to-morrow, he would still be called a Chauhán Rájpút by both himself and his neighbours of both religions. But his Hindu brethren would also call him Rángar, which he would resent as only slightly less abusive than *chotikat,* a term of contempt applied to those who have, on conversion to Islám, cut off the *choti* or Hindu scalplock. The Rángar or Musalmán Rájpúts bear the worst possible reputation for turbulence and cattle-stealing, and gave much trouble in the mutiny. Many proverbs concerning them are quoted under the head of Gújar. Here is another—" A Rángar is best in a wineshop, or " in a prison, or on horseback, or in a deep pit." I believe that in Central India the term Rángar is applied to any uncouth fellow.[1]

The Baria (No. 11).—The Baria of Jálandhar are said to be Solar Rájpúts, descended from Rája Karan of the Mahábhárat. Their ancestor Mal (!) came from Jal Káhra in Patiála about 500 years ago. Those of Siálkot, where they are found in small numbers, but considered to be Jats, not Rájpúts, say they are of Lunar Rájpút descent. The tribe is practically confined to Patiála and Nábha, and the name of the ancestor Mal, if common to the tribe, looks as if they were not Rájpúts at all, though it is unusual in the Sikh States for Jats to claim the title of Rájpút. I have no further information regarding the tribe. There are Barhaiya Rájpúts in the Azimgarh and Gházípur neighbourhood.

The Atiras (No. 12).—This tribe is returned from Patiála only. I cannot find it mentioned in any of the authorities.

The Naipal (No. 13).—The Naipál are a clan of the great Bhatti tribe, who are found on the Satluj above Fírozpur. They once held the river valley as far down as that town, but were driven higher up by the Dogars, and in their turn expelled the Gújars. Mr. Brandreth says of them:— " They resemble very much in their habits the Dogars and Gújars, and are probably greater " thieves than either. They appear almost independent under the Ahlúwália rulers and to have " paid a small rent in kind only when the Kárdár was strong enough to compel them to it, which " was not often the case. They have lost more of their Hindu origin than either the Dogars or " Gújars, and in their marriage connections they follow the Muhammadan law, near blood relations " being permitted to enter into the marriage compact." All the Naipál have returned themselves as Bhatti as well, and it is possible that many of them have shown Bhatti only as their tribe, and are therefore not returned under the head Naipál.

The Rathor (No. 14).—The Ráthor are one of the 36 royal races, and Solar Rájpúts. Their old seat was Kanauj, but their more modern dynasties are to be found in Márwár and Bíkáner. They are returned from many districts in the Panjáb, but are nowhere numerous.

447. The Rajputs of the Western Plains.—The next group of Rájpút tribes that I shall discuss are those of the great Western Plains. I have already said much regarding the position of the Rájpút in this part of [P. 241] the Panjáb, and the difficulty of drawing any line between him and the Jat of the neighbourhood. Here the great Rájpút tribes have spread up the river valleys as conquerors. Traditionally averse from manual labour and looking upon the touch of the plough handle as especially degrading, they have been wont to content themselves with holding the country as dominant tribes, pasturing their great herds in the broad grazing grounds of the west, fighting a good deal and plundering more, and leaving agriculture to the Aráín, the Mahtam, the Kamboh, and such small folk. The old tradition is not forgotten; but the rule of the Sikh, if it afforded ample opportunity for fighting, destroyed much of their influence, and the order and equal justice which have accompanied British rule have compelled all but the most wealthy to turn their attention, still in a half-hearted sort of way, to agriculture.

* P. 140-43 Abstract No. 80 on the next page* shows the distribution of these tribes. They are roughly arranged according to locality. First come the royal races

[1] Mr. Wilson notes that he has heard Rángar applied to Hindu Rájpúts. This is, I think unusual. The word is often spelt and pronounced Rángbar.

Abstract No. 80, showing the Rajput [P.242]

	RAJPUTS OF THE					
	1		2		3	
	PUNWAR.		BHATTI.		WATTU.	
	Rájpút.	Jat.	Rájpút.	Jat.	Rájpút.	Jat.
Dehli	566	79	5,935	100	...	...
Gurgaon	1,236	862	118	...	...	...
Karnal	1,795	43	466	107	...	...
Hissar	4,301	362	3,775	214	401	...
Rohtak	11,789	329	292	14	...	...
Sirsa	5,571	122	7,232	126	3,786	24
Ambala	829	114	2,179	649	...	...
Ludhiana	267	10	2,038	1,004	...	...
Jalandhar	2,043	87	3,027	367	...	...
Hushyarpur	237	...	3,767	43	...	...
Kangra	...	...	55	...	...	...
Amritsar	71	653	10,610	205	...	...
Gurdaspur	426	2,287	9,749	5	...	...
Sialkot	137	117	12,875	3,677	...	...
Lahore	1,598	311	15,854	10,287	86	739
Gujranwala ...	94	538	9,477	7,722	5	312
Firozpur	3,587	716	12,372	590	1,509	704
Rawalpindi ...	7,174	814	30,304	2,056	...	...
Jhelam	646	524	10,430	6,241	...	7
Gujrat	125	145	2,022	9,926	...	...
Shahpur	1,008	71	13,476	396	134	43
Multan	4,995	2,563	14,890	9,682	100	...
Jhang	490	284	17,392	2,874	246	107
Montgomery ...	3,083	726	12,600	3,528	11,190	454
Muzaffargarh ...	363	1,561	2,878	6,988	27	110
Derah Ismail Khan ...	193	1,317	76	13,767	...	107
Derah Ghazi Khan ...	262	1,919	23	12,971	...	13
Bannu	4	405	780	1,057	...	283
British Territory ...	**53,151**	**16,959**	**204,569**	**94,665**	**17,484**	**2,963**
Patiala	867	864	3,035	587	95	...
Nabha	3	...	676	1	1	...
Kapurthala ...	141	...	10,632	...	8	...
Jind	1,065	...	485	...	...	...
Faridkot	380	19	1,282	3	46	241
Total Eastern Plains...	2,836	887	16,323	619	155	241
Bahawalpur ...	4,435	...	21,657	569	3,442	3
Total Hill States ...	582	...	282	5	107	...
British Territory ...	**53,151**	**16,959**	**204,569**	**94,665**	**17,484**	**2,963**
Native States ...	**7,853**	**887**	**38,262**	**1,193**	**3,704**	**244**
Province... ...	**61,004**	**17,846**	**242,831**	**95,858**	**21,188**	**3,207**

Tribes of the Western Plains.

WESTERN PLAINS.

4		5		6		7
Joya.		Khichi.		Dhudhi.		
Rájpút.	Jat.	Rájpút.	Jat	Rájpút.	Jat.	Hináj.
...	...	5,100	...	3	4	...
...	...	...	...	...	145	..
...	...	3	...	3	17	...
1,533	100	46	3	30	626	...
...	...	2	2	...	162	...
5,439	55	147	16	450	544	...
142	...	...	...	8	2	...
...	...	...	...	9	8	...
...	...	...	...	...	348	...
...	...	...	...	308	...	...
...	...	...	...	...	...	...
...	...	5	...	112	...	...
...	...	...	...	129	...	...
...	205	...	13	...	99	...
1,284	390	489	518	1,063	710	...
10	995	40	432	...	561	...
4,174	782	421	36	299	264	...
43	49	..	...	489	27	...
...	...	2	74	...	733	...
4	54	6	...	3	1,524	...
2,195	516	514	57	593	426	...
5,059	473	2,573	54	1,356	1,875	3,885
670	1,533	983	483	1,090	1,578	345
4,397	2,165	2,363	373	1,507	1,349	28
343	1,[illegible]33	22	44	180	505	...
...	1,788	...	877	...	605	...
8	1,421	3	355	...	66	...
...	479	...	...	...	136	...
25,301	12,338	12,724	3,337	7,649	12,315	4,258
170	...	...	...	...	502	...
38	...	...	...	...	...	...
...	...	...	...	30	...	...
5	...	...	...	...	...	...
340	...	2	...	35	89	...
569	...	2	...	65	599	...
4,684	...	606	254	48	479	...
9	...	...	...	...	9	...
25,301	12,338	12,724	3,337	7,649	12,315	4,258
5,262	...	608	254	113	1,087	...
30,563	12,338	13,332	3,591	7,762	13,402	4,258

Abstract No. 80, showing the Rajput

RAJPUTS OF THE

	8		9		10	
	SIAL.		RANJHA.		GONDAL.	
	Rájpút.	Jat.	Rájpút.	Jat.	Rájpút.	Jat.
Dehli	...	...	...	...	2	...
Gurgaon	5	2	...	...	...	3
Karnal	2	1	...	...	...	6
Hissar	51	1	...	...	2	1,437
Rohtak	6	4	...	...	2	2,714
Sirsa	246	13	1	...	2	3
Ambala	33	76	...	...	...	8
Ludhiana	35	5	...	...	...	...
Jalandhar	...	31	...	...	...	24
Hushyarpur ...	...	333	...	...	5,301	203
Kangra	1,593	...	...	...	17,154	1,661
Amritsar	...	221	...	...	82	65
Gurdaspur ...	5	137	11	230	...	443
Sialkot	7	719	...	...	11	1,791
Lahore	193	1,243	16	53	18	859
Gujranwala ...	349	433	102	1,166	[illegible]	3,953
Firozpur	367	285	...	14	51	161
Rawalpindi ...	828	141	14	8	139	611
Jhelam	576	256	103	1,601	69	6,354
Gujrat	78	1,091	...	6,924	...	24,825
Shahpur	2,403	71	6,789	258	19,272	305
Multan	23,037	560	152	148	26	196
Jhang	36,374	437	151	162	868	649
Montgomery ...	6,684	1,202	115	1	[illegible]	122
Muzaffargarh ...	2,520	2,453	10	168	...	155
Derah Ismail Khan ...	571	4,648	21	161	6	388
Derah Ghazi Khan ...	706	2,536	...	9	24	53
Bannu	207	189	...	5	13	48
British Territory ...	**76,957**	**17,093**	**7,490**	**10,903**	**43,220**	**47,276**
Patiala	...	...	...	10	...	...
Nabha	4	...	...	...	1	2
Kapurthala ...	10	269	...	17	...	...
Jind	1	...	...	...	2	...
Faridkot	91	4	...	22	3	46
Total East. Plains ...	113	273	...	49	6	86
Bahawalpur ...	133	...	...	...	4	107
Total Hill States ...	10	...	...	4	...	132
British Territory ...	76,957	1[illegible],093	7,490	10,903	43,220	47,276
Native States ...	256	273	...	53	10	325
Province	77,213	17,366	7,490	10,956	43,230	47,601

Tribes of the Western Plains—concluded.

WESTERN PLAINS—CONCLUDED.

11		12	13	14	15	16	17
MEKAN.							
Rájpút,	Jat.	Tiwána.	Chhádhar.	Virk.	Bhutta.	Lángáh.	Súmra.
...	...	...	...	...	...	...	...
...	...	...	...	...	...	...	...
...	...	...	...	...	...	...	...
...	...	...	...	2	...	1	...
...	...	8	...	...	...	...	...
30	...	...	...	4	31	12	11
...	...	89	...	...	...	...	76
..	...	1	...	...	7	...	...
...	...	...	...	...	9	...	...
...	...	...	...	...	691	...	...
...	...	...	...	...	...	...	...
...	...	9	...	...	241	91	6
...	...	...	...	...	...	936	...
...	67	...	...	...	98	1	...
...	101	6	4	2	159	196	16
...	12	...	333	6,871	...	...	7
2	52	12	...	2	57	25	1
24	...	1	...	...	...	464	...
30	1,125	8	131	...	11	284	...
...	918	...	...	...	...	2	...
5,181	160	3,202	1,877	66	162	20	...
352	19	45	638	28	169	96	88
99	220	18	13,390	64	3,231	41	1
62	...	23	61	79	20	174	5
39	119	...	...	...	3	1	5
...	65	...	...	...	...	4	2
...	131	...	...	...	...	...	...
149	168	37	1	...	...	...	...
5,968	3,157	3,598	16,435	7,118	4,891	2,348	218
...	...	2	...	...	194	...	1,564
...	...	...	...	...	...	...	199
...	...	...	...	...	...	...	...
...	...	...	...	...	...	...	23
...	...	...	...	...	...	1	301
...	...	9	...	...	194	1	2,101
...	...	...	1,311	...	...	...	...
...	...	...	...	...	...	...	...
5,968	3,157	3,598	16,435	7,118	4,891	2,348	218
...	...	9	1,311	...	194	1	2,101
5,968	3,157	3,607	17,746	7,118	5,085	2,349	2,316

of Punwár and Bhatti, who have held between them from time immemorial the country of the lower Satluj and the deserts of Western Rájpútána. They are the parent stocks whence most of the other tribes have sprung, though as they have moved up the river valleys into the Panjáb plains they have taken local tribal names which have almost superseded those of the original race. Thus the figures for all these tribes are more or less imperfect, some having returned the local and some the original tribe only, while others have shown both and are entered in both sets of figures. Next to these races follow the Wattu, Joya, Khíchi, and Dhúdhi, who hold the Satluj valley somewhat in that order. They are followed by the Hiráj and Siál of the Chenáb and Lower Jahlam, and these again by the tribes of the Upper Jahlam and the Sháhpur *bár*. Of these last the Ránjha, Gondal, and Mekan would probably not be recognised as Rájpúts by their neighbours the Tiwána, Janjúa, and the like. Last of all come five tribes who have already been considered under Jats. From what has already been said as to the confusion between Jat and Rájpút in these parts, it might be expected that many of these people will have been returned as Jats; and in such cases the figures are shown side by side. But in the case of at any rate the Bhatti and Punwár, it does not follow that these men are not Jats; for in many instances they have given their Jat tribe, and added to it the Rájpút tribe from which they have a tradition of origin.

448. **Rajput tribes of the Western Plains. The Punwar (No. 1).**—The Punwár or Pramara was once the most important of all the Agnikula Rájpúts. "The world is the Pramara's" is an ancient saying denoting their extensive sway; and the *Nau Kot Márústhali*, extending along and below the Satluj from the Indus almost to the Jamna, signified the *máru asthal* or arid territory occupied by them, and the nine divisions of which it consisted. But many centuries have passed since they were driven from their possessions, and in 1826 they held in independent sway only the small State of Dhát in the desert. It will be seen from the Abstract that the Punwár are found in considerable numbers up the whole course of the Satluj and along the Lower Indus, though in the Deraját all and in the Multán division many of them are shown as Jats. They have also spread up the Beás into Jálandhar and Gurdáspur. There is also a very large colony of them in Rohtak and Hissár and on the confines of those districts; indeed they once held the whole of the Rohtak, Dádri, and Gohána country, and their quarrels with the Játu Túnwar of Hissár have been noticed under the head Játu.

The Bhatti (No. 2).—Bhatti, the Panjáb form of the Rájpútáná word Bháti, is the title of the great modern representatives of the ancient Jádúbansi royal Rájpút family, descendants of Krishna and therefore of Lunar race. Their traditions tell that they were in very early times driven across the Indus; but that returning, they dispossessed the Langáh, Joya, and others of the country south of the Lower Satluj some seven centuries ago, and founded Jaisalmer. This State they still hold, though their territory has been greatly circumscribed since the advent of the Ráthor; but they still form a large proportion of the Rájpút subjects of the Ráthor Rájas of Bíkáner. At one time their possessions in those parts included the whole of Sirsa and the adjoining portions of Hissár, and the tract is still known as Bhattiána. The story current in Hissar is that Bhatti, the leader under whom the Bhattis recrossed the Indus, had two sons Dusal and Jaisal, of whom the latter founded Jaisalmer while the former settled in Bhattiána. From Dusal sprang the Sidhu and Barár Jat tribes (see section 436), while his grandson Rájpál was the ancestor of the Wattu. (But see further, section 449 *infra*.) According to General Cunningham the Bhattis originally held the Salt-range Tract and Kashmír, their capital being Gajnipur, or the site of modern Ráwalpindi; but about the second century before Christ they were driven across the Jahlam by the Indo-Scythians, and their leader, the Rája Rasálu of Panjáb tradition, founded Siálkot. The invaders however followed them up and dispersed them, and drove them to take refuge in the country south of the Satluj, though their rule in the Kashmír valley remained unbroken till 1339 A.D.

The Bhatti is still by far the largest and most widely distributed of the Rápút tribes of the Panjáb. It is found in immense numbers all along the Lower Satluj and Indus, though on the former often and on the latter always classed as Jat. It is hardly less numerous on the Chenáb, the Upper Satluj, and the Beás, it is naturally strong in Bhattiána, there is a large colony in the Dehli district, while it is perhaps most numerous of all in the seats of its ancient power, in Siálkot, Gujrát and the Salt-range country. And if we reckon as Bhatti the Sidhu and Barár Jats of the Málwa, who are admittedly of Bhatti origin, we shall leave no portion of the Panjáb proper in which a large Bhatti population is not to be found. Many of those returned as Bhatti are also returned as belonging to other tribes, but these form a wholly insignificant fraction of the whole; and the only large numbers appearing twice over appear to be the 1,100 Naipál of Fírozpur already alluded to, 2,000 Bhatti Túnwar (*sic*) in Ráwalpindi, 2,400 Khokhar and 1,600 Kharral in Baháwalpur, 1,700 Kashmíri Jats in Gújránwála. In this last case the word is probably Bhat, a great Kashmír tribe, and not Bhatti. But if the Bhatti formerly held Kashmír, it is not impossible that the two words are really identical. Perhaps also Bhatti has in many cases been given as their tribe by Jats or low-class Rájpúts, or even by men of inferior castes who returned themselves as Jats or Rájpúts for their own greater exaltation. But if this be so, it only shows how widespread is the fame of the Bhatti within the Panjáb. Almost every menial or artisan caste has a Bhatti clan, and it is often the most numerous of all, ranking with or above the Khokhar in this respect.

Yet it is strange, if the Bhatti did hold so large a portion of the Panjáb as General Cunningham alleges, how almost universally they trace their origin to Bhatner in Bhattiána or at least to its neighbourhood. Either they were expelled wholly from the Upper Panjáb and have since returned to their ancient seats, or else the glory of their later has overshadowed that of their earlier dynasties, and Bhatner and Bhattiána have become the city and country of the Bhatti from which all good Bhatti trace their origin. The subject population of Bíkáner is largely composed of Bhatti, while Jaisalmer is a Bhatti State; and it seems impossible that if the Bhatti of the Higher Satluj are immigrants and not the descendants of the residue of the old Bhatti who escaped expulsion, they should not have come largely from both these States, and moreover should not have followed the river valleys in their advance. Yet the tradition almost always skips all intermediate steps, and carries us straight back to that ancient city of Bhatner on the banks of the long dry Ghaggar, in the Bíkáner territory bordering on Sirsa. The Wattu Bhatti of Montgomery, while tracing their origin from Rája Salváhan, the father of Rája Rasálu of Siálkot, say that their more immediate ancestors came from Bhatner; the Nún Bhatti of Multán trace their origin to the Dehli country; while the Bhatti of Muzaffargarh, Jhang, Gújránwála, Siálkot, Jahlam, and Pindi, all look to Bhatner as the home of their ancestors. It is probable either that Bhatner is used merely as a traditional expression, or that when the Ghaggar dried up or the Ráthor conquered Bíkáner, the Bhatti were driven to find new homes in the plains of the Panjáb. Indeed Mr. Wilson tells me that in Sirsa, or the old Bhattiána, the term Bhatti is commonly applied to any Musalmán Jat or Rájpút from the direction of the Satluj, as a generic term almost synonymous with Ráth or Pachháda.

[P. 243] In Multán the Nún, a Bhatti clan, are the dominant tribe in the Shújábád *tahsíl*, where they settled some four or five hundred years ago. The Mittru Bhatti of Multán came from Bíkáner. The Bhatti of Montgomery are probably Wattu and Khíchi who will be described presently. The Bhatti of Jhang hold a considerable tract called Bhattiora in the Chiniot uplands north of the Chanáb. They came first from Bhatner to the right bank of the Jahlam near the Sháhpur border, and thence to Bhattiora. They are described as "a fine race of men, industrious agriculturists, "hardly at all in debt, good horse-breeders, and very fond of sport. They do very little cattle-"lifting, but are much addicted to carrying off each other's wives." The Bhatti of the Gújránwála *bár*, where they are the "natural enemies of the Virk," are descended from one Dhír who eighteen generations ago left Bhatner, and settled in the Núr Mahal jungles as a grazier and freebooter. His grandson went further on to the banks of the Rávi, and his son again moved up into the uplands of Gújránwála. The modern descendants of these men are described as "a muscular and noble-"looking race of men, agriculturists more by constraint than by natural inclination, who keep "numerous herds of cattle which graze over the pasture lands of the *bár*, only plough just sufficient "to grow food for their own necessities, and are famous as cattle-lifters and notorious thieves." The Bhatti of Gújránwála enjoyed considerable political importance in former times, and they still hold 86 villages in that district. In Siálkot the Bhatti claim descent from Bhoni seventh in descent from their eponymous ancestor Bhatti, who came to Gújránwála from Bíkáner, and thence to Siálkot. None of these Bhatti of the *bár* will give their daughters to the neighbouring Jat tribes, though they will take wives from among them without scruple. In the Salt-range Tract the Bhatti seem to hold a very subordinate position as Bhatti, though it may be that some of the innumerable Rájpút tribes of those tracts may consider themselves Bhatti as well as whatever their local name may be. In Kapúrthala and Jálandhar they have lost position greatly in recent times. Till dispossessed by the Ahlúwália Sikhs, the Rais of Kapúrthala were Bhatti Rájpúts.

449. Rajput Tribes of the Satluj.—The Wattu (No. 3).—The Wattu are a Bhatti clan, of whose origin the Hissár story has been given in section 448 above. The Sirsa tradition appears to be that one Rája Júnhar, a descendant of the Bhatti Rája Salváhan of Siákot, was settled in Bhatner, where he had two sons Achal and Batera. From the latter sprang the Sidhu and Barár Jats. The former again had two sons Jaipál and Rájpál, of whom Jaipál was the ancestor of the Bhatti proper, and Rájpál of the Wattu. The Wattu date their conversion to Islám by Bába Faríd, from the time of Khíwa who ruled at Haveli in Montgomery, and was succeeded by the famous Wattu Chief Lakhe Khán. They hold both banks of the Satluj in the Sirsa district, and the adjoining parts of Montgomery and Baháwalpur, from Baggehi 16 miles above Fázilka, to Phuláhi 70 miles below it. Above them lie the Dogars, below them the Joya. They are said to have crossed from the right bank of the river and spread into the then almost uninhabited prairies of Sirsa only some five generations ago, when Fázil Dalel Rána came from Jhang near Haveli and settled the unoccupied riverain. There is also a small section of them on the Rávi in the Montgomery district. It is not impossible that some of the Wattu have returned themselves as Bhatti simply, for some few have returned themselves under both heads. The tribe was formerly almost purely pastoral, and as turbulent and as great marauders as other pastoral tribes of the neighbourhood; and the habits of the Rávi Wattu, who gave trouble in 1857, have hardly changed. But the Satluj Wattu who possess but little jungle have taken very generally to agriculture, and Captain Elphinstone says that "some of their estates are well cultivated, their herds have diminished, and many of "them cannot now be distinguished in appearance from peaceful Aráíns or Khokhars. The change "in their habits has indeed been remarkable, as they still speak with exultation of the Kárdárs they "used to kill during the Sikh rule, and the years in which they paid no revenue because the Sikhs "were unable or afraid to collect it." Mr. Purser describes the Wattu as "priding themselves "upon their politeness and hospitality. They are of only moderate industry, profuse in expenditure "on special occasions, indifferent to education and exceedingly fond of cattle." He classes them however with the Káthia, Kharral, Siál, Bahniwál, Biloch and Joya as "essentially robber tribes "and more or less addicted to cattle-stealing." This I suspect simply means that these are the dominant tribes of the tract, who look upon a pastoral as higher than an agricultural life.

The Joya (No. 4) and Mahar.—The Joya is one of the 36 royal races of Rájpúts, and is described in the ancient chronicles as "Lords of the Jangal-des," a tract which comprehended Hariána, Bhattiána, Bhatner, and Nagor. They also held, in common with the Dehia with whom their name is always coupled, the banks of the Indus and Satluj near their confluence. Some seven centuries ago they were apparently driven out of the Indus tract and partly subjugated in the Bágar country by the Bhatti; and in the middle of the 16th century they were expelled from the Joya canton of Bíkáner by the Ráthor rulers for attempting to regain their independence. Tod remarks that "the Rájpúts carried fire and sword into this country, of which they made a desert. Ever since "it has remained desolate, and the very name of Joya is lost, though the vestiges of considerable "towns bear testimony to a remote antiquity." The Joya however have not disappeared. They still hold all the banks of the Satluj from the Wattu border nearly as far down as its confluence with the Indus, though the Bhatti turned them out of Kahror, and they lost their semi-independence when their possessions formed a part of the Baháwalpur State; they hold a tract in Bíkáner on the bed of the old Ghaggar just below Bhatner, their ancient seat; and they are found in no inconsiderable numbers on the middle Satluj of Lahore and Fírozpur and on the lower Indus of the Deraját and Muzaffargarh, about a third of their whole number being returned as Jats. The Multán *bár* is known to this day as the Joya *bár*. General Cunningham says that they are to be found in some numbers in the Salt-range or mountains of Júd, and identifies them with the Jodia or Yodia, the warrior class of India in Panini's time (450 B.C.), and indeed our figures show some 2,700 Joya in Sháhpur. But Panini's Jodia would perhaps more probably be the modern Gheba, whose original tribal name is said to be Jodra, and Gheba a mere title. The Joya of the Satluj and of Hissár trace their origin from Bhatner, and have a curious tradition current apparently from Hissár to Montgomery, to the effect that they cannot trace their Rájpút descent in the main line. The Hissár Joya make themselves descendants in the female line of Sameja, who accompanied the eponymous ancestor of the Bhatti from Mathra to Bhatner. The Montgomery Joya have it that a lineal descendant of Benjamin, Joseph's brother, came to Bíkáner, married a Rája's daughter, begot their ancestor, and then disappeared as a *faqír*. The tradition is perhaps suggested by the word *joí* meaning "wife." The Montgomery Joya say that they left Bíkáner in the middle of the 14th century and settled in Baháwalpur, where they became allies of the Langáh dynasty of Multán, but were subjugated by the Dáúdpotra in the time of Nádir Sháh. The Multán Joya say that they went from Bíkáner to Sindh and thence to Multán. This is probably due to the fact of their old possessions on the Indus having died out of the tribal memory, and been replaced by their later holdings in Bíkáner. They are described by Captain Elphinstone as "of smaller stature than the great Rávi "tribes, and considered inferior to them in regard of the qualities in which the latter especially "pride themselves, namely bravery and skill in cattle-stealing. They possess large herds of cattle "and are bad cultivators."

The Mahar are a small tribe on the Satluj opposite Fázilka, and are said to be descended from Mahar, a "brother of the Joya. They are said to be quarrelsome, silly, thievish, fond of cattle, "and to care little for agricultural pursuits."

The Khichi (No. 5).—The Khichi are a Chauhán clan, and are said to have come originally from Ajmer, the old seat of the Chauhán power, thence to Dehli, and from Dehli to the Satluj during the Mughal rule. This is probably a mere tradition of the movement of the Chauhán centre from Ajmer to Dehli. They are found along the lower and middle Satluj, and the Rávi from Multán to Lahore, there are a few of them on the Chanáb, and there are considerable numbers of them in the Dehli district. In Montgomery they are found chiefly on the Rávi, where they used to be hand-in-glove with the Kharral but mended their ways under the later Sikh rule and are now peaceful husbandmen.

The Dhudhi (No. 6).—I suspect that there is some confusion in these figures, and that some of the Dád or Dádhwál Rájpúts of the eastern sub-montane have been included with the Dhúdhi of the Satluj. The former will be described in their proper place. The latter are a small Punwár clan found with their kinsmen the Ráthor scattered along the Satluj and Chanáb. Their original seat is said to have been in the Maílsi *tahsíl* of Multán, where they are mentioned as early as the first half of the 14th century. When the Dehli empire was breaking up they spread along the rivers. One of them, Háji Sher Muhammad, was a saint whose shrine in Multán is still renowned. They are said to be "fair agriculturists and respectable members of society."

450. Rajput tribes of the Chanab. The Hiraj (No. 7).—The Hiráj is a Siál clan which holds a tract on the banks of the Rávi just above its junction with the Chanáb. It is possible that some of the clan have returned themselves as Siál simply, and are therefore not represented in the figures. The Hiráj of Multán have returned themselves as Siál Hiráj to the number of 3,380, and are shown in both columns.

The Sial (No. 8).—The Siál is politically one of the most important tribes of the Western
P. 244] Plains. As Mr. Steedman observes, the modern history of the Jhang district is the history of the Siál. They are a tribe of Punwár Rájpúts who rose to prominence in the first-half of the 18th century.[1] Mr. Steedman writes: "They were till then probably a pastoral tribe, but little given to
"husbandry, dwelling on the banks of river, and grazing their cattle during the end of the cold and
"the first months of the hot weather in the low lands of the Chanáb, and during the rainy season in
"the uplands of the Jhang *bár*. The greater portion of the tract now occupied by them was prob-
"ably acquired during the stormy century that preceded the conquest of Hindustán by the
"Mughals. During this period the country was dominated from Bhera, and sometimes from
"Multán. The collection of revenue from a nomad population inhabiting the fastnesses of the *bár*
"and the deserts of the *thal* could never have been easy, and was probably seldom attempted. Left
"alone, the Siál applied themselves successfully to dispossessing those that dwelt in the land—the
"Nols, Bhangus, Mangans, Marrals, and other old tribes—amusing themselves at the same time with
"a good deal of internal strife and quarrelling, and now and then with stiffer fighting with the
"Kharrals and Biloches.

"Then for 200 years there was peace in the land, and the Siáls remained quiet subjects of the
"Lahore Súbah, the seats of local government being Chiniot and Shorkot. Walídád Khán died in
"1747, one year before Ahmad Sháh Abdáli made his first inroad and was defeated before Dehli.
"It is not well known when he succeeded to the chieftainship, but it was probably early in the
"century; for a considerable time must have been taken up in the reduction of minor chiefs and
"the introduction of all the improvements with which Walídád is credited. It was during
"Walídád's time that the power of the Siáls reached its zenith. The country subject to Walídád
"extended from Mankhera in the Thal eastwards to Kamália on the Rávi, from the confluence of the
"Rávi and Chanáb to the iláka of Pindi Bhattián beyond Chiniot. He was succeeded by his
"nephew Ináyatulla, who was little if at all inferior to his uncle in administrative and military
"ability. He was engaged in constant warfare with the Bhangi Sikhs on the north, and the
"chiefs of Multán to the south. His near relations, the Siál chiefs of Rashídpur, gave him constant
"trouble and annoyance. Once indeed a party of forty troopers raided Jhang, and carried off the
"Khán prisoner. He was a captive for six months. The history of the three succeeding chieftains
"is that of the growth of the power of the Bhangis and of their formidable rival the Sukarchakia
"misl, destined to be soon the subjugator of both Bhangis and Siáls. Chiniot was taken in 1803,
"Jhang in 1806. Ahmad Khán, the last of the Siál Kháns, regained his country shortly after in
"1808, but in 1810 he was again captured by the Mahárája, who took him to Lahore and threw him
"into prison. Thus ended whatever independence the Siál Kháns of Jhang had ever enjoyed.

"The Siáls are descended from Rai Shankar, a Punwár Rájpút, a resident of Dáranagar
"between Alláhábád and Fattahpur. A branch of the Punwárs had previously emigrated from their
"native country to Jaunpur, and it was there that Rai Shankar was born. One story has it that
"Rai Shankar had three sons, Seo, Teo, and Gheo, from whom have descended the Siáls of Jhang,
"the Tiwánas of Sháhpur and the Ghebas of Pindi Gheb. Another tradition states that Siál was
"the only son of Rai Shankar, and that the ancestors of the Tiwánas and Ghebas were only
"collateral relations of Shankar and Siál. On the death of Rai Shankar we are told that great
"dissensions arose among the members of the family, and his son Siál emigrated during the reign
"of Allauddín Ghori to the Panjáb. It was about this time that many Rájpút families emigrated
"from the Provinces of Hindustán to the Panjáb, including the ancestors of the Kharrals,
"Tiwánas, Ghebas, Chaddhars, and Punwár Siáls. It was the fashion in those days to be converted
"to the Muhammadan religion by the eloquent exhortations of the sainted Báwa Faríd of
"Pák Pattan; and accordingly we find that Siál in his wanderings came to Pák Pattan, and there
"renounced the religion of his ancestors. The Saint blessed him, and prophesied that his son's
"seed should reign over the tract between the Jhelam and Chanáb rivers. This prediction was not

---

[1] General Cunningham states that the Siál are supposed to be descended from Rája Húdi, the Indo-Scythian opponent of the Bhatti Rája Rasálu of Siálkot; but I do not find this tradition mentioned elsewhere.

"very accurate. Bába Faríd died about 1264-65. Siál and his followers appear to have wandered "to and fro in the Rechna and Jetch doábs for some time before they settled down with some "degree of permanency on the right bank of the Jhelam. It was during this unsettled period that "Siál married one of the women of the country, Soháq daughter of Bhai Khán Mekhan, of Saiwál "in the Sháhpur district, and is also said to have built a fort at Siálkot while a temporary resident "there. At their first settlement in this district, the Siáls occupied the tract of country lying "between Mankhera in the *thal* and the river Jhelam, east and west, and from Khusháb on the "north to what is now the Garh Maháraja iláka on the south."

The political history of the Siál is very fully described in the Jhang Settlement Report from which I have made the above extract, while their family history is also discussed at pages 502 *ff* and 520 of Griffin's *Panjáb Chiefs*. The clans of the Siáls are very numerous, and are fully described by Mr. Steedman in his Jhang Report, who remarks "that it is fairly safe to assume that "any tribe (in Jhang only I suppose) whose name ends in *ána* is of Siál extraction."

The head-quarters of the Siáls are the whole southern portion of the Jhang district, along the left bank of the Chanáb to its junction with the Rávi, and the riverain of the right bank of the Chanáb between the confluences of the Jahlam and Rávi. They also hold both banks of the Rávi throughout its course in the Multán and for some little distance in the Montgomery district, and are found in small numbers on the upper portion of the river. They have spread up the Jahlam into Sháhpur and Gújrát, and are found in considerable numbers in the lower Indus of the Deraját and Muzaffargarh. Who the Siáls of Kángra may be I cannot conceive. There is a Siál tribe of Ghiraths ; and it is just possible that some of these men may have returned their *caste* as Siál, and so have been included among Rájpúts. Mr. Purser describes the Siál as "large in stature and of a "rough disposition, fond of cattle and caring little for agriculture. They observe Hindu ceremonies "like the Kharral and Káthia, and do not keep their women in *pardah*. They object to clothes of "a brown (*úda*) colour, and to the use of brass vessels."

451. Rajput tribes of the Jahlam.—The Ranjha (No. 9).—The Ránjha are chiefly found in the eastern uplands of Sháhpur and Gújrát between the Jahlam and Chanáb, though they have in small numbers crossed both rivers into the Jahlam and Gújránwála districts. They are for the most part returned as Jats except in Sháhpur. They are however Bhatti Rájpúts ; and though they are said in Gújrát to have laid claim of late years to Qureshi origin as descendants of Abú Jáhil uncle of the Prophet, whose son died at Ghazni whence his lineage emigrated to the Keràna *bár*, yet they still retain many of their Hindu customs. They are described by Colonel Davies as "a peaceable and well-disposed section of population, subsisting chiefly by agriculture. In physique "they resemble their neighbours the Gondals, with whom they intermarry freely." They would perhaps better have been classed as Jats.

The Gondal (No. 10).—The Gondal hold the uplands known as the Gondal *bár*, running up the centre of the tract between the Jahlam and Chanáb in the Sháhpur and Gújrát districts. They are also numerous in the riverain of the right bank of the former river in the Jahlam district, and a few have spread eastwards as far as the Rávi. They are said to be Chauhán Rájpúts, and 1,388 in Jahlam and 6,674 in Sháhpur have shown themselves as Gondal Chauhán, and appear in both columns in consequence. But I do not think these men have any connection with the Gondal whom our figures show as so numerous in Kángra and Hushyárpur. I have had the figures for these last districts examined, and there is no mistake about the name. Who the Gondal of the hills are I do not know, as I can find no mention of them ; but 3,451 of the Kángra Gondal have also returned themselves as Pathiál.[1] The Gondal of the plains are probably as much Jats as Rájpúts, as they appear to intermarry with the surrounding Jat tribes. Colonel Davies writes of them : "Physically "they are a fine race, owing doubtless to the free and active life they lead and the quantities of "animal food they consume ; and if we except their inordinate passion for appropriating the cattle "of their neighbours which in their estimation carries with it no moral taint, they must be pro- "nounced free from vice." They say that their ancestor came from Naushahra in the south to Pák Pattan, and was there converted by Bába Faríd ; and if this be so they probably occupied their present abodes within the last six centuries.

The Mekan (No. 11).—The Mekan are a small tribe said to be of Punwár origin and spring from the same ancestor as the Dhúdhi already described. They occupy the Sháhpur *bár* lying to the west of the Gondal territory, and are also found in smaller numbers in Jahlam and Gujrát. They are a pastoral and somewhat turbulent tribe.

The Tiwana (No. 12).—The Tiwána hold the country at the foot of the Sháhpur Salt-range and have played a far more prominent part in the Panjáb history than their mere numbers would render probable. They are said to be Punwár Rájpúts, and descended [P. 245 from the same ancestor as the Siál and Gheba (see Siál *supra*). They probably entered the

[1] Mr. Anderson suggests that Gondal may be the name of one of the Brahminical *gotras*. This would explain the extraordinarily large numbers returned under this heading ; but I cannot find a *gotra* of that name in any of the lists to which I have access. This much appears to be certain ; that there is no Gondal tribe of Rájpúts in Kángra which numbers over 17,000 souls.

Panjáb together with the Siál, and certainly before the close of the 15th century. They first settled at Jahángír on the Indus, but eventually moved to their present abodes in the Sháhpur *thal*, where they built their chief town of Mitha Tiwána. The subsequent history of the family is narrated at pages 519 to 534 of Griffin's *Panjáb Chiefs* and at pages 40 *ff* of Colonel Davies' Sháhpur Report. The Tiwána resisted the advancing forces of the Sikhs long after the rest of the district had fallen before it. They are now " a half pastoral, half agricul- " tural tribe, and a fine hardy race of men who make good soldiers, though their good qualities " are sadly marred by a remarkably quarrelsome disposition, which is a source of never-ending " trouble to themselves and all with whom they are brought in contact."

452. The Rajputs of the Western Hills.—I have already described the position occupied by Rájpúts in the Salt-range Tract. The dominant tribes, such as the Janjúa, have retained their pride of lineage and their Rájpút title. But many of the minor tribes, although probably of Rájpút descent, have almost ceased to be known as Rájpúts, and are not unfrequently classed as Jat. Especially the tribes of the Hazára, Murree, and Kahúta hills, though almost certainly Rájpúts, are, like the tribes of the Chibhál and Jammu hills, probably of very impure blood. The tribes of the Salt-range Tract are exceedingly interesting, partly because so little is known about them. The names of many of them end in *ál*, which almost always denotes that the name is taken from their place of origin[1]; and a little careful local enquiry would probably throw much light on their migrations. The great Janjúa tribe appears to be Ráthor; and from the fact of the old Bhatti rule which lasted for so long in Kashmír, we should expect the hill tribes, most of whom come from the banks of the Jahlam, to be Bhatti also. But there is perhaps some slight ground for believing that many of them may be Punwár (see Dhúnd *infra*). If these tribes are really descendants of the original Jádúbansi Rájpúts who fled to the Salt-range after the death of Krishna, they are probably, among the Aryan inhabitants of the Panjáb proper, those who have retained their original territory for the longest period, unless we except the Rájpúts of the Kángra hills. The grades and social divisions of the Hill Rájpúts are dwelt upon in the section treating of the tribes of the eastern hills. The same sort of classification prevails, though to a much less marked extent, among the western hills; but the Janjua are probably the only one of the tribes now under consideration who can be ranked as Mián
'. 150- Sáhu or first-class Rájpúts. Abstract No. 81 on the next page* shows the distribution of these tribes. They are divisible into three groups, roughly arranged in order from north and west to south and east. First came the tribes of the hills on the right bank of the Jahlam, then the Salt-range tribes, then those of the cis-Jahlam sub-montane, and last of all the Tárars who have been already discussed as Jats. I had classed as separate castes those persons who returned themselves as Dhúnds and Kahúts, under Nos. 74 and 103 in Table VIII A. But I have brought those figures into this Abstract alongside of the Dhúnds and Kahúts who returned themselves as Rájpúts.

The figures for these tribes are probably more imperfect than those for any other group of the same importance, at any rate so far as the tribes of the Salt-range are concerned. In that part of the Panjáb it has become the fashion to be Qureshi or Mughal or Awán, rather even than Rájpút; and it is certain that very many of these men have returned themselves as such. Till the detailed clan tables are published the correct figures will not be ascertainable.

453. Rajput tribes of the Murree and Hazara Hills.—The Dhund and Satti (Nos. 1, 2).—The Dhúnd, Satti, and Ketwál occupy nearly the whole of the lower hills on the right bank of the

[1] This is not so, indeed, in the case of the Gakkhars, whose clan names all end in *ál*, and are pure patronymics.

Abstract No. 81, showing Rajput [P. 24

	RAJPUTS OF THE									
	1		2	3	4		5		6	7
	DHUND.				DHANTAL.		BHAKRAL.			
	Rájpút.	Dhúnd (caste No. 74).	Satti.	Ketwál.	Rájpút.	Jat.	Rájpút.	Jat.	Kaniál.	Kahút (caste No. 103).
Hissar	...	...	...	34	...	...	...	..	...	...
Ambala	...	...	...	...	...	...	...	...	.	...
Hushyárpur	...	...	...	...	...	...	...	...	...	...
Kángra	...	...	18	188	109	...	17	..	2	...
Amritsar	...	...	27	...	...	...	...	...	...	...
Gurdáspur	...	...	...	...	...	...	...	...	...	...
Siálkot	...	...	7	14	...	...	54	21	.	...
Lahore	...	...	39	4	7	...	20	...	...	2
Gujránwála	..	...	...	13	...	...	...	...	...	...
Firozpur	...	...	41	...	...	...	...	...	...	1
Ráwalpindi	11,720	223	1,407	1,291	4,235	6,340	4,778	1,576	3,218	62
Jhelam	15	...	31	3	31	3,680	207	1,253	191	8,766
Gujrát	...	...	10	88	6	6	...	1,965	1,156	...
Shahpur	...	...	...	...	...	...	42	48	35	377
Multan	1	...	5	...	.	...	...	...	28	22
Jhang	...	...	1	...	...		...	...	...	25
Muzaffargarh	...	...	...	...	...	...	...	...	...	153
Derah Ismail Khan ...	...	...	...	...	...	...	1	...	...	...
Bannu	3	...	45	...	...	...	3	...	2	...
Hazara	17,548	20,085	664	...	...	...	10	...	...	...
British Territory ...	29,314	20,315	2,373	1,642	4,388	10,026	5,144	4,863	4,640	9,468
Total East. Plains ...	...	...	..	...	...	...	69	13	...	34
Baháwalpur	...	...	...	...	...	...	3,309	...	...	...
Total Hill States ...	...	...	28	...	...	...	..	...	...	...
British Territory ...	29,314	20,315	2,373	1,642	4,388	10,026	5,144	4,863	4,640	9,468
Native States ...	...		28		...	...	3,378	13	..	34
Province	29,314	20,315	2,401	1,642	4,388	10,026	8,522	4,876	4,640	9,502

Tribes of the Western Hills.

WESTERN HILLS. 8 Janjua. Rajpút.	8 Janjua. Jat.	9 Manhas. Rajpút.	9 Manhas. Jat.	10 Chibh.	11 Thakar.	12 Salahria.	13 Kátil.	14 Raghbansi.	15 Tirat.	
...	..	...	...	2	..	...	...	1,615	...	Hissar.
16	...	18	2	...	3	..	...	890	...	Ambala.
2,944	60	3,877	90	..	21	...	...	101		Hushyárpur.
128	65	2,058	...	84	563	...	..	154	...	Kángra.
	11	316	524	20	63	422	...	..	...	Amritsar.
136	610	5,500	67	168	937	7,611	2,645	3,716	...	Gurdáspur.
620	1,110	4,836	1,156	295	5,037	28,114		1,058	...	Siálkot.
203	643	444	669	20	481	1,883	...	23	...	Lahore.
133	1,018	1,9[illegible]2	1,724	84	7	39	..	8	2,832	Gujránwála.
109	44	44	158	2	15	205		10	...	Firozpur.
16,236	92	12,549	113	811	9	78	...	1	...	Ráwalpindi.
9,964	232	15,199	1,711	614	35	19	..	4	5	Jhelam.
1,363	732	1,110	48	6,994	19	93	...	7	.	Gujrát.
3,727	30	340	...	66	...	30	..	...	1,173	Shahpur.
896	253	6	74	7	4	28	.	8	...	Multan.
1,078	366	8	..	3	2	...	..	21	70	Jhang.
152	966	24	...	1	...	5	...	3	...	Muzaffargarh.
3	963	773	...	...	1	..	...	...	...	Derah Ismail Khan.
475	255	21	1	29	6	18	...	8	...	Bannu.
158	1	5	...	2	6	...	...	...	...	Hazara.
38,552	8,419	49,424	6,570	9,245	8,158	38,698	2,645	8,646	4,228	**British Territory.**
4	...	82	15	..	920	5	...	577	...	Total East. Plains.
...	15		...	.	..	...	...	...	...	Bahawalpur.
7	...	134	...	.	218	...	...	1,355	...	Total Hill States.
38,552	8,419	49,424	6,570	9,245	8,158	38,698	2,645	8,646	4,228	**British Territory.**
11	15	216	15		1,147	5		1,932	.	**Native States.**
38,563	8,434	49,640	6,585	9,245	9,305	38,703	2,645	10,578	4,228	**Province.**

Jahlam in the Hazára and Ráwalpindi districts. Of the three the Dhúnd are the most northern, being found in the Abbottábád *tahsíl* of Hazára and in the nothern tracts of Ráwalpindi, while below them come the Satti. In Hazára I have classed as Dhúnd 2,776 persons who returned themselves as Andwál, which appears to be one of the Dhúnd clans. They claim to be descendants of Abbás, the paternal uncle of the Prophet; while another tradition is that their ancestor Takht Khán came with Taimur to Dehli where he settled; and that his descendant Zoráb Khán went to Kahúta in the time of Sháh Jahán, and begat the ancestors of the Jadwál, Dhúnd, Sarrára and Tanáoli tribes. His son Khalúra or Kulu Rai was sent to Kashmír and married a Kashmíri woman from whom the Dhúnd are sprung, and a Ketwál woman. From another illegitimate son of his the Satti, who are the bitter enemies of the Dhúnd, are said to have sprung; but this the Satti deny and claim descent from no less a person than Nausherwán. These traditions are of course absurd. Kulu Rai is a Hindu name, and one tradition makes him brought up by a Bráhman. Major Wace writes of the Dhúnd and Karrál: "Thirty years ago their acquaintance with the "Muhammadan faith was still slight, and though they now know more of it, and are more careful "to observe it, relics of their Hindu faith are still observable in their social habits." This much appears certain, that the Dhúnd, Satti, Bib, Chibh, and many others, are all of Hindu origin, all originally occupants of the hills on this part of the Jahlam, and all probably more or less connected. I find among the Punwár clans mentioned by Tod, and supposed by him to be extinct, the Dhoonda, Soruteah, Bheeba, Dhúnd, Jeebra, and Dhoonta; and it is not impossible that these tribes may be Punwár clans.

The history of these tribes is told at pages 592*ff* of Sir Lepel Griffin's *Panjáb Chiefs*. They were almost exterminated by the Sikhs in 1837. Colonel Cracroft considers the Dhúnd and Satti of Ráwalpindi a "treacherous, feeble, and dangerous population," and rendered especially, dangerous by their close connection with the Karrál and Dhúnd of Hazára. He says that the Satti are a finer and more vigorous race and less inconstant and volatile than the Dhúnd, whose traditional enemies they are. Sir Lepel Griffin remarks that the Dhúnd "have ever been a lawless untractable race, but their courage is not equal to their disposition to do evil." On the other hand Major Wace describes both the Dhúnd and Karrál as "attached to their homes and fields, "which they cultivate simply and industriously. For the rest their character is crafty and "cowardly." Both tribes broke into open rebellion in 1857, and the Dhúnd were severely chastised in Ráwalpindi, but left unpunished in Hazára. Mr. Steedman says: "The hillmen of Ráwalpindi are not of very fine physique. They have a good deal of pride of race, but are rather squalid in appearance. The rank and file are poor, holding but little land and depending chiefly on their cattle for a livelihood. They have a great dislike to leaving the hills, especially in the hot weather, when they go up as high as they can, and descend into the valleys during the cold weather. They stand high in the social scale."

The Ketwal (No. 3).—The Ketwál belong to the same group of tribes as the Dhúnd and Satti, and hold the hills to the south of the Satti country. They claim descent from Alexander the Great (!) and say that they are far older inhabitants of these hills than either the Dhúnd or Satti; but the tribe was apparently almost exterminated by the Dhúnd at some time of which the date is uncertain, and they are now few and unimportant.

The Dhanial (No. 4).—The Dhaniál also appear to belong to the group of hill tribes of the Salt-range Tract and of probable Rájpút blood which we are now discussing. It is from them that the Dhani country in the Chakwál *tahsíl* of Jahlam takes its name; and there appears still to be a colony of them in those parts, though they are now chiefly found in the lower western hills of the Murree range, being separated from the Satti by the Ketwál. They claim to be descended from Ali, son-in-law of the Prophet. They are a fine martial set of men and furnish many recruits for the army, but were always a turbulent set, and most of the serious crime of the surrounding country used to be ascribed to them. Most of them have been returned as Jats.

The Bhakral (No. 5) and Budhal.—These are two more members of the same group of tribes, [P. 247] who hold considerable areas in the south-east portion of the Ráwalpindi district. The Bhakrál are also found in some numbers in Jahlam and Gújrát. I had not taken out separate figures for the Budhál. Of the Ráwalpindi Bhakrál 5,099 show themselves as Punwár also, and are included in both figures. The Budhál, like the Dhaniál, claim descent from Ali. Both these tribes probably came from the Jammu territory across the Jahlam. They do not approve of widow-marriage. Who the 3,000 odd Bhakrál returned for Baháwalpur may be I do not know; but it is improbable that they should be of the same tribe as those of the Salt-range Tract. Perhaps there has been some confusion of names.

The Alpial.—Here again I did not take out separate figures. But I find that 8,685 of the Manj Rájpúts of Ráwalpindi (see Abstract No. 82, page 250*) are Alpiál of the Fatah Jhang *tahsíl*. *P. 158-59.
The Alpiál hold the southern corner of the Fatah Jhang *tahsíl* of Ráwalpindi. They are admittedly a Rájpút tribe, and their marriage ceremonies still bear traces of their Hindu origin. They seem to have wandered through the Khusháb and Talagang country before settling in their present abodes, and if so, probably came up from the south. They are "a bold lawless set of men "of fine physique and much given to violent crime."

The Kharwal.—The Kharwál, for whom I have no separate figures, claim to be a Janjúa clan and descendants of Rája Mal, and Mr. Steedman sees no reason to doubt the tradition. They occupy the hills of the eastern half of the Kahúta *tahsíl* in Ráwalpindi, and are "a fine strong "race, decidedly superior to the ordinary Rájpúts, and socially hold much the same position as "other Janjúas." They do not approve of widow-marriage.

The Kanial (No. 6).—The Kaniál belong, according to Mr. Steedman, to that miscellaneous body of men who call themselves Rájpúts, and hold a large portion of the south-eastern corner of the Ráwalpindi district; and are of much the same class as the Budhál and Bhakrál. They also appear to stretch along the sub-montane as far east as Gújrát.

454. The Rajput tribes of the Salt-range.—The Kahut (No. 7) and Mair.—I have classed the Kahút as a separate caste under No. 103 of Table VIII A. But they probably belong to the group we are now considering, and I therefore show them in Abstract No. 81 and discuss them here. With them I notice the Mair, for whom I have no separate figures; and with these two are commonly associated the Kasar, who will be described under the head Mughal. These three tribes occupy the Dhani country in *tahsíl* Chakwál of Jahlam; the Kahúta holding Kahútáni or its southern portion, the Mair the centre, and the Kasar the north. All three state that they came from the Jammu hills, joined Bábar's army, and were located by him in their present abodes which were then almost uninhabited. They seem to have been ever violent and masterful, and to have retained their independence in a singular degree. A graphic description of their character by Mr. Thomson is quoted at length under the head Mughal, to which I must refer the reader. They most probably belong to the group of Rájpút or *quasi*-Rájpút tribes who hold the hills on either bank of the Jahlam, and the Kahúta hills of Ráwalpindi now held by the Ketwal and Dhaniál, and the town of Kahúta now in the hands of the Janjúa, still bear their name. They now belong to the Salt-range and not to the Jahlam hills, but I have put them in the Abstract among the tribes with whom they are probably connected by origin. They are sometimes said to be Awán, as indeed are the Dhúnd also. Their bards claim for them Mughal origin, and it is quite possible that some of them may have returned themselves as either Awán or Mughal. Of the 8,766 Kahút returned from Jahlam, all but 293 have shown Mughal as their clan. Besides the Kahút shown under No. 103, Table VIII A., 177 Rájpúts have returned their tribe as Kahút. The more respectable Mair call themselves Minhás, probably the same word as the well-known Manhás tribe presently to be described; and it may be that the Mair have been returned as Manhás Rájpúts.

The Jodra and Gheba.—I have no separate figures for these tribes, the only Gheba who have returned themselves as such being apparently 105, of whom 89 are in the Peshâwar division. They may have returned themselves as Mughal or some caste other than Rájpút, or as some other Rájpút tribe, or as Rájpút simply without specifying any tribe. The tradition which makes the Siál, Tiwána, and Gheba descendants of Saino, Teno, and Gheo, the three sons of Rai Shankar Punwár, has already been noticed under the head of Siál. An amended genealogy is given at page 520 of Griffin's *Punjáb Chiefs*. The Siál and Tiwána appear to admit the relationship, and, as already noticed under the head Dhúnd, it is not at all impossible that this group of Rájpút tribes may be of Punwár origin. The Gheba are said to have come to the Panjáb some time after the Siál and Tiwána, and to have settled in the wild hilly country of Fateh Jhang and Pindi Gheb in Ráwalpindi. Here they held their own against the Awáns, Gakkhars, and neighbouring tribes till Ranjít Singh subdued them. The Jodra are said to have come from Jammu, or according to another story from Hindústán, whence also Colonel Cracroft says that the Gheba traditions trace that tribe, and to have held their present tract before the Gheba settled alongside of them. They now occupy the eastern half of the Pindi Gheb, and the Gheba the western half of the Fateh Jhang *tahsíl* in Ráwalpindi, the two tracts marching with each other. I am informed, though unfortunately I cannot remember who was my authority, that the Gheba is really a branch of the original Jodra tribe that quarrelled with the others, and took the name of Gheba which till then had been simply a title used in the tribe; and the fact that the town of Pindi Gheb was built and is still held by the Jodra, and not by the Gheba, lends some support to the statement. The history of the Gheba family is told at pages 538 *ff* and of the Jodra family at pages 535 *ff* of Sir Lepel Griffin's *Punjáb Chiefs*. Colonel Cracroft describes the Jodra as "fine, spirited fellows who delight in field sports, have horses and hawks, are often "brawlers, and are ever ready to turn out and fight out their grievances, formerly with swords, "and now with the more humble weapons of sticks and stones." The same writer says that the Gheba are "a fine, hardy race of men, full of fire and energy, not addicted to crime, though their "readiness to resent insult or injury, real or imagined, or to join in hand-to-hand fights for their "rights in land, and their factions with the Jodra and Alpiál, are notorious."

The Januja (No. 8).—The head-quarters of the Janjúa are the eastern Salt-range, but they are found in small numbers throughout the Multán and Deraját divisions, and in Hushyárpur General Cunningham thinks that they are Aryan, and a branch of the Anuwán, Awán, or sons of Anu, and connects Janj the first syllable of their name, and Chach a tract in Ráwalpindi, with the old kings of the Hund on the Indus who are said by Masaudi to have borne the name of Chach or Jaj. Sir Lepel Griffin is inclined to think that they are a branch of the Yádúbansi

Rájpúts, now chiefly represented by the Bhatti, who held Kashmír till the Mahommedan conquest of the Panjáb, and whose history has been briefly sketched under the head Bhatti; and Abu Fazl also makes them a branch of the Yádu stock. They themselves say they are descendants of Rája Mal Ráthor, who migrated about 980 A. D. either from Jodhpur or from Kanauj to the Jahlam and built Malot; and the Janjúa genealogies show a striking uniformity in only giving from 18 to 23 generations since Rája Mal. One of his sons is said to have been called Júd, the old name of the Salt-range; and Mr. Brandreth states that only the descendants of his brother Wír are now known as Janjúa. If this be so, and if the identification by General Cunningham of Bábar's Júd with the Awán be accepted, the connection of the two tribes by traditional descent from a common ancestor follows. The Janjúa once held almost the whole of the Salt-range Tract, but were gradually dispossessed by the Gakkhars in the north and by the Awáns (if they be a separate people) in the west; and they now hold only the central and eastern parts of the range as tribal territory, which is exactly what they held at the time of Bábar's invasion. They still occupy a social position in the tract which is second only to that of the Gakkhars, and are always addressed as Rája. They do not permit widow marriage. The history of the tribe is told fully at paragraphs 50 *ff* of Brandreth's Jahlam Report, and that of its leading family at pages 602 *ff* of the *Panjáb Chiefs*. The tribe is very fully described by Mr. Thomson in his Jahlam Report. He too makes them Ráthor Rájpúts from Jodhpur, and says they are the only undoubtedly and admittedly Rájpút tribe in Jahlam. He describes them as physically well-looking, with fine hands and feet; much given to military service, especially in the cavalry; poor agriculturists, bad men of business, and with great pride of race.

455. Rajput tribes of the Jammu border.—The Manhas (No. 9).—The Manhás or Jamwál claim Solar origin by direct descent from Rám Chandra. They say that their ancestor came from Ajudhia and conquered Jammu, and founded the city of that name. Some say that before this conquest they first settled in Siálkot; others, that they went first to Kashmír, then to Siálkot, and then to Jammu. All seem agreed that they moved into Jammu from the plains. The name Jamwál appears to have been the old name of the whole tribe, but to be now confined to the royal branch who do not engage in agriculture, and look down upon their cultivating brethren who are commonly styled Manhás. The Manhás intermarry with the Salahria and other second-class Rájpúts of the neighbourhood. They call their eldest son Rája and the younger ones Mián, and use the salutation *Jai*! They are for the most part Hindus, at least in the cis-Jahlam tract. [P. 248] They pour water on a goat's head at *mukláwa*, and consider that his shaking his head in consequence is pleasing to their ancestors. The Manhás are found in large numbers throughout the country below the Jammu border, in Ráwalpindi, Jahlam, Siálkot, and Gurdáspur, but especially in the two first. In Siálkot 763 Manhás have returned themselves also as Bhatti, 741 as Salahria, and 775 as Raghbansi; while in Gurdáspur 2,060 are also shown as Raghbansi. So of the Jat Manhás of Gújránwála, 1,325 are Virk who have shown themselves as Manhás also. The Manhás are real husbandmen, and therefore occupy a very inferior position in the local scale of Rájpút precedence.

The Chibh (No. 10).—The Chibh claim to be descended from the Katoch Rájpúts of Kángra, at least on the female side.[2] If so, their position must once have been much higher than it now is; but the story is probably untrue. I have suggested under the head Dhúnd that the Chibh may perhaps be Punwár. Their ancestor Chib Chand is said to have left Kángra some 1,400 years ago, and have settled at Bhimbar in the Jammu hills. The first Chibh to become a Musalmán was one Súr Sadi of the time of Aurangzeb. He died a violent death and is still venerated as a martyr, and the Mahomedan Chibh offer the scalplocks of their male children at his tomb, till which ceremony the child is not considered a true Chibh, nor is the mother allowed to eat meat. Within the Panjáb the Chibh are found almost entirely in the northern portion of Gújrát under the Jammu hills. The hills above this territory are their proper home, and are attached to the State of Kashmír. The tribe has also given its name to the Chibhál, or hill country of Kashmír on the left bank of the Jahlam along the Hazára border, though I believe that they do not now occupy those hills. The Chibh is a tribe of good position; they, like the Janjúa, enjoy the title of Rája; Saiyads and Gakkhars do not hesitate to marry their daughters; and till the Sikh rule they did not cultivate themselves. Now-a-days, however, they follow the plough. The history of the Chibh chiefs is related at page 583 of the *Panjáb Chiefs*. The Chibh are identified by some with the Sibæ of the ancients.

The Thakar (No. 11).—The Thakar Rájpúts shown in the Abstract are almost all Salahria Rájpúts of Siálkot, where 5,279 men returned themselves as Rájpút Salaria Thakar. They are shown again under the head Salahria. So 921 of the Nábha Thakar are Chauhán. The significance of the expression Thakar is discussed under the head of Rájpúts of the Eastern Hills; but

[1] Mr. Brandreth says that Major Tod comes to the same conclusion; but I have been unable to find the passage.

[2] They have however a wonderful story about a son of one of the kings of Persia marrying the daughter of a Rája in the Deccan, and having by her descendants, one of whom Nahar Chand (?) became king of Kángra. His son Chibh Chand became ruler of Bhimbar; hence the Chibh.

Thákur is also sometimes used by the high Rájpúts of the hills as a title of dignity, and the two words are often confused.

The Salahria (No. 12).—The Salahria are Sombansi Rájpúts who trace their descent from one Rája Saigal of fabulous antiquity, and from his descendant Chandra Gupta. They say that their eponymous ancestor came from the Deccan in the time of Sultán Mamdúh as commander of a force sent to suppress the insurrection of Shúja the Khokhar, and settled at Siálkot; and that his descendants turned Musalmán in the time of Bahlol Lodi. They are for the most part Mahomedan, but still employ Bráhmans, and do not marry within the tribe. They mark the foreheads of the bride and bridegroom with goats' blood at their weddings. Their head-quarters are in the eastern portion of Siálkot, but they are also found in Gurdáspur and Lahore. The Thakar returned from Siálkot under No. 11 of the Abstract are for the most part Salahria, and have been included in the figures for both tribes; while 741 of the Siálkot Salahria show themselves as Manhás and 347 as Bhatti. In all these cases the men are shown under both headings. In Gurdáspur 3,712 of the Salahria are shown also as Bágar or Bhágar, and have been included under both Salahria and Bágri.

The Katil (No. 13).—The Kátil are a Rájpút clan in Gurdáspur, regarding whom I have no information save that they intermarry with the Salahria.

The Raghbansi (No 14).—The Raghbansi Rájpúts are perhaps most numerous in the eastern part of the North-Western Provinces. In the Panjáb they are chiefly found in the Hill States and the sub-montane of Gurdáspur and Siálkot, though there are a few in the Jamna districts also. But the name would appear to imply little more than traditional origin. Thus of the Gurdáspur Raghbansi 2,080, and 775 of those of Siálkot, have returned themselves as Manhás also, and are shown under both headings.

456. The Rajputs of the Eastern Hills.—The last, and in many respects the most interesting group of Rájpút tribes that I have to discuss, are those of the Kángra and Simla Hills and the sub-montane tract at their foot between the Beás and the Jamna. Not only are the Hill Rájpúts probably those among all the peoples of the Panjáb who have occupied from the most remote date their present abodes, but they have also retained their independence longest. Often invaded, often defeated, the Rájas of Kángra Hills never really became subjects of the Musalmán; and it was reserved to Ranjít Singh to annex to his dominions the most ancient principalities in Northern India. Thus the Kángra Hills are that portion of the Panjáb which is most wholly Hindu, not merely by the proportion which the number of real or nominal Hindus bears to the total population, but still more because there has never been any Musalmán domination, which should either loosen the bonds of caste by introducing among the converted people the absolute freedom of Islám in its purity, or tighten them by throwing the still Hindu population, deprived of their Rájpút rulers, more wholly into the hands of their priests. It is here then that we may expect to find caste existing most nearly in the same state as that in which the first Musalman invaders found it when they entered the Panjáb. It is certainly here that the Bráhman and Kshatriya occupy positions most nearly resembling those assigned them by Manu.

The constitution of Rájpút society in these hills will best be explained by the following extract from Mr. Barnes' Kángra Report, and by the further extracts which I shall make under the head Thakar and Ráthi. The extracts are long; but the matter is so important as bearing upon the whole question of caste, that I do not hesitate to give them. Mr. Barnes writes :—

"Any member of a royal house, whether belonging to the Dogar circle of municipalities across "the Rávi, or to the Jálandhar circle on this side of the river, is essentially Rájpút. Those also "with whom they condescend to marry are included under this honourable category. The name "is assumed by many other races in the hills; but by the general feeling of the country the "appellation of Rájpút is the legitimate right of those only to whom I have here restricted "it.

"The descendants of all these noble houses are distinguished by the honorary title of 'Miáns.' "When accosted by their inferiors they receive the peculiar salutation of 'Jai Dya,' offered to no "other caste.[1] Among themselves the same salutation is interchanged; and as there are endless "gradations even among the Míáns, the inferior first repeats the salutation and the courtesy is "usually returned. In former days great importance was attached to the Jai Dya: unautho-"rized assumption of the privilege was punished as a misdemeanour by heavy fine and imprison-"ment. The Rája could extend the honour to high-born Rájpúts not strictly belonging to a Royal "clan, such, for instance, as the Soukla or the Manhás. Any deviation from the austere rules "of the caste was sufficient to deprive the offender of this salutation, and the loss was "tantamount to excommunication. The Rájpúts delight to recount stories of the value of "this honour, and the vicissitudes endured to prevent its abuse. The Rája Dhián Singh, the "Sikh Minister, himself a Jamwál Mián, desired to extort the Jai Dya from Rája Bhír Singh, "the fallen chief of Núrpur. He held in his possession the grant of a jágír valued at Rs. 25,000, "duly signed and sealed by Ranjít Singh, and delayed presenting the deed until the Núrpur "chief should hail him with this coveted salutation. But Bhír Singh was a Rája by a long line "of ancestors, and Dhián Singh was a Rája only by favour of Ranjít Singh. The hereditary "chief refused to compromise his honour, and preferred beggary to affluence rather than "accord the Jai Dya to one who by the rules of the brotherhood was his inferior. The derivation "of the phrase is supposed to be *Jai*, victory, and *Deb*, king; being synonymous, when used [P. 249] "together, to the national expression of *Vive le Roi*, or 'the king for ever.'

"A Mián, to preserve his name and honour unsullied, must scrupulously observe four fundamental "maxims:—*first*, he must never drive the plough; *secondly*, he must never give his daughter in "marriage to an inferior, nor marry himself much below his rank; *thirdly*, he must never accept money "in exchange for the betrothal of his daughter; and *lastly*, his female household must observe strict "seclusion. The prejudice against the plough is perhaps the most inveterate of all; that step can "never be recalled. The offender at once loses the privileged salutation; he is reduced to the second "grade of Rájpúts; no Mián will marry his daughter, and he must go a step lower in the social scale "to get a wife for himself. In every occupation of life he is made to feel his degraded position. In "meetings of the tribe and at marriages the Rájpúts undefiled by the plough will refuse to sit at "meals with the *Hal Báh*, or plough driver, as he is contemptuously styled; and many, to avoid the "indignity of exclusion, never appear at public assemblies. This prejudice against agriculture is as "old as the Hindu religion; and I have heard various reasons given in explanation of it. Some "say it is sacrilegious to lacerate the bosom of mother-earth with an iron plough-share; others de-"clare that the offence consists in subjecting sacred oxen to labour. The probable reason is that the "legitimate weapon of the Kshatria, or military class, is the sword; the plough is the insignia of a "lower walk in life, and the exchange of a noble for a ruder profession is tantamount to a renuncia-"tion of the privileges of caste.

"The giving one's daughter to an inferior in caste is scarcely a more pardonable offence than "agriculture. Even Ranjít Singh, in the height of his prosperity and power, felt the force of "this prejudice. The Rája of Kángra deserted his hereditary kingdom rather than ally his "sisters to Dhián Singh, himself a Mián of the Jammu stock, but not the equal of the Katoch "prince. The Rájpúts of Katgarh, in the Núrpur pargaunah, voluntarily set fire to their houses "and immolated their female relatives to avoid the disgrace of Ranjít Singh's alliance; and when "Mián Padma, a renegade Patháuia, married his daughter to the Sikh monarch, his brethren, un-"deterred by the menaces of Ranjít Singh, deprived him and his immediate connexions of the Jai "Dya, and to this day refuse to associate with his descendants. The seclusion of their women "is also maintained with severe strictness. The dwellings of Rájpúts can always be recognised by "one familiar with the country. The houses are placed in isolated positions, either on the crest of "a hill which commands approaches on all sides, or on the verge of a forest sedulously preserved "to form an impenetrable screen. When natural defences do not exist, an artificial growth is promot-"ed to afford the necessary privacy. In front of their dwellings, removed about fifty paces from "the house, stands the 'mandi' or vestibule, beyond whose precincts no one unconnected with the "household can venture to intrude. A privileged stranger who has business with the master of the "house may by favour occupy the vestibule. But even this concession is jealously guarded, and "only those of decent caste and respectable character are allowed to come even as far as the "'mandi.' A remarkable instance of the extremes to which this seclusion is carried occurred under "my own experience. A Katoch's house in the Mandi territory accidentally caught fire in broad "day. There was no friendly wood to favour the escape of the women, and rather than brave "the public gaze they kept their apartments and were sacrificed to a horrible death. Those who "wish to visit their parents must travel in covered palanquins, and those too poor to afford a con-"veyance travel by night, taking unfrequented roads through thickets and ravines.

"It is melancholy to see with what devoted tenacity the Rájpút clings to these deep-rooted "prejudices. Their emaciated looks and coarse clothes attest the vicissitudes they have undergone to "maintain their fancied purity. In the quantity of waste land which abounds in the hills, a "ready livelihood is offered to those who will cultivate the soil for their daily bread; but this "alternative involves a forfeiture of their dearest rights, and they would rather follow any pre-

[1] Hence the word Jaikári commonly used to denote first-class Rájpúts in the hills.

"carious pursuit than submit to the disgrace. Some lounge away their time on the tops of the "mountains, spreading nets for the capture of hawks; many a day they watch in vain subsisting on "berries and on game accidentally entangled in their nets; at last when fortune grants "them success they despatch the prize to their friends below, who tame and instruct the bird "for the purpose of sale. Others will stay at home, and pass their time in sporting either "with a hawk, or, if they can afford it, with a gun: one Rájpút beats the bushes, and the "other carries the hawk ready to be sprung after any quarry that rises to the view. At the close "of the day, if they have been successful, they exchange the game for a little meal, and thus pro-"long existence over another span. The marksman armed with a gun will sit up for wild pigs "returning from the fields, and in the same manner barter their flesh for other necessaries of life. "However the prospect of starvation has already driven many to take the plough, and the number "of seceders daily increases. Our administration, though just and liberal, has a levelling ten-"dency; service is no longer to be procured; and to many the stern alternative has arrived of tak-"ing to agriculture and securing comparative comfort, or enduring the pangs of hunger and death. "So long as any resource remains the fatal step will be postponed, but it is easy to foresee that "the struggle cannot be long protracted; necessity is a hard task-master, and sooner or later the "pressure of want will eventually overcome the scruples of the most bigoted.

"Next to the royal clans in social importance are those races with whom they are connected "by marriage. The honour of the alliance draws them also within the exclusive circle. It is not "easy to indicate the line which separates the Rájpúts from the clans immediately below him, and "known in the hills by the appellation of Ráthi; the Mián would restrict the term (Rájpút) "to those of royal descent; the Ráthi naturally seeks a broader definition, so as to include his own "pretensions. Altogether, I am inclined to think that the limit I have fixed will be admitted to "be just, and those only are legitimately entitled to rank as Rájpúts who are themselves the mem-"bers of a royal clan, or are connected in marriage with them. Among these (second-class) tribes "the most eminent are the Manhás, Juriál, and Sonkla Rájpúts. The two former are indeed "branches of the Jammuwál clan, to which they are considered but little inferior. They occasional-"ly receive the salutation of Jai Dya, and very few of them engage in agriculture. Another class "of Rájpúts who enjoy great distinction in the hills are the descendants of ancient petty chiefs or "Ránas whose title and tenure generally preceded even the Rájas themselves. These petty chiefs "have long since been dispossessed, and their holdings absorbed in the larger principalities which "I have enmerated. Still the name of Rána is retained, and their alliance is eagerly desired by "the Miáns. All these tribes affect most of the customs of Rájpúts. They select secluded spots "for their dwellings, immure their women, are very particular with whom they marry or betroth "in marriage, but have generally taken to agriculture. In this particular consists their chief dis-"tinction from the Miáns."

On this Mr. Lyall notes that there are now-a-days not many even of the better Rájpút families who do not themselves do every kind of field work other than ploughing. He also points out that the Rájpúts of the second grade might more properly be called Thakars of the first grade. For the absence of any definite line of demarcation between Rájpút and Thakar, see the extracts quoted under the head Thakar (section 459). Finally I may state that throughout the Hill States, the Rájpúts of proximate descent from ruling chiefs entered themselves in the present Census as Kshatriyas, to distinguish themselves from mere Rájpúts. I have taken two figures together. The Rájpúts of the sub-montane of Hushyárpur, Jálandhar, and Ambála differ little if at all from those of the Eastern Plains who have already been described. The following Kángra proverbs illustrate Mr. Barnes' description of the Hill Rájpúts: "It is bad to deal with a Rájpút; sometimes you get double value, "and sometimes nothing at all:" and "A Rájpút's wedding is like a fire of "maize stalks; great rolling of drums, and very little to eat."

P. 158-59. Abstract No. 82 on the next page gives the figures for the several tribes roughly grouped by locality, those of the higher hills coming first, then those of Hushyárpur, and then those of Jálandhar and Ambála. Many of these are mere local clans named after their principal seats. It is probable that all these royal families sprang from a common stock, but all traces of what that stock was seem to be lost in obscurity. Unfortunately the Settlement Reports give little or no information regarding these tribes or clans; while Mr. Coldstream's report, from which I had hoped for much information, is wholly silent on the

Abstract No. 82, showing the Rajput

	RAJPUTS OF THE							
	1	3	3	4	5	6	7	8
	Katoch.	Goleria.	Dharwál.	Chandel.	Pathiál.	Patháni̇a.	Jaswál.	Dádwal.
Ambala ...	1	...	...	29	4	10	24	...
Ludhiana ..	..	...	...	10	4	.	10	2
Jalandhar ..	...	...	...	292	214	...	766	190
Hushyarpur ...	5	...	...	81	291	6,601	4,118	7,028
Kangra ...	3,038	3,035	7,368	26	6,070	3,466	2,289	1,166
Amritsar ...	1	...	...	4	...	...	...	12
Gurdaspur ...	...	...	...	17	7	...	161	38
Sialkot ...	...	...	...	...	37	...	...	155
Lahore ...	1	...	...	3	4	17	4	35
Firozpur ...	...	...	...	42	...	...	5	2
Rawalpindi ...	43	...	...	5	302	619	25	6
British Territory	**3,121**	**3,037**	**7,368**	**690**	**7,101**	**10,777**	**7,423**	**8,706**
Patiala ...	...	...	...	148	4	1	...	..
Nabha ...	...	...	...	...	...	...	1	...
Kapurthala ...	...	...	...	.	...	...	34	...
Maler Kotla ...	...	...	...	...	...	...	...	...
Kalsia ...	...	...	...	4	...	...	1	...
Total East. Plains	...	...	...	155	4	1	47	...
Mandi ...	133	...	...	...	412	154	51	14
Bilaspur ...	...	37	...	3,006	24	67	3	...
Total Hill States	632	37	...	3,377	440	378	58	14
British Territory	**3,121**	**3,037**	**7,368**	**690**	**7,101**	**10,777**	**7,423**	**8,706**
Native States ...	**632**	**37**	**...**	**3,532**	**444**	**379**	**105**	**14**
Province ...	**3,753**	**3,074**	**7,368**	**4,222**	**7,545**	**11,156**	**7,528**	**8,720**

tribes of the Eastern Hills.

EASTERN HILLS.

9	10	11	12	13	14		15	
					Manj.			
Laddu.	Kilchi.	Khoja	Náru.	Ghorewáha.	Rájpút.	Jat.	Táoni.	
81	...	...	945	2,351	38	...	12,982	Ambala.
20	..	...	2,020	4,254	5,680	...	...	Ludhiana.
37	..	...	4,628	8,848	5,754	...	113	Jalandhar.
6,596	6,346	5,819	8,787	2,716	1,[illegible]45	...	63	Hushyarpur.
405	...	...	3	...	..	...	...	Kangra.
...	...	...	805	32	1,170	58	...	Amritsar.
...	...	.	1,565	...	1,151	1,599	...	Gurdaspur.
...	...		612	62	266	81	...	Sialkot.
...	...	...	1,269	146	103	557	...	Lahore.
2	314	...	611	58	1,488	43	35	Firozpur.
...	...	...	311	2	8,930	...	...	Rawalpindi.
7,144	**6,754**	**5,819**	**22,107**	**18,493**	**26,309**	**2,654**	**13,284**	**British Territory.**
...	...	...	362	886	653	...	6,092	Patiala.
	...	...	126	265	...	...	210	Nabha.
...	...	...	930	...	1,628	...	...	Kapurthala.
...	...	.	...	157	393	...	7	Maler Kotla.
...	...	...	5	86		...	1,001	Kalsia.
...	3	...	1,493	1,443	2,676	1	7,310	Total East. Plains.
...	...		...	...	...	...	...	Mandi.
...	..	...	...	45	...	...	6	Bilaspur.
..	...	...	1	45	...	...	8	Total Hill States.
7,144	**6,754**	**5,819**	**22,107**	**18,493**	**26,309**	**2,654**	**13,284**	**British Territory.**
..	**3**	**...**	**1,562**	**1,488**	**2,676**	**1**	**7,318**	**Native States.**
7,144	**6,757**	**5,819**	**23,669**	**19,981**	**28,985**	**2,655**	**20,602**	**Province.**

subject. The figures for tribal divisions of the Rájpúts of the Hill States appear to be exceedingly imperfect. Indeed the divisions themselves do not seem to be very clearly marked. Mr. Barnes writes :—

"Each class comprises numerous sub-divisions. As the family increased, individuals left the [P. 250]
"court to settle on some estate in the country, and their descendants, though still retaining the "generic appellation of the race, are further distinguished by the name of the estate with which "they are more immediately identified. Sometimes, though not so frequently, the designation of "the ancestor furnishes a surname for his posterity. Thus among the Pathánias or Núrpur Míáns "there are twenty-two recognised sub-divisions ; the Golerias are distributed into thirteen distinct "tribes ; the Katoch clan has four grand divisions, each of which includes other subordinate de-"nominations. A Rájpút interrogated by one who he thinks will understand these refined distinc-"tions, will give the name, not of his clan but of his patronymic. To a stranger he gives no "detail, but ranges himself under the general appellation of Kshatriya or Rájpút."

457. Rajput tribes of the Eastern Hills.—The Katoch, Goleria, and Dharwal (Nos. 1, 2, 3).—The Katoch is the family of the Kángra dynasty, a dynasty which dates from certainly some centuries before Christ, whose tree shows an unbroken line of four hundred and seventy kings, and whose kingdom once included the whole of the Hoshyárpur and Jálandhar districts. The ancient name of the kingdom is said to have been Katoch. Sir Lepel Griffin writes thus of the Katoch of Kángra, and the neighbouring Hill Rájas :—

"Antecedent to what are called historic times, conjecture must take the place of truth ; but "it is not difficult to imagine that those long genealogies, by the side of which the noblest names "of Europe seem but as of yesterday, contain some semblance of the truth. These quiet mountain "valleys, guarded by difficult passes, by ice and by snow, lay altogether out of the path of the "invading armies which, one after another, in quick succession, poured down upon the plains of "Hindustán from the north-west. Here a peaceful race, with no ambition urging them to try "their strength against their neighbours, and with little wealth to tempt invasion, may have quietly "lived for thousands of years, and their royal dynasties may have been already ancient when "Moses was leading the Israelites out of Egypt, and the Greeks were steering their swift ships to "Troy."

Their pride is expressed in the following proverb :—"In the house of the Katoch the work-"man gets coarse flour, and the flatterer fine rice." The Katoch claim to form a third section of the great Rájpút stock, Súrajbansi and Chandrabansi being the other two. They say they are descended from an ancestor called Bhúmi who was formed from the sweat on Bhágwatí's forehead ; and as *bhúmia* means earth, it may be that their division completes the triplet of the Sun, the Moon, and the Earth-born races.

The Goleria are the ruling family of Goler, and a branch of the Katoch stock ; the Dharwál I cannot identify. Some of the Kángra Ráthor have returned their clan as Dharwál.

The Chandel and Pathial (Nos. 4, 5).—The Chandel are one of the 36 royal races, and are fully described in Elliott's *Races of the N.-W. Provinces.* It is not impossible that they are the same stock as the Chandál, outcastes where subjects, Rájpúts where dominant. They are returned chiefly from the Native State of Biláspur. It would be interesting to know how this lowest of all the Rájpút races finds a place among the Simla States, and whether the ruling family of Biláspur is Chandel. The Pathiál appears to be among the most distinguished of the second class Rájpúts, and might, according to Mr. Lyall, more properly be classed as first-class Thakars. In Kángra 3,451 persons have entered themselves as Gondal Pathiál, and are shown under both headings.

The Pathania (No. 6).—This is the tribe to which the ruling family of Núrpur in Kángra belonged, and is said to take its name from Pathánkot in Gurdáspur, "the first possession which "the family occupied on their emigration to this neighbourhood from Hindústán ;" though in this case it would seem more probable that they gave their name to the town. I have, however, received a tradition, though not from good authority, that the Pathánia Rájpúts only occupied Pathánkot some five or six centuries ago. They are chiefly found in the Hushyárpur and Kángra districts. They are said to be of the same stock as the Katoch.

The Jaswal (No. 7).—The Jaswál are the ancient ruling family of the Jaswán *dún* in the low hills of Hushyárpur. They are nearly allied with the Katoch house of Kángra.

The Dudwal (No. 8).—The Dúdwál are the ancient ruling family of Dutárpur, and are said to take their name from Dáda in Kángra on the Hushyárpur border. The Ránas of the Bít Mánaswál or tableland of the Hushyárpur Siwáliks were Dúdwál Rájpúts, and the clan still holds the tract. They are chiefly found in Hushyárpur.

The Laddu Kilchi and Khoja (Nos. 9, 10, 11).—The Kilchi is said to be a clan of the Manj Rájpúts, which see further on ; but the Hushyárpur Kilchi have returned their second sub-division as follows : Bhatti, 240 ; Chauhán, 255 ; Ghorewáha, 134 ; Laddu, 905 ; Manj, 127 ; Náru, [P. 251]
1,279 ; Pathánia, 86. Of the Khoja 2,278 have shown themselves as Janjúa and 1,189 as Náru. Of the Laddu 905 have shown themselves as Kilchi also. All these are confined almost entirely to Hushyárpur, and are probably local clans.

The Naru (No. 12).—The Náru are with the exception perhaps of the Manj, the most widely spread of the Hill Rájpúts; but their head-quarters are the districts of Jálandhar and Hushyárpur. The Náru would appear to differ in their accounts of their own origin. Those of Hushyárpur, many or most of whom are still Hindu, and those of the adjoining northern portions of Jálandhar say that they are Chandrabansi and came from the hills; while those of the east of Jálandhar about Philaur, who are all Musalmáns, say their ancestor was a Raghbansi Rájpút who came from Ajudhia, entered the service of Shaháb-ul-dín Ghori, and eventually settled near Philaur. A third story makes the common ancestor a son of a Rája of Jaipur or Jodhpur, who was converted in the time of Mahmúd Ghaznavi, and settled at Bajwára in Hushyárpur. The Náru held the Hariána tract on the Jálandhar and Hushyárpur border till the Sikhs dispossessed them. The original settlement of the Jálandhar Náru was Mau, a name which, as Mr. Barkley points out, suggests an origin from eastern Hindústán or Central India. Of the Hushyárpur Náru 1,279 have also shown themselves as Kilchi, 556 as Manhás, and 903 as Gondal.

The Ghorewaha (No. 13).—The head-quarters of the Ghorewáha are the Jálandhar district, of which they occupy the eastern corner, and are found in small numbers in all the adjoining districts. To the west of them are the Manj, and to the north of them the Náru. They are almost all Musalmán. They are Kachwáha Rájpúts, descendants of Kash, the second son of Ráma. They say that Rája Mán, sixth in descent from Kash, had two sons Kachwáha and Hawáha, and that they are of the lineage of Hawáha. The two brothers met Shaháb-ul-dín Ghari (!) with an offering of a horse, and received in return as large a territory as they could ride round in a day; hence their name. The division of their country took place while they were yet Hindus, so that their settlement in their present tract was probably an early one. The Ráhon Ghorewáha, who are still Hindus, would seem to have immigrated more lately than the rest of the tribe, as they trace their origin from Jaipur, and their genealogists still live in Kota and Bundi in Rájpútána. Mr. Barkley is disposed to put the Ghorewáha conquest of their present territory at some five centuries ago. In the time of Akbar their possessions would seem to have been more extensive than they are now.

The Manj (No. 14)[1].—The Manj are the most widely distributed of all the sub-montane Rájpúts, if our figures are to be accepted as correct. They hold the south-western portion of the Jálandhar and the north-western portion of the Lúdhiána district, and are to be found in all the adjoining districts and States. There are also some 9,000 of them shown in the Pindi district. These last are the Alpiál of that district who have returned themselves as Manj Alpiál; but whether they are of the same stock as the Manj of Lúdhiána and Jálandhar, I cannot say. The Manj say that they are Bhatti Rájpúts, and descended from Rája Salváhan, father of Rája Rasálu of Siálkot. Some 600 years ago Shekh Cháchu and Shekh Kilchi, two Manj Rájpúts, are said to have settled at Hatúr in the south-west of Lúdhiána, whence their descendants spread into the neighbouring country; and the Jálandhar traditions refer their conquest of the tract to the time of Ala-ul-dín Khilji. As however they state that Shekh Cháchu was converted by Makhdúm Shah Jahánia of Uchh, who died in 1383 A.D., it would appear that if the tradition has any foundation, Ala-ul-dín Saiyad must be meant. After the dissolution of the Dehli Empire the Manj Rais of Talwandi and Raikot ruled over a very extensive territory south of the Satluj, till dispossessed of it by the Ahlúwália Sikhs and Ranjít Singh; and even earlier than this the Manj Nawábs of Kot Isa Khán had attained considerable importance under the Emperors. North of the Satluj the Manj never succeeded in establishing a principality; but they held a large tract of country in the south-west of the Jálandhar district about Talwan, Nakodar, and Malsián, and held much of it in *jágir* under the Mughals, but were dispossessed by Tára Singh Gheba and the Sindhánwála Sikhs. The Manj are now all Musalmán, though many were still Hindu after the time of Shekh Cháchu. Their genealogists live in Patiála, as do those of the Bhatti of Jálandhar. In the *Ayín-i-Akbari* the Manj are wrongly shown as Main, a title which is said to belong properly to the Ghorewáha of Lúdhiána.

The Taon (No. 15).—The Táoni are also Bhatti and descendants of Rája Salváhan, whose grandson Rai Tán is their eponymous ancestor One of his descendants, Rai Amba, is said to have built Ambála. They occupy the low hills and sub-montane in the north of Ambála district including the Kalsia State, and some of the adjoining Patiála territory. They are said to have occupied their present abode for 1,800 years.

CASTES ALLIED TO THE RAJPUTS.

458. The Thakar, Rathi, and Rawat (Caste Nos. 60, 39, and 82).—The
P. 98-9. figures for these castes are given in Abstract No. 71 on page 219. The Ráwat has already been described in section 145. The Thakar (or, as I believe it more properly should be, Thakkar) and Ráthi, are the lower classes of Hill

[1] For the greater part of the description of the Rájpúts of the Jálandhar district, I am indebted to the kindness of Mr. Barkley, who has given me access to a most valuable collection of MS. notes made when he was Deputy Commissioner of that district.

Rájpúts who, though they are admittedly Rájpúts and give their daughters to Rájpúts, who are styled by that title, do not reach the standard defined in section 456 which would entitle them to be *called* Rájpút, but are on the other hand above the Ráwat. The line between Rájpút and Thakar is defined, so far as it is capable of definition, in the following section. The line between Thakar and Ráthi may be roughly said to consist in the fact that Ráthis do and Thakars do not ordinarily practise widow-marriage; though the term Ráthi is commonly applied by Rájpúts of the ruling houses to all below them. Again the line between Ráthi and Kanet is exceedingly difficult to draw: in fact in Chamba Ráthi and Kanet are considered identical and are said to eat and marry together, and it is said that Ráthi is in Chamba and Jammu only another name for the same people who are called Kanet in Kúlu and Kángra. Thus no Kanets but numerous Ráthis are returned from Chamba. On the other hand, no other of the Hill States returns either Thakars or Ráthis, having probably included the former with Rájpúts and the latter with Kanets. Even Mr. Lyall says: "Our Kángra term Ráthi is a rough word to apply to any but the lowest class;" and speaking of Kúlu, he says: "The "children of a Bráhman or Rájpút by a Kanet wife are called Bráhmans and "Rájpúts, the term Ráthi being often added as a qualification by any one who "himself pretends to unmixed blood."

459. Mr. Barnes writes thus of the distinction between Thakar and Ráthi:—

"The Ráthis are essentially an agricultural class, and prevail throughout the Núrpur and "Nádáon parganahs. The Ráthis and the Ghiraths constitute the two great cultivating tribes in "these hills; and it is a remarkable fact that in all level and irrigated tracts, wherever the soil "is fertile and produce exuberant, the Ghiraths abound; while in the poorer uplands, where the "crops are scanty and the soil demands severe labour to compensate the husbandmen, the Ráthis "predominate. It is as rare to find a Ráthi in the valleys as to meet a Ghirath in the more "secluded hills. Each class holds possession of its peculiar domain, and the different habits and "associations created by the different localities have impressed upon each caste a peculiar "physiognomy and character. The Ráthis generally are a robust and handsome race; their "features are regular and well-defined; the colour usually fair; and their limbs athletic, as if "exercised and invigorated by the stubborn soil upon which their lot is thrown. On the other "hand, the Ghirath is dark and coarse featured; his body is stunted and sickly; goitre is fearfully "prevalent among his race; and the reflection occurs to the mind that, however teeming and "prolific the soil, however favourable to vegetable life, the air and climate are not equally adapted "to the development of the human frame.

"The Ráthis are attentive and careful agriculturists. Their women take little or no part in [P. 252] "the labours of the field. In origin they belong neither to the Kshatriya nor to the Súdra class, "but are apparently an amalgamation of both. Their ranks are being constantly increased by "defections from the Rájpúts, and by illegitimate connections. The offspring of a Rájpút father "by a Súdra mother would be styled a Ráthi, and accepted as such by the brotherhood. The sects "of the Ráthis are innumerable; no one could render a true and faithful catalogue of them. "They are as numerous as the villages they inhabit, from which indeed their distinguishing names "are generally derived. A Ráthi is cognizant only of the sects which immediately surround him. "They form a society quite sufficient for his few wants, and he has little idea of the extent and "ramifications of his tribe. The higher sects of the Ráthis are generally styled Thakars. They "are affronted at being called Ráthis, although they do not affect to be Rájpúts. The best "families among the Thakars give their daughters in marriage to the least eligible of the Rájpúts, "and thus an affinity is established between these two great tribes. The Ráthis generally assume "the thread of caste. They avoid wine, and are extremely temperate and frugal in their habits. "They take money for their daughters, or exchange them,—a practice reprobated by the Shástras "and not countenanced by the highest castes. On the death of an elder brother the widow lives "with the next brother, or, if she leaves his household, he is entitled to recover her value from "the husband she selects. Altogether, the Ráthis are the best hill subjects we possess;—their "manners are simple, quiet, and unaffected; they are devoted to agriculture, not unacquainted with "the use of arms; honest, manly, industrious and loyal."

Here he makes Thakars first class Ráthis. Mr. Lyall on the other hand seems inclined to class Thakars as second or third class Rájpúts. Speaking of the caste tables which he appends to his reports, in which he classes the Hindu population under the heads of first grade Bráhman; second grade Bráhman; first grade Rájpút; second grade Rájpút; Khatris, Mahájans, Kirárs, &c.; first grade Súdras, Thakars, Ráthis, &c.; second grade Súdras; he writes:—

"The Rájpút clans of the second grade might more properly be called first grade Thakars: "among the most distinguished and numerous of them are the Habrols, the Pathiáls, the Dhatwáls, "the Indaurias, the Nángles, the Gumbaris, the Ránes, the Paniáls, the Ranats, the Mailes. "They marry their daughters to the Miáns, and take daughters in marriage from the Ráthis. In "the statements most of the Thakars have been entered as second class Rájpúts, and a few as "first class Súdras. Most of the Thakars entered in this last class might more properly have been "classed as Ráthis. The Núrpur Thakars are all no better than Ráthis. A Thakar, if asked in "what way he is better than a Ráthi, will say that his own manners and social customs, "particularly in respect of selling daughters, marrying brother's widow, &c, are more like "those of the Mián class than those of the Ráthis are. The best line of distinction however "is the marriage connection; the Mián will marry a Thakar's daughter, but not a Ráthi's. "The Ráthi's daughter marries a Thakar, and her daughter can then marry a Mián. No "one calls himself a Ráthi, or likes to be addressed as one. The term is understood to convey "some degree of slight or insult; the distinction between Thakar and Ráthi is however very loose. "A rich man of a Ráthi family, like Shib Diál Chaudhri of Chetru, marries his daughter to an "impoverished Rája, and his whole clan gets a kind of step and becomes Thakar Rájpút. So "again a Rája out riding falls in love with a Pathiál girl herding cattle, and marries her "whereupon the whole clan begins to give its daughters to Miáns. The whole thing reminds one "of the struggles of families to rise in society in England, except that the numbers interested "in the struggle are greater here, as a man cannot separate himself entirely from his clan, and "must take it up with him or stay where he is, and except that the tactics or rules of the game "are here stricter and more formal, and the movement much slower."

P. 101. And the quotation from the same report given on page 221 may be referred to. The Ráthi does not seem to be a favourite in Kángra. Here are two proverbs about him: "The Ráthi in the stocks, the barley in the mill;" and "A "Ráthi, a goat, a devotee, and a widow woman; all need to be kept weak, for "if strong they will do mischief."

Of the Thakars of Kángra 2,273 have shown their tribe as Phúl, and 4,304 as Jarautia. In Gurdáspur 1,007 are shown as Pangláua and 294 as Balotra. Some 6,000 altogether show Kásib as their clan, which is probably only their Brahminical gotra. Among the Ráthis of Kángra there are 1,078 Balotra, 1,716 Barhái, 3,029 Chángra, 1,879 Dharwál, 1,632 Gurdwál, 1,113 Goital, 1,101 Mangwál, 518 Phawál, and 1,774 Rákor. In Chamba there are 2,350 Chophal. Altogether 15,000 show themselves as Kásib. There is a local saying that there are as many clans of Ráthis as there are different kinds of grass.

459a. The Dhund and Kahut (Caste Nos. 74 and 103).—These have been already discussed together with the Rájpúts of the Western Hills in sections 453, 454.

PART IV.—MINOR LAND-OWNING AND AGRICULTURAL CASTES.

460. Introductory and General.—I have roughly grouped the tribes and castes which I propose to discuss in this part of the present chapter under three heads, Minor Dominant Tribes, Minor Agricultural and Pastoral Tribes, and Foreign Races. The figures for each group will be found prefixed to the detailed discussion of the castes which compose it. No very definite line can be drawn between the several groups; but the general idea of the classification has been to include in the first such tribes or castes as, while not of sufficient magnitude or general importance to rank with the four great races which have been discussed in the two preceding parts of the chapter, yet occupy a social position somewhat similar to theirs, and either are or have been within recent times politically dominant in their tribal territories. In the second group I have included those cultivating tribes who, while forming a very large and important element in the agricultural section of the population, occupy a subject or subordinate position, and have not, at least within recent times, risen to political prominence. The third group includes that miscellaneous assortment of persons who bear titles, such as Shekh or Mughal, which purport to denote foreign origin. Many, perhaps most of them, are really of Indian origin, and many of them are neither agriculturists nor land-owners. But no general grouping of castes in the Panjáb can hope to be exact; and this appeared to be the most convenient place in which to discuss them. The tribes discussed in this part of the chapter complete the essentially land-owning or agricultural tribes of the Panjáb. The Bráhmans and Saiyads cultivate largely, while the mercantile classes own large areas; but they will be more conveniently dealt with under a separate head in the next part of the chapter. [P. 253]

MINOR DOMINANT TRIBES.

461. Minor dominant tribes.—The tribes or castes which I have included in Abstract No. 83 on the next page* are those which are, like the Jats and Rájpúts, dominant in parts of the Panjáb, but are not so numerous or so widely spread as to rank with those great races. Indeed many of them are probably tribes rather than castes or races; though in some cases their origin has been forgotten, while in others an obviously false origin has been invented. They are divided into four groups, the Karrál, Gakkhar, Awán, and Khattar of the Salt-range Tract, the Khokhar, Kharral and Dáúdpotra of the Western Plains, and the Dogar, Ror, Taga, Meo and Khánzádah of the Eastern Plains; while the Gújar, who is more widely distributed than the rest, comes last by himself. With the Western Plains group are included the Káthia, Háns, and Khagga, for whom I have no separate figures: indeed it will be apparent from a perusal of the following paragraphs that the figures for all these minor castes in the western half of the Province are exceedingly imperfect. Not only are the lax use of the word Jat and the ill-defined nature of the line separating Jats from Rájpúts already alluded to sources of great confusion, but many of these tribes have set up claims to an origin which shall connect them with the founder of the Mahomedan religion, or with some of the great Mahomedan conquerors. *P. 166-67.

Thus we find many of them returned or classed as Shekh, Mughal, or what not; and the figures of the Abstract alone are exceedingly misleading. I have in each case endeavoured to separate the numbers thus returned, and to include them under their proper caste headings; and it is the figures thus given in the text, and not those of the tables, that should be referred to. Even these are not complete, for till we have the full detail of clans we cannot complete the classification.

The ethnic grouping of the tribes discussed in this section is a subject which I had hoped to examine, but which lack of time compels me to pass by unnoticed. I will only note how the tendency on the frontier and throughout the Salt-range Tract is to claim Arab or Mughal, and in the rest of the Province to claim Rájpút origin. The two groups of tribes which occupy the mountain country of the Salt-range and the great plateaus of the Western Plains are the most interesting sections of the Panjáb land-owning classes, need the most careful examination, and would reward it with the richest return.

462. The Karral (Caste No. 101).—The Karráls are returned for Hazára only; and I have no information concerning them save what Major Wace gives in his Settlement Report of that district. He writes: "The Karrál country "consists of the Nára *ildqah* in the Abbottábád *tahsíl*. The Karráls were "formerly the subjects of the Gakkhars, from whom they emancipated them-"selves some two centuries ago. Originally Hindus, their conversion to Islám "is of comparatively modern date. Thirty years ago their acquaintance with "the Mahomedan faith was still slight; and though they now know more of "it, and are more careful to observe it, relics of their former Hindu faith are "still observable in their social habits. They are attached to their homes and "their fields, which they cultivate simply and industriously. For the rest, "their character is crafty and cowardly." Major Wace further notes that the "Karráls are identical in origin and character with the Dhúnds." This would make the Karráls one of the Rájpút tribes of the hills lying along the left bank of the Jahlam; and I have been informed by a native officer that they claim Rájpút origin. They are said too to have recently set up a claim to Kayáni Mughal origin, in common with the Gakkhars; or, as a variety, that their ancestor came from Kayán, but was a descendant of Alexander the Great! But the strangest story of all is that a queen of the great Rája Rasálu of Panjáb folklore had by a paramour of the scavenger class four sons, Seo, Teo, Gheo, and Karu, from whom are respectively descended the Siáls, Tiwánas, Ghebas, and Karráls. They intermarry with Gakkhars, Saiyads, and Dhúnds.

[P. 255] **463. The Gakkhar (Caste No. 68).**—The Gakkhars are the ancient rulers of the northern portion of the cis-Indus Salt-range Tract, just as are the Awáns and Janjúas of the southern portion of the same tract; and it appears probable that they at one time overran Kashmír, even if they did not found a dynasty there. Their own story is that they are descended from Kaigohar of the Kayáni family then reigning in Ispahán; that they conquered Kashmír and Tibet and ruled those countries for many generations, but were eventually driven back to Kábul, whence they entered the Panjáb in company with Mahmúd Ghaznavi early in the 11th century. This last is certainly untrue, for Ferishtah relates that in 1008 Mahmud was attacked by a Gakkhar army in the neighbourhood of Pesháwar. Sir Lepel Griffin thinks that they were

Abstract No. 83, showing the Minor [P. 254]

	MINOR DOMINANT									
	FIGURES.									
	101	68	12	162	58	77	79	46	55	86
	Karrál.	Gakkhar.	Awán.	Khattar.	Khokhar.	Kharral.	Dáúdpotra.	Dogar.	Ror.	Taga.
Dehli	...	...	...	...	1	...	...	48	666	9,954
Gurgaon	...	...	...	...	1	...	...	..	..	140
Karnál	...	...	1	...	1	...	...	1,960	34,094	4,162
Hissar	...	...	...	...	...	...	...	4,723	...	...
Rohtak	...	...	...	...	...	...	...	213	...	36
Sirsa	...	...	...	...	...	...	...	236	...	...
Ambala	...	...	...	...	...	...	...	1,417	1,861	4
Ludhiána	...	...	3,312	...		...	...	2,214	26	...
Jalandhar	...	...	9,420	...	...	...	...	4,079	...	...
Hushyárpur ...	...	...	9,771	...	...	...	...	4,073	...	...
Kangra	...	...	88	...	...	...	...	4	...	...
Amritsar	...	...	1,383	..	9	...	...	4,067	...	...
Gurdáspur	...	...	153	...	...	...	...	1,853	...	...
Siálkot	...	...	19,753	...	...	...	...	2,006	...	..
Lahore	...	...	2,470	...	...	70	...	6,783	...	...
Gujránwála ...	...	...	569	...	...	...	...	566	...	...
Firozpur	...	...	60	...	...	...	...	14,143	...	...
Ráwalpindi ...	119	10,667	124,834	...	438	4	1	6	...	...
Jahlam	...	9,920	92,856	..	1,745	1	...	...	...	...
Gujrát	..	75	13,029	..	393	...	...	...	...	...
Shahpur	...	114	48,485	...	10,265	1	...	7	...	...
Multan	...	..	2,399	235	7,606	2,402	1,315	186	...	...
Jhang	...	...	1,496	...	11,239	489	1	1	...	...
Montgomery ...	...	14	515	7	2,866	15,643	27	358	...	...
Muzaffargarh ...	...	65	626	...	951	112	108	6	...	...
Derah Ismail Khan ...	...	6	825	...	...	...	...	...	...	...
Derah Ghazi Khan ...	...	5	286	...	...	...	99	...	...	...
Bannu	...	50	20,908	...	...	...	...	.	...	...
Pesháwar	6	242	97,445	399	191	27	...	148	...	...
Hazara	10,288	4,613	65,606	600	302	...	...	...	...	...
Kohát	...	18	16,163	4	24	...	...	...	...	...
British Territory	10,418	25,789	582,457	1,245	36,126	18,839	1,551	49,338	39,647	14,305
Patiála	...	...	14	...	11	...	...	8,475	36	...
Nábha	...	...	7	...	...	6	...	185	...	...
Kapurthala ...	...	...	412	...	...	...	...	3,815	...	...
Jínd	...	...	...	...	...	...	..	189	1,048	...
Farídkot	...	...	...	...	...	...	...	1,009	...	...
Maler Kotla ...	...	...	4	...	...	...	...	75	...	...
Kalsia	...	...	1	...	...	...	...	347	...	...
Total East. Plains ...	...	...	438	...	11	6	...	14,095	1,094	...
Baháwalpur ...	...	...	...	...	...	...	10,612	4	...	...
Mandi	...	...	...	...	...	...	...	...	...	..
Chamba	...	...	...	...	...	...	...	...	...	...
Náhan	...	...	...	...	...	...	...	...	...	...
Biláspur	...	...	...	...	...	...	...	...	...	...
Nálagarh	...	...	...	...	...	...	...	...	...	...
Total Hill States ...	...	...	...	...	...	..	...	...	...	...
British Territory	10,418	25,789	582,457	1,245	36,126	18,839	1,551	49,338	39,647	14,305
Native States ...	...	..	438	...	11	6	16,612	14,099	1,084	..
Province ...	10,413	25,789	582,855	1,245	36,137	18,845	18,168	63,437	40,731	14,305

Dominant Tribes for Districts and States.

TRIBES.

			Proportion per 1,000 of total Population.																	
34 Meo.	123 Khánzádah.	8 Gújar.	101 Karrál.	68 Gakkhar.	12 Awán.	162 Khattar.	Total.	58 Khokhar.	77 Kharral.	79 Dáúdpotra.	Total.	46 Dogar.	55 Ror.	86 Taga.	34 Meo.	123 Khánzádah.	Total.	8 Gújar.	Grand Total.	
9,567	64	25,836	...	...	...	...	...	...	...	...	...	...	1	15	15	...	31	40	71	Dehli.
103,678	3,671	20,955	...	...	...	...	...	...	...	...	...	...	...	...	161	6	167	33	200	Gurgaon.
351	1	21,808	...	...	...	...	...	...	...	...	...	3	55	7	1	...	66	35	101	Karnál.
449	...	8,426	...	...	...	...	...	...	...	...	...	9	...	...	1	...	10	17	27	Hissar.
234	...	3,032	...	...	...	...	...	...	...	...	...	...	...	...	...	...	...	5	5	Rohtak.
219	...	750	...	...	...	...	...	...	...	...	...	1	...	...	1	...	2	3	5	Sirsa.
889	7	51,077	...	...	...	...	...	...	...	...	...	...	4	...	1	...	5	48	53	Ambala.
9	...	30,759	...	...	5	...	5	...	...	...	...	4	...	...	...	...	4	50	59	Ludhiána.
...	...	18,394	...	...	12	...	12	...	...	...	...	5	...	...	...	...	5	23	40	Jalandhar.
...	...	68,302	...	...	11	...	11	...	...	...	...	5	...	...	...	...	5	76	92	Hushyárpur.
...	...	8,460	...	...	...	...	...	...	...	...	...	...	...	...	...	...	...	12	13	Kangra.
...	...	4,168	...	...	2	...	2	...	...	...	...	5	...	...	...	...	5	5	12	Amritsar.
...	...	43,571	...	...	...	...	...	...	...	...	...	1	...	...	...	...	1	53	54	Gurdáspur.
...	...	11,642	...	...	19	...	19	...	...	...	...	2	...	...	...	...	2	11	32	Siálkot.
...	4	7,079	...	...	3	...	3	...	...	...	...	7	...	...	...	...	7	8	18	Lahore.
...	...	1,986	...	...	1	...	1	...	...	...	...	1	...	...	...	...	1	3	5	Gujráuwála.
...	...	12,013	...	...	...	...	...	...	...	...	...	22	...	...	...	...	22	10	41	Firozpur.
...	...	25,403		13	152	...	165	1	...	...	1	...	...		...	...	...	31	197	Ráwalpindi.
...	...	18,924	...	17	158	...	175	3	...	...	3	...	...	...	...	...	...	32	210	Jahlam.
...	...	93,442	...	...	19	...	19	1	...	...	1	...	...	...	...	...	...	136	156	Gujrát.
...	...	886	...	...	115	...	115	24		...	24	...	...	...	...	...	...	2	141	Shahpur.
3	5	604	...	...	4	...	4	14	5	2	21	...	...	...	...	...	...	1	26	Multan.
...	...	238	...	...	4	...	4	28	1	...	29	...	...	...	...	...	...	1	34	Jhang.
...	...	365	...	...	1	...	1	7	37	...	44	1	...	...	...	...	1	1	47	Montgomery.
...	...	63	...	...	2	...	2	3	...	...	3	...	...	...	...	...	...	...	5	Muzaffargarh.
...	...	77	...	...	2	...	2	...	...	...	...	...	...	...	...	...	...	...	2	Derah Ismail Khan.
...	...	37	...		1	...	1	...	...	...	...	...	...	...	...	...	...	...	1	Derah Ghazi Khan.
...	...	50	...		63	...	63	...	...	...	...	...	...	...	...	...	...	...	63	Bannu.
...	3	13,514	...	...	164	1	165	...	...	...	...	...	...	...	...	...	...	23	188	Peshávar.
...	...	60,948	25	11	161	1	198	1		...	1	...	...	...	...	...	...	159	349	Hazara.
...	...	206	...	...	89		89	...	...	...	...	...	...	...	...	...	...	1	90	Kohát.
115,399	**8,755**	**553,417**	**1**	**1**	**28**	...	**30**	**2**	**1**	...	**3**	**3**	**2**	**1**	**6**	...	**12**	**29**	**24**	**British Territory.**
62	1	35,359	...	...	...	...	...	...	...	...	...	6	...	...	...	...	6	24	30	Patiála.
374	1	5,456	...		...	...	...	...	...		...	1	...	...	1	...	2	21	23	Nábha.
...	...	5,805	...	...	2	...	2	...		...		15	...		...	...	15	23	40	Kapurthala.
6	...	1,740	...	...	...	...		...		...	...	1	4	...	...	...	5	7	12	Jínd.
335	...	645		...	...		...	...	...	...	...	10	...		4	...	14	7	21	Farídkot.
...	...	2,376	...	...	...	...	...	...	...	...	...	1	...	...	...	...	1	33	34	Maler Kotla.
25	...	4,491	...	...	...	...	...	...	...	...	...	5	...	...	...	...	5	66	71	Kalsia.
828	2	56,066	...	...	...	...	...	...	...	...	...	6	...	...	...	...	6	22	28	Total East. Plains
...	...	456	...	...	...	...	...	...	...	29	29	...	...	...	...	...	...	1	30	Baháwalpur.
...	...	1,259	...	...	...	...	...	...	...	...	...		...		...	...	...	9	9	Mandi.
...	...	907	...	...	...	...	...		...	...	...	...	...	...	...	...	...	8	8	Chamba.
...	...	2,445	...	...	...	...	...	...	...	...	...	...	...	...	...	...	...	22	22	Náhan.
...	...	3,083	...	...	...	...	...	...	...	...	...	...	...	...	...	...	...	36	36	Bilaspur.
...	...	8,952	...	...	...	...	...	...	...	...	...	...	...	...	...	...	...	168	168	Nálagarh.
...	...	17,445	...	...	...	...	...	...	...	...	...		...		...	...	...	23	23	Total Hill States.
115,999	**3,755**	**553,317**	**1**	**1**	**28**	...	**30**	**2**	**1**	.	**3**	**3**	**2**	**1**	**6**		**12**	**29**	**74**	**British Territory**
828	2	73,987	...	...	...	...	...	...	...	4	4	4	...	...	...		4	19	27	**Native States.**
116,226	**3,757**	**627,304**	...	**1**	**28**	...	**24**	**2**	**1**	**1**	**4**	**3**	**2**	**1**	**5**	...	**11**	**18**	**67**	**Province.**

emigrants from Khorásán who settled in the Panjáb not later than 300 A.D., and points out that, like the Persians and unlike the other tribes of the neighbourhood, they are still Shíahs. It is at any rate certain that they held their present possessions long before the Mahomedan invasion of India. Ferishtah writes of them during Muhammad Ghori's invasion in 1206 A.D. :—

" During the residence of Muhammad Ghori at Lahore on this occasion, the Ghakkars who " inhabit the country along the banks of the Níláb up to the foot of the mountains of Siwálik, " exercised unheard of cruelties on the Muhammadans and cut off the communication between the " provinces of Peshávar and Multán. These Ghakkars were a race of wild barbarians, without " either religion or morality. It was a custom among them as soon as a female child was born, to " carry her to the door of the house and there proclaim aloud, holding the child in one hand and a " knife in the other, that any person who wanted a wife might take her otherwise she was im- " mediately to be put to death. By this means they had more men than women which occasioned " the custom of having several husbands to one wife. When this wife was visited by one of her " husbands she left a mark at the door, which being observed by any of the other husbands, he with- " drew till the signal was taken away. This barbarous people continued to make incursions on the " Muhammadans till in the latter end of this king's reign their chieftain was converted to the true " faith while a captive. A great part of these mountaineers, having very little notion of any " religion, were easily induced to adopt the tenets of the true faith ; at the same time most of the " infidels who inhabited the mountains between Ghazni and the Indus were also converted, some " by force and others by persuasion, and at the present day (1609 A.D.) they continue to profess " the faith of Islám." *Briggs' Ferishtah, i.* 183 *f.*

The Gakkhars however did not hesitate to assassinate Muhammad Ghori on his return from Lahore.

General Cunningham identifies the Gakkhars with the Gargaridæ of Dionysius, and holds them to be descendants of the great Yueti or Takhari Scythians of the Abár tribe, who moved from Hyrkania to Abryán on the Jahlam under either Darius Hystaspes (circa 500 B.C.), or still earlier under one of the Scytho-Parthian Kings. The whole origin and early history of the tribe will be found discussed at pages 22 to 33, Vol. II of the Archæological Reports, and at pages 574 to 581 of Griffin's *Panjáb Chiefs ;* while much information as to their early history is given in Brandreth's Settlement Report of the Jahlam District. As Mr. Thomson says : " The " Turanian origin of the Gakkhars is highly probable ; but the rest of the " theory is merely a plausible surmise. On the whole there seems little use in " going beyond the sober narrative of Ferishtah, who represents the Gakkhars " as a brave and savage race, living mostly in the hills, with little or no religion, " and much given to polyandry and infanticide." They have now, in apparent imitation of the Awáns, set up a claim to Mughal origin ; and many of the Ráwalpindi Gakkhars returned themselves as Mughals, while I am told that some of the Gakkhars of Chakwál entered themselves as Rájpúts.

464. At present the Gakkhars are practically confined to the Ráwalpindi, Jahlam, and Hazára Districts, where they are found all along the plateaus at the foot of the lower Himálayas, from the Jahlam to Harípur in Hazára. To the figures given in Table VIII-A should be added 1,543 persons who returned themselves in Ráwalpindi as Mughal Gakkhar, and perhaps 4,549 others who returned themselves as Mughal Kayáni, of whom 3,861 were in Ráwalpindi, 592 in Jahlam, and 93 in Kohát. This would raise the total number of Gakkhars to 31,881, of whom about half are in Ráwalpindi. They are described by Mr. Thomson as compact, sinewy, and vigorous, but not large boned ; making capital soldiers and the best light cavalry in Upper India ; proud and self-respecting, but not first-class agriculturists; with no contempt for labour, since many work as coolies on the railway; but preferring service in the army or police. Their race feeling is strong, and a rule of inheritance disfavours Gakkhars of the half-blood. Colonel Cracroft notes that they refuse to give their daughters in marriage to any other class except Saiyads, that they keep their women very strictly secluded, and marry only among the higher Rájpúts, and among them only when they cannot find a suitable match among themselves. "Some of their "principal men are very gentlemanly in their bearing, and show unmistake-"ably their high origin and breeding. They still cling to their traditions "and, though the Sikhs reduced them to the most abject poverty, are looked "up to in the district as men of high rank and "position, and in times of commotion they would "assuredly take the lead one way or the other." Thus the character of the "savage Gargars" seems to have been softened and improved by time. The Gakkhars do not seem always to have returned their clans, which are very well marked. I give in the margin the figures for a few of the largest. Their local distribution in the Jahlam District is fully described in Mr. Thomson's Settlement Report.

GAKKHAR CLANS.	
Bugiál	7,117
Iskandrál	2,668
Fírozál	1,822
Admál	1,801
Surangál	1,681

465. The Awan (Caste No. 12).—The Awáns, with whom have been included all who returned themselves as Qutbsháhi, are essentially a tribe of the Salt-range, where they once held independent possessions of very considerable extent, and in the western and central portions of which they are still the dominant race. They extend along the whole length of the range from Jahlam to the Indus, and are found in great numbers throughout the whole country beyond it up to the foot of the Sulemáns and the Safed Koh; though in Trans-Indus Bannu they partly and in Dehra Ismáíl almost wholly disappear from our tables, being included in the term Jat which in those parts means not very much more than *et cætera*. Thus we find among the Jats of our tables no fewer than 30,015 who returned Awán as their tribe and who should probably be classed as Awán, of whom the details are given in the margin.

AWAN JATS.			
Hushyarpur ...	2,400	Derah Ismail Khan ...	8,444
Lahore ...	831	Derah Ghazi Khan ...	1,015
Gajranwala ...	611	Bannu ...	9,147
Jahlam ...	668	Other places ...	2,015
Gujrat ...	715		
Multan ...	1,178		
Jhang ...	559		
Muzaffargarh ...	2,017	TOTAL ...	30,015

[P. 256] The eastern limits of their position as a dominant tribe coincide approximately with the western border of the Chakwál and Pind Dádan Khán *tahsíls*. They have also spread eastwards along the foot of the hills as far east as the Sutlej, and southwards down the river valley into Multán and Jhang. They formerly held all the plain country at foot of the western Salt-range, but have been gradually driven up into the hills by Patháns advancing from the Indus and Tiwánas from the Jahalm.

Their story is that they are descended from Qutb Sháh of Ghazni, himself a descendant of Ali, the son-in-law of Mahomet, but by a wife other than the Prophet's daughter, who came from Hirát about 1035 A.D. and settled in the neighbourhood of Peshâwar. Thence they spread along the

Salt-range, forming independent clans by whom the Chief of Kálábágh was acknowledged as the head of the tribe. Mr. Brandreth is of opinion that they are more probably "descendants of the Bactrian Greeks driven south "from Balkh by Tartar hordes, and turning from Hírát to India," and that they entered the Panjáb not more than some 250 years ago as a conquering army under leaders of their own, and dispossessed the Janjúa Rájpúts of the Salt-range country. General Cunningham, on the other hand, is inclined to identify them with the Júd, whom Bábar mentions as being descended from the same ancestor as the Janjúas and occupying the western Salt-range at the time of his invasion, and who were so called from the old name of Mount Sakesar which is still the tribal centre of the Awán race. He would make both the Awáns and the Janjúas Anúwán or descendants of Anu; and thinks it probable that they held the plateaus which lie north of the Salt-range at the time of the Indo-Scythian invasion which drove them southwards to take refuge in the mountains. (*Archæological Reports*, Vol. II, page 17*ff.*) Bábar describes the Júd and Janjúas as having been from of old the lords of the Salt-range and of the plain country at its foot between the Indus and the Jahlam, and mentions that their minor Chiefs were called Malik, a title still used by the headmen of those parts. The Jálandhar Awáns state that they came into that district as followers of one of the early Emperors of Dehli who brought them with him from the Salt-range; and it is not impossible that they may have accompanied the forces of Bábar. Many of them were in former times in the imperial service at Dehli, keeping up at the same time their connection with their Jálandhar homes. It is almost certain that Mr. Brandreth's theory is incorrect. The Awáns have been almost the sole occupants of the Miánwáli Salt-range Tract for the last 600 years. Mr. Thomson considers the whole question in sections 73-74 of his Jahlam Settlement Report, and adduces many strong reasons in support of his conclusion that the Awáns are a Jat race who came through the passes west of Derah Ismáíl Khán and spread northwards to the country near Sakesar, a conclusion towards which some of the traditions of Derah Ismáíl Khán also are said to point. I may add that some of the Awáns of Gújrát are said to trace their origin from Sindh. Major Wace also is inclined to give the Awáns a Jat origin. In the genealogical tree of the Kálábágh family which used to be the chief family of the tribe, in which tree their descent is traced from Qutb Sháh, several Hindu names, such as Rai Harkaran, occur immediately below the name of Qutb Sháh. The Awáns still employ Hindu Bráhmans as family priests.

466. Mr. Thomson describes the Awáns as frank and pleasing in their manners, but vindictive, violent, and given to faction; strong and broad shouldered, but not tall; strenuous but slovenly cultivators; and essentially a peasant race. Colonel Davies thinks scarcely more favourably of them. He writes: "The Awáns are a brave high-spirited race but withal exceeding-"ly indolent. In point of character there is little in them to admire; headstrong "and irascible to an unusual degree, and prone to keeping alive old feuds, they "are constantly in hot water; their quarrels leading to affrays and their affrays "not unfrequently ending in bloodshed. As a set-off against this it must "be allowed that their manners are frank and engaging, and although they "cannot boast of the truthfulness of other hill tribes, they are remarkably "free from crime." Mr. Steedman says: "The Awáns hold a high, but "not the highest place among the tribes of the Ráwalpindi District. As a rule "they do not give their daughters in marriage to other tribes, and the "children of a low-caste woman by an Awán are not considered true Awáns." In Jahlam their position would scarcely seem to be so high as in Ráwalpindi, as Mr. Thomson describes them as distinctly belonging to the *zamíndár* or peasant class, as opposed to the Gakkhars and Janjúas who are *Sahú* or gentry. The history of the Awáns is sketched by Sir Lepel Griffin at pages 570*ff* of his *Panjáb Chiefs*. The Awáns have returned very few large sub-divisions. I give the figures for some of the largest in the margin. Of the Khokhar 5,663 are in Ráwalpindi, 2,362 in Jahlam, 3,949 in Sháhpur, 2,438 in Bannu, and 3,301 in Hazára; while of the Khattar 10,916 are in Ráwalpindi. These men are probably really Khattars and Khokhars rather than Awáns, but have returned themselves thus in pursuance of the tradition of all the three tribes having a common origin.

AWAN CLANS.

1.	Khokhar ...	18,368	7.	Babkál ...	6,118
2.	Madhwál ...	11,903	8.	Khurána...	6,105
3.	Khattar ...	11,278	9.	Darhál ...	5,299
4.	Kalghán ...	11,166	10.	Gulsháhi...	3,450
5.	Rehán ...	8,394	11.	Kang ...	2,979
6.	Jand ...	6,288	12.	Chahán ...	2,326

467. The Khattar (Caste No. 162).—The Khattars are a tribe which claims kinship with the Awáns, and to be, like them and the western Khokhars, descended from one of the sons of Qutb Sháh Qureshi of Ghazni. But the Awáns do not always admit the relationship, and the Khattars are said often to claim Rájpút origin. Mr. Steedman however accepts their Awán origin, and says that an Awán admits it, but looks upon the Khattars as an inferior section of the tribe to whom he will not give his daughters in marriage. Sir Lepel Griffin, who relates the history of the principal Khattar families at pages 561 to 569 of his *Panjáb Chiefs*, thinks that they were originally inhabitants of Khorásán who came to India with the early Mahomedan invaders. But Colonel Cracroft notes that the Khattars of Ráwalpindi still retain marriage customs which point to an Indian origin; and they themselves have a tradition of having been driven out of their territory on the Indus near Attak into Afghánistán, and returning thence with the armies of Muhammad Ghori. General Cunningham, on the other hand, would identify them with a branch of the Kator, Cidaritæ, or little Yúchi, from whom the Gújars also are descended and whose early history is related in section 480. (*Archæological Reports*, Vol. II, page 80). They now hold the tract known by their name which extends on both sides of the Kála Chitta Pahár from the Indus to the boundary of the Ráwalpindi *tahsíl*, and from Usmán Kátar on the north to the
P. 257] Khair-i-Múrat hills on the south, and which they are said to have taken from Gújars and Awáns. The figures of Table VIII-A are very imperfect, as the Khattars of Ráwalpindi have returned themselves as Awáns. Under the caste heading of Awán no fewer than 11,278 persons have shown their clan as Khattar, of whom all but 362 are in the Ráwalpindi district, thus bringing up the total numbers for the Province to 12,523. Colonel Cracroft writes: "The Khattars enjoy an unenviable notoriety in regard to crime. Their "tract has always been one in which heavy crime has flourished; they are bad "agriculturists, extravagant in their habits, keep hawks and horses, and are "often backward in paying their revenue. They do not allow their daughters "to inherit excepting in cases of intermarriage with members of the family "and even then only for some special reason." On this Steedman notes

" Since then they have become more civilised and less addicted to deeds of " violence. Socially the Khattars hold an intermediate place, ranking below " Gakkhars, Awáns, Ghebas, Jodras, and other high class Rájpúts."

468. The Khokhar (Caste No. 58).—The figures of Table VIII A under the head Khokhar only represent a fraction of the Khokhars in the Panjáb. The Khokhars are ordinarily considered a Rájpút tribe, and most of the Khokhars of the central districts have so returned themselves. Many of the Khokhars of the western districts again, and all those of the frontier, have been returned as Jats; while only in the Ráwalpindi and Multán divisions are separate figures shown for the Khokhar caste. How far this inclusion is due to Khokhars having actually returned themselves as Rájpút or Jat by caste and Khokhar by tribe, and how far to the action of the divisional offices, I cannot say exactly till the detailed clan tables are ready. But from local enquiry it would appear that Khokhars did very generally return themselves as Jats or Rájpúts, especially the latter, and Mr. Thomson tells me that in Pind Dádan Khán the Jat Khokhars are said to be entirely distinct from the Rájpút Khokhars. The figures in the margin show those who are returned as Khokhar, Rájpút Khokhar, and Jat Khokhar respectively. In the east of the Panjáb Khokhars appear to be admittedly of Rájpút origin, though in Jálandhar at least they are said to intermarry rather with their own clan, Shekhs, Awáns, and the like, than with their Rájpút neighbours. But in the west the Khokhars have set up a claim to be descended from Muhammad the eldest son of Qutb Sháh of Ghazni, the traditional ancestor of the Awáns; and the claim is often admitted by the Awáns themselves, though of course as mythical as the Awán's own story. Thus no fewer than 18,388 men, of whom the detail has already been given in section 466, have returned themselves as Awán by caste and Khokhar by clan, and should probably be counted as Khokhars and added to the figures given above. Mr. Barkley points out

KHOKHARS.
(Small numbers omitted in the details but included in the totals.)

District or State.	Caste Khokhar.	Caste Rájpút.	Caste Jat.	Total.
Rohtak	...	27	1,675	1,702
Sirsa	...	1,100	276	1,376
Jálandhar	...	3,682	...	3,682
Amritsar	9	3,016	134	3,159
Gurdáspur... ...	...	1,785	1,310	3,095
Siálkot	...	1,870	1,243	3,113
Lahore	...	8,349	2,184	10,533
Gujránwála ...	...	961	3,767	4,728
Firozpur	...	2,404	427	2,831
Ráwalpindi ...	438	295	161	894
Jahlam	1,745	2,208	2,011	5,964
Gujrát	393	5,208	1,745	7,346
Sháhpur	10,265	4,524	1,800	16,589
Multán	7,696	236	963	8,895
Jhang	11,239	6,605	5,040	22,884
Montgomery	2,866	1,058	2,157	6,081
Muzaffargarh ...	951	18	2,937	3,906
Derah Ismail Khán ...	...	20	8,013	8,033
Derah Ghazi Khán ...	...	12	4,690	4,702
Bannu	...	70	1,115	1,185
Kapúrthala ...	...	2,375	10	2,385
Baháwalpur ...	...	6,310	...	6,310
British Territory ...	36,126	45,731	42,110	123,967
Native States ...	11	9,649	221	9,881
Province	36,137	55,380	42,331	133,848
Add Awán Khokhar ...	...	...	...	18,388
GRAND TOTAL ...	...	...	...	152,236

that the annals of Jaisalmer given by Major Tod narrate the quarrels between the Khokhars and the Bhattis of Jaisalmer long before the time of Mahomet; though I should add that Major Tod thinks Khokhar may be a misreading for Gakkhar. Major Tod gives Khokra as one of the clans of the Ráthor Rájpúts. In Baháwalpur I find that 2,412 of the Khokhar Rájpúts have returned their main tribe as Bhatti. On the whole it would appear most probable that they are really Rájpúts, perhaps not of the purest descent; while the low repute in which Rájpúts are held on the frontier would account for the rise of the claim to Qureshi origin, which would quickly spread among a Musalmán tribe. In Sirsa, where the prohibition against marriage out of the caste is very strictly observed, the Khokhars intermarry with the local Rájpút tribes. Sir Lepel Griffin indeed separates the Khokhar Rájpúts from those Khokhars who claim kindred origin with the Awáns; but it is doubtful whether this is allowable, for the Awán tradition is apparently spreading, even among those Khokhars who are still recognised as Rájpúts throughout the country side. At the same time the Khokhars are so widely spread, and have been at one time or another so powerful that Khokhar is almost as favourite a name as Bhatti for the clans of the lower castes in the Panjáb; and it may be that there is a distinct Khokhar caste apart from the Khokhar Rájpúts, just as both are certainly distinct from the Khokhar Chúhras. Colonel Davies notes that many of the social customs of the Khokhars of Sháhpur denote Hindu origin; and this would be quite decisive against the Qutb Sháhi myth.

469. The Khokhars are most numerous along the valleys of the Jahlam and Chanáb, and especially in the Jhang and Sháhpur districts; but they are also found, though in smaller numbers, on the lower Indus and the Satluj, and especially in Lahore, and also all along the foot of the hills from the Jahlam to the Satluj. Pind Dádan Khán is said to have taken its name from a Khokhar Chief who founded it and was Rája of those parts in the time of Jahángír; and the history of the family, which at one time possessed some importance, and of the struggles between the Janjúas and the Khokhars for the possession of the tract, is told at pages 589*ff* of Griffin's *Panjáb Chiefs*. In Jhang too they once ruled over an extensive tract lying east of the Jahlam. The Khokhars of Gújrát and Siálkot have a tradition that they were originally settled at Garh Karánah, which they cannot identify,[1] and were ejected
P. 258] by Tamerlane; and that they then went to Jammu, whence they spread along the hills; and the concentration of the Khokhars of the plains on the Jahlam and the Chanáb, and the wide diffusion of those of the sub-montane tract, lend some colour to the theory that they spread downwards from the hills, and not upwards from the south. In Akbar's time the Khokhars were shown as the principal tribe of the Dasúya parganah of Hushyárpur; and the Mahomedan historians tell us that the Khokhars held Lahore and were powerful in the Upper Bári *Doáb* at the time of Taimur's invasion.[2]

The Khokhars of Sháhpur are said to be split up into innumerable clans, among whom the Nissowána, notorious for their thieving propensities and generally lawless character, are alone important; but in Jhang Mr. Steedman describes the Khokhars as among the best of the agricultural classes, hardworking, thrifty, and not given to crime.

---

[1] Mr. Steedman suggests Koh Kerána, lying south of Sháhpur, in the Jhang district.

[2] The English Editors generally suggest Gakkhar as an emendation: probably because they do not know the word Khokhar.

470. The Kharral (Caste No. 77).—The Kharrals would appear to be a true Rájpút tribe, though a very considerable portion of them have been returned as Jat. The figures in the margin show the total number returned under the several headings of Jat, Rájpút, and Kharral. Of the Rájpút Kharrals of Baháwalpur 1,613 have returned their main tribe as Bhatti. The few Kharrals of Jálandhar are there recognised as Rájpúts, and the Kharrals of Montgomery claim descent from Rája Karan. They are found in large numbers only along the valley of the Rávi, from its junction with the Chanáb to the boundary between Lahore and Montgomery; while a few have spread up the Deg river into the Lahore and Gújránwála *bár*, and smaller numbers are found all along the Satluj valley as high up as Fírozpur. The tribes of this portion of the Rávi are divided into two classes, the Great Rávi tribes and the Little Rávi tribes. The former are pastoral rather than agricultural, and include the Kharrals, Káthias, and many of the great tribes of Mahomedan Jats. They look down upon the little Rávi tribes who live within their limits, and who are agricultural rather than pastoral, consisting of Aráíns, Kambohs, and similar tribes common in the Eastern Panjáb. The great Rávi tribes are notorious for their propensity to cattle-stealing, and among them a young man is not allowed to wear a turban or to marry a wife till he shows by stealing a buffalo that he is able to support her, while a headman who has not a number of dependants ready to steal for or with him is popularly known as "an "orphan."

KHARRALS.
(Small numbers omitted in the details, but included in the totals.)

DISTRICTS.	KHARRALS.			
	Kharral.	Jat.	Rájpút.	TOTAL.
Sirsa	...	35	2,026	2,061
Amritsar	...	1,001	...	1,001
Lahore	70	5,992	35	6,097
Gujránwála ...	..	3,070	4,470	7,540
Firozpur	...	1,441	278	1,719
Multán	2,492	364	500	3,356
Jhang	489	673	2,054	3,216
Montgomery ...	15,643	2,361	3,444	21,448
Derah Ismail Khan ...	...	1,300	...	1,300
Baháwalpur ...	...	237	2,042	2,279
British Territory ...	18,839	18,582	14,242	51,663
Native States ...	6	237	2,042	2,285
Province	18,845	18,819	16,284	53,948

471. Among the tribes of the great Rávi the Kharrals are the most northernly and one of the most important. They are themselves divided into two factions, the upper Rávi and lower Rávi, the head-quarters of the latter being at Kot Kamália. The two are at bitter feud, and the only tie between them is their hatred of their common enemy, the Siál Rájpúts of Jhang. The Kamália Kharrals rose to some prominence in the time of Alamgír, and still hold remains of grants then made them, but the upper Kharrals are now the more powerful branch of the two. The Kharrals have ever been notorious for turbulence, and Mr. Purser's Montgomery Report contains details of their doings before and under Sikh rule, while the history of the family is narrated in full at pages 509*ff* of Griffin's *Panjáb Chiefs*. They trace their origin from one Bhúpa a descendant of Rája Karan, who settled at Uchh and was there converted by Makhdúm Sháh Jahánia. From Uchh they moved up to their present territory. There are now very few in the Multán district; but the fact of their being found along the Satluj, though in small numbers only, lends some support to the story of their having come upwards from below. Captain Elphinstone thus describes the Kharrals in his Gugaira Report :—

> "The 'Kharrals' are the most northernly of the 'Great Ravi' tribes. They occupy a great "portion of the land between Gugaira and the Lahore district, on both sides of the river, and "extend some distance into the Gujránwála district. In turbulence and courage they have been "always considered to excel all the others except the Káthias; but the tract occupied by them "has been gradually denuded by the rapid extension of cultivation, of what formerly constituted "their greatest strength,—heavy jungle. In case of disturbances, therefore, they have had at more "recent periods to evacuate their own lands on the approach of large military forces, thus "sustaining much damage by the destruction of their villages. Their most celebrated leader, "Ahmad Khan, who was killed in September 1857 by a detachment under Captain Black, headed "the combined tribes, however, in no less than five insurrections, which to a certain extent all "proved successful, their chief object—the plunder of the Khatris and Hindus—having usually "been accomplished at the expense of a moderate fine imposed on them under the name of "'Nazarána,' after the conclusion of peace. This success had spread his renown far and wide, "and had given him a great influence over the whole of the 'Great Ravi,' as was proved by the "outbreak of 1857, which appears to have been mainly planned and organized by him. In "stature the Kharrals are generally above the average height, their features are very marked, and "their activity and endurance are remarkable. Like all the other Jats they pretend to a descent "from the Rájpúts, and like that class look down with some contempt upon men who handle the "plough. The cultivation in their villages is, therefore, almost exclusively left to the Vysiwáns "and inferior castes, the Kharral proprietors contenting themselves with realizing their share of "the produce. They only possess land in tracts inundated by the rivers, mere well-cultivation "being too laborious a task even for their dependants."

Mr. Purser adds that they are wasteful in marriage expenditure, hospitable to travellers, thievish, and with little taste for agriculture; and that they still follow many Hindu customs, especially on the occasion of marriage. In Lahore they appear to bear a no better character than in Montgomery; and there is a Persian proverb: "The Dogar, the Bhatti, the Wattu, and the "Kharral are all rebellious and ought to be slain." Sir Lepel Griffin writes of them: "Through all historic times the Kharrals have been a "turbulent, savage, and thievish tribe, ever impatient of control, and "delighting in strife and plunder. More fanatic than other Mahomedan "tribes, they submitted with the greatest reluctance to Hindu rule; and
[P. 259] "it was as much as Díwán Sáwan Mal and the Sikhs could do to restrain them; "for whenever an organised force was sent against them they retired into the "marshes and thick jungles, where it was almost impossible to follow them." In Gújránwála they are said to be "idle, troublesome, bad cultivators and "notorious thieves, their persons generally tall and handsome, and their habits "nomad and predatory."

472. The Kathia, Khagga, and Hans.—The Káthia is another of the Great Rávi tribes, and comes next in importance among them to the Kharral. It is not shown in our tables as a separate caste, and nobody seems to have returned himself as Káthia. But there are 3,878 men in Montgomery and 1,972 in Multán who have returned their *caste* as Punwár; and as the Káthias claim to be Punwár Rájpúts, and were so entered in the settlement, it is probable that these are the Káthias. This is the explanation given by the Deputy Commissioner of Montgomery after local inquiry. These men have been included under the head Rájpút in our tables. The Káthias are almost confined to the Rávi valley of the Multán and Montgomery districts; but they hold a considerable area in the south of Jhang, which they are said to have acquired from the Siál in return for aid afforded to the latter against the Nawáb of

Multán. They are supposed to be the same people as the Kathæi, who in their stronghold of Sangala so stoutly resisted the victorious army of Alexander. The question is elaborately discussed by General Cunningham at pages 33 to 42 of volume II of his *Archæological Reports*, and in Volume I, pages 101*ff* of Tod's *Rájasthán* (*Madras Reprint*, 1880). Captain Elphinstone thus describes them in his Montgomery report :—

"The remarkable fact that a people called 'Kathaioi' occupied a part of the Gugaira district "when Alexander invaded the Panjab, invests the Kathia tribe with a peculiar interest. After much "enquiry on the subject, I have come to the conclusion that the Kathias of the present day have a "strong claim to be considered the descendants of the same 'Kathaioi' who so gallantly resisted the "Macedonian conqueror. Their own account of their origin is, of course, far different. Like all "Jats they take a particular pride in tracing their descent from a Rajput prince about the time of "their conversion to Muhammadanism under the Emperor Akbar. But an examination of their "alleged pedigree shows that, like many other popular traditions of this kind, this account of their "origin must be altogether fictitious. They state that a prince named 'Khattya' reigning in "Rajputana, was compelled to yield up one of his sisters in marriage to the Emperor of Dehli. "After brooding for some time over this great outrage to Rajput honour, he contrived to assemble "a large army with which he attacked the imperial forces: he was, however, overcome by "superior numbers, and was made a prisoner after nearly all his adherents had been slain. He was "then conducted with great honour to the Court of Dehli, where the Emperor treated him with "kindness, and at last induced him to embrace the Muhammadan faith, and placed under his charge "an important post near the Court. Some time afterwards he was sent with a force to subdue a "portion of the Ravi tribes who had risen in insurrection, and after conquering them was so much "attracted by the beauty of the country, that he remained and received a grant of the whole tract "for himself and his descendants. All the Kathias claim descent from this prince, but, unfortunate-"ly for the credibility of this story, the only way that his 8,000 descendants manage to arrange the "matter is by assuming that the prince had no less than 150 sons; whilst in a pedigree prepared by "the chief mírási of the tribe, in which the increase of offspring in the different generations is "arranged with more accordance to probability, the line is only brought down to a few of the princi-"pal families of the tribe.

"In their habits the Kathias differ little from the other Jat tribes. Before the accession of "Ranjit Singh they lived chiefly on cattle grazing and plunder. Like the Kharrals and Fattianas "they still keep up Hindu '*Parohits*,' who take a prominent part at all marriage festivities, an "undoubted sign of their conversion to Muhammadanism having been of recent date. They are "a handsome and sturdy race, and like nearly all Jats of the 'Great Ravi' do not allow their children "of either sex to marry until they have attained the age of puberty, because, as they justly consider, "too early marriages would be detrimental to the 'physique' of the race. Their chief and favourite "article of food is buttermilk; the consumption of wheat among them is very inconsiderable."

Mr. Purser, however, gives a somewhat different account of their migrations. He says :—

"The Káthias have been identified with the 'Kathaioi' of Alexander's time. According to "their account they are descended from Rája Karan, Súrajbansi. Originally they resided in Bíkáner, "whence they emigrated and founded the State of Káthiáwár. From there they went to Sirsa and "then to Baháwalpur. Next they crossed over to Kabula and went on to Daira Dínpanah. Here they "quarrelled with the Bilochis and had to leave. They then settled at Mírah Siál in Jhang. They "stole the cattle of Aláwal Khán of Kamália, who was killed pursuing them. Saádat Yár Khán "obtained the release of their leaders (who were imprisoned on account of this affair) on condition of "their settling on the Rávi. Thus the Káthias obtained a footing in this district. They always held "by the Kamália Kharrals, but plundered the others whenever they could get a chance. The "Káthias are Punwár Rájpúts. There are two main divisions; the Kathias proper, and the "Baghelas."

This would make the Káthias of the Rávi immigrants from Káthiawár. But a Pandit of Gújarát who was sent into the Panjáb by the Rája of Jazdán, one of the principal Káthiawár States, to make enquiries on the subject, tells me that the Káthiawár Rájpúts, who also claim descent from Rája Karan, have a tradition that they came to their present territory from the Panjáb *viâ* Sindh and Kach. The Káthia tradition is that they were driven out of Sarsa Ránia, or the valley of the lower Ghaggar, about the time of Tamerlane's invasion.

The Khagga and Háns appear to have returned themselves as Qureshi, and are described in section 503 under the head Shekh.

473. The Daudpotra (Caste No. 79).—The Dáúdpotra are the reigning family of Baháwalpur, and usually claim to be Qureshi Arabs, though occasionally said to be Rájpúts; but all that is certain about their origin is that their ancestor Dáúd Khán was a Juláha by occupation, if not by caste. Besides the numbers shown in Table VIII A as Dáúdpotras, 1,421 persons have returned themselves as Shekh Dáúdpotra, of whom 1,287 are in the Multán district. The tribe is practically confined to Baháwalpur and the neighbouring portions of Multán, part of which was once included in the Baháwalpur State.

Their founder Dáúd Khán is said to have been the son of one Jám Junjar of Shikárpur, and brother of Muhammad the ancestor of the Kalhora dynasty of Sindh; while another story makes him a Wattu Rájpút. Both accounts are very probably false. Cunningham relates their origin thus: "When "Nádir Sháh proceeded to establish his authority in Sindh, he found the an"cestor of the family a man of reputation in his native district of Shikarpur. "The Sháh made him deputy of the upper third of the province; but, becoming "suspicious of the whole clan, resolved on removing it to Ghazni. The tribe "then migrated up the Satluj and seized lands by force. They fabulously trace "their origin to the Caliph Abbás; but may be regarded as Biloches changed by "long residence in Sindh. In establishing themselves on the Satluj, they "reduced the remains of the ancient Langáhs and Joyas to still further insigni"ficance." (*History of the Sikhs*,—113, note.)

474. The Dogars (Caste No. 46).—The Dogars of the Panjáb are found in the upper valleys of the Satluj and Beás above the lower border of the
[P. 260] Lahore district, and have also spread westwards along the foot of the hills into Siálkot. There are also considerable colonies of them in Hissár and Karnál

They are thus described by Mr. Brandreth in his Fírozpur Report:—

"In my account of the Firozpur ilaqua I have already alluded to the Dogars, who are supposed "to be converted Chauhan Rajputs from the neighbourhood of Dehli. They migrated first to the "neighbourhood of Pák Pattan, whence they spread gradually along the banks of the Satluj, and "entered the Firozpur district about 100 years ago. The Firozpur Dogars are all descended from "a common ancestor named Bahlol, but they are called Mahu Dogars, from Mahu the grandfather "of Bahlol. Bahlol had three sons, Bambu, Langar, and Sammu. The Dogars of Firozpur and "Mullanwala are the descendants of Bambu; those of Khai the descendants of Langar; the descen"dants of Sammu live in the Kasúr territory. There are many other sub-castes of the Dogars in "other districts along the banks of the Satluj, as the Parchats, the Topuras, the Chopuras, &c. "The Chopura Dogars occupy Mandot. The Firozpur Dogars consider themselves superior in rank "and descent to the other sub-castes. They are very particular to whom they give their daughters "in marriage though they take wives from all the other families. At one time infanticide is said "to have prevailed among them, but I do not think there is much trace of it at the present day.

"Sir H. Lawrence, who knew the Dogars well, writes of them that 'they are tall, handsome, "'and sinewy, and are remarkable for having, almost without exception, large aquiline noses; they "'are fanciful and violent, and tenacious of what they consider their rights, though susceptible to "'kindness, and not wanting in courage; they appear to have been always troublesome subjects, and "'too fond of their own free mode of life to willingly take service as soldiers.' The Jewish face "which is found among the Dogars, and in which they resemble the Afgháns, is very remarkable, "and makes it probable that there is very little Chauhan blood in their veins, notwithstanding the "fondness with which they attempt to trace their connection with that ancient family of Rajputs. "Like the Gujars and Naipáls they are great thieves, and prefer pasturing cattle to cultivating. "Their favourite crime is cattle-stealing. There are, however, some respectable persons among them, "especially in the Firozpur ilaqua. It is only within the last few years that the principal Dogars "have begun to wear any covering for the head; formerly the whole population, as is the case with "the poorer classes still, wore their long hair over their shoulders without any covering either of "sheet or turban. Notwithstanding the difference of physiognomy, however, the Dogars preserve "evident traces of some connection with the Hindus in most of their family customs, in which they "resemble the Hindus much more than the orthodox Muhammadans."

475. Mr. Purser notes that they are divided into two tribes, one of which claim to be Chauhán and the other Punwár Rájpúts, and he notes their alleged advent from Pák Pattan, but not their previous migration from Dehli. If they ever did move from Dehli to the Montgomery district, it can hardly have been since the Ghaggar ceased to fertilize the intervening country, and the date of the migration must have been at least some centuries back; and the Dogars of Hissár came to those parts from the Panjáb, probably from the Satluj across the Sirsa district. The Dogars of Lahore and Fírozpur are essentially a riverside tribe, being found only on the river banks: they bear the very worst reputation, and appear from the passage quoted above to have retained till quite lately some at least of the habits of a wild tribe. I suspect that their origin was probably in the Satluj valley. They appear to have entered the Fírozpur district about 1760 A.D., and during the next forty years to have possessed themselves of a very considerable portion of the district, while their turbulence rendered them almost independent of the Sikh Government. In 1808 we recognised the Dogar State of Fírozpur, and took it under our protection against Ranjít Singh; but it lapsed in 1835.

The Rájpút origin of the Dogars is probably very doubtful, and is strenously denied by their Rájpút neighbours, though I believe that Dogar, or perhaps Doghar, is used in some parts of the Province to denote one of mixed blood. Another derivation of the name is *doghgar* or milkman. The Dogars seem to be originally a pastoral rather than an agricultural tribe, and still to retain a strong liking for cattle, whether their own or other people's. They are often classed with Gújars, whom they much resemble in their habits. In Lahore and Fírozpur they are notorious cattle-thieves, but further north they seem to have settled down and become peaceful husbandmen. They are not good cultivators. Their social standing seems to be about that of a low-class Rájpút; they are practically all Musalmáns. The Dogars have returned hardly any large clans; some of the largest are shown in the margin.

DOGAR CLANS.	
Mattar ...	5,325
Chína ...	2,268
Tagra ...	2,232
Máhu ...	1,802
Chokra ..	1,627

476. The Ror (Caste No. 55).—The real seat of the Panjáb Rors is in the great *dhák* jungles south of Thánesar on the borders of the Karnál and Ambála districts, where they hold a *chaurási* nominally consisting of 84 villages, of which the village of Amín, where the Pándavas arranged their forces before their last fight with the Kauravas, is the *tíka* or head village. But the Rors have spread down the Western Jamna Canal into the lower parts of Karnál and into Jínd in considerable numbers. They are said also to hold 12 villages beyond the Ganges. They are fine stalwart men, of very much the same type as the Jats, whom they almost equal as husbandmen, their women also working in the fields. They are more peaceful and less grasping in their habits than the Jats, and are consequently readily admitted as tenants where the latter would be kept at arm's length.

Of their origin I can say nothing certain. They have the same story as the Aroras, of their having been Rájpúts who escaped the fury of Paras Rám by stating that their caste was *aur* or "another." The Aroras are often called Roras in the east of the Panjáb; yet I can hardly believe that the frank and stalwart Ror is of the same origin as the Arora. The Amín men say that they came from Sambhal in Murádábád; but this may only be in order to connect themselves with their neighbours the Chauhán Rájpúts, who certainly came from there. But almost all the Rors alike seem to point to Bádli in the Jhajjar *tahsíl* of Rohtak as their immediate place of origin, though some of them say they came from Rájpútána. Their social status is identical with that of Jats; and they practise *karewa* or widow-marriage, though only, they say, within the caste. Their sub-divisions seem to be exceedingly numerous. A few of the largest are given in the margin. The Ambála Rors would appear to be mostly Sagwál.

Ror clans.		
Sagwál	...	1,848
Malpla	...	1,567
Khíchi	...	1,207
Jográn	...	1,193

477. The Taga (Caste No. 86).—The Tagas of the Jamna Khádir of Dehli and Karnál, the only part of the Province in which they are found, are said to be Gaur Bráhmans by origin, and to have acquired their present name because they "abandoned" (*tág dena*) priestly functions and took to agriculture. Their origin is discussed at great length in Vol. I of Elliott's *Races of the North-West Provinces*, pages 106 to 115; and they are there identified with the Takkas, a possibly Scythian race who had the snake for their totem, and whose destruction by Rája Janamajáya is supposed to be commemorated
P. 231] in the tradition of that monarch's holocaust of serpents. The difficulty felt by Sir H. Elliott in accounting for their tracing their origin to Hariána is perhaps explained by the fact that they give Safídon in Jínd on the border of Hariána as the place where the holocaust took place; and the name of the town is not improbably connected with *sámp* or snake. The Tagas are probably the oldest inhabitants of the upper Jamna Khádir, holding villages which have been untouched by changes in the course of the stream for a far longer period than most of their neighbours. They are of superior social standing and seclude their women, but are bad cultivators, especially the Mahomedans. About three-fourths of the total number have adopted Islám and ceased to wear the sacred thread. The Hindus still wear it, but Bráhmans do not intermarry with them, and they employ Bráhmans to officiate for them in the usual manner. They are poor agriculturists. They must be carefully distinguished from the Tágus or criminal Bráhmans of the same tract discussed in section 586.

478. The Meo (Caste No. 34).—The Meos are the people who have given its name to Mewát or the hill country of Alwar, Gurgáon, and Bhartpur. They are found within the Panjáb chiefly in Gurgáon, though a considerable number have spread into the south of the Dehli district. They are all Mahomedan, though, as will be seen presently, their religion is of a very impure type. They are so excellently described by Captain Powlett in his Gazetteer of Alwar, that I cannot do better that quote the passage almost in full, adding to it Mr. Channing's remarks upon it. Captain Powlett writes as follows:—

"The Meos are numerically the first race in the State, and the agricultural portion of them is "considerably more than double any other class of cultivators except Chamars. They occupy about "half the Ulwar territory, and the portion they dwell in lies to the north and east.

"They are divided into fifty-two clans, of which the twelve largest are called 'Páls,' and the "smaller 'Gots.' Many of these are not settled in Ulwar, but would be found in Mathra, Bhartpur, "and Gurgaon. Of the 448 villages belonging to the Meos the *Ghaseria* clan holds 112, the "*Dhingal* 70, the *Landáwat* 64, the *Nai* 63, the *Singal* 54, the *Dulot* 53, and the *Pundlot* 22.

"It has already been set forth in the historical sketch that the Meos—for they no doubt are "often included under the term Mewatti—were, during the Muhammadan period of power, always "notorious for their turbulence and predatory habits: however, since their complete subjection by

" Bakhtáwar Singh and Banni Singh (during the first-half of this century), who broke up the " large turbulent villages into a number of small hamlets, they have become generally well " behaved; but they return to their former habits when opportunity occurs.

" In 1857 they assembled, burnt state ricks, carried off cattle, &c., but did not succeed in " plundering any town or village in Ulwar. In British territory they plundered Firozpur and " other villages, and when a British force came to restore order many were hanged.

" Though Meos claim to be of Rajput origin, there are grounds for believing that many spring " from the same stock as the Mínas. The similarity between the words Meo and Mína suggest " that the former may be a contraction of the latter. Several of the respective clans are identical " in name (Singal, Nai, Dulot, Pundlot, Diugal, Balot); and a story told of one Daria Meo, and his " ladylove Sisbadani Míni seems to show that they formerly intermarried. In Bulandshahr a caste " called Meo Mínas is spoken of in the Settlement Report, which would seem farther to connect the " two. However, it is probable enough that apostate Rajputs and bastard sons of Rajputs founded " many of the clans, as the legends tell.

" The Meos are now all Musalmans in name; but their village deities are the same as those of " Hindu zamindars. They keep too several Hindu festivals. Thus the Holi is with Meos a season " of rough play, and is considered as important a festival as the Moharram, Id, and Shabrát; and " they likewise observe the Janamashtami, Dusehra and Diwáli. They often keep Brahmin priests " to write the *píli chitthi*, or note fixing the date of a marriage. They call themselves by Hindu " names, with the exception of 'Rám;' and 'Singh' is a frequent affix though not as common as " 'Khan.'

" On the Amáwas, or monthly conjunction of the sun and moon, Meos, in common with Hindu " Ahirs, Gujars, &c., cease from labour; and when they make a well the first proceeding is to " erect a 'Chabútra' to 'Bairúji' or 'Hanúmán.' However, when plunder was to be obtained, " they have often shown little respect for Hindu shrines and temples; and when the sanctity of a " threatened place has been urged, the retort has been '*Tum to Deo, Ham Meo*!' You may be a " Deo (God), but I am a Meo!

" As regards their own religion Meos are very ignorant. Few know the *kalima*, and fewer " still the regular prayers, the seasons of which they entirely neglect. This, however, only applies " to Ulwar territory; in British, the effect of the schools is to make them more observant of religious " duties. Indeed, in Ulwar, at certain places where there are mosques, religious observances " are better maintained, and some know the *kalima*, say their prayers, and would like a school.

" Meos do not marry in their Pál or clan, but they are lax about forming connections with " women of other castes, whose children they receive into the Meo community. As already stated " Brahmins take part in the formalities preceding a marriage, but the ceremony itself is performed " by the Kazi.

" As agriculturists, Meos are inferior to their Hindu neighbours. The point in which they " chiefly fail is working their wells, for which they lack patience. Their women, whom they do " not confine, will, it is said, do more field work than the men; indeed one often finds women at work " in the crops when the men are lying down. Like the women of low Hindu castes they tattoo " their bodies, a practice disapproved by Musalmans in general. Meos are generally poor and live " badly; they have no scruples about getting drunk when opportunity offers. The men wear the " *dhoti* and *kumri*, and not *pahjamás*. Their dress is, in fact, Hindu. The men often wear " gold ornaments, but I believe the women are seldom or never allowed to have them."

To this Mr. Channing adds:—

" My own enquiries on the subject were imperfect when they were interrupted by my transfer " from Gurgaon; but they led me to a conclusion which I find has also been adopted by Major " Powlett, that the Mínas and Meos are connected, and I should be inclined to add that both are " probably representatives of the earlier non-Aryan inhabitants of the country. In Tod's " Rájasthán, Vol. II, page 76, I find it stated that Mewas o is a name given to the fastnesses in " the Aravalli hills, to which Mínas, Kolis and others make their retreat. Pál is, on the same " authority, the term for a community of any of the aboriginal mountain races; its import is a " defile or valley, fitted for cultivation and defence; and Pál is the term given to the main Sub- " Divisions of the Meos and also of the Mínas. These latter, who in Gurgaon are known only as a " body of professional criminals, were the original masters of the State of Amber or Jaipur, " the Rájpút kingdom of which was founded by Dhole Rae about A.D. 967 after subduing the Mínas. " Tod also states that in Jaipur the Mínas are still the most numerous tribe, and possess large " immunities and privileges; formerly the tíka of sovereignty was marked by blood taken from " the great toe of a Mína of Kalikho, another token, as I intepret it, of the ancient sovereignty of " the tribe. Meos are often mentioned, although not in Gurgaon, as Mína Meos: and in the " older Muhammadan historians and in Tod, I find expeditions against their country spoken of as " expeditions against the Mawasat, and in later time as against the Mawas. These facts incline " me to the belief that the Meos are such of the aborginal Mína population of the Aravalli hills as " were converted to Muhammadanism, and that their name is probably a corruption of Mewasati " or the men of the mountain passes. Perhaps other enquiries may be able to confirm or refute this " theory, which I only put forward tentatively.

"Any Meo will tell glibly enough that the tribe is divided into twelve Páls and fifty-two "Gots; but no two enumerations of the Páls that I have seen correspond precisely; and the "fifty-two Gots include the Páls, and are not, as would at first appear, in addition to them. The "following enumeration of the Páls is perhaps correct :—

1. Balant.	5. Chirklot.	9. Yunglot.
2. Ratáwat.	6. Dimrot.	10. Dahngal.
3. Darwál.	7. Dulot.	11. Signal
4. Landáwat.	8. Nái.	12. Kalesa or Kalsákhi.

[P. 262] "Besides these there is a thirteenth Palákhra or little Pál Páhat. The Páls which are strongest "in Gurgáon are the Dahngals in the north of Núh; the Chirklots in the south-east of Núh and "in the country round Punahána; the Landáwats, Dimrots, and Dulots in the Firozpur "valley, and the Darwáls in the country south of Núh. These Meo sub-tribes still possess "a strong feeling of unity and the power of corporate action."

MEO CLANS.

1.	Chirklot ...	26,467	8.	Bálot ...	2,849
2.	Dhangal ...	21,075	9.	Tanúr or Tunwar ...	2,432
3.	Dimrot ...	10,277	10.	Nái ...	2,035
4.	Gurwál ...	5,511	11.	Badgújar ...	2,003
5.	Landáwat ...	3,294	12.	Golwál ...	2,003
6.	Dulot ...	2,999	13.	Páhut ...	1,639
7.	Dherwál ...	2,944	14.	Bailána ...	1,380

The principal Meo subdivisions returned in Gurgáon are shown in the margin. In Ambála and perhaps elsewhere the word Meo seems commonly to be used as equivalent to Men or fisherman; and it may be that some of the Meos returned from other districts than Gurgáon and those bordering upon it, are not true Meos.

479. The Khanzadah (Caste No. 123).—The Khánzádahs are practically confined to Gurgáon so far as the Panjáb is concerned. Captain Powlett describes them thus :—

"They are the Mewáti Chiefs of the Persian historians, who were probably the representatives "of the ancient Lords of Mewát. These Mewátis are called Khánzádahs, a race which, "though Musalmán like the Meos, was and is socially far superior to the Meos, and has no love for "them; but who in times past have united with them in the raids and insurrections for which "Mewát was so famous, and which made it a thorn in the side of the Dehli Emperors. In fact, the "expression Mewáti usually refers to the ruling class, while Meo designates the lower orders. The "latter term is evidently not of modern origin, though it is not, I believe, met with in history; and "the former is, I think, now unusual, Khánzádah having taken its place.

"The Khánzádahs are numerically insignificant, and they cannot now be reckoned among the "aristocracy. In social rank they are far above the Meos, and though probably of more recent "Hindu extraction, they are better Musalmans. They observe no Hindu festivals, and will not "acknowledge that they pay any respect to Hindu shrines. But Brahmins take part in their "marriage contracts, and they observe some Hindu marriage ceremonies. Though generally as "poor and ignorant as the Meos, they unlike the latter say their prayers, and do not let their "women work in the fields.

"They are not first rate agriculturists, the seclusion of their women giving them a disadvan-"tage beside most other castes. Some have emigrated and taken to trade in the Gangetic cities, "but these have no connection now with the original Khánzádah country. Those who have not "abandoned the traditions of their clan are often glad of military service, and about fifty are in "British regiments. In the service of the Ulwar State there are many. There are 26 Khánzádah "villages in the State, in most of which the proprietors themselves work in the field and follow the "plough.

"The term Khánzádah is probably derived from Khánazád, for it appears that Bahádur Náhar "the first of the race mentioned in the Persian histories, associated himself with the turbulent "slaves of Firoz Sháh after the death of the latter, and, being a pervert, would contemptuously "receive the name of Khánazád (slave) from his brethren. The Khánzádahs themselves indig-"nantly repudiate this derivation, and say the word is Khán Jádú (or Lord Jádú), and was intend-"ed to render still nobler the name of the princely Rajpút race from which they came. Con-"verted Jádús were called by the old Musalman historians Mewátis, a term Chand applies to a "Mewát chief of the Lunar race, of which race the Jádú Maharaja of Karauli calls himself the "head."

To this Mr. Channing adds :—

"Khánzádas are a race who were formerly of much more importance than at present; they "claim to have been formerly Jádu Rájpúts, and that their ancestors Lakhan Pál and Sumitr "Pál, who dwelt at Tahangarh in Bharatpur, were converted to Islam in the reign of Firoz Shah "(A.D. 1351 to 1388), who gave Lakhan Pál the name of Náhir Khan and Sumitr Pál the name of "Bahadur Khan, and in recognition of their high descent called them Khánzádahs and made them "bear rule in Mewat. At first they are said to have lived at Sarahta near Tijára, and afterwards "according to tradition, they possessed 1,484 villages. However this may be, there is no doubt "that they were the ruling race in Mewat down to the time of Bábar; since then they have "gradually declined in importance, and now in this district own only a few villages near Núh and "to the north of Firozpur. Traces of their former importance exist at Sohna, Bundsi, and Kotila. "Kotila was one of their chief fortresses; the village is situated in a small valley, wholly "surrounded by the hill, except where a small funnel-like pass gives entrance to it. In front of "this pass is the Kotila jhíl, and when this is filled with water the only road to the pass lies "along a narrow strip of land between the lake and the hill. The remains of a breastwork along "the face of the hill and across the mouth of the pass still exist, while on the hill above the "village is a small ruined fort. The village now belongs to Meos. Some of the buildings bear "witness to its former greater importance. I have a suspicion that they are more intimately "connected than they acknowledge with the Meos, whom they seem to me to resemble in personal "appearance. They do not ordinarily intermarry with Meos, but the Meo inhabitants of five "villages in the Firozpur tahsil profess to have been formerly Khánzádahs, and to have become Meos "by intermarriage. Their traditions also, which point to Sarahta as their ancient home, agree, I "think it will be found, with those of more than one clan of Meos. If my supposition that the "Meos are converted Mínas is correct, I am inclined to suspect that the Khánzádas are the repre- "sentatives of the noble class among the aboriginal population. Tod mentions an Asíl or un- "mixed class among the Mínas known as Mainas."

The Khánzádahs of Gurgaon have returned themselves as Jádúbansi in the column for clan, and they commonly say that this is their only *got*. Khánzádah, or "the son of a Khán" is precisely the Musalmán equivalent to the Hindu Rájpút or "son of a Rája;" and there can be little doubt that the Khánzádahs are to the Meos what the Rájpúts are to the Jats.

480. The Gujjar (Caste No. 8).—The Gújars are the eighth largest caste in the Panjáb, only the Jats, Rájpúts, and Patháns among dominant castes, the mixed caste of Aráíns, and the Bráhmans, Chamárs, and Chúhras exceeding them in point of number. They are identified by General Cunningham with the Kushán or Yúchi or Tochari, a tribe of Eastern Tartars. About a century before Christ their Chief conquered Kábul and the Pesháwar country; while his son Híma Kadphises, so well known to the Panjáb Numismatologist, extended his sway over the whole of Upper Panjáb and the banks of the Jamna as far down as Mathra and the Vindhyas, and his successor the no less familiar king Kanishka, the first Buddhist Indo-Scythian prince, annexed Kashmír to the kingdom of the Tochari. These Tochari or Kushán are the Kaspeiræi of Ptolemy; and in the middle of the second century of our æra, Kaspeira, Kasyapapura, or Multán, was one of their chief cities. Probably about the beginning of the 3rd century after Christ, the attacks of the White Huns recalled the last king of the united Yúchi to the west, and he left his son in charge of an independent province whose capital was fixed at Pesháwar; and from that time the Yúchi of Kábul are known as the Great Yúchi, and those of the Panjáb as the Kator or Little Yúchi. Before the end of the 3rd century a portion of the Gújars had begun to move southwards down the Indus, and were shortly afterwards separated from their northern brethren by Indo-Scythian wave from the north. In the middle of the 5th century there was a Gújar kingdom in south-western Rájpútána, whence they were driven by the Balas into Gújarát of the Bombay Presidency; and about the end of the 9th century, Ala Khána the Gújar king of Jammu, ceded the present Gújar-des, corresponding very nearly with the the Gújrát district, to the king of Kashmír. The town of Gújrát is [P. 263] said to have been built or restored by Ali Khán Gújar in the time of Akbar. The grounds for General Cunningham's identification will be found in full detail at pages 61 to 82 of Vol. II. of the *Archæological Reports*.

The present distribution of the Gújars in India is thus described by General Cunningham :—

> "At the present day the Gujars are found in great numbers in every part of the North-West of India, from the Indus to the Ganges, and from the Hazara mountains to the Peninsula of Gujrat. They are specially numerous along the banks of the Upper Jamna, near Jagádri and Buriya, and in the Saharanpur district, which during the last century was actually called Gujarat. To the east they occupy the petty State of Samptar in Bundelkhand, and one of the northern districts of Gwalior, which is still called Gujargár. They are found only in small bodies and much scattered throughout Eastern Rajputana and Gwalior; but they are more numerous in the Western States, and specially towards Gujarat, where they form a large part of the population. The Rajas of Rewári to the south of Dehli are Gujars. In the Southern Panjab they are thinly scattered, but their numbers increase rapidly towards the north, where they have given their name to several important places, such as Gujranwala in the Rechna-Doab, Gujrat in the Chaj Doab, and Gujar Khan in the Sindh Sagar Doab. They are numerous about Jahlam and Hassan Abdál, and throughout the Hazara districts; and they are also found in considerable numbers in the Dardu districts of Chilás, Kohli, and Pálas, to the east of the Indus, and in the contiguous districts to the west of the river."

In the Panjáb they essentially belong to the lower ranges and sub-montane tracts; and though they have spread down the Jamna in considerable numbers, they are almost confined to the riverain lowlands. In the higher mountains they are almost unknown. The figures showing their distribution are given
P. 166-67. in Abstract No. 83 at page 254. Gújrát is still their stronghold, and in that district they form 13½ per cent. of the total population. There alone have they retained their dominant position. Throughout the Salt-range Tract, and probably under the eastern hills also, they are the oldest inhabitants among the tribes now settled there; but in the west the Gakkhars, Janjúas, and Patháns, and in the east the Rájpúts have always been too strong for them, and long ago deprived them of political importance. In the Pesháwar district almost any herdsman is called a Gújar, and it may be that some of those who are thus returned are not true Gújars by race.[1] But throughout the hill country of Jammu, Chibhál, and Hazára, and away in the Independent Territory lying to the north of Pesháwar as far as the Swát river, true Gújar herdsmen are found in great numbers, all possessing a common speech, which is a Hindi dialect quite distinct from the Panjábi or Pashto current in those parts. Here they are a purely pastoral and almost nomad race, taking their herds up into the higher ranges in summer and descending with them into the valleys during the cold weather; and it may be said that the Gújar is a cultivator only in the plains. Even there he is a bad cultivator, and more given to keeping cattle than to following the plough.

It is impossible without further investigation to fix the date of the Gújar colonization of the lower districts. They are almost exclusively Musalmán except in the Jamna districts and Hushyárpur, and they must therefore have entered those districts before the conversion of the great mass of the caste. The Jálandhar Gújars date their conversion from the time of Aurangzeb, a very probable date. The Fírozpur Gújars say that they came from Dáránagar in the south of India, that they moved thence to Ránia in Sirsa, and thence again to Fírozpur *viá* Kasúr. The Musalmán Gújars of all the eastern half

---

[1] On the other hand, Mr. Steedman is of opinion that the figures for the Gújars of Ráwalpindi are very much under the mark, and that many of them must have been returned as Jats, Rájpúts, or perhaps even Mughals.

of the Province still retain more of their Hindu customs than do the majority of their converted neighbours, their women, for instance, wearing petticoats instead of drawers, and red instead of blue. It is noticeable that Gújrát is to the Gújars what Bhatner and Bhattiána are to the Bhatti, a place to which there is a traditional tendency to refer their origin.

481. The Gújar is a fine stalwart fellow, of precisely the same physical type as the Jat; and the theory of aboriginal descent which has sometimes been propounded, is to my mind conclusively negatived by his cast of countenance. He is of the same social standing as the Jat, or perhaps slightly inferior; but the two eat and drink in common without any scruple and the proverb says: "The Jat, Gújar, Ahír, and Gola are all four hail fellows well met." But he is far inferior in both personal character and repute to the Jat. He is lazy to a degree, and a wretched cultivator; his women, though not secluded, will not do field-work save of the lightest kind; while his fondness for cattle extends to those of other people. The difference between a Gújar and a Rájpút cattle-thief was once explained to me thus by a Jat: "The Rájpút will steal "your buffalo. But he will not send his father to say he knows where it is "and will get it back for Rs. 20, and then keep the Rs. 20 and the buffalo too. The Gújar will." The Gújars have been turbulent throughout the history of the Panjáb, they were a constant thorn in the side of the Dehli Emperors, and are still ever ready to take advantage of any loosening of the bonds of discipline to attack and plunder their neighbours. Their character as expressed in the proverbial wisdom of the countryside is not a high one: "A desert is better than a Gújar: wherever you see a Gújar, hit "him." Again: "The dog and the cat two, the Rángar and the Gújar "two; if it were not for these four one might sleep with one's door "open:" so "The dog, the monkey, and the Gújar change their minds "at every step;" and "When all other castes are dead make friends with a "Gújar." As Mr. Maconachie remarks: "Though the Gújar possesses two "qualifications of a highlander, a hilly home and a constant desire for "other people's cattle, he never seems to have had the love of fighting and "the character for manly independence which distinguishes this class elsewhere. "On the contrary he is generally a mean sneaking cowardy fellow; and I "do not know that he improves much with the march of civilization, though "of course there are exceptions; men who have given up the traditions of "the tribe so far as to recognize the advantage of being honest— "generally."

Such is the Gújar of the Jamma districts.[1] But further west his character would seem to be higher. Major Wace describes the Gújars of Hazára as "a simple all-enduring race, thrifty and industrious, with no "ambition but to be left alone in peace with their cattle and fields;" and "many of them are fine men in every way." Mr. Thomson says that the Gújars of Jahlam are the best farmers in the district (perhaps not exces- [P. 265] sive praise in a district held by Gakkhars, Awáns, and Rájpúts), though the Maliár or Aráin is a better market gardener; and that they are quiet and industrious, more likeable than (Salt-range) Jats, but with few attractive qualities. Mr. Steedman gives a similar account of the Gújars of

[1] Mr. Wilson, however, writes: The Gújar villages in Gurgáon have on the whole stood "the late bad times better than those of almost other caste—better than the Játs, and almost as "well as the Ahírs. Our Gurgáon Gújars are very little given to thieving, and I have rather "a high opinion of them."

Ráwalpindi, calling them "excellent cultivators." So the Gújars of Hushyárpur are said to be "a quiet and well-behaved set." In Jálandhar Sir Richard Temple describes them as "here as elsewhere of pastoral habits, but "more industrious and less predatory than usual;" and Mr. Barkley writes: "At present, after thirty years of British rule, they are probably as little "given to crime as any other large class in the agricultural population. It is "still generally true that they occupy themselves more with grazing than "with agriculture; but this is by no means invariably the case." But in Fírozpur again Mr. Brandreth describes them as "unwilling cultivators, and "greatly addicted to thieving," and gives instances of their criminal propensities. Thus it would appear that the further the Gújar moves from his native hills, the more he deteriorates and the more unpleasant he makes himself to his neighbours. The following description of the Gújars of Kángra by Mr. Barnes is both graphic and interesting: —

"The Gujars of the hills are quite unlike the caste of the same designation in the plains. "There they are known as an idle, worthless and thieving race, rejoicing in waste, and enemies to "cultivation and improvement; but above and below they are both addicted to pastoral habits. In "the hills the Gujars are exclusively a pastoral tribe,—they cultivate scarcely at all. The Gadis keep "flocks of sheep and goats and the Gujar's wealth consists of buffaloes. These people live in the "skirts of the forests, and maintain their existence exclusively by the sale of the milk, ghee, and "other produce of their herds. The men graze the cattle, and frequently lie out for weeks in the "woods tending their herds. The women repair to the markets every morning with baskets on their "heads, with little earthen pots filled with milk, butter-milk and ghee, each of these pots "containing the proportion required for a day's meal. During the hot weather the Gujars usually "drive their herds to the upper range, where the buffaloes rejoice in the rich grass which the "rains bring forth, and at the same time attain condition from the temperate climate and the "immunity from venomous flies which torment their existence in the plains. The Gujars are a fine, "manly race, with peculiar and handsome features. They are mild and inoffensive in manner, and "in these hills are not distinguished by the bad pre-eminence which attaches to their race in the "plains. They are never known to thieve. Their women are supposed to be not very scrupulous. "Their habits of frequenting public markets and carrying about their stock for sale unaccompanied "by their husbands undoubtedly expose them to great temptations; and I am afraid the imputa-"tions against their character are too well founded. They are tall, well-grown women, and may be "seen every morning entering the bazaars of the hill towns, returning home about the afternoon "with their baskets emptied of their treasures. The Gujars are found all over the district. They "abound particularly about Jowala Mukhi, Tira, and Nadaun. There are some Hindu Gujars "especially towards Mandi; but they are a small sect, compared to the Musalmans."

It has been suggested, and is I believe held by many, that Jats and Gújars, and perhaps Ahírs also, are all of one ethnic stock; and this because there is a close communion between them. It may be that they are the same in their far-distant origin. But I think that they must have either entered India at different times or settled in separate parts, and my reason for thinking so is precisely because they eat and smoke together. In the case of Jat and Rájpút the reason for differentiation is obvious, the latter being of higher rank than the former. But the social standing of Jats, Gújars, and Ahírs being practically identical, I do not see why they should ever have separated if they were once the same. It is, however, possible that the Jats were the camel graziers and perhaps husbandmen, the Gújars the cowherds of the hills, and the Ahírs the cowherds of the plains. If this be so, they afford a classification by occupation of the yeoman class, which fills up the gap between and is absolutely continuous with the similar classification of the castes above them as Bráhmans, Banyas, and Rájpúts, and of the castes below them as Tarkháns, Chamárs, and so forth. But we must know more of the early distribution of the tribes before we can have any opinion on the subject. I have noticed in the early historians a connection between the migrations and location of Gújars and Rájpúts which has struck me as being more than accidental; but the

Abstract No. 84, showing [P. 264]

	GUJAR								
	1	2	3	4	5	6	7	8	9
	Túnwar.	Chokhar.	Rawál.	Kalsán.	Kathána.	Kasánah.	Kálas.	Gorsí.	Chechí.
Dehli ...	2,555	744	100	1	336	676	7	8	51
Gurgaon ...	324	1	...	8	1,620	797	...	...	274
Karnal ...	...	2,325	4,417	1,588	21	92	...	122	307
Hissar ...	116	34	8	20	380	508	180	10	308
Rohtak ...	...	10	3	1	101	128	4	41	42
Ambala ...	...	240	10	...	1,401	2,280	1,208	1,504	2,810
Ludhiána ...	...	...	...	...	749	605	1,175	3,462	3,285
Jálandhar ...	...	...	...	...	546	388	565	1,457	1,152
Hushyárpur ...	...	...	...	...	546	2,200	1,111	3,301	3,171
Kángra ...	...	...	...	...	60	135	118	209	418
Amritsar ...	...	...	...	...	153	134	...	180	615
Gurdáspur ...	1,140	336	...	...	2,750	1,533	...	1,772	4,010
Siálkot ...	...	3	10	...	1,020	439	...	277	602
Lahore ...	...	1	13	...	445	82	...	200	1,020
Gujránwala ...	...	...	17	...	125	25	60	38	205
Firozpur ...	...	...	...	...	1,168	312	166	870	779
Ráwalpindi ...	...	280	...	...	5,046	612	1,318	1,232	3,207
Jahlam ...	...	20	...	...	3,684	882	1,260	300	1,621
Gujrát ...	...	260	...	...	21,449	3,048	3,560	3,312	8,002
Peshawar ...	...	13	3	...	...	2	13	119	167
Hazara ...	...	195	...	...	8,526	11	1,314	319	7,156
States of East. Plains.	134	167	30	...	2,782	456	652	2,036	5,258
British Territory.	4,143	4,524	4,600	1,627	51,065	15,126	12,194	19,279	39,562
Native States...	134	167	67	...	3,080	1,014	1,209	2,824	6,427
Province ...	4,277	4,691	4,667	1,627	54,145	16,140	13,403	22,103	45,989

Gujar tribes for districts.

TRIBES.

10	11	12	13	14	15	16	17	18	19	
Dhedar.	Poswál.	Lawí.	Bijár.	Khatindar.	Melu.	Thakaria.	Chauhán.	Monan.	Bhumla.	
1	6	4	...	...	...	...	87	...	...	Dehli.
10	762	17	...	...	...	...	155	...	2,602	Gurgaon.
48	208	...	33	...	118	...	172	...	...	Karnál.
83	70	42	70	...	602	...	86	...	...	Hissar.
2	24	1	...	...	9	...	52	...	...	Rohtak.
1,318	4,467	554	3,504	...	6	...	1,280	...	...	Ambala.
1,130	1,690	613	1,681	...	400	29	518	30	...	Ludhiána.
86	1,130	173	683	...	1	...	682	278	...	Jálandhar.
...	6,910	2,825	3,230	1,172	2,357	1,200	4,530	2,585	...	Hushyárpur.
52	211	851	190	...	...	13	645	142	...	Kángra.
...	197	...	180	...	...	...	146	60	...	Amritsar.
215	1,687	30	710	...	...	860	1,151	4,740	...	Gurdáspur.
167	541	1	176	...	...	...	517	...	...	Siálkot.
54	198	40	178	...	47	4	104	91	...	Lahore.
...	27	...	126	...	...	13	221	...	...	Gujránwala.
338	380	114	215	...	...	...	332	170	...	Firozpur.
340	2,417	4	1,041	...	25	975	2,361	344	...	Ráwalpindi.
451	1,340	36	907	...	...	758	1,287	62	35	Jahlam.
1,021	3,401	150	3,592	...	1,380	3,524	7,086	382	2,180	Gujrát.
2	31	2	230	...	...	...	...	...	...	Peshávar.
800	2,684	...	2,501	...	...	2,362	5,132	221	21	Hazara.
908	1,005	416	1,664	...	382	183	981	403	328	States of East. Plains.
7,055	28,539	5,461	19,159	1,172	4,968	9,770	27,554	9,123	4,937	British Territory.
1,261	1,441	1,258	2,186	...	956	183	2,238	403	370	Native States
8,316	29,980	6,719	21,345	1,172	5,924	9,953	29,792	9,526	5,307	Province.

subject needs an immense deal of work upon it before it can be said to be even ready for drawing conclusions.

482. Gujar Tribes.—The Gújar tribes and clans appear to be very numerous, and apparently new local sub-divisions have sprung up in many places. Still the distribution of the main tribes for which I give figures on the opposite page* in Abstract No. 84 is far more general than is the case with other castes of equal importance. The figures only include 47 per cent. of the Gújars of the Province; but they comprise 69 per cent. of those of Gújrát, and probably include most of the great original tribes. The Khatána and Chechi far surpass the others in number. *P. 186-87.

MINOR AGRICULTURAL AND PASTORAL TRIBES.

483. The minor agricultural and pastoral tribes.—The group of castes for which the figures are given in Abstract No. 85 on page 266† are not separated from the castes and tribes already discussed by any clearly defined line. Indeed it is quite a matter of opinion whether some of these should not have been ranked with the major and some of those with the minor tribes. But the group now to be discussed very generally hold an inferior position among the agricultural community, and seldom if ever occupy the position of the dominant tribe in any considerable tract of country. They may be divided into three classes, though here again the lines of the demarcation are indistinct. The first consists of the market gardeners proper or growers of vegetables, and includes the Máli, Saini, Aráin, and Bághbán, all four of whom are probably closely connected, and some of them almost undistinguishable. The cultivation of vegetables is looked upon as degrading by the agricultural classes, why I know not, unless it be that nightsoil is generally used for their fertilisation; and a Rájpút would say: "What! Do you take "me for an Aráin?" if anything was proposed which he considered derogatory. The second class comprises the Kanet and Ghirath, the low-class cultivators of the hills, and the Kamboh, Ahír, Mahtam, and other cultivators of inferior status. Some of these are closely allied to the vegetable-growers; others again to the Ghosi and Gaddi which constitute the third class, and are pastoral rather than agricultural. The class as a whole is to be found in largest number in the fertile districts of the eastern plains and sub-montane tract, and in the hills where the proud Rájpúts look upon labour at the plough as degrading. It is least numerous in the Derajját where the comprehensive name of Jat embraces all cultivators of this class. †P. 190-93.

484. The Mali and Saini (Caste Nos. 45 and 31).—The Sainis would appear to be only a sub-division of the Mális. In Bijnor they are said to be identical, and I am informed that the two intermarry in many, but not in all, parts of the North-West Provinces. It is probable that the Sainis are a Máli tribe, and that some of the higher tribes of the same caste will not marry with them. The Máli, the *Málakára* or florist of the Puráns, is generally a market or nursery gardener, and is most numerous in the vicinity of towns where manure is plentiful and there is a demand for his produce. He is perhaps the most skilful and industrious cultivator we possess, and does wonders with his land, producing three or even four crops within the year from the same plot. He is found under the name of Máli only in the Jamna zone, including the [P. 267]

[1] Mr. Wilson notes that the Gújars and the Bargújar tribe of Rájpúts are often found together; and suggests that the latter may be to the Gújars what the Khánzádahs are to the Meos and what most Rájpúts are to the Jats.

eastern portions of Hissár, his place being taken by the Saini in the eastern sub-montane districts, and by the Aráin or Bághbán in the remainder of the Province. He is almost always a Hindu. Most of the few Mális shown for the western districts were returned as Maliár, the Panjábi form of Máli; and some of them as Phulára or Phulwára (but see section 485 for the inclusion of Maliár under Aráin).

The Sainis, who, as I have just explained, are probably a Máli tribe, are said to claim Rájpút origin in Jálandhar; but Mr. Barkley writes of the Sainis of that district: "They consider themselves the same as the Mális of the "North-West Provinces, and to be connected with the Aráins, though the "latter know nothing of the relationship. They are not found west of the "Chanáb, but are numerous in some parts of the Ambála district." They appear from our figures to lie all along the foot of the hills between the valleys of the Jamna and Rávi, but not to have reached the Chanáb valley. Both they and the Mális are properly tribes of Hindústán rather than of the Panjáb. About 10 per cent. of the Sainis are Sikhs, and the remainder Hindus. In Ráwalpindi no fewer than 3,655 Mughals have returned their tribe or clan as Saini; but it is probable that these have no connection with the caste under discussion, as it would not appear to have penetrated so far westwards. The Sainis of Rúpar in Ambála are described "an ill-conditioned set, first-rate cultivators, but refractory and intriguing."

The Mális and Sainis, like all vegetable growers, occupy a very inferior position among the agricultural castes; but of the two the Sainis are probably the higher, as they more often own land or even whole villages, and are less generally mere market gardeners than are the Mális.

The largest of the Máli sub-divisions are the Phúl with 11,646, and the Bhagarti with 15,658 persons. The Sainis do not appear to have returned any large clans except in Hushyárpur, of which district some of the largest clans are shown in the margin, and in Gurdáspur where 1,541 Sainis showed their clans as Salahri. Mr. Barkley notes that some of the clans of Aráins and of Sainis in Jálandhar bear the same names, and those not always merely names of other and dominant tribes.

SAINI CLANS IN HUSHYARPUR.

Clan		Number	Clan		Number
Boli	...	3,462	Alagni	...	2,182
Pawán	...	2,980	Mangar	...	1,692
Gaddi	...	2,708	Badyál	...	1,142
Hamarti	...	2,506	Baráyat	...	1,120
Badwál	...	2,226			

485. The Arain, Baghban, and Maliar (Caste Nos. 7 and 65).—The word Bághbán is the Persian equivalent of the Hindi word Máli, and means simply a gardener. But it is commonly used for the Aráin in the west of the Panjáb; and even as far east as Jálandhar there are two villages of the same name, of which the one which is held by Aráins is often distinguished by the addition of *Bághbánán* to its name. Unfortunately the Peshávar divisional officer has included those who returned themselves as Aráin or Maliár under Bághbán, and I cannot give separate figures for them. The Bághbáns of the Ráwalpindi division are discussed below.

The Aráins, or as they are called on the Jamna Ráins, are probably a true caste in the Satluj valley and throughout the Eastern Plains. But in the western half of the Panjáb excepting on the Satluj, the word seems to be used for any market-gardener. Mr. Steedman writes: "Aráin, Ráin, Bághbán, "Máli, and Maliár are in Jhang and Ráwalpindi a very mixed body of men,

Abstract No. 85, showing Minor [P. 266]

	MINOR AGRICULTURAL AND						
							FIG
	45	31	7	65	20	29	147
	Máli.	Saini.	Aráin.	Bághbán.	Kanet.	Ghirath.	Reya.
Dehli	12,714	1,672	1,585	..	...	...	1,993
Gurgaon	9,673	..	1	..	...	...	...
Karnal	10,124	21	7,118	...	..	...	...
Hissar	9,777	...	1,907	...	...	...	...
Rohtak	7,949	...	36	...	...	...	...
Sirsa	885	...	4,742	..	...	...	...
Ambala	...	63,054	30,881	...	2,602	296	..
Ludhiána	...	304	27,229	...	20	4	.
Simla	...	50	24	...	9,090	101	...
Jalandhar	11	14,324	123,323	...	60	389	..
Hushyárpur ...	195	48,790	38,901	...	1,639	41,793	...
Kángra . ..	407	1,911	1,067	..	61,141	108,716	...
Amritsar	...	565	44,709	...	...	210	..
Gurdáspur	..	13,842	55,983	...	...	6,142	...
Sialkot	...	433	65,241	...	...	14	...
Lahore	122	2	94,964	...	...	20	..
Gujránwála ...	...	...	21,740	...	...	...	...
Firozpur	52	...	51,043	...	...	4	...
Báwalpindi ...	106	7	2	41,701	1	...	..
Jahlam	...	...	15,470	11,414	...	6	...
Gujrat	...	...	20,386	...	...	...	...
Shahpur	...	...	8,574	...	...	...	...
Multan	49	53	23,981	20	...	4	...
Jhang	...	...	6,077	...	...	...	...
Montgomery ...	...	...	22,889	...	..	...	...
Muzaffargarh ...	13	...	3,991	...	...	...	...
Derah Ismail Khan ..	...	...	1,068	...	..	8	...
Derah Ghazi Khan ...	22	..	59	...	...	12	...
Bannu	...	3	3,941	...	...	9	...
Pesháwar	...	...	...	21,240	...	12	...
Hazara	...	...	...	5,532	...	...	...
Kohát	...	...	...	1,154	...	...	...
British Territory	**52,102**	**140,031**	**676,831**	**81,063**	**74,553**	**157,740**	**1,993**
Patiála	6,052	7,854	41,500	153	14,203	328	...
Nábha	269	22	3,182	...	...	...	...
Kapurthala ...	1	2,061	39,095	...	...	...	..
Jínd	3,104	7	2,353	...	33	314	...
Farídkot	12	73	2,294	..	...	...	...
Maler Kotla ...	...	...	1,738	..	1	...	...
Kalsia	3,069	...	2,879	...	14	...	...
Total Eastern Plains ...	13,180	10,017	93,011	153	14,251	642	...
Baháwalpur ...	...	...	29,031	...	...	...	...
Mandi	...	435	391	...	68,681	719	...
Chamba	5	1	...	...	...	96	...
Náhan	354	...	232	...	37,817	180	...
Biláspur	...	58	29	...	20,593	116	..
Bashahr	...	...	...	...	38,094	...	...
Nálagarh	2	1,015	92	...	13,613	680	...
Suket	...	169	370	...	21,830	21	...
Total Hill States ...	434	2,594	1,138	...	256,971	1,670	...
British Territory	52,102	140,031	676,831	81,063	74,553	157,740	1,998
Native States ..	13,614	12,601	123,210	153	271,222	2,512	
Province .	65,716	152,632	800,041	81,216	345,775	160,252	1,993

Agricultural and Pastoral Tribes.

PASTORAL TRIBES.

UBES.

105 Lodha.	142 Káchhi.	33 Kamboh.	27 Ahír.	51 Mahtam.	118 Sarrára.	123 Ghosi.	81 Gaddi.	
3,825	1,323	46	14,514	...	...	876	267	Dehli.
226	1	...	64,884	...	...	16	...	Gurgaon.
1,659	284	9,082	1,007	...	...	490	2,729	Karnal.
7	61	11	7,861	...	...	300	...	Hissar.
18	1	...	15,824	...	...	309	...	Rohtak.
1	16	...	922	1,988	...	67	...	Sirsa.
1,528	55	12,988	1,561	...	...	224	901	Ambala.
48	7	951	1	...	...	201	...	Ludhiána.
17	8	11	536	...	...	...	...	Simla.
...	42	7,120	259	3,314	...	...	...	Jalandhar.
...	10	466	30	230	...	...	5	Hushyárpur.
...	11	...	26	1	...	...	2,036	Kángra.
...	66	13,051	356	1,872	...	...	...	Amritsar.
...	...	275	53	...	...	...	303	Gurdáspur.
...	...	10	448	1,052	...	1	...	Siálkot.
152	34	17,694	1,213	9,551	..	99	...	Lahore.
8	...	604	85	17	...	...	...	Gujránwála.
174	1	5,208	1,100	5,954	...	83	...	Firozpur.
385	...	8	941	...	...	235	...	Ráwalpindi.
2	...	14	195	...	...	...	...	Jahlam.
...	...	...	58	2,022	...	...	...	Gujrat.
...	...	128	962	...	...	...	...	Shahpur.
375	...	687	887	4,193	...	332	...	Multan.
...	..	3	45	29	...	...	...	Jhang.
...	...	14,673	186	13,147	...	...	...	Montgomery.
3	...	11	73	2,943	...	6	...	Muzaffargarh.
11	...	...	...	...	...	...	...	Derah Ismail Khan.
...	1	1	6	822	...	...	...	Derah Ghazi Khan.
1	...	7	...	...	...	...	...	Bannu.
92	6	3	436	4	...	23	...	Peshávar.
...	...	...	37	...	4,426	...	...	Hazara.
2	1	1	62	...	...	...	1	Kohát.
8,537	**1,928**	**83,656**	**114,633**	**47,140**	**4,426**	**3,351**	**6,242**	**British Territory.**
27	27	23,417	31,512	...	...	181	...	Patiála.
1	8	8,649	14,711	21	...	...	...	Nábha.
...	9	12,937	28	2,347	...	...	...	Kapurthala.
2	291	529	5,023	...	...	8	3	Jínd.
...	...	4	153	106	...	...	...	Farídkot.
...	...	4,570	24	...	...	...	...	Maler Kotla.
3	...	740	39	...	...	...	...	Kalsia.
42	330	45,855	58,946	2,474	...	189	3	Total Eastern Plains.
...	...	...	...	5,766	...	...	...	Baháwalpur.
...	...	4	...	...	...	...	...	Mandi.
...	...	...	...	...	...	...	11,161	Chamba.
48	...	7	33	...	..	...	...	Náhan.
...	...	...	...	...	...	...	16	Biláspur.
...	...	...	3	...	..	...	...	Bashahr.
...	...	40	...	...	...	3	...	Nálagarh.
...	...	1	...	...	...	...	...	Suket.
48	...	78	61	...	...	3	11,177	Total Hill States.
8,537	**1,928**	**83,656**	**114,638**	**47,140**	**4,426**	**3,351**	**6,242**	**British Territory.**
90	**330**	**45,983**	**59,007**	**8,240**	**...**	**192**	**11,180**	**Native States.**
8,627	**2,258**	**129,589**	**173,640**	**55,380**	**4,426**	**3,543**	**17,422**	**Province.**

Abstract No. 85, showing Minor

	MINOR AGRICULTURAL AND									
	PROPORTION PER 1,00									
	45	31	7	65		20	29	147	105	112
	Máli.	Saini.	Aráin.	Bághbán.	TOTAL.	Kanet.	Ghirath.	Reya.	Lodha.	Káchhi.
Dehli ..	20	3	2	...	25	...	...	3	6	2
Gurgaon ...	15	...	...	...	15	...	...	...	...	...
Karnal ...	16	...	11	...	27	...	...	...	3	...
Hissar ...	19	...	4	...	23	...	...	...	...	...
Rohtak ...	14	...	...	...	14	..	...	...	...	...
Sirsa ...	3	...	19	...	22	...	...	...	...	...
Ambala ...	...	59	29	...	88	3	...	...	1	...
Ludhiána ...	...	...	44	...	44	...	...	...	...	...
Simla ...	...	1	1	...	2	212	2	...	...	...
Jalandhar ...	...	18	156	...	174	...	...	...	...	...
Hushyárpur ...	...	49	43	...	92	2	46	...	...	...
Kángra ...	1	3	1	...	5	84	149	...	...	...
Amritsar ...	...	1	50	...	51	...	...	...	...	...
Gurdáspur ...	...	17	68	...	85	...	7	1	...	...
Siálkot ...	...	...	65	...	65	...	...	...	...	...
Lahore ...	...	...	103	...	103	...	...	...	...	...
Gujránwála ...	...	...	35	...	35	...	...	...	...	...
Firozpur ...	...	...	78	...	78	...	...	...	...	...
Rawalpindi ...	...	...	...	51	51	...	...	...	...	...
Jahlam ...	...	...	35	19	54	...	...	...	...	...
Gujrat ...	...	...	30	...	30	...	...	...	...	...
Shahpur ...	...	...	20	...	20	...	...	...	...	...
Multan ...	...	...	43	...	43	...	...	...	1	...
Jhang ...	...	...	15	...	15	...	...	...	...	...
Montgomery ...	...	...	54	-	54	...	...	...	...	...
Muzaffargarh	...	...	12	...	12	...	...	...	...	...
Derah Ismail Khan	...	...	2	...	2	...	..	...	...	...
Derah Ghazi Khan	...	...	...	...	...	...	...	...	...	...
Bannu ...	...	...	12	...	12	.	...	...	...	...
Peshawar ...	...	...	...	30	30	...	...	...	...	...
Hazara ...	...	...	...	14	14	...	...	...	...	...
Kohát ...	...	...	...	6	6	...	...	...	...	...
British Territory.	3	7	36	4	50	4	8	...	...	...
Patiála ...	4	5	28	...	37	10	...	...	...	...
Nábha ...	1	...	12	...	13	...	...	...	..	...
Kapurthala ...	...	8	155	...	163	...	1	...	...	...
Jínd ...	12	...	9	...	21	...	...	...	...	1
Farídkot ...	...	1	23	...	24	...	...	...	...	...
Máler Kotla ...	...	...	24	...	24	...	...	...	...	...
Kalsia ...	45	...	43	...	88	...	...	...	...	...
Total Eastern Plains.	5	4	37	...	46	6	...	...	...	...
Bahâwalpur ...	...	...	51	...	51	...	..	...	...	...
Mandi ...	...	3	3	...	6	467	5	...	...	...
Chamba ...	...	...	...	...	...	...	1	...	..	..
Náhan ...	3	...	2	...	5	338	2	...	...	...
Bilâspur ...	...	1	...	..	1	238	1	...	...	...
Bashahr ...	...	...	...	...	...	606	...	...	...	...
Nálagarh ...	...	36	2	...	38	255	13	...	...	...
Suket ...	...	3	7	...	10	416	...	...	...	...
Total Hill States	1	3	1	...	5	335	2	...	...	...
British Territory.	3	7	36	4	50	4	8	...	...	-
Native States	4	3	32	...	39	70	1	...	...	...
Province ...	3	7	36	4	50	15	7	...	...	-

Agricultural and Pastoral Tribes—*concluded.*

PASTORAL TRIBES—CONCLUDED.

OF TOTAL POPULATION.

33	27	51	118		125	81			
Kamboh.	Ahír.	Mahtam.	Sarrára.	Total.	Ghosi.	Gaddi.	Total.	GRAND TOTAL.	
...	23	...	...	34	1	...	1	60	Dehli.
...	101	...	...	101	...	...	...	116	Gurgaon.
15	2	...	...	20	1	4	5	52	Karnal.
...	16	...	...	16	1	...	1	40	Hissar.
...	29	...	...	29	1	...	1	44	Rohtak.
...	4	8	...	12	...	...	..	34	Sirsa.
12	1	...	...	17	...	1	1	106	Ambala.
2	...	...	...	2	...	...	...	46	Ludhiána.
...	12	...	...	226	...	...	...	228	Simla.
9	...	4	...	13	...	...	...	187	Jalandhar.
1	...	...	...	49	...	2	2	143	Hushyárpur.
1	...	...	...	234	...	3	3	212	Kángra.
15	...	2	...	17	...	...	...	68	Amritsar.
...	...	...	..	8	...	...	...	93	Gurdáspur.
...	...	1	...	1	...	...	...	66	Siálkot.
19	1	10	...	30	...	...	...	133	Lahore.
1	...	...	...	1	...	...	...	36	Gujránwála.
8	2	9	...	19	...	...	...	97	Firozpur.
...	1	...	...	1	...	...	...	52	Rawalpindi.
...	...	...	...	...	...	...	...	54	Jahlam.
...	...	3	...	3	...	...	...	33	Gujrat.
...	2	...	...	2	...	...	...	22	Shahpur.
1	2	8	...	12	1	...	1	56	Multan.
...	...	...	...	...	...	...	...	15	Jhang.
34	...	31	...	65	...	...	...	119	Montgomery.
...	...	9	...	9	...	...	...	21	Muzaffargarh.
...	...	...	...	...	...	...	...	2	Derah Ismail Khan.
...	...	2	...	2	...	...	...	2	Derah Ghazi Khan.
...	...	...	...	...	...	...	...	12	Bannu.
...	1	...	...	1	...	...	...	37	Peshάwar.
...	...	...	11	11	...	...	...	25	Hazara.
...	...	...	...	...	...	...	...	6	Kohát.
4	6	8	...	25	...	...	...	75	British Territory.
16	21	...	...	47	...	...	...	84	Patiála.
14	56	...	...	70	...	...	...	83	Nábha.
51	...	9	...	61	...	...	...	224	Kapurthala.
2	20	...	...	23	...	...	...	44	Jínd.
...	2	1	...	3	...	...	...	27	Farídkot.
64	...	...	...	64	...	...	...	88	Máler Kotla.
11	1	...	...	12	...	...	..	100	Kalsia.
18	23	1	...	48	...	...	...	94	Total Easter Plains.
...	...	3	...	3	...		...	54	Bahάwalpur.
...	...	...	...	472	...	...	...	478	Mandi.
...	...	...	...	1	...	96	96	97	Chamba.
...	...	...	...	340	...	...	...	345	Náhan.
...	...	...	...	239	...	...	...	240	Bilάspur.
...	...	...	...	606	...	...	...	606	Bashahr.
1	...	...	...	260	...	...	...	307	Nálagarh.
...	...	...	...	416	...	...	.	426	Suket.
...	...	...	...	337	...	..	...	342	Total Hill States.
4	6	8	...	25	...	...	...	75	British Territory.
12	15	2	...	100	...	8	8	142	Native States.
6	8	2	...	88	...	1	1	89	Province.

"the names denoting occupation rather than caste, and are invariably held in "very low repute." The Maliár of the Ráwalpindi division for the most part returned their clan as Janjúa, Qutbsháhi (Awán), Khokhar, or Bhatti, though some of them give what are apparently true Aráin clans, such as Wáhand. Table VIII A gives no Aráins or Bághbáns in the Ráwalpindi district, but the fact is that by an unfortunate error, not detected till after the tables were in print, the Maliárs of Ráwalpindi and Jahlam were entered as Maniárs under Caste No. 47. I have added them to the figures for Bághbán in the Abstract, and it follows that all the Ráwalpindi and Jahlam Bághbáns of the Abstract were returned as Maliár, and not as Bághbán. So too, the figures for Muzaffargarh and the two Derahs are very imperfect, as Abstract No. 72 on page 224* shows that some thousands of Aráins or Maliárs in those districts * P. 106-107.
returned their caste as Jat. On the whole it would appear that Máli and Aráin are true castes in the eastern half of the Province, but that in the Western Panjáb, Aráin, Maliár, and Bághbán are commonly used as mere names of one and the same occupation. The detailed clan tables, when published, will throw much light upon the real affinities of these three castes.

486. The Aráins are found in great numbers throughout the northern, central, and western portions of the Eastern Plains and throughout the Ráwalpindi and Multán divisions; but west of Lahore the name must be taken to refer, except on the Satluj, to an occupation rather than a caste. Their strongholds are the Jálandhar, Amritsar, and Lahore divisions, and more especially the districts of Jálandhar and Lahore and the State of Kapúrthala where they form respectively 17·4, 10·3, and 16·3 per cent. of the total population. They are admirable cultivators, skilful and industrious, but like all vegetable growers of low standing among the cultivating classes. Where, however, they are found in very large numbers their position is higher, as there they are general cultivators rather than market gardeners. They are almost without exception Musalmáns, and would appear to be a true Panjáb tribe, to have come from the neighbourhood of Multán, and to have some affinity with the Kamboh. Mr. Purser writes: "The Aráins of Montgomery know nothing "of their origin. They claim to be Súrajbansi Rájpúts, and to have come "up to this district from the Dehli part of the country. They are usually "supposed to be Mahomedan Kambohs, and the latter undoubtedly came "from the west, so it is likely the Aráins did too. This is rendered more pro-"bable by the fact that the Aráins of Sahâranpur are said to have come from "Afghánistán. They do not seem to have got much below the Lahore border. [P. 268]
"Their chief divisions are Gahlán, Chandor, Chάchar, Sindhu, and Barár." I find that the Aráins of Fírozpur and Lahore also trace their origin from Uchh or Multán, and are supposed to be akin to the Kamboh. In Sirsa the Satluj Aráins meet those of the Ghaggar. They two do not intermarry, but the Aráins of the Ghaggar valley say they were Rájpúts living on the Panjnad near Multán, but were ejected some four centuries ago by Saiyad Jalál-ud-dín of Uchh. They claim some sort of connection with Jaisalmer. Till the great famines of 1759 and 1783 A.D. they are said to have held all the lower valleys of the Choya and Ghaggar, but after the latter date the Bhattis harassed the Sumras, the country became disturbed, and many of the Aráins emigrated across the Ganges and settled near Bareli and Rámpur. They marry only with the Ghaggar and Bareli Aráins. The Satluj Aráins in Sirsa say that they are, like the Aráins of Lahore and Montgomery, connected by origin with the Hindu Kambohs. Mr. Wilson thinks it probable that both classes are really

Kambohs who have become Musalmáns, and that the Ghaggar Aráins emigrated in a body from Multán, while the others moved gradually up the Satluj into their present place. He describes the Aráins of the Ghaggar as the most advanced and civilised tribe in the Sirsa district, even surpassing the Sikh Jats from Patiála; and he considers them at least equal in social status with the Jats, over whom they themselves claim superiority. The Aráins of Fírozpur, Ludhiána, Ambála, and Hissár also trace their origin from Uchh or its neighbourhood, though the Hissár Aráins are said to be merely Mahomedan Mális.

Of the Aráins of Jálandhar Mr. Barkley says that they are commonly believed to be descended from Kambohs, and that even those who are ashamed of so commonplace an origin are not prepared altogether to disclaim the relationship, but state that the Kambohs are the illegitimate and they the legitimate descendants of a common ancestor. He further states that they are settlers from the south, that none of their settlements are much older than 250 years, and that their original country is said to extend from Hánsi to Multán, while those of the Jálandhar Aráins whose history he has traced have come from the direction of Hissár. The Jálandhar Aráins themselves say they are descended from Rai Chajju of Ujjain who held the whole of the Sirsa district in *jágír;* while the Karnál Ráins also trace their origin from Sirsa. On the whole it would appear probable that the Aráins originally came from the lower Indus and spread up the five rivers of the Panjáb; and that at an early stage in their history a section of them moved up the Ghaggar, perhaps then a permanent river flowing into the Indus, and there gained for themselves a position of some importance. As the Ghaggar dried up and the neighbouring country became more arid, they moved on into the Jamna districts and Cis-Satluj tract generally, and perhaps spread along the foot of the hills across the line of movement of their brethren who were moving up the valleys of the larger rivers. Their alleged connection with the Mális is probably based only upon common occupation; but there does seem some reason to think that they may perhaps be akin to the Kambohs, though the difference must be more than one of religion only, as many of the Kambohs are Musalmán.

P. 196-97. Abstract No. 86 on the opposite page shows some of the largest Aráin clans. I have included under the head Aráin 987 persons who have returned themselves as Bhohar, which I am informed is an Aráin clan. Of these 850 were in Multán, 34 in Montgomery, and 103 in Muzaffargarh.

487. The Kanet (Caste No. 20).—The Kanets are the low-caste cultivating class of all the eastern Himálayas of the Panjáb and the hills at their base, as far west as Kúlu and the eastern portion of the Kángra district, throughout which tract they form a very large proportion of the total population. Beyond this tract, in Kángra proper, their place is filled by Ghiraths. The country they inhabit is held or governed by Hill Rájpúts of prehistoric ancestry, the greater part of whom are far too proud to cultivate with their own hands, and who employ the Kanets as husbandmen. The Kanets claim to be of impure Rájpút origin, but there is little doubt that they are really of aboriginal stock. At the same time it is most difficult to separate them from
†P. 161-62. Ráthis (*q. v.*, page 251†), and in Chamba both have been included under the latter head. The whole question of their origin is elaborately discussed by General Cunningham at pages 125 to 135 of Vol. XIV of his Archæological

Abstract No. 86, [P. 269]

	Arain.											
	1	2	3	4	5	6	7	8	9	10	11	12
	Multáni.	Ghalar.	Múnda.	Hánsi.	Ráhman.	Bhedu.	Goher.	Balgoria.	Galra.	Maláni.	Nain.	Chandor.
Ambala ...	6,421	47	...	...	...	...	...	.	...	217	34	270
Ludhiána ...	8	1,714	1,291	862	282	423	24	...	...	153	571	1,037
Jalandhar ...	...	1,821	...	4,704	3,912	7,372	5,255	...	...	1,792	4,619	5,141
Hushyárpur ..	...	...	164	1,951	120	455	91	2,809	4,485	1,116	...	973
Amritsar ...	150	514	41	142	123	...	...	...	..	278	1,128	5,428
Gurdáspur ...	10	127	...	935	34	253	360	...	...	251	895	1,167
Siálkot ...	36	...	...	382	1,804	155	75	..	...	23	571	1,340
Lahore ...	6,486	32	8	89	113	48	10	..	...	697	9,081	6,113
Gujránwála ...	130	...	...	18	305	...	58	...	..	...	184	333
Firozpur ...	3	40	...	500	2	37	377	...	...	1,070	4,862	3,867
Gujrát ...	...	33	...	...	412	...	...	...	...	...	668	...
Shahpur ...	...		4	1	...	...	...	..	...	1	...	...
Multan ...	1	...	...	60	...	...	...	...	...	6	...	258
Jhang ...	...	...	...	...	...	...	...	...	...	...	...	...
Montgomery ...	...	...	..	14	...	86	...	...	...	188	7	70
Muzaffargarh ...	...	...	..	...	...	...	...	...	..	...	...	...
British Territory.	**13,286**	**4,337**	**1,508**	**9,658**	**7,107**	**8,829**	**6,250**	**2,809**	**4,485**	**5,826**	**21,622**	**26,119**
Native States	**607**	**26**	**790**	**54**	**13**	**7**	**13**	...	..	**424**	**302**	**1,387**
Province ...	**13,893**	**4,363**	**2,298**	**9,712**	**7,120**	**8,836**	**6,263**	**2,809**	**4,485**	**6,250**	**21,934**	**27,506**

showing Arain Clans.

13	14	15	16	17	18	19	20	21	23	23	
Dhange.	Bhatti.	Bhutta.	Janjua.	Dhúdhi.	Rámí.	Ghalán.	Wáhand.	Qutbshálí.	Jatálí.	Cháchar.	
130	655	7	3	88	...	208	...	...	1,004	7	Ambala.
36	34	405	14	628	463	1,860	...	...	1,537	77[illegible]	Ludhiána.
377	331	3,134	1,487	1,215	13,004	7,213	...	..	4,031	858	Jalandhar.
113	150	922	12	1,054	342	3,892	...	..	1,031	636	Hushyárpur.
...	1,282	12	26	...	3,272	504	178	8	2,884	1,429	Amritsar.
5,784	2,295	352	31	159	1,864	3,561	...	...	3,937	757	Gurdáspur.
350	1,988	895	801	786	.	...	329	4	2,644	7	Siálkot.
815	1,080	7,646	521	422	2,630	8,628	...	...	5,099	3,715	Lahore.
...	1,210	580	1,641	88	71	278	1,076	16	901	9	Gujranwála.
947	2,262	2,580	10	217	2,704	3,856	...	335	3,243	1,9[illegible]5	Firozpur.
...	495	24	980	...	...	363	814	110	1,131	...	Gujrát.
...	162	85	350	...	...	...	352	3	203	...	Shahpur.
22	830	,711	668	78	..	...	3	12	2,053	...	Multan.
...	208	17	1,422	130	.	...	63	69	...	...	Jhang.
520	772	4,014	185	1,585	...	3	...	.	987	10	Montgomery.
...	1,385	1,409	32	...	...	..	...	...	..	...	Muzaffargarh.
9,295	15,684	24,477	8,098	6,559	24,355	30,479	2,815	557	32,153	10,233	British Territory.
956	1,002	8,126	8	69	46	2,708	..	...	1,114	383	Native States.
10,251	16,686	32,603	8,106	6,628	24,401	33,187	2,815	557	33,267	10,616	Province.

Reports. He identifies them with the Kunindas or Kulindas of the Sanskrit classics and of Ptolemy, and is of opinion that they belong to that great Khasa race which, before the Aryan invasion, occupied the whole Sub-Himalayan tract from the Indus to the Brahmaputra, and which, driven up into the hills by the advancing wave of immigration, now separates the Aryans of India from the Turanians of Tibet. But the Kanets are divided into two great tribes, the Khasia and the Ráo, and it is probable that the Khasias are really descended from intercourse between the Aryan immigrants and the women of the hills. The process by which the great Khas tribe of Nepal thus grew up is admirably described by Mr. Hodgson in his Essay in the Military tribes of that country, which is quoted at some length by General Cunningham, and, less fully, by me at page 236* *supra*. The distinction between Khasia and Ráo is still sufficiently well marked. A *P. 131. Khasia observes the period of impurity after the death of a relation prescribed for a twice-born man; the Ráo that prescribed for an outcast. The Khasia wears the *janeo* or sacred thread, while the Ráo does not. But the distinction is apparently breaking down, at least in Kúlu where the two tribes freely eat together and intermarry, though the Khasia, if asked, will deny the fact.

488. Mr. Lyall thus describes the Kanets of Kúlu :—

"The Kanets are often classed by other Hindus as on a par with the Rathis of Kangra. Just "as the Rathis claim to be Rajputs who have lost grade by taking to the plough, or the offspring "of Rájputs by Sudra women, so the Kanets say that they are the children of women of the hills "by Rajputs who came up from the plains. By one story both Kanets and Dagis were originally "of the same stock. Two sons of the demi-god, Bhim Sen Pándab, had each a son by the "daughter of a Kulu rakhas or demon. One of these sons married a Bhotanti, or woman of Tibet, "who fed him with yak's flesh, so he and his children by her became Dagis. The other son was "ancestor of the Kanets.

"Both of these stories perhaps point to the conclusion that the Kanets and Dagis are of mixed "Mughal and Hindu race. General Cunningham says as much of the Kanets of Kanawar, and "connects the caste name with the word Karána, which implies mixed blood. The Kanets are "divided into Kassiyas and Raos. The Raos say that the origin of this division was that a Raja "of Kulu ordered the Kanets to reform their loose practices, and conform altogether to Hinduism; "those who obeyed were called Kassiyas, and those who stuck to their old ways Raos. It is a fact "that at the present day the former are more Hindu in all observances than the latter, and the story "is otherwise probable, as one can see that the foreign priests round the Rajas were always "striving to make the Kulu people more orthodox Hindus, greater respectors of Brahmins, and "less devoted to the worship of their local divinities. The Kassiyas wear the *janeo*, and pretend "to some superiority, which, however, is not admitted by the Raos. They intermarry and eat "and drink together out of the same cooking pot, but not out of the same dish or plate."

He adds that they are not tall, but strong and active, and generally have [P. 270] handsome figures. Some are hardly darker than Spaniards in complexion, with a ruddy colour showing in their cheeks; others are as dark as the ordinary Panjábi. Of the "so called Kanets of Láhul" he writes that they "are "a mixed race, but the Mongolian element predominates over the Indian. "Many of those who live in the lower valley are no doubt descendants of "Kanet settlers from Kúlu and Bangáhal; the rest are pure Tibetan, or nearly "so." In Láhul the Kanets, like all other classes of the people, will eat cows and bullocks which have died a natural death. They never wear the sacred thread. The social status of the Kanet appears to be very low. A Sunár will marry a Kanet woman, but he will not give his daughter to a Kanet, nor will he eat from the hand of a Kanet, though his wife will do so. In Láhul even a Bráhman or Thakar will take a Kanet woman as a second-class wife, and the offspring of the latter, who are known as *Garu*, will in a few generations rank as Thakar. Those of the former however can never rise to full equality with the pure Bráhman, though they are commonly known as Bráhmans. The fathers will not eat from the hands of sons begotten in this manner, but will smoke with them.

General Cunningham says that the Kanets have three principal clans—Mangal, Chauhán, and Ráo. The Chauhán will almost certainly be Khasia. With respect to the Mangal I have no information, nor do I find it in my papers, unless Pangalána be a misreading for Mangalána or Mangal. The principal Kanet divisions returned in our papers are shown in the margin. More than half the Kásib are in Bashahr. The name belongs to a Brahminical *gotra*, and is probably no tribe at all and only returned because the heading of the schedule was misunderstood. The Chauhán are principally returned from Mandi, Suket, Náhan, Keonthal, and Jubbal; the Khasia from Bashahr and Kángra; the Pangalána from Suket; and the Punwár from Náhan. General Cunningham assigns the upper valley of the Pabar to the Chauhán, the lower Pabar, the Rúpin, and the Tons valleys to the Ráo and the tract west of the Pabar basin to the Mangal. Mr. Anderson notes that the Khasia are more common in Kúlu proper, and the Ráo in Seoráj.

KANET TRIBES.

1.	Kásib ...	67,233	5.	Pangalána...	12,067
2.	Chauhán ...	38,585	6.	Thakar ...	7,356
3.	Ráo ...	32,218	7.	Punwár ...	7,129
4.	Khasia ...	29,285	8.	Lastúri ...	3,859

489. The Ghirath, Bahti, and Chang (Caste No. 29).—The Ghiraths fill much the same position in Kángra proper and the hills below it as do the Kanets in the part to the east. With them I have included the Báhti and the Cháng, as it appears that one and the same people are known as Ghirath in Kángra, and as Bahti in the eastern and Cháng in the western portion of the lower ranges. All three intermarry freely, and are considered by Mr. Lyall as identical. In the Amritsar division all the Ghiraths except 128 were returned as Cháng. The Jálandhar divisional office took the three names together. The Ghiraths of Kángra and Hushyárpur are thus described by Mr. Barnes :—

P. 161-62. "My previous remarks (quoted on page 251 under the head Ráthi) will have introduced the "reader to the Girths. They form a considerable item in the population of these hills, and in "actual numbers exceed any other individual caste. With the Girths I have associated the few "Jats that reside in this district, and the Changs, which is only another name for Girths, prevalent "about Haripur and Nurpur. They amount altogether to 111,507 souls. The Girths are sub-"divided into numerous sects. There is a common saying that there are 360 varieties of rice, and "that the sub-divisions of the Girths are equally extensive, the analogy arising from the Girths "being the usual cultivators of rice. The Girths predominate in the valleys of Palum, Kangra, and "Riblo. They are bound again in the 'Hul Doon,' or Haripur valley. These localities are the "strongholds of the caste, although they are scattered elsewhere in every portion of the district, and "generally possess the richest lands and the most open spots in the hills. The Girths belong to the "Sudra division of Hindus, and this fact apparently accounts for the localities wherein they are "found. The open valleys, although containing the finest lands, are also the only accessible "portions of the hills. The more refined castes preferred the advantages of privacy and seclusion, "although accompanied by a sterner soil and diminished returns. They abandoned the fertile "valleys to less fastidious classes, whose women were not ashamed to be seen nor to work in the "fields, and the men were not degraded by being pressed as porters.

"The Girths are a most indefatigable and hard-working race. Their fertile lands yield "double crops, and they are incessantly employed during the whole year in the various processes "of agriculture. In addition to the cultivation of their fields, the Girth women carry wood, "vegetables, mangoes, milk and other products to the markets for sale; many sit half the day "wrangling with customers until their store is disposed of. The men are constantly seized for "begár, or forced labour, to carry travellers' loads, or to assist in the various public buildings in "course of construction. From these details it will be perceived that the Girths have no easy "time of it, and their energies and powers of endurance must be most elastic to bear up against "this incessant toil.

"To look at their frames, they appear incapable of sustaining such fatigue. The men are "short in stature, frequently disfigured by goitre (which equally affects both sexes), dark and sickly "in complexion, and with little or no hair on their faces. Both men and women have coarse "features, more resembling the Tartar physiognomy than any other type, and it is rare to see a "handsome face, though sometimes the younger women may be called pretty. Both sexes are "extremely addicted to spirituous drinks. Although industrious cultivators, they are very litigious "and quarrelsome; but their disputes seldom lead to blows; and though intemperate, they are still "thrifty,—a Girth seldom wastes his substance in drink. In their dealings with one another they "are honest and truthful, and altogether their character, though not so peaceable and manly as the "Rathi, has many valuable and endearing traits. The Girths being Sudras do not wear the *janeo* or "thread of caste. They take money for their daughters, but seldom exchange them. The younger "brother takes his brother's widow; if she leave his protection, he was entitled by the law of "the country to her restitution and under us he should at all events receive money com-"pensation."

The Ghiraths are said to be of Rájpút origin by mixed marriages or illegitimate intercourse, but I have no trustworthy information on the subject. They are essentially agricultural, and the proverb says:—"As the rice bends "in the ear the Ghirath lifts his head." Their social position is low. "You "can no more make a saint of a Ghirath than expect chastity of a buffalo," and they practise widow-marriage, for "You can't make a Ghirathni a widow, "any more than you can turn a hill buffalo into a barren cow."

The Ghiraths have returned few large sub-divisions. The eight largest are given in the margin. Bhárdwáj is another Brahminical *gotra*, and probably returned through misapprehension. Chhábru is found only in Hushyárpur, and Chhora and Bhattu only in Kángra. The others occur in both districts.

GHIRATH TRIBES.					
1.	Kandal ...	24,392	5.	Reru ...	2,532
2.	Bhárdwáj ...	8,330	6.	Badiál ...	2,058
3.	Pathári ...	3,091	7.	Chhora ...	1,695
4.	Chhábru ...	2,717	8.	Battu ...	1,623

490. The Reya (Caste No. 147).—Having thus disposed of the two great inferior cultivating castes of the hills, I shall take the others as far as possible in order of locality from east to west. The Reyas are a small Hindu caste found only in the Dehli district. They say they were Rájpúts but were excluded from the caste because they took to practising *karewa* or widow-marriage. They are now quite separate. They eat and smoke with [P. 271] Jats and agricultural castes of similar standing, but will not marry them except by *karewa*. They own nine villages in Dehli, and the names of their clans are sometimes Rájpút and sometimes not. They trace their origin from Mahrauli where the Qutb pillar stands.

491. The Lodha and Kachhi (Caste Nos. 105 and 142).—These are two well-known cultivating castes of Hindústán, and are found in the Panjáb chiefly in the Jamna districts, though a few of them have moved on westwards to the great cantonments. They are almost without exception Hindus. The Lodhas are said to be numerous in Hushangábád, and to be distinct from the Lodhi outcasts of Central India; but the Lodhas of Dehli would appear to be of very low social standing. It is said that there are two distinct castes of Lodhas, one spelled with the hard and the other with the soft *d*, and perhaps this may account for the apparent confusion. The Ambála Lodhas cultivate hemp largely, and work it up into rope. The Káchhis are said to be the market gardeners of Hindústán, and of low standing. In the Panjáb I believe they are generally engaged in the cultivation of water-nuts and similar produce; indeed in many parts they are called Singhári (from *Singhára*, a water-nut) as commonly as Káchhi.

492. **The Kamboh (Caste No 33.)**—The Kambohs are one of the finest cultivating castes in the Panjáb. They seldom engage in market-gardening, but they are no less industrious and skilful than the Aráins. They are found in the upper Satluj valley as low down as Montgomery, throughout the northern portion of the Eastern Plains, and as low down the Jamna valley as Karnál. They are especially numerous in Kapúrthala. The Jamna Kambohs seem to have come into the valley from the west, and there has quite lately been a very large influx of Kambohs from the northern tracts of Patiála into the great *dhák* jungles between Thánesar and the river. The Satluj Kambohs of Montgomery are divided into two branches, one of which came up the river from the Multán country and the other down the valley from the neighbourhood of Kapúrthala, both movements having taken place under the Sikh rule. They claim descent from Rája Karan, and say that their ancestor fled to Kashmír. The Kambohs of Bijnor also trace their origin to the trans-Indus country, and Mr. Purser accepts this tradition as evidently true. They are said by some to be ancient inhabitants of Persia, and the Karnál Kambohs trace their origin from Garh Ghazni; but the fact that 40 per cent. of them are Hindus and 23 per cent. Sikhs is conclusive against their having had any extra-Indian origin, unless at a very remote period. I have in section 486 noted the fact that Aráins and Kambohs are commonly supposed to be closely related. Indeed in Montgomery a man appears to be called Aráin if he is Musalmán and Kamboh if Hindu. But that this is not always the case is evident from the fact of a very considerable proportion of the Kambohs of Amritsar, Lahore, Fírozpur, Patiála, Nábha, and Maler Kotla having returned themselves as Musalmáns, although Musalmán Aráins are also numerous in those tracts. In Jálandhar the village of Bhalowál is owned partly by Kambohs and partly by Aráins, both being Musalmán. It is perhaps doubtful whether the supposed relationship has any further basis than the fact that they both came from the west, and are both of much the same social standing and agricultural repute. The detailed clan tables will probably throw light on the question, though in Kapúrthala, the stronghold of the Kambohs, their clans were not recorded. It is said by some that the chief distinction is that the Kambohs take money for their daughters, while the Aráins do not. But the social standing of the Kamboh is on the whole superior to that of the Aráin, and very markedly so where the latter is a vegetable-grower. The Kamboh, moreover, is not a mere agriculturist. He not unfrequently engages in trade, and even takes service in the army or in offices or even as a private servant, while his wife not unfrequently lends money even where he is a mere husbandman; and under Akbar a Kamboh General called Sháhbáz Khán commanded 5,000 men and distinguished himself greatly in Bengal. Musalmán Kambohs held Sohna in Gurgáon some centuries ago; and the tombs and mosques that they have left show that they must have enjoyed a considerable position. The military, mercantile, and clerkly Kambohs are said to be distinguished as Qalmi or "men of the pen," and not to intermarry with the agricultural section of the caste. But this is probably a mere social custom and not a caste rule. The Kambohs do not seem to bear as high a character for honesty as they do for skill. There is a Persian proverb current in the North-West Provinces: "The Afgháns, the Kambohs, and the Kashmíris; all three

rogues (*badzát*)," and Mr. Benton of Karnál describes them as "notoriously deceitful and treacherous." On the other hand Sardár Gurdiál Singh states, I know not on what authority, that "during the reign of terror in India, it "was the Kambohs who were trusted by the rich bankers for carrying "their cash in the disguise of *faqírs*." The Kambohs are said to be exceptionally numerous in Mírat. Their location under the hills lends some slight support to their tradition of origin from Kashmír.

KAMBOH CLANS.			
1. Thind ...	10,394	6. Sando ...	4,321
2. Jausan ...	6,635	7. Jammún	2,515
3. Jaura ...	5,420	8. Jhande ...	2,028
4. Dahút ...	4,063	9. Unmál ...	2,001
5. Mahrok ...	4,880		

The Kambohs seem to have returned very few large sub-divisions. The figures for the nine largest are given in the margin.

493. The Ahír (Caste No. 27).—The Ahírs are properly a pastoral caste, their name being derived from the Sanskrit *Abhíra*, or "milkman." But in the Panjáb they are now almost exclusively agricultural, and stand in quite the first rank as husbandmen, being as good as the Kamboh and somewhat superior to the Jat. They are of the same social standing as the Jat and Gújar, who will eat and smoke with them; but they do not seem ever to have been, at any rate within recent times, the dominant race in any considerable tract. Perhaps their nearest approach to such a position was in Rewári and the country to the west of it still locally known as Hírwáti, where they held nearly three quarters of the *parganah* in 1838. A very full description of them will be found in Elliott's *Races of the North-West Provinces*, and also in Sherring, I, 332*ff*. The west coast of India and Gújarát would appear to be their ancient homes, but they are numerous in Behar and Gorakhpur, and at one time there was an Ahír dynasty in Nepal. In the Panjáb they are chiefly found in the south of Dehli, Gurgáon, and Rohtak and the Native States bordering upon these districts, and in this limited tract they form a considerable proportion of the whole population. They are almost all Hindus, and [P. 272]
are said to trace their origin from Mathra. They are industrious, patient, and orderly; and though they are ill spoken of in the proverbs of the countryside, yet that is probably only because the Jat is jealous of them as being even better cultivators than himself. Thus they say in Rohtak: "Kosli (the head village of the Ahírs) has fifty brick houses and several thousand swaggerers." So in Dehli: "Rather be kicked by a Rájpút or stumble uphill, "than hope anything from a jackal, spear grass, or an Ahír;" and again: "All castes are God's creatures, but three castes are ruthless. When they "get a chance they have no shame; the whore, the Bauya, and the Ahír." But these stigmas are now-a-days at least wholly undeserved.

The Ahírs of the North-West Provinces have three great sections, the Nandbans of the central *doáb*, the Jádúbans of the upper *doáb* and the Mathra country, and the Gwálbans of the lower *doáb* at Benares. The Ahírs of the Panjáb have returned themselves as shown in the margin. Of the Gwálbans more than 16,000 are found in Patiála. Within these tribes they have numerous clans, among which the Kosali of Rohtak and Gurgáon number 7,322.

AHIR TRIBES.			
Jádúbans	...	...	43,961
Nandbans	...	...	24,998
Gwálbans	...	...	25,187

494. The Mahtam (Caste No. 51).—There has been a confusion in the figures of Table VIIIA owing to the fact that the Mahtams are also called Bahrúpias. The Mahtams of Gújrát and Siálkot returned themselves under that name, and were included under Bahrúpia in Table VIIIA. I have
'P. 190- restored them to their proper place in Abstract No. 85, page 266.* The Mah-
93. tams, or as they are called in the Jálandhar division Mahton (nasal *n*), are found chiefly in the Satluj valley, and along the foot of the hills between Jálandhar and Gújrát. They are of exceedingly low caste, being almost out-casts; by origin they are vagrants, and in some parts they apparently retain their wandering habits, while everywhere they are still great hunters, using nooses like those of the Báwarias described in section 575. But in many districts, and especially on the middle Satluj, they have devoted themselves to husbandry and are skilful and laborious cultivators. The great majority of them are classed as Hindus, but about one-fifth are Musalmán, and as many again Sikh. But the Musalmán section, even in the Multán division, eat wild pig and retain most of their Hindu customs, and are consequently not admitted to religious equality by the other Musalmáns. They appear, however, to bury their dead. They live, in Muzaffargarh, in grass huts on the river banks, whence the saying—"Only two Mahtam huts and calls itself Khairpur." Mr. Purser thus describes the Mahtams of Montgomery:—

"They are a low Hindu caste, and are looked down on by their neighbours. Their story is "that they were Rajputs, and one of their ancestors was a kanungo. Akbar was then on the "throne. Kanungos were called *mahta*, and thus they got their name. The first mahta was dis-"missed, and then settled at Mahtpur in Jalandhar. His descendants emigrated and settled along "the banks of the rivers as they found quantities of *sarr* in such situations, and working in *sarr* "was their chief occupation. It was not till the Nakkai chiefs held sway that they settled down "permanently in this district. They adopted the custom of marriage with widows according to the "form of *chaddar dálna*, and so became Sudras. They are also called 'Bahrupias,' which name "is a corruption of '*Bho-rúp-ias*,' and means people of many modes of life, because they turned "their hands to any business they could find (yet *cf.* Select Glossary, I, 17 & 54). Cunningham "(History of the Sikhs, page 17) says, 'the hardworking Hindu Mahtams are still moving family "'by family and village by village eastward away from the Ravi and Chanab.' This would seem "to give the Mahtams a western instead of eastern origin as claimed by them. They own a good "many villages (19), most of which are in good condition. Where they are not proprietors of the "whole village, they reside in a separate group of huts at some distance from the main *ábádi*. "They are great hands at catching wild pigs; but it is in cutting down the jungle on inundated "lands that they excel. Though industrious they do not care much for working wells, and prefer "cultivating lands flooded by the rivers. They are quarrelsome and addicted to petty thieving. "They are of medium stature and stoutly made."

495. There is a Bahrúp tribe of Banjáras or, as they are called in the Panjáb, Labánas; and the Labánas and Mahtams of the Satluj appear closely to resemble each other. Elliott's description of the Bahrúp Banjáras at page 54, Volume I of his *Races of the North-West Provinces*, tallies curiously in some respects with that of the Bahrúpia Mahtams of Gújrát given by Captain Mackenzie at section 71 of his settlement report of that district; and on the whole it seems probable that the Mahtams are Banjáras or Labánas, in which case it is possible that the Satluj group have come up from Rájpútána, while the sub-montane group are merely a western continuation of the Banjáras of the lower hills. This is the more probable as I find that the Jálandhar Mahtams trace their origin from Jammu, conquered Ráhon from the Gújars, and were in turn deprived of it by the Ghorewáha Rájpúts probably not less than five centuries ago. At the same time I should note that the Mahton of Hushyárpur and the neighbourhood appear to hold a much higher social position than the Mahtams of the Satluj; and it may be that the two are really distinct. Sardár Gurdiál Singh indeed goes so far as to say that the

Mahton of Hushyárpur are of good Rájpút blood, though they have lost caste by taking to ploughing and practising widow-marriage, and that their social standing is not much below that of Rájpúts. He thinks that the name may be derived from *Mahta*, which he says is a title of honour current among the Rájpúts of the hills; and this agrees with the Montgomery tradition quoted above. Mr. Anderson also gives the Hushyárpur Mahtons high social standing. On the other hand, Mr. Wilson says that the Labánas of Sirsa would scout the idea of connection with the Mahtams of the Satluj, whom they consider utterly inferior to themselves. The point needs to be cleared up by further enquiry, especially in the districts where the classes come into contact. Our detailed tables of clans will doubtless throw light on the question.

496. The Sarrara (Caste No. 118).—It is perhaps probable that these men are the same as those discussed under the head "Sarera" in the section on Hill Menials. But I have separated them, as their identity is not at all certain. The Sarráras which are found in Hazára belong to a race inhabiting Chibhál, or the hill country of Kashmír on the Hazára border, and according to Major Wace belong to the same ethnic group as the Dhúnd, Satti, and Kharrál of the same tract. It might perhaps have been better to take them with the Kharráls. They are chiefly found in the Abbottábád *tahsíl*, where they are purely agricultural. They are all Musalmán.

497. The Ghosi (Caste No. 125).—The Ghosi is I believe an Ahír tribe; but in the Panjáb the name is only used for Musalmáns, and is often applied to any cowherd or milkman of that religion, whether Gújar, Ahír, or of any other caste, just as Gwála is used for a Hindu cowherd. The Ghosi proper is only found in the eastern districts, though a few have strayed into the large cantonments to the west. But the 235 persons shown as Ghosi in the Ráwal- [P. 273]
pindi division are, according to my papers, entered as Ghasiára or "grass-cutter," while the 337 of the Multán division are shown as Her, probably for Ahír. How these came to be classed as Ghosi I cannot explain. It was not done by my orders. It is said that Hindus will buy pure milk from the Musalmán Ghosi, but will reject it if there is any suspicion of its having been watered by the latter, as they must not drink water at his hands! The Ghosis are a purely pastoral caste, at any rate in the Panjáb. They are however sometimes butchers.

498. The Gaddi (Caste No. 81).—These figures appear to include two entirely distinct classes of people. The Musalmán Gaddis of Dehli, Karnál, and Ambála are apparently a tribe found in the upper *doáb* of the Jamna and Ganges, closely resembling the Ghosi, and perhaps like them a subdivision of the Ahírs. They are called Gádi almost as often as Gaddi. They are by hereditary occupation milkmen; but in Karnál, where they are most numerous, they have settled down as cultivators and own several villages. They are poor husbandmen. And a further confusion may possibly have taken place from the fact that a descendant of a Rájpút father by a widow of another caste married by *karewa* is called Garra with the hard *r*. Indeed it is not quite impossible that here we may have the connecting link between the two classes. At any rate the word Gaddi, as used in the Panjáb proper, is applied to the inhabitants of the mountain range between Kángra and Chamba and of its continuation in the latter State. The term is commonly applied to almost any inhabitant of that region; but the true Gaddis, whom General Cunningham is inclined to identify with the ancient Gandaridæ, or Gangaridæ, are apparently of Khatri origin. Mr. Barnes thus describes them :—

"The Gadis are the most remarkable race in the hills. In features, manners, dress, and dialect "they differ essentially from all the rest of the population. The Gadis reside exclusively upon the "snowy range which divides Chamba from Kangra. A few of them have wandered down into "the valleys which skirt the base of this mighty chain, but the great majority live on the "heights above; they are found from an elevation of 3,500 or 4,000 feet up to 7,000 feet. "Above this altitude there is little or no cultivation, the increasing acclivity of the range "opposing insurmountable obstacles. They preserve a tradition among themselves that their "ancestors originally came from the Panjab, and that during the horrors of the Mahomedan "invasions the population of the cities fled from the open country before their invaders and "took refuge in these ranges, at that period almost uninhabited. The term 'Gadi' is a "generic name, and under this appellation are included Brahmins, Khatris, and a few Rajputs and "Rathis. The majority, however, are Khatris, and the sub-divisions of the caste correspond "exactly with the tribes among the Khatris existing in the plains of the Panjab at the "present day. Impure castes are not styled Gadis, but are known by the names of Badi, "Sipi, Háli, &c. They are a semi-pastoral, semi-agricultural race. The greater portion of "their wealth consists of flocks of sheep and goats, which they feed half the year (the "winter months) in the valleys of Kangra, and for the other half drive across the range "into the territories of Chamba. They hold lands on this side and also in Chamba, and in "former days were considered subject to both States. At present our rule has materially "weakened the tenure of the Chamba Chief, and many continue all the year round on this "side of the range acknowledging no allegiance whatever to Chamba. It was a rule with "these simple people, whenever fined by the Kangra authorities, to pay a similar penalty "into the Chamba treasury. I am afraid our institutions have taught them greater independence, "and the infraction of this custom is now more frequent than the observance. Many Gadis "cultivate the winter crops or wheat in Kangra, and returning with their flocks grow the "summer or rain crop at 'Barmor,' as the province on the other side of the snow is designated. "They all wear woollen clothes, which they make up at home out of the wool from their own "flocks. The men don a remarkable high-peaked cap, with flaps to pull down over the ears "in case of severe weather. The front is usually adorned with a garland of dried flowers, "or with tufts of the Impeyan pheasant, or red beads, the seeds of parasitical plants growing "in the forests. The rest of their dress is a frock, made very capacious and loose, secured "round the waist, with a black woollen cord. In the body of this frock the Gadi stores "the most miscellaneous articles; his own meal, tied up in an untanned leather pouch, with "two or three young lambs just born, and perhaps a present of walnuts or potatoes for his "master are the usual contents. His legs are generally bare, but occasionally he wears woollen "trowsers very loose at the knee, to allow free motion in walking, and fitting tight at the ankle "over which it lies in folds so as not to restrict the action of the limbs. The women "wear the same frock, only reaching to their ankles, secured with the same woollen cord. "Their garment fits rather tighter about the body, and is both modest and becoming. The "head-dress is a 'chaddur,' or sheet, thrown loosely over the upper portion of the body, "and sometimes fastened in the shape of a turban, with a loose streamer behind by way "of ornament. The Gadis are a very simple and virtuous race; they are remarkable, even "among the hill population, for their eminent regard for truth; crime is almost unknown "among them; their women are chaste and modest, seldom deserting their husbands. Like "all the inhabitants of mountainous regions they are frank and merry in their manners,—they "constantly meet together, singing and dancing in a style quite peculiar to themselves. "They are great tipplers, and at these festive meetings the natural hilarity is considerably "enhanced by deep potations. In person they are a comely race. The women frequently are "very fair and beautiful,—their features are regular, and the expression almost always mild "and engaging. The Gadis wear the thread of caste, and are much stricter in Hindu customs "and observances than most of the inhabitants of the higher ranges of the Himalaya. They "are not a very widely-diffused race. They extend over the greater part of Chamba, "inhabit the skirts of the Kangra snowy range, and are found also on the southern face "of the Badrawar hills across the Ravi. Their peculiar caste, 'Khatri,' and their posi- "tion in the ranges immediately above Lahore favour the tradition that originally they were "fugitives from the cities of the plains before the Mahomedan inroads."

They are almost all shepherds, and do not in any way resemble the Khatris of the plains. They are all Hindus, but locally distinguished from the *jándre* or cotton-clad Hindus. The Khatri and Rájpút Gaddis intermarry; and in some places the Bráhman Gaddi will marry the Khatri Gaddi. The Khatri or true Gaddis are the best of the classes, and "number among them the best shepherds, and the richest and most influential men." It is not improbable that in Chamba, their true home, the Rájpút and Bráhman Gaddis are less numerous than in Kángra. The Gaddi are a simple and rustic people. The proverb says: "The Gaddi is a good natured fool; ask for his cap and he gives "you his coat." And again: "In no-man's-land one makes friends with "Gújars and Gaddis."

FOREIGN RACES.

409. Foreign Races.—I have called the groups of which the figures are given on the next page* in Abstract No. 87 Foreign Races, because they bear titles properly foreign to India and for the most part lay claim to foreign origin. It will presently be seen how little real right many of them have to the names they bear. The Saiyads might have been included in the group, but they have been classed with the priestly castes. The present group is divisible into three sections, the Arab and Shekh, the Túrk and Mughal, and the Ghulám and Qizilbásh. The last two and probable many of the Arabs and Túrks are true foreigners, and have a good claim to the names they bear; but the Shekhs and Mughals are for the most part mere pretenders. What Rájpút is to the Hindu, Sheikh, Saiyad, and in the west of the Panjáb Mughal, are to the Musalmán; and every convert of low caste who wishes to glorify himself assumes one of these titles, while tribes whose origin is lowly or has been forgotten, trace their descent from the people of the Prophet or of one of the Mahomedan conquerors of India. As Mr. Thompson puts it: "Pride of race "leads to the invention of some royal progenitor, and pride of religion is a "perpetual inducement to escape from the admission of an idolatrous ancestry." *P. 207. [P. 274]

500. The Arab (Caste No. 140).—Arabs are returned in the Panjáb chiefly from the Multán and Pesháwar divisions. They are probably Arab merchants from Bombay, where I believe men of true Arab extraction are somewhat numerous. That they have not come direct from Arabia is shown by the language table, in which Arabic is returned as the mother-tongue of only 63 persons. More than half the Arabs in the Panjáb are to be found in Peshávar itself. This is hardly to be wondered at, for Peshávar is a city in which may be found representatives of almost every Eastern nation, and is the half-way house between India and Asia. It is possible that some of our Shekhs, whether truly or falsely so called, may have returned themselves as Arabs, but I do not think it likely. The true Shekhs are of course of Arab origin; but I believe that such men when their settlement in the Panjáb is of any long standing, always call themselves Shekh or Qureshi, and not Arab. [P. 275]

501. The Shekh (Caste No. 17).—*Shekh* is an Arabic word meaning an elder or Chief, and probably corresponds very closely among the tribes of Arabia with *Chaudhri* among those of the Panjáb. Thus the title should properly be confined to, and is very generally assumed by tribes of true Arab descent. But it has been degraded to a much more vulgar use. If a Rájpút or Jat turn Mahomedan he retains his caste name, and is still a Rájpút or Jat; though I have known Musalmán Rájputs who had fallen in life and taken to weaving call themselves Shekhs, though still recognized as relations by their brethren of the village whence they came. So if an outcast or man of impure calling becomes Musalmán and retains his occupation, or at least substitutes for it another only slightly less degrading, he also retains his caste name or is known by an entirely new one, such as Díndár or Musalli. But the class which lie between these two extremes, and are neither so proud of their origin as to wish, nor so degraded by their occupation as to be compelled to retain their original caste name, very generally abandon that name on their conversion to Islám and adopt the title of Shekh.

[P. 274]

Abstract No. 87, showing Foreign Races.

	Figures.						Proportion per 1,000 of Total Population.						
	140	17	126	37	130	181	14	17	126	37	130	181	
	Arab.	Shekh.	Túrk.	Mughal.	Ghulám.	Qizilbásh.	Arab.	Shekh.	Túrk.	Mughal.	Ghulám.	Qizilbásh.	Total.
Dehli	...	50,195	5	5,806	...	...	...	78	...	9	...	...	87
Gurgaon	...	10,157	...	1,317	...	...	...	16	...	2	...	...	18
Karnál	...	13,789	...	597	...	...	...	22	...	1	...	...	23
Hissar	...	3,983	...	492	...	...	..	8	..	1	...	...	9
Rohtak	..	6,334	...	414	...	...	...	15	...	1	...	...	16
Sirsa	...	2,733	...	604	...	..	...	11	...	3	...	...	14
Ambala	...	28,920	...	855	...	...	..	27	...	1	..	...	28
Ludhiána	19	6,129	...	677	...	...	...	10	...	1	..	...	11
Simla	...	3,676	...	160	...	..	...	86	...	4	...	...	90
Jullundur	...	9,720	...	1,662	...	...	...	12	...	2	...	...	14
Hoshiárpur	...	6,839	..	1,400	...	...	...	8	...	2	...	...	10
Kángra	...	1,792	...	289	...	..	...	2	...	...	...	...	2
Amritsar	...	8,280	...	2,546	...	...	...	9	...	3	...	...	12
Gurdáspur	...	10,468	157	2,450	...	..	..	13	...	3	...	...	16
Siálkot	...	11,636	2	4,537	...	...	...	12	...	4	...	...	16
Lahore	3	17,853	95	3,676	...	33	...	10	...	4	...	..	23
Gujránwála	...	8,557	...	827	...	...	...	14	...	1	...	...	15
Ferozepore	...	6,806	...	1,103	..	...	...	10	...	2	...	...	12
Rawalpindi	17	25,524	188	25,109	...	...	...	31	...	31	...	...	62
Jhelum	...	8,412	...	11,222	...	...	...	14	...	19	...	...	33
Gujrát	...	7,906	...	5,290	...	...	...	11	...	8	...	...	19
Shahpur	...	7,499	..	2,335	...	..	...	18	...	6	...	...	24
Mooltan	475	12,649	1	4,601	99	...	1	23	...	8	...	...	32
Jhang	...	5,337	...	3,122	...	...	...	14	...	8	...	...	22
Montgomery	35	4,740	1	1,620	...	...	...	11	...	4	...	...	15
Muzaffargarh	297	5,046	...	576	...	..	1	15	...	2	...	...	18
D. I. Khan	23	5,713	1	676	...	10	...	13	...	2	...	...	15
D. G. Khan	32	4,060	5	405	...	...	...	13	...	1	...	...	14
Bannu	...	11,391	...	759	...	...	...	34	...	2	...	...	36
Peshâwar	1,418	9,576	83	4,538	3,347	389	2	16	...	8	5	1	32
Hazara	23	5,098	2,996	5,297	...	.	...	13	7	13	...	...	33
Kohát	...	4,428	1	153	...	9	...	24	...	1	...	...	25
British Territory	2,842	327,928	3,535	95,861	3,446	441	...	17	...	5	...	...	22
Patiála	...	14,603	...	1,854	...	...	...	10	...	1	...	...	11
Nábha	...	2,229	...	341	...	...	...	8	...	1	...	...	9
Kapurthala	...	3,447	...	606	...	...	...	10	...	2	...	...	12
Jínd	...	3,150	...	926	...	...	...	13	...	4	...	...	17
Total East. Plains	..	26,214	...	4,517	...	...	...	10	...	2	...	...	12
Bahâwalpur	...	14,248	...	2,523	...	...	...	25	...	4	...	...	29
Chamba	..	2,169	...	119	...	...	...	19	...	1	...	...	20
Total Hill States	...	3,945	...	578	..	...	...	5	...	1	...	...	6
British Territory ...	2,842	327,928	3,535	95,861	3,446	441	...	17	...	5	...	...	22
Native States	...	44,407	...	7,618	...	...	...	12	...	2	...	...	14
Province	2,842	372,335	3,535	102,979	3,446	441	...	16	...	5	...	...	21

There is a Persian proverb: "The first year I was a weaver (Juláha); the "next year a Shekh. This year if prices rise I shall be a Saiyad." Moreover many of the inferior agricultural Musalmán tribes of Indian descent have, especially in the west of the Province, set up a claim to Arab origin; and though they are still known by their tribal name, have probably or almost certainly returned themselves as Shekhs in the present Census. In these last cases they will in all probability have often shown their tribal name as the sub-division of the Shekhs to which they belong, and it is to be hoped that the detailed clan tribes will, when published, throw much light upon the true composition of our figures for Shekhs. Meanwhile only a few of the largest sub-divisions can be examined. In one respect I myself am responsible for the uncertainty of meaning which attaches to these figures. There are certain agricultural tribes whose claims to Qureshi origin appear to be valid, such as the Khagga and Háns of Montgomery; and these men I included under the head Shekh. It was most certainly a mistake to do so, and I shall give separate figures for them below. With them I shall discuss some of the larger sub-divisions of Shekhs which have been returned in our papers. In many cases the titles here given are no less misleading than the original title of Shekh. The Shekhs who have returned themselves as Jats in the Multán and Deraját division are shown in Abstract No. 72, page 224.* *P. 106. 107.

Shekhs do not bear the best of characters in some parts. In Rohtak they are said to "supply recruits to our armies and jails with praiseworthy indifference," and in Derah Ismáíl Khán the Naumuslim Shekhs are described as "a lazy thriftless set of cultivators." The true Qureshis of the south-western districts, however, are often possessed of great influence, and hold a high character for sanctity. Such are the descendants of Bahá-ul-haqq the renowned saint of Multán, who are known as Háshmi Qureshis, and whose family is described at pages 490*ff* of Griffin's *Punjáb Chiefs*. They are chiefly found in the Multán, Jhang, and Muzaffargarh districts.

502. Tribes and castes included under Shekh—Qureshi.—The figures below show the number of people who have returned themselves as Qureshi:—

QURESHI SHEKHS.

District and State.	Number.	District and State.	Number.	District and State.	Number.
Dehli	19,355	Siálkot	2,103	Muzaffargarh ...	3,265
Gurgaon	3,977	Lahore	13,330	Derah Ismail Khán ...	2,436
Rohtak	1,212	Gujránwála ...	2,343	Derah Ghazi Khán ...	1,730
Sirsa	1,701	Firozpur	3,461	Bannu	8,666
Ambála	16,629	Ráwalpindi	12,420	Peshávar	3,001
Ludhiána	1,076	Jahlam	3,634	Hazára	2,433
Simla	1,322	Gujrát	4,000	Kohát	2,342
Jalandhar	3,616	Sháhpur	4,276	Patiála	5,874
Hushyárpur... ...	1,977	Multán	6,100	Baháwalpur ...	3,001
Amritsar	12,309	Jhang	3,987	Other Districts and States.	4,536
Gurdáspur	2,013	Montgomery ...	2,199		161,854

The Qureshi is the Arab tribe to which the Prophet belonged. Consequently it is the favourite tribe from which to claim descent, and it is to be feared that comparatively few of those who have returned themselves as

Qureshi have any real title to the name. Among those who so style themselves many claim to belong to the Farúqis or descendants of Umar the second Caliph, or to the Sadíqis or descendants of Abul Bakar the first Caliph, both of whom were Qureshi by tribe. But the term Sadíqi is often confused with Sidqi, a title derived from the same root and meaning "the true;" but which, in the east of the Panjáb at any rate, is commonly used as an equivalent to Naumuslim to distinguish converts of Indian descent from original Mahomedan immigrants.

Naumuslim—means nothing more than a new Musalmán; and only 3,491 of our Shekhs have, by returning themselves as Shekh Naumuslim, admitted their true origin. These men are scattered in small numbers about the Province, but 1,437 of them are in Baháwalpur.

Ansari.—Ansári or "auxiliaries" was the title given to the believers of Medina who welcomed Mahomet after his flight from Mecca; and those who claim descent from these men style themselves Ansári. As many as 7,215 of our Shekhs have so returned themselves, of whom 1,501 are in Ambála, 1,539 in Multán, and the rest scattered about the Province. One large section of the Shekhs of Pánípat commonly style themselves Ansári; but they would appear to have now returned themselves as Muhájarín.

Muhajarin.—The faithful who accompanied Mahomet in his *Hajirah* or flight from Mecca were called Muhájarín or "the fugitives or emigrants," and their descendants still retain the title. In the Karnál district 8,560 persons have so returned themselves, and are doubtless the men of Pánípat just alluded to.

P. 276] 503. **The Hans and Khagga.**—The Háns is one of the tribes which I regret having included among the Shekhs. The numbers according to our returns are given in the margin; but it is very probable that many of the Háns have returned themselves as Shekh or Qureshi and not as Háns, since they claim Qureshi origin. They say they emigrated from Arabia to Afghánistán and thence to the Panjáb, where they settled at Pakka Sidhár in the Montgomery district. In the time of Alamgír the Háns tribe, under their chief Shekh Qutb, attained independent rule over a portion of that district and retained their independence till the time of the Sikhs, when about the middle of the 18th century the streams which fertilized their country dried up and they lost their home. At present they do not own a single entire village, and have preserved none of their former influence.

THE HANS.	
District.	Numbers.
Multan ...	622
Jhang ...	7
Montgomery ...	268
TOTAL ...	897

Khaggas.—The Khaggas are another tribe which I have classed as Shekh, but had better have kept separate. The numbers returned are shown in the margin. But here again many of them have probably returned themselves as Shekhs or Qureshi. Mr. Purser thus describes them: "The Khaggas came to the Montgomery district "after the conquest of Multán by Ranjít Singh. "They claim to be Qureshi, and name as the first "Khagga, Jalál-ul-din, disciple of Muhammad Irák. "Khagga is said to mean a peculiar kind of fish; and "the name was given to Jalál-ud-din by his spiritual "teacher on the occasion of his rescuing a boat over-"taken by a storm."

THE KHAGGAS.	
District.	Numbers.
Multan ...	672
Jhang ...	5
Montgomery ...	172
Muzaffargarh...	54
TOTAL ...	903

504. The Nekokara and Jhandir.—The Kokára or Nekokára, who are chiefly found in the Jhang district, claim to be Hashmi Qureshis, who came from Baháwalpur some 450 years ago. They hold land in Gújránwála also, but are not a very important tribe. In Gújránwála many of them are *faqírs*, and they generally bear a semi-religious character.

The Jhandir—are also said to be of Qureshi origin, and though they do not openly profess to be religious directors, there is a certain odour of sanctity about the tribe. Most of them can read and write, and they are "particularly free from ill deeds of every description." They own land in the extreme south of the Jhang district. They are said to have been the standard-bearers of one of the great saints, whence their name.

505. The Sarai, Miana, and others.—**Sarai.**—The Sarai family are the descendants of the Kalhora Kings of Sindh who have settled at Hájípur in Derah Gházi Khán. Some account of their history will be found in Mr. Fryer's report on that district, and in Mr. O'Brien's *Glossary*. They were included with Shekh in the divisional office, and I have no separate figures for them as yet. Tod makes the Sarai descendants, or perhaps only namesakes, of Sehl, a Kaurava Rájpút and in ancient times prince of Sindh and founder of Aror on the Indus. He says: "Sehl or Sehr became a titular "appellation of the country, its princes, and its inhabitants the Sehrai." (See further Sarai under Jats of the western sub-montane, section 433).

Miana.—Mián is used in the west of the Panjáb to denote any holy man and his descendants will often style themselves Miána. Thus the head of the Sarai family just described is known as the Mián Sáhib Sarai. But in Hazára at least and probably in other parts of the frontier, any new convert to Mahomedanism is often called a Miána, and most of them are cultivators. I have with some hesitation classed them as Shekh rather than with Ulama. There are 3,282 in the Ráwalpindi and 188 in the Deraját division.

RETURNED AS SHEKHS.

Name of Castes.	Number returned as Shekhs.
Bodla ...	2,435
Dáúdpotra ...	1,421
Kalál ...	270
Awán ...	449
Maliár ...	221
Tarkhán ...	118
Mochi ...	107
Rájpút	106
29 other castes, mostly low.	685

Besides the classes discussed above, the castes shown in the margin appear from a rough examination of the Shekh sub-divisions to have returned themselves as Shekhs in the numbers shown against each. They are described in their proper places. Of the Bodlas returned as Shekhs 144 are in Hissár, 749 in Sirsa, 339 in Fírozpur, 349 in Montgomery, and 254 in Baháwalpur. Of the Dáúdpotras 1,287 are in Multán. Besides these, men returning themselves under the following names have been classed as Shekh: Shekhra, a contemptuous diminutive of Shekh; Pírzádah, or descendants of a *pir* or Musalmán spiritual guide; Shekhzádah, or son of a Shekh. There appear to have been only 383 of the first, 19 of the second, and 17 of the third. In the Lahore division the Bharáis (caste No. 48) have been most erroneously classed as Shekh, to the number of 1,444 in Lahore, 2,256 in Gújránwála, and 1,646 in Fírozpur.

506. The Turk (Caste No. 126).—I shall not attempt to touch upon the much debated question of the distinction between Túrks and Mughals. It will be sufficient to say that a Túrk in the Panjáb means, probably invariably, a Túrkomán native of Túrkistán and of Mongolian race. In the Dehli territory indeed the villagers, accustomed to describe the Mughals of the Empire as Túrks, use the word as synonymous with "official"; and I have heard my Hindu clerks of Káyath caste described as Túrks merely because they were in Government employ. On the Biloch frontier also the word Túrk is commonly used as synonymous with Mughal. The Túrks of the Panjáb are practically confined to the Hazára district, and are doubtless the representatives of the colony of Kárlagh Túrks who came into the Panjáb with Tamarlane (1399 A.D.) and possessed themselves of the Pakhli tract in the Hazára district, which apparently included the Tanáwal, Dhamtaur, and Swáti country, and was politically attached to Kashmír. These men were dispossessed of their territory by Swátis and Tanáolis from across the Indus about the beginning of the 18th century; and the Túrks now returned are doubtless their descendants. The word Túrk is a Tartar word meaning a "wanderer"; thus in poetry the Sun is called "the Túrk of China," that is of the East, or "the Túrk of the Sky." The Túrks of Gurdáspur are said to be rope-makers by occupation (see further sections 412 and 416).

[P. 277] **507. The Mughal (Caste No 37).**—The Mughals proper or Mongols, for the two words are only different forms of the same name, probably either entered the Panjáb with Bábar, or were attracted thither under the dynasty of his descendants. They are probably to be found in greatest number in the neighbourhood of Dehli, the capital of that dynasty; and I believe that the great majority of those who have returned themselves as Mughals in the Eastern Punjáb really belong to that race. They are also numerous in the Ráwalpindi division and on the upper frontier, along the route of the Mughal armies, and where they find a more kindred people than in the great Panjáb plains. But as will be presently explained, the number of true Mughals in these parts is certainly much smaller than would appear from our figures. The Mughals of Gújrát are described by Mr. Monckton as "an unhappy "race. Puffed up with pride of birth, they account themselves above all "other classes except Saiyads, and even among themselves each house reckons "itself higher than its neighbour. Among the clans, though of high descent, "they are now at a discount. Those that might be admitted their equals, "such as Chibs or Gakkhars, despise them; while to lower classes they "themselves will not stoop; and the consequence is that social relations are "sometimes at a dead-lock." The description applies with equal truth to the Mughals of the Dehli territory. Even on the frontier the Mughals do not bear a good name. "The Mughals tyrannize over the cultivator, and the "cultivator over the earth"; and again: "Trust not the Mughal's letters. "Of the Mughals, first letters, then armies."

The Mughals are distributed very widely over the Province; but are, excepting Dehli, most numerous in the western districts, and more especially in Ráwalpindi, Jahlam, and Hazára. It is certain that a very large number of these men are not Mughals at all. Some, probably a considerable number of them, belong to agricultural tribes locally known by tribal names, such as Gakkhars, Sattis, Ghebas, and the like, who have set up an almost certainly groundless claim to Mughal origin. Many of these have already been noticed. But more than this, there is a tendency, apparently confined to Dehli and the Ráwalpindi and Peshâwar divisions, for men of low caste to call themselves Mughals just as throughout the Province they call themselves Shekhs. Thus we find among the sub-divisions of those returned as Mughals 1,512 Kahárs in Hazára, and in Ráwalpindi 3,655 Sainis and 1,263 Rawáls;

while in the eight districts just specified no fewer than 2,724 other members of 41 separate castes, for the most part of low standing, have been detected among the Mughals by a rough examination of the detailed clan tables, and this is doubtless only a specimen of what has taken place on a very extensive scale. Major Wace is of opinion that recent Jat converts to Mahomedanism often take the title of Mughal. On the other hand no fewer than 2,510 persons have returned themselves as Pathán by caste and Mughal by tribe, of whom 1,169 are in the Peshâwar district, 746 in the Deraját, and 401 in Ráwalpindi and Jahlam. Further light will doubtless be thrown upon the composition of the so-called Mughals when the detailed tables are published. Of the true Mughal tribes, only the Chughatta and the Barlás seem to be numerously represented in the Panjáb, the former numbering 23,593 and the latter 12,137. Men so returned are probably true Mughals. Their numbers for the districts in which they are shown as numerous are given in the margin. Besides these 1,543 of the Ráwalpindi Mughals return themselves as Gakkhar and 3,861 as Kayáni, the latter also of which names perhaps refer to the Gakkhars, who sometimes claim to be Kayáni.[1] In 1864, Colonel Cracroft gave the number of true Mughals in the Ráwalpindi district at 2,767 souls. At last Census there were 8,205.

District.	Mughal tribes.	
	Chughatta.	Barlás.
Dehli	1,618	..
Amritsar	1,140	...
Siálkot	...	1,554
Ráwalpindi	1,613	1,661
Jahlam	2,735	2,304
Gújrát	590	3,633
Shahpur	1,143	179
Multán	3,083	34
Jhang	2,471	4
Hazára	1,014	141
Baháwalpur	1,488	...

508. The Kasars of Jahlam.—The Gakkhars, Sainis, and other castes mentioned above are described in their proper places. But the Kasars of Jahlam have apparently returned themselves in a body as Mughals, for no fewer than 8,527 of the Jahlam Mughals show Kasar as their clan. These Kasars occupy the north of the Dhani country about Bubiál and Chaupeda. They say that their old home was in Jammu, and that they joined the armies of Bábar and so obtained possession of their territory which was then almost uninhabited. Their present claim to Mughal origin is evidently suggested by their association with the Mughal power, and is apparently a new idea; for up to the time of the Census itself they seem to have enjoyed the rare distinction of being one of the few Salt-range tribes who claimed neither Rájpút, Awán, nor Mughal descent. They are described by Mr. Thomson as a passionate and revengeful race, careless of human life, but good cultivators though somewhat exacting landlords. "Envy is their most odious quality; every "family is distracted with mean jealousies wich are sometimes prosecuted with "astonishing rancour, and not unseldom degenerate into criminal greed. It "is fair to add that their vices seem to be gradually losing strength. Many

[1] I have not been able to obtain satisfactory information regarding this word. The city of Kayán was the capital of Kai Kayús, Kai Kubád, and Kai Khasru; and some say that the Gakkhars call themselves Kayáni because they claim descent from these three Kings. Others say that the Mughals proper, and especially the Chughattas and Qizilbáshes, are Kayánis; and that the Gakkhars call themselves Kanáni or Canaanites because they claim descent from Jacob and Joseph who lived in Canaan; and that it is this word which has been misread Kayáni.

"of the headmen are personally very engaging, good horsemen, keen sportsmen, "with frank manners and a good presence; and it is sometimes difficult to "understand how they should have such a mean side to their character."

509. Ghulam (Caste No 130).—These men are returned from the Peshâwar district to the number of 3,347 under the name of Ghulám Khánazád, and from Multán to the number of 99 to the name of Khánazád simply. The latter may be an error for Khánzádah. The Peshâwar men show their clans as Turkhel Ghulám and Malekhel. They are said to be descendants of captives in war who were made slaves (*ghulám*), whence their name. They are still chiefly employed in domestic service, and are generally attached to their hereditary masters, though some of them have taken to shop-keeping and other occupations.

[P. 278] Since writing the above, which is based upon the information of a highly educated gentleman in our political service, himself a Native of Peshâwar, I find that Muhammad Haiyát Khán states in his *Haiyát-i-Afgháni* that the Qizilbásh of Kábul described below are collectively known as Ghulám-khánah. If so, our Ghulám Khánazáds are probably nothing more than Qizilbáshes. But the class described above does exist in Peshâwar in considerable numbers.

509a. The Qizilbash (Caste No. 181).—The Qizilbásh[1] are a tribe of Tartar horsemen from the eastern Caucasus, who formed the backbone of the old Persian army and of the force with which Nádir Sháh invaded India. Many of the great Mughal ministers have been Qizilbásh, and notably Mír Jumlah the famous minister of Aurangzeb. They are said to take their name from a red cap of peculiar shape which they wear, which was invented by the founder of the Sophi dynasty of Persia, an intolerant Shíah, as the distinguishing mark of that sect, and which his son Sháh Tumásp compelled Humáyún to wear when a refugee at the Persian Court. There are some 1,200 families of Qizilbásh in the city of Kábul alone, where they were located by Nádir Sháh, and still form an important military colony and exercise considerable influence in local politics. They are not uncommon throughout Afghánistán. Besides the number of Qizilbásh returned as such, 66 were entered as Patháns, of whom 48 were in Derah Ismáíl Khán. See also the preceding paragraph under the head Ghulám.

---

[1] In the caste table the word is spelt *Kizal*, but I believe *Qizil* is correct.

PART V.—RELIGIOUS, PROFESSIONAL, MERCANTILE, AND MISCELLANEOUS CASTES. [P. 279]

510. General and Introductory.—The classes discussed in this part of the chapter form an exceedingly heterogeneous collection. They are in fact all those that are left after separating the landowning and agricultural castes on the one hand, and the vagrant, artisan, and menial classes on the other. They include some of the highest and some of the lowest castes in the Province, yet there is a connection between the priestly Bráhman and the semi-priestly Nái, between the merchant Khatri and the pedlar Maniár. I have divided the castes now to be considered into six groups. The first includes the priestly castes such as the Bráhman and Saiyad ; the second the various ascetic, religious, and mendicant orders of *faqírs* ; the third the minor professional castes such as the Nái, the Mirási, and the Bhát ; the fourth the great mercantile castes such as the Khatri and Arora ; the fifth the carriers and pedlars such as the Banjára and Maniár ; while in the sixth are included those miscellaneous castes, such as the Kashmíri and Káyath, for whom I have been unable to find a place elsewhere. The line between the merchants and shop-keepers on the one hand and the carriers and pedlars on the other is exceedingly ill-defined, both in the figures and in the facts. The groups are too diverse in their character for any general discussion of them to be profitable ; and I shall consider each under its separate heading, where also will be found the figures showing their distribution throughout the Panjáb.

PRIESTLY CLASSES.

511. Priestly castes.—The group of castes which I am about to discuss, and of which the figures are given in Abstract No. 88 on the next page,* may be divided into three classes, Hindu priests, Muhammadan priests, and *faqírs*. *P. 216-17.
The last I give in this abstract so as to complete the group ; but they will be discussed further on, and I shall confine my remarks at present to the priestly and religious castes, as distinct from orders. The Bráhmans are of course the very type of a Hindu caste, while the pujáris of our tables probably belong for the most part to what is now a real caste, though the word itself is merely the name for an occupation. But the Muhammadan group is not so homogeneous. The title of a Saiyad should be, but notoriously is not, confined to the descendants of a common ancestor ; while the Ulama are professedly a miscellaneous collection of persons returned under entries most of which should never have appeared at all in the caste column. The Chishtis again probably include both spiritual and carnal descendants of their Chief, as is the case with so many of the religious orders next to be discussed ; while the Bodlas are almost certainly a clan of Rájpúts who have acquired a character for sanctity. Theoretically, the two groups should occupy very different positions among the followers of their respective faiths. The Bráhman is a priest, and entitled as such to reverence and support by the ordinances of the Hindu religion : the Saiyad merely claims respect in virtue of his descent from the son-in-law of the Prophet, and the Muhammadan religion as such has no organised priesthood. But it has already been pointed out in the Chapter on Religion that there is really

little to choose between the Hindu and the Musalmán as regards the spiritual bondage in which their superstition enfolds them; and indeed that if either has the advantage, it is the former rather than the latter. The classes included under the present group are by no means purely priestly; they are also large owners and cultivators of land. But their most distinctive characteristic is their saintly character, and I have therefore separated them from the land-owning and agricultural classes. At the same time the distinction between the Saiyad and the Qureshi Shekh as regards the spiritual reverence paid them is probably, at least in the south-western districts, exceedingly small.

512. **The Brahman (Caste No. 3).**—The Bráhman or Levite of the Hindu caste system is the third most numerous caste in the Panjáb, outnumbering all but Jats and Rájpúts. I shall not attempt to discuss his origin and theoretical position; much has been written and published concerning him, the first hundred pages of Sherring's first volume and the whole of the second volume of Wilson's *Indian Caste* are devoted to him alone, and Colebrooke's Essays contain much valuable information on the subject. The figures of Abstract No. 88 showing the distribution of the caste in the Panjáb are very striking. The proportion of Bráhmans to total population reaches its maximum in the hills of Kángra and Simla, the most Hindu portion of the Province, where it rises as high as from 13 to 15 per cent. Throughout the remainder of the Panjáb the proportion steadily changes with the prevailing religion. It is highest in the sub-montane and Jamna tracts where the people are essentially Hindus; it gradually decreases from east to west, being markedly smaller in the central and Sikh districts; it is still smaller in the cis-Indus Salt-range Tract; while in the Western Plains and beyond the Indus the Bráhmans may be said comparatively speaking to disappear. The Bráhmans have no territorial organisation. They accompany their clients in their migrations, settle with them in their new homes, and receive grants of land to hold or cultivate

[P. 280] The function and position of the Bráhman in his sacerdotal character have been already described in the Chapter on Religion, section 236. He concerns himself but little with the spiritual guidance of the people, but he is consulted as to omens and auspicious names, dates, and events, and he officiates at all ceremonial functions. These duties however employ, except perhaps in the west of the Province, but a small proportion of the total number; and the remainder are pure Levites, ready to be fed or receive offerings in the name of God, but their sacerdotal functions being purely passive. These men supple-
[P. 281] ment the offerings of their clients by practising agriculture very extensively; and it may be said that wherever the Bráhmans are numerous they are, excepting only the educated Pandits or Pádhas, land-owners and cultivators. They are poor husbandmen, for their pride of caste and the fact that a large part of their subsistence comes to them without the necessity of toil render them impatient of manual labour; and like the Rájpúts they look upon the actual operation of ploughing as degrading, insomuch that in the hills a Bráhman who ploughs is scarcely recognised as a brother by the higher classes of the caste. In social position the Bráhman is of course pre-eminently first in the Hindu portion of the Panjáb, though he is thought but meanly of on the frontier. Yet even where his position is most readily admitted he has failed to make himself beloved. He is grasping, quarrelsome, and overbearing, inflated with pride in his own descent and contempt for that of others, while he holds himself aloof from the clients whose pockets he preys upon, and declines to

Abstract No. 88, showing the Priestly and Ascetic Classes for Districts and States.

	Priestly Castes.																
	Figures.							Proportion per 1,000 of total Population.									
	3	120	24	70	116	172		3	120		24	70	116	172			
	Bráhman.	Pujari.	Saiyad.	Ulama.	Chishti.	Bodla.	Faqír.	Bráhman.	Pujári.	Total.	Saiyad.	Ulama.	Chishti.	Bodla.	Total.	Faqír.	Grand Total.
Dehli	61,007	...	8,800	1	76	...	12,359	95	...	95	14	...	...	...	14	19	128
Gurgaon	52,642	...	3,518	416	506	...	17,283	82	...	82	5	1	1	...	7	27	116
Karnal	55,168	...	4,309	...	305	...	14,916	89	...	89	7	...	...	...	7	24	120
Hissar	31,613	...	1,706	...	8	111	7,328	63	...	63	4	...	...	...	4	15	82
Rohtak .	58,211	...	880	...	2	...	11,405	105	...	105	2	...	...	...	2	21	128
Sirsa	5,559	...	634	...	...	...	2,740	22	...	22	3	...	...	...	3	11	36
Ambala	65,035	...	8,513	6	...	43	20,771	61	...	61	8	...	...	...	8	19	88
Ludhiana	25,121	...	3,655	30	...	...	19,185	41	...	41	6	...	...	...	6	31	78
Simla	2,567	227	315	...	...	...	157	60	5	65	7	...	...	...	7	4	76
Jalandhar	30,535	45	6,909	251	...	...	18,629	30	...	30	9	...	...	...	9	24	72
Hushyarpur	77,412	15	4,060	109	...	...	16,233	86	...	86	4	...	...	...	4	18	108
Kangra	109,881	836	157	6	...	...	6,329	150	1	151	...	...	...	...	...	9	160
Amritsar	34,753	203	5,003	542	3	...	20,026	39	...	30	6	1	...	...	7	22	68
Gurdaspur	47,890	...	6,077	241	309	...	11,774	58	...	53	7	...	...	...	7	14	79
Sialkot	36,100	...	12,840	1,946	...	...	12,105	36	...	36	13	2	...	...	15	12	63
Lahore	20,813	135	7,930	401	132	110	7,965	23	...	23	9	...	...	...	9	8	40
Gujranwala	18,060	...	6,339	4,289	8	15	5,074	29	...	29	10	7	...	...	17	8	54
Firozpur ...	12,079	...	3,134	38	429	520	7,366	19	...	19	5	...	1	1	7	11	37
Rawalpindi	18,523	...	20,422	26	...	...	1,861	23	...	23	25	...	...	...	25	2	50
Jahlam	10,010	...	14,663	111	21	...	1,493	17	...	17	25	...	...	...	25	3	45
Gujrat	8,668	...	16,428	1,701	135	...	1,369	13	...	13	24	3	...	...	27	2	42
Shahpur	5,462	...	8,625	754	137	...	2,303	13	...	13	20	2	...	...	22	5	40

[P. 280]

Multan	4,183	...	8,903	2,311	451	54	3,889	8	...	8	16	4	1	...	21	7	36
Jhang	5,319	1	5,944	706	421	...	3,497	13	...	13	15	2	1	...	18	9	40
Montgomery	3,168	...	4,225	760	674	102	3,709	7	...	7	10	2	2	...	14	9	30
Muzaffargarh... ...	1,841	...	6,928	1,268	97	...	1,932	5	...	5	20	4	...	...	24	6	35
Dera Ismail Khan ...	3,549	...	8,771	170	110	...	1,233	8	...	8	20	...	...	...	20	3	31
Dera Ghazi Khan ...	2,164	...	6,223	2,563	41	...	603	6	...	6	17	7	...	...	24	2	32
Bannu	2,027	...	11,943	181	132	...	574	6	...	6	36	1	...	...	37	2	45
Peshawar	3,746	5	4,515	2,216	1	...	525	6	...	6	8	4	...	...	12	1	19
Hazara	4,662	...	15,235	574	...	...	487	11	...	11	37	1	...	...	38	1	50
Kohat	883	...	7,770	222	...	...	126	5	...	5	43	1	...	...	44	1	50
British Territory ...	818,814	1,467	225,446	21,759	3,998	955	235,231	43	...	43	12	1	...	...	13	12	68
Patiala	94,483	...	7,870	340	532	15	35,855	64	...	64	5	...	...	...	5	24	93
Nabha	17,980	...	709	15	167	...	6,646	69	...	69	3	...	1	...	4	25	98
Kapurthala	8,059	10	2,704	115	10	...	7,058	32	...	32	11	...	...	...	11	29	72
Jind	27,253	...	354	13	...	...	5,949	110	...	110	1	...	...	...	1	21	135
Faridkot	2,078	...	93	37	8	...	1,640	21	...	21	1	...	...	...	1	17	39
Maler Kotla ...	2,570	...	823	...	...	...	1,734	36	...	36	12	...	...	...	12	24	72
Kalsia	3,525	...	172	...	...	...	1,647	52	...	52	3	...	...	...	3	23	78
Total East. Plains ...	161,419	10	13,258	520	117	15	61,203	64	...	64	5	...	...	...	5	24	93
Bahawalpur	3,677	...	9,065	1	...	...	1,953	6	...	6	16	...	...	...	16	3	25
Mandi	16,014	...	35	...	...	...	785	109	...	109	...	...	...	...	...	5	114
Chamba	15,450	...	52	...	...	...	676	133	...	133	...	...	...	...	...	6	139
Nahan	5,538	53	124	...	...	...	477	49	...	49	1	...	...	...	1	4	54
Bilaspur	24,462	290	...	...	...	...	564	283	3	286	...	...	...	...	...	6	292
Bashahr	4,805	212	3	...	...	...	116	75	3	78	...	...	...	...	...	2	80
Nalagarh	5,730	...	80	...	...	...	589	107		107	1	...	...	...	1	11	119
Suket	6,670	...	5	...	...	...	249	127	...	127	...	...	...	...	...	5	132
Total Hill States ...	293	2,454	333	...	...	...	3,938	131	3	134	1	...	...	...	1	5	140
British Territory ...	818,814	1,467	225,446	21,759	3,998	955	235,231	43	...	43	12	1	...	...	13	12	68
Native States ...	265,379	2,464	22,656	521	717	15	67,093	69	1	70	6	...	...	...	6	17	93
Province ...	1,084,193	3,931	248,102	22,280	4,715	970	302,324	48	...	48	11	1	...	...	12	18	73

associate himself with the community upon which he lives. "A Dúm, a "Bráhman, and a goat are of no avail in time of need." Where Bráhmans hold any considerable share of a village trouble and disputes are sure to follow; and the villages have a proverb: "As famine from the desert, so comes "evil from a Bráhman." So their avarice is expressed in the saying—"The "Mulla, the Bhát, the Bráhman, and the Dúm; these four castes were not "born on giving day," and their love of good living by the proverb: "Dine "with a Bráhman and jog along the road with a Kirár" (the Kirárs being great talkers). On the whole the Bráhman has but little real influence over the Hindu peasant, and the reverence paid him is largely traditional or due to the conservative tendency of the women. The Bráhmans of the hills have a social and tribal organisation almost exactly corresponding with that of the hill Rájpúts. The quotations from Mr. Barnes given at pages 175* and *P. 6
179† bear upon the subject. They too are divided into grades, each grade †P. 16
marrying from the one below and giving their daughters to the one above, while the lower classes will marry Káyath or Banya, and in Kúlu even Kanet women. The mixed class of Pahári Mahájans is described below under mercantile castes. In the hills of Hazára on the banks of the Jahlam these Mahájans, who are also called Dhakochi, seem to include the whole Bráhman caste. In the Peshávar division 185 persons are returned as Bráhman-Mahájans, and these I have classed as Bráhmans. It is probable that some of the Pahári Mahájans also are really Bráhmans. The Hill Bráhmans universally eat meat, from which the Bráhmans of the plains, except perhaps in the extreme west, scrupulously abstain. Of the total number of Bráhmans only about 7,000 are returned as Sikh, the denial of the superiority claimed by the higher castes which distinguished the teaching of Guru Govind not being acceptable to the Bráhman. The Sikhs employ Hindu Bráhmans as their *parohits* or family priests in exactly the same way as do the Hindus and Jains. There are also 3,500 Musalmán Bráhmans, chiefly in the Dehli district. These men are known as Huseni Bráhmans, and are said to receive oblations in the name of the Hindu gods from Hindus and in the name of Alláh from Musalmáns.

513. The divisions of the Brahmans.—The Brahminicial *gotras* have already been described in section 353. The Bráhman caste or class is divided into ten great sections, all based upon geographical distribution, which differs in customs and standing and do not intermarry. They again are divided into two groups each containing five sections, as follows:—

A.—The five Dravidas (south of the Vindhyas).

1. The Maharáshtra (of the Mahratta country).
2. The Tailanga or Andhra (of the Telugu country).
3. The Dravida (of the Tamil or Dravida country).
4. The Karuáta (of the Carnatic).
5. The Gurjara or Gújaráti (of Gújarát in Sindh)

B.—The five Gaurs (north of the Vindhyas).

6. The Gaur (of Gaur, probably not Bengal, *see below*).
7. The Sáraswat or Sársút (of the Panjáb, beyond the Saruswati).
8. The Kanyakubja (of Kanauj).
9. The Maithila (of the Mithila country).
10. The Utkala (of Orissa).

Of these great divisions the Panjáb Bráhmans belong for the most part to the Gaur in the Jamna and south-eastern districts and the eastern hills, and to the Sársút in the remainder of the Province. The figures are given below in Abstract No. 89, a few districts in which only small numbers are shown being omitted. It may be said that a line drawn north-east and south-west through Simla and Patiála roughly divides the Gaur from the Sársút. I append a description of some of the principal divisions of the Bráhmans to be met with in the Panjáb, and must refer the reader for fuller details to the authorities quoted in the beginning of section 512.

[P. 282]

Abstract No. 89, showing Brahman Divisions for Districts and States.

BRAHMAN.

	1	2	3	4	5
—	Gaur.	Sársút.	Achárj.	Dákaut or Dakótra.	Gújaráti.
Dehli	58,648	1,260	340	558	190
Gurgaon	46,287	123	285	811	95
Karnál	51,656	2,459	381	356	338
Hissar	28,119	1,077	408	426	218
Rohtak	51,955	157	317	490	493
Sirsa	2,119	1,310	232	196	11
Ambala	42,803	15,339	1,254	950	357
Ludhiána	1,951	21,114	287	219	474
Simla	655	2,015	...	...	1
Jalandhar	1,886	26,058	201	20	1
Hushyárpur	840	11,166	271	90	242
Kangra	5,177	83,012	285	39	74
Amritsar	412	32,543	22	...	144
Gurdáspur	725	19,155	1,467	7	413
Siálkot	724	32,262	672	26	...
Lahore	707	5,970	626	...	13
Gujránwála	118	16,099	469	30	51
Firozpur	1,569	8,404	175	64	8
Ráwalpindi ...	286	7,288	227	198	...
Jahlam	77	5,256	180	95	...
Gujrát	113	6,041	150	106	...
Shahpur	48	3,254	60	...	...
Multan	262	1,537	119	55	1
Jhang	19	3,478	78	1	...
Montgomery	163	1,396	99	28	10
Muzaffargarh	42	932	58	...	...
Derah Ismail Khan ...	36	1,791	63	...	...

	1	2	3	4	5
—	Gaur.	Sársút.	Achárj.	Dákaut or Dakótra.	Gújaráti.
Derah Ghazi Khan ...	91	1,106	40	...	...
Bannu	53	1,120	58	43	...
Peshâwar	168	1,446	70	...	111
Kohát	37	453	18	17	1
British Territory ...	297,779	318,767	8,965	4,867	3,244
Patiála	42,735	48,393	645	1,559	404
Nabha	8,104	8,471	200	249	53
Jínd	23,312	2,568	...	286	365
Farídkot	226	1,742	42	60	...
Maler Kotla	193	2,277	...	...	7
Kalsia	1,887	759	48	154	19
Total East. Plains ...	80,798	64,304	1,038	3,396	1,017
Baháwalpur	215	1,892	158	...	...
Mandi	1,941	13,928	9	...	...
Náhan	2,844	1,567	67	39	4
Biláspur	57	24,287	18	...	3
Rashahr	1,153	876	2	...	...
Nálagrah	108	5,113	91	...	...
Suket	1,564	4,854	...	...	...
Total Hill States ...	13,418	67,024	320	39	24
British Territory ...	297,779	318,767	8,965	4,867	3,244
Native States ...	94,431	138,220	1,516	2,435	1,041
Province ...	392,210	451,987	10,481	7,302	4,285

The Gaur Brahman.—There has been much dispute about the position of the Gaur from which this section is named. Their traditional place of origin is Hariána, and their present home is the portion of the North-West Provinces lying west of Alígarh and Mathra, and the part of the Panjáb defined above; and they are separated from Bengal by other sections of the caste. General Cunningham suggests that Gaur is the old name of Gonda, while Sir George Campbell would make it another form of the word Ghaggar. The Gaur Bráhmans are far more strict in all caste observances than the Sársút Bráhmans, from whose hands they will not eat bread, and upon whom they look down.

The Sarsut Brahman is the Bráhman of the Panjáb Proper, and takes his name from the Saraswati which lies near his eastern boundary. He is said to be less grasping and quarrelsome than the Gaur, and he is certainly much less rigid in his observance of caste rules, eating and smoking with most of the stricter Hindu castes, such as Banyas, Khatris, Súds, and Káyaths. He eats flesh in the hills, and perhaps in some parts of the plains also.

The Gujarati and Dakaut Brahmans.—These men are scattered in small numbers all over the Province. The Gújarati Bráhmans probably belong to the Gurjara section already mentioned. The Dákaut or Dakotra Bráhmans are fortune-tellers and astrologers, and came from Northern Rájpútána. They belong to the Panj Gaur group, of which they are sometimes, in Rájpútána which is their home, reckoned as a separate section. The following description is taken from my Karnál Report:—

"Offerings to Bráhmans are divided into *bár* and *graha* for the days of the week, and two "*grahin* for Ráhu and Ket, the two demons who cause eclipses by attacking the sun and moon. "These two are parts of a jin (Rákshas), who, when sitting at dinner with the gods and jins, "drank of the nectar of the gods instead of the wine of the jins. The sun and moon told of him "and Bhagwán cut him into two parts, of which Ráhu, including the stomach and therefore the "nectar, is the more worthy. When anybody wishes to offer to Bráhmans from illness or other "cause, he consults a Bráhman who casts his horoscope and directs which offering of the seven "*grahas* should be made. The *grahins* are most commonly offered during an eclipse, that to "Ráhu being given at the beginning, and that to Ket at the end of the transit. The Gaur "Bráhmans will not take any black offerings, such as a buffalo or goat, iron, sesame (*til*) or *urad*, "black blankets or clothes, salt, &c., nor oil, second-hand clothes, green clothes, nor *satnaja*, "which is seven grains mixed with a piece of iron in them; those belonging to the *grahe* whose "offerings are forbidden to them. An exception, however, is made in favour of a black cow.

"The Gújaráti or Biás Bráhmans who came from Gújarát in Sindh are in some respects "the highest class of all Bráhmans; they are always fed first; and they bless a Gaur when they "meet him, while they will not eat ordinary bread from his hands. They are fed on the 12th "day after death, and the Gaurs will not eat on the 13th day if this has not been done. But "they take inauspicious offerings. To them appertain especially the Ráhu offerings made at an "eclipse. They will not take oil, sesame, goats, or green or dirty clothes; but will take old clothes "if washed, buffaloes, and *satnája*. They also take a special offering to Ráhu made by a sick "person, who puts gold in ghi, looks at his face in it, and gives it to a Gújráti, or who weighs "himself against *satnája* and makes an offering of the grain. A buffalo which has been possessed "by a devil to that degree that he has got on to the top of a house (no difficult feat in a village) "or a foal dropped in the month of Sáwan, or buffalo calf in Mág, are given to the Gújaráti as "being unlucky. No Gaur would take them. At every harvest the Gújaráti takes a small allow- "ance (*seori*) of grain from the thrashing floor, just as does the Gaur. [P. 282]

"The Dákauts came from Agroha in the Dakhan. Rája Jasrat, father of Rámchandar, "had excited the anger of Saturday by worshipping all the other *graha* but him. Saturday "accordingly rained fire on Jasrat's city of Ajudhia. Jasrat wished to propitiate him, but the "Bráhmans feared to take the offering for dread of the consequences; so Jasrat made from the "dirt of his body one Daka Rishi who took the offerings, and was the ancestor of Dákauts by a "Súdra woman. The other Bráhmans, however, disowned him; so Jasrat consoled him by pro- "mising that all Bráhmans should in future consult his children. The promise has been fulfilled. "The Dákauts are pre-eminent as astrologers and soothsayers, and are consulted by every class "on all subjects but the dates of weddings and the names of children, on which the Gaurs advise. "They are the scape-goats of the Hindu religion; and their fate is to receive all the unlucky "offerings which no other Bráhman will take, such as black things and dirty clothes. Especially "they take the offerings of Wednesday, Saturday, and Ket. They are so unlucky that no Bráh- "man will accept their offerings; and if they wish to make them they have to give them to their "own sister's sons. No Hindu of any caste will eat any sort of food at their hands, and at "weddings they sit with the lower castes; though of course they only eat food cooked by a "Bráhman. In old days they possessed the power of prophecy up to 10-30 A.M.; but this has "now failed them. They and the Gújarátis are always at enmity, because, as they take many "of the same offerings, their interests clash."

The Pushkarna Brahmans take their name from the sacred lake of Pushkar or Pokhar near Ajmer. One section of them is said to have been originally Beldárs or Ods who were raised to Brahminical rank as a reward for excavating the tank. They still worship the pickaxe. They are the hereditary Bráhmans of the Rájpútána Bhátias. and are more strict in caste matters than the Sársút. They are found in some numbers in the western districts of the Panjáb.

The Mahabrahman or Acharj.—This is the Bráhman who performs the funeral ceremonies. After the cremation he is seated on the dead man's bedstead and the sons lift him up, bedstead and all, and make obeisance to him. He then receives the bedstead and all the wearing apparel of the dead man. He rides on a donkey, and is considered so impure that in many villages he is not allowed to come inside the gate.

The Muhial, Moyal or Mial Brahmans.—This is a sub-section of the Sársút section, who are said to be so named from the seven *Múhins* or clans of which they consist. They are almost confined to the sub-montane Salt-range Tract. They say that certain of their ancestors rose to high position under the Mughals, since when they have abandoned all performance of priestly functions or claim to a sacerdotal character, and cultivate land, but especially take service in the army or as clerks. They object to be called Bráhmans, as the enlistment of Bráhmans is said to be forbidden in our army. This is their own account; but in Hazára proper the Muhiáls perform priestly functions and receive alms and oblations just like other Bráhmans. Another story derives their name from a place called Mava, 'now deserted.'

Dharukra Brahmans are Gaur Bráhmans of the Dehli Territory who have taken to widow-marriage, and with whom other Bráhmans will not intermarry. They are much the same as the Dasa or Doghla Bráhmans."

Chamarwa and Gurra Brahmans.—These are the Bráhmans who minister to the Chamárs,
[P. 283] Aheris, and other outcastes. They are not recognized as Bráhmans by the other classes; and though they wear the sacred thread it is perhaps possible that their claim to Bráhman origin is unfounded. Yet on the whole it seems most probable that they are true Bráhmans by descent, but have fallen from their high position. They are often called Chamarwa Sádhs.

514. The Pujaris and Bhojkis (Caste No. 120).—Pujári means really nothing but an officiating priest at a temple or shrine, and in the majority of cases would be a Bráhman or *faqír*. But the Pujáris of the shrines in the Kángra and Simla hills have grown into a distinct caste, composed originally, it is said, of a mixed collection of Náis, Bráhmans, Rájpúts, and Jogis, who all intermarried. Those of the great shrines, such as Jawálamukhi and Báwan, are called Bhojkis; and I have included under the head Pujári 1,274 persons returned as Bhojkis, of whom the distribution is shown in the margin. They are all priests of Devi, and their name is said to be a corruption of Pújki. The Bhojkis are said by Mr. Barnes to be "not "Bráhmans, though they are the hereditary priests "of these celebrated temples. They all wear the "sacred thread; they intermarry among themselves alone, eat flesh, drink wine "and are a debauched and profligate set; the men are constantly in the "Courts involved in litigation, and the women are notorious for their loose "morality." Colonel Jenkins of Kángra writes of them as follows:—

BHOJKIS.		
Jalandhar	...	45
Hushyarpur	...	15
Kangra	...	729
Amritsar	...	203
Lahore	...	135
Jhang	...	1
Kapurthala	...	10
Bilaspur	...	136
		1,274

"The Bhojkis are perhaps a unique feature of this district. They are attached to the great "temples at Kángra and Jawálamukhi and are supported by the income. They claim to be "Sársút Brahmins; but if so, have certainly sunk in the social scale, as no ordinary Brahmins "would eat 'kachi rasoi' with them. They appear to occupy much the same position as the "Ganga Putras of Benares, and the probability is that they are mere 'Jogis' who have obtained "a reflected sanctity from the goddesses whose service they have entered The word is evidently "connected with the Sanskrit root 'bhoj' to feed, and is taken from the nature of their duties. "They intermarry among themselves and with a class of Jogis called 'Bodha Pandits.' They are "very quarrelsome, litigious, and profligate, and may be well characterized by the famous epithet "ορθροφοιτοσυκοφαντοδικοταλαιπωρος, which, if I remember right, was translated 'Early "rising, base informing, sad litigious, plaguy fellows'"

Of the 3,931 Pujáris and Bhojkis shown in Table VIII A, 394 Pujáris are Mahomedan. These are almost certainly Bukháris or people, or perhaps

Saiyads, of Bukhára, the words Pujári and Bukhári being identical if written without dots. They are found only in Jálandhar, Lahore, and Amritsar, the three great commercial towns.

515. **The Saiyads (Caste No. 24)**.– The true Saiyads are the descendants of Ali, the son-in-law of Mahomet, and I believe that the word properly includes only those descended from him by Fátima, Mahomet's daughter. But there are Ulavi Saiyads who are said to be descended through other wives. Our tables show 248,102 Saiyads in the Panjáb, but it is impossible to say how many of these are of true Saiyad stock. Certainly an immense number of those returned as such have no real claim to the title. The saying is "Last year I was a Juláha; this year I am a Shekh; next year if prices rise I shall be a Saiyad;" and if "generation" be substituted for "year," the process is sufficiently common. The Saiyads are found scattered throughout the Province. In the eastern half of the Panjáb they form a comparatively small element in the population, except in Dehli itself. These men for the most part came in with the Mahomedan conquerors or under their dynasties, and were granted lands or revenue which their descendants still hold and enjoy. The Bára Saidát of the Jamna-Ganges *Doáb*, with whom many of these Eastern Saiyads are connected, enjoyed considerable political importance during the latter days of the Mughal empire. But directly the meridian of Lahore is passed the Saiyads form a markedly larger portion of the population, being largest of all on the Pathán frontier and in the Salt-range Tract, and only slightly smaller on the lower Indus. Many of the Pathán tribes, such as the Bangash of Kohát and the Mishwáni, claim Saiyad origin, and it may be that some of these have returned themselves as Saiyads instead of as Patháns. The Apostles who completed the conversion of the Patháns to Islám were called Saiyads if they came from the west and Shekhs if from the east, and it is probably to the descendants of the former, and to false claims to Saiyad origin set up most commonly in a wholly Musalmán tract, that the large number of Saiyads in the north-west of the Panjáb is due. At the same time the Biloches, who were originally Shíahs and were called "the friends of Ali," reverence and respect Saiyads far more than do those bigoted Sunnis the Patháns; and I am surprised to find Saiyads more numerous among the latter than among the former. The Saiyads of Kágán who came into Hazára with Saiyad Jalál Bába hold the whole of the Kágán valley, and the Saiyads of the Multán district occupy a prominent position, and will be found described at length in Mr. Roe's Settlement Report. The abject state of bondage in which the Saiyads and other holy men hold the frontier races has been described in the Chapter on Religion, section 277. The Saiyad is, no less than the Bráhman, a land-owner and cultivator on a large scale. Indeed, while the Bráhman is by birth a priest, or at the least a Levite, the Saiyad as such is neither; though he makes use of his supposed saintliness, at any rate in the west of the Panjáb, to compel offerings to which the ordinances of his religion give him no sort of claim. The Saiyad of Karnál is thus described in my Settlement Report. "The Saiyad is emphatically the worst cultivator I know. Lazy, thriftless, and intensely ignorant "and conceited, he will not dig till driven to it by the fear of starvation, and "thinks that his holy descent should save his brow from the need of sweating. At the best he has no cattle, he has no capital, and he grinds down "his tenants to the utmost. At the worst he is equally poor, dirty, and holy. "He is the worst revenue payer in the district; for to him a lighter assess-

"ment only means greater sloth." Mr. Thorburn thus describes the Saiyads of Bannu:—

"As a rule the Saiyads are land-owners not tenants, and bad, lazy, land-owners they make "too. In learning, general intelligence, and even in speech and appearance, they are hardly dis-"tinguishable from the Patháns or Jats amongst whom they live. Here and there certainly "honourable exceptions are to be found. The way the lands now held by them were originally "acquired was in most cases by gift. Though many of them still exercise considerable influence, "their hold as a class on the people at large is much weaker than it was thirty years ago. The "struggle for existence caused by the increase of population since annexation has knocked much "of the awful reverence the Pathán zamíndár used to feel towards holy men in general out of "him. He now views most matters from rather a hard worldly than a superstitious standpoint. "Many a family or community would now cancel the ancestral deed of gift under which some "Saiyad's brood enjoys a fat inheritance. But for the criminal consequences which would ensue "from turning them out neck and crop, the spiritual consequences would be risked willingly "enough."

In Afghánistán the Saiyads have much of the commerce in their hands, as their holy character allows them to pass unharmed where other Patháns
[P. 284] would infallibly be murdered. Even the Biloches do not love the Saiyad: they say, "May God not give kingship to Saiyads and Mullas." The Saiyads as a rule follow the Mahomedan law of inheritance, and do not give their daughters to other than Saiyads. But in the villages of the east many of them have adopted the tribal customs of their neighbours, while in the west the Hindu prejudice against widow-marriage has in many cases extended to them.

516. Divisions of the Saiyads.—The Panjáb Saiyads are primarily divided into Hasani descended from Hasan and Husaini descended from Husain the sons of Ali, Hasan-Husaini the descendants of Abdul Qádir Giláni who sprang from an intermarriage between the two branches, Ulavi descended from Ali by other wives than Fátima, and Zaidi who are descended from Zaid Shahíd, a grandson of Husain. But they also have a second set of divisions named after the places whence their ancestors came. Thus the descendants of Abdul Qádir are often known as Giláni: so the Gardezi or Bághdádi Saiyads are an important branch of the Husainis, and once owned a large portion of the Sarai Sidhu *tahsíl* of Multán, while the Zaidis are said to be a branch of the Gardezis. The Bukhári Saiyads seem to be of the Husaini section. The numbers returned are given in the margin. The Saiyads of the Western Plains are chiefly Bukhári and Husaini; the Giláni Saiyads are found chiefly in the centre of the Panjáb and the Salt-range and western sub-montane, the Shirázi in Jahlam and Shábpur, the Jáfiri in Gújrát, the Husaini in Jahlam, the Bákhari in Ráwalpindi, and the Mashaidi in the Salt-range Tract.

SAIYAD SECTIONS.

1.	Hasani ...	11,746	6.	Bákhari ...	13,324
2.	Husaini ...	86,831	7.	Mashaidi	24,271
3.	Zaidi ...	4,089	8.	Giláni ...	18,967
4.	Jáfiri ...	6,386	9.	Shirázi ...	7,933
5.	Bukhári ...	96,378	10.	Gardezi ...	1,902

517. The Ulama (Caste No. 70).—This is a perfectly miscellaneous assortment of people, many of whom cannot claim to have any priestly character. Any divine learned in the faith of Islám claims the title of Alim, the plural of which is Ulama or "the learned men." But on the frontier any person who can read and write and possesses sufficient religious knowledge to enable him to conduct the devotions in a mosque claims the title. Besides the people who have returned themselves as Ulama, I have included under this heading a large number of persons who have denoted their caste by some word which expresses nothing more than a certain degree of religious knowledge or standing among the Mahomedans. The terms so included and the numbers returned under each are shown in the margin. The mean-

ULAMA.

Ulama ...	7,396	Muláná ...	1,053
Mujáwir ...	3,480	Makhdúmána	301
Qázi ...	2,623	Mián ...	714
Mulla ...	2,479	Mullázádah ...	158
Mulla-Mulwána	2,879	Others ...	197

ing of Ulama has just been described. Those who returned themselves as such are almost wholly in the Lahore and Ráwalpindi divisions, and 4,129 are in Gurdáspur and 1,701 in Gujrát. Mujáwir is the hereditary guardian of a shrine. Of those returned as such 2,479 are in Derah Ghází, and are very possibly the attendants of the celebrated shrine of Sakhi Sarwar at Nigáha. Qázi is the Mahomedan law-doctor who gives opinions on all religious and legal questions. But the descendants of a famous Qázi often retain the title, and there are several well-known Qázi families. Of our Qázis 1,725 are in Síálkot, 542 in Amritsar, and 241 in Gurdáspur. In Derah Ghází the Qázis are said all to be Awáns, and to call themselves Ulama. The Mulla or Maulvi is a doctor of divinity who teaches tho precepts of the faith. Mulwána or Mulána appear to be merely other forms of Mulla; all these people are returned from the Deraját, Pesháwar, and Multán divisions. Makhdúm means the head of a shrine, generally a descendant of the saint who presides over the management; and the title used to be almost confined to the heads of the more celebrated shrines; but it is now used by those of smaller shrines also, and by any who claim descent from any saint. Makhdúmána is another form of the same word, or perhaps rather denotes the descendants of a Makhdúm. In the Deraját Mián means any saint or holy man or teacher, but is now often used by the descendants of such persons. Miána has been discussed under Shekh. Mullázádah is of course nothing more than the descendant of a Mulla. Under this head of Ulama should probably be included the Akhúndzádah and Akhúnd Khel. Akhúnd is a title given to any spiritual chief of renown, and the descendants of these men are known by the above names. Indeed Major Wace says that among the Hazára Patháns any one who has studied the religious books is called Akhúndzádah or Mulla indifferently. Under the head Patháns 3,665 men have shown their tribe as Akhúnd Khel; 2,128 in Pesháwar, 946 in Hazára, 354 in Ráwalpindi, and 166 in Bannu. But Mr. Beckett points out that many of these are men who cannot show any claim to the title. "They are mostly Gújars and "Awáns, but are slow to admit this, and very often pretend that they are "Saiyads. They should not be classed as Mullas or priests, as they perform "no priestly functions. They cultivate land or graze cattle like any other "Patháns, but cling to the title, as it carries with it a certain amount of "consideration." I suspect there are very many of those classed in our tables as Ulama who have no better claim to the title. The popular opinion of the Ulama is expressed in the proverbs quoted at pages 143-4 in the Chapter on Religion.

518. The Chishti (Caste No. 116).—This heading includes two different classes of people. The Chishti or Chishtia is an order of Mahomedan *faqírs* founded by Banda Nawáz who is buried at Kalbargah They are much given to singing, and are generally Shíahs. The Indian Chishtis are also said to be followers of Khwájah Múín-ul-dín of Chisht, who died in 471 Hij and was perhaps the same man as or a disciple of Banda Nawáz. At any rate there are members of the Chishtia order in the Panjáb, and these are Chishtia *faqírs* by reason of their belonging to that order. But the celebrated Bába Faríd of Pák Pattan was a Chishtia *faqír;* and the descendants of his relations and children, whether carnal or spiritual, have developed into a caste which is found in the lower Satluj and chiefly in the Montgomery district, though they would appear to be found in other parts of the Panjáb also, and which in many respects much resembles the Bodlas next to be described. Of the

Chishtis of our table the whole 887 of the Dehli division and 140 of those of the Lahore division returned themselves as Chishtia *faqírs*, and are probably mere members of the order. The other figures I cannot separate. Mr. Purser says that the ancestors of the Montgomery Chishtis are supposed to have come from Kábul to Lahore 600 years ago, and then moved to Montgomery where Bába Faríd settled at Pák Pattan. Like the Bodlas they were till lately wholly nomad, and like them they claim Qureshi origin; and it is not impossible that some of them have returned themselves as Shekh. They take Rájpút girls to wife. There is a saying—"You can tell a Chishti by his squint-eye"; but what the origin of it may be I know not.

519. The Bodla (Caste No. 172).—The Bodlas are a small section of the [P. 285] Wattu Rájpúts of the lower and middle Satluj, who have for some generations enjoyed a character for peculiar sanctity, and who now claim Qureshi origin from Abu Bakr Sadiq; and 2,435 of them have entered themselves as Qureshi and not as Bodla, and are included under the head Shekh. Of these 144 are in Hissár, 749 in Sirsa, 339 in Fírozpur, 349 in Montgomery, and 254 in Baháwalpur. They still marry Wattu girls, though they give their daughters only to Bodlas. They were till lately a wholly pastoral tribe, and still hold a *jágír*, the proceeds of which they now supplement by cultivation. They came up from Multán through Baháwalpur to Montgomery, where they are described by Mr. Purser as "lazy, silly, and conceited." From Montgomery they spread into Sirsa, where they occupied the Bahak *parganah* which they still hold. They are credited with the power of curing disease by exorcism, and especially snake-bite and hydrophobia; they are recognised saints, and can curse with great efficacy. They have no relations with the other Qureshis of the neighbourhood, and their Wattu origin is undoubted.

ASCETIC AND MENDICANT ORDERS.

520. The ascetic and mendicant orders.—I now turn to the consideration of that section of the community which is commonly included under the generic term of Faqír. I must first point out that our figures, though representing with fair accuracy the total numbers of this class, are wholly imperfect so far as the details are concerned. The divisional offices included the various orders under the general term, but that was easily remedied. I have had them picked out again, and have given the numbers to be added on this account to the figures of Table VIIIA in each case in the following paragraphs. But the real reason of the failure of our figures to show details is, that the great mass of these *faqírs* entered the name of their order not under "tribe" but under "sect"; and as we were forbidden to tabulate any sects except Shiah, Sunni, Wahábi, and Farázi, the details were not worked out at all. If I had known how largely this had been the case, I should not have tabulated separately even the few orders that are shown in Table VIIIA, as the figures are utterly misleading; and for this reason I do not give details of Faqírs in my Abstract on *P. 216-17. page 280.*

The figures for Faqírs comprehend at least three if not four very different classes of people. First come the religious orders pure and simple. Many of these are of the highest respectability; the members are generally collected in monasteries or shrines where they live quiet peaceful lives, keeping open house to travellers, training their neophytes and exercising a wholesome influence upon the people of the neighbourhood. Such are many at least of the Bairágis and Gosáins. Some of the orders do not keep up regular monasteries, but travel about begging and visiting their disciples; though even here they generally have permanent head-quarters in some village, or at some shrine or temple where one of their order officiates. So too the monasterial orders travel about among their disciples and collect the offerings upon which they partly subsist. There is an immense number of these men whose influence is almost wholly for good. Some few of the orders are professedly celibate, though even among them the rule is seldom strictly observed; but most of the Hindu orders are divided into the Sanyogi and Viyogi sections of which the latter only takes vows of celibacy, while among the Musalmán orders celibacy is seldom even professed. Such however as live in monasteries are generally if not allways celibate. The professed ascetics are called Sádhs if Hindu and Pírs if Musalmán. The Hindus at any rate have their neophytes who are undergoing probation before admission into the order, and these men are called *Chela.* But besides these both Hindu and Musalmán ascetics have their disciples, known respectively as *Sewak* and *Muríd*, and these latter belong to the order as much as do their spiritual guides; that is to say a Káyath clerk may be a Bairági or Pathán soldier a Chishti, if they have committed their spiritual direction respectively to a Bairági and Chishti *guru* and *pír*. Now it is not probable that such men have returned the name of the order as their caste, though this may occasionally have happened; and it is certain that none of them have returned themselves as Faqír. Thus so far the orders are made up of men who have voluntarily entered them, renouncing caste and worldly pursuits. But these men marry and have *bindi* or carnal children; while their *nadi* or spiritual children, the *chelas* just mentioned, may after admission to the order return to their homes. And it often happens that the descendants whether carnal or spiritual of a Bairági, for instance, will grow into a separate caste known by the name of Bairági, but having no connection whatever save by origin with the order of that name. Such men would return their caste as Bairági, and will have been included under Faqír. How far this custom is general I cannot say ; but we have just discussed one instance of it in the case of the Chishti of Montgomery, and I know of villages held by Bairágis under precisely similar circumstances in Karnál.

I have said that many of the members of these orders are pious, respectable men whose influence is wholly for good. But this is far from being the case with all the orders. Many of them are notoriously profligate debauchers, who wander about the country seducing women, extorting alms by the threat of curses, and relying on their saintly character for protection. Still even these men are members of an order which they have deliberately entered, and have some right to the title which they bear. But a very large portion of the class who are included under the name Faqír are ignorant men of low caste, without any acquaintance with even the general outlines of the religion they profess, still less with the special tenets of any particular sect, who borrow the garb of the regular orders and wander about the country living on the alms of the credulous, often hardly knowing the names of the orders to which the external signs they wear would show them to belong. Such men are mere beggars, not ascetics; and though their numbers are unfortunately large, we have no means of separating them. Besides the occupations described above, the Faqír class generally have in their hands the custody of petty shrines, the menial service of village temples and mosques, the guardianship of cemeteries, and similar semi-religious offices. For these services they often receive small grants of land from the village, by cultivating which they supplement the alms and offerings they receive.

The subject of the religious orders of the Hindus is one of the greatest [P. 286] complexity; the cross divisions between and the different meanings of such words as Jogi, Sanyási, and Sádh are endless; and no one who was not deeply versed in the sectarian system of Hinduism could hope to deal with the subject fully. I shall therefore not attempt to do more than jot down a few rough notes on some of the most important orders. The student will find a mass of information on the subject in Wilson's *Sects of the Hindus;* while Trumpp in his introduction to his *Adi Granth*, and Cunningham in an Appendix to his *History of the Sikhs* give many particulars about the Sikh sects and orders.

521. **The Hindu orders of ascetics.—The Bairagi (Caste No. 53).**—Bairági, or as it is more correctly spelled Vairági, signifies any one devoid of passion. But the word is usually applied in the Panjáb to a regular order of Vaishnava devotees, said to have been founded by Sri Anand, the 12th disciple of Rámanand. They are divided into several sections, among which may be mentioned the Rámanandi who worship Rám Chandra, the Rádhabalabhi who especially affect the worship of Rádha the wife of Krishna, the Nímanandi whose chief object of reverence is Sálig Rám, and the Rámanúji who adore Mahádeo; though these last two would appear to be Saiva rather than Vaishnava. They are for the most part collected in monasteries and are an exceedingly respectable class of *faqírs*, but many of the wandering mendicants also call themselves Bairágis. Their distinctive mark is a string of brown crinkled beads. They are most numerous in the Jamna districts, though to the figures of Table VIII A must be added 2,238 males and 1,621 females who returned themselves as *faqírs*, and who are to be found in almost equal numbers in the Amritsar, Lahore, and Fírozpur districts. The Bairágis of the monasteries are often but not always celibate. But there are in Karnál, and perhaps in other parts of the Province, villages held by descendants of both the children and the disciples of the Bairági monks, who have dropped their original castes and are now known as Bairágis, though they have no longer any connection with the order.

The Sanyasi Caste (No. 95).—The word Sanyási really means nothing more than the ascetic stage through which every Bráhman should properly pass. But as commonly used it corresponds among the followers of Siva with Bairági among the followers of Vishnu, and is as indefinite in its meaning. It is indeed specially applied to the Tridandi Rámanújas, a Vaishnava sect; but it is also used to include all Saiva classes of ascetics except perhaps the Jogi. In the Panjáb the word is commonly used to denote the followers of Shankar Achárj, and would include the Gosáins. The Sanyásis are said to be ordinarily buried in a sitting posture, and not burnt. To the figures of Table VIII A must be added 1,824 males and 727 females, about half of whom are in the Amritsar and another quarter in the Lahore division. The Sanyásis, so far as our figures go, seem specially to affect the districts of the eastern sub-montane.

The Gosain (Caste No. 102).—The Gosáin is a Saiva order corresponding in many ways with the Bairágis among Vaishnavas. Like them the Gosáins are often collected in monasteries, while many of them officiate as priests in the temple of Siva. They are also like the Bairágis one of the most respectable of the Hindu orders. They are very commonly but not at all necessarily celibate. To the figures of the table must be added 1,368 males and 594 females, almost all in the Hissár district. The Gosáin appears to be almost confined to the South-eastern districts.

The Sadh (Caste No. 155).—Sádh is properly nothing more than the Hindu equivalent of the Musalmán word *Pír;* or rather Sádh applies only to a Hindu devotee, while *Pír* includes any Mahomedan holy man. But the word is especially applied to a set of Hindu Unitarians who are chiefly found in the Upper Ganges-Jamna *doab*, from Farrúkhábád upwards. The sect was founded by one Bírbhán some 200 years ago. The Sádhs do not smoke, and affect great personal cleanliness, and their religious ceremonies consist in eating together. It is a sect rather than an order and the Jats of a large village in Karnál are Sádhs by sect, though Jats by caste. (*See* Wilson's *Hindu Sects*, pages 227*ff*). To the figures of the tables must be added 100 men and 13 women, mostly in the Hissár district. Our figures show Sádhs chiefly for the Dehli district and Rohtak, which would appear to connect them with the Sádh sect; yet the paucity of females show that the figures refer to a religious order. The priests of the menial classes are often called Sádh, as the Chamarwa Sádhs of the Chamárs, or the Charandási Sádhs and the Kabírbansi Sádhs of the Juláhas.

The Jogi.—The Jogi will presently be discussed under the head of *Minor Professional Castes.* It will there be explained that the word originally means nothing more than one who has by the practice of mental abstraction acquired the power of clairvoyance and similar faculties. But besides the low-class Jogi Ráwal there described there are two sets of exceedingly respectable Jogi Faqírs, the Kanphatta who pierce their ears and the Augar who do not. The former are priests of Siva and are generally to be found in Shiválas. The latter too are Saiva, but are more secular. The Kanphatta is also called Darshana. The figures for Jogi given in Table VIII A include 3,658 males and 1,750 females of the Kanphatta, and 1,720 males and 1,273 females of the Augar clan, but these figures are of course exceedingly incomplete. The Jogis bury their dead in a sitting posture.

The Aghori or Aghorpanthi.—Is an order which has happily almost died out. My figures show 316 only; but I have been told by an intelligent native that he can remember that in his youth they were common objects, wandering about the streets stark naked leading a jackal by a string, smeared with blood and human ordure, and carrying the same substances in a skull with which to bespatter him who refused them alms. Not two years ago one of these wretches was caught at Rohtak in the act of devouring the body of a newly buried child which he had dug out.[1]

522. **The Sikh orders of ascetics.—The Suthra Shahi (Caste No. 163).**—This order was founded by a Bráhman called Sucha under the auspices of Guru Har Rai.[2] They are now numerous and widely distributed, though our figures, to which must be added 112 males and 15 females, show only a small number scattered through the Sikh tract. They are notorious for gambling, thieving, drunkenness, and debauchery, and lead a vagabond life, begging and singing songs of a mystic nature. They wear ropes of black wool on the head and neck, and beat two small black sticks together as they beg. Although a Sikh order, they are all entered as Hindus, use the Hindu *tilak* or sectarian mark, and follow the Hindu rites throughout. They were founded before the time of Guru Govind, which probably accounts for their calling themselves Hindus. They generally add Sháh to their names. Trumpp says of them "there is no order or regular discipline among them, and profligates and vagabonds join them. They are a public nuisance and disavowed by the Sikhs."

The Udasi (Caste No. 84).—The Udási or Nánakputra [illegible] founded by Sri Chand, the eldest son of Bába Nának, and excommunicated by the second Guru, Amr Dás. They again, being founded before the time of Guru Govind, have for the most part returned themselves as Hindus. To the figures of Table VIII A must be added 7,127 males and 1,944 females. They are almost confined to the Sikh tract. They are for the most part celibate, and the naked section or Udási Nanga are always so. They practise Hindu rites, wear the *tilak* or sect-mark, and reject the Granth of Guru Govind but revere the Adi Granth of Bába Nának. They are hardly recognised as Sikhs. They are said to bear a high character, and are sometimes collected in monasteries, though not usually so. Many live at home, engage in worldly pursuits, and differ little from their neighbours. So at least says Trumpp.

The Nirmala (Caste No. 152).—The Nirmalas or 'without stain' were originally strict Sikhs and followers of Guru Govind. They wore white clothes, lived chiefly at the centres of Sikhism, and had considerable influence in the Sikh councils. But they have of late years relapsed into Hinduism, and have taken to wearing red clothes and practising Hindu rites, and they are now hardly true Sikhs. The greater part of them, however, have returned themselves as Sikhs. They live almost entirely in monsateries and are almost always celibate. They do not beg, but live on the offerings of the faithful. They have a high reputation for morality, and used to be much respected at Amritsar, where there is a considerable Nirmala community, for purity of morals, though it is said that they are now degenerating. They are governed by a Council known as the Akhára which makes periodical visitations of the Nirmala Societies thoughout the Panjáb, and is controlled by a head abbot or *Mahant.* To the figures of the table must be added 1,587 males and 500 females, of whom 500 are in Amritsar and 300 in Jálandhar. They are confined to the Sikh tract. It is said that the Nirmalas and the Udásis are not unfrequently confused.

The Akali or Nihang.—These famous soldier fanatics, who were the Gházis of the Sikhs, are represented in my tables by a total of 547 which is of course absurd. They were *nihang* or 'reckless' soldiers of the *akál* or 'Immortal;' and Phula Singh Akáli was Ranjít Singh's great leader. The order was founded by Guru Govind in person, and it was they who withstood the attempted innovations of Banda. They wear blue chequered clothes, bangles of steel on the wrist, and quoits of steel on their conical blue turbans, together with miniature daggers, knives, and an iron chain. [P. 287]

---

1 *Query.* What is the derivation of ogre?

2 Wilson says they look up to Teg Bahádur, the father of Guru Govind, as their founder; but Trumpp, who is quoted in the text, is more probably right.

Their head-quarters used to be at Amritsar, where they assumed the direction of religious ceremonies and the duty of convoking the council of the Khálsa. They were dreaded even by the Sikh Chiefs for their fanaticism and turbulence, and often levied offerings by force. They were warrior-priests, and political rather than religious, and the order is now fast dwindling away. Their present head-quarters are said to be at Anandpur in Hushyárpur. They still pride themselves upon the purity with which they preserve the original ordinances of their religion, rejecting all Hindu rites even in their marriage ceremonies. They still bear in their memories the ancient glory of the Sikhs, and an Akáli who wishes to imply that he is alone will say that he is 'with 125,000 Khálsa.'

The Diwana Sadh or "mad saints" wear uncut hair, a necklace of shells, and a very large feather in their turbans. They are chiefly recruited from low castes, and are for the most part married. In their habits they resemble Sikhs, but they revere the Adi Granth only. My figures show 495 males and 346 females, most of whom are in the Kángra district.

523. **The Musalman order of ascetics—The Bharai (Caste No. 48).**—The Bharáis, or Pirháis or Piráhis as they are often called, are the priests of Sakhi Sarwar Sultán, and have been already alluded to in section 221 in the chapter on Religion. The Bharáis of the Lahore division were included under Shekh in the divisional office; they number 1,444 in Lahore, 2,256 in Gújránwála and 1,646 in Fírozpur. The Bharáis are almost confined to the central and sub-montane districts and states, where the Sultáni belief is most prevalent. There are however a few in the districts of the Western Plains. They go about beating a drum and begging in the name of Sakhi Sarwar, and conduct parties of pilgrims to the shrine at Nigáha. They also receive the offerings of the local shrines. They circumcise boys in the western districts, and often act as Mírásis with whom they are sometimes confused. Indeed on the lower Indus they supersede the Nái as circumcisors, and are said to take their name from the fact that the Prophet gave his coat (*pairáhan*) to one of their ancestors as a reward for circumcising a convert after a barber had refused to do so! The real origin of the name is probably to be found in the fact that the pilgrims to Nigáha call each other *Pír bhra* or "Saint-brothers."

The Madari caste No. 63).—The Madáris are followers of Zindah Sháh Madár, the celebrated saint of Makanpur in Oudh. His name was Bázi-ul-din Sháh, and he was a converted Jew who was born at Aleppo in A. D. 1050, and is said to have died at Makanpur at the mature age of 383 years after expelling a demon called Makan Deo from the place. He is supposed by some to be still alive (whence his name), Mahomet having given him the power of living without breath. His devotees are said never to be scorched by fire, and to be secure against venomous snakes and scorpions, the bites of which they have power to cure. Women who enter his shrine are said to be seized by violent pain as though they were being burnt alive. To the figures of Table VIII A must be added 20,968 males and 17,476 females, of whom some 5,700 are in Ambála, 5,400 in Lúdhiána, 6,600 in Jálandhar, 2,000 in Hushyárpur, 3,200 in Amritsar, 2,300 in Siálkot, and 1,500 in Fírozpur. Thus they are very generally distributed throughout the eastern half of the Panjáb. In the four western divisions they seem to be almost unknown. They wear their hair matted and tied in a knot, and belong to the *be shara* section of Mahomedan orders who regard no religion, creed, or rules of life, though they call themselves Musalmán.

The Malang are said to be a branch of the Madári. My tables show only 851 males and 659 females under that head, mostly in Patiála, Maler Kotla, Jálandhar and Fírozpur.

The Benawa (Caste No. 111).—The Benawa *faqírs* are the followers of Khwájah Hasan Básri; but who he is I cannot say unless he be the same as Hasan Básri of Básra near Baghdád, the founder of the Sarwardia order. To the figures of the table must be added 2,483 males and 2,153 females. The Benawa are almost entirely confined to the Jumna districts and Rohtak.

The Darvesh (Caste No. 136).—Darvesh is simply another word for *faqír*, and means one who begs from door to door (*dar* "door"). But the Darvesh of our tables, to the figures of which 84 males and 106 females, chiefly from Siálkot, must be added, are a peculiar class found only in Batála and Pathánkot and in Amritsar and Kapúrthala. There seems to be a colony of these men who are distinguished by the title of Darvesh. They cultivate a little land, play musical instruments, beg, make ropes, go to a house where there has been a death and chaunt the praises of the deceased, hang about mosques, and so forth. They are hardly ascetics, yet the small number of women seem to show that they have not yet formed into a separate caste, and are still recruited from outside.

The Jalali (Caste No. 143).—The Jaláli order was founded by Saiyad Jalál-ul-dín of Bukhára, though the Panjáb Jalális are sometimes said to be followers of Sher Sháh Saiyad Jalál of Uchh, himself a Jaláli *faqír*. To the figures of the table must be added 2,322 males and 1,928 females, mostly from the Jálandhar, Amritsar, and Lahore divisions. Candidates for admission to the orders shave completely, burn their clothes, and are branded on the right shoulder. The Jalális are common in Central Asia.

The Husaini (Caste No. 160).—The Husainis are confined to Gurgáon, and present the peculiarity of having more females than males among their numbers. I have no information regarding them. They may perhaps be Husaini Saiyads.

The Qadiri (Caste No. 175).—The Qádiri are the followers of the celebrated Saiyad Abdul Qádir Pír Dastagír, whose shrine is at Bághdád; most of the Sunni divines of the North-West Frontier are Qádri, and the Akhúnd of Swát belongs to the order. To the numbers shown in Table VIII A must be added 2,710 males and 2,181 females, for the most part in the Ambála, Amritsar, and Lahore divisions. They sit for hours repeating the following declaration: "Thou "art the guide, thou art the truth, there is none but thee!"

The Naqshbandia are followers of Khwájah Pír Muhammad Naqshband. My figures only show 287 males and 219 females, chiefly in the Amritsar Division. They worship by sitting perfectly silent and motionless, with bowed head and eyes fixed on the ground.

The Sarwardia.—(*See above under "Benawa"*).—"They are the followers of Hasan Básri of Básra near Bághdád. They worship seated, chaunting at short intervals and in measured tones the word *Alláhu*, which is articulated with a suppressed breath and as if ejaculated by a powerful effort. The devotee often faints with the exertion.

The Chishti.—(*See Section* 518 *above*).—Besides those classed under Chishti, my figures give 2,329 males and 2,014 females, almost all in the eastern half of the Province. The Chishti *faqírs* are the followers of Banda Nawáz whose shrine is at Kalbargah. They worship by leaping up and gesticulating, and repeating '*Alláh Yá-allá-hú*,' till they work themselves into a frenzy and at last sink down exhausted.

MINOR PROFESSIONAL CASTES.

524. The minor professional castes.—I have felt great doubt as to how I should class and where I should place the castes which I have included in this group, and the distribution of which is shown in Abstract No. 90 on the next page.* Many of them are in some measure allied to the priestly classes, * P. 232-33. they have functions to perform in connection with weddings and similar ceremonies, they receive customary fees for the peformance of those functions, and they are invested with a sort of *quasi*-sacred character. On the other hand, they have many points in common with the menials; their social status is very low, and many of them are retained by the villagers on the same footing as the ordinary village servants, their rights and duties being regulated by custom. The castes of the group may be divided into three classes, the Nái, Bhát, and Mírási who are real village servants though of a very special character; the Jogis and Ráwals who are for the most part astrologers and semi-religious; and the Bahrúpias and Bhánds who are actors and story-tellers, and purely professional.

525. The Nai (Caste No. 21).—The Nái is the barber of the country, and [P. 288] when a Musalmán, and in the cities, is often called Hajjám. In respect of his being a barber he is a true village menial, and he shaves and shampooes the villagers, prepares tobacco for the village rest-house, and attends upon the village guests. But he is much more than a barber. He is the hereditary bearer of formal messages from one village to another, such as news of auspicious events, formal congratulations, letters fixing the dates of weddings, and the like. News of a death is never carried by him, however, but always by a Chúhra. He forms moreover, in company with a Bráhman, the embassy sent to conclude a betrothal, and he is generally the agency through which the preliminaries of match-making are conducted. At wedding ceremonies too he plays an important part, next indeed to that of the Bráhman himself, and on all these occasions receives suitable gratuities. He is also the leech of the country, the Jarráh or surgeon is usually a Nái by caste, and circumcision is commonly performed by a Nái. Notwithstanding all this he is one of the impure castes, standing much on the same level as the washerman, far above the Chamár, and somewhat below the Lohár, for his occupation as a barber [P. 289] proper is considered degrading. At the same time every Nái is not prepared

to handle everybody's poll. The outcast tribes have their own Náis, for a Nái who had shaved a Chúhra would not be permitted to touch a Jat. I believe that all our own barbers are Musalmáns because a Hindu Nái who shaved a Christian would be considered as polluted. The Náis are popularly known as a class of great astuteness, and the proverb says: "the jackal is the sharpest "among beasts, the crow among birds, and the Nái among men." The Náis are very uniformly distributed over the Province, being least common in the Deraját, where however some of them appear to have returned themselves as
P. 106-107. Jats (see Abstract No. 72, page 224). They are apparently Hindu among Hindus and Musalmán among Musalmáns, and in a less degree Sikh among Sikhs. On the whole about 55 per cent. are Musalmáns, 6 per cent. Sikhs, and the remainder Hindus. A Sikh barber would appear a contradiction in terms; but besides the functions enumerated above, he shampooes, cuts the nails, and cleans the ears of his patients. He appears to be known as Jájak in the west of the Province, and as Kangera or "comb-man" in the Hills. In Gurgáon Musalmán barbers are sometimes called Ustán, as well as by the more common term Hajjám.

The Nái tribes and clans are very numerous. I show a few of the largest in the margin. The first two are most numerous in the Dehli and Hissár divisions, the next two in the central districts, and the last two in the west of the Province. The Musalmán Náis of Karnál are said to be divided into two sections, the Túrkia who came in with the Mahomedan conquerors and the Gagrel or converts from Hinduism, so called because their women wear or once wore the Hindu petticoat or *gágra*.

DIVISIONS OF NAIS.

1.	Gola ...	10,981	4.	Bahgu ...	2,555
2.	Bhanbheru ...	14,816	5.	Bhatti ...	16,221
3	Basi ...	1,605	6.	Khokhar ...	12,026

526. The Bhat (Caste No. 62).—The Bhát or Bhat as he is often called in the Panjáb is, like the Mírási, a bard and genealogist, or as some people call him panegyrist. But he is a bard of a very superior sort, and far removed above the level of the Mírási. He is *par excellence* genealogist of the Rájpúts and Bráhmans, though he performs the same office for some Jat tribes; he is himself of admitted Bráhman origin; and he is found in largest numbers in the eastern and sub-montane districts where Hindu Rájpúts form the largest proportion of the population. The Hill State of Náhan indeed returns Bháts as forming 11·4 per cent. of its total population, but this seems hardly possible, though the entry in the original table is clear enough.

I have included under the head of Bhát the following entries—Cháran, 13 in the Hissár division; Mádho, 217 in the Ambála division; Jága, 13 in the Jálandhar division; Rai, 202 in the Ráwalpindi, Multán, and Peshówar divisions. Rai is a mere honorific title for a Bhát. The other three entries are names of great Bhát tribes; and it appears that while the Jága or Bhát proper is the genealogist and historian, the Cháran and Birm Bháts are bards and heralds and compose verses in honour of the ancestors of great men—so at least say Sherring and Elliott, both of whom give a good deal of information concerning the caste. The Jága or Bhát genealogist, to which class the great mass of our Bháts belong, is a hereditary servant, each local clan having its own Bhát who pays them periodical visits, writes up its genealogies to date, and receives his fees. At great weddings he attends and recites the history and praises of ancestors, and the genealogy of the bridegroom. But as he often lives too far off to be summoned to ordinary weddings, a Mírási or Dúm

Abstract No. 90, showing the Minor Professional Castes.

	MINOR PROFESSIONS.																		
	FIGURES.							PROPORTION PER 1,000 OF TOTAL POPULATION.											
	21	62	25	40	80	128	141	21	62	25		40	80		128	141		
	Náí.	Bhát.	Mírásí.	Jogí.	Ráwal.	Bahrúpia.	Bhánd.	Náí.	Bhát.	Mírásí.	TOTAL.	Jogí.	Ráwal.	TOTAL.	Bahrúpia.	Bhánd.	TOTAL.	GRAND TOTAL.
Dehli	11,080	1,019	1,756	5,006	2	1	46	17	2	8	22	8	...	8	...	...	...	30
Gurgaon	12,342	832	3,499	4,009	...	2	71	19	1	5	25	6	...	6	...	...	...	31
Karnál	10,307	1,390	2,974	9,287	5	32	9	17	2	5	24	15	...	15	...	...	...	39
Hissar	8,698	785	3,659	1,919	31	3	...	17	1	7	25	4	...	4	...	...	...	29
Rohtak	10,618	337	2,780	3,765	5	12	27	19	1	5	25	7	...	7	...	...	...	32
Sirsa	4,150	447	3,015	388	...	...	9	16	2	12	30	2	...	2	...	...	...	32
Ambála	14,932	1,273	4,695	11,897	22	...	273	14	1	4	19	11	...	11	...	...	...	30
Lúdhiána	11,065	109	5,480	1,022	18	...	...	18	...	9	27	2	...	2	...	...	...	29
Jálandhar	12,301	193	7,170	517	2,842	...	...	16	...	9	25	1	4	5	...	...	...	30
Hushyárpur	12,143	1,355	4,955	313	2,761	167	...	13	2	5	20	...	3	3	...	...	...	23
Kángra	7,838	323	1,927	5,043	764	1	...	11	...	3	14	7	1	8	...	...	...	22
Amritsar	14,694	339	11,046	1,727	2,325	...	...	17	...	12	29	2	3	5	...	...	...	34
Gurdáspur	14,413	912	7,273	2,216	3,337	58	...	18	2	9	29	3	4	7	...	...	...	36
Siálkot	20,569	1,646	12,921	3,282	1,214	...	...	20	2	13	35	3	1	4	...	...	...	39
Lahore	13,840	381	11,747	343	1,508	...	109	15	...	13	28	...	2	2	...	...	...	30
Gujránwála	14,474	135	12,251	205	2,048	...	120	23	...	20	43	...	3	3	...	...	...	46
Firozpur	9,794	240	7,434	175	168	...	59	15	...	11	26	...	...	...	...	...	...	26

[P. 288]

Ráwalpindi	11,996	582	6,205	2,081	...	...	3	15	1	8	24	3	...	3	...	...	...	27
Jahlam	10,569	320	7,643	1,290	...	10	54	18	...	13	31	2	...	2	...	...	...	33
Gújrát	13,553	276	7,885	1,033	1	...	2	20	...	11	31	1	...	1	...	...	...	32
Shahpur	7,541	70	8,341	428	...	22	31	18	...	20	38	1	...	1	...	...	...	39
Multán	6,036	336	7,510	691	...	...	508	11	1	14	26	1	...	1	...	1	1	28
Jhang	6,307	110	7,741	573	...	...	106	16	...	20	36	1	...	1	...	...	...	37
Montgomery	6,477	147	9,695	513	...	...	118	15	...	23	38	1	...	1	...	...	...	39
Muzaffargarh	4,064	123	3,634	450	...	...	5	12	...	11	23	1	...	1	...	...	...	24
Dera Ismail Khan ...	2,687	103	2,700	50	...	...	...	6	...	6	12	...	...	...	...	...	...	12
Dera Gházi Khan ...	407	239	1,007	129	...	4	...	1	1	3	5	..	...	...	...	...	...	5
Bannu ...	3,596	85	3,918	63	...	...	67	11	...	12	23	...	...	...	...	...	...	23
Peshâwar ...	5,648	106	3,866	55	78	...	6	10	...	7	17	...	...	..	...	...	...	17
Hazara ...	4,218	28	1,856	77	60	...	...	10	...	5	15	...	...	...	...	...	...	15
Kohát ...	2,202	4	1,185	15	23	...	...	12	...	9	21	...	...	...	...	...	...	21
British Territory ...	288,738	14,171	177,707	58,715	17,266	321	1,620	15	1	...	25	3	1	4	...	...	...	29
Patiála ...	25,021	918	10,131	6,992	27	38	430	17	1	7	25	5	...	5	...	...	...	30
Nábha ...	5,277	160	2,169	767	...	3	...	20	1	8	29	3	...	3	.	...	...	32
Kapurthala ...	4,340	4	2,539	79	530	24	...	17	...	10	27	..	2	2	...	...	...	29
Jínd ...	4,911	421	1,956	1,823	...	...	13	20	2	8	30	7	...	7	.	...	...	37
Farídkot ...	1,568	19	1,147	11	7	...	...	16	...	12	28	...	...	...	...	...	...	28
Maler Kotla ...	1,414	4	686	126	...	...	...	20	...	10	30	2	...	2	...	...	...	32
Total Eastern Plains ...	44,594	1,878	19,264	11,077	564	65	461	18	1	8	27	4	...	4	...	...	...	31
Baháwalpur ...	6,437	655	7,429	96	...	...	...	11	1	13	25	...	...	...	...	...	...	25
Mandi ...	299	200	16	477	...	...	2	3	1	...	3	3	...	3	...	...	...	6
Chamba ...	325	133	113	1,412	15	...	...	3	1	1	5	12	...	12	...	...	...	17
Náhan ...	199	12,745	63	230	...	...	100	2	114	1	117	2	...	2	...	1	1	120
Total Hill States ...	2,354	13,318	541	2,945	23	...	194	3	17	...	20	4	15	19	...	...	...	39
British Territory ...	288,738	14,171	177,707	58,715	17,266	321	1,620	15	1	9	25	3	1	4	...	...	...	29
Native States ...	53,385	15,851	27,234	14,018	587	65	655	14	4	7	25	4	...	4	...	...	...	29
Province ...	342,123	30,022	204,941	72,733	17,853	386	2,275	15	1	9	25	3	1	4	...	...	...	29

is often retained in addition, who takes the place of the Bhát on such occasions. The status of the Bhát is high; and in Rájpútána they are said to possess great influence. The Bhát is almost always Hindu, even where his clients have become Mahomedans. A few are Sikhs, and still fewer Musalmáns; and it is doubtful whether these last are not really Mírásis. There are said to be Musalmán Bháts in Siálkot who have migrated from the Jhang uplands and are much addicted to thieving; but I much doubt whether they belong to the Bhát caste. I have said that the Bháts are of undoubted Bráhman origin, and this is true of the Jága and Cháran, who are ordinarily called Bháts. Whether it is true of the Mádho Bháts also I am not so certain. The Mádhos would appear to be named after Mádho, the founder of the Mádhavi sect of minstrel mendicants; and the Bhátra, who however claims Bráhman origin, is called Mádho in Ráwalpindi. Besides the 217 persons mentioned above who returned their caste as Mádho, a very considerable number of those who have given their caste as Bháts show Mádho as their tribe.

527. **The Dum and Mirasi (Caste No. 25).**—Under this head have been included both Dúm and Mírasi, the former being the Hindu and Indian and the latter the Musalmán and Arabic name, and the whole class being commonly called Dúm-Mírási by the people. It fact no one of my divisional offices separated the two entries, and the two words are used throughout the Province as absolutely synonymous. The Dúms, however, must be carefully distinguished from the Dom or Domra, the executioner and corpseburner of Hindústán, and the type of all uncleanliness to a Hindu; as also from the Dúm of the Hill States, whom I have classed as Dúmna and not as Mírási, as I understand that the word Dúm is there applied to workers in bamboo. The class is distributed throughout the Province, but is most numerous in the Amritsar, Lahore, Ráwalpindi, and Multán divisions, and in Baháwalpur and the other States which march with them. On the lower Indus many of them would seem to have returned themselves as Jats—see Abstract No. 72,* page 224. *P. 106-107.
The word Mírási is derived from the Arabic *mirás* or inheritance; and the Mírási is to the inferior agricultural cases and the outcast tribes what the Bhát is to the Rájpúts. Even Játs employ Mírásis, though the hereditary genealogist of many of the Ját tribes is the Sánsi; and, as just stated, Rájpúts often employ Mírásis in addition to Bháts. But the Mírási is more than a genealogist; he is also a musician and minstrel; and most of the men who play the musical instruments of the Panjáb are either Mírásis, Jogis, or *faqirs.* "The Dúm does not make a good servant, nor a fiddle-bow a good weapon."

The social position of the Mírási, as of all the minstrel castes, is exceedingly low, but he attends at weddings and on similar occasions to recite genealogies. Moreover there are grades even among Mírásis. The outcast tribes have their Mírásis who, though they do not eat with their clients and merely render them professional service, are considered impure by the Mírásis of the higher castes. The Mírási is generally a hereditary servant like the Bhát; and is notorious for his exactions, which he makes under the threat of lampooning the ancestors of him from whom he demands fees. "These "four were not born on giving day; the Mulla, the Bhát, the Bráhman, and [P. 290]
"the Dúm." The Mírási is almost always a Musalmán. The few Hindus returned from the hilly and sub-montane districts are very possibly Dúmnas returned as Dúms. I have included under the head of Mírási the following schedule entries; Dhádhi, 37 in Ambála, 478 in Multán, and 77 in the

Deraját; Khariála, 371, and Sarnai, 3 in Jálandhar; Rabábi, 109 in Lahore. Besides these numbers, the above terms, as well as Naqárchi, have all been included with Mírási in the offices of one or more divisions. The last three are simply words meaning players upon the flageolet, the flute, and the kettle drum. The Dhádhi appears only to sing and not to play any instrument, and in the Deraját at least is said not to intermarry with the Dúm, so probably he should not have been included. The Khariála is said to be a sort of Mírási, but I have no further information concerning him. The two largest tribes returned for Mírásis seem to be the Chúnhar with 13,493, and the Kalet with 4,897 persons. The detailed tables of clans will, when published, give complete information on the subject.

528. The Jogi, Rawal and Nath (Caste Nos. 40 and 80).—The figures under the head Jogi include two very distinct classes of persons. First are the Jogis proper, a regular religious order of Hindus, which includes both the Augar Jogis and the Kanphatta Jogi ascetics, who are followers of Gorakhnáth and priests and worshippers of Siva. These men are fully as respectable as the Bairágis, Gosáins, and other religious orders. So far as the sub-divisional tables help us, the present figures include 9,143 of this class, of whom 5,769 are males, but the real number is probably greater. They are all Hindus. They
P. 228 have been discussed in the earlier portion of this section, at page 286. The second class is that miscellaneous assortment of low-caste *faqírs* and fortune-tellers, both Hindu and Musalmán but chiefly Musalmán, who are commonly known as Jogis. The word Jogi or Yogi means a student of the Joga school of philosophy, which teachs how, by suppression of the breath, mental abstraction, and the like, to obtain supernatural powers of divination, second sight, and so forth;[1] and the result is that every rascally beggar who pretends to be able to tell fortunes, or to practise astrological and necromantic arts in however small a degree, buys himself a drum and calls himself and is called by others a Jogi. These men include all the Musalmáns, and probably a part of the Hindus of the eastern districts who have been returned as Jogis. They are a thoroughly vagabond set, and wander about the country beating a drum and begging, practising surgery and physic in a small way, writing charms, telling fortunes, and practising exorcism and divination; or, settling in the villages, eke out their earnings from these occupations by the offerings made at the local shrines of the malevolent godlings or of the Saiyads and other Musalmán saints (see sections 216 and 226) ; for the Jogi is so impure that he will eat the offerings made at any shrine. These people, or at least the Musalmán section of them, are called in the centre of the Panjáb Ráwals, or sometimes Jogi-Ráwals, from the Arabic *Rammál* a diviner, which again is derived from *ramal* "sand" with which the Arab magicians divine; and the two sets of figures must be taken together, always remembering that those for Jogis include respectable Jogis, while those for Ráwals, who are all Musalmáns, do not. The Jogi-Ráwals of Káthiawár are said to be exorcisers of evil spirits, and to worship a deity called Koriál. In Siálkot the Jogis pretend to avert storms from the ripening crops by plunging a drawn sword into the field or a knife into a mound, sacrificing goats, and accepting suitable offerings. Mr. Benton writes:—"The Jogi is a favourite character in Hindústáni "fiction. He there appears as a jolly playful character of a simple disposition,

[1] See Wilson's *Sects of the Hindus*, pages 130*ff* for a very interesting account of both classes of Jogis, and for references to further authorities.

who enjoys the fullest liberty and conducts himself in the most eccentric fashion under the cloak of religion without being called in question."

The Ráwals of the Panjáb are notorious cheats. One of their favourite devices is to personate a long lost relative. In the Province itself they seldom venture upon open crime; but they travel about the Central Provinces and the Deccan and even visit Bombay and Calcutta, and there pilfer and rob. They are often absent for long periods on these expeditions; and meanwhile the Banyas of their villages support their families on credit, to be repaid with interest on the return of the father. Some interesting information regarding them will be found in Selected Papers, No. XVIII of 1869 of the Panjáb Police Department. The town of Ráwalpindi is named after the Ráwals; but the Ráwals of the district appear to have returned themselves either as Jogis or more probably as Mughals, as 1,263 of the Mughals of Ráwalpindi give Ráwal as their clan. There they are said, in addition to their usual pursuits, to recite at the Muharram stories of the doings of Mahomet, accounts of his miracles, and hymns in his praise.

The Náths of the higher hills, where the worship of Siva is prevalent, correspond very closely with the Jogis of the plains, though they make little pretence to an ascetic character and live chiefly by growing vegetables; but they also perform certain semi-sacerdotal function, taking the place of the Achárj of the plains in the funeral ceremonies of the Kanets, and receiving like him the clothes of the deceased. They also consecrate new houses, and purify them when they have been defiled. They now form a true caste, and are not recruited from without. One or more in almost every Náth household has his ears pierced in honour of Siva, and is called a Kanphatta Náth. They occupy much the same social position as the Jogi-Ráwal of the plains. They are understood to have returned themselves as Jogis and to be included in the figures now under discussion.

RAWALS CLASSED AS JOGIS.

Jálandhar ...	2,842	Siálkot ...	1,244
Hushyárpur ...	2,781	Lahore ...	1,508
Kángra ...	764	Gujránwála ...	2,048
Amritsar ...	2,325	Kapurthala ...	530
Gurdáspur ...	3,337	Other places ...	434
			17,853

Of the figures given in Table VIII A, all the Hindus are men returned as Jogis. Of the Musalmáns the numbers shown in the margin were returned as Ráwals, the remainder being Jogis.

529. The Bahrupia (Caste No. 128).—The Bahrúpia is in its origin a purely occupational term; it is derived from the Sanskrit *bahu* "many" and *rúpa* "form," and denotes an actor, a mimic, or one who assumes many forms or characters. One of their favourite devices is to ask for money, and when it is refused, to ask that it may be given on condition of the Bahrúpia succeeding in deceiving the person who refuses it. Some days later the Bahrúpia will again visit the house in the disguise of a pedlar, a milkman, or what not, sell his goods without being detected, throw off his disguise, and [P. 291] claim the stipulated reward. They may be drawn from any caste, and in Rohtak there are Chúhra Bahrúpias. But in some districts a family or colony of Bahrúpias has obtained land and settled down on it, and so become a caste as much as any other. Thus there is a Bahrúpia family in Pánípat who hold a village revenue-free, though these men have apparently returned themselves as Shekhs. It is probable that the figures do not include all who follow the profession of acting in the Panjáb, many of them having returned their true caste and not their occupation. On the other hand, it is certain that the returns for Bahrúpias in Siálkot and Gújrát do not refer at all to what I here call Bahrúpias, but are Mahtams, who are commonly known as Bahrúpias in those districts—see section 494 on Mahtams. The exclusion of these figures reduces the total number of Bahrúpias in the Province to 386, and I have altered the figures of Abstract No. 90 accordingly. The Bahrúpias of Gurdáspur are said to work in cane and bamboo.

530. The Bhand (Caste No 141).—The Bhánd or Naqqál is the story-teller, joker, and buffoon, and is often also called Básha. The name comes from the Hindi *Bhánda* "buffooning." He is separate from and of a lower professional status than the Bahrúpia. Both are commonly kept by Rájas and other wealthy men like the jester of the early English noble, but both also wander about the country and perform to street audiences. The Bhánd is not a true caste any more than the Bahrúpia, and I understand that they are often Mírásis by caste and probably have in many cases so returned themselves. Elliott seems to imply that Bahrúpia is a caste and Bhánd an occupation; but the former statement is certainly not true in the Panjáb. The entries under this head include both Básha and Naqqál.

MERCANTILE AND SHOP-KEEPING CASTES.

531. Merchants and Shop-keepers.—The group of mercantile castes for
P. 238-41. which the figures will be found in Abstract No. 91 on the next page practically hold the whole commerce of the Panjáb in their hands. They do not engage in the carrying trade, nor do they traffic in cattle; being for the most part Hindus they will not sell liquor or meat; and being of fair social standing they do not sell vegetables; but with these exceptions almost the whole of the mercantile and commercial transactions of the Province, excepting as a general rule petty hawking and pedling, are conducted by one or other of the castes which I have included in this abstract. They may be divided into five groups, the first consisting of Banyas, Dhúnsars, Bohras, and Pahári Mahájans; the second of Súds and Bhábras; the third of Khatris, Khakhas, and Bhátias; the fourth of Aroras; and the fifth of Khojahs and Paráchas.

The territorial distribution of these groups is very well marked. The first or Banya group is almost confined to the eastern and south-eastern divisions of Dehli, Hissár, and Ambála, and to the central Native States, though a few of them have spread along the north of the Eastern Plains and into the Hill States. West of Lahore they are practically unknown. The second or Súd and Bhábra group is found only in the districts that lie under the hills on the northern border of the Province from Ambála to Káwalpindi. The third or Khatri group constitutes a large proportion of the mercantile classes of all the centre and, excluding the frontier, of the north-west of the Province, being most numerous in the Jálandhar, Amritsar, Lahore, and Káwalpindi divisions. The fourth or Arora group have the Multán and Deraját divisions and Baháwalpur almost to themselves, extending also into Pesháwar and Kohát, and crossing the Satluj in Sirsa to meet the Banya group of the east. Finally, the fifth or Mahomedan group is confined to the central and western districts and the Salt-range Tract.

On the whole this class constitutes 7 per cent. of the population of the Province. But in the districts of the Multán and Deraját divisions and in Baháwalpur the proportion rises to from 11 to 17 per cent. This however is

Abstract No. 91, showing the [P. 292]

	MERCAN					
	Fr					
	14	173	124	112	75	88
	Banya.	Dhúnsar.	Bohra.	Mahájan Pahári.	Súd.	Bhábra.
Dehli	42,414	57	245	...	...	414
Gurgaon	36,801	494	75	...	...	...
Karnál	40,699	4	240	...	4	5
Hissar	43,309	...	...	...	...	...
Rohtak	41,470	23	...	...	..	...
Sirsa	10,496	...	...	...	1	...
Ambala	40,069	10	...	...	1,637	675
Ludhiána	8,722	...	...	...	2,075	1,325
Simla	1,042	...	...	...	401	47
Jálandhar	3,126	6	...	837	1,756	687
Hoshyárpur	1,591	2	...	76	1,602	1,119
Kángra	89	3	50	4,120	5,775	133
Amritsar	2,686	...	...	...	1,084	1,309
Gurdaspur	14,804	7	...	...	118	134
Siálkot	10,796	...	...	...	1	1,773
Lahore	2,093	1	...	...	479	949
Gujránwála	160	11	...	...	5	577
Firozpur	11,451	77	...	...	617	721
Rawalpindi	2,597	9	...	...	40	1,015
Jahlam	219	...	...	...	..	...
Gujrát	288	...	...	...	16	12
Shahpur	9	...	...	...	3	...
Multan	562	3	...	...	...	248
Jhang	20	12	...	...	...	...
Montgomery	122	1	...	...	...	6
Muzaffargarh	24	...	...	...	...	3
Derah Ismail Khan	37	...	...	...	...	4
Derah Ghazi Khan	98	1	...	...	...	38
Bannu	116	...	...	...	...	62
Peshâwar	389	...	...	...	55	3
Hazara	475	...	...	...	...	...
Kohát	121	...	...	...	...	41
British Territory	316,823	711	610	5,033	15,669	11,300
Patiála	75,238	138	1	...	2,743	1,329
Nábha	13,693	40	...	...	177	225
Kapurthala	481	6	...	...	708	...
Jínd	16,801	17	...	...	2	31
Farídkot	1,604	...	...	...	7	345
Maler Kotla	3,245	...	...	...	132	124
Kalsia	3,274	...	...	...	36	5
Total East. Plains	118,564	219	1	...	3,805	2,059
Baháwalpur	486	...	...	...	...	368
Mandi	4	...	926	...	41	...
Chamba	498	...	...	...	2	...
Náhan	1,335	...	3	...	96	2
Biláspur	3	...	333	...	11	...
Bashahr	33	...	129	...	3	...
Nálagarh	32	...	171	...	11	325
Suket	14	...	618	...	3	...
Total Hill States	2,081	...	3,054	...	421	327
British Territory	316,823	711	610	5,033	15,669	11,300
Native States	121,121	219	3,055	...	4,226	1,754
Province	437,944	930	3,665	5,033	19,895	14,054

Mercantile and Shop-keeping Castes.

TILE.

GURES.

16	179	69	10	44	104	
Khatri.	Khakha.	Bhátia.	Arora.	Khojah.	Parácha.	
4,657	...	...	210	6	...	Dehli.
179	...	...	...	3	...	Gurgaon.
1,170	...	...	8	...	.	Karnál.
187	...	...	1,858	91	...	Hissar.
62	...	...	17	5	...	Rohtak.
295	...	...	5,554	149	...	Sirsa.
8,154	...	..	102	190	...	Ambala.
15,944	...	...	354	...	...	Ludhiána.
331	...	...	29	...	...	Simla.
22,868	...	...	762	1,068	...	Jálandhar.
19,780	...	...	316	922	...	Hoshyárpur.
7,760	...	...	110	67	...	Kángra.
31,411	...	780	20,613	6,934	...	Amritsar.
15,778	...	6	1,216	2,312	...	Gurdáspur.
18,440	...	5,784	15,793	5,550	...	Siálkot.
32,970	..	296	33,136	12,813	177	Lahore.
21,301	...	748	30,079	3,458	...	Gujránwála.
9,174	...	23	13,306	2,486	...	Firozpur.
41,135	49	213	12,181	1,220	1,944	Rawalpindi.
35,941	1	1,100	12,345	2,672	318	Jahlam.
17,794	...	5,318	23,964	2,215	1	Gujrát.
15,015	...	734	35,017	1,551	424	Shahpur.
9,798	...	1,995	76,842	5,640	7	Multan.
15,196	...	461	45,041	3,352	2	Jhang.
4,402	...	1	51,260	4,440	...	Montgomery.
1,[illegible]08	...	202	33,827	714	...	Muzaffargarh.
3,077	...	1,478	44,146	904	...	Derah Ismail Khan.
2,863	...	266	37,041	204	...	Derah Ghazi Khan.
1,746	...	2,084	24,286	996	...	Bannu.
9,578	1	241	13,333	1,780	2,903	Pesháwar.
10,267	603	52	2,455	9	1,569	Hazara.
1,383	...	67	5,233	40	878	Kohát.
380,399	**654**	**21,790**	**589,957**	**61,297**	**8,223**	**British Territory.**
17,603	...	7	1,692	285	221	Patiála.
3,998	...	...	176	3	...	Nábha.
5,613	...	...	799	820	215	Kapurthala.
235	...	...	35	2	...	Jínd.
1,162	...	...	2,163	40	2	Farídkot.
638	...	...	99	296	...	Maler Kotla.
501	...	...	12	...	...	Kalsia.
29,883	...	7	4,976	1,446	438	Total East. Plains.
1,069	...	1,068	56,483	3,138	...	Baháwalpur.
2,960	...	...	...	...	...	Mandi.
1,378	...	...	10	...	...	Chamba.
231	...	...	1	...	...	Náhan.
1,487	...	...	10	...	...	Biláspur.
45	...	...	...	...	...	Bashahr.
570	...	...	...	1	...	Nálagarh.
466	...	...	...	...	...	Suket.
7,788	...	6	24	1	...	Total Hill States.
380,399	654	21,790	589,957	61,297	8,223	British Territory.
38,740	...	1,081	61,483	4,585	438	Native States.
419,139	654	22,871	601,440	65,882	8,661	Province.

Abstract No. 91, showing the Mercantile

	MERCAN							
	PROPORTION PER 1,000							
	14	173	124	112		75	88	
	Banya.	Dhúnsar.	Bohra.	Mahájan Pahári.	TOTAL.	Súd.	Bhábra.	TOTAL.
Dehli	66	...	...	...	66	...	1	1
Gurgaon	57	1	...	...	58	...	...	...
Karnál	65	...	...	...	65	...	...	...
Hissar	86	...	...	...	86	...	...	...
Rohtak	75	...	...	...	75	...	...	...
Sirsa	41	...	...	...	41	...	...	...
Ambala	38	...	...	...	38	2	1	3
Ludhiána	14	...	...	...	14	3	2	5
Simla	24	...	...	...	24	9	1	10
Jálandhar	4	...	...	1	5	2	1	3
Hushyárpur	2	...	...	...	2	2	1	3
Kángra	...	...	...	6	6	8	...	8
Amritsar	3	...	...	...	3	1	2	3
Gurdáspur	18	...	...	...	18	...	...	...
Siálkot	11	...	...	...	11	...	2	2
Lahore	2	...	...	...	2	1	1	2
Gujránwála	...	...	...	...	...	...	1	1
Firozpur	18	...	...	...	18	1	1	2
Rawalpindi	3	...	...	...	3	...	1	1
Jahlam	...	...	...	...	...	...	...	...
Gujrát	...	...	...	...	...	...	...	...
Shahpur	...	...	...	...	...	...	...	...
Multan	1	...	...	...	1	...	...	...
Jhang	...	...	...	...	...	...	...	...
Montgomery	...	...	...	...	...	...	...	...
Muzaffargarh	...	...	...	...	...	...	...	...
Derah Ismail Khan ...	...	...	...	...	...	...	...	...
Derah Ghazi Khan ...	...	...	...	...	...	...	...	...
Bannu	...	...	...	...	...	...	...	...
Peshawar	1	...	...	...	1	...	...	...
Hazara	1	...	...	...	1	...	...	...
Kohát	1	...	...	...	1	...	...	...
British Territory ...	17	...	...	...	17	1	1	2
Patiála	51	...	...	...	51	2	1	3
Nábha	52	...	...	...	52	1	1	2
Kapurthala	2	...	...	...	2	3	...	3
Jínd	67	...	...	...	67	...	...	...
Faridkot	17	...	...	...	17	...	4	4
Maler Kotla	46	...	...	...	46	2	2	4
Kalsia	49	...	...	...	49	1	...	1
Total East. Plains ...	47	...	...	...	47	2	1	3
Baháwalpur	1	...	...	...	1	...	1	1
Mandi	...	...	6	...	6	...	...	...
Chamba ...	4	...	...	...	4	...	...	...
Náhan	12	...	...	...	12	1	...	1
Bilaspur	...	...	4	...	4	...	...	...
Bashahr	1	...	2	...	3	...	...	...
Nálagarh	1	...	3	...	4	...	6	6
Suket	...	...	12	...	12	...	...	...
Total Hill States ...	3	...	4	...	7	1	...	1
British Territory ...	17	...	-		17	1	1	2
Native States ...	31	...	1	...	32	1	1	2
Province	19	...	...	...	19	1	1	2

and Shop-keeping Castes—*concluded.*

TILE.

OF TOTAL POPULATION.

16	179	69		10	44	104			
Khatri.	Khakha.	Bhátia.	Total.	Arora.	Khojah.	Paráchá.	Total.	Grand Total.	
7	...	...	7	...	...	...	...	74	Dehli.
...	...	...	...	...	...	...	...	58	Gurgaon.
2	...	...	2	...	...	...	...	67	Karnál.
...	...	...	...	3	...	...	...	89	Hissar.
...	...	...	...	...	...	...	...	75	Rohtak.
1	...	...	1	22	1	...	1	65	Sirsa.
8	...	...	8	1	...	...	...	50	Ambala.
26	...	...	26	1	...	...	...	46	Ludhiána.
8	...	...	8	1	...	...	...	48	Simla.
29	...	...	29	1	1	...	1	30	Jálandhar.
22	...	...	22	...	1	...	1	28	Hushyárpur.
11	...	...	11	...	...	...	...	25	Kángra.
35	...	1	36	23	8	...	8	78	Amritsar.
19	...	...	19	1	3	...	3	41	Gurdáspur.
18	...	6	24	16	5	...	5	58	Siálkot.
36	...	...	36	36	13	...	13	89	Lahore.
35	...	1	36	40	6	...	6	93	Gujránwála.
14	...	...	14	20	4	...	4	58	Firozpur.
50	...	...	50	15	1	2	3	72	Rawalpindi.
61	...	2	63	21	5	1	6	90	Jahlam.
26	...	8	34	35	3	...	3	72	Gujrát.
36	...	2	38	83	4	1	5	126	Shahpur.
18	...	4	22	139	10	...	10	172	Multan.
38	...	3	41	114	9	...	9	164	Jhang.
11	...	...	11	120	10	...	10	141	Montgomery.
5	...	1	6	100	2	...	2	108	Muzaffargarh.
7	...	3	10	100	2	...	2	112	Derah Ismail Khan.
8	...	1	9	102	1	...	1	112	Derah Ghazi Khan.
5	...	6	11	73	3	...	3	87	Bannu.
5	...	...	5	22	3	5	8	36	Peshâwar.
25	1	...	26	6	...	4	4	37	Hazara.
8	...	...	8	29	...	5	5	48	Kohát.
20	...	**1**	**21**	**29**	**3**	...	**3**	**72**	**British Territory.**
12	...	...	12	1	...	...	...	67	Patiála.
15	...	...	15	1	...	...	...	70	Nábha.
22	...	...	22	3	3	1	4	34	Kapurthala.
1	...	...	1	...	...	...	...	68	Jínd.
12	...	...	12	22	...	...	...	55	Farídkot.
9	...	...	9	1	4	...	4	64	Maler Kotla.
7	...	...	7	...	...	...	...	57	Kalsia.
12	...	...	12	2	1	...	1	65	Total East. Plains.
2	...	2	4	98	5	...	5	109	Baháwalpur.
20	...	...	20	...	...	...	...	26	Mandi.
12	...	...	12	...	...	...	...	16	Chamba.
2	...	...	2	...	...	...	...	15	Náhan.
17	...	...	17	...	...	...	...	21	Biláspur.
1	...	...	1	...	...	...	...	4	Bashahr.
11	...	...	11	...	...	...	...	21	Nálagarh.
9	...	...	9	...	...	...	...	21	Suket.
10	...	...	10	...	...	...	...	18	Total Hill States.
20	...	1	21	29	3	...	3	72	British Territory.
10	...	...	10	16	1	...	1	61	Native States.
18	...	1	19	26	3	...	3	69	Province.

due, not to the fact that a larger proportion of the population of these parts is engaged in commerce, but to the peculiar versatility of the Arora of the south-western Panjáb, who is a trader first indeed, but after that anything and everything. Throughout the Eastern Plains the proportion is very uniform, naturally rising highest in the districts which include large cities. Throughout the hills and submontane districts the proportion is singularly low, for these tracts include none of the commercial centres of the Panjáb, and the needs of the people are simple and easily supplied. In the central districts and the Salt-range Tract the proportion is large, probably because the Khatris like the Aroras by no means confine themselves to commerce as an occupation.

532. The Banya (Caste No. 14).—The word Banya is derived from the Sanskrit *bánijya* or trade; and the Banya, as the name implies, lives solely for and by commerce. He holds a considerable area of land in the east of the Province; but it is very rarely indeed that he follows any other than mercantile pursuits. The commercial enterprises and intelligence of the class is great, and the dealings of some of the great Banya houses of Dehli, Bíkáner, and Márwár are of the most extensive nature. But the Banya of the village, who represents the great mass of the caste, is a poor creature, notwithstanding the title of Mahájan or "great folk," which is confined by usage to the caste to which he belongs. He spends his life in his shop, and the results are apparent in his inferior physique and utter want of manliness. He is looked down upon by the peasantry as a cowardly money grubber; but at the same time his social standing is from one point of view curiously higher than theirs, for he is, what they are not, a strict Hindu, he is generally admitted to be of pure Vaisya descent, he wears the *janeo* or sacred thread, his periods of purification are longer than theirs, he does not practise widow-marriage, and he will not eat or drink at their hands; and religious ceremonial and the degrees of caste proper are so interwoven with the social fabric that the resulting position of the Banya in the grades of rustic society is of a curiously mixed nature. The Banya is hardly used by the proverbial wisdom of the countryside: "He who has a Banya for a friend is not in want of an "enemy;" and, "First beat a Banya, then a thief." And indeed the Banya has too strong a hold over the husbandman for there to be much love lost between them. Yet the money-lenders of the villages at least have been branded with a far worse name than they deserve. They perform functions of the most cardinal importance in the village œconomy, and it is surprising how much reasonableness and honesty there is in their dealings with the people so long as they can keep their business transactions out of a court of justice.

The Banya class forms the main commercial element of the population [P. 293] of Northern and North-Western India up to the meridian of Lahore, and of Rájpútána. Indeed the origin and stronghold of at any rate those sections of the caste which are most numerously represented in the Panjáb is North-Western Rájpútána, and it is curious that while spreading so far to the east of Bíkáner, they should have obtained so little hold to the west of that country. In the Panjáb they are practically found in any great numbers only in the Dehli and Hissár divisions, Ambála, and in the Central States of the Eastern Plains, and Fírozpur; though curiously enough there appears to be a considerable colony of them in Gurdáspur and Siálkot. But the word Banya is generically used for "shop-keeper" all over the Panjáb, not excepting even the frontier where Kirár is the more usual term; and it is just possible that in some cases other mercantile castes have been included in the figures. This however cannot have happened to any considerable extent, or the figures for the sub-divisions of each caste would at once show what had happened. Of the Banyas of the Panjáb about 92 per cent. are Hindus. Only 0·84 per cent. are Sikhs, most of whom are to be found in Patiála, Nábha and Ráwalpindi. The Jains constitute 7 per cent. of the whole, and are confined to the Dehli division, Hissár, and Rohtak, or the tract bordering upon Rájpútána, the great stronghold of Western Jainism. It is curious that the proportion of Jain Banyas should not be larger in Sirsa. Only some 500 souls are returned as Musalmáns, and these may perhaps be Banyas by occupation rather than by caste.

It is sometimes said that Banya is no true caste at all, but merely an occupational term equivalent to "shop-keeper," and that the great divisions of the Banyas, the Aggarwáls, Oswáls, and the like, really occupy the position of castes; and this is in a sense true. The great sections do not intermarry, and very possibly represent stocks of different origin; and if caste is used in the same sense as tribe, these sections are doubtless separate castes. But if the word is used in its purely Brahminical sense, I do not think the Aggarwál and Oswál Banyas are separate castes any more than are the Gaur and Sársút Bráhmans. The two cases seem to me analagous. In all the non-agricultural castes who are found distributed widely among the population, anything corresponding with compact tribal divisions, such as we find among Rájputs, Patháns, or Jats, is impossible. They do not move into and occupy a large tract of country; they rather spread from centres of origin, diffusing themselves among and accompanying the agricultural tribes in their movements. But the great divisions of the Banya caste occupy identical social and religious positions, and recognise each other, whether rightly or wrongly, as of common origin distinct from that of the Khatris and other castes whose avocations are the same as their own; and, save in the sense in which such caste names as Chamár and Chúhra are only occupational terms, I think that the term Banya must be taken to describe a true caste of supposed common blood, and not a collection of tribes of distinct descent united only by identity of occupation (see further section 351 *supra*).

533. The divisions of the Banya Caste.—The divisions of the Banya caste with which we are concerned in the Panjáb are shown in the margin.

BANYA SECTIONS.	
Aggarwál ...	364,355
Oswál	3,863
Mahesri	5,755
Sarália	11,899
Dasa	2,473
TOTAL ...	388,345
Others and unspecified	49,599
TOTAL ...	437,944

The **Aggarwals** or north-eastern division of Banyas include the immense majority of the caste in every district throughout the Province. They have, according to Sherring, a tradition of of a far distant origin on the banks of Godavery. But the place to which all Aggarwáls refer the origin of the section, and from which they take their name, is Agroha in the Hissár district, once the capital of a Vaisya Rája of the name of Agar Sen, and whence they are said to have spread over Hindústán after the taking of that place by Shaháb-ul-dín Ghori in 1195; and Elliott points out that the fact that throughout the North-Western Provinces the Aggarwál Banyas are supposed to be specially bound to make offerings to Gúga Pír, the great saint from the neighbourhood of Agroha, bears testimony to the truth of the tradition. The eighteen sons of Agar Sen are said to have married the eighteen snake-daughters of Rája Básak, and Gúga Pír is the greatest of the snake-gods. The Aggarwáls are often Jain, especially in Dehli and among the more wealthy classes of the cities; and when Jains, are generally of the Digambara sects (see section 259, Chapter IV). But the great mass of them are Hindus, and almost invariably of the Vaishnava sect.

The **Oswals** or south-western section of the caste trace their origin from Osia or Osnagar, a town in Márwár. Their distribution in the Panjáb is shown in the margin; their real home is in Gújarát and South-Western Rájpútána, where they are exceedingly numerous. They are very generally Jains, and when Jains, almost always of the Swetámbara sect.

OSWAL.			
Dehli ...	467	Sirsa ...	1,378
Gurgaon	51	Patiala	262
Karnal...	1,088	Other places...	70
Hissar ...	527		
Rohtak	20	TOTAL	3,863

The third or north-western section is **Mahesri** who are most numerous in Bíkáner. Mr. Wilson says that those of Sirsa claim Rájpút origin, and still have sub-divisions bearing Rájpút names. They say that their ancestor was turned into stone for an outrage upon a *faqír*, but was restored to life by Mahesh or Mahádeo; hence their name. Their distribution in the Panjáb is shown in the margin. They are for the most part Vaishnava Hindus, though occasionally Jains. Their relations with the Aggarwáls are much closer than are those of the Oswáls.

MAHESRI.			
Dehli ...	525	Firozpur	145
Gurgaon	490	Multán	177
Hissar ...	530	Other places...	198
Rohtak	285		
Sirsa ...	920	TOTAL	5,755
Amritsar	2,485		

The **Saralia Banyas** are returned in the localities shown in the margin. They are a branch of the Aggarwáls, but owing to some dispute left Agroha and settled in Sarála, a town not far from Agroha, from which they take their name. They are as strict as other Aggarwáls, and not in any way *dasa* or impure. They do not intermarry with other Aggarwáls. I have been able to discover nothing regarding their origin or the distinction between them and the other sections of the caste.

SARALIA.	
Ambala	9,841
Simla	28
Patiala	971
Kalsia	868
Hill States ...	191
TOTAL	11,899

The **Dasa Banyas** are not properly a distinct section of the caste. The word means 'hybrid,' and is used for members of other castes who have departed from the custom of the caste, or whose descent is not pure. The Dasa Banyas are said to be descendants of an illegitimate son of an Aggarwál. To the figures given for them above should be added 1,664 in Ambála who have returned themselves as Gáta, which is a synonym for Dasa.

Little appears to be known of the minor sub-divisions. It is to be hoped that the detailed tables of sub-divisions of castes now in course of preparation from the papers of the Panjáb Census will tell us something about them. The three great sections, Aggarwál, Oswál and Mahesri, are said not to intermarry. The Banyas possess the Bráhminical *gotras*, but it appears that they also have other sub-divisions of the main sections of the caste.

534. The Dhunsar (Caste No. 173).—The head-quarters of the Dhúnsar are at Rewári in Gurgáon. The total number in the Panjáb is under 1,000, and all but three are Hindus. They take their name from Dhosi, a flat-topped hill near Nárnaul, where their ancestor Chimand performed his devotions. They are of Bráhminical origin, as is admitted by the Bráhmans [P. 294]
themselves, and it is possible that some of them may have recorded themselves as Bráhmans in the schedules. Indeed, I find 1,608 Dhúsar Bráhmans returned, of whom 1,560 are in Gurdáspur; but whether these are the same men as the Dhúnsars of Rewári I cannot say. The detailed tables when ready will clear up this point. In any case, they are no longer Bráhmans, any more than are the agricultural Tagas; and like the latter they employ Bráhmans to minister to them. They are almost exclusively clerks or merchants, though, like the Khatris, some of them have risen to eminence in the army and the Court. The great Hemu, the leader of the Indian army at the second battle of Pánípat, was a Dhúnsar of Rewári. Sherring states that the Dhúnsars have a tradition of origin in the neighbourhood of Benares before migrating to Dehli, that they excel as minstrels, and are exceedingly

strict Hindus of the Vaishnava sect. They seem to be numerous in the North-West Provinces.

535. The Bohra (Caste No. 124).—The figures under the heading of Bohra include two very distinct classes of men. Of the 3,665 Bohras shown in our tables, 560 are found in the Dehli division, and 3,105 in the Hill States of Kángra. The first are Bráhman money-lenders from Márwár, who have of late years begun to settle in the districts on the Jamna, and have already acquired a most unenviable notoriety for unscrupulous rapacity. There is a rustic proverb: "A Bohra's 'good morning!' is like a message from the angel "of death;" and another: "A Jat to guard crops, a Bráhman as a money-"lender, and a Banya as a ruler:—God's curse be on you!"

In the hills any money-lender or shop-keeper is apparently called a Bohra (from the same root as *beohár* or "trade,"[1]) and the word is used in the same general sense in the south of Rájpútána and in Bombay, taking the place of the "Banya" of Hindustán, though in Gújrat it is specially applied to a class of Shíah traders who were converted to Islám some 600 years ago. In the Panjáb all the Bohras are Hindus. It will be noticed that in those Hill States in which Bohras are numerous, Banyas are hardly represented in the returns, and *vice versâ;* and there can be little doubt that both the Banyas and the Bohras shown for the Hill States are the same as the Pahári Mahájans next to be discussed. The Hill Bohras are said to be exceedingly strict Hindus, and to be admitted to intermarriage with the lower classes of Rájpúts, such as Ráthis and Ráwats. In Gurdáspur I am told that there is a small class of traders called Bohras who claim Jat origin, and who are notorious for making money by marrying their daughters, securing the dower, and then running away with both, to begin again *da capo*.

536. The Pahari Mahajans (Caste No. 112).—As I have just remarked, the Banyas and Bohras returned for the Hill States should probably be included with these people. They appear to be a mixed caste sprung from the intermarriage of immigrants from the plains belonging to the Banya and Káyath castes and are generally either traders or clerks. But the term is in the hills really occupational rather than the name of any caste; and it appears that a Bráhman shop-keeper would be called a Mahájan, while a Mahájan clerk would be called a Káyath. Thus Mr. Barnes says that "the "Káyath of the hills, unlike his namesake of the plains, belongs to the "Vaisya or commercial class and wears the *janeo* or sacred thread," and Major Wace writes of Hazára: "The Hill Bráhmans or Mahájans keep "shops, cultivate, or take service, as well as act as priests." The true Banya of Hindústán, who is found in the hills only as a foreigner, will not intermarry with these Pahári Mahájans.

537. The Sud (Caste No. 75)[2].—The Súds are almost entirely confined to the lower hills, and the districts that lie immediately under them as far west as Amritsar. Their head-quarters are at Lúdhiána and the neighbouring town of Máchhíwára, and they are, I believe, unknown outside the Panjáb. They are almost wholly mercantile in their pursuits though occasionally taking service as clerks, and occupy a social position markedly inferior to that of either the Banya or the Khatri. They wear a *janeo* or sacred thread made

[1] Mr. Beames gives *Wohora* as the true form of the word.
[2] I am indebted to the kindness of Mr. Gordon Walker, Settlement Officer of Lúdhiána, for much of the information recorded below.

of three instead of six strands, and many of them practise widow-marriage. With the exception of a few who are Sikhs they are almost all Hindu, but are, in comparison with the other mercantile castes, very lax in the observance of their religion. They indulge freely in meat and wine, and in habits, customs, and social position resemble very closely the Káyaths. The tribe is apparently an ancient one, but I can obtain no definite information as to its origin. Various fanciful derivations of the tribal name are current, for the most part of an opprobrious nature. I attempted to make inquiries from some leading Súds; but the result was the assembling of a Pancháyat, the ransacking of the Sanskrit classics for proof of their Kshatriya origin, and a heated discussion in the journal of the Anjúman.

They are divided into two main sections, the Uchándia or Súd of the hills and the Newandia or Súd of the plains. I find however that some of the Súds of Hushyárpur trace their origin from Sarhind. They also distinguish the Súds who not do practise widow-marriage from those who do, calling the former *khara*, and the latter and their offspring *gola, doghla* (hybrid) or *chichán*. These two sections, of which the latter corresponds exactly with the *Dasa* and *Gata* Banyas already described, do not intermarry. The Súds forbid marriage in all four *góts*, and here again show how much less their tribal customs have been affected by their religion than have those of the Banyas and Khatris. They are of good physique, and are an intelligent and enterprising caste with great power of combination and self-restraint; and they have lately made what appears to be a really successful effort to reduce their marriage expenses by general agreement. The extensive sugar trade of Lúdhiána, and generally the agricultural money-lending of the richest part of that district, are almost entirely in their hands. They are proverbially acute and prosperous men of business, and there is a saying: "If a Súd is "across the river, leave your bundle on this side." The husbandman of the villages is a mere child in their hands.

538. The Bhabra (Caste No. 88).—The Bhábras appear to be a purely Panjáb caste, and have their head-quarters in the towns of Hushyárpur and Siálkot. They occupy very much the same territorial position as do the Súds, except that they do not penetrate so far into the hills, and extend as far west as Ráwalpindi instead of stopping short at Amritsar. Indeed there seems to be some doubt whether the word **Bhábra** is not as much a [P. 295] religious as a caste term, and whether it signifies anything more than a Súd, or perhaps a Banya also, of the Jain religion. No Súds have returned themselves as Jains; and though some 11 per cent. of the Bhábras have returned themselves as Hindus, yet, as already explained in Part IV of the Chapter on Religion, they belong almost exclusively to the Swetámbara or more lax sect of the Jains, and consider themselves Hindus first and Jains afterwards. A precisely similar difficulty with regard to the significance of the term Oswál is discussed in section 259. As a fact I believe that *all* Bhábras are Jains. Some of them are said to be Oswáls; but whether this means that they are Oswál Banyas by caste or Swetámbara Jains by religion I cannot say. They are all traders. Further information regarding this caste is greatly needed. I have only come across two facts which seem to throw light on their origin. The Bhábras of Hushyárpur make annual pilgrimages to a village called Fattahpur in the hills, some 20 miles from Hushyárpur, where there are remains of a very ancient and extensive town, and there worship at an ancestral shrine. The Bhábras of Jálandhar attribute their name to their refusal to wear the *janeo* or sacred thread at the solicitation of one Bír Swámi, who thereupon said that their faith (*bhú*) was great. This would separate them from the Banyas. On the other hand many of the Gurdáspur Bhábras are said to be Oswál and Kandelwál Banyas; and Mr. Wilson says that in Sirsa the Sikh immigrants from Patiála call the Oswál Banyas Bhábra. The Bhábras have a curious rule against one man marrying two wives under any circumstances whatever.

539. The Khatri (Caste No. 16).—The Khatri occupies a very different position among the people of the Panjáb from that of the castes which we have just discussed. Superior to them in physique, in manliness, and in energy, he is not, like them, a mere shop-keeper. He claims, indeed, to be a direct representative of the Kshatriya of Manu, but the validity of the claim is as doubtful as are most other matters connected with the four-fold caste system. The following extract from Sir George Campbell's *Ethnology of India* describes the position of the Khatri so admirably that I shall not venture to spoil it by condensation. The Aroras whom he classes with the Khatris I shall describe presently :—

"Trade is their main occupation; but in fact they have broader and more distinguishing "features. Besides monopolising the trade of the Panjab and the greater part of Afghanistan, "and doing a good deal beyond those limits, they are in the Panjab the chief civil administrators, "and have almost all literate work in their hands. So far as the Sikhs have a priesthood, they "are, moreover, the priests or gurus of the Sikhs. Both Nanak and Govind were, and the "Sodis and Bedis of the present day are, Khatris. Thus then they are in fact in the Panjab, "so far as a more energetic race will permit them, all that Mahratta Brahmins are in the Mahratta "country, besides engrossing the trade which the Mahratta Brahmins have not. They are "not usually military in their character, but are quite capable of using the sword when necessary. "Diwan Sáwan Mal, Governor of Multan, and his notorious successor Múlraj, and very many "of Ranjit Singh's chief functionaries, were Khatris. Even under Mahomedan rulers in the "west, they have risen to high administrative posts. There is a record of a Khatri Dewan of "Badakshan or Kunduz; and, I believe, of a Khatri Governor of Peshawar under the Afghans. "The Emperor Akbar's famous minister, Todur Mal, was a Khatri; and a relative of that man "of undoubted energy, the great Commissariat Contractor of Agra, Joti Parshad, lately in"formed me that he also is a Khatri. Altogether there can be no doubt that these Khatris are "one of the most acute, energetic, and remarkable races in India, though in fact, except locally "in the Panjáb, they are not much known to Europeans. The Khatris are staunch Hindus; "and it is somewhat singular that, while giving a religion and priests to the Sikhs, they them"selves are comparatively seldom Sikhs. The Khatris are a very fine, fair, handsome race. "And, as may be gathered from what I have already said, they are very generally educated.

"There is a large subordinate class of Khatris, somewhat lower, but of equal mercantile "energy, called Rors, or Roras. The proper Khatris of higher grade will often deny all con"nexion with them, or at least only admit that they have some sort of bastard kindred with "Khatris; but I think there can be no doubt that they are ethnologically the same, and they "are certainly mixed up with Khatris in their avocations. I shall treat the whole kindred as "generically Khatris.

"Speaking of the Khatris then thus broadly, they have, as I have said, the whole trade of "the Panjab and of most of Afghanistan. No village can get on without the Khatri who keeps "the accounts, does the banking business and buys and sells the grain. They seem, too, to get "on with the people better than most traders and usurers of this kind. In Afghanistan, among "a rough and alien people, the Khatris are as a rule confined to the position of humble dealers, "shop-keepers, and money-lenders; but in that capacity the Pathans seem to look at them as a "kind of valuable animal; and a Pathan will steal another man's Khatri, not only for the sake "of ransom, as is frequently done on the Peshawar and Hazara frontier, but also as he might "steal a milchcow, or as Jews might, I dare say, be carried off in the middle ages with a view to "render them profitable.

"I do not know the exact limits of Khatri occupation to the west, but certainly in all "Eastern Afghanistan they seem to be just as much a part of the established community as they "are in the Panjáb. They find their way far into Central Asia, but the further they get the "more depressed and humiliating is their position. In Turkistan, Vambery speaks of them with "great contempt, as yellow-faced Hindus of a cowardly and sneaking character. Under Tur"coman rule they could hardly be otherwise. They are the only Hindus known in Central

"Asia. In the Panjáb they are so numerous that they cannot all be rich and mercantile; and "many of them hold land, cultivate, take service, and follow various avocations.

"The Khatris are altogether excluded from Brahmin Kashmir. In the hills however the "'Kakkas,' on the east bank of the Jahlam, are said to have been originally Khatris (they are "a curiously handsome race), and in the interior of the Kangra hills there is an interesting "race of fine partiarchal-looking shepherds called Gaddis, most of whom are Khatris. Khatri "traders are numerous in Dehli; are found in Agra, Lucknow, and Patna; and are well known "in the Bara Bazaar of Calcutta, though there they are principally connected with Panjab "firms.

"The Khatris do not seem, as a rule, to reach the western coast: in the Bombay market I "cannot find that they have any considerable place. In Sindh, however, I find in Captain "Burton's book an account of a race of pretended Kshatriyas who are really Banias of the "Nanak-Shahi (Sikh) faith and who trade, and have a large share of public offices. These are "evidently Khatris. Ludhiana is a large and thriving town of mercantile Khatris, with a "numerous colony of Kashmiri shawl-weavers."

Within the Panjáb the distribution of the Khatri element is very well marked. It hardly appears east of Lúdhiána, the eastern boundary of the Sikh religion, nor does it penetrate into the eastern hills. It is strongest in the central districts where Sikhism is most prevalent, and in the Ráwalpindi division and Hazára, and occupies an important position in the western Hill States. Although the Khatris are said to trace their origin to Multán, they are far less prominent in the southern districts of the Western Plains, and least of all on the actual frontier; but this would be explained if the Aroras be considered a branch of the Khatris.

As Sir George Campbell remarked, it is curious that, intimately connected as the Khatris always have been and still are with the Sikh religion, only 9 per cent. of them should belong to it. Nor do I understand why the proportion of Sikhs should double and treble in the Jahlam and Ráwalpindi districts. Some 2,000 are Musalmán, chiefly in Multán and Jhang where they are commonly known as Khojahs; and these men are said to belong chiefly to the Kapúr section. The rest are Hindus.

540. **The divisions of the Khatri Caste.** - The question of the sub-divisions of the Khatris is exceedingly complicated. Within recent times there has sprung up a system of social gradua- [P. 296]
tion in accordance with which certain Khatri tribes refuse to intermarry with any save a certain specified number of their fellow tribes, and the distinctions thus created have been formulated in a set of names such as *Dhaighar*, "he who only marries into two and a half houses;" *Chárzati*, "he who marries into four tribes;" *Chhezáti*, "he who marries into six tribes;" and so on. This purely artificial and social classification has obscured the original tribal divisions of the caste; for Khatris of the same tribe may be in one part of the Province Chárzátis, and in another Bárázátis and so forth. It has also terribly confused the entries in the schedules, assisted by an unfortunate mistake in the sample schedules issued with the instructions to enumerators, in which, owing to my own ignorance of the matter, one of the *pancháyati* or artificial divisions was shown as a tribe. The distribution of the main sections is shown in Abstract No. 92 below*. It will be noticed that *P. 249
they include more than three-quarters of the total Khatris of the Province, but that the percentage unclassified is very large in some districts. In others again the number classified is larger than the total Khatri population. This is due to the same figures being in some cases repeated twice over. Thus in Gújránwála 963 Khatris have returned themselves as Kapúr Chárzáti, and so appear under both heads; and so in other cases also.

The headings of the Abstract include three different kinds of divisions, first the four real tribal sections, then the four most important of the artificial divisions alluded to above, and finally six of the most important clans. The origin of the division into the four sections called Bunjáhi, Sarín, Báhri, and Khokhrán, is said to be that Ala-ul-dín Khilji attempted to impose widow-marriage upon the Khatris. The Western Khatris resolved to resist the innovation, and sent a deputation of 52 (*báwan*) of their members to represent their case at court; but the Eastern Khatris were afraid to sign the memorial. They were therefore called followers of *Shara Ayín* or the Mahomedan customs—hence Sarín—while memorialists were called *Báwanjai* from the number of the deputation or of the clans respectively represented by the members of the deputation; hence Banjáhí. The Khokhrán section is said to consist of the descendants of certain Khatris who joined the Khokhars in rebellion, and with whom the other Khatri families were afraid to intermarry; and the Báhri section, of the lineage of Mahr Chand, Khan Chand, and

Abstract No. 92, showign the Divisions of the Khatris.

	Khatris.													
	1	2	3	4	5	6	7	8	9	10	11	12	13	14
	Bunjáhi.	Sarín.	Báhri.	Khokrán.	Dhaighar.	Chárzáti.	Panjzáti.	Chhezáti.	Sodhi.	Bedi.	Kapúr.	Khanno.	Marhotra.	Seth.
Ambála	6,604	1,046	355	...	...	81	...	...	...	103	91	97	1	40
Lúdhiána	10,103	1,825	766	45	139	503	74	..	124	48	370	223	134	60
Jalandhar	720	3,137	1,732	...	...	776	301	...	2,624	1,978	329	3	1,323	...
Hushyárpur	5,645	6,665	564	5	18	58	...	5	8	186	198	160	26	...
Kangra	483	1,059	1,232	...	50	595	...	...	2	5	623	48	...	6
Amritsar	12,097	10,516	106	...	140	3,859	...	...	114	328	1,615	1,725	1,171	247
Gurdaspur	583	503	..	240	...	...	...	...	117	1,302	411	401	100	42
Sialkot	7,880	3,038	4,137	4,307	...	36	3	...	203	563	299	72	256	...
Lahore	9,126	1,271	3,928	321	449	2,038	134	47	396	294	2,807	2,547	3,466	474
Gujranwala	11,179	226	4,413	1,872	135	1,962	5	...	29	652	1,164	296	1,010	81
Firozpur	3,779	419	474	..	16	48	236	...	186	34	131	122	135	18
Rawalpindi	10,195	15	3,868	7,596	70	10	56	...	77	126	1,429	407	790	8
Jahlam	13,362	182	3,596	16,578	606	430	...	141	89	166	776	348	814	...
Gujrat	5,222	2,742	1,668	4,189	...	1,174	..	...	35	122	752	269	475	...
Shahpur ... ... — ...	6,009	3	444	2,810	506	1,269	20	13	9	18	903	458	1,726	...
Multan	476	5	320	1	44	163	84	25	2	...	936	929	1,465	4
Jhang	6,634	6	1,594	16	250	2,322	740	...	1	2	1,162	469	1,614	21
Peshawar	2,778	174	1,217	...	312	1,083	...	...	20	317	743	62	603	...
Hazara	3,271	16	170	2,627	...	...	...	...	...	138	391	39	254	...
British Territory	118,985	32,893	33,053	41,080	2,950	16,926	1,609	230	4,082	6,671	15.951	9,121	16,030	1,193
Native States	10,405	3,935	698	..	55	357	4	...	402	133	1,542	895	1,667	239
Province	127,390	36,828	33,751	41,080	3,005	17,283	1,613	230	4,484	6,804	17,493	10,016	17,697	1,432

Kapúr Chand, three Khatris who went to Dehli in attendance upon one of Akbar's Rajpút wives, and who, thus separated from the rest of the caste, married only within each other's families. But these are fables, for the same division into Báhri and Bunjáhi appears among the Bráhmans of the Western Plains. The number of clans is enormous. The most important in point of social rank are the Marhotra or Mahra, the Khanna, the Kapúr, and the Seth, the first three of which are said to be called after the names of the three men just mentioned, while Seth is a term now used for any rich banker. These four clans belong to the Báhri section of the caste, and constitute the Dhaighar and Chárzáti divisions which stand highest of all in the social scale. The origin of the term Dhaighar lies in the fact that the families of that division exclude not only the father's clan, but also such families of the mother's clan as are closely connected with her; and thus reduce the clans available for intermarriage to two and a half. I should say that each division will take wives from the one below it, though it will not give its daughters to it in marriage. The Bedi and Sodhi clans belong to the Bunjáhi tribe, and owe most of their influence and importance to the fact that Bába Nának belonged to the former and Guru Rám Dás and Guru Hargovind to the latter. They are commonly said to be the descendants of these men, but this appears to be a mistake, the two clans dating from long before Bába Nának. The Sodhis played an important part during the Sikh rule. They claim descent from Sodhi Rai, son of Kál Rai King of Lahore, and the Bedis from Kálpat Rai, brother of Kál Rai and King of Kasúr, who being deprived of his kingdom by his nephew, studied the Vedas at Benares and was known as Vedi. The modern head-quarters of the Bedis is at Dera Nának in Gurdáspur where Bába Nának settled and died, and of the Sodhis at Anandpur in Hushyárpur, which is also the great centre of the Nihang devotees. [P. 297]

541. The Khakha (Caste No. 179).—Khakha is said to be a not uncommon epithet to apply to any petty Khatri trader. But the people to whom our figures refer are now sufficiently distinct, though their Khatri origin is, I believe, undoubted. They are in fact converted Khatris, and are found in greatest numbers in the Kashmir hills lying along the left bank of the Jahlam; whence a few have made their way into Hazára and Ráwalpindi. Sir George Campbell calls them "a curiously handsome people."

542. The Bhatia (Caste No. 69).—The Bhátias are a class of Rájpúts, originally coming from Bhatner, Jaisalmer, and the Rájpútána desert, who have taken to commercial pursuits. The name would seem to show that they were Bhátis (called Bhatti in the Panjáb); but be that as it may, their Rájpút origin appears to be unquestioned. They are numerous in Sindh and Gújarát where they appear to form the leading mercantile element, and to hold the place which the Aroras occupy higher up the Indus. They have spread into the Panjáb along the lower valleys of the Indus and Satluj, and up the whole length of the Chenáb as high as its debouchure into the plains, being indeed most numerous in Siálkot and Gújrát. In this Province however they occupy an inferior position, both in a social and in a mercantile sense. They stand distinctly below the Khatri and perhaps below the Arora, and are for the most part engaged in petty shop-keeping, though the Bhátias of Derah Ismáil Khán are described as belonging to a "widely spread and enterprising mercantile community." They are often supposed to be Khatris, and in Jahlam they are said to follow the Khatri divisions of Báhri, Bunjáhi, Dhaighar, Chárzáti, &c. They are very strict Hindus; far more so than the other trading classes of the Western Panjáb; and eschew meat and liquor. They do not practise widow-marriage.

543. The Arora (Caste No. 10).—The Arora, or Rora as he is often called, is the trader *par excellence* of the Jatki-speaking or south-western portion of Panjáb, that is to say of the lower valleys of our five rivers; while higher up their courses he shares that position with the Khatri. East of the upper Satluj he is only found in the immediate neighbourhood of the river. More than half the Aroras of the Panjáb dwell in the Multán and Deraját divisions. Like the Khatri, and unlike the Banya, he is no mere trader; but his social position is far inferior to theirs, partly no doubt because he is looked down upon simply as being a Hindu in the portions of the Province which are his special habitat. He is commonly known as a Kirár, a word almost synonymous with coward, and even more contemptuous than is the name Banya in the east of the Province. The word Kirár, indeed, appears to be applied to all the Western or Panjábi traders, as distinct from the Banyas of Hindústán, and is so used even in the Kángra Hills. But the Arora is the person to whom the term is most commonly applied, and Khatris repudiate the name altogether as derogatory. The Arora is active and enterprising, industrious and thrifty. "When an Arora girds up his loins, he makes it only two miles (from Jhang) to Lahore." He will turn his hand to any work, he makes a most admirable cultivator, and a large proportion of the Aroras of the lower Chenáb are purely agricultural in their avocations. He is found throughout Afghánistán and even Túrkistán, and is the Hindu trader of those countries; while in the Western Panjáb he will sew clothes, weave matting and baskets, make vessels of brass and copper, and do goldsmith's work. But he is a terrible coward, and is so branded in the proverbs of the countryside: "The thieves were four "and we eighty-four; the thieves came on and we ran away. Damn the thieves! "Well done us!" And again: "To meet a Ráthi armed with a hoe makes a "company of nine Kirárs feel alone." Yet the peasant has a wholesome dread of the Kirár when in his proper place. "Vex not the Jat in his jungle, or the "Kirár at his shop, or the boatman at his ferry; for if you do they will break "your head." Again: "Trust not a crow, a dog, or a Kirár, even when asleep." So again: "You can't make a friend of a Kirár any more than a *Satti* of a "prostitute." The Arora is of inferior physique, and his character is thus summed up by Mr. Thorburn: "A cowardly, secretive, acquisitive race, very "necessary and useful it may be in their places, but possessed of few manly "qualities, and both despised and envied by the great Musalmán tribes of Bannu." A few of the Aroras are returned as Musalmán, some 7 per cent. as Sikh, and the rest as Hindu. But many of the so-called Hindus, especially on the lower Chanáb and Satluj, are really Munna (shaven) Sikhs, or followers of Bába Nának, while the Hindu Aroras of the Indus worship the river. Further details will be found in sections 240 and 264 of Chapter IV on the Religions of the people.

544. **Origin and divisions of the Aroras.**—The Aroras claim to be of Khatri origin, and it will presently be seen that they follow some of the Khatri sub-divisions.[1] The Khatris however reject the claim. Sir George Campbell (see section 539) is of opinion that the two belong to the same ethnic stock. They say that they became outcasts from the Kshatriya stock during the persecution of that people by Paras Rám, to avoid which they denied their caste and described it as *Aur* or another, hence their name. Some of them fled northwards and some southwards, and hence the names of the two great sections of the caste, Uttarádhi and Dakhana. But it has been suggested with greater probability that, as the Multán and Lahore Khatris are Khatris of Multán and Lahore, so the Aroras are Khatris of Aror the ancient capital of Sindh, now represented by the modern Rori. The number of clans is enormous, and many of them are found in both sections. The Uttarádhi and Dakhana do not intermarry, the section being endogamous and the clan, as usual, exogamous. All Aroras are said to be of the Kásib *gotra*. The

[1] The detailed figures, when published, will show how far the identity of divisions extends.

women of the northern or Uttarádhi section wear red ivory bracelets and the section is divided into two sub-sections called Báhri and Bunjáhi (see Khatri divisions, section 540). The women of the southern or Dakhana section wear white ivory bracelets, and the section is divided into two sub-sections, the Dahra and the Dakhanadháin ; but the Dahra sub-section is so important that it is often counted as a third section, and the term Dakhana applied to the Dakhanadháins alone. So it is said that in some places the Dahra women alone wear white, and the Dakhana women spotted bracelets of both colours. The Báhri and the Dakhanadháin claim social superiority, and will take wives from, but not give daughters to, the other sub-section of their respective sections. The figures are given in Abstract No. 93 on the next page.* It will be noticed that the Dakhanas are far strongest in the southern and south-western districts. *Below.

Abstract No. 93, showing the Divisions of the Aroras. [P. 298]

	Aroras.				Aroras.		
	1	2	3		1	2	3
	Uttarádhi.	Dakhana.	Dahra.		Uttarádhi.	Dakhana.	Dahra.
Sirsa	1,522	3,875	120	Muzaffargarh ...	909	20,166	2,241
Amritsar	5,716	142	8	D. I. Khán ...	10,434	3,165	8
Sialkot	7,604	...	5,787	D. G. Khán ...	10,611	22,587	1,016
				Bannu	11,275	10,580	57
Lahore	12,141	4,422	4,983				
Gujránwála	21,872	5	6,753	Peshávar	4,152	33	2,818
Firozpur	5,079	3,432	46	Hazára	1,787	12	207
				Kohát	3,763	212	27
Rawalpindi	2,966	72	4,836				
Jahlam	5,335	15	5,608				
Gújrát	9,[illegible]98	63	11,771	Baháwalpur ...	4,307	44,075	6,703
Shahpur	20,193	5,348	9,482				
Multán	8,793	34,389	6,455	British Territory	166,036	123,940	102,241
Jhang	18,004	2,185	23,541	Native States ...	6,397	45,507	6,707
Montgomery ...	3,108	13,101	16,283	Province ...	172,433	169,447	108,948

545. The Khojah and Paracha (Castes Nos. 44 and 104).—The word Khojah is really nothing more than our old friend the Khwájah of the *Arabian Nights*, and means simply a man of wealth and respectability. In the Panjáb it is used in three different senses : for a eunuch, for a scavenger converted to Islám, and for a Mahomedan trader.[1] It is in the last sense that it is used in our tables. There does not appear to be any true *caste* of Khojahs, any Hindu trader converted to Mahomedanism being known by that name. Thus the Khojahs of Sháhpur are almost entirely Khatris, and a Khatri now becoming a Musalmán in that district would be called a Khojah. The Khojahs of Jhang, on the other hand, are said to be converted Aroras ; while some at least of the Lahore Khojahs claim Bhátia origin, and one section of the Ambála

[1] The Khojahs of Bombay are well known for their wealth and commercial enterprise.

Khojahs are Káyaths. Now the Paráchas also are Mahomedan traders; and there is at least a very definite section of them with head-quarters at Mukhad on the Indus in Ráwalpindi who are a true caste, being converted Khatris, and marrying only among themselves. But unfortunately the word Parácha is also used in the central districts for any petty Mahomedan trader. The fact seems to be that in the Ráwalpindi and Peshâwar divisions, where Paráchas are a recognised and wealthy caste, Khojah is used for miscellaneous Mahomedan traders, chiefly hawkers and pedlars, or at least petty traders; while in the eastern districts and in the Deráját, where Khojahs are commercially important, Parácha is used for the Mahomedan pedlar. Thus in our tables the divisional offices have in many cases included Parácha under Khojah and Khojah under Parácha, and the figures cannot safely be taken separately.

These Mahomedan traders, whether called Khojah or Parácha, are found all along the northern portion of the Province under the hills from Amritsar to Peshâwar, and have spread southwards into the central and eastern districts of the Western Plains, but have not entered the Deraját or Muzaffargarh in any numbers; though to the figures of Abstract No. 91 must be added those *P. 106-107. of Abstract No. 72 (page 224*) for these last districts. Their eastern boundary is the Satluj valley, their western the Jahlam-Chanáb, and they are found throughout the whole of the Salt-range Tract. Probably it is hardly correct to say of them that they have "spread" or "entered;" for they apparently include many distinct classes who will have sprung from different centres of conversion. They appear to be most numerous in Lahore. A very interesting account of a recent development of trade by the Khojahs of Gújrát and Siálkot is given in Panjáb Government Home Proceedings No. 10 of March 1879. It appears that these men buy cotton piece-goods in Dehli and hawk them about the villages of their own districts, selling on credit till harvest time, and the business has now assumed very large proportions. The Khojahs of the Jhang district are thus described by Mr. Monckton: "They do not cultivate "with their own hands, but own a great many wells and carry on trade to a "considerable extent. They are supposed to have been converted from "Hinduism. They do not practise cattle-stealing, but are a litigious race, "and addicted to fraud and forgery in the prosecution of their claims."

The Paráchas of the Salt-range Tract require a word of separate notice. Their head-quarters are at Mukhad in Pindi, and there are also large colonies at Attak and Peshâwar, whence they carry on an extensive trade with the cities of Central Asia, chiefly in cloth, silk, indigo, and tea. They say that their place of origin is the village of Dangot in the Bannu district, and that they moved to Mukhad in Sháhjahán's time; but another account is that they were Khatris of Lahore, deported by Zamán Sháh. They have seven clans and give their daughters only to Paráchas, though they will occasionally take wives of foreign origin. They still retain the Hindu title of Rája. They will not marry with Khojahs and have dropped the Hindu ceremonial at their weddings, which they say the Khojahs of those parts still retain. They account for their name by deriving it from *párcha* "cloth" one of the principal staples of their trade. Some of the Paráchas of Ambála seem to have returned themselves as Parácha Khel, and to have been not unnaturally classed as Patháns by the tabulators. I cannot give separate figures for these.

CARRIER AND PEDLAR CASTES.

[P. 299] **546. Carriers, Cattle-merchants, Pedlars, &c.**—I have said that the commerce of the Panjáb was in the hands of the group just discussed, with the exception of the trade in meat, liquor, and vegetables, the traffic in cattle, the carrying trade, and petty pedling and hawking. The sellers of meat and liquor will be discussed under the head of miscellaneous artisans; and the group which I am now about to describe consists of the traders in cattle, the carriers, and the pedlars and hucksters of the Province. I have divided it into three sections, though I shall presently show that the first two overlap considerably, and that the third is incomplete. The first section includes the Banjáras, the Labánas, the Rahbáris, and the Untwáls; and these castes include most of the professional carriers and cattle-dealers, and some of the pedlars of the Panjáb. The second class consists of the Maniárs, the Bhátras, and the Kangars, and includes the rest of the pedlars of the Province save only such as belong to the Khoja and Parácha castes just discussed. The third class includes the Kunjras and the Tambolis, both Greengrocers.

But it must be understood that, though there are no castes in the Panjáb besides those above mentioned whose hereditary occupation it is to trade in cattle and carry merchandise, yet an immense deal of traffic in cattle goes on quietly among the villagers without the intervention of any outsider; while in the early months of the hot weather, when the spring harvest has been cut, and before the early rains of autumn have softened the ground sufficiently for ploughing to be possible, the plough oxen of the unirrigated Eastern Plains find employment in carrying the produce of their villages to the line of rail or to the great city marts, and in bringing back salt and other products not indigenous to the tract.

547. **The Banjara (Caste No. 94).**—This and the following or Labána caste are generally said to be identical, being called Banjára in the eastern districts and Labána in the whole of the Panjáb proper. But Banjára, derived from *banij* "a trader" or perhaps from *banji* "a pedlar's pack," is used in the west of the Panjáb as a generic term for "pedlar," and I have therefore kept the figures distinct. Indeed it is to be feared that in that part of the Province many persons have been shown as Banjára in consequence of their occupation only.

The Banjáras of the eastern districts are a well-marked class, of whom a long and very complete description will be found in Elliott's *Races of the N. W. P.*, Vol. I, pages 52-56. They are the great travelling traders and carriers of Central India, the Deccan and Rájpútána; and under the Afghán and Mughal Empires were the commissariat of the imperial forces. There is a simile applied to a dying person; "The Banjára goes into the jungle with "his stick in his hand. He is ready for the journey, and there is no body "with him." From Sir H. Elliott's description they seem to be a very composite class, including sections of various origin. But the original Banjára caste is said to have its habitat in the sub-montane tract from Gorakhpur to Hardwár. The Banjáras of the North-West Provinces come annually into the Jamna districts and Eastern States in the cold weather with letters of credit on the local merchants, and buy up large numbers of cattle which they take back again for sale as the summer approaches; and it is principally these men and the Banjára carriers from Rájputána to whom our figures for Hindu Banjáras refer. The Musalmán Banjáras are probably almost all pedlars. The headmen of the Banjára parties are called *Naik* (Sanskrit Náyaka "chief") and Banjáras in general are not uncommonly known by this name. The Railway is fast destroying the carrying trade of these people except in the mountain tracts. The word Banjára is apparently sometimes used for an oculist, so at least Mr. Baden-Powell states. (See further under Mahtam, section 495 *supra.*)

548. The Labana (Caste No. 52).—These men are generally associated with the caste just discussed. With the exception of Muzaffargarh and Baháwalpur, which will be discussed presently, they are almost wholly confined to the hill and sub-montane districts. They are the carriers and hawkers of the hills, and are merely the Panjábi representatives of that class of Banjáras already alluded to who inhabit the sub-montane tracts east of the Ganges. The Labánas of Gújrát are thus described by Captain Mackenzie :—

"The Labanas are also a peculiar people. Their status amongst Sikhs is much the same as "that of the Mahtams. They correspond to the Banjáras of Hindustan, carrying on an extensive "trade by means of large herds of laden bullocks. Latterly they have taken to agriculture, but "as an additional means of livelihood, not as a substitute for trade. As a section of the com-"munity they deserve every consideration and encouragement. They are generally fine substan-"tially built people. They also possess much spirit. In anarchical times when the freaks or "feuds of petty Governors would drive the Jats or Gujars to seek a temporary abiding place away "from their ancestral village, the Labánas would stand their ground, and perhaps improve the "opportunity by extending their grasp over the best lands in the village, in which their shorter-"sighted and less provident lords of the Manor had, in some former period, permitted them to "take up their abode for purposes of commerce. Several cases of this nature came to light during "settlement, and in most of them the strength and spirit of progress were as apparent in the "Labánas as were the opposite qualities conspicuous in their Gujar opponents Their principal "village is Tanda (which means a large caravan of laden bullocks) and is an instance of what I "have above alluded to. Allowed to reside by the Gujar proprietors of Mota, they got possession "of the soil, built a kasba, and in every point of importance swamped the original proprietors. "They have been recognized as proprietors, but feudatory to their former landlords the Gujars of "Mota, paying to them annually in recognition thereof, a sum equal to one-tenth of the Govern-"ment demand."

There is a curious colony of Labánas on the lower Indus who are said to have settled there under the Sikh rule, and who are almost all Munna Sikhs or followers of Bába Nának, though many of them are returned in the Baháwalpur tables as Hindus. These men have almost entirely given up traffic and trade, and settled on the banks of the river where they lead a sort of semi-savage life, hunting and making ropes and grass mats for sale. They hardly
P. 256-57. cultivate at all. Their numbers are much under-stated in Abstract No. 94, as
†P. 106-107. Abstract No. 72 (page 224†) shows that 4,317 of the Baháwalpur Labánas were returned as Jats. The Labánas of Jhang are said to have come from Jaipur and Jodhpur, and to be the same as the Mahtams of Montgomery. On the whole the Labánas appear to be by origin closely allied with, if not actually belonging to, the vagrant and probably aboriginal tribes whom we shall discuss in the next part of this chapter ; and it may be that at least some sections of the Labánas are of the same stock as they. (See further under Mahtam, section 495 *supra.*) About 30 per cent. of the Labánas are returned as Sikhs and almost all the rest as Hindus, there being only some 1,500 Musalmáns among them. Little is known of the sub-divisions of the caste. The largest seems to be the Ajráwat with 4,400 souls, chiefly in Gújrát and Lahore ; the Dátla with 4,173 souls, chiefly in Lahore ; the Maliána with 2,537 and the Bhagiána with 2,015 persons, both in the Amritsar and Lahore divisions ; and the Gáhri with 1,925 persons along the whole foot of the hills. But the greater part of the caste have returned no large divisions.

[P. 301] **549. The Rahbari (Caste No. 122).**—This is a camel-breeding caste found only in the eastern and south-eastern districts of the Panjáb and in the adjoining Native States. In the extensive jungles of these tracts they pasture large herds of camels, while they also carry merchandise from place to place

Abstract No. 94, showing Castes of Carriers, Pedlars, &c.

	CARRIERS AND HAWKERS.																					
	FIGURES.									PROPORTION PER 1,000 OF TOTAL POPULATION.												
	94	52	122	144	47	174	180	114	165	94	52	122	144		47	174	180		114	165		
	Banjára.	Labána.	Rahbári.	Untwál.	Maniár.	Bhátra.	Kangar.	Kunjra.	Tamboli.	Banjára.	Labána.	Rahbári.	Untwál.	TOTAL.	Maniár.	Bhátra.	Kangar.	TOTAL.	Kunjra.	Tamboli.	TOTAL.	GRAND TOTAL
Dehli ...	1,854	44	308	7	742	...	...	459	120	3	...	...	...	3	1	...	...	1	1	...	1	5
Gurgaon ...	763	...	46	...	1,102	...	10	1,150	49	1	...	...	...	1	2	...	...	2	2	...	2	5
Karnál ...	617	5	1,125	...	789	...	...	426	13	1	...	2	...	3	1	...	...	1	1	...	1	5
Hissar ...	272	54	643	...	1,231	...	...	501	...	...	...	1	...	1	2	...	...	2	1	...	1	4
Rohtak ...	102	...	509	...	957	...	...	557	...	...	...	1	...	1	2	...	...	2	1	...	1	4
Sirsa ...	...	9	51	...	235	...	...	39	...	...	...	...	...	...	1	...	...	1	...	...	...	1
Ambála ...	1,909	1,310	96	...	797	40	...	283	136	2	1	...	...	3	1	...	...	1	...	...	...	4
Lúdhiána ...	942	923	45	...	94	146	...	82	14	2	1	...	...	3	...	...	...	...	...	...	.	3
Jálandhar ...	...	1,204	...	29	2	...	...	94	26	...	2	...	...	2	...	...	...	...	...	...	...	2
Hushyárpur ...	2	3,736	...	...	178	...	...	52	...	...	4	...	...	4	...	...	...	...	...	...	...	4
Kángra ...	1	2,198	...	...	75	...	...	...	...	...	3	...	...	3	...	...	...	...	...	...	...	3
Amritsar ...	67	566	...	...	...	...	284	...	1	...	1	...	...	1	..	...	...	...	...	..	...	1
Gurdáspur ...	...	5,492	...	...	...	...	77	...	...	...	7	...	...	7	...	...	...	...	...	...	...	7
Siálkot ...	267	6,584	...	...	...	...	278	...	17	...	7	...	...	7	...	...	...	...	...	...	...	7
Lahore ...	162	10,116	...	...	1	95	...	11	36	...	11	...	...	11	...	...	...	...	...	...	...	11
Gujránwála ...	74	356	...	...	...	59	...	58	2	...	...	...	...	...	...	...	...	...	...	...	...	...
Firozpur ...	11	138	...	...	6	...	...	191	29	...	...	...	...	...	...	...	...	.	...	...	...	

Ráwalpindi ...	69	191	...	...	...	29	...	1	505	...	...	...	...	...	...	...	...	...	...	1	1	1
Jahlam ...	...	74	...	...	...	45	...	...	10	...	...	...	...	...	...	...	...	...	...	...	...	...
Gújrát ...	30	5,203	...	...	...	...	...	47	...	...	8	...	...	8	...	...	...	...	...	...	...	8
Multán ...	457	307	...	794	...	...	...	1	51	1	1	...	1	3	...	...	...	...	...	...	...	3
Montgomery ...	385	80	...	1	...	...	...	...	...	1	...	...	...	1	...	...	...	...	...	...	.	1
Muzaffargarh ...	33	2,315	...	45	...	...	...	...	...	...	7	...	...	7	...	...	...	...	...	...	...	7
Derah Ismail Khán	...	541	...	54	...	...	...	...	1	...	1	...	...	1	...	...	...	...	...	...	...	1
Derah Ghazi Khán	2	82	...	176	...	...	...	...	2	...	...	...	...	...	...	...	...	...	...	...	...	...
Bannu ...	...	62	...	125	...	...	...	...	...	...	...	...	...	...	...	...	...	...	...	...	...	...
Pesháwar ...	158	64	...	354	...	...	...	16	32	...	...	...	1	1	...	...	...	...	...	...	...	1
Hazara ...	...	446	...	19	...	...	...	...	...	...	1	...	...	1	...	...	...	...	...	...	...	1
Kohàt ...	...	158	...	425	...	...	...	...	6	...	1	...	2	3	...	...	...	...	...	...	...	3
British Territory	8,216	42,495	2,825	2,033	6,209	421	649	4,019	1,114	...	2	...	...	2	...	...	...	...	...	...	...	...
Patiála ...	1,101	1,156	485	13	821	287	4	656	7	1	1	...	...	2	1	...	...	1	...	...	...	3
Nábha ...	15	...	230	...	190	4	...	46	...	...	...	1	...	1	1	...	...	1	...	...	...	2
Kapurthala ...	...	1,766	...	44	...	6	...	8	5	...	7	...	...	7	...	...	...	...	...	...	...	7
Jind ...	80	...	335	...	244	...	...	166	5	...	...	1	...	1	1	...	...	1	1	...	1	3
Total Eastern Plains.	2,040	2,922	1,056	62	1,350	369	4	981	17	1	1	...	...	2	1	...	...	1	...	...	...	3
Baháwalpur ...	...	1,730	...	...	...	...	...	...	...	...	...	...	...	...	...	...	...	...	...	...	...	...
Mandi ...	...	634	...	...	...	...	...	...	...	...	4	...	...	4	...	...	...	...	...	...	...	4
Náhan ...	955	11	...	...	...	...	...	1	13	9	...	...	...	9	...	...	...	...	...	...	...	9
Biláspur ...	4	304	...	...	...	...	...	...	...	...	4	...	...	4	...	...	...	...	...	...	...	4
Nálagarh ...	...	303	...	...	4	...	...	...	...	...	6	...	...	6	...	...	...	...	...	...	...	6
Total Hill States	961	1,342	...	...	15	129	...	1	15	1	2	...	...	3	...	...	...	...	...	...	...	3
British Territory	8,216	42,495	2,825	2,038	6,209	421	649	4,019	1,114	...	2	...	...	2	...	...	...	...	...	...	...	2
Native States ...	3,001	5,994	1,056	62	1,365	498	4	982	32	1	2	...	...	3	...	...	...	...	...	...	...	3
Province ...	11,217	48,489	3,881	2,100	7,574	919	653	5,001	1,146	...	2	...	...	2	...	...	...	...	...	...	...	2

for hire. Their proper home appears to be Bíkáner and the Rájpútána desert.

550. Untwal (Caste No. 144).—This is a purely occupational term and means nothing more than a camel-man. Under this head have been included Shutarbán and Sárbán, both words having the same meaning. But Malik has been classed as Biloch, as the title is chiefly confined to the Biloch camelman. Indeed many of the persons returned as Biloches in the Central Panjáb would probably have been more properly described as Untwál, since the term Biloch throughout the central districts is used of any Musalmán camelman. It will be noticed that the Untwáls are returned only from those parts of the Province where the real meaning of Biloch is properly understood. In those parts they are said to be all Jats ; but Jat means very little, or rather almost anything, on the Indus.

551. The Maniar (Caste No. 47).—Here again we meet with an occupational term, and with resulting confusion in the figures. The Maniár of the eastern districts is a man who works in glass and sells glass bangles, generally hawking them about the villages. But throughout the rest of the Panjáb Maniár is any pedlar, *maniári bechhna* being the common term for the occupation of carrying petty hardware about for sale. Thus we have Khojah, Parácha, Banjára, and Maniár, all used in different parts and some of them in the same part of the Province for a pedlar ; and the result is that the figures have probably been mixed up. The extraordinary number of Maniárs returned for the Jahlam and Ráwalpindi districts in Table VIII A is due to an unfortunate error, not detected till after the table was printed, by which Maliár was read Maniár. These people are really vegetable-growers, and have been classed in their proper place in the Abstracts of this chapter.

552. The Bhatra (Caste No. 174).—The Bhátra is also a pedlar ; but he belongs to a true caste. He claims Bráhman origin, and his claim would appear to be good, for he wears the sacred thread, applies the *tilak* or forehead mark, and receives offerings at eclipses in that capacity. He is probably a low class of Gújaráti or Dákaut Bráhman, and like them practises as an astrologer in a small way. The Bhátras of Gújrát are said to trace their origin to the south beyond Multán. The Bhátras hawk small hardware for sale, tell fortunes, and play on the native guitar, but do not beg for alms. It is their function to pierce the noses and ears of children to receive rings. Mr. Baden-Powell describes the instruments used at page 268 of his *Panjáb Manufactures*. The Ramaiya of the east of the Panjáb appears to correspond exactly with the Bhátra and to be the same person under a different name, Ramaiya being used in Dehli and Hissár, Bhátra in Lahore and Pindi, and both in the Ambála division ; and I directed that both sets of figures should be included under the head Bhátra. Unfortunately the order was not carried out. The number of Ramaiyas returned is shown in the margin. But in any case the figures are incomplete. The Bhátra is essentially a pedlar and has probably been returned by one of the names for pedlars just referred to more often than by his caste name. He is said to be called Mádho in Ráwalpindi, but this is probably due to some confusion of Bhátra with Bhát.

Dehli division ...	419
Hissár division ...	19
Ambála division ...	16
	454

553. The Kangar (Caste No. 180).—The Kangar is also a travelling hawker, but he confines his traffic to small articles of earthenware such as pipe-bowls, and especially to those earthen images in which native children delight. These he makes himself and hawks about for sale. He is returned in the tables from the Amritsar division only. But Baden-Powell gives at page 267 of *Panjáb Manufactures* a long account of an operation for a new nose said to be successfully performed by the Kangars of Kángra

554. The Kunjra (Caste No. 114).—Here again is a purely occupational term, and again confusion as the consequence. Kunjra is nothing more or less than the Hindústáni, as *Sabzi farosh* is the Persian for greengrocer. The big men generally use the latter term, the small costermongers the former. But in no case is it a caste. The Kunjra belongs as a rule to one of the castes of market gardeners which have been described under minor agricultural tribes. I do not know why Kunjra should have been returned under that name only in the east. It may be that in other parts of the Province it is more usual to call the seller of vegetables an Aráin or Bághbán as the case may be, and that the word Kunjra is little used. This probably is the true explanation, as the figures for Native States show the same peculiarity.

555. The Tamboli (Caste No. 165).—A Tamboli is a man who sells pân and betel-nut; but whether the sale of those commodities is confined to a real caste of that name I cannot say. It is probable that the term is only occupational. If Tamboli were a real caste we should have it returned from every district, as the word seems to be in use throughout the Province. Sherring, however, gives it as a separate caste in the neighbourhood of Benares. *Tambúli* is the Sanskrit name of the betel plant.

MISCELLANEOUS CASTES.

556. Miscellaneous Castes.—The castes which I have included in Abstract
P. 260-61 No. 95 on the next page are of a miscellaneous nature, and would not conveniently fall under any of the main divisions under which I have grouped my castes. I have divided them into two classes. The first, which includes Kashmíris, Dogras, Gúrkhas, and Pársis, are Indian castes who live on the borders of the Panjáb but are only present in the Province as immigrants; though indeed some of the Kashmíri colonies are now permanent and contain large numbers of people. The second, which includes Káyaths, Bishnois, Cháhzangs, and Kanchans are inhabitants of the Panjáb, though no one of them except the Káyath of the plains can be said to be a true caste.

[P. 302] **557. The Kashmiri and Dogra (Castes Nos. 26 and 182).**—The word Kashmíri is perhaps applicable to the members of any of the races of Kashmír; but it is commonly used in Kashmír itself to denote the people of the valley of Srínagar. Our figures however probably include some Chibhális, or the race who inhabit the Kashmír hills and the borders of Gújrát, Ráwalpindi, and Hazára. But they do not include either Dogras or the Paháris of Kishtwár and Badarwáh, as these last are Hindus, while our Kashmíris are Musalmáns. In any case the term is a geographical one, and probably includes many of what we should in the Panjáb call separate castes. The cultivating class who form the great mass of the Kashmíris proper are probably of Aryan descent, though perhaps with an intermixture of Khas blood, and possess marked characters.

Abstract No. 95, showing Miscellaneous Castes for Districts and States.

	MISCELLANEOUS CASTES.																		
	FIGURES.									PROPORTION PER 1,000 OF TOTAL POPULATION.									
	26	182	148	168	184	90	106	138	96	26	148	168		90	106	138	96		
	Kashmíri.	Dogra.	Gúrkha.	Bangáli.	Pársi.	Káyath.	Bishnoi.	Cháhzang.	Kanchan.	Kashmíri.	Gúrkha.	Bangáli.	TOTAL.	Káyath.	Bishnoi.	Cháhzang.	Kanchan.	TOTAL.	GRAND TOTAL.
Dehli	82	...	...	6	27	3,887	1	...	323	...	...	...	...	6	...	...	1	7	7
Gurgaon	...	...	...	...	...	664	...	...	238	...	...	...	...	1	...	...	...	1	1
Karnál	21	1	...	...	...	737	...	...	275	...	...	...	...	1	...	...	...	1	1
Hissar	...	...	...	...	...	404	8,118	...	122	...	...	...	...	1	16	..	...	17	17
Rohtak	...	...	...	...	...	673	7	...	210	...	...	...	...	1	...	...	...	1	1
Sirsa	...	...	...	...	...	304	417	...	5	...	..	...	...	1	2	...	...	3	3
Ambala	58	...	...	616	6	1,641	...	...	745	...	...	1	1	2	...	...	3	5	6
Ludhiána	2,492	...	...	10	...	112	...	...	202	4	...	...	4	...	...	...	...	...	4
Simla	205	...	12	...	...	130	...	...	27	5	...	...	5	3	...	...	1	4	9
Jalandhar	1,291	...	...	241	2	237	...	...	391	2	...	...	2	...	...	...	...	...	2
Hushyarpur	315	...	...	...	2	192	...	...	262	...	...	...	...	...	...	...	...	...	...
Kangra	1,661	...	1	...	4	105	...	2,624	10	2	...	...	2	...	...	4	...	4	6
Amritsar	32,495	...	...	...	9	366	...	...	767	36	...	...	36	...	...	...	1	1	37
Gurdaspur	6,662	...	921	...	...	183	...	...	191	8	...	...	8	...	...	...	...	...	8
Sialkot	19,153	...	...	...	7	138	1	...	450	19	...	...	19	...	...	...	...	...	19

[P. 302]

Lahore	11,659	...	8	...	92	1,157	...	...	1,285	13	...	...	13	1	...	...	1	2	15
Gujranwala	6,186	...	...	...	...	72	...	...	478	10	...	...	10	...	...	...	1	1	11
Firozpur	1,637	...	...	...	9	378	...	...	689	3	...	...	3	1	...	..	1	2	5
Rawalpindi	23,803	115	...	10	169	211	...	...	167	29	...	...	29	...	...	...	...	...	29
Jahlam	9,672	40	...	...	16	84	...	...	219	16	...	...	16	...	...	...	...	...	16
Gujrat	33,319	5	26	...	...	23	...	...	227	48	...	...	48	...	...	...	...	...	48
Shahpur	143	...	1	...	...	48	...	...	89	...	...	...	...	...	...	...	...	...	...
Multan	92	...	6	8	63	84	1	...	1,003	...	...	...	...	...	...	...	2	2	2
Jhang	15	...	...	...	2	24	...	...	286	...	...	...	...	...	...	...	1	1	1
Montgomery	35	...	...	...	2	11	1	...	347	...	...	...	...	...	...	...	1	1	1
Muzaffargarh	17	...	...	...	...	18	...	...	242	...	...	...	...	...	...	...	1	1	1
Peshawar	13,082	148	9	13	39	...	...	...	183	22	...	...	22	...	...	...	...	...	22
Hazara	13,997	...	761	1	...	...	...	...	...	34	2	...	36	...	...	...	...	...	36
British Territory ...	**178,253**	**393**	**1,759**	**918**	**462**	**11,910**	**8,550**	**2,624**	**9,648**	**9**	...	...	**9**	**1**	...	...	**1**	**2**	**11**
Patiala	144	4	1	34	...	1,016	8	...	736	...	...	...	...	1	...	...	...	1	1
Total East. Plains ...	735	4	4	34	...	1,423	26	...	1,183	...	...	...	...	1	...	...	...	1	1
Bahawalpur	4	...	...	...	...	8	...	...	...	...	...	...	...	...	...	...	...	...	...
Total Hill States ...	28	...	149	92	...	79	...	...	79	...	...	...	...	...	...	...	...	...	...
British Territory ...	178,253	393	1,759	918	462	11,910	8,550	2,624	9,648	9	...	...	9	1	...	...	1	2	11
Native States	767	4	153	126	...	1,510	26	...	1,262	...	...	...	...	...	...	...	..	...	...
Province	179,020	397	1,912	1,044	462	13,420	8,576	2,624	10,910	8	...	...	8	1	...	...	...	1	9

Drew describes them as "large made and robust and of a really fine cast "of feature," and ranks them as "the finest race on the whole Continent "of India." But their history is, at any rate in recent times, one of the most grievous suffering and oppression; and they are cowards, liars, and withal quarrelsome, though at the same time keen-witted, cheerful and humorous. A good account of them will be found in Drew's *Jummoo and Kashmir*. The Chibhális are for the most part Musalmán Rájpúts, and differ from the Dogras only in religion, and perhaps in clan.

The Kashmíris of the Panjáb may be broadly divided into three classes. First the great Kashmíri colonies of Lúdhiána and Amritsar, where there are nearly 35,000 Kashmíris permanently settled and engaged for the most part in weaving shawls and similar fine fabrics. These men are chiefly true Kashmíris. Secondly, the recent immigrants driven from Kashmír by the late famine into our sub-montane districts, or attracted by the special demand for labour in the Salt-range Tract and upper frontier which was created by works in connection with the Kábul campaign. It is impossible to say how many of these men are Chibhális and how many Kashmíris. [P. 303] Thirdly, the Chibhális who have crossed the border and settled in our territories in the ordinary course of affairs. These men are probably confined to Gújrát and the trans-Salt range Tract. Besides those who are returned as Kashmíris, I find no fewer than 7,515 persons returned as Kashmíri Jats, of whom 1,152 are in Lahore and 5,081 in Gújránwála. Those are probably Kashmíris who have settled and taken to cultivation. The Kashmíri weavers of Amritsar are described as "litigious, deceitful, "and cowardly, while their habits are so unclean that the quarter of the "city which they inhabit is a constant source of danger from its liability to "epidemic disease." The Kashmíris have returned numerous sub-divisions, of which the few largest are shown in the margin. Their distribution does not appear to follow any rule; and it is hardly worth while giving detailed figures in this place. The Kashmíris of our cities are as a rule miserably poor.

KASHMIRI TRIBES.

1. Bat	... 24,463	6. Shekh	... 14,902
2. Lun	... 4,818	7. Batti	... 14,725
3. Dár	... 16,215	8. Mahar	... 3,083
4. Wáin	... 7,419	9. Warde	... 4,863
5. Mír	... 19,855	10. Mán	... 2,656

558. The Dogra (Caste No. 181).—The Dogras are Rájpúts who inhabit Jammu, and have returned themselves as such to the number of 1,415 scattered about the Province, the largest number in one district being 391 in Ráwalpindi. Thus our separate figures mean little, and might well have been included with Rájpúts. The word Dogra, however, is commonly used for any inhabitant of Jammu whatever be his caste, Dogar being another word for the Jammu territory. Dogras are probably present in the Panjáb as settlers from across the border, as famine fugitives, and in the Dogra regiments of our army. I believe their Rájpút origin is undoubted; but that it is equally certain that they are not pure Rájpúts.

559. The Gurkha, Parsi, and Bangali (Caste Nos. 148, 184, and 168).—The Gúrkhas are the ruling and military race of Nepal, and are only found in the Panjáb as members of our Gúrkha regiments. They are of mixed Aryan and Turanian blood, and an admirable and interesting account of them will be found in that one of Hodgson's *Essays* which deals with the military tribes of Nepal. The Pársis are the Zoroastrian class of that name who have come from the Bombay Presidency into the Panjáb as merchants and shop-keepers. The Bangális are the Bengali Baboos of our offices. They are I believe for the most part either Bráhmans or Káyaths, Bengali being of course a purely geographical term. They are only found in offices and counting-houses.

560. The Kayaths (Caste No. 90).—The Káyath is the well-known writer class of Hindústán. He does not appear to be indigenous in the Panjáb, and is found in decreasing numbers as we go westwards. He is only to be found in the administrative or commercial centres and is being rapidly displaced, so far as Government service is concerned, by Panjábi clerks. His origin is discussed in Colebrook's *Essays*.

But in the Panjáb hills Káyath is the term of an occupation rather than of a caste, and is applied to members of a mixed caste formed by the inter-marriage of Bráhmans and Káyaths proper, and even of Banyas who follow clerkly pursuits. Their caste would be Mahájan (Pahári) and their occupation Káyath. Mr. Barnes says: "The Káyath of the hills is not identical with the Káyath of the plains. He belongs to the Vaisya or commercial class, and is entitled to wear the *janeo* or sacred thread. The Káyath of the plains is a Sudra, and is not entitled to assume the *janeo*.[1]" (See also Pahári
P. 245. Mahájan, page 294.)

561. The Bishnoi (Caste No. 106).—The Bishnois are really a religious sect and not a true caste. Their tenets and practice have been briefly sketched at page 123 in the Chapter on Religion. Almost all the followers of this sect are either Jats or Tarkháns by caste, and come from the Bágar or Bíkáner prairies; but on becoming Bishnois they very commonly give up their caste name and call themselves after their new creed. This is, however, not always so; and many of the Bishnois will doubtless have returned themselves under their caste names. I do not know whether the Jat and Tarkhán Bishnois intermarry or not. But a Bishnoi will only marry a Bishnoi. They are only found in Hariána, and are all Hindus.

562. The Chazang (Caste No. 138).—This again is not a true caste, for it is confined to the Buddhists of Spiti, among whom caste is said to be unknown. The word Cháhzang means nothing more or less than "land-owner," from *cháh* "owner" and *zang* "land," and includes all the land-owning classes of Spiti, where everybody owns land except Hesis and Lohárs. These people are by nationality Tibetan, or as they call themselves Bhoti, and should perhaps have been returned as such. Mr. Anderson says: "Cháhzang means the "land-holding class, and the people towards Tibet, Ladákh, and Zanskár are "known as Cháhzang. It appears to be used in a very wide sense to mean "all that speak Bhoti, just as Monpa means 'the people that do not know,' "that is, the Hindus."

563. The Kanchan (Caste No. 96).—This again is hardly a caste, Kanchan simply meaning a Musalmán pimp or prostitute, and being the Hindustáni equivalent for the Panjábi Kanjar. The figures for Kanjar, except in the Dehli, Hissár, and Ambála divisions, have been included under this heading (see section 590). The word *kanchan* is said to mean "pure and "illustrious." The Hindu prostitute is commonly known as Rámjani and

[1] This last assertion is contested in a pamphlet called *Kayastha Ethnology* (Lucknow, 1877).

it appears that they have generally returned themselves under their proper castes.[1] Such few as have not shown themselves as Rámjani have been included with Kanchan. Randi is also used for a prostitute in the east of the Province, but it means a "widow" throughout the Panjáb proper. It will be observed that two-fifths of the Kanchans are males. These people form a distinct class, though not only their offspring, but also girls bought in infancy or joining the community in later life and devoting themselves to prostitution, are known as Kanchans.

563a. **Miscellaneous Castes of Table VIII B.**—In Table VIII B I have given the figures for a number of miscellaneous castes which I did not think it worth while to show in detail in Table VIII A. Many of these I cannot identify, and cannot even be sure that I have got the names right. And many more would properly fall under some one of the various groups into which I have divided my castes for the purposes of this chapter. But the numbers are so small and time so pressing that I shall take them as they come in Table VIII B. and give briefly the infor- [P. 304]
mation I possess regarding such of them as I know anything about. Many of them are not castes at all, but either occupational or geographical terms. *Toba* (*Caste No. 186*)—literally means a diver, but is used for the men who dig and clean wells, in which process diving is necessary. They generally belong to the Jhínwar and Máchhi caste, and are often fishermen as well as well-sinkers. *Patwa* (*Caste No. 187*).—From *pat* silk, and means any worker in silk, but is generally used only for those who make silken cord and waistbands, thread beads and silk, and so forth. They are called *Patoi* in the west. They are said often to be Khatris. *Bágri* (*Caste No. 188*)—means any one from the Bágar or prairies of Bíkáner, but is usually confined to Jats from those parts. *Gwálpa* (*Caste No. 189*).—These men are apparently Tibetans, but I cannot define the meaning of the word. *Kharásia* (*Caste No. 190*).—The men who work the water mills so common in the hills. They are said often to be Dáolis. *Pachháda* (*Caste No. 192*)—used in Bhattiána and Hariána for Musalmán Jat and Rájpút immigrants from the Satluj country to the west (*pachham*), just as Bágri is used for similar Hindu immigrants from the South. *Tará ora* (*Caste No. 193*).—These people came to Hazára from Amb and the Buner and Chagharza hills. They trace their descent from a Káfir convert to Islám called Dúman. They all are agricultrual by occupation. *Palledár* (*Caste No. 194*)—A porter, generally found in the bazaars and markets. *Kamáchi* (*Caste No. 196*).—A class of vagrant minstrels who beg and play at weddings. *Kúchband* (*Caste No. 197*).—Makers of *kuch* or weaver's brushes. They belong to the outcast and vagrant classes. *Dárúgar* (*Caste No. 198*).—A man who makes gunpowder. Under this head is included *Atishbáz*, a man who makes fireworks. *Páli* (*Caste No. 199*).—Páli is the ordinary village word for cowherd in the east of the Panjáb. But in Multán there is a separate Páli caste who have lately been converted from Hinduism and still retain many of their Hindu customs. They follow all sorts of handicrafts, and especially that of oil-pressing, and engage in trade in a small way. *Jarrah* (*Caste No. 200*).—The Native Surgeon who applies plasters, draws teeth, sets fractures, and so on. He is almost always a Nái. *Kápri* (*Caste No. 201*).—A caste who claim Bráhman origin, and whose occupation is that of making the ornaments worn by the bridegroom at weddings, artificial flowers, and similar article made of talc, tinsel, and the like. They are apparently connected, in Dehli at least, with the Jain temples, where they officiate as priests and receive offerings. They also act as Bháts at weddings. They are said to come from Rájpútána. *Pánda* (*Caste No. 202*).—A name commonly given to any educated Bráhman who teaches or officiates at religious functions. Probably of the same origin as Pandit. In the hills it is said to be used for Dakaut Bráhmans. *Sapela* (*Caste No. 203*).—A snake-catcher and charmer, generally belonging to one of the vagrant tribes. *Marátha* (*Caste No. 204*).—An inhabitant of Maharásthra or the Mahratta Country. *Akhúndzadah* (*Caste No. 205*).—See Ulama, section 517. *Sapándi* (*Caste No. 206*).—Probably the same as Sapela No. 203 *q.v.* *Díwán*. (*Caste No. 207*).—This is the title of the revenue minister at a Native Court. There is also a Sikh order called Díwána. *Hesi* (*Caste No. 208*)—should have been included with No. 167 described under Gipsy tribes in the next part of this chapter. *Arya* (*Caste No. 209*).—Probably followers of the Arya Samáj. *Attár* (*Caste No. 210*).—A dispensing druggist, as distinct from the *Pansári* from whom the drugs are bought, and the *Gándi*, a distiller of essences and perfumes. The Attár however makes arracks and sherbets. *Qarol* (*Caste No. 211*).—These are the descendants of the hunters and menagerie keepers of the old Mughal Court at Dehli. They are of several castes, but probably for the most part Pathán; but they have now formed a separate caste, marry only among themselves, and have taken to agriculture. They are called after their weapon, the hunting-knife or *qarol*. *Marejha* (*Caste No. 212*).—A class of wandering beggars who come from Rájpútána and Sindh. *Márwári* (*Caste No. 213*).—Inhabitants of Márwár, but generally applied in the Panjáb to Bráhman money-lenders or Bohras from that tract. *Láhori* (*Caste No. 214*).—Residents of Lahore; but perhaps Khatris, of whom there is a great Láhori section. *Lánia*

[1] But see Sherring, Vol. I., p. 274.

(Caste No. 215)—Probably salt-makers, and should have been included with Núngar No. 176. ***Gargajje*** *(Caste No 216)*.—The same as ***Garzmár***, a class of ***faqirs*** who thurst iron spikes into their flesh. ***Bodhi*** *(Caste No. 217)*.—As it stands the word would mean a Buddhist. But it is perhaps a misreading for Bhoti, an inhabitant of Bhot or Thibet, who also would be a Buddhist. ***Nánbai*** *(Caste No. 218)*.—A baker. ***Jatojha*** *(Caste No. 219)*.—A Púrbi caste who keep milch kine. ***Múnhband*** *(Caste No. 220)*.—The Jain ascetic who hangs a cloth over his mouth (***múnh***). ***Bisáti*** *(Caste No. 221)*.—A dealer in petty hardware who spreads (***basat***) his mat (***bisát***) in front of him and displays his wares upon it. ***Pahári*** *(Caste No. 222)*.—A generic term for a hill man. ***Hijra*** *(Caste No. 226)*.—A eunuch, distinct from the Hinjra which is a large Jat tribe and separately described in its proper place. ***Saknsar*** *(Caste No. 227)*.—A small caste in Hushyárpur who were only a few generations ago Punwár Rájpúts, but have been driven by poverty to growing vegetables and working in grass, and are now a separate caste ranking with the Aráins. ***Ghardmi*** *(Caste No. 229)*.—Thatchers, generally Jhínwars. ***Chhatarsaz*** *(Caste No. 231)*.—Umbrella makers. ***Sangtarásh*** *(Caste No. 233)*.—Stone-cutters. ***Chirímár*** *(Caste No. 234)*.—Bird catchers, who almost always belong to the vagrant tribes. ***Chíníqar*** *(Caste No 239)*.—Sugar refiners. ***Suthár*** *(Caste No 259)*.—The Bombay word for carpenters, ***cf***, Tarkhán No. 11. ***Dhai Sirkiband*** *(Caste No. 263)*.—The men who make ***sirki*** or roof-ridges of grass to protect carts and the like. Almost always of the vagrant classes. ***Hindki*** *(Caste No. 271)*.—A generic term on the Upper Indus for all Musalmáns of Indian descent who speak Panjábi dialects. ***Kamera*** *(Caste No. 280)*.—An agricultural labourer hired by the day, month, or year on fixed pay, not receiving a share of the produce. ***Guru*** *(Caste No 297)*.—A Hindu spiritual preceptor. ***Karár*** *(Caste No. 300)*.—More properly Kirár. Any Hindu trader in the west or in the hills. ***Uzbak*** *(Caste No. 301)*.—A Túrk tribe, and should have been included with Túrk No. 125. ***Gwála*** *(Caste No. 306)*.—The term for a Hindu cowherd and shepherd, generally an Ahír. ***Tabákhia*** *(Caste No 308)*.—A man who keeps a cook-shop and hawks cooked food about the streets. ***Kharol*** *(Caste No 317)*.—Probably the same as Qarol, No. 211, described above.

PART VI.—THE VAGRANT, MENIAL AND ARTISAN CASTES.

564. Division of the subject.—Having discussed the land-owning and agricultural, and the priestly, mercantile, and professional castes, I now turn to the lowest strata of Panjáb society, the vagrant and criminal tribes, the gipsies, the menials, and the artisans. These classes form in many respects one of the most interesting sections of the community. Politically they are unimportant; but they include the great mass of such aboriginal element as is still to be found in the Panjáb, their customs are not only exceedingly peculiar but also exceedingly interesting as affording us a clue to the separation of the non-Aryan element in the customs of other tribes, and while the industries of the Province are almost entirely in their hands an immense deal of the hardest part of the field,work is performed by them. At the same time they are precisely the classes regarding whom it is most difficult to obtain reliable information. They are not pleasant people to deal with and we are thrown but little into contact with them, while the better class of native groups most of them under one or two generic terms, such as Chúhra, Dúm, or Nat, and thinks it would degrade him to show any closer acquaintance with their habits. I have roughly divided these castes into eleven groups. First I have taken the vagrant, hunting, and criminal tribes, then the gipsy tribes, then the scavenger classes, the leather-workers and weavers, the water-carriers, fishermen and boatmen, the carpenters, blacksmiths, stone-masons and potters, the goldsmiths and saltmakers, the washermen, dyers, and tailors, the oilmen, butchers, cotton scutchers, wine distillers, and other miscellaneous artisans, the menials peculiar to the hills, and finally the Púrbi menials of our cantonments. [P. 303]

These classes may be grouped in two different ways, according as the classification is based upon their ethnic and occupational affinities, or upon their position in the industrial œconomy of the country. I shall first consider them from the former point of view.

565. Origin and evolution of the lower menials.—It appears to me that starting with an aboriginal and vagrant stock, there are two continuous series of gradations leading from that stock to the weavers at least on the one hand and probably to the water-carriers on the other, and that no line can be drawn anywhere in either series which shall distinctly mark off those above from those below it. For specific instances of the manner in which these occupations shade off one into another I must refer the reader to the following pages. But I will endeavour to exemplify what I mean by an imaginary series. Suppose an aboriginal tribe of vagrant habits, wandering about from jungle to jungle and from village to village, catching for the sake of food the vermin which abound such as jackals, foxes, and lizards, and eating such dead bodies as may fall in their way, plaiting for themselves rude shelter and utensils from the grasses which fringe the ponds, living with their women very much in common and ready to prostitute them for money when occasion offers, and always on the watch for opportunities of pilfering, and you have the lowest type of gipsy and vagrant tribes as we now find them in the Panjáb. Now imagine such a tribe abandoning its vagrant habits and settling as menials in a village. Being no longer nomads they would cease to hunt and eat vermin; but they would still eat carrion, they would still plait grass, and being what they were, the filthiest work to be performed, namely that of scavengering, would fall to their share. They would then be the Chúhra or scavenger caste as they exist in every village. Suppose again that a section of them, desirous of rising in life, abandoned plaiting grass and scavengering and took to tanning and working in leather, the next less filthy work available, as their occupation, and modified their primitive creed so as to render it somewhat more like that of their Hindu neighbours, but being still specially concerned with dead animals, continued to eat carrion: we should then have the Chamár or tanner and leather-worker. And finally if, desiring to live cleanly, they gave up eating carrion and working in leather and took to weaving, which is (I know not why, unless it be that weavers' implements are made from grass by the outcast classes of grass-workers) considered only less degrading, they would become the Juláha of our towns and villages and be admitted under semi-protest within the pale of Hinduism. Or they might skip the leather-working stage and pass direct from scavengering to weaving. Now if all this were merely speculation upon what is *possible*, it would mean little or nothing. But when we see that changes of this sort are actually in progress, it seems to me that the suggestion may mean a good deal. We see the vagrant classes such as the Báwaria and Aheri tending to settle down in the villages and perform low menial offices; we see the Dhának converted from the hunter of the jungles into a scavenger and weaver; we see the Chúhra refuse to touch night-soil and become a Musalli, or substitute leather-working and tanning for scavengering and become a Rangreta; we see the Khatík who is a scavenger in the east turn into a tanner in the west; we see the Koli Chamár abandon leather-working and take to weaving, and turn into a Chamár-Juláha or Búnia; we see that in some districts most of the Mochis are weavers rather than leather-workers; and we find that it is impossible to draw a hard and fast line anywhere between vagrancy and scavengering at the bottom and weaving at the top or to say that such a caste is above and such a caste is below the line, but that each caste throws out off-shoots into the grade above that which is occupied by the greater number of its members.

566. Origin of the water-carrying classes.—In the second series of changes we have not so many examples of the intermediate steps. But it is natural that the upward movement in the social scale which every tribe is fain to make if possible should not be confined to one definite direction only. Some of the vagrant castes have like the Báwaria abandoned the eating of carrion and become hunters of higher game, though not perhaps quite relinquishing their taste for vermin; some while retaining their nomad habits have taken to specified forms of labour like the Od or Changar; others have settled down to cultivation like the Mahtam or to crime like the Mína; while others again have taken to the carrying trade like some sections of the Banjáras, or to the pedlar's business. But there is a group of these tribes who are distinctly water-hunters; who catch, not deer and jackals, but water fowl, fish, and crocodiles or tortoises, who [P. 306] live in the fens or on the river-banks, weave huts for themselves from the pliant withies of the water-loving shrubs, and make twine and rope for their nets from the riverside grasses. Such are the Kehal, the Mor, the Jhabel. And on giving up eating crocodiles and tortoises and confining themselves to fish, these men are as it were received into society, as is the case with the Kehals. The Jhabels again have advanced a step further, and are a respectable class of boatmen and fishermen. Now the Jhínwar, Kahár, and Máchhi caste are the basket-makers, boatmen, fishermen, and water-carriers, and among the Musalmáns the cooks of country. Is it not possible that they may be but a step, a long one perhaps, in advance of the Jhabel? I find that in the hills, where Hindu customs have probably preserved their primitive integrity most completely, Bráhmans will drink from the hands of very many people from whose hands they will not eat; and the Sanskrit Scriptures make the fisherman the descendant of a Súdra woman by a Bráhman father. It is stated that the Rámdásia or Sikh Chamárs have taken largely to the occupation of "Kahárs or bearers," though this may not and probably does not include water-carrying. The series of steps is not so close as in the former case; but I think that the suggestion is worthy of further examination.

567. Effect of religion upon occupation.—I have pointed out that with the rise in the social scale, the original religion would be gradually modified so as to bring it more into accord with the religion of the respectable classes. As a fact it is curious how generally the observances, if not the actual religion of these lower menials, follow those of the villagers to whom they are attached. Chúhras and the like will bury their dead in a Musalmán and burn them in a Hindu village, though not recognised by their masters as either Hindu or Musalmán. But it is not uncommonly the case that the open adoption of a definite faith, the substitution of Islám or Sikhism for that half-Hindu half-aboriginal religion which distinguishes most of these outcast classes, is the first step made in their upward struggle; and it is very commonly accompanied by the abandonment of the old occupation for that which stands next higher in the scale. The scavenger on becoming a Musalmán will refuse to remove night soil, and on becoming a Sikh will take to tanning and leather-working. The tanner and leather-worker on becoming a Musalmán will give up tanning, and on taking the Sikh *páhul* will turn his hand to the loom, and so forth. I quote a very interesting note on this subject by Sardár Gurdiál Singh, one of our Native Civilians:—

"Of the Bhagats enumerated in Bhagatmál several were of low castes. They were all "reformers of the dark ages of Hindustan. They addressed the people in their vernaculars "and did away with the secrecy observed by the Brahmanical teachings and removed the "barrier in the way of reform presented by the difficulty of the language (Sanskrit) through "which the Brahmins taught their system of religion. Among others was Kabír a Juláha, "Sadhna a Kasai, Nám Deo a Chhímba, and Ravi Dás a Chamár. Their writings have "been quoted in the Adi Granth, the Sikh scriptures. One of the reforms contemplated and "partially carried out by Sikhism was the abolition of caste system and opening the study "of Theology and the scriptures (Hindu) to every class, even the Chúhras and Chamárs who were "mentioned in Dharm Shastras as having no adhikár.[1] Taking advantage of this, some of the

[1] The word adhikár means "fitness"; and those castes were said to have no adhikár who were not fit to listen to the Hindu Scriptures.

"lowest classes received Sikh baptsim (*pahul*) and became Sikhs. They gave up their mean "occupation and took to other means of livelihood. They also changed their name and gave "up as much social intercourse with the unconverted members of their tribe as they pos-"sibly could. Thus the Chamárs on their conversion to Sikhism took the name of Ravi "Dás, the first Bhagat of their tribe, to show that they followed his example. Ravdásia is "the correct form of the word. But it was soon confounded with the name of Rám Das, "the 4th Sikh Guru, and pronounced Rámdásia.[1] The word is still pronounced as Ravdásia "by most of the Sikhs. Similarly Chhímba Sikhs call themselves Námabansis from Nám "Deo.

"The Chúhras on becoming Sikhs took the names of Mazhabi ((just as that of Díndár "on conversion to Islám) and Rangreta. No one of the Rangretas follows the occupation of a "Chúhra, but they have been rightly classed with Chúhras. Similarly if the Rámdásias do "not follow the occupation of Chamárs, it is no reason to separate them from that caste. "So if a Rámdásia is Juláha, that is a weaver, and if he is a 'Bazzaz' that is a draper, "his caste remains unchanged. If a Chamár, a leather-worker becomes a Sikh and receives "the '*pahul*' to-day, he at once joins the Rámdásias. The Rámdásias do receive the "daughters in marriage of ordinary Chamárs, but give them '*pahul*' before associating with "them. A Rámdásia would not drink water from the hands of an ordinary Chamár un-"less he becomes a Sikh. The Mazbi Sikhs also keep themselves aloof from the Chúhras, "in exactly the same manner as Rámdásias do from Chamárs."

It is quite true, as the Sardár points out, that the Rámdási is still a Chamár and the Rangreta still a Chúhra. The change has been recent and is still in progress. But how long will they remain so? Their origin is already hotly disputed and often indignantly denied, though the fact of new admissions still taking place puts it beyond the possibility of doubt. But there can be little doubt that they will in time grow into separate castes of a standing superior to those from which they sprang; or more probably perhaps, that they will grow to be included under the generic name of the caste whose hereditary occupation they have adopted, but will form distinct sections of those castes and be known by separate sectional names, even after the tradition of their origin has faded from the memory of the caste. And there can, I think, be as little doubt that some of the sections which now form integral parts of these lower occupational castes would, if we could trace back their history, be found to have been formed in a precisely similar manner. The tradition of inferior origin and status has survived, and the other sections, perhaps themselves derived from the same stock but at a more remote date, will hold no communion with them; but the precise reason for the distinction has been forgotten. The absence of the hereditary theory of occupation among the people of the frontier and its effect by example upon those of the Western Plains, have already been discussed in sections 343 and 348.

568. Growth of sections among the menial castes.—But if these occupational castes are recruited by new sections coming up from below, they also receive additions from above. The weavers especially may be said to form a sort of debateable land between the higher and the lower artisan castes, for a man of decent caste who from poverty or other circumstances sinks in the scale often takes to weaving, though he perhaps rarely falls lower than this. The barber, carpenter, and blacksmith classes have in Sirsa been recruited from the agricultural castes within

[1] I do not think this is quite correct. The Rabdási or Raidási Chamárs are Hindus and the Rámdási are Sikhs. But it may be that the Ravdási are analogous with the Nának-panthi Sikhs who are commonly reckoned as Hindus, while the Rámdási correspond with the Singhi or Govindi Sikhs proper. As the Sardár points out presently, the Rámdásis receive the *páhul*, an institution of Guru Govind; while the Rabdásis do not. (See further section 606 *infra*.)

the memory of the present generation, and it is hardly possible that what has so lately happened there should not have earlier happened elsewhere. When a hitherto uninhabited tract is settled by immigrants of all classes pouring in from all directions, as has been the case with Sirsa during the last fifty years, [P. 307] the conditions are probably especially favourable to social change. People who have hitherto been separated by distance but who have the same caste name or the same occupation, meet together bringing with them the varying customs and distinctions of the several neighbourhoods whence they came. They do not as a rule fuse together, but remain distinct sections included under a common caste-name, though often reluctant to admit that there is any community of origin or even of caste, and refusing to associate or to intermarry with each other. There is a great demand for agricultural labour and the artisan tends to become a cultivator; old distinctions are sometimes forgotten, and new sections are continually formed. To use technical language, society is more colloid than in older settled tracts where the process of crystallisation, for which rest and quiet are necesssary, is more advanced; and diffusion and osmose are correspondingly more easy and more active. But what is now taking place in Sirsa must have taken place elsewhere at some time or other. Almost all the menial and artisan castes are divided into sections which are separate from each other in custom and status; and though in many cases these distinctions are probably based upon geographical distribution and consequent variation of customs, yet in other cases they probably result from the fact that one section has risen and another fallen to its present position.

569. The higher and hill menials.—The higher menial classes present, so far as I see, no such continuity of gradation as we find among the outcasts. The Kumhár or potter with his donkey is perhaps the lowest of them, and may not improbably belong by origin and affinity to the classes just discussed. The blacksmith, carpenter, and stonemason class form a very distinct group, as also do the washermen and dyers. The oilman and butcher is perhaps lower than any of them, and it appears that he should rank with the weavers, though I do not know that there is at present any connection between the two classes. The goldsmiths seem to stand alone, and to have descended from above into the artisan classes, probably being by origin akin to the mercantile castes. Among the menials of the hills, on the contrary, the continuity of the whole class now under consideration is almost unbroken. The outcast classes are indeed separate from the higher artisans in the lower hills; but as we penetrate further into the Himálayas we find the scavenger class working as carpenters and blacksmiths, and the whole forming one body which it is almost impossible to separate into sections on any other basis than the present calling of the individual.

570. The œconomical divisions of the menial classes.—The second or œconomical basis upon which these menial and artisan castes may be classified will be dismissed with a very few words. The whole group may be broadly divided into three sections, the vagrant classes, the village menials, and the independent artisans. The vagrant classes serve no man and follow no settled calling. The independent artisans work, like the artisans of Europe, by the piece or for daily hire; and in urban communities, as distinct from the village community which is often found living in a town the lands attached to which they hold and cultivate, include all industrial classes and orders. But in the villages there is a very wide distinction between the village menial and the independent artisan. The carpenter, the blacksmith, the potter, the scavenger, the leather-worker, the water-carrier, and in villages where the women are secluded the washerman,—all classes in fact whose services are required in husbandry or daily domestic life —are paid not by the job, but by customary dues usually consisting of a fixed share of the produce of the fields; and the service they are bound to perform is often measured by kind and not by quantity. Thus the potter has to supply all the earthen vessels, and the leather-worker all the leathern articles that are required by his clients. Those artisans, however, whose services are only occasionally required, such as the weaver, the oilman, and the dyer, are paid by the job; not usually indeed in cash, but either in grain, or by being allowed to retain a fixed proportion of the raw material which their employers provided for them to work upon. The goldsmith occupies in the village a semi-mercantile position, and is a pawnbroker as much as an artisan; while the other crafts are scarcely represented among the rural communities.

571. The internal organization of the menial classes.—The elaborate organisation of the menial and artisan classes, whether based upon the tribal organisation of the agricultural communities whom they serve, or following the type of the trades-guilds proper of the towns, has already been alluded to in sections 352 and 356. The subject is one of which we know little, yet a more accurate knowledge of the details of these two types of organisation could hardly fail to throw much light upon the evolution of caste. Especially would it be interesting to trace the points of similarity and of difference between the respective systems where the occupation is hereditary and partakes of the nature of other castes, and where it is individual and the guild is little more than a voluntary association. The question of how caste and guild rules are reconciled in cases where the guild includes men of many castes, and what happens when they conflict, is also one of considerable interest. That the organisation is singularly complete and the authority wielded by it exceedingly great, is beyond the possibility of doubt; and it is a common observation that disputes between members of these classes rarely come before our courts for adjudication, being almost invariably settled by the administrative body of the caste or guild. This may be a survival from old times, when such courts or officers of justice as existed would probably have declined to be troubled with the disputes of low caste men.

VAGRANT AND CRIMINAL TRIBES.

572. The Wandering and criminal tribes.—The figures for the wander-
P. 272-3 ing and criminal tribes are given in Abstract No. 96 on page 309.* This group and that of the gipsy tribes which I shall discuss next are so much akin that it is impossible to draw any definite line of demarcation. I have attempted to include in the former the vagrant, criminal, and hunting tribes, and in the latter those who earn their living by singing, dancing, tumbling, and various kinds of performances. The two together form an exceedingly interesting section of the population, but one regarding which I have been able to obtain singularly little information. They are specially interesting, not only because almost every tribe included in these two groups is probably aboriginal in its ultimate origin, for so much could be said, I believe, of some even of our Jat tribes; but also because they have in a special degree retained
P. 308] their aboriginal customs and beliefs and in fact are at the present moment the Panjáb representatives of the indigenous inhabitants of the Province A

Abstract No. 96, showing Wandering and [P. 309]

	WANDERING AND												
	FIGURES.												
	65	129	64	71	91	100	72	117	107	161	133	106	159
	Od.	Beldár.	Changar.	Báwaria.	Aheri.	Thori.	Sánsi.	Pakhíwára.	Jhabel.	Kehal.	Gágra.	Mína.	Hárni.
Dehli ...	223	...	...	...	88	...	53	...	...	..	...	41	...
Gurgaon ..	113	...	..	618	529	...	2	...	...	...	...	691	...
Karnal ...	629	...	...	3	100	...	1,309	...	...	...	49	7	...
Hissar ...	202	356	...	788	4,487	1,550	179	...	...	...	...	...	...
Rohtak ...	776	...	13	242	843	3	140	...	...	...	...	...	...
Sirsa .	198	...	39	3,335	527	2,811	92	...	987	...	...	23	...
Ambála ...	84	155	...	...	292	27	905	...	...	...	109	...	...
Ludhiana ...	101	...	323	265	...	...	1,330	...	...	...	169	...	160
Jalandhar ...	...	2	4,499	...	...	...	403	52	...	...	49	...	22
Hushyarpur ...	...	515	164	...	...	...	159	...	200	...	115	...	342
Kángra ...	47	473	336	...	...	...	18	...	...	...	15	...	...
Amritsar ...	22	...	4,712	...	...	...	2,853	190	...	...	368	...	...
Gurdáspur ...	...	...	3,063	...	...	...	1,973	470	546	...	308	...	186
Siálkot ...	...	173	7,139	...	...	...	1,736	2,441	...	...	421	...	424
Lahore ...	1,873	791	4,279	2,000	...	1	2,163	29	570	...	426	...	1
Gujránwála ..	29	...	741	2	...	...	2,887	175	...	...	677	...	...
Firozpur ...	156	2	1,513	8,130	...	1	492	...	1,876	...	54	...	37
Ráwalpindi ...	...	376	474	...	...	...	5	...	...	...	...	...	...
Gujrat ...	...	279	64	...	...	...	1,090	213	...	...	...	...	...
Shahpur ...	6	110	63	...	...	...	491	25	...	...	...	...	...
Multan ...	3,459	38	79	...	...	...	116	727	1,868	232	...	...	...
Jhang ...	2	...	87	...	...	...	151	...	7	143	...	...	...
Montgomery ...	706	...	243	...	...	...	430	8	318	123	...	...	...
Muzaffargarh ...	1,862	79	...	...	...	...	18	...	1,351	723	...	...	...
D. I. Khan ...	602	17	...	...	...	...	...	...	...	...	...	...	...
D. G. Khan ...	1,353	...	...	...	22	...	...	1	17	23	...	...	...
British Territory.	**12,470**	**3,409**	**28,011**	**15,394**	**6,928**	**4,535**	**19,035**	**4,311**	**7,754**	**1,243**	**2,759**	**768**	**1,162**
Patiala ...	457	...	84	2,184	3,998	1,579	1,121	...	...	...	46	200	9
Nabha ...	30	...	13	482	98	...	223	...	...	...	...	124	3
Kapurthala ...	...	...	614	...	...	...	68	191	137	...	62	...	17
Jind ...	214	..	8	122	1,083	...	108	...	...	...	...	...	...
Faridkot ...	470	...	105	3,072	...	...	123	..	23	...	2	...	129
Total Eastern Plains.	1,184	...	820	6,121	6,159	1,579	2,032	191	160	...	117	349	176
Bahawalpur ...	1,973	...	20	509	...	1,408	162	...	149	8	231	...	..
Nahan ...	...	...	25	...	...	781	7	...	...	...	...	...	...
Bilaspur ..	...	25	...	...	...	268	32	...	...	...	...	...	...
Bashahr ...	...	...	...	...	...	672	...	...	...	...	...	...	...
Nalagarh .	...	15	4	...	..	175	18	...	...	...	3	...	...
Total Hill States	...	40	29	...	...	3,072	80	...	...	...	3	...	...
British Territory.	**12,470**	**3,409**	**28,011**	**15,394**	**6,928**	**4,535**	**19,035**	**4,311**	**7,754**	**1,243**	**2,759**	**768**	**1,162**
Native States.	**3,157**	**40**	**875**	**6,630**	**6,158**	**6,059**	**2,274**	**191**	**309**	**8**	**351**	**348**	**176**
Province ...	**15,627**	**3,449**	**28,886**	**22,024**	**13,086**	**10,594**	**21,309**	**4,502**	**8,063**	**1,251**	**3,110**	**1,116**	**1,338**

Criminal Tribes for Districts and States.

CRIMINAL TRIBES.

PROPORTION PER 1,000 OF TOTAL POPULATION.

85	120	64		71	91	100	72	117	107	161	133		166	159		
Od.	Beldár.	Changar.	TOTAL.	Báwaria.	Aheri.	Thori.	Sánsi.	Pakhiwára.	Jhabel.	Kehal.	Gágra.	TOTAL.	Mína.	Hárni.	TOTAL.	GRAND TOTAL.
...	...	...	...	...	...	...	...	...	...	...	...	...	...	...	...	...
...	...	...	...	1	1	...	...	...	...	...	...	2	1	...	1	3
1	...	...	1	...	...	...	2	...	...	...	...	2	...	...	...	3
...	1	...	1	2	9	3	...	...	...	...	...	14	...	...	...	15
1	...	...	1	...	2	...	...	...	...	...	...	2	...	...	...	3
1	...	...	1	13	2	11	...	...	4	...	...	30	...	...	...	31
...	...	...	...	...	...	...	1	...	...	...	...	1	...	...	...	1
...	...	1	1	...	...	...	2	...	...	...	...	2	...	...	...	3
...	...	6	6	...	...	...	1	...	...	...	...	1	...	...	...	7
...	...	...	...	...	...	...	...	...	...	...	...	...	...	...	...	...
...	1	...	1	...	...	...	...	...	...	...	...	...	...	...	...	1
...	...	5	5	...	...	...	3	...	...	...	...	3	...	...	...	
...	...	4	4	...	...	...	2	1	1	...	...	4	...	...	...	8
...	...	7	7	...	...	...	2	2	...	...	...	4	...	...	...	11
2	1	5	8	2	...	...	2	...	1	...	...	5	...	...	...	13
...	...	1	1	...	...	...	5	...	...	...	1	6	...	...	...	7
...	...	2	2	12	...	...	1	...	3	...	...	16	...	...	...	18
...	...	1	1	...	...	...	...	...	...	...	...	...	...	...	...	1
...	...	...	...	...	...	...	2	...	...	...	...	2	...	...	...	2
...	...	...	...	...	...	...	1	...	...	...	...	1	...	...	...	1
6	...	...	6	...	...	...	...	1	3	...	...	4	...	...	...	10
2	...	...	2	...	...	...	1	...	1	...	...	2	...	...	...	4
6	...	...	6	...	...	...	...	...	4	2	...	6	...	...	...	12
1	...	...	1	...	...	...	...	...	...	...	...	...	...	...	...	1
4	...	...	4	...	...	...	...	...	...	...	...	...	...	...	...	4
1	...	1	2	1	...	...	1	...	...	...	...	2	...	...	...	4
...	...	...	...	1	3	1	1	...	...	...	...	6	...	...	...	6
...	...	...	...	2	...	...	1	...	...	...	...	3	...	...	...	3
...	...	2	2	...	...	...	...	1	1	...	...	2	...	...	...	4
1	...	...	1	...	8	...	1	...	...	...	...	9	...	...	...	10
5	...	1	6	32	...	...	1	...	...	...	...	33	...	1	1	40
...	...	...	...	2	2	1	1	...	...	...	...	6	...	...	...	6
3	...	...	3	1	...	3	...	...	...	...	...	4	...	...	...	7
...	...	...	...	...	...	7	...	...	...	...	...	7	...	...	...	7
...	...	...	...	...	...	3	...	...	...	...	...	3	...	...	...	3
...	...	...	...	...	...	9	...	...	...	...	...	9	...	...	...	9
...	...	...	...	...	...	3	...	...	...	...	...	3	...	...	...	3
...	...	...	...	...	...	4	...	...	...	...	...	4	...	...	...	4
1	...	1	2	1	...	...	1	...	...	...	...	2	...	...	...	4
1	...	...	1	2	2	2	1	...	...	...	...	7	...	...	...	8
1	...	1	2	1	1	...	1	...	...	...	...	3	...	...	...	5

complete record of their manners and customs would probably throw much light upon the ethnology of the Punjab, as it would enable us to discriminate aboriginal from Aryan customs, and thus assist us in determining the stock to which each of those many castes whose origin is so doubtful should be referred.

The tribes under discussion are for the most part outcasts, chiefly because they feed on the fox, jackal, lizard, tortoise, and such like unclean animals. They are, like the scavengers, hereditary workers in grass, straw, reeds, and the like. Many of them appear to use a speech peculiar to themselves, regarding which Dr. Leitner has collected some information, while a sort of glossary has been published by the darogha of the Lahore Central Jail. In some cases this speech appears to be a true language or dialect peculiar to the tribe; in others to be a mere *argot* consisting of the language current in the locality, thinly disguised, but sufficiently so to render it unintelligible to the ordinary listener. A copious glossary of the Rámási or *lingua franca* of the thieving classes is said to have been published in 1855 as Volume I of the "Selections from the Records of the Agra Govern-"ment." Much information regarding the criminal tribes may be gleaned from the published reports of the Thuggee and Dacoity Department, and especially from Colonel Sleeman's report published in 1849. The wandering tribes included in the group now under discussion have been divided into three classes. The first, including the Ods, the Beldárs and the Changars are those who have a fixed occupation, though no fixed dwelling-place. The last, which comprises the Mínas and the Hárnis, are not hunters, and are rather criminal than wandering, the families at least usually having fixed abodes, though the men travel about in search of opportunities for theft. The middle group, consisting of the Báwaria, the Aheri, the Thori, the Sánsi, the Pakhíwára, the Jhabel, the Kehal, and the Gágra, are hunters and fishermen living a more or less vagrant life in the jungles and on the river banks; and often, though by no means always, addicted to crime. The distribution of each tribe is noted under its separate head; but the action of the Criminal Tribes Act, which is enforced against a given tribe in some districts but not in others, has probably modified their distribution by inducing them to move from the former to the latter class of the districts. At the end of this section I notice various castes of criminal habits who either have not been distinguished in our tables, or have been treated of elsewhere.

573. The Od and Beldar (Caste Nos. 85 and 129).—These two sets of figures should probably be taken together, as they appear to refer to the same caste. Indeed in several of the divisional offices the two terms have been treated as synonymous. Beldár is properly the name of an occupation merely; it is derived from *bel* a mattock, and it denotes all whose calling it is to work with that instrument. But though the common coolie of the Province will often turn his hand to digging, the Od is the *professional* navvy of the Panjáb; and the word Beldár is seldom applied, at least as a tribal name, to the members of any other caste, though it seems in more common use in the west than in the east, the Od of the west being generally known as Beldár [1].

[1] Mr. Christie, however, assures me that there are large communities of professional Beldárs who are *not* Ods. They are generally Musalmán in the Punjáb proper and Hindu in the eastern districts; they are not outcasts, have fixed habitations, and work as carriers with their animals when earth-work is not forthcoming. It may be that the Musalmáns returned in our tables belong to this class; as Od and Beldár have been confused.

The Od or Odh is a wandering tribe whose proper home appears to be Western Hindústán and Rájpútána; at least the Ods of the Panjáb usually hail from those parts. They are vagrants, wandering about with their families in search of employment on earthwork. They will not as a rule take petty jobs, but prefer small contracts on roads, canals, railways, and the like, or will build a house of adobe, and dig a tank, or even a well. They settle down in temporary reed huts on the edge of the work; the men dig, the women carry the earth to the donkeys which they always have with them, and the children drive the donkeys to the spoilbank. In the Salt-range Tract they also quarry and carry stone; and in parts of the North-West Provinces they are said to be wandering pedlars. They eat anything and everything, and though not unfrequently Musalmáns, especially in the west, are always outcast. They have a speech of their own called Odki of which I know nothing, but which is very probably nothing more than the ordinary dialect of their place of origin. They wear woollen clothes, or at least one wollen garment. They claim descent from one Bhagírat who vowed never to drink twice out of the same well, and so dug a fresh one every day till one day he dug down and down and never came up again. It is in mourning for him that they wear wool, and in imitation of him they bury their dead even when Hindu, though they marry by the Hindu ceremony. Till the re-appearance of Bhagírat they will, they say, remain outcasts. They are said to claim Rájpút or Kshatriya origin and to come from Márwár. They worship Ráma and Siva (*cf.* Pushkárna Brahmans. Wilson's *Indian Caste*, Vol. II, pp. 114, 139, 169). They are, for a vagrant tribe, singularly free from all imputation of crime. They are distributed pretty generally throughout the Province, but are most numerous in Lahore and along the lower Indus and Chanáb, and least numerous in the hills and sub-montane districts.

574. The Changar (Caste No. 64).—The Changars are outcasts of probably aboriginal descent, who are most numerous in the Amritsar division, Lahore, Firozepur, and Faridkot, but especially in Siálkot; and they say that their ancestors came from the Jammu hills. They are originally a vagrant tribe who wander about in search of work; but in the neighbourhood of large cities they are to be found in settled colonies. They will do almost any sort of work, but are largely employed in agriculture, particularly as reapers; while their women are very generally employed in sifting and cleaning grain for the graindealers. They are all Musalmáns and marry by *nikáh*, and they say that they were converted by Shams Tabríz of Multán. Their women still wear petticoats and not drawers; but these are blue, not red. They are exceedingly industrious, and not at all given to crime. They have a dialect of their own regarding which, and indeed regarding the tribe generally, Dr. Leitner has published some very interesting information. He says that they call themselves not Changar but Chúbna, and suggests that Changar is derived from *chhánna* to sift. It has been suggested that Changar is another form of Zingari; but Dr. Leitner does not support the suggestion.

P. 310] **575. The Bawaria (Caste No. 71).**—The Báwarias are a hunting tribe who take their name from the *báwar* or noose with which they snare wild animals.[1]

[1] The Mahtams hunt with similar nooses; but theirs are made of *múnj* rope, while the Báwaria nooses are made of leather.

They set long lines of these nooses in the grass across the jungles: from this line they arrange two rows of scarecrows consisting of bits of rag and the like tied on to the trees and grass; they then drive the jungle, and the frightened deer and other animals, keeping between the lines of scarecrows, cross the line of nooses in which their feet become entangled. In addition to hunting they make articles of grass and straw and reeds and sell them to the villagers. The Báwarias are a vagrant tribe whose proper home appears to be Mewár, Ajmer, and Jodhpur; in the Panjáb they are chiefly found along the middle Satluj valley in Sirsa, Fírozpur, Farídkot, Lahore, and Patiála, though they occur in smaller numbers in Hissár, Rohtak, and Gurgáon, all on the Rájpútána border. They are black in colour and of poor physique.

But though they are primarily vagrants, they have settled down in some parts, and especially in the Fírozpur District are largely employed as field labourers and even cultivate land as tenants. Their skill in tracking also is notorious. They are by no means always, or indeed generally criminal, in this Province at least; and in Lahore and Sirsa seem to be sufficiently inoffensive. But in many parts of the Panjáb, and generally I believe in Rájpútána, they are much addicted to crime. I am indebted to the kindness of Mr. MacCracken, Personal Assistant to the Inspector-General of Police, for the figures of Abstract No. 97 on page 312,* which shows the number of *P. 280-81 each criminal caste registered under the Criminal Tribes Act in each district of the Panjáb. From these figures it appears that the Báwarias are registered as professional criminals only in Fírozpur and Lúdhiána, and that in the former district only a small portion of the caste is so registered. Even where they are criminal they usually confine themselves to petty theft, seldom employing violence. About one-tenth of them are returned as Sikhs, but hardly any as Musalmáns. They eat all wild animals, including the pig and the lizard, and most of them will eat carrion. But it is said that the ordinary Bráhman officiates at their weddings, so that they can hardly be called outcast. They, like most thieving classes, worship Devi, and sacrifice to her goats and buffaloes with the blood of which they mark their foreheads; and they reverence the cow, wear the *choti*, burn their dead, and send the ashes to the Ganges. It is said that the criminal section of the tribe will admit men of other castes to their fraternity on payment. They have a language of their own which is spoken by the women and children as well as by the men. They are said to be divided into three sections: the Bidáwati of Bíkáner who trace their origin to Bidáwar in Jaipur, do not eat carrion, disdain petty theft but delight in crimes of violence, will not steal cows or oxen, and affect a superiority over the rest; the Jangali or Kálkamalia[1] generally found in the Jangaldes of the Sikh States, Fírozpur, and Sirsa, and whose women wear black blankets; and the Káparia who are most numerous in the neighbourhood of Dehli, and are notoriously a criminal tribe. The three sections neither eat together nor intermarry. The Kálkamalia is the only section which are still hunters by profession, the other sections looking down upon that calling. The Káparia are for the most part vagrant; while the Bidáwati live generally in fixed abodes.

576. The Aheri and Thori (Caste Nos. 91 and 100).—It appears almost certain that, so far as the plains of the Panjáb are concerned, these two sets of figures refer to the same caste and should be taken together. In the hills the

[1] Also called Kaldhaballia, from *dhabla* a skirt, the blanket forming a petticoat.

men who carry merchandise on pack animals are known as Thoris; and it is probable that the Thoris returned for the Hill States are nothing more than persons who follow this occupation, for it is improbable that the Aheri of Rájpútána should be found in the Simla hills, and the word seems to be applied to anybody who carries on beasts of burden without regard to caste. Still, the Thoris do seem to have a connection with the Banjáras. They are said by Tod to be carriers in the Rájpútána deserts; and the headmen of both Thoris and Banjáras are called Náik. The question needs further examination. It is not at all impossible that the Thoris may be allied to or identical with the lower class of Banjáras, while the Aheris are true hunters. But in the Panjáb plains the two words seem to be used indifferently, and I shall consider them as synonymous for the present. Mr. Wilson says that an Aheri is called Náik as a term of honour, and Thori as a term of contempt.

The Aheris or Heris or Thoris are by heredity hunters and fowlers, and Sir Henry Elliott says that they have proceeded from the Dhánaks, though they do not eat dead carcasses as the Dhánaks do. Their name is said to signify "cowherd," from *her*, a herd of cattle. They are vagrant in their habits, but not unfrequently settle down in villages where they find employment. They catch and eat all sorts of wild animals, pure and impure, and work in reeds and grass. In addition to these occupations they work in the fields, and especially move about in gangs at harvest time in search of employment as reapers; and they cut wood and grass and work as general labourers, and on roads and other earthworks. In Sirsa they occasionally cultivate, while in Karnál they often make saltpetre, and in Rájpútána they are employed as out-door servants, and even as musicians. Their home is Rájpútána, and especially Jodhpur and the prairies of Bíkáner, and they are found in the Panjáb only in Dehli and Hissár divisions, Jínd, and Patiála. In appearance and physique they resemble the Báwaria just described; but they have no special dialect of their own. A few in the Sikh States are returned as Sikhs; but the remainder are Hindus. They are considered outcasts, and made to live beyond the village ditch. They do not keep donkeys nor eat beef or carrion, and they worship the ordinary village deities, but especially Bábaji of Kohmand in Jodhpur and Khetrpál of Jodpur. The Chamarwa Bráhmans officiate at their marriages and on like occasions. They burn their dead and send the ashes to the Ganges. Mr. Christie says "What beef is to the Hindu and pork to the Musalmán, horse-flesh is to the Aheri." They have clans with Rájpút names, all of which intermarry one with another. They are said in some parts to be addicted to thieving; but this is not their general character.

[P. 311] **577. The Sansi (Caste No. 72).**—The Sánsis are the vagrants of the centre of the Panjáb, as the Aheris are of its south-eastern portions. They are most numerous in the Lahore and Amritsar divisions, and are also found in considerable numbers in Lúdhiána, Karnál and Gújrát. They trace their origin from Márwár and Ajmer where they are still very numerous. They are essentially a wandering tribe, seldom or never settling for long in any one place. They are great hunters, catching and eating all sorts of wild animals, both clean and unclean, and eating carrion. They keep sheep, goats, pigs and donkeys, work in grass and straw and reeds, and beg; and their women very commonly dance and sing and prostitute themselves. They have some curious connection with the Jat tribes of the Central Panjáb, to most of whom they are the hereditary genealogists or bards; and even in Rájpútána they commonly call themselves *bhart* or "bards." They are said also to act as genealogists to the

Dogars of Fírozpur, the Rájpúts of Hushyárpur and Jálandhar, and the Sodhis of Anandpur. Ahout 11 per cent. are returned as Musalmáns and a very few as Sikhs. The rest are Hindus, but they are of course outcasts. A slight sketch of their religion is given in section 296. They trace their descent from one Sáns Mal of Bhartpur whom they still revere as their Guru, and are said to worship his patron saint under the name of Malang Sháh. Their marriage ceremony is peculiar, the bride being covered by a basket on which the bridegroom sits while the nuptial rites are being performed. They are divided into two great tribes, Kálka and Málka which do not intermarry. They have a dialect peculiar to themselves; and their women are especially depraved.

The Sánsis are the most criminal class in the Panjáb; and it will be seen from Abstract No. 97 on the next page* that they are registered under the Act in nine districts. Still though the whole caste is probably open to suspicion of petty pilfering, they are by no means always professional thieves. The Panjáb Government wrote in 1881: "Their habits vary greatly in "different localities. A generation ago they were not considered a criminal "class at Lahore, where they kept up the genealogies of the Jat land-holders "and worked as agricultural labourers. In Gurdáspur on the other hand "they are notorious as the worst of criminals." Where they are professional criminals they are determined and fearless, and commit burglary and highway robbery, though their gangs are seldom large. The thieving Sánsis are said to admit any caste to their fraternity on payment except Dhedhs and Mhangs; and the man so admitted becomes to all intents and purposes a Sánsi.

*P. 280-81

578. The Pakhiwara (Caste No. 117).—The Pakhíwáras are often said to be a branch of the Sánsis, whom they resemble in many respects; but this is more than doubtful. They take their name from the word *pakhi*, which means a "bird," and also a "straw hut," either meaning being appropriate, as the Pakhíwáras live in straw huts and are hunters and fowlers. They are found chiefly in the Amritsar division, Gújrát, and Multán, but especially in Siálkot. They are all Musalmán, but eat vermin and are therefore outcasts.[1] They are by hereditary occupation fowlers and hunters; but they seem to have taken very generally to hawking vegetables about for sale, and in some parts the word Pakhíwára is almost synonymous with *kunjra* or "greengrocer." They are a very criminal tribe, and in Siálkot they are (see Abstract No. 97) registered as such and have been settled by Government in small villages and given land to cultivate. Excepting the persons so settled the Pakhíwáras are essentially vagrant in their habits.

579. The Jhabel (Caste No. 107).—The Jhabel, or as he is often called Chabel, is said to take his name from *Chamb*, the Panjábi for a *jhíl* or marsh.[2] Mr. O'Brien describes the Jhabel in his *Glossary* as a "tribe of fishermen who "came originally from Sindh, and still speak pure Sindhi among themselves; "and who are addressed by the title of *Jám*, which is Sindhi for 'Prince.' "They are Musalmáns and are considered orthodox, because they do not, like "the Kehals and other fishing tribes, eat turtles and crocodiles[1]." This refers

[1] Mr. Christie says that, of the four great Sunni schools (see section 283), the Hambali are most restricted as to what is lawful to eat, the Hanifi rules follow very closely the Mosaic customs, the Sháfai teach that all animals which inhabit the water are clean, while the Máliki pronounce everything pure, whether on earth or in the water, and exclude only such animals as have been specially declared unclean, as the dog, the pig, and birds that use their talons when feeding. He tells me that all Pakhíwáras belong to the Máliki, and all Jhabels and Malláhs to the Sháfai school.

[2] Another derivation is from *jham*, the dredger used in sinking wells.

to the neighbourhood of Multán, where they are a purely fishing and hunting caste of vagrant habits, living on the banks of the river. But they have spread up the Satluj as high as Fírozpur and Lahore, and on the upper parts of the river work chiefly as boatmen though they still fish and are great hunters. In fact Mr. Wilson says that all the Sirsa Malláhs or boatmen are Jhabels, and it is very probable that many Jhabels have in that district, and perhaps elsewhere, returned themselves as Malláh.

There are small colonies of Jhabels in Hushyárpur, Gurdáspur, and Kapúrthala, who are hunters and fishermen, divers and well-sinkers, and sometimes own a little land. They look upon the calling of boatman as degrading, and will not intermarry with the Jhabels of the Satluj. In Gurdáspur the word is said to include men of any caste who make their living from the fens or swamps; but I doubt the accuracy of this statement. (See also next paragraph under Kehal.)

580. The Kehal or Mor (Caste No. 161).—The Kehals or Mors, for the two appear to be identical and I have joined the figures together, are a vagrant fishing tribe found on the banks of the lower Satluj, Chenáb, and Indus. Mr. O'Brien writes of them in his *Glossary*:—

"They profess Mahomedanism, but eat alligators, turtles and tortoises, which they justify "by a text of Imám Sháfi.[1] They derive their name from *kehara*, Sindhi for lion; but perhaps "the Sanskrit *kewada* or 'fisherman' is a more probable derivation."

And in his Settlement Report he writes:—

"The Kehals and Mors are said to be one tribe. In the north of the district they are "called Mors, eat crocodiles and tortoises, and no Mahomedan will associate with them. In the "south they do not eat these animals, and are considered good Mahomedans. The Kehals and "Mors live by fishing, but some of them, as well as of the Jhabels, have taken to agriculture, and "are fond of cultivating *samáka*, a grain that is sown in the mud left by the retreating river. "These tribes live separately in villages near the river, called Miáni, from *me*, a 'fisherman.' "There is an old report in the Deputy Commissioner's office, which says that these three tribes "were cannibals; but modern observation does not confirm this."

The Kehals also catch and eat lizards. It is said that a crocodile can [P. 313] smell a Mor from a long distance, and will flee at his approach; and some officers who have come into contact with the tribe tell me that they are inclined to believe the statement, for that they would do the same. Of the 1,251 Kehals entered in the tables, 390 returned themselves as Mor and 861 as Kehal.

581. The Gagra (Caste No. 133).—Gágra is a small caste, for the most part Musalmáns and chiefly found in the central districts, who wander about catching and eating vermin. But their hereditary occupation is that of catching, keeping, and applying leeches; and they are often called Jukera, from *jouk*, a "leech." They also make matting and generally work in grass and straw, and in some parts the coarse sacking used for bags for pack animals and similar purposes is said to be made almost entirely by them. The Musalmán Gágras marry by *nikáh*. They seem to fulfil some sort of functions at weddings, and are said to receive fees on those occasions. It is said that they worship Bála Sháh, the Chúhra *Guru*.

582. The Mina (Caste No. 166).—The Mina is, in the Panjáb at least, almost invariably criminal. In Alwar and Jaipur, however, which are his home, this does not appear to be the case. Indeed the Jaipur State is said to be "really made up of petty Mína States, now under the chieftaincy of the Kachwáha Rájputs." In Gurgáon indeed he cultivates land, but this does

[1] *Vide* note [1] on previous page.

Abstract No. 97 showing Classes registered [P. 312]

1	2				3				4			
	MINAS.				BILOCHIS.				BAWARIAS.			
	MALES.		FEMALES.		MALES.		FEMALES.		MALES.		FEMALES.	
DISTRICT.	Adults.	Children.	Adults.	Children.	Adults.	Children.	Adults.	Children.	Adults.	Children.	Adults.	Children.
Gurgáon [1]	301	133	298	8	...	...	...	...	...	...	...	...
Karnál [2]	...	...	...	...	70	...	52	...	...	...	...	...
Ambála [2]	...	...	...	..	408	...	...	...	...	...	...	...
Lúdhiána [3]	...	...	...	...	...	...	...	...	270	20	256	
Firozpur [1], [2]	...	...	...	...	...	...	...	...	893	71	...	...
Jálandhar [2]	...	...	...	...	...	...	...	...	...	...	...	...
Hushyárpur [4]	...	...	...	...	...	...	...	...	...	...	...	...
Gurdáspur	...	...	...	...	...	.	...	...	...	...	...	...
Lahore [2]	...	..	...	...		...	...	...	...	...	..	...
Siálkot [2]	...	...	...	...	...	...	..	...	...	...	...	...
Gujránwála [2]	..	...	...	...	...	...	...		...	...	...	...
Ráwalpindi [2]	...	...	...	...	...	...	...	...	..	...	.	...
Gújrát	...	...	...	...	...	...	...	...	...	...	...	...
TOTAL ...	301	133	208	8	478	...	52	...	1,063	91	256	2

[1] Under or ders of Government,
[2] Children below the age of 12
[3] Children under 6 years of age
[4] No children have been re

under the Criminal Tribes Act for Districts.

				6				7				8			
HARNIS.				SANSIS.				PAKHIWARAS.				GURMANGS.			
MALES.		FEMALES.		MALES.		FEMALES.		MALES.		FEMALES.		MALES.		FEMALES.	
Adults.	Children.	Adults.	Children.	Adults.	Children.	Adults.	Children.	Adults.	Children.	Adults.	Children.	Adults.	Children.	Adults.	Children.
...	...	...	...	...	...	...	...	...	...	...	...	...	...	...	...
...	...	...	...	459	...	343	...	...	...	...	...	..	...	...	...
...	...	...	...	...	...	...	...	...	...	...	...	...	...	...	...
1,048	153	910	148	390	55	310	68	...	...	...	...	...	...	...	...
...	...	...	...	...	.	...	...	...	...	...	...	...	...	...	...
38	...	41	...	247	...	233	...	...	...	...	...	...	...	...	...
199	..	194	...	93	...	83	...	...	...	...	..	...	...	...	...
...	...	...	...	753	...	644	...	...	...	...	...	...	...	...	...
...	...	...	...	539	362	487	...	..	...	...	..	...	...	..	...
...	...	...	...	711	...	538	...	587	...	426	...	...	...	...	...
...	...	...	..	1,283	...	1,030	...	...	...	...	...	...	...	...	...
...	..	...	...	...	...	...	...	...	...	...	...	23	...	20	...
...	...	..	...	294	209	257	179	1	4	1	1	...	...	...	...
1,285	153	1,145	148	4,767	626	3,923	217	588	4	427	1	23	...	20	...

the names of the females have now been removed from the registers.
years are not registered.
are omitted from the registers.
gistered.

not prevent his being a professional thief. I extract the following description of the caste from Major Powlett's Gazetteer of Alwar:—

"Minas were formerly the rulers of much of the country now held by the Jaipur Chief. "They still hold a good social position, for Rájputs will eat and drink from their hands, and they "are the most trusted guards in the Jaipur State. The Minas are of two classes, the 'Zemindari' "or agricultural, and the 'Chaukidari,' or watchmen. The former are excellent cultivators, and "are good, well-behaved people. They form a large portion of the population in Karauli, and are "numerous in Jaipur.

"The 'Chaukidari' Minas, though of the same tribe as the other class, are distinct from it. "They consider themselves soldiers by profession, and so somewhat superior to their agricultural "brethen, from whom they take, but do not give, girls in marriage. Many of the 'Chaukidari' "Minas take to agriculture, and, I believe, thereby lose caste to some extent. These Chaukidari "Minas are the famous marauders. They travel in bands, headed by a chosen leader, as far "south as Haidarabad in the Deccan, where they commit daring robberies; and they are the "principal class which the Thaggi and Dacoiti Suppression Department has to act against. In "their own villages they are often charitable; and as successful plunder has made some rich, "they benefit greatly the poor of their neighbourboood, and are consequently popular But "those who have not the enterprise for distant expeditions, but steal and rob near their own "homes, are numerous and are felt to be a great pest. Some villages pay them highly as Chaukidars to refrain from plundering and to protect the village from others. So notorious are they "as robbers that the late Chief of Alwar, Banni Singh, was afraid lest they should corrupt "their agricultural brethren, and desirous of keeping them apart forbade their marrying or even "smoking or associating with members of the well-conducted class.

"In April 1863, Major Impey, then Political Agent of Alwar, issued orders placing the "Chaukidari Minas under surveillance; and under Major Cadell's direction lists of them have been "made out, periodical roll-call enforced in the villages and absence without leave certificate "punished.

"I am not sure that, although speaking generally, Minas are divided into Chaukidari and "Zamindari, there is any hard and fast line between the two classes. There is, I believe, an "intermediate class, for Maharaja Banni Singh's attempts to keep the two apart were not very "successful.

"There are said to be 32 clans of Minas. Out of 59 Minas apprehended for dacoity by the Dacoity Suppression Department, I found that the Jeb clan furnished 17, the Kagot 8, the Sira 8 and the Jarwál and Bágri 5 each. The Susawat was, I believe, formerly the most powerful clan, and that which held Ajmere."

The Mínas are the boldest of our criminal classes. Their head-quarters, so far as the Panjáb is concerned, are the village of Sháhjahánpur, attached to the Gurgáon district but surrounded on all sides by Rájpútána territory. There they till lately defied our police, and even resisted them with armed force. Their enterprises are on a large scale, and they are always prepared to use violence if necessary. In Márwár they are armed with small bows, which do considerable execution. They travel great distances in gangs of from 12 to 20 men, practising robbery and dacoity even as far as the Deccan. The gangs usually start off immediately after the Díwáli feast, and often remain absent the whole year. They have agents in all the large cities of Rájpútána and the Deccan who give them information, and they are in league with the carrying castes of Márwár. After a successful foray they offer one-tenth of the proceeds at the shrine of Káli Devi. The criminal Mínas are said to inhabit a tract of country about 65 miles long and 40 broad, stretching from Sháhpurah 40 miles north of Jaipur to Guráora in Gurgáon on the Rohtak border, the most noted villages being Koti Putli, Bhairor, and Sháhjahánpur, each of which contains some 500 robbers. Their claim to Rájpút descent is probably well-founded, though they are said to spring from an illegitimate son of a Rájpút; and in woman's slang one woman is said to "give Mína" (*mina dena*) to another when she accuses her of illicit intercourse.[1] They practise *karewa* or widow-marriage. They have a

[1] This is as I find the fact stated. But the word *mihna* or *mahna* seems to be commonly used in the same sense throughout the Panjab; and it is very probable that the expression quoted has nothing to do with the name of the Mína caste.

dialect of their own ; or rather perhaps, a set of slang words and phrases which are common to the criminal classes. In the Panjáb the Mína is almost confined to Gurgáon and the neighbouring portions of the Patiála and Nábha States. They are almost all Hindus and belong to the Chaukídári section and the Kagot clan (see further under Meo, section 478).

583. The Harni (Caste No. 159).—This again is one of the most criminal castes in the Province, and as will be seen from the figures of Abstract No. *P. 280-81 97 on page 312,* a greater number of them are registered under the Criminal Tribes Act than of any other caste except Sánsi. They are found in the districts lying under the hills from Lúdhiána to Siálkot, and also in Fírozpur and Farídkot. They are said to have been Rájpúts driven from Bhatner by famine, who were employed by the Rai of Raikot in Lúdhiána for purposes of theft and to harass his enemies. They are also said to be Bhíls or Gonds and to have come from the Rájpútána desert. Their chief crimes are burglary, and highway robbery, to effect which they travel in gangs, often under the disguise of carriers with pack-oxen. Their women also wander about as pedlars to pilfer and collect information. They are all returned as Musalmán.

584. The Bilochi (Caste No. 18).—The Biloch of the frontier has already been described at pages 193*ff*. But there is a small criminal tribe called Bilochi who [P. 314] may be noticed here. They seem to be found chiefly, if not entirely, in Ambála and Karnál, numbering some 1,000 souls in the former and 150 in the latter district, inhabiting the banks of the Saruswati from Pehoa downwards, and infesting the Cháchra or dense *dhák* jungle of that neighbourhood. Mr. Stone writes :—"During the rainy season the whole country is inundated for months. "Village roads are washed away or concealed under the luxurious growth of "grass, and dense masses of jungle shut in the view on every side. No "stranger could possibly penetrate to the Biloch village through such a clueless "maze without a guide. The only road open to the traveller is the raised one "between Tháuesar and Pehoa; the moment he leaves that he is lost. A "more suitable stronghold for a criminal tribe can hardly be imagined." They are almost certainly of true Biloch origin, and still give their tribal names as Rind, Lashári, Jatoi, and Korai. But they are by their habits quite distinct from both the land-owning Biloch and the camel-driver who is so commonly called Biloch simply because he *is* a camel-driver (see section †P. 280-81 375.) Abstract No. 97 on page 312† shows the numbers registered as professional criminals. They are described as coarse-looking men of a dark colour living in a separate quarter, and with nothing to distinguish them from the scavenger caste except a profusion of stolen ornaments and similar property. They say that their ancestors once lived beyond Kasúr in the Lahore district but were driven out on account of their marauding habits. The men still keep camels and cultivate a little land as their ostensible occupation ; but during a great part of the year they leave the women, who are strictly secluded, at home, and wander about disguised as *faqírs* or as butchers in search of sheep for sale, extending their excursions to great distances and apparently to almost all parts of India. Further information will be found in a very interesting report by Mr. Stone in Punjab Government Home Proceedings, No. 16 of March 1877.

585. The Bangali.—The word Bangáli is applied to any native of Bengal, and especially to the Bengali Baboo of our offices. The figures given in our tables under Caste No. 168 evidently refer to these men and are not properly caste statistics, the Bengalis of the Panjáb being of various castes, though generally I believe either Bráhmans or Káyaths. But in the Panjáb there is a distinct criminal tribe known as Bangáli, who are said to have emigrated from Hushyárpur to Kángra in which district they are chiefly to be found. They are not registered under the Criminal Tribes Act. None of these people have been returned in our Census tables as Bangáli by caste ; and as th y are sometimes said to be a Sánsi clan and as the word Bangáli seems to be applied in some districts to all Kanjars and in others to all Sipádas or snake-charmers, it is probable that the Kángra Bangális are not a separate caste. I see that in the Dehli division Bangális have been included with Sánsis. Mr. Christie writes: "The Bangális have very probably been included with Jogis in "the returns. There are a vagrant tribe of immigrants from Bengal. They "keep dogs and donkeys and exhibit snakes, eat all sorts of vermin, and have "a dialect of their own. Their women dance, sing, and prostitute them-"selves. They are not criminals in the ordinary sense, but are in the habit "of kidnapping boys to sell to Hindu mahants (*sic*). The name is also "applied generally to Musalmán jugglers."

586. **Other criminal tribes.**—The **Tagus** of Karnál and the upper *doáb* of the Ganges and Jamna are admittedly Bráhmans, and have probably returned themselves as such.[1] Tágu is merely used to denote a section of that caste which has taken to picking pockets and petty theft. They steal only by day and seclude their women. They wear the *janeo* or sacred thread. They have lately been declared under the Criminal Tribes Act. They must be distinguished from the Tagas, also a Brahminical tribe of the same parts, who are peaceful agriclturists. It is said that the name is properly Táku, but Tágu is the form in common use.

The Gurmangs are an insignificant class of criminals found in the Ráwalpindi district, where some of them are registered as criminals. They do not appear in our returns, nor can I say under what caste they have returned themselves.

The Kanjars (Caste No. 135) will presently be described in section 590. They appear to be often criminal in their habits, more especially in the neighbourhood of Dehli.

The Dumnas and Chuhras (Caste Nos. 41 and 44) are described in sections 597 to 600. Many of the Dúmnas of the Jammu hills and the there plains immediately below them are professional thieves. Of criminal Chuhrás appear to be two distinct classes, those of the Dehli territory and those of the western sub-montane districts, each of which uses a separate *argot* peculiar to itself.

The Rawals (Caste No. 80) have been described in section 528, and are often professional criminals. In fact the same may be said of almost every one of the lowest castes, as well as of the vagrant classes next to be discussed.

THE GIPSY TRIBES.

587. **The Gipsy tribes.**—The gipsy tribes, for which the figures will be found in Abstruct No. 98 on the opposite page,* are hardly to be distinguished from those whom I called the wandering and criminal tribes. They too are vagrants and outcasts, and they too are hereditary workers in grass, straw, and *P. 286-87

[1] Mr. Christie states, however, that the term Tágu is often used to include Jhínwars, or rather Dhínwars, as well as Bráhmans.

the like. But I have classed as Gipsies, for want of a better distinction, those tribes who perform in any way, who practise tumbling or rope-dancing, lead about bears and monkeys, and so forth. The gipsy, and apparently all the vagrant tribes, are governed by tribal councils and often appeal to ordeals. A common form of ordeal is that the accused stands in a pond with a pole in his hand. At a given signal he ducks his head; while another man, honest and true, starts running at a fair pace for a spot 70 paces distant. If the accused can keep under water while the 140 paces there and back are accomplished, he is acquitted. If not, he has to submit to such penalty as the council may impose.

[P. 315] **588. The Nat and Bazigar (Caste Nos. 98 and 89).**—The Nat is the typical gipsy of the Panjáb. It is possible that there may be properly some distinction between the Nat and the Bázígar; but the two words are synonymous in general parlance, and I shall discuss the figures together. In the Lahore division indeed, and in some other districts, the two have not been returned separately. Bázígar is a Persian word meaning "he who does *bázi*" or any sort of game or play, but it is applied only to jugglers and acrobats. Some say that the Bázígar is a tumbler and the Nat a rope-dancer; others that the Bázígar is a juggler as well as an acrobat, while the Nat is only the latter, and it is possible that those who reach the higher ranks of the profession may call themselves by the Persian name; others again say that among the Nats the males only, but among the Bázígars both sexes perform; and this latter distinction is reported from several districts. On the whole it is perhaps more probable that the Nat is the caste to which both classes belong, and Bázígar an occupational term. In the Dehli and Hissár divisions the word used for Bázígar is Bádi, a term which is apparently quite unknown in any other part of the Panjáb except Ambála; and I have classed Bádi and Bázígar together.

The Nats then, with whom I include the Bázígars, are a gipsy tribe of vagrant habits who wander about with their families, settling for a few days or weeks at a time in the vicinity of large villages or towns, and constructing temporary shelters of grass. In addition to practising acrobatic feats and conjuring of a low class, they make articles of grass, straw, and reeds for sale; and in the centre of the Panjáb are said to act as Mírásis, though this is perhaps doubtful. They often practise surgery and physic in a small way, and are not free from the suspicion of sorcery. They are said to be divided into two main classes; those whose males only perform as acrobats, and those whose women, called Kabútri, perform and
[P. 316] prostitute themselves. About three-quarters of their number returned themselves as Hindus, and most of the rest as Musalmáns. They mostly marry by *phera*, and burn the dead; but they are really outcasts, keeping many dogs with which they hunt and eat the vermin of the jungles. They are said especially to reverence the goddess Devi, Guru Teg Bahádur, the Guru of the Sikh scavengers, and Hanúmán or the monkey god, the last because of the acrobatic powers of monkeys. They very generally trace their origin from Márwár; and they are found all over the Province except on the frontier, where they are apparently almost unknown. The large numbers returned in Baháwalpur and Montgomery, in the former as Nats and in the latter as Bázígars, is very striking. Their different tribes are governed by a Rája and Ráni, or King and Queen, like the gipsy tribes of Europe. The Musalmán Nats are said to prostitute their unmarried, but not their married women; and

Abstract No. 98, showing the Gipsy [P. 315.]

	FIGURES.								
	98	89	164	135	167	177	121	158	150
	Nat.	Bázígar.	Perna.	Kanjar.	Hesi.	Garri.	Qalandari.	Gandhila.	Baddún.
Dehli ...	266	1	...	591	...	...	147	...	...
Gurgaon ...	629	719	102	692	...	...	1,806	...	...
Karnál ...	815	248	...	30	...	...	14	67	...
Hissar ...	576	294	...	1	...	...	30	...	...
Rohtak ...	106	318	13	...	...	...	...	...	...
Sirsa ...	287	...	28	265	...	...	8	...	...
Ambála ...	1,990	489	...	114	...	...	6	343	9
Lúdhiána ...	161	935	...	...	...	...	2	...	121
Jálandhar ...	112	254	...	...	...	...	9	113	339
Hushyárpur ...	75	...	...	...	18	...	45	14	56
Kangra ...	360	...	...	...	424	...	...	7	...
Amritsar ...	163	442	...	...	...	...	...	...	164
Gurdaspur ...	8	160	83	...	...	...	...	...	91
Siálkot ...	28	36	...	...	...	685	...	...	...
Lahore ...	...	1,361	147	...	...	...	185	186	339
Gujránwála ...	...	930	5	...	...	...	400	8	151
Firozepur ...	...	1,188	18	...	...	...	16	...	170
Ráwalpindi ...	580	667	17	...	...	...	5	...	...
Jahlam ...	281	238	8	...	...	...	145	...	...
Gújrát ...	139	68	19	...	...	...	800	...	...
Shahpur ...	320	594	1	...	...	...	16	...	...
Multan ...	369	130	130	...	...	...	16	...	...
Jhang ...	276	1	85	...	...	...	122	...	...
Montgomery ...	398	2,349	277	...	...	...	69	55	...
Muzaffargarh ...	97	72	...	...	...	...	...	...	...
British Territory ...	**8,190**	**11,504**	**933**	**1,694**	**442**	**685**	**3,841**	**793**	**1,440**
Patiála ...	1,052	1,598	45	5	...	...	54	165	26
Nábha ...	57	296	15	...	...	...	...	...	...
Kapurthala ...	39	2	38	85	...	...	...	...	270
Jínd ...	183	152	...	...	...	...	...	...	...
Faridkot ...	90	124	...	...	...	...	...	...	...
Malerkotla ...	1	76	...	...	...	...	...	...	...
Kalsia ...	85	53	...	...	...	...	...	18	...
Total East. Plains ...	1,548	2,301	123	90	...	...	54	183	296
Bahawalpur ...	1,919	...	101	1,041	...	...	...	472	...
Total Hill States ...	83	36	...	47	668	...	...	1	...
British Territory ...	**8,190**	**11,504**	**933**	**1,694**	**442**	**685**	**3,841**	**793**	**1,440**
Native States ...	**3,550**	**2,337**	**224**	**1,178**	**668**	...	**54**	**656**	**296**
Province ...	**11,740**	**13,841**	**1,157**	**2,872**	**1,110**	**685**	**3,895**	**1,449**	**1,736**

. ri es for Districts and States.

Proportion per 1,000 of total Population.									
98	89	164	135	167	177	121	158		
Nat.	Bázígar.	Perna.	Kanjar.	Hesi.	Garri.	Qalandari.	Gandhila.	Total.	
...	...	...	1	...	...	...	...	1	Dehli.
1	1	...	1	...	...	3	...	6	Gurgaon.
1	...	...	...	..	...	...	...	1	Karnál.
1	1	...	...	...	...	...	...	2	Hissar.
...	1	...	...	...	...	...	...	1	Rohtak.
1	...	...	1	...	...	...	...	2	Sirsa.
2	...	...	...	...	...	...	...	2	Ambála.
...	2	...	...	...	...	...	...	2	Lúdhiána.
...	...	...	...	...	...	...	...	...	Jálandhar.
...	...	...	...	...	...	...	...	...	Hushyárpur.
...	...	...	...	...	...	...	...	...	Kangra.
...	...	...	...	...	...	...	.	...	Amritsar.
...	...	...	...	...	...	...	...	...	Gurdaspur.
...	...	...	...	...	1	...	...	1	Siálkot.
...	2	...	...	...	...	...	...	2	Lahore.
...	1	..	...	..	...	1	...	2	Gujránwála.
...	2	...	...	...	...	...	...	2	Firozepur.
1	1	...	...	...	...	...	...	2	Ráwalpindi.
...	...	...	...	...	...	...	...	...	Jahlam.
...	...	...	...	...	...	1	...	1	Gújrát.
1	1	...	...	...	...	...	...	2	Shahpur.
1	...	...	...	...	...	...	...	1	Multan.
1	...	...	...	...	...	...	...	1	Jhang.
1	6	1	...	...	...	...	...	8	Montgomery.
...	...	...	...	...	...	...	...	...	Muzaffargarh.
...	1	...	...	...	...	...	...	1	**British Territory.**
1	1	...	...	...	...	...	...	2	Patiála.
...	1	...	...	...	...	...	...	1	Nábha.
...	...	...	...	...	...	...	...	...	Kapurthala.
1	1	...	...	...	...	...	...	2	Jínd.
1	1	...	...	...	...	...	...	2	Faridkot.
...	1	...	...	...	...	...	...	1	Malerkotla.
1	1	...	...	...	...	...	...	2	Kalsia.
1	1	...	...	...	...	...	...	2	Total East Plains.
3	...	...	2	...	...	...	1	6	Baháwalpur.
...	...	...	...	1	...	...	...	1	Total Hill States.
...	1	...	...	...	...	...	...	1	**British Territory.**
1	1	...	...	...	...	...	...	2	**Native States.**
...	1	..	...	...	...	...	...	1	**Province.**

when a Nat woman marries, the first child is either given to the grandmother as compensation for the loss of the mother's gains as a prostitute, or is redeemed by payment of Rs. 30. But this is perhaps the custom with the Pernas rather than with the Nats (see below). Another, and more probable account is, that the first wife married is one of the tribe, and is kept secluded; after which the Musalmán Nat, who is usually to be found in the towns, will marry as many women as he can procure by purchase from the vagrant tribes or otherwise, and these latter he prostitutes.

589. The Perna (Caste No. 164).—The Pernas are also a vagrant tribe of gipsies, exceedingly similar to the Nats or Bázígars. But there is said to be this great distinction, that the Pernas habitually and professedly prostitute their women, which the Nats do not.[1] The Perna women are said to be jugglers and tumblers, and generally perform their acrobatic feats holding a sword or knife to their throats; but their characteristic occupation is dancing and singing rather than tumbling. The men apparently do not perform, but merely play the drum for the women to dance to. It is not quite clear that the word is anything more than the name of an occupation like Bázígar, for some Pernas are said to be Chúhra by caste. It is possible that they are a true caste, but like many of the vagrant tribes will admit strangers to their fraternity on payment. They are almost all Musalmáns, and are said to marry by *nikáh*. They are said to be divided into two classes, *báratáli* and *teratáli*, from the sort of music to which they dance, *tál* meaning a "beat" in music. If so, the music with thirteen beats in a bar must be worth listening to as a curiosity. They are probably found almost all over the Province except in the frontier districts; but in the Lahore division they have been included with Bázígar, and perhaps the same has happened elsewhere, though my papers do not show it.

590. The Kanjar (Caste No. 135).—I have taken a liberty with these figures which is I think justified by my information. The Kanjar of the Dehli territory, or as he seems to be called in the Ambála division the Jallád, is a wandering tribe very similar to the Perna; and in that part of the country a pimp or prostitute is called Kanchan or by some similar name, and never Kanjar. In the remainder of the Panjáb the word Kanchan is not used, the wandering tribe of Kanjars is apparently not found, and Kanjar is the ordinary word for pimp or prostitute. Thus I found Kanchan and Kanjar (including Jallád) separately returned for the Dehli, Hissár, and Ambála divisions, and Kanjar only for the rest of the Province. Now prostitutes are found all over the Province. Accordingly I classed the Kanchan of the three divisions just named, together with the Kanjar of the remainder of the Panjáb, under the head Kanchan (Caste No. 96), and left only the Kanjar of the Dehli territory under the head we are now discussing. The Kanchans are almost all Musalmáns, while the Kanjars are all Hindus except in Sirsa; and it is probable that the Musalmán Kanjars shown for Sirsa should also have been classed as Kanchan, and that the Hindus shown as Kanchan are really Kanjars.

The Kanjars of the Dehli territory are a vagrant tribe who wander about the country catching and eating jackals, lizards and the like, making rope and other articles of grass for sale, and curing boils and other diseases. They parti-

---

[1] Mr. Christie, on the other hand, who is a good authority, says that the fact is exactly the reverse of this.

cularly make the grass brushes used by weavers.[1] They are said to divide their girls into two classes; one they marry themselves, and them they do not prostitute; the other they keep for purposes of prostitution. The Jalláds of Ambála are said to be the descendants of a Kanjar family who were attached to the Dehli Court as executioners, and who, their duty being to flog, mutilate, and execute, were called Jallád or "skinners," from *jild*, "skin." The Kanjars appear to be of a higher status than the Nat, though they are necessarily outcasts. They worship Máta, whom they also call Káli Mái; but whether they refer to Káli Devi or to Sítala does not appear; most probably to the former. They also reverence Gúga Pír. Dehli is said to be the Panjáb head-quarters of the tribe. But the word Kanjar seems to be used in a very loose manner; it is by no means certain that these Kanjars are not merely a Báwaria tribe; and it is just possible that they have received their name from their habit of prostituting their daughters, from the Panjábi word Kanjar. The words Kanjar and Bangáli also seem often to be used as synonymous. A good deal of information regarding the Kanjars will be found in No. X of 1866 of the Selected Cases of the Panjáb Police. In that pamphlet they are called Báwarias. I should probably have done better had I grouped Kanjar with Báwaria, and not with Nat and Perna.

591. **The Hesi (Caste No. 167).**—The Hesi appears to share with the Lohár the distinction of being the only castes recognised among the Buddhists of Spiti, the other classes of that society eating together and intermarrying freely, but excluding these two from social intercourse. The Hesis of Spiti, however, or rather the Bedas as they are there called, the two names referring to the same people, do not appear to have returned themselves as of that caste, as all our Hesis are Hindus, whereas all the people of Spiti except two are returned as Buddhists.

317] The Hesis are the wandering minstrels of the higher Himalayan valleys. "The men play the pipes and kettle-drum, while the women dance and sing "and play the tambourine. They are (in Láhul and Spiti) the only class that "owns no land. 'The Beda no land and the dog no load' is a proverbial "saying." He is called "the 18th caste," or the odd caste which is not required, for no one will eat from the hands of a Hesi. Yet he has his inferiors for he himself will not eat from the hands of a Lohár or of a Náth, the Kúlu equivalent for Jogi. He is ordinarily a beggar, but sometimes engages in petty trade; and to call a transaction "a Hesi's bargain" is to imply that it is mean and paltry. The Hesi or Hensi, as the word is sometimes spelt, is found in Kángra, Mandi, and Suket. To the figures of Table VIII A should be added 201 Hesis in Suket who were left out by mistake, and are shown under Caste No. 208, Table VIII B.

592. **The Garris (Caste No. 177).**—The Garris are returned in Siálkot only. They are said to be a poor caste of strolling actors and mountebanks, mostly Hindu, who have their head-quarters in Jammu, but are not unfrequently found in the Baijwát or plain country under the Jammu hills.

593. **The Qalandari (Caste No. 121).**—The Qalandari is the Kalender of the *Arabian Nights*. He is properly a holy Mahomedan ascetic who abandons the world and wanders about with shaven head and beard. But the

[1] The Kúchband, who make these brushes, are said to be a section of the Kanjars who have given up prostitution, form a separate guild, and will not marry with the other sections of the tribe.

word is generally used in the Panjáb for a monkey-man; and I have classed him here instead of with *faqírs*. I believe that some of them have a sort of pretence to a religious character; but their ostensible occupation is that of leading about bears, monkeys, and other performing animals, and they are said, like the Kanjars, to make clay pipe-bowls of superior quality The numbers returned are small except in Gurgáon, where the figures are suspiciously large[1]; but it is probable that many of these men have returned themselves simply as *faqírs*. The detailed tables of sub-divisions will when published throw light upon the subject.

594. The Baddun (Caste No. 150).—A gipsy tribe of Musalmáns returned from the centre of the Panjáb, chiefly in the upper valleys of the Sutlej and Beás. They, like the Kehals, are followers of Imám Shafi, and justify by his teaching their habit of eating the crocodile, tortoise and frog. They are considered outcasts by other Mahomedans. They work in straw, make pipe-bowls, and their women bleed by cupping. They also are said to lead about bears, and occasionally to travel as pedlars. They are said to have three clans, Wáhle, Dhara, and Balare, and to claim Arab origin.

595. The Gandhila (Caste No. 158).—The Gandhílas are a low vagrant tribe, who are said by Elliott to be "a few degrees more respectable than the Báwarias," though I fancy that in the Panjáb their positions are reversed. They wander about bare-headed and bare-footed, beg, work in grass and straw, catch quails, clean and sharpen knives and swords, cut wood, and generally do odd jobs. They are said to eat tortoises and vermin. They also keep donkeys, and even engage in trade in small way. It is said that in some parts they lead about performing bears; but this I doubt. They have curious traditions which are reported to me from distant parts of the Province. regarding a kingdom which the tribe once possessed, and which they seem inclined to place beyond the Indus. They say they are under a vow not to wear shoes or turbans till their possessions are restored to them.

THE SCAVENGER CASTES.

596. The Scavenger Castes.—Abstract No. 99* on the next page shows *P. 291-
the distribution of this class, in which I have included Chúhra, Dhának, and 92.
Khatík. The class is numerically and economically one of the most important in the Province, for the Chúhras are only exceeded in number by the Jat, Rájpút, and Bráhman, while they occupy a very prominent position among the agricultural labourers of the Panjáb. But socially they are the lowest of the low, even lower perhaps than the vagrant Sánsi and the gipsy Nat, and as a rule can hardly be said to stand even at the foot of the social ladder, though some sections of the clan have mounted the first one or two steps. Their hereditary occupation is scavengering, sweeping the houses and streets, working up, carrying to the fields, and distributing manure, and in cities and in village houses where the women are strictly secluded, removing night soil. They alone of all classes keep those impure animals, pigs and fowls; and they and the leather-workers alone eat the flesh of animals that have died of disease or by natural death. Together with the vagrants and gipsies they are the hereditary workers in grass and reeds, from which they make winnow-

[1] Mr. Channing suggests that these men may be the *faqírs* of the shrine of Sháh Chokha, a saint much venerated by the Meos; insomuch that the abduction of a married woman from the fair of the saint is held to be allowable, Sháh Chokha being said to have given the woman to the abductor.

P. 318]

Abstract No. 99, showing the Scavenger Castes.

	SCAVENGER CLASS,						
	FIGURES.			PROPORTION PER 1,000 OF TOTAL POPULATION.			
	4	43	87	4	43	87	
	Chúhra.	Dhának.	Khatík.	Chúrah.	Dhának.	Khatík.	TOTAL.
Dehli	26,087	6,700	1,867	40	11	3	54
Gurgaon	17,783	5,693	1,398	28	9	2	39
Karnál	31,288	3,369	1,093	50	5	2	57
Hissar	12,126	13,529	950	24	27	2	53
Rohtak	19,901	18,692	832	36	34	2	72
Sirsa	16,051	1,491	1,100	63	6	4	73
Ambala	41,755	44	1,200	39	...	1	40
Ludhiána	18,525	...	196	30	...	...	30
Simla	1,845	...	2	43	...	...	43
Jalandhar	31,849	16	697	40	...	1	41
Hushyárpur	17,287	...	570	19	...	1	20
Kángra	896	1	131	1	...	...	1
Amritsar	107,011	...	...	120	...	...	120
Gurdáspur	56,985	...	...	69	...	...	69
Siálkot	78,980	...	93	78	...	...	78
Lahore	99,025	43	242	107	...	...	107
Gujránwála	57,911	...	93	94	...	...	94
Firozpur	68,905	144	389	106	...	1	107
Ráwalpindi	22,046	8	263	27	...	...	27
Jahlam	25,027	4	52	42	...	...	42
Gujrát	38,231	...	444	55	...	1	56
Shahpur	28,297	...	6	67	...	...	67

Abstract No. 99, showing the Scavenger Castes—*concluded.*

	SCAVENGER CLASS.						
	FIGURES.			PROPORTION PER 1,000 OF TOTAL POPULATION.			
—	4	43	87	4	43	87	
	Chúhra.	Dhának.	Khatík.	Chúhra.	Dhának.	Khatík.	TOTAL.
Multan	29,489	31	18	53	...	...	53
Jhang	20,944	...	2	53	...	...	53
Montgomery	28,857	...	8	68	..	...	68
Muzaffargarh... ...	11,312	...	114	33	...	...	33
Dera Ismail Khan ...	9,041	2	...	20	..	...	20
Dera Ghazi Khan ...	4,633	16	6	13	...	...	13
Bannu	5,940	8	1	18	...	...	18
Peshávar	7,653	79	22	13	...	...	13
Hazara	2,279	...	48	6	...	...	6
Kohát	1,221	2	3	7	...	...	7
British Territory ...	939,572	49,876	11,845	50	3	1	54
Patiála	66,183	5,548	1,254	45	4	1	50
Nábha	10,429	1,378	148	40	5	1	46
Kapurthala	16,334	...	61	65	...	...	65
Jind	7,006	7,090	315	29	28	1	58
Farídkot	13,369	42	...	138	...	...	138
Maler Kotla	1,465	...	89	21	...	1	22
Kalsia	3,008	...	117	44	...	2	46
Total Eastern Plains ...	118,667	16,165	2,120	47	6	1	54
Baháwalpur	18,604	...	182	32		...	32
Total Hill States ...	1,896	18	34	2	...	...	2
British Territory ...	939,572	49,876	11,845	50	3	1	54
Native States ...	139,167	16,183	2,336	36	4	1	41
Province ...	1,078,739	66,059	14,181	48	3	1	52

ing pans and other articles used in agriculture; and like them they eat jackals, lizards, tortoises, and pigs. Many of them have abandoned scavengering and taken to leather-work and even to weaving, and by doing so have mounted one or even two steps in the social grades, as in the latter case they pass over the leather-workers. But to secure the full benefit of this change of occupation they must relinquish the habit of eating carrion. Their agricultural functions will be presently described. It is probable that they are essentially of aboriginal origin; but there is little doubt that the aboriginal nucleus has received additions from other sources, of those who have gradually sunk in the scale of occupations or have in any way been degraded to the lowest level. The distribution of the class will be noticed as each of the three castes is discussed. In the hills they are replaced by menials who will be described in the separate section on the menials of those parts.

597. The Chuhra (Caste No. 4).—The Chúhra or Bhangi of Hindústán[1] is the sweeper and scavenger *par excellence* of the Panjáb, is found throughout the Province except in the hills, where he is replaced by other castes presently to be described. He is comparatively rare on the frontier, where he is, I believe, chiefly confined to the towns; and most numerous in the Lahore and Amritsar divisions and Farídkot where much of the agricultural labour is performed by him, as he here fills the position with respect to field-work which is held in the east of the Province by the Chamár. For the frontier, however, *P. 106-107 the figures of Abstract No. 72 (page 224*) must be added, which shows the Chúhras and Kutánas who have returned themselves as Jats. He is one of the village menials proper, who receive a customary share of the produce and perform certain duties. In the east of the Province he sweeps the houses and village, collects the cowdung, pats it into cakes and stacks it, works up the manure, helps with the cattle, and takes them from village to village. News of a death sent to friends is invariably carried by him, and he is the general village messenger (*Lehbar, Balái, Baláhar, Daura*). He also makes the *chháj* or winnowing pan, and the *sirki* or grass thatch used to cover carts and the like. In the centre of the Province he adds to these functions actual hard work at the plough and in the field. He claims the flesh of such dead animals as do not divide the hoof, the cloven-footed belonging to the Chamár. But his occupations change somewhat with his religion; and here it will be well to show exactly what other entries of our schedules I have included under the head of Chúhra:—

Divisions.	Mazbi.	Rangreta.	Musalli.	Kutána.
Dehli	39	...	...	...
Hissár	...	...	...	...
Ambála	1,761	245	...	...
Jalandhar	1,314	14	70	...
Amritsar	3,758	...	...	...
Lahore	3,780	...	3,109	...
Ráwalpindi	1,411	...	84,539	...
Multan	364	...	...	14,297
Deraját	...	...	...	6,766
Peshâwar	305	...	7,171	...

[1] They prefer to call themselves Chúhra, looking upon the term Bhangi as opprobrious.

These various names denote nothing more than a change of religion sometimes accompanied by a change of occupation. Table VIII shows that the Hindu Chúhra, that is to say the Chúhra who follows the original religion of the caste and has been classed by us as Hindu, is found in all the eastern half of the Panjáb plains: but that west of Lahore he hardly exists save in the great cities of Ráwalpindi, Multán and Peshávar. His religion is sketched in Part VIII of the Chapter on Religion. I may add that since writing that chapter, I have received traditions from distant parts of the Province which leave little doubt that Bála Sháh, one of the Chúhra *Gurus*, is another name for Bál Mík, a hunter of the Karnál district, who was converted by a holy Rishi, and eventually wrote the Rámáyana. The Rishi wished to prescribe penance, but reflected that so vile a man would not be able to say RAM RAM. So he set him to say MRA MRA which, if you say it fast [P. 319]
enough, comes to much the same thing. Their other *guru* is Lál Beg; and they still call their priests Lálgurus. They generally marry by *phera* and bury their dead face downwards, though they not unseldom follow in these respects the custom of the villagers whom they serve.

598. The Sikh Chuhra – Mazbi and Rangreta.—The second and third entries in the table of the last paragraph, *viz.*, Mazbi and Rangreta, denote Chúhras who have become Sikhs. Of course a Mazbi will often have been returned as Chúhra by caste and Sikh by religion; and the figures of Table VIIIA are the ones to be followed, those given above being intended merely to show how many men returned to me under each of the heads shown I have classed as Chúhras. Sikh Chúras are almost confined to the district and states immediately east and south-east of Lahore, which form the centre of Sikhism. Mazbi means nothing more than a member of the scavenger class converted to Sikhism (*see further, page* 154). The Mazbis take the *páhul*, wear their hair long, and abstain from tobacco, and they apparently refuse to touch night-soil, though performing all the other offices hereditary to the Chúhra caste. Their great *Guru* is Teg Bahádur, whose mutilated body was brought back from Dehli by Chúhras who were then and there admitted to the faith as a reward for their devotion. But though good Sikhs so far as religious observance is concerned, the taint of hereditary pollution is upon them; and Sikhs of other castes refuse to associate with them even in religious ceremonies. They often intermarry with the Lál Begi or Hindu Chúhra. They make capital soldiers and some of our regiments are wholly composed of Mazbis. The Rangreta are a class of Mazbi apparently found only in Ambála, Lúdhiána and the neighbourhood, who consider themselves socially superior to the rest. The origin of their superiority, I am informed, lies in the fact that they were once notorious as highway robbers! But it appears that the Rangretas have very generally abandoned scavengering for leather work, and this would at once account for their rise in the social scale. In the hills Rangreta is often used as synonymous with Rangrez, or Chhímba or Lílári to denote the cotton dyer and stamper; and in Sirsa the Sikhs will often call any Chúhra whom they wish to please Rangreta, and a rhyme is current *Rangreta, Guru ká beta*, or "the Rangreta is the son of the Guru."

599.—The Musalman Chuhra—Musalli, Kutana, &c.—Almost all the Chúhras west of Lahore are Musalmáns, and they are very commonly called Musalli or Kutána, the two terms being apparently almost synonymous, but Kutána being chiefly used in the south-west and Musalli in the north-west.

In Sirsa the converted Chúhra is called Díndár or "faithful" as a term of respect, or Khojah, a eunuch, in satirical allusion to his circumcision, or, as sometimes interpreted, Khoja, one who has found salvation. But it appears that in many parts the Musalmán Chúhra continues to be called Chúhra so long as he eats carrion or removes night-soil, and is only promoted to the title of Musalli on his relinquishing those habits, the Musalli being considered distinctly a higher class than the Chúhra. On the other hand the Musalli of the frontier towns does remove night-soil. On the Pesháwar frontier the Musalli is the grave-digger as well as the sweeper, and is said to be sometimes called Sháhi Khel, though this latter title would seem to be more generally used for Chúhras who have settled on the upper Indus and taken to working in grass and reeds like the Kutánas presently to be described.

Kutána, or as it is more commonly called in the villages Kurtána[1], is the name usually given to a class of Musalmán sweepers who have settled on the bank of the lower Indus, have given up scavengering and eating carrion, and taken to making ropes and working in grass and reeds; though the word is also applied to any Mahomedan sweeper. Some of the Kurtánas even cultivate land on their own account. So long as they do no scavengering the Kurtánas are admitted to religious equality by the other Mahomedans. I think it is not impossible that the Kurtánas of the Indus banks are a distinct caste from the Bhangi and Chúhra of the Eastern Panjáb. The detailed table of clans will doubtless throw light on the point.

600. Divisions of the Chuhras.—The Chúhra divisions are very numerous, but the larger sections returned in our schedules only include about half the total number. Some of the largest are shown in the margin. The greater number of them are evidently named after the dominant tribe whom they or their ancestors served. The Sahotra is far the most widely distributed, and this and the Bhatti and Khokhar are the principal tribs in the Multán and Ráwalpindi divisions. The others seem to be most largely returned from the Lahore and Amritsar divisions. Those who returned themselves as Chúhras and Musallis respectively showed some large tribes, and the above figures include both. The Kurtánas returned no large tribes.

CHUHRA TRIBES.

Tribe		Number	Tribe		Number
Sahotra	...	79,551	Sindhu		22,895
Gil	...	77,618	Chhapriband		18,872
Bhatti	...	44,486	Untwál	...	18,781
Khokhar		39,751	Kandabári		17,623
Mattu	...	36,746	Hánsi	..	13,234
Kháru	...	26,654	Khosar	...	13,180
Kaliyána	.	25,814	Borat	..	12,535
Ladhar	..	24,199	Dháríwál	...	5,617

601. The Dhanak (Caste No. 43).—The Dhának is found only in the Dehli and Hissár divisions and the eastern portion of the Phúlkián States. He is essentially a caste of Hindústán and not of the Panjáb proper. Sir H. Elliott says that they are most numerous in Behar, and that they are fowlers, archers, and watchmen, besides performing other menial service. He says that the Aheri tribe of hunters is an offshoot from the Dhánaks, and Wilson derives the name from the Sanskrit *dhanushka*, a bowman. The Panjáb Dhánaks, however, are not hunters, and the only difference between their avocations and those of the Chúhras would appear to be that the Dhánaks, while they will do general scavengering, will not remove night-

[1] There is said to be a respectable agricultural caste of this name in Derah Ismáíl Khán, who must be distinguished from the sweeper Kurtána.

soil, and that a great deal of weaving is done by them in the villages. Like the Chúhras, they are generally village menials proper, having customary rights and duties. The Chúhras are said to look down upon the Dhánaks; but they are apparently on an equality, as neither will eat the leavings of the other, though each will eat the leavings of all other tribes except Sánsis, not excluding Khatíks. There are practically speaking no Sikh or Musalmán Dhánaks, and their religion would appear to be that of [P. 320] the Chúhras, as the only considerable tribe the Dhánaks have returned is Lál Guru, another name for Lál Beg the sweeper Guru. But they are said to burn their dead. They marry by *phera* and no Bráhman will officiate.

602. The Khatik (Caste No. 87).—This also is a caste of Hindústán, and is found in any numbers only in the Jamna zone, Patiála, and Sirsa. But it has apparently followed our troops into the Panjáb, and is found in most of the large cantonments or in their neighbourhood. Many of these latter have adopted the Musalmán religion. They appear to be closely allied to the Pásis, and indeed are sometimes classed as a tribe of that caste. They form a connecting link between the scavengers and the leather-workers, though they occupy a social position distinctly inferior to that of the latter. They are great keepers of pigs and poultry, which a Chamár would not keep. At the same time many of them tan and dye leather, and indeed are not seldom confused with the Chamrang. The Khatík, however, tans only sheep and goat skins (so at least I am informed by some Lahore Khatíks and Chamrangs) using salt and the juice of the Madár (*Calotropis procera*), but no lime; while the Chamrang tans buffalo and ox hides with lime, and does not dye leather. It is probable, however, that Chamrang is more the name of an occupation than of a caste. The Khatík is said sometimes to keep sheep and goats and twist their hair into waistbands for sale; and even occasionally to act as butcher, but this last seems improbable from his low position, unless indeed it be as a pork-butcher. At the same time the information that I have received is very conflicting, and it may be that I have put the Khatík too low, and that he would have better been classed with the leather-workers. So far as I can make out, the fact is that the Khatík of the east is a pig-keeper and the Khatík of the west a tanner, the latter occupying a higher position than the former (see further under Chamrang, section 609). Mr. Christie tells me that the Hindu Khatík pig-keeper is a Púrbi immigrant; while the Musalmán Khatík tanner of the Panjáb proper is nothing more than a Chamár who has adopted Islám and given up working in cowhide.

THE LEATHER-WORKERS AND WEAVERS.

603. The leather-workers and weavers.—Next above the scavenger classes in social standing come the workers in leather, and above them again the weavers. Abstract No. 100 on the opposite page* gives the distribution *P. 298, 99 of both groups. I have taken them together; for though there is a wide distinction between the typical leather-worker or Chamár and the typical weaver or Juláha, yet they are connected by certain sections of the leather-working classes who have taken to weaving and thus risen in the social scale, just as we found in the case of some of the scavengering classes. It is probable that our figures for Chamár and Mochi really refer to the same caste, while Chamrang and Dabgar are perhaps merely names of occupations.

The group forms an exceedingly large proportion of the population in the eastern districts and States and under the hills, where the Chamár is the field-labourer of the villages. But in the central districts his place in this respect is taken, as already remarked, by the Chúhra. In the west, too, the leather-worker, like all other occupational castes, is much less numerous than in the east. The weaver class, on the other hand, is naturally least numerous in the eastern districts where much of the weaving is done by the leather-working castes.

604. The Chamar (Caste No 5).—The Chamár is the tanner and leather-worker of North-Western India, and in the western parts of the Panjáb he is called Mochi whenever he is, as he generally is, a Musalmán, the caste being one and the same. The name Chamár is derived from the Sanskrit *Charmakára* or " or worker in hides." But in the east of the Province he is far more than a leather-worker. He is the general coolie and field labourer of the villages; and a Chamár, if asked his caste by an Englishman at any rate, will answer "Coolie" as often as "Chamár."[1] They do all the *begár*, or such work as cutting grass, carrying wood and bundles, acting as watchmen, and the like; and they plaster the houses with mud when they need it. They take the hides of all dead cattle and the flesh of all cloven-footed animals, that of such as do not divide the hoof going to Chúhras. They make and mend shoes, thongs for the cart, and whips and other leather work; and above all they do an immense deal of hard work in the fields, each family supplying each cultivating association with the continuous labour of a certain number of hands. All this they do as village menials, receiving fixed customary dues in the shape of a share of the produce of the fields. In the east and southeast of the Panjáb the village Chamárs also do a great deal of weaving, which however is paid for separately. The Chamárs stand far above the Chúhras in social position, and some of their tribes are almost accepted as Hindus. Their religion is sketched in section 294. They are generally dark in colour, and are almost certainly of aboriginal origin though here again their numbers have perhaps been swollen by members of other and higher castes who have fallen or been degraded. The people say: "Do "not cross the ferry with a black Bráhman or a fair Chamár," one being as unusual as the other. Their women are celebrated for beauty, and loss of caste is often attributed to too great partiality for a Chamárni. Sherring has a long disquisition on the Chamár caste, which appears to be much more extensive and to include much more varied tribes in Hindústán than in the Panjáb.

Rahtia	... 572	Bilái	... 423
Búnia	... 512	Dhed	... 242

605. Miscellaneous entries classed as Chamars.—Under the head Chamár, I have included the schedule entries shown in the margin.

The **Dhed** appears to be a separate caste in the Central Provinces though closely allied with the Chamár. But in the Panjáb, as also I understand in the Central Provinces, the word is often used for any "low fellow," and is especially applied to a Chamár.

[1] Why is a Chamár always addressed with "Oh Chamár ke" instead of "Oh Chamár," as any other caste would be?

Abstract No. 100, showing Caste of Leather-workers and Weavers.

	LEATHER-WORKERS AND WEAVERS.															
	FIGURES.							PROPORTION PER 1,000 OF TOTAL POPULATION.								
	5	19	113	169	9	73	170	5	19	113		9	73	170		
	Chamár.	Mochi.	Chamrang.	Dabgar.	Juláha.	Gadaria.	Kanera.	Chamár.	Mochi.	Chamrang.	TOTAL.	Juláha.	Gadaria.	Kanera.	TOTAL.	GRAND TOTAL.
Dehli	63,407	128	...	27	6,673	2,457	...	98	...	...	98	10	4	...	14	112
Gurgaon	71,504	51	...	...	2,339	4,424	...	111	...	...	111	4	7	...	11	122
Karnál	54,067	197	...	20	9,090	3,725	...	87	...	...	87	15	6	...	21	108
Hissar	49,269	782	...	93	1.265	1	...	98	1	...	99	3	...	...	3	102
Rohtak ...	50,081	106	...	...	1.275	3	...	90	...		90	2	...	...	2	92
Sirsa	18,022	3,073	...	57	2,817	...	...	71	12	...	83	11	...	...	11	94
Ambála	140,751	932	...	...	24.931	6,671	...	131	1	...	132	23	6	...	29	161
Ludhiána	59,655	6,171	...	...	14,723	29	...	96	13	...	109	24	...	...	24	133
Simla	3,384	174	...	...	700	242	...	79	4	...	83	16	6	...	22	105
Jálandhar	79,155	16,517	...	4	15,790	56	...	100	21	...	121	20	...	...	20	141
Hushyárpur	100,207	14,726	...	6	20,841	...	...	111	16	...	127	23	...	...	23	150
Kángra	51,679	151	...	1	28,129	...	...	71	...	...	71	38	...	...	38	109
Amritsar	1,049	24,311	338	8	41,598	...	...	1	27	...	28	47	...	...	47	75
Gurdáspur	20,572	14,716	806	10	4,456	...	...	25	18	1	44	49	...	...	49	93
Siálkot	8,076	15,003	2,602	...	27,140	39	...	8	15	3	26	27	...	...	27	53
Lahore	4,775	18,527	15	115	35,742	276	...	5	20	...	25	39	...	...	39	64
Gujránwála ...	183	22,260	...	90	26,230	6	...	...	36		36	43	...	...	43	79
Firozpur	13,501	18,386	180	36	20.434	312	17	21	28	...	40	31	...	...	31	80
Ráwalpindi	2,069	20,385	2	...	37,001	203	...	3	25	...	28	45	...	...	45	73
Jahlam	294	21,844	...	23	28,620	22	...	...	37	...	37	49	...	...	49	86

[P. 321]

Gújrát	440	32,461	...	107	23,870	...	...	1	47	...	48	35	...	...	35	83
Shahpur	16	15,314	...	38	22,472	4	...	...	36	...	36	53	...	...	53	89
Multan	1,946	16,596	155	69	23,753	91	109	4	30		34	43	...	...	43	77
Jhang	34	14,132	...	36	24,176	7	...	...	36	...	36	61	...	...	61	97
Montgomery	256	14,118	...	68	20,454	...	...	1	33	...	34	48	...	...	48	82
Muzaffargarh	78	11,103	...	...	13,625	...	346	...	33	...	33	40	...	1	41	74
Derah Ismail Khan ...	4	4,903	...	22	5,673	...	106	...	11	...	11	13	...	...	13	24
Derah Gházi Khan ...	3	1,013	...	...	726	9	13	...	3	...	3	2	...	...	2	5
Bannu	...	3,890	...	...	3,357	5	421	...	12	...	12	10	...	1	11	23
Peshávar	4,156	3,263	111	...	15,372	98	...	7	6	...	13	26	...	...	26	39
Hazara	2,292	4,285	...	...	11,985	...	...	6	10	...	16	29	...	...	29	45
Kohát	652	1,349	...	...	1,781	10	...	4	7	...	11	10	...	...	10	21
British Territory ...	801,995	322,873	4,209	835	552,944	18,693	1,012	42	17	..	59	29	1	...	30	8
Patiála	143,093	3,227	752	30	19,910	964	5	97	2	1	100	14	1	...	15	115
Nábha	24,817	922	...	...	4,694	2	...	95	3	...	98	18	...	...	18	116
Kapurthala	10,061	6,302	...	9	7,399	...	...	40	25	...	65	29	...	...	29	94
Jínd	22,212	145	...	15	1,160	112	...	89	1	...	90	5	...	...	5	95
Faridkot	2,065	2,441	...	...	2,661	...	...	21	25	...	46	27	...	...	27	73
Maler Kotla	7 282	181	...	...	1,682	...	...	102	3	...	105	24		...	24	129
Kalsia	9,508	165	...	...	3,141	636	...	140	2	...	142	46	9	...	55	197
Total Eastern Plains ...	223,972	13,388	752	63	40,735	1,714	5	89	5	...	94	16	1	...	17	111
Baháwalpur	5,383	12,830	...	141	17,397	...	...	9	22	...	31	30	...	..	30	61
Mandi	8,178	2	...	...	3,575	...	...	56	...	...	56	24	...	...	24	80
Chamba	4,799	65	...	...	2,266	...	...	41	1	...	42	20	...	...	20	62
Náhan	4,354	1	67	...	592	75	...	39	...	1	40	5	1	...	6	46
Biláspur	8,275	...	...	...	4,750	...	...	96	...	...	96	55	...	...	55	151
Nálagarh	5,753	26	...	...	664	1	...	108	...	...	108	12	...	...	12	120
Suket	2,498	...	...	...	909	...	...	48	...	...	48	17	...	...	17	65
Total Hill States ...	41,349	181	67	...	13,236	93	...	54	...	...	54	17	...	...	17	71
British Territory ...	801,995	322,873	4,209	835	552,944	18,693	1,012	42	17	...	59	29	1	..	30	89
Native States ...	270,704	26,399	819	204	71,368	1,807	5	70	7	...	77	19	...	...	19	96
Province ...	1,072,699	349,272	5,028	1,039	624,312	20,500	1,017	47	15	...	62	28	1	...	29	91

The **Bunia** appears only in the Lúdhiána district, and is applied to a Sikh Chamár who has given up leather-work and taken to weaving, and accordingly stands in a higher rank than the leather-worker. [P. 322]

The **Bilai** is apparently the village messenger of the Dehli division. He is at least as often a Chúhra as a Chamár, and might perhaps better have been classed with the former. But there is a Chamár clan of that name who work chiefly as grooms.

The **Dosad** is a Púrbi tribe of Chamárs, and has apparently come into the Panjáb with the troops, being returned only in Dehli, Lahore, and Ambala.

The **Rahtia** is said by several of my informants to be a Sikh Chamár who, like the Búnia, has taken to weaving; but unfortunately part of my Rahtias are Musalmán. In Sirsa the word seems to be applied to the members of any low caste, such as Chamár or Chúhra.[1]

606. **The Sikh Chamar or Ramdasia.**—It will be seen from Table VIII A that in the north and centre of the Eastern Plains a very considerable number of Chamárs have embraced the Sikh religion. These men are called Rámdásia after Guru Rám Das, though what connection they have with him I have been unable to discover. Perhaps he was the first Guru to admit Chamárs to the religion. Many, perhaps most of the Rámdásia Chamárs have abandoned leather-work for the loom; they do not eat carrion, and they occupy a much higher position than the Hindu Chamárs, though they are not admitted to religious equality by the other Sikhs. The Rámdásia are often confused with the Raidási or Rabdási Chamárs. The former are true Sikhs, and take the *páhul*. The latter are Hindus, or if Sikhs, only Nánakpanthi Sikhs and do not take the *páhul;* and are followers of Bhagat Rav Dás or Rab Dás, himself a Chamár. They are apparently as true Hindus as any Chamárs can be, and are wrongly called Sikhs by confusion with the Ramdásias. (See further, paragraph 608.)

607. **The Musalman Chamar or Mochi** (**Caste No. 19**).—The word Mochi is properly the name of an occupation, and signifies the worker in tanned leather as distinguished from the tanner. The Mochi not only makes leather articles, but he alone grains leather and gives it a surface colour or stain, as distinguished from a colour dyed throughout. In the east of the Panjáb the name is usually applied only to the more skilled workmen of the towns. In the west however it is simply used to designate a Mussalmán Chamár; and the Mochi there is what the Chamár is in the east and belongs to the same caste, though his change of religion improves, though only slightly, his social position. He does not ordinarily weave, though in Hushyárpur the majority of the Mochis are said to be weavers, and he is not admitted to religious or social communion by the other Musalmáns. In the west of the Panjáb, however, the Chamár or Mochi no longer occupies that important position as an agricultural labourer that he does in the east. In the west he is merely a tanner and leather-worker, and his numbers are proportionally less than when a large part of the field-work is done by him. Moreover, he no longer renders menial service; and it may be that his improved social position is partly due to this fact. Mr. Christie, indeed, says that so soon as a Chamár, whether Hindu or Musalmán, abandons menial offices and confines himself to working in leather, he rises in the social scale and assumes the more respectable

[1] So I am told. Mr. Wilson, however, says that he has never heard the word used.

name of Mochi. The Mochi is proverbially unpunctual in rendering service, and there is a saying, "The Mochi's to-morrow never comes." To the figures for Mochis must be added those who are shown in Abstract No. 72 (page

P. 106-107 224) as having returned themselves as Jats.

608. **Divisions of Chamars and Mochis.**—The tribes of the Chamár caste are innumerable, and some of them very large. It does not seem worth while to give any tabular statement, as to include anything like even half the total number a very long list would have to be shown. But it is worth while comparing the figures for Chamárs and Mochis for a few of the largest tribes. This is done in the margin. Only the first seven tribes are found in any numbers among the Chamárs of the Dehli and Hissár divisions. Nos. 4 and 7 are the principal ones of the Ambála division while these two last, together with Nos. 8 to 18, are found in the Jálandhar division. Among the Mochis the Bhatti and Chauhán tribes are the most numerous.

Tribe.		Chamar and Mochi tribes.	
		Chamárs.	Mochis.
1. Jatia	...	53,088	...
2. Raidási	...	61,616	...
3. Chándar	...	32,061	...
4. Chauhán	...	21,390	12,188
5. Chamár	...	7,893	...
6. Golia	...	1,178	...
7. Bhatti	...	16,286	40,286
8. Mahmi	...	7,340	819
9. Phúndwál	...	5,328	...
10. Jál	...	8,326	3,137
11. Batoi	...	19,096	...
12. Badhan	...	13,753	1,167
13. Sindhu	...	13,889	3,426
14. Hír	...	12,860	767
15. Bains	...	6,591	442
16. Ghameri	...	2,715	...
17. Rámdásia	...	28,634	...
18. Bhúti	...	648	2,770
19. Kathána	...	...	3,585

It is obvious that many of these tribal names are merely taken from the dominant race in whose service the tribe was formed. Rámdásia is of course a religious and not a tribal division; and doubtless many of the sub-divisions returned are merely clans, and included in the larger tribes. This last point will be shown in the detailed tables. But it appears that the Chamárs of the Eastern Panjáb may be broadly divided into five great sections, the Jatia, the Raidási, the Chamár, the Chándar, and the Golia or Raigar, no one of which intermarries with the others. The Jatia are found in greatest numbers about the neighbourhood of Dehli and Gurgáon. They work in horse and camel hides, which are an abomination to the Chándar, probably as having the foot uncloven; and are perhaps named from the word *Jat* (hard *t*), a camel-grazier. On the other hand, they are said to obtain the services of Gaur Bráhmans, which would put them above all other Chamárs, who have to be content with the ministrations of the outcast Chamarwa Bráhman. The Raidási or Rabdási Chamárs are named after Rai Dás Bhagat, himself a Chamár, a contemporary of Kabír, and like him a disciple of Rámánand. They are the prevalent tribe in Karnál and the neighbourhood. The Golia is the lowest of all the sections; and indeed the word Golia is the name of a section of many of the menial castes in the Eastern Panjáb, and in almost all cases carries with it an inferior standing in the caste. The Chamár comes between the Jatia and the Golia, and is the prevalent tribe further west, about Jálandhar and Ludhiána. The Chándar is the highest of all, and is said in Dehli to trace its origin from Benares, probably from some association with Kabír. It is the principal section in Hissár and Sirsa. They do not tan, leaving that to the Chamrangs and Khatíks, and working only in ready prepared leather. There are doubtless similar tribal distinctions among the Chamárs of the central districts; but I have no information regarding them.

609. **The Chamrang (Caste No. 113).**—Chamrang is probably a purely occupational term, Chamrangs being Chamárs by caste. The figures of Table VIII A however would seem to show that Chamrang and Khatík have been confused in our returns, Chamrang being returned in largest numbers for the Amritsar division, for which no Khatíks are shown. The Chamrang does not

[P. 323] stain or dye leather, but only tans it, *rangna*, as applied to leather, meaning nothing more than to "tan." He tans ox and buffalo hides only, and does not work in the leather which he tans. (See further Khatík, section 602.)

610. **The Dabgar (Caste No 169).**—The Dabgar is the man who makes the raw hide jars in which oil and *ghi* are carried and stored. He is said to be a separate caste in the North-West Provinces; but the word implies, at

least in many parts of the province, nothing more than an occupation which, in Siálkot, is followed chiefly by Khojahs, Chamrangs and Chúhras.

611. The Koli of the plains (Caste No. 66).—The Koli of the hills will be discussed when the hill menials are treated of; but the figures include a certain number of people who probably belong to a wholly different caste from them. The former are probably of true Kolian origin; while the latter, that is to say all those returned as Kolis for the Dehli and Hissár divisions, belong in all probability to the great Kori or Koli tribe of Chamárs, the head-quarters of which is in Oudh, and whose usual occupation is weaving. These men are commonly classed with Chamárs in the district in which they are found, but are distinguished from the indigenous Chamárs by the fact of their weaving only, and doing no leather-work. Indeed they are commonly known as Chamár-Juláhas. Mr. Benton says: "The Chamár-Juláhas have no "share in the village skins, and do no menial service; but they would be very "glad to be entered among the village Chamárs, who have anticipated them and driven them to weaving as an occupation." I very much doubt whether this is generally true. As a rule the substitution of weaving for leather-work is made voluntarily, and denotes a distinct rise in the social scale. The Karnál Kolis do not obtain the services of Bráhmans. (See further Koli, section 657, and Kori, section 663).

612. The Julaha and Paoli (Caste No. 9).—The weavers proper, of which the Juláha as he is called in the east and the Páoli as he is called in the villages of the west is the type, are an exceedingly numerous and important artisan class, more especially in the western districts where no weaving is done by the leather-working or scavenger castes. It is very possible that the Juláha is of aboriginal extraction. Indeed Mr. Wilson, who has had while making the settlement of Sirsa district unequalled opportunities of comparing different sections of the people, is of opinion that the Juláhas and Chamárs are probably the same by origin, the distinction between them having arisen from divergence of occupation. Be this as it may, there is no doubt that the present position of the two is widely dissimilar. The Juláha does not work in impure leather, he eats no carrion, he touches no carcases, and he is recognised by both Hindu and Musalmán as a fellow believer and admitted to religious equality. In a word, the Chamár is a menial, the Juláha an artisan. The real fact seems to be that the word Juláha, which is a pure Persian word, the equivalent Hindi term being Tánti, is the name of the highest occupation ordinarily open to the outcast section of the community. Thus we find Koli-Juláhas, Chamár-Juláhas, Mochi-Juláhas, Ramdási-Juláhas, and so forth; and it is probable that after a few generations these men drop the prefix which denotes their low origin, and become Juláhas pure and simple.

The Juláha proper is scantily represented in the Dehli and Hissár divisions, where his place is taken by Koli or Chumár-Juláha and Dhának; and is hardly known in the Deraját, where probably the Jat does most of the weaving. (See also figures of Abstract No. 72, page 224*). In the rest of the Province he constitutes some 3 to 4 per cent. of the total population. He is generally Hindu in Kángra and Dehli, and often Hindu in Karnál, Ambala, and Hoshyárpur; but on the whole some 92 per cent. of the Juláhas are Musalmán. The Sikhs are few in number. *P. 106-107

The Juláha confines himself, I believe, wholly to weaving. He is not a true village menial, being paid by the piece and not by customary dues.

He is perhaps the most troublesome of the artisan classes. Like the shoemaker of Europe, he follows a wholly sedentary occupation, and in the towns at least is one of the most turbulent classes of the community. There is a proverbial saying: "How should a weaver be patient?" Indeed the contrast between the low social standing and the obtrusive pretentiousness of the class is often used to point a proverb: "A weaver by trade, and his name is Fatah "Khán ('victorious chief.')" "Lord preserve us! The weaver is going out "hunting!" "Himself a weaver, and he has a Saiyad for his servant!" "What! Patháns the bond servants of weavers!" and so forth.

613. **Divisions of Julahas.**—The Juláha sub-divisions are exceedingly numerous, but the names of most of the larger ones are taken from dominant land-owning tribes. I note some of the largest in the margin. The Bhattis are very widely distributed; the Khokhars are chiefly found west of Lahore: the Janjúas and Awáns in the Ráwalpindi division, the Sindhus in the Amritsar and Lahore divisons, and the Jaryáls in Kángra. The Kabírbansi are returned for Ambála and Kángra, and apparently this word has become a true tribal name and now includes Musalmán Juláhas. It is derived from the great Bhagat Kabír of Benares who was himself a Juláha, and whose teaching most of the Hindu Juláhas profess to follow. The eastern Juláhas are said to be divided in two great sections, Deswáli, or those of the country, and Tel, the latter being supposed to be descended from a Juláha who married a Teli woman. The latter are socially inferior to the former. In the Jamna districts there are also a Gangapuri (? Gangapári) and a Multáni section, the former being found only in the Jamna valley and the latter on the borders of the Málwa. The weaver appears to be called Golah in Peshâwar and Kásbi in Hazára.

JULAHA DIVISIONS.

1.	Bhatti	50,558
2.	Khokhar ...	33,672
3.	Janjua	22,150
4.	Sindhu	18,724
5	Kabírbansi	11,222
6.	Awán	8,832
7.	Jaryál ...	5,984

614. **The Gadaria (Caste No 73).**—The Gadaria is the shepherd and goatherd of Hindústán, and is almost confined to the Jamna zone of the Panjáb. But even in that part of the Province he has almost ceased to be distinctively a shepherd, as the cultivating classes themselves often pasture their own flocks, and has become rather a blanket weaver, being indeed as often called Kambalia as Gadaria. The Gadarias are Hindu almost without exception.

615. **The Kanera (Caste No. 170).**—A small Muhammadan caste, found only on the lower courses of the Satluj, Chanáb, and Indus. They must be distinguished from the Kandera or Penja of Dehli. They are a river tribe, and their original occupation was plaiting mats from grass and leaves, making string, and generally working in grass and reeds; but they have now taken to weaving generally, and even cultivate land. They are a low caste, slightly but only slightly superior in standing and habits to the other grass-workers and tribes of the river banks. "A Kaneri by caste, and her name is Ghulám "Fátimah, and she is an associate of the gentlemen of the desert (wild-"pigs.)!"

WATERMEN, BOATMEN, AND COOKS.

[P. 324] 616. **Watermen, boatmen, and cooks.**—Abstract No. 101 below* gives
*P. 304-305 the figures for this great group, in which I have included the Jhínwar, the Máchhi, the Bhatyára, the Bharbhúnja, and the Malláh. It is generally believed that all these men are of the same caste, Kahár being their usual name in the North-West Provinces, Jhínwar in the east of the Panjáb where they are for the most part Hindu, and Máchhi in the west of province where they are mostly Musalmán. Being essentially fishermen and watermen, they are most numerous in proportion to total population in the western and central districts

Abstract No. 101, showing Castes of Watermen

	WATER-CARRIERS.				
	FIGURES.				
	15	23	92	108	43
	Jhínwar.	Máchhi.	Bhatyára.	Bharbhúnja.	Malláh.
Dehli	14,497	1	519	1,223	740
Gurgaon	10,223	70	1,120	1,047	1,385
Karnál	31,200	...	405	1,257	1,277
Hissar	4,144	384	127	248	116
Rohtak	9,878	9	365	1,029	3
Sirsa	898	2,839	5	24	58
Ambala	47,104	31	648	1,102	1,009
Ludhiána	15,834	23	132	75	463
Simla	337		...	8	8
Jalandhar	24,717	996	...	64	1,212
Hushyárpur	22,168	224	...	20	1,399
Kangra	10,500	...	...	...	2,661
Amritsar	45,360	...	...	...	2,304
Gurdáspur	34,300	...	...	...	2,925
Siálkot	35,314	...	...	...	1,831
Lahore	20,941	24,747	103	172	2,398
Gujranwala	4,958	17,091	8	15	970
Firozpur	9,945	13,935	...	93	1,209
Ráwalpindi	82,632	120	...	...	994
Jahlam	3,413	6,120	...	19	2,145
Gujrát	5,131	14,942	...	...	549
Shahpur	187	11,156	...	...	1,278
Multan	303	9,610	1,964	32	6,011
Jhang	37	9,517	100	...	3,006
Montgomery	126	22,059	...	2	199
Muzaffargarh	19	3,350	2,354	...	7,976
Dera Ismail Khan	362	3,495	...	...	3,176
Dera Ghazi Khan	438	411	157	...	1,101
Bannu	339	2,029	...	...	1,546
Peshávar	3,056	104	...	...	1,024
Hazara	1,328	...	...	...	532
Kohát	1,080	40	...	...	59
British Territory	**368,004**	**144,121**	**8,007**	**6,429**	**51,614**
Patiála	36,477	413	403	291	120
Nábha	5,744	28	48	...	9
Kapurthala	7,769	2,712	...	52	1,751
Jínd	4,033	12	27	152	55
Faridkot	849	1,431	...	...	52
Maler Kotla	1,658	16	...	...	...
Kalsia	2,997	129	1	163	1
Total East. Plains	60,604	4,741	533	740	1,088
Baháwalpur	128	19,115	3,436	...	14,056
Náhan	1,806	...	...	15	47
Biláspur	1,764	...	...	...	...
Total Hill States	5,058	30	...	25	277
British Territory	**368,004**	**144,121**	**8,007**	**6,429**	**51,614**
Native States	**65,880**	**23,886**	**3,969**	**765**	**16,321**
Province	**433,884**	**168,007**	**11,976**	**7,194**	**67,935**

for Districts and States.

BOATMEN AND COOKS.

Proportion per 1,000 of total population.						
15	23	92	108	42		
Jhínwar.	Máchhi.	Bhatyára.	Bhar-bhúnja.	Malláh.	Total.	
22	...	1	2	1	26	Dehli.
16	..	2	2	2	22	Gurgáon.
60	...	1	2	2	65	Karnál.
8	1	...	...	...	9	Hissar
18	...	1	2	...	21	Rohtak.
4	11	...	...	.	15	Sirsa.
44	..	1	1	1	47	Ambala.
26	...	...	..	1	27	Ludhiána.
8	...	...	...	1	9	Simla.
31	1	...	...	2	34	Jalandhar.
25	1	...	...	2	28	Hushyárpur.
14	...	...	...	4	18	Kangra.
51	...	...	...	3	54	Amritsar.
42	...	...	...	4	46	Gurdáspur.
35	...	..	...	2	37	Siálkot.
23	27	...	...	3	53	Lahore.
8	28	...	...	1	37	Gujranwala.
15	22	...	..	2	39	Firozpur.
11	...	...	...	1	12	Ráwalpindi.
6	6	...	...	4	16	Jahlam.
7	22	...	..	1	30	Gujrát.
...	26	...	...	3	29	Shahpur.
1	17	4	...	11	33	Multan.
...	24	...	...	8	32	Jhang.
...	52	...	...	...	52	Montgomery.
...	10	7	...	24	41	Muzaffargarh.
1	8	..	...	7	16	Dera Ismail Khan.
1	1	...	...	3	5	Dera Ghazi Khan.
1	9	...	...	5	15	Bannu.
1	...	—	..	2	3	Peshá war.
3	...	...	...	1	4	Hazara.
6	...	...	...	...	6	Kohát.
19	8	—	..	3	30	**British Territory.**
25	..	...	...	...	25	Patiála.
22	...	...	...	...	22	Nábha.
31	11	..	...	7	40	Kapurthala.
10	...	...	1	...	20	Jind.
9	15	...	...	1	25	Faridkot.
23	...	...	...	...	23	Maler Kotla.
44	2	...	2	..	48	Kalsia.
24	2	...	.	1	27	Total East. Plains.
...	33	6	..	25	64	Baháwalpur.
16	...	...	...	...	16	Náhan.
21	...	...	...	...	21	Biláspur.
7	...	...	...	...	7	Total Hill States.
19	8	...	...	3	30	**British Territory.**
17	6	1	...	4	28	**Native States.**
19	8	1	...	3	31	**Province.**

which are traversed by the great Panjáb rivers, where too they assist largely in agricultural labour, besides finding more extensive occupation as cooks among a Musalmán population with no prejudices against eating food prepared by others. On the frontier proper, like most of the occupational castes, they are few in number. In the Eastern Plains and hills these people are returned as Jhínwars; west of Lahore as Máchhis. They are one of the pleasantest and most willing of the menial classes, and the Bhíshti is proverbially a good servant. Bhatyára, Bharbhúnja, and Malláh are names of occupations merely, but of occupations which are followed almost if not quite exclusively by the Jhínwar caste.

617. The Jhinwar (Caste No. 15).—The Jhínwar, also called Kahár in [P 325]
the east, and Mahra[1], where a Hindu, in the centre of the Province, is the carrier, waterman, fisherman, and basket-maker of the east of the Panjáb. He carries palanquins and all such burdens as are borne by a yoke on the shoulders; and he specially is concerned with water, insomuch that the cultivation of water-nuts and the netting of water fowl are for the most part in his hands, and he is the well-sinker of the Province. He is a true village menial, receiving customary dues and performing customary service. In this capacity he supplies all the baskets needed by the cultivator, and brings water to the men in the fields at harvest time, to the houses where the women are secluded, and at weddings and other similar occasions. His occupations in the centre and west of the Province are described below under the head Máchhi. His social standing is in one respect high; for all will drink at his hands. But he is still a servant, though the highest of the class.

Division.	Saqqáb.	Máshki.
Dehli	12,870	...
Hissár	7,604	...
Ambála	1,104	...
Jalandhar	29	...
Lahore	11,893	...
Ráwalpindi	...	321
Multán	...	125
Pesháwar	...	194
States of East Plains...	5,303	...

I have included under Jhínwar such men as returned themselves as Bhíshtis, Mashkis, or Saqqáhs, the terms for Musalmán water-carriers. It is just possible that some of these men may be of other castes than Jhínwar, but the number of such will be exceedingly small. The numbers so included are given in the margin, except for the Amritsar division which made no separate returns.

618. Divisions of Jhinwar, Machhi, and Mallah.—The sub-divisions of both Jhínwar and Máchhi are very numerous. I show one or two of the largest in the margin, adding the figures for Malláhs. These tribes do not appear to be found in any numbers among the Bhatyára and Bharbhúnja, and we must wait for the detailed tables of clans before we can compare the sub-divisions of those castes, and thus throw light upon the question of their identity or diversity.

Division.	Divisions of the Jhinwar group.		
	Jhínwar.	Máchhi.	Maláh.
Khokar	8,657	43,865	2,362
Mahár	27,337	115	...
Bhatti	6,000	15,961	3,496
Manhás	3,112	7,619	329
Tánk	8,587	2	13
Suhál	3,923	14	...

[1] Mahra seems to be a title of respect, just as a Bhíshti is often addressed as Jamadár. *Mahár* is a synonym for "chief" in the south-west of the Province.

619. The Machhi and Men (Caste No. 28).—Máchhi is, as I have said, only the western name for the Musalmán Jhínwar. In the Amritsar division those returning themselves as Máchhi have been included under Jhínwar. In the Lahore and Ráwalpindi divisions both names are used; and in the western districts both, where used at all, are applied indifferently to the same person. But in parts of the Central Panjab, where the eastern Hindu meets the western Musalmán, the two terms are generally used distinctively. The Máchhi occupies in the centre and west the same position which the Jhínwar fills in the east, save that he performs in the former parts of the Province a considerable part of the agricultural labour, while in the east he seldom actually works in the fields, or at least not as a part of his customary duties; though of course all classes work for pay at harvest time, when the rice is being planted out, and so forth. But besides the occupations already described for the Jhínwar,[1] the Máchhi is the cook and midwife of the Punjáb proper. All the Dáyas and Dáyis, the accoucheur, midwife, and wetnurse class, are of the Jhínwar or Máchhi caste. So too the common oven which forms so important a feature in the village life of the Panjáb proper, and at which the peasantry have their bread baked in the hot weather, is almost always in the hands of a Máchhi for Musalmáns and a Jhínwar for Hindus. In some parts he is also the wood-cutter of the village. In the Deraját he is sometimes called Mánjhi or Manjhera, more particularly when following the occupation of a fisherman; and the name Men is often given him under the same circumstances in the rest of the Central and Western Panjáb, along the banks of our great rivers. Both these castes, where returned separately, have been classed as Máchhi, as have also the Sammi or fisherman and quail-catcher, and the Mahígír, Machhahra, Machhiyánia, or fisherman. The details are given below. Of the Mens in the Lahore division, 7,035 are in Lahore and 3,095 in Gújránwála, while of those of the Multán division all but 180 are in Montgomery. Thus the Mens seem almost confined to the middle Satluj. On the lower Indus, in Gújarát and lower Sindh Máchhi seems to mean nothing more
P. 106-107. than fisherman. The figures of Abstract No. 72 (page 224) show that many of the Máchhis of the Deraját have returned themselves as Jats.

ENTRIES CLASSED AS MACHHI.

Entry.	Dehli.	Hissar.	Jalandhar.	Lahore.	Pindi.	Multan.	Derajat.
Men	...	...	756	10,743	70	5,195	...
Manchera	...	...	...	...	...	...	48
Mahígír, Machhahra, &c....	70	85	...	...	...	89	...
Sammi	...	...	...	168	...	...	...

620. The Bhatyara and Bharbhunja (Caste Nos. 92 and 108).—The Bhatyára is the baker and seller of ready-cooked food, who is to be found in all the caravanserais of our towns and encamping grounds. He is, I believe

[1] The carriage of burdens slung from a *bangi* or yoke seems to be almost unknown in the west of the Punjab.

almost without exception, a Jhínwar by caste; and in many districts those who have returned themselves as Bhatyáras have been classed either as Jhínwar or as Máchhi, so that our figures do not completely represent the entries in the [P. 326] schedules. They are said to be divided in the North-West Provinces at any rate into two classes, Shersháhi and Salímshahi, the women of the former wearing petticoats and of the latter drawers. They date the division from the time of Sultán Sher Sháh and his son Salím Sháh. Now that the railway has diminished their trade, the Bhatyáras are said to have taken to letting out *yekkas* and ponies for hire; and in the Deraját they are said to be the donkey-keepers of the district and to do petty carriage. This would connect them with the kiln rather than with the oven. In any case the name appears to be purely an occupational one, derived from *bhatti*, an oven or kiln; but like so many occupational guilds, the Bhatyáras appear in some parts to marry only among those following the same avocation.[1] The same may be said of the Bharbhúnja, who is as his name implies a grain-parcher. He too is almost always a Jhínwar, but a small section of the Bharbhúnjas are Káyaths. He does not appear to occur as a separate class in the west of the Province, where probably the grain parching is done at the public oven of the Jhínwar or Máchhi. The Bharbhúnja is also occasionally called Bhojwa, and on the Indus Chatári.

621. The Mallah and Mohana (Caste No. 42).—The Malláh is the boatman of the Panjáb, and is naturally found in largest numbers in those districts which include the greatest length of navigable river. It appears from Abstract No. 72 (page 224*) that on the Indus he has often returned *P. 106-
himself as Jat. He is, I believe, almost invariably a Jhínwar by caste, and 107.
very generally a Musalmán by religion; though Mr. Wilson believes that in Sirsa most of the Malláhs on the Satluj are by caste Jhabel *q. v.* He generally combines with his special work of boat management some other of the ordinary occupations of his caste, such as fishing or growing water-nuts; but he is *not* a village menial.

Division.	Classed as Mallah.		
	Moháná.	Táru.	Dren.
Hushyarpur ...	...	...	69
Kangra	...	145	2,151
Hill States ...	...	5	73
Jahlam	979	...	...
Multan	4,750	...	...
Jhang	677	...	...
Muzaffargarh ...	6,641	...	...
Derah Ismail Khan	3,176	...	...
Derah Ghazi Khan	1,101	...	...
Bannu	1,375	...	...
Bahawalpur ...	9,180	...	...

Under the head Malláh have been included those returning themselves as Moháná, Táru, or Dren, the figures for which entries are given on the margin. In Lahore and Pesháwar no separate returns were made for Moháná. The Moháná is said to be the fisherman of Sindh; but in the Panjáb he is at least as much a boatman as a fisherman. The word in Sanskrit means an estuary or confluence of waters. The Dren and Táru are found in the hills only, where they carry travellers across the rapid mountain torrents on inflated hides. The former are said to be Musalmán and the latter Hindu. The word *dren* appears originally to mean the buffalo hide upon which the transit is made. In the Hill States 55 men returned as Daryái have also been included. Broadly speaking, it may perhaps be said that the Jhínwar

[1] It is noticeable that all those returned as Bhatyára are Musalmán; probably because most Hindus, in the east of the Panjáb at least, will not eat bread made and cooked by a Jhínwar.

and Máchhi follow their avocations on land and the Malláh and Mohána on water, all belonging to the same caste.

622. **The Dhinwar of the Jamma.**—Along the left bank of Jamna below Dehli are settled a certain small number of people who call themselves Dhínwars. They work as fishermen and boatmen and some of them as Bharbhúnjas, and have returned themselves in the present Census, partly as Jhínwars, but mostly as Malláhs. They appear to have moved up the river from the neighbourhood of Agra, and to keep themselves distinct from the indigenous Jhínwars. They are much addicted to thieving, and it has been proposed to treat them as a criminal tribe. Violent crime is however rare among them. They cultivate and even own a certain area of land. They generally travel about in the disguise of musicians, singing, begging, pilfering, and committing burglary and theft on a large scale when opportunity offers. They apparently extend all along the banks of the river in Aligarh, Bulandshahr, and other districts of the North-West Provinces. Men of this class seem to travel all over the Panjáb, as they have been convicted even in the frontier districts. All Hindus drink at their hands,—a sufficient proof that they are true Jhínwars by caste.

WORKERS IN WOOD, IRON, STONE, AND CLAY.

623.—**The workers in wood, iron, stone, and clay.**—This group, of which
P. 310-11. the figures are given in Abstract No. 102 on the opposite page, completes, with the scavenger, leather-worker, and water-carrier classes, the castes from which village menials proper are drawn. It is divided into four sections, the workers in iron, in wood, in stone, and in clay. The workers in iron and wood are in many parts of India identical, the two occupations being followed by the same individuals. In most parts of the Panjáb they are sufficiently well distinguished so far as occupation goes, but there seems reason to believe that they really belong to one and the same caste, and that they very frequently intermarry. True workers in stone may be said hardly to exist in a Province where stone is so scarce; but I include among them the Ráj who is both a mason and a bricklayer and is said generally to be a Tarkhán by caste, and they are connected with the carpenters by the Thávi of the hills, who is both carpenter and stone-mason. The potters and brickmakers are a sufficiently distinct class, who are numerous in the Panjáb owing to the almost universal use of the Persian wheel with its numerous little earthen pots to raise water for purposes of irrigation.

[P. 327] 624. **The Lohar (Caste No. 22).**—The Lohár of the Panjáb is, as his name implies, a blacksmith pure and simple. He is one of the true village menials, receiving customary dues in the shape of a share of the produce, in return for which he makes and mends all the iron implements of agriculture, the materials being found by the husbandman. He is most numerous in proportion to total population in the hills and the districts that lie immediately below them, where like all other artisan castes he is largely employed in field
†P. 106-107. labour. He is, even if the figures of Abstract No. 72 (page 224†) be included, present in singularly small numbers in the Multán and Deraját divisions and in Baháwalpur; but why so I am unable to explain. Probably men of other castes engage in blacksmith's work in those parts, or perhaps the carpenter and the blacksmith are the same. His social position is low, even for a menial; and he is classed as an impure caste in so far that Jats and others of similar standing will have no social communion with him, though not as an outcast like the

Abstract No. 102, showing the Blacksmith, [P. 327]

	WORKERS IN WOOD, IRON,								
	Figures								
	22	157	163	11	132	149	93	171	12
	Lohár.	Siqligar.	Dhogri.	Tarkhán.	Kamángar.	Thávi.	Ráj.	Khumra.	Kumhár.
Delhi	5,934	4	...	9,622	107	...	389	131	13,724
Gurgaon	5,503	1	...	10,655	...	...	64	114	14,261
Karnal	9,190	12	...	13,787	208	...	583	55	14,712
Hissar	5,682	31	...	12,627	16	...	310	2	19,662
Rohtak	7,447	7	...	10,821	71	...	294	169	12,031
Sirsa	1,652	1	...	7,222	..	...	126	...	16,114
Ambala	16,550	157	...	25,265	30	...	917	449	15,508
Ludhiána	8,520	47	2	18,809	12	...	120	...	8,226
Simla	715	...	...	1,042	...	...	3	...	173
Jalandhar	13,396	17	...	26,232	5	...	533	...	12,904
Hushyárpur ...	15,033	12	...	28,033	15	...	1,146	...	10,661
Kángra	15,655	34	1,412	16,286	265	...	527	...	7,897
Amritsar	18,778	1	...	34,984	61	...	717	...	29,175
Gurdáspur	16,601	...	...	29,621	11	...	675	...	17,029
Siálkot	18,584	...	...	41,781	..	...	817	...	29,713
Lahore	13,767	144	..	31,009	239	...	876	...	31,524
Gujránwála ...	12,364	12	...	26,872	58	...	324	...	26,931
Firozpur	7,097	84	...	21,424	39	...	134	...	15,254
Ráwalpindi ...	12,236	165	...	22,450	290	...	...	...	14,668
Jahlam	9,970	23	...	14,824	42	...	1	...	10,031
Gujrát	12,934	66	...	21,828	33	...	260	...	16,401
Shahpur	5,074	49		10,270	131	...	...	...	11,760
Multan	2,768	...	...	11,915	441	...	...	...	13,716
Jhang	3,062	...	...	8,418	173	...	49	...	15,381
Montgomery ..	3,673	...	...	9,499	158	...	4	...	17,865
Muzaffargarh ..	1,477	..	...	8,024	165	...	...	...	6,629
Derah Ismail Khan ...	1,289	...	...	3,93[illegible]	9	...	...	...	2,674
Derah Ghazi Khan ...	220	...	...	782	11	...	3	...	[illegible]
Bannu	4,754	...	..	5,574	101	...	...	...	4,303
Peshawar	6,521	144	...	12,504	49	...	84	...	7,583
Hazára	5,899	48	...	8,271	178	...	...	...	3,687
Kohát	2,374	81	...	3,615	12	...	15	...	1,186
British Territory	**264,720**	**1,140**	**1,414**	**508,008**	**2,930**	...	**9,080**	**910**	**421,588**
Patiala	17,768	155	...	41,454	132	0	1,202	94	27,464
Nábha	2,858	12	...	9,208	1	...	57	...	5,002
Kapurthala ...	4,106	2	...	7,715	6	...	471	...	4,797
Jind	3,034	64	...	5,358	32	...	138	...	5,333
Faridkot	1,180	...	...	3,944		...	8	...	1,636
Maler Kotla ...	1,325	...	...	1,929	...	...	100	...	1,154
Kalsia	1,177	16	...	1,683	...	...	177	...	1,014
Total East. Plains	**32,827**	**258**	...	**72,468**	**172**	**9**	**2,162**	**94**	**47,771**
Baháwalpur ...	2,833	21	...	9,996	56	...	...	...	10,883
Mandi	1,632	...	...	270	...	610	...	...	1,508
Chamba	1,537	...	302	1,570	...	...	...	...	1,540
Náhan	1,707	...	...	1,336	...	...	1	...	278
Bilaspur	1,014	35	...	238	...	178	..	...	844
Bashahr	916	...	...	1,106	...	...	...	...	63
Nálagarh	773	10	...	527	...	123	...	...	457
Suket	1,201	...	...	56	..	781	...	...	313
Total Hill States...	**11,902**	**64**	**302**	**6,469**	..	**1,895**	**48**	...	**5,783**
British Territory	264,720	1,140	1,414	508,008	2,930	...	9,080	910	421,588
Native States ...	47,062	343	302	88,933	228	1,904	2,210	94	64,437
Province ...	311,782	1,483	1,716	596,941	3,158	1,904	11,290	1,004	486,025

Carpenter, and Potter Castes.

STONE AND CLAY.											
PROPORTION PER 1,000 OF TOTAL POPULATION.											
22	153		11	132		140	93		13		
Lohár.	Dhogri.	Total.	Tarkhán.	Kamángar.	Total.	Thávi.	Ráj	Total.	Kumhár	Grand Total.	
10	..	10	15	...	15	...	1	1	21	47	Dehli.
9	.	9	16	...	16	...	...	...	23	47	Gurgaon.
15	...	15	23	...	23	...	1	1	24	62	Karnál.
11	...	11	25	...	25	..	1	1	30	76	Hissar.
13	...	13	20	...	20	...	...	...	22	55	Rohtak.
6	...	6	29	...	29	...	...	...	64	90	Sirsa.
15	..	15	24	...	24	...	1	1	15	55	Ambala.
14	...	14	30	...	30	...	...	...	13	57	Ludhiána.
17	...	17	24	...	24	...	...	...	4	45	Simla.
17	...	17	33	...	33	...	1	1	16	67	Jalandhar.
17	...	17	31	...	31	..	1	1	12	61	Hushyárpur.
21	2	23	23	...	22	...	1	1	14	60	Kángra.
21	...	21	30	...	30	...	1	1	33	94	Amritsar.
20	...	20	36	...	36	...	1	1	21	78	Gurdáspur.
18	...	18	41	...	41	.	1	1	29	89	Siálkot.
15	...	15	34	...	34	...	1	1	34	84	Lahore.
20	...	20	44	...	44	...	1	1	44	109	Gujránwála.
11	...	11	33	...	33	...	...	...	23	67	Firozpur.
15	...	15	27	...	27	...	...	...	18	60	Ráwalpindi.
17	.	17	25	...	25	...	...	...	17	59	Jahlam.
19	...	19	32	...	32	...	...	...	24	75	Gujrát.
12	...	12	24	...	24	...	...	..	28	64	Shahpur.
5	...	5	23	1	23	...	...	...	25	53	Multan.
8	...	8	21	...	21	...	...	...	39	68	Jhang.
9	..	9	22	...	23	..	...	..	42	51	Montgomery.
7	...	7	24	...	24	...	...	...	20	73	Muzaffargarh.
3	...	3	9	...	9	...	...	...	6	18	Derah Ismail Khan.
1	...	1	2	...	2		...	...	...	3	Derah Ghazi Khan.
14	...	14	17	...	17	...	...	..	13	14	Banuu.
11	...	11	21	...	21	...	...	...	13	45	Peshâwar.
14	...	14	20	...	20	...	...	...	9	43	Hazára.
13	...	13	20	...	20	...	...	...	7	40	Kohat.
14	...	**14**	**27**	...	**27**	...	...	...	**22**	**68**	**British Territory.**
12	.	12	28	...	28	...	1	1	19	60	Patiála.
11	..	11	35	..	35	...	...	...	19	65	Nábha.
16	...	16	30	...	30	...	2	3	19	67	Kapurthala.
15	...	15	22	...	22	...	1	1	21	59	Jind.
12	...	12	41	...	41	...	...	...	17	70	Faridkot.
19	...	19	27	...	27	...	2	2	16	64	Maler Kotla.
17	...	17	25	...	25	...	3	3	15	60	Kalsia.
13	...	**13**	**29**	..	**29**	...	**1**	**1**	**19**	**62**	**Total East. Plains.**
5	...	5	17	...	17	...	...	...	19	41	Baháwalpur.
11	...	11	2	...	2	4	...	4	10	27	Mandi.
13	3	16	14	..	14	...	...	...	13	43	Chamba.
15	...	15	12	...	12	...	...	...	2	29	Náhan.
22	...	22	3	...	3	1	...	1	10	36	Bilaspur.
14	...	14	18	...	18	...	...	...	1	33	Bashahr.
14	...	14	10	...	10	2	...	2	8	34	Nálagarh.
23	...	23	1	...	1	15	...	15	6	45	Suket.
16	...	**16**	**8**	...	**8**	**2**	..	**2**	**8**	**34**	**Total Hill States.**
14	...	**14**	**27**	...	**27**	...	...	...	**22**	**63**	**British Territory.**
12	..	**12**	**23**	...	**23**	...	**1**	**1**	**17**	**58**	**Native States.**
14	...	**14**	**26**	...	**26**	...	...	...	**21**	**61**	**Province.**

scavenger. His impurity, like that of the barber, washerman, and dyer, springs solely from the nature of his employment; perhaps because it is a dirty one, but more probably because black is a colour of evil omen, though on the other hand iron has powerful virtue as a charm against the evil eye. It is not impossible that the necessity under which he labours of using bellows made of cowhide may have something to do with his impurity.[1] He appears to follow very generally the religion of the neighbourhood and some 34 per cent. of the Lohárs are Hindu, about 8 per cent. Sikh, and 58 per cent. Musalmán. Most [P. 328] of the men shown as Lohárs in our tables have returned themselves as such, though some few were recorded as Ahngar, the Persian for blacksmith, and as Nálband or farrier. In the north of Sirsa, and probably in the Central States of the Eastern Plains, the Lohár or blacksmith and the Kháti or carpenter are undistinguishable, the same men doing both kinds of work; and in many, perhaps in most parts of the Panjáb the two intermarry. In Hushyárpur they are said to form a single caste called Lohár-Tarkhán, and the son of a blacksmith will often take to carpentry and *vice versâ;* but it appears that the castes were originally separate, for the joint caste is still divided into two sections who will not intermarry or even eat or smoke together, the Dhamán, from *dhamna* "to blow," and the Khatti from *khát* "wood." In Gújránwála the same two sections exist; and they are the two great Tarkhán tribes also (see section 627). In Karnál a sort of connection seems to be admitted, but the castes are now distinct. In Sirsa the Lohárs may be divided into three main sections; the first, men of undoubted and recent Jat and even Rájpút origin who have, generally by reason of poverty, taken to work as blacksmiths; secondly the Suthár Lohár or members of the Suthár tribe of carpenters who have similarly changed their original occupation; and thirdly, the Gádiya Lohár, a class of wandering blacksmiths not uncommon throughout the east and south-east of the Province, who come up from Rájpútána and the North-West Provinces and travel about with their families and implements in carts from village to village, doing the finer sorts of iron work which are beyond the capacity of the village artisan. The tradition runs that the Suthár Lohárs, who are now Musalmán, were originally Hindu Tarkháns of the Suthár tribe (see section 627); and that Akbar took 12,000 of them from Jodhpur to Dehli, forcibly circumcised them, and obliged them to work in iron instead of wood. The story is admitted by a section of the Lohárs themselves, and probably has some substratum of truth. These men came to Sirsa from the direction of Sindh, where they say they formerly held land, and are commonly known as Multáni Lohárs. The Jat and Suthár Lohárs stand highest in rank, and the Gádiya lowest. Similar distinctions doubless exist in other parts of the Panjáb, but unfortunately I have no information regarding them. Our tables show very few Lohár tribes of any size, the only one at all numerous being the Dhamán found in Karnál and its neighbourhood, where it is also a carpenter tribe.

The Lohár of the hills is described in section 651 (see also Tarkhán, section 627).

625. The Siqligar (Caste No. 157).—The word Siqlígar is the name of a pure occupation, and denotes an armourer or burnisher of metal. They are shown chiefly for the large towns and cantonments; but many of them probably returned themselves as Lohárs.

---

[1] Colebrooke says that the Karmakára or blacksmith is classed in the Puráns as one of the polluted tribes.

626. The Dhogri (Caste No. 153).—These are the iron miners and smelters of the hills, an outcast and impure people, whose name is perhaps derived from *dhonkni* "bellows," and it is possible that their name is rather Dhonkri than Dhogri. Their status is much the same as that of the Chamár or Dúmna. They are returned only in Kángra and Chamba.

627. The Tarkhan (Caste No. 111).—The Tarkhán, better known as Barhái in the North-West Provinces, Bárhi in the Jamna districts, and Kháti in the rest of the Eastern Plains, is the carpenter of the Province. Like the Lohár he is a true village menial, mending all agricultural implements and household furniture, and making them all except the cart, the Persian wheel, and the sugar-press, without payment beyond his customary dues. I have already pointed out that he is in all probability of the same caste with the Lohár; but his social position is distinctly superior. Till quite lately Jats and the like would smoke with him though latterly they have begun to discontinue the custom. The Kháti of the Central Provinces is both a carpenter and blacksmith, and is considered superior in status to the Lohár who is the latter only. The Tarkhán is very generally distributed over the Province, though, like most occupational castes, he is less numerous on the lower frontier than elsewhere. The figures of
P. 106-107. Abstract No. 72 (page 224) must however, be included. In the hills too his place is largely taken by the Thávi (*q. v.*) and perhaps also by the Lohár. I have included under Tarkhán all who returned themselves as either Bárhi or Kháti; and also some 600 Kharádis or turners, who were pretty equally distributed over the Province. I am told that in the Jamna districts the Bárhi considers himself superior to his western brother the Kháti, and will not intermarry with him; and that the married women of latter do not wear nose-rings while those of the former do. The Tarkhán of the hills is alluded to in the section on Hill Menials. The Ráj or bricklayer is said to be very generally a Tarkhán.

TRIBES OF TARKHANS.

1.	Jhángra ...	9,518	7.	Netál ...	2,764
2.	Dhamán ...	71,519	8.	Janjúa ...	12,576
3.	Khatti ...	19,071	9.	Tháru ...	2,822
4.	Siáwan ...	1,932	10.	Khokhar...	27,534
5.	Gáde ...	2,209	11.	Bhatti ...	18,837
6.	Mathárn ...	6,971	12.	Begi Khel	2,212

The tribes of Tarkhán are numerous, but as a rule small. I show some of the largest in the margin, arranged in the order as they occur from east to west. No. 1 is chiefly found in the Dehli and Hissár divisions; Nos. 2 and 3 in Karnál, the Ambála and Jálandhar divisions, Patiála, Nábha, Farídkot, and Firozpur; No. 4 in Jálandhar and Siálkot; No. 5 in Amritsar; No. 6 in Ludhiána, Amritsar, and Lahore; No. 7 in Hushyárpur; No. 8 in the Rawálpindi division; No. 9 in Gurdáspur and Siálkot; Nos. 10 and 11 in the Lahore, Ráwalpindi, and Multán divisions; No. 12 in Hazára. The carpenters of Sirsa are divided in two great sections, the Dhamán and the Kháti proper, and the two will not intermarry. These are also two great tribes of the Lohárs (*q. v.*). The Dhamáns again include a tribe of Hindu Tarkháns called Suthár, who are almost entirely agricultural, seldom working in wood, and who look down upon the artisan sections of their caste. They say that they came from Jodhpur, and that their tribe still holds villages and revenue-free grants in Bíkáner. These men say that the Musalmán Multáni Lohárs described in section 624 originally belonged to their tribe; the Suthár Tarkháns, though Hindus, are in fact more closely allied with the Multáni Lohárs than with the Khátis, and many of their clan sub-divisions are identical with those of the former; and some of the Lohárs who have immigrated from Sindh admit the community of caste. Suthár is in Sindh the common term for any carpenter. It is curious that the Bárhis of Karnál are also divided into two great sections, Dese and Multáni. The Sikh Tarkháns on the Patiála border of Sirsa claim Bágri origin, work in iron as well as in wood, and intermarry with the Lohárs. (See *supra* under Lohárs.)

628. The Kamangar (Caste No. 132)—The Kamángar, or as he is commonly called in the Panjáb Kamagar, is as his name implies a bow-maker; and with him I have joined the Tírgar or arrow-maker, and the Pharera which appears to be merely a hill name for the Rangsáz. These men are found chiefly in the large towns and cantonments, and, except in Kángra, appear to be always Musalmán. Now that bows and arrows are no longer used save for purposes of presentation, the Kamángar has taken to wood decorating. Any colour or lacquer that can be put on in a lathe is generally applied by the Kharádi; but flat or uneven surfaces are decorated either by the Kamángar or by the Rangsáz; and of two the Kamángar does the finer sorts of work. Of course rough work, such as painting doors and window-frames, is done by the ordinary Mistri who works in wood, and who is generally if not always a Tarkhán. I am not sure whether the Kamángar can be called a distinct caste; but in his profession he stands far above the Tarkhán, and also above the Rangsáz. [P. 329]

629. The Thavi (Caste No. 149).—The Thávi is the carpenter and stone-mason of the hills, just as the Ráj of the plains, who is a bricklayer by occupation, is said to be generally a Tarkhán by caste. His principal occupation is building the village houses, which are in those parts made of stone; and he also does what wood work is required for them. He thus forms the connecting link between the workers in wood or Tarkháns on the one hand, and the bricklayers and masons or Rájs on the other. Most unfortunately my offices have included the Thávis under the head Tarkhán, so that they are only shown separately for the Hill States; and indeed many of the Hill States themselves have evidently followed the same course, so that our figures are very incomplete In Gurdáspur 1,722 and in Síalkot 1,063 Thávis are thus included under Tarkhán. The Thávi is always a Hindu, and ranks in social standing far above the Dági or outcast menial, but somewhat below the Kanet or inferior cultivating caste of the hills. Sardár Gurdiál Singh gives the following information taken down from a Thávi of Hushyárpur :—" An old man said he and his people " were of a Bráhman family, but had taken to stone-cutting and so had " become Thávis, since the Bráhmans would no longer intermarry with them. " That the Thávis include men who are Bráhmans, Rájputs, Kanets, and the " like by birth, all of whom intermarried freely and thus formed a real Thávi " caste, quite distinct from those who merely followed the occupation of Thávi " but retained their original caste." The Thávi of the hills will not eat or intermarry with the Barhái or Kharadi of the neighbourhood. Further details regarding his social position will be found in section 650, the section treating of hill menials.

630. The Raj (Caste No. 93).—Ráj is the title given by the guilds of bricklayers and masons of the towns to their headmen, and is consequently often used to denote all who follow those occupations. Mimár is the corresponding Persian word, and I have included all who so returned themselves under the head of Ráj. The word is probably the name of an occupation rather than of a true caste, the real caste of these men being said to be almost always Tarkhán. The Ráj is returned only for the eastern and central districts, and seems to be generally Musalmán save in Dehli, Gurgáon and Kángra. Under Ráj I have included Batahra, of whom 66 are returned from the Jálandhar and 20 from the Amritsar division. But I am not sure that this is right; for in Chamba at any rate the Batahra seems to be a true caste, working generally as stone-masons, occasionally as carpenters, and not unfrequently cultivating land. In Kúlu, however, the Batahra is said to be a Koli by caste who has taken to slate quarrying.

631. The Khumra (Caste No. 171).—The Khumra is a caste of Hindustán, and is found only in the eastern parts of the Panjáb. His trade is dealing in and chipping the stones of the hand-mills used in each family to grind flour; work which is, I believe, generally done by Tarkháns in the Panjáb proper. Every year these men may be seen travelling up the Grand Trunk Road, driving buffaloes which drag behind them millstones loosely cemented together for convenience of carriage. The millstones are brought from the neighbourhood of Agra, and the men deal in a small way in buffaloes. They are almost all Musalmán.

632. The Kumhar (Caste No. 13).—The Kumhár, or, as he is more often called in the Panjáb, Gumiár, is the potter and brick-burner of the country. He is most numerous in Hissár and Sirsa where he is often a husbandman, and in the sub-montane and central districts. On the lower Indus he has returned
P. 106-107. himself in some numbers as Jat—(see Abstract No. 72, page 224). He is a true village menial, receiving customary dues, in exchange for which he supplies all earthen vessels needed for household use, and the earthenware pots used on the Persian wheel wherever that form of well gear is in vogue. He also, alone of all Panjáb castes, keeps donkeys; and it is his business to carry grain within the village area, and to bring to the village grain bought elsewhere by his clients for seed or food. But he will not carry grain out of the village without payment. He is the petty carrier of the villages and towns, in which latter he is employed to carry dust, manure, fuel, bricks, and the like. His religion appears to follow that of the neighbourhood in which he lives. His social standing is very low, far below that of the Lohár and not very much above that of the Chamár; for his hereditary association with that impure beast the donkey, the animal sacred to Sitala the small-pox goddess, pollutes him; as also his readiness to carry manure and sweepings. He is also the brick-burner of the Panjáb, as he alone understands the working of kilns; and it is in the burning of pots and bricks that he comes into contact with manure, which constitutes his fuel. I believe that he makes bricks also when they are moulded; but the ordinary village brick of sun-dried earth is generally made by the coolie or Chamár. The Kumhár is called Pazáwagar or kiln-burner, and Kúzagar (vulg. Kujgar) or potter, the latter term being generally used for those only who make the finer sorts of pottery. On the frontier he appears to be known as Gilgo.

The divisions of Kumhárs are very numerous, and as a rule not very large. I show a few of the largest in the margin. The first two are found in the Dehli and Hissár, the third in the Amritsar and Lahore, and the last two in the Lahore, Ráwalpindi, and Multán divisions. In Pesháwar more than two-thirds of the Kumhárs have returned themselves as Hindki.

KUMHAR DIVISIONS.

Division	Number	Division	Number
1. Gola ...	20,059	4. Dhodi ...	3,786
2. Mahár ...	12,649	5. Khokhar ...	15,039
3. Dol ...	6,777		

The Mahár and Gola do not intermarry. The Kumhárs of Sirsa are divided into two great sections, Jodhpuria who came from Jodhpur, use furnaces or *bhattis*, and are generally mere potters; and the Bíkáneri or Dese who came from Bíkáner and use *pajáwas* or kilns, but are chiefly agricultural, looking down upon the potter's occupation as degrading. The Kumhárs of those parts are hardly to be distinguished from the Bágri Jats. The two [P. 330] sections of the caste appear to be closely connected.

WORKERS IN OTHER METALS AND MINERALS.

633. Workers in other metals and minerals.—Having discussed the blacksmiths, stone-masons, and potters, I next turn to the group for which figures will be found in Abstract No. 103 on the opposite page*. It is *P. 318-19 divisible into four classes, the Sunár, the Nyária, and the Dáoli who work in the precious metals, the Thathera who works in brass, bell-metal and the like, the Agari, Núngar, and Shorágar who make salt and saltpetre, and the Chúrigar or glass-blower and bracelet-maker. The workers in precious metals are found all over the Province, though they are less numerous among the rustic and comparatively poor population of the Western Plains, and most numerous in those districts which include the great cities, and in the rich central districts. The salt-workers are naturally almost confined to the eastern and south-eastern portions of the Province and to the great grazing plains of the Multán division, where the saline water of the wells, the plains covered with soda salts, and the plentiful growth of the barilla plant afford them the means of carrying on their occupation. The salt of the Salt-range is quarried ready for use, indeed in a state of quite singular purity; and the work of quarrying and carrying is performed by ordinary labourers and does not appertain to any special caste or calling.

634. The Sunar (Caste No. 30).—The Sunár, or Zargar as he is often called in the towns, is the gold and silver smith and jeweller of the Province. He is also to a very large extent a money-lender, taking jewels in pawn and making advances upon them. The practice, almost universal among the villagers, of hoarding their savings in the form of silver bracelets and the like makes the caste, for it would appear to be a true caste, an important and extensive one; it is generally distributed throughout the Province, and is represented in most considerable villages. The Sunár is very generally a Hindu throughout the Eastern Plains and the Salt-range Tract, though in the Multán division and on the frontier he is often a Musalmán. In the central division there are a few Sikh Sunárs. The Sunár prides himself upon being one of the twice-born, and many of them wear the *janeo* or sacred thread; but his social standing is far inferior to that of the mercantile and of most of the agricultural castes, though superior to that of many, or perhaps of all other artisans. In Dehli it is said that they are divided into the Dase who do and the Deswále who do not practise *karewa*, and that the Deswála Sunár ranks immediately below the Banya. This is probably true if a religious standard be applied; but I fancy that a Jat looks down upon the Sunár as much below him.

635. The Nyaria (Caste No. 131).—The Nyária or refiner (from *nyára* "separate") is he who melts the leavings and sweepings of the Sunár and extracts the precious metal from them. In the west of the Panjáb he seems to be known as Shodar or Sodar; and as one of the Sunár clans is called

Sodari, it may be that the Nyária is generally or always a Sunár by caste. The books are silent on the subject; and I have no other information. The Nyária however is, unlike the Sunár, generally a Musalmán; though curiously enough he is shown as Hindu only in Peshawar.

636. The Daoli (Caste No. 134).—Under this head I have included 87 men who have returned themselves as Sansoi, as this appears to be the usual name in the higher ranges for the Dáoli of the low hills. The Dáolis are men who wash gold from the beds of mountain streams, and are naturally found only in the hills, those returned from Patiála being inhabitants of the hill territory which belongs to that State. They also work the water-mills which are so common on the mountain torrents. Most of them are Hindu, a few Sikh, and none Musalmán. These men are outcasts of about the same status as the Dúmna; indeed they are said by many to belong to the Dúmna caste, and it appears that they also make matting and the like.

637. The Thathera (Caste No. 115).—The Thathera is the man who sells, as the Kasera is the man who makes vessels of copper, brass, and other mixed metals. He is generally a Hindu. The word seems to be merely the name of an occupation, and it is probable that most of the Thatheras have returned themselves as belonging to some mercantile caste. Those shown in the tables are for the most part Hindus. The Thathera is also known as Thathyár. He is said to wear the sacred thread.

638. The Agari (Caste No. 109).—The Agari is the salt-maker of Rájpútána and the east and south-east of the Panjáb, and takes his name from the *ágar* or shallow pan in which he evaporates the saline water of the wells or lakes at which he works. The city of Agra derives its name from the same word. The Agaris would appear to be a true caste, and are said in Gurgáon to claim descent from the Rájpúts of Chitor. There is a proverb: "The Ak, "the Jawása, the Agari, and the cartman; when the lightning flashes these four "give up the ghost," because, I suppose, the rain which is likely to follow would dissolve their salt. The Agaris are all Hindus, and are found in the Sultánpur tract on the common borders of the Dehli, Gurgáon, and Rohtak districts, where the well water is exceedingly brackish, and where they manufacture salt by evaporation. Their social position is fairly good, being above that of Lohárs, but of course below that of Jats.

639. The Nungar and Shoragar (Caste Nos. 76 and 154).—Núngar, or as it is often called Núnia or Lúnia or Núnári, is derived from *nún* "salt," and denotes an occupation rather than a true caste. This is true also of the Shorágar or saltpetre-maker, who is sometimes called Rehgar from *reh* or saline efflorescence. But the two terms are commonly applied to the same class of men,[1] who indeed, now that the making of salt is prohibited in most parts of the Panjáb, manufacture either saltpetre from the debris of old village sites, or crude soda (*sajji*) from the barilla plant which is found in the arid grazing grounds of the Western Plains. Many of them have settled down to agricultural pursuits, and this is especially true in the Multán and Deraját divisions. They also appear to carry goods from place to place on donkeys, which would seem to indicate a very low social status, though these men are said to consider themselves superior to the Núngars who still work at their hereditary calling, and to refuse to intermarry with them. They are generally Hindus in the east and Musalmáns in the west of the Province.

[1] Núnia is said to signify a maker of saltpetre in Oudh and its neighbourhood.

Abstract No. 103, showing Castes working in other Metals and Minerals.

	WORKERS IN OTHER METALS AND MINERALS.																	
	FIGURES.								PROPORTION PER 1,000 OF TOTAL POPULATION.									
	30	131	134	115	109	76	154	139	30	131	134	115		109	76	154		
	Sunár.	Nyária.	Dáoli.	Thathera.	Agari.	Núngar.	Shorágar.	Chúrígar.	Sunár.	Nyária.	Dáoli.	Thathera.	TOTAL.	Agari.	Núngar.	Shorágar.	TOTAL.	GRAND TOTAL.
Dehli	4,085	...	...	166	1,300	203	2	55	6	...	...	...	6	2	...	...	2	8
Gurgaon	2,255	3	...	379	2,788	1	...	128	4	...	...	1	5	4	...	...	4	9
Karnál	4,021	13	...	166	7	887	272	...	7	...	...	...	7	...	1	...	1	8
Hissar	3,975	61	...	557	...	...	575	...	6	...	...	1	7	...	...	1	1	8
Rohtak	2,773	48	...	159	940	6	405	153	5	...	...	...	5	2	...	1	3	8
Sirsa	2,479	...	...	...	...	...	...	...	10	...	...	...	10	...	...	...	...	10
Ambala	7,323	102	66	21	...	5,126	20	...	7	...	...	...	7	...	5	...	5	12
Ludhiána	5,962	19	...	73	...	1	...	...	10	...	...	...	10	...	...	...	...	10
Simla	330	...	...	46	...	...	...	...	8	...	...	1	9	...	...	...	...	9
Jalandhar	6,900	28	6	27	...	1	236	6	9	...	...	...	9	...	...	...	...	9
Hushyárpur	6,689	8	797	178	...	1	44	47	7	...	1	...	8	...	...	...	...	8
Kángra	3,071	3	331	267	...	...	...	119	4	...	1	...	5	...	...	...	...	5
Amritsar	8,605	17	...	419	...	...	...	159	10	...	...	...	10	...	...	...	...	10
Gurdáspur	6,008	179	...	261	...	...	...	105	7	...	...	...	7	...	...	...	...	7
Siálkot	8,947	72	...	27	...	...	...	206	9	...	...	...	9	...	...	...	...	9
Lahore	8,317	258	...	107	...	1	...	73	9	...	...	...	9	...	...	...	...	9
Gujránwála	6,141	442	...	342	...	1	...	72	10	1	...	1	12	...	...	...	...	12
Firozpur	4,812	18	...	3	..	44	...	13	7	...	...	...	7	...	...	...	...	7

Ráwalpindi	6,523	176	5	12	...	...	...	138	8	...	...	...	8	...	...	...	...	8
Jahlam	5,806	354	...	308	...	...	...	180	10	1	...	1	12	...	...	...	...	12
Gujrat	5,446	118	...	80	...	...	...	231	8	...	...	...	8	...	...	...	...	8
Shahpur	3,597	40	...	19	...	...	...	97	9	..	...	...	9	...	...	...	...	9
Mooltan	2,044	...	...	274	...	2,303	...	83	4	...	...	1	5	...	4	...	4	9
Jhang	1,697	27	...	73	...	375	..	32	4	...		...	4		1	...	1	5
Montgomery	3,265	71	...	13	...	1,138	...	2	8	...	...	...	8	...	3	...	3	11
Muzaffargarh	946	63	...	11	...	999	...	52	3	...	...	...	3	...	3	...	3	6
D. I. Khan	1,080	3	...	...	...	...	...	1	2	...	...	...	2	...	...	...	...	2
D. G. Khan	292	1	...	...	...	146	...	1	1	...	...	...	1	...	...	...	...	1
Bannu	3,722	59	...	...	...	...	...	...	11	...	...	...	11	...	...	...	...	11
Peshâwar	3,079	905	...	...	...	...	...	5	5	2	...	...	7	...	...	...	...	7
Hazara	1,320	...	...	8	...	...	..	95	3	...	...	...	3	...	...	...	...	3
Kohát	832	15	...	...	...	...	...	58	5	...	...	...	5	...	...	...	...	5
British Territory	**132,345**	**3,114**	**1,255**	**3,996**	**5,035**	**11,228**	**1,554**	**2,111**	**7**	...	..	...	**7**	...	**1**	...	**1**	**8**
Patiála	10,709	17	252	230	84	6,283	91	170	7	...	...	...	7	...	4	...	4	11
Nábha	1,811	...	...	26	...	201	...	...	7	...	...	...	7	...	1	...	1	8
Kapurthala	2,162	14	...	160	...	11	...	45	9	...	...	...	9	...	...	...	...	9
Jínd	1,423	28	...	...	...	446	3	...	6	...	...	...	6	.	2	...	2	8
Total East. Plains ...	18,034	81	252	464	87	7,012	94	215	7	...	...	...	7	...	3		3	10
Baháwalpur	2,284	145	...	139	...	1,385	...	122	4	...	...	...	4	..	2	...	2	6
Mandi	335	...	115	5	...	...	...	...	2	...	1	...	3	...	...	...	...	3
Chamba	217	...	...	28	...	...	...	...	2	...	...	...	2	...	...	...	...	2
Náhan	451	...	896	8	...	3	...	...	4	...	8	...	12	...	...	...	...	12
Biláspur	265	...	169	...	...	...	...	...	3	...	2	...	5	...	...	...	...	5
Nálagarh	274	...	136	4	...	14	...	...	5	...	2	...	7	...	...	...	...	7
Total Hill States ...	2,238	...	1,396	281	...	18	...	...	3	...	2	...	5	...	1	...	1	6
British Territory	**132,345**	**3,114**	**1,255**	**3,996**	**5,035**	**11,228**	**1,554**	**2,111**	**7**	...	...	...	**7**	...	**1**	...	**1**	**8**
Native States	**22,556**	**226**	**1,648**	**884**	**87**	**8,415**	**94**	**337**	**6**	...	...	...	**6**	...	**2**	...	**2**	**8**
Province	**154,901**	**3,340**	**2,903**	**4,880**	**5,122**	**19,643**	**1,648**	**2,448**	**7**	...	...	...	**7**	...	**1**	...	**1**	**8**

640. The Churigar (Caste No. 139).—The Chúrígar, or as he is called in the west Bangera or Wangrígar, is the maker of bracelets, generally of glass or lac. He is also sometimes called Kachera or glass-worker. In the east of the Province the Maniár sells these bracelets, but in the west he is a general pedlar; and I understand that there the Bangera sells as well as makes bracelets. It is also said that the term Chúrígar is extended to men who make bracelets of bell-metal, or of almost any material except silver or gold. The word appears to be merely the name of an occupation, and it is probable that many of these bracelet-makers have returned their true caste. It may be too that in the east of the Province the distinction between Chúrígar and Maniár has not always been observed.

WASHERMEN, DYERS, AND TAILORS.

641. Washermen, Dyers, and Tailors.—The next group I shall discuss is that of the washermen, dyers, calico printers, and tailors. In it [P. 332]
I have included the Dhobi, the Chhímba, the Rangrez, the Lílári, and the Charhoa, and the figures for these castes will be found in Abstract No. 104, below.* But the group is a curiously confused one; and I regret to say that *P. 322-23
the confusion has extended to our tables. The terms, at any rate in the west of the Panjáb, denote occupations rather than true castes; and the line of distinction between the various occupations is not only vague, but varies greatly from one part of the Province to another, the Lílári doing in some parts what the Chhímba does in others, and the Charhoa combining the occupations of the whole group in the Multán and Deraját divisions; while the Darzi is often a Chhímba and the Chhímba a Darzi. Thus it is impossible to say that these terms denote separate castes, though the caste to which the group belongs, of which the Dhobi in the east and the Charhoa in the west may be taken as types, is a very distinct one. At the same time, where the occupations are separate they are in the hands of separate trades-guilds with separate rules and organisation, and it is probable that intermarriage is at any rate unusual. Like most occupational castes, those of this group are less numerous on the frontier than elsewhere.

642. The Dhobi and Chhimba (Caste Nos. 32 and 33).—The Dhobi is [P. 333]
perhaps the most clearly defined and the one most nearly approaching a true caste of all the castes of the group. He is found under that name throughout the Panjáb, but in the Derajàt and Multán divisions he is undistinguishable from the Charhoa, and I regret to say that here the divisional officers have included those who returned themselves as Dhobis under the head of Charhoa. Some of the Charhoas seem also to have returned themselves as Jats (see Abstract No. 72, page 224†). The Dhobi is the washerman †P. 106-107
of the country. But with the work of washing he generally combines, especially in the centre and west of the Province, the craft of calico-printing; and in the Lahore and Rávalpindi divisions the Chhímba has been classed as Dhobi, while in the Jálandhar division most of the Dhobis have been classed as Chhímbas. In fact the two sets of figures must be taken together. The Dhobi is also a true village menial in the sense that he receives a fixed share of the produce in return for washing the clothes of the villages where he performs that office. But he occupies this position only among the higher castes of the land-owners, as among the Jats and castes of similar standing the women generally wash the clothes of the family. The Dhobi is there-

fore to be found in largest number in the towns. His social position is very low, for his occupation is considered impure; and he alone of the tribes which are not outcast will imitate the Kumhár in keeping and using a donkey. He stands below the Nái, but perhaps above the Kumhár. He often takes to working as a Darzi or tailor. He is most often a Musalmán. His title is *Bareta* or *Khalífah*, the latter being the title of the heads of his guild.

The Chhímba, Chhaimpa, Chhípi or Chhímpi is properly a calico-printer, and stamps coloured patterns on the cotton fabrics of the country; and he is said occasionally to stamp similar patterns on paper. But, as before remarked, he can hardly be distinguished from the Dhobi. Besides printing in colour, he dyes in madder, but as a rule in no other colour. He is purely an artisan, never being a village menial except as a washerman. He is sometimes called Chhápegar, and I have classed 45 men so returned as Chhímbas. I have also thus classed 23 men returned as Chhaperas. Wilson, at page 111 of his *Glossary*, gives these two words as synonymous with Chhímpi; but I am informed that in some places, though not in all, Chhápegar is used to distinguish those who ornament calico with patterns in tinsel and foil only. The Chhímba often combines washing with dyeing and stamping, and he very commonly works as a Darzi or tailor, insomuch that Chhímba is not unfrequently translated by "tailor."

Divisions.	Divisions of Washermen.		
	Dhobi.	Chhímba.	Charhoa.
1. Bhalam ...	1,826	...	74
2. Mahmal ...	1,318	...	...
3. Koháns ...	1,032	...	...
4. Agrai ...	49	...	1,050
5. Rikhrai ...	682	...	2,264
6. Akthra ...	943	...	...
7. Sárli ...	737	...	...
8. Sippal ..	6,200	3,704	5,799
9. Bhatti ...	4,207	2,995	4,306
10. Khokhar ...	3,419	3,107	3,313
11. Kamboh ...	216	533	2,335

But few large divisions are returned for these castes. I give in the margin the figures for a few of the largest, showing the Dhobi, Chhímba, and Charhoa side by side. The divisions are roughly arranged in the order in which they are found from east to west.

643. The Lilari and Rangrez (Caste Nos. 67 and 110).—These two classes have been hopelessly mixed up in the divisional offices, and the two sets of figures must be taken together. They are both dyers, and both artisans and not menials, being chiefly found in the towns. But the distinction is said to be that the Lílári dyes, as his name implies, in indigo only; while the Rangrez dyes in all country colours except indigo and madder, which last appertains to the Chhímba. It is noticeable that, with the exception of a few returned as Hindus by the Native States, both of these castes are exclusively Musalmáns. The Hindu indeed would not dye in blue, which is to him an abomination; and madder-red is his special colour, which perhaps accounts for the Chhímbas, most of whom are Hindus, dyeing in that colour only. In Peshávar the Dhobi and Rangrez are said to be identical. The Lílári is often called Nílári or Níráli; while I have included under this heading 251 men returned as Púngar from Multán, where I am informed that the term is locally used for Lílári.

644. The Charhoa (Caste No. 54).—The Charhoa is the Dhobi and Chhímba of the Multán and Deraját divisions; and, as far as I can find out,

Abstract No. 104, showing Washermen, Dyers, and Tailors

	WASHERMEN, DYERS AND TAILORS.												
	FIGURES.						PROPORTION PER 1,000, OF TOTAL POPULATION.						
	32	36	110	67	59	61	32	36	110	67	59	61	
	Dhobi.	Chhímba.	Rangrez.	Lílári.	Charhoa.	Darzi.	Dhobi.	Chhímba.	Rangrez.	Lílári.	Charhoa.	Darzi.	TOTAL.
Dehli	4,157	2,626	681	...	...	583	6	4	1	...	...	1	12
Gurgaon	3,446	1,389	1,468	...	...	970	5	2	2	...	...	2	11
Karnal	2,748	4,856	1,662	...	...	1,238	4	8	3	...	...	2	17
Hissar	1,785	5,156	...	1,959	.	580	4	10	...	4	...	1	19
Rohtak	2,763	4,786	...	1,960	...	78	5	9	...	4	...	...	18
Sirsa	347	2,825	...	410	...	142	1	11	...	2	...	1	15
Ambala	5,036	5,618	...	1,382	...	913	5	5	..	1	...	1	12
Ludhiana	1,167	7,158	...	585	...	171	2	12	...	1	...	...	15
Simla	732	69	...	10	...	81	17	2	...	2	...	2	23
Jalandhar	1,107	9,743	...	602	...	436	2	14	...	1	...	1	18
Hushyarpur	288	7,662	...	607	...	1,551	...	9	...	1	...	2	12
Kangra	364	2,867	...	532	...	3,682	...	4	...	1	...	5	10
Amritsar	2,555	13,379	...	1,817	...	1,227	3	15	...	1	...	2	21
Gurdaspur	5,395	5,778	...	695	...	714	7	7	...	1	...	1	16
Sialkot	13,988	1,577	...	2,599	...	1,206	14	2	...	3	...	1	20
Lahore	15,596	...	...	1,107	...	1,026	17	...	...	1	...	1	19
Gujranwala	7,901	...	...	2,286	...	1,685	13	...	...	4	...	3	20
Firozpur	11,649	...	...	376	...	161	18	...	...	1	...	...	19

Rawalpindi	5,751	2	...	1,285	...	6,109	7	...	...	2	...	7	16
Jahlam	6,686	...	...	1,156	20	2,222	11	...	...	2	...	4	17
Gujrat	7,674	...	...	2,279	17	1,476	11	...	...	3	...	2	16
Shahpur	5,624	42	...	115	...	437	13	...	...	...	...	1	14
Multan	423	484	...	412	11,452	532	1	1	...	...	21	1	24
Jhang	7	36	128	61	5,234	387	...	...	...	..	13	1	14
Montgomery	1,429	153	21	111	6,049	342	3	...	...	...	14	1	18
Muzaffargarh	8	47	24	106	6,318	125	...	...	...	...	19	...	19
Dera Ismail Khan	...	2	53	5	2,639	87	...	...	...	...	6	...	6
Dera Ghazi Khan ...	...	13	3	4	592	12	...	...	...	...	2	...	2
Bannu	...	12	127	...	2,270	45	...	...	...	...	7	...	7
Peshawar	5,467	136	...	1,077	...	737	9	...	...	1	...	1	11
Hazara	2,694	...	...	59	...	1,076	7	...	...	...	...	3	10
Kohat	1.019	...	...	260	...	112	6	...	...	1	...	...	7
British Territory	**117,815**	**76,416**	**4,167**	**23,887**	**734,591**	**30,143**	**6**	**4**	...	**1**	**2**	**2**	**15**
Patiala	2,074	15,045	...	1,954	...	471	1	10	...	1	...	...	12
Nabha	629	2,784	...	223	...	59	2	11	...	1	...	...	14
Kapurthala	762	2,750	...	84	...	719	3	11	...	...	...	3	17
Jind	1,028	2,351	...	1,013	...	137	4	9	...	4	...	1	18
Faridkot	17	1,624	...	...	...	8	...	17	...	...	...	...	17
Total East. Plains	5,174	25,967	30	3,520	...	1,515	2	10	...	1	...	1	14
Bahawalpur	9,163	...	825	102	...	393	16	...	...	...	...	1	18
Total Hill States	1,063	1,108	38	190	...	412	1	1	...	...	...	1	3
British Territory	**117,815**	**76,416**	**4,167**	**23,887**	**34,591**	**30,143**	**6**	**4**	...	**1**	**2**	**2**	**15**
Native States	**15,400**	**27,075**	**893**	**3,812**	...	**2,320**	**4**	**7**	...	**1**	...	**1**	**13**
Province	**133,215**	**103,491**	**5,060**	**27,639**	**34,591**	**32,463**	**6**	**5**	...	**1**	**2**	**1**	**15**

not unseldom carries on the handicrafts of the Líllári and Rangrez also. In his capacity of washerman he is, like the Dhobi and under the same circumstances, a recognised village menial, receiving customary dues in exchange for which he washes the clothes of the villagers. In Baháwalpur he has been returned as Dhobi.

645. The Darzi (Caste No. 61).—Darzi, or its Hindi equivalent Súji, is purely an occupational term, and though there is a Darzi guild in every town there is no Darzi caste in the proper acceptation of the word. The greater number of Darzis belong perhaps to the Dhobi and Chhímba castes, more especially to the latter; but men of all castes follow the trade, which is that of a tailor or sempster. The Darzis are generally returned as Hindu in the east and Musalmán in the west.

MISCELLANEOUS ARTISANS.

646. Miscellaneous artisans.—A group of miscellaneous artisans completes the artisan and menial class. It includes the Penja or cotton scutcher, the Teli or oil-presser, the Qassáb or butcher, and the Kalál or spirit-distiller. The figures are given in Abstract No. 105 on the next page.* The first three *P. 326-27 form a fairly coherent group, inasmuch as they very often belong to one caste. The last is quite distinct. The distribution of each caste will be noticed under its separate head.

647. The Penja, Teli, and Qassab (Castes Nos. 83, 23 and 38).—The Penja, as often called Pumba or Dhunia, and in the cities Naddáf, is the cotton scutcher who, striking a bow with a heavy wooden plectrum, uses the vibrations of the bow-string to separate the fibres of the cotton, to arrange them side by side, and to part them from dirt and other impurities. The Teli is the oil-presser; and the Qassáb the butcher who slaughters after the Mahomedan fashion, dresses the carcase, and sells the meat. But while the Teli appears to be a true caste, the Qassáb and Penja are only names of occupations which are almost invariably followed by Telis. In Multán and the [P. 334] Deraját the Teli is commonly called Cháki or Chakáni, and a quaint story concerning him is related by Mr. O'Brien at page 93 of his *Multáni Glossary*. The Teli, including the Penja and Qassáb, is very uniformly distributed over the Province save in the hills proper, where oil and cotton are imported and the Hindu population need no butchers. He is naturally most numerous in great cities, while on the frontier he is, like most occupational castes, less common. In the Deraját, however, many of the Qassábs would appear to have been returned as Jats (see Abstract No. 72, page 224†). †P. 106-107.

The numbers returned for Gurgáon under the head Qassáb seem extraordinarily large; but I can detect no error in the tables.[1] The Teli is almost exclusively a Musalmán; and the Hindu Penja of the eastern districts is said to be known by the name of Kandera, a word, however, which appears to be applied to Musalmán Penjas also in Rájpútána.

The Teli is of low social standing, perhaps about the same as that of the [P. 335] Juláha with whom he is often associated, and he is hardly less turbulent and

[1] Is it possible that a large portion of the Gurgáon Julábas have returned themselves as Telis? The Julábas are not nearly as numerous in Gurgáon as one would expect. Mr. Wilson suggests that the very numerous cattle-dealers or Beopáris who are found about Fírozpur Jhirka in the south of the district, and who are perhaps Meos by caste, may very probably have returned themselves as Qassábs. He points out that so much of the weaving in Gurgáon is done by Chamárs that Julábas would naturally not be very numerous.

troublesome than the latter. Mr. Fanshawe notes that in Rohtak " the butcher " class is the very worst in the district, and is noted for its callousness in " taking human life, and general turbulence in all matters " ; and there is a proverb, " He who has not seen a tiger has still seen a cat, and he who has " not seen a Thug has still seen a Qassáb." In Karnál the Qassábs are said often to practise market-gardening.

648. The Kalal (Caste No. 56).—The Kalál, or Kalwár as he is called in the west of the Panjáb, is the distiller and seller of spirituous liquors. The word, however, seems to mean a potter in Pesháwar. He is commonly known as Neb in Nábha and Patiála, and when a Mahomedan often calls himself Kakkezai and when a Sikh Ahlúwália, the origin of which names will presently be explained. I have said that the Kalál is a distiller; and that is his hereditary occupation. But since the manufacture of and traffic in spirits have been subjected to Government regulation a large portion of the caste, and more especially of its Sikh and Musalmán sections, have abandoned their proper calling and taken to other pursuits, very often to commerce, and especially to traffic in boots and shoes, bread, vegetables, and other commodities in which men of good caste object to deal. They are notorious for enterprise, energy, and obstinacy. " Death may budge; but a Kalál won't." They are, owing to circumstances presently to be mentioned, most numerous in the Sikh portions of the Panjáb, and especially in Kapúrthala. In the western districts they seem to be almost unknown. Rather more than half of them are still Hindu, about a quarter Sikh, and the other quarter Musalmán. The original social position of the caste is exceedingly low, though in the Panjáb, it has been raised by special circumstances.

The reigning family of Kapúrthala is descended from Sada Singh Kalál who founded the village of Ahlu near Lahore. The family gradually rose in the social scale, and Badar Singh, the great-grandson of Sada Singh, married the daughter of a petty Sardár of the district. From this union sprang Jassa Singh, who became the most powerful and influential Chief that the Sikhs ever possessed till the rise of Ranjít Singh. He adopted the title of Ahlúwália from his ancestral village Ahlu, the title is still borne by the Kapúrthala royal family, and a Sikh Kalál will commonly give his caste as Ahlúwália. The caste was thus raised in importance, many of its members abandoned their hereditary occupation, and its Musalmán section also grew ashamed of the social stigma conveyed by the confession of Kálal origin. It accordingly fabricated a story of Pathán origin, and, adding to the first letter of the caste name the Pathán tribal termination, called itself Kakkezai. The name was at first only used by the more wealthy members of the caste; but its use is spreading, and the cultivating owners of a village in Gújrát entered themselves as Kalál in the first and as Kakkezai in the second settlement. The well-known Shekhs of Hoshyárpur are Kaláls who, while claiming Pathán origin, call themselves Shekhs and forbid widow-marriage. Some of the Musalmán Kaláls claim Rájput or Khatri origin, and it is probable that many of the caste have returned themselves as Shekhs. The commercial Kaláls are said not to intermarry with those who still practise distillation.

MENIALS OF THE HILLS.

649. The Menials of the Hills.—The figures for such of the menial castes
P. 328· as are peculiar to the hills are given in Abstract No. 106 on page 337. To
29 these must of course be added those members of the menial castes already

Abstract No. 105, showing Miscellaneous Artisans.

	MISCELLANEOUS ARTISANS.									
	Figures.				Proportion per 1,000 of total population.					
	83	23	38	56	83	23	38		56	
	Penja.	Teli.	Qassáb.	Kalál.	Penja.	Teli.	Qassáb.	Total.	Kalál.	Grand Total.
Dehli	145	5,593	4,320	758	...	9	7	16	1	17
Gurgaon	616	4,799	13,352	481	1	7	21	29	1	30
Karnál	756	9,777	4,587	878	1	16	7	24	1	25
Hissar	...	6,891	2,857	360	...	14	6	40	1	41
Rohtak	...	6,313	6,318	268	...	11	11	22	...	22
Sirsa	...	3,914	842	401	...	16	3	19	2	21
Ambala	6,684	17,577	2,881	5,057	6	16	3	25	5	30
Ludhiána	188	10,883	1,621	1,955	...	18	3	21	3	24
Simla	33	59	42	99	1	1	1	3	2	5
Jalandhar	...	10,829	1,603	1,624	...	14	2	16	2	18
Hushyárpur	4	10,758	2,077	2,695	...	12	3	14	3	17
Kángra	2	5,495	190	2,505	...	7	...	7	4	11
Amritsar	...	20,654	1,971	2,121	...	23	2	25	2	27
Gurdaspur	...	17,644	846	1,209	...	21	1	22	1	23
Siálkot	...	13,652	1,927	1,987	...	13	2	15	2	17
Lahore	...	23,066	2,464	1,909	...	25	2	27	2	29
Gujránwála	...	9,523	2,384	551	...	15	4	19	1	20
Firozpur	...	10,938	714	1,929	...	17	1	18	3	21

Ráwalpindi	...	12,384	789	280	...	15	1	16	...	16
Jahlam	...	8,302	2,003	1,076	...	14	3	17	2	19
Gujrát	...	8,562	1,169	552	...	12	2	14	1	15
Shahpur	210	2,112	5,202	123	...	5	12	17	...	17
Multan	91	484	5,914	580	...	1	11	12	1	13
Jhang	...	250	4,979	...	...	1	13	14	...	14
Montgomery	...	1,557	5,170	275	...	4	12	16	1	17
Muzaffargarh	67	238	3,136	19	...	1	9	10	...	10
Dera Ismail Khan	12	149	1,584	20	...	...	4	4	...	4
Dera Ghazi Khan	8	40	221	3		...	1	1	...	1
Bannu	...	95	2.967	...	...	...	9	9	...	9
Peshāwar	1,344	3,250	2,636	472	2	6	6	14	1	15
Hazara	164	2,480	412	18	...	6	1	7	...	7
Kohát	94	311	1,179	30	1	2	6	9	...	9
British Territory	**10,418**	**228,585**	**88,357**	**30,237**	**1**	**12**	**5**	**18**	**2**	**20**
Patiála	4,827	21,097	4,390	4,609	3	14	3	20	3	23
Nábha	280	3,250	468	643	1	12	2	15	2	17
Kapurthala	53	3,718	918	1,644	...	15	4	19	7	26
Jínd	29	3,193	1,306	708	...	13	5	18	3	21
Farídkot	...	1,548	92	1,043	...	16	1	17	10	27
Maler Kotla	...	1,192	503	29	...	17	7	24	...	24
Kalsia	651	1,196	204	147	10	18	3	31	2	33
Total East. Plains	5,840	35,770	8,719	8,875	2	14	3	19	4	23
Baháwalpur	630	727	3,217	319	1	1	6	8	1	9
Total Hill States	212	1,806	75	719	...	2	...	2	1	3
British Territory	**10,418**	**228,585**	**88,357**	**30,237**	**1**	**12**	**5**	**18**	**2**	**20**
Native States	**6,682**	**38,303**	**12,011**	**9,913**	**2**	**10**	**3**	**15**	**3**	**18**
Province	**17,100**	**266,888**	**100,368**	**40,150**	**1**	**12**	**4**	**17**	**2**	**19**

Abstract No. 106, showing [P. 337]

	MENIALS OF							
	FIGURES.							
	49	78	57	41	137	97	66	50
	Barwála.	Batwál.	Meg.	Dúmna.	Baráru.	Sarera.	Koli.	Dági.
Dehli	7	...	...	...	...	...	4,400	...
Gurgaon	72	...	...	..	...	...	5,810	...
Hissar	...	...	...	...	...	...	400	...
Ambala	...	...	926	128	23	...	1,130	197
Ludhiana...	5	...	...	9	...	...	205	...
Simla	...	...	...	457	...	...	3,791	264
Jalandhar	1,339	1	...	278	93	198	95	77
Hushyarpur	1,740	85	...	3,629	199	4,520	370	31
Kangra	1,514	3,630	...	11,095	089	5,122	11,301	10,743
Amritsar	13,180	80	237	260	361	...	...	...
Gurdaspur	9,530	964	6,373	27,270	337	481	238	...
Sialkot	16,901	13,190	28,705	...	79	...	14	...
Lahore	3,745	146	496	181	...	55	2	...
Gujranwala	5,029	19	80	105	...	...	...	...
Gujrat	904	...	1,373	...	...	...	...	...
British Territory ...	54,128	18,121	38,371	43,424	2,070	10,407	27,837	20,311
Patiala	...	6	...	1,163	70	2	10,018	...
Kapurthala	508	...	...	30	101	116	...	...
Total Eastern Plains ...	511	6	...	1,193	171	119	10,107	...
Mandi	...	...	...	11,540	...	15	10,673	4,475
Chamba	119	537	96	1,881	18	272	1,609	17,934
Nahan	...	...	...	4,126	203	...	24,230	2,213
Bilaspur	...	...	...	1,653	12	...	2,947	...
Bashahr	...	...	...	97	...	...	14,149	...
Nalagarh	...	...	...	1,006	15	...	1,435	3,051
Suket	...	...	...	3,133	...	...	7,753	1,680
Total Hill States ...	119	657	96	25,916	434	287	85,227	32,682
British Territory	54,128	18,121	38,371	43,424	2,070	10,407	27,837	20,311
Native States	630	663	96	27,109	605	406	95,334	32,682
Province	54,758	18,784	38,467	70,533	2,675	10,813	123,171	52,093

Menials of the Hills.

THE HILLS.

				Proportion per 1,000 of total Population.												
176	178	185	161	10	78	57	41	137	97		66	50	176	151		
Rehar.	Dosáli.	Hádi.	Ghái.	Barwála.	Batwál.	Meg.	Dúmna.	Barára.	Sarera.	Total.	Koli.	Dági.	Rehar.	Ghái.	Total.	Grand Total.
...	...	...	...	...	...	...	...	...	...	...	7	...	...	...	7	7
...	...	...	...	...	...	...	...	...	...	...	9	...	...	...	9	9
...	...	...	...	...	...	...	...	...	...	...	1	...	...	...	1	1
...	...	...	...	...	...	1	...	...	...	1	1	...	...	...	1	2
...	...	...	...	...	...	...	...	...	...	...	...	...	...	...	...	...
67	...	...	...	...	...	...	11	...	...	11	88	6	1	...	95	106
...	30	...	6	2	...	...	...	...	...	2	...	...	...	...	...	2
...	212	...	3	2	...	...	4	...	5	11	...	...	...	...	...	11
...	276	295	1,570	2	6	..	15	1	7	30	15	27	...	2	44	74
...	16	...	...	15	...	...	...	...	...	15	...	...	...	...	...	15
...	9	...	...	12	1	8	33	...	1	55	...	...	...	...	...	55
...	...	...	...	17	13	28	...	...	..	58	...	...	...	...	...	58
...	..	...	...	4	...	1	...	...	...	5	...	...	...	...	...	5
...	...	...	...	8	...	...	...	...	...	8	...	...	...	...	...	8
...	...	...	...	1	...	2	...	..	...	3	...	...	...	...	...	3
64	622	305	1,588	3	1	2	2	...	1	9	1	1	...	..	2	11
...	...	...	...	...	...	...	1	...	...	1	7	...	...	...	7	8
...	...	...	...	2	...	...	...	...	...	2	...	...	...	...	...	2
...	...	...	...	...	...	...	...	...	...	...	4	...	...	...	4	4
...	...	..	...	...	...	...	70	...	...	79	73	30	...	...	103	182
147	45	...	...	1	5	1	16	...	2	25	14	155	...	...	169	194
...	...	...	...	...	...	...	37	2	...	30	216	20	...	...	236	275
...	...	...	62	...	...	...	19	...	...	19	31	...	...	...	34	53
29	...	...	...	...	...	...	2	...	..	2	220	...	...	...	220	222
...	...	...	71	...	...	...	20	...	...	20	27	57	...	1	85	105
...	...	...	...	...	...	...	60	...	...	60	148	32	...	..	180	240
750	45	...	138	...	...	...	34	1	...	35	111	43	1	...	155	190
64	622	305	1,588	3	1	2	2	...	1	9	1	1	...	...	2	1.
750	45	...	138	...	...	...	7	..	...	7	25	8	...	...	33	40
814	667	305	1,726	2	1	2	3	...	...	8	5	2		...	7	-

described as are to be found in the hill tracts, such as the Chamár, Tarkhán, Lohár, and the like. I have divided the class into two groups. The first includes those castes which are found among the lower hills and in the tract at their foot. Even here it will be found that occupations tend to merge one into another in the most confusing manner, and that, even more than in the plains proper, it is difficult to distinguish between one outcast class and another. The second group is more strictly confined to the actual mountains; and here all seems to be confusion.

The Chamár, the Jhínwar, and the artisans appear to be tolerably distinct, and have already been described with the groups under which they fall. But even this is not the case everywhere; while throughout the hills we find a mixed class known as Kolí, Dági, or Chanál, who not only perform the usual services demanded of outcasts, but also follow the occupations of very many of the artisan and higher menial castes. It is impossible to say how many of the people who have returned themselves as Barhái or some other caste which is sufficiently distinct in the plains, are really Koli by caste and have adopted the occupation merely of the caste under whose name they are shown. And even the inferior castes which bear the same name in the hills as in the plains, often adopt very different habits and occupy very different positions in the two tracts, as will be seen from the extracts I shall presently give from the reports of Messrs. Barnes and Anderson. One difference is probably almost universal, and that is that in the hills almost *all* menial castes occupy themselves very largely in field-labour; and it will be seen that in some parts the Kolis are generally known as Hális or Sepis, words in common use in the plains for two classes of agricultural labourers. At the same time it would appear that the services performed and dues received by village menials are less commonly regulated by custom in the hills than in the plains. The social position of the menial classes in the hills is thus described by Mr. Barnes in his Kángra Report :—

> "Those classes who are too proud or too affluent to plough and yet hold lands, generally entertain *Kámas*, or labourers from these outcast races, whose condition is almost analogous to that of slavery. He gets bread to eat, and a few clothes a year, and is bound to a life of thankless exertion. These castes are always first impressed for begar, or forced labour, and, in addition to carrying loads, have to provide grass for the camp. In the hills the depression of these castes is more marked than I have observed elsewhere;—their manner is subdued and deprecatory; they are careful to announce their caste; and an accidental touch of their persons carries defilement, obliging the toucher to bathe before he can regain his purity. If any person of this caste has a letter to deliver, he will throw or deposit his charge on the ground, but not transmit it direct from hand to hand. He is not allowed to approach near, and in Court when summoned, he will stand outside, not venturing unless bid to intrude within the presence. If encouraged to advance he does so with hesitation; while all the neighbours fall back to avoid the contamination of his touch. Under the rule of the Rájas they were subjected to endless restrictions. The women were not allowed to wear flounces deeper than four inches to their dress, nor to [P. 336]
> use the finer metal of gold for ornaments. Their houses were never to exceed a certain size, nor to be raised above one floor; the men were interdicted from wearing long hair; and in their marriages the bride was forced to go on foot, insead of riding in a *jampán* or chair, as allowed to every other class. Certain musical instruments, such as the *Dufúl* or drum, and the *Nikára*, or trumpet, were positively prohibited. Many of these restrictions are still maintained, although, of course, there has been no sanction given or implied by the officers of Government."

650. As for the confusion I have mentioned, it is so clearly brought out in a report by Mr. Anderson, and that report gives such a valuable and interesting picture of the curious condition of the lower stratum of society in Kúlu and the higher hills, that I need not apologize for quoting it at some length. I should explain that the paragraphs I am about to quote were not meant by Mr. Anderson as a complete report upon any section of Kúlu society, but were merely hasty notes written in reply to enquiries made by me concerning certain specified castes :—

"I have said that a Kanet will smoke with a Náth and with a Nai, but in Kulu no good inference can be drawn from the fact that the *hukka* is common. I believe that not many years ago all castes would have smoked from one pipe. It is still not a matter of much importance, and under ordinary circumstances, a Kanet will smoke with a Thawi, a Náth or a Nai, though he might probably, if taxed with doing so, deny it. He would not eat with them. In some places as in Monáli Kothi, Kanets smoke with Dagis, but this is not common in Kulu, though the exclusiveness has arisen only within the last few years, as caste distinctions became gradually more defined.

"Then as to the identity of Dagi and Chanal. In Kulu proper there are no Chanals, that is, there are none who on being asked to what caste they belong will answer that they are Chanals; but they will describe themselves as Dagi Chanals or Koli Chanals, and men of the same families as these Dagi Chanals or Koli Chanals will as often merely describe themselves as Dagis or Kolis. In Kulu Dagi, Koli, and Chanal mean very nearly the same thing, but the word Koli is more common in Seoraj and Chanal is scarcely used at all in Kulu; but Chanals are, I believe, numerous in Mandi, and in the Kangra valley. A Dagi who had been out of the Kulu valley told me he would call himself a Dagi in Kulu, a Chanal in Kangra and a Koli in Plach or Seoraj, otherwise these local castes would not admit him or eat with him. Again and again the same man has called himself a Dagi and also a Koli. If a Kanet wishes to be respectful to one of this low caste he will call him a Koli, if angry with him a Dagi. A Chanal of Mandi Territory will not intermarry with a Kulu Dagi.

"The popular explanation of the word Dagi is that it is derived from *dág* cattle, because they drag away the carcases of dead cattle and also eat the flesh. If a man says he is a Koli, then a Kanet turns round on him and asks him whether he does not drag carcasses; and on his saying he does the Kanet alleges he is a Dagi, and the would-be Koli consents. There are very few in Kulu proper that abstain from touching the dead. There are more in Seoraj, but they admit they are called either Dagis or Kolis, and that whether they obtain from touching carcasses or not, all eat, drink and intermarry on equal terms. It is a mere piece of affectation for a man who does not touch the dead to say he will not intermarry with the family of a man who is not so fastidious. This is a social distinction, and probably also indicates more or less the wealth of the individual who will not touch the dead.

"From the natural evolution of caste distinctions in this direction, I would reason that once all the lower castes in Kulu ate the flesh of cattle, but as Hindu ideas got a firmer footing, the better off refrained and applied to themselves the name of Koli. Popular tradition seems however to go in the opposite direction, for according to it the Kolis came from Hindustan and gradually fell to their present low position. The real Koli, or as he is called in Kulu the *Sachcha Koli*, is found in Kotlehr, Lambagraon, &c., of Kangra proper. There the caste is also very low, but tradition ascribes to it a much higher position than it now holds. The Kolis of Kangra will not have intercourse with the Kolis of Kulu on equal terms; the latter admit their inferiority and ascribe it to their being defiled by touching flesh. But it is the same with Brahmans of the plains and of the hills; they will not intermarry.

"I am not aware what position the Kolis of Kangra hold to the Chanals of Kangra, but I believe they are considered inferior to them, and that they will not eat together nor intermarry. The Chanals of Kangra will not, I understand, touch dead cattle, and will not mix on equal terms with those that do. There are some Chanals in Outer Seoraj who are considered inferior to the Kolis there.

"A Chamar in Seoraj will call himself a Dagi, and men calling themselves Kolis said they would eat and drink with him. They said he was a Chamar merely because he made shoes, or worked in leather. Most Dagis in Kulu proper will not eat with Chamars, but in some places they will. It depends on what has been the custom of the families.

"The Kolis of Nirmand keep themselves separate from the Dagis in that direction, that is from those that touch dead cattle. The reason is that they are more or less under the influence of the Brahmins who form a large part of the population of that village. These Kolis of Nirmand will however intermarry with a family of Kolis that lives at a distance in Inner Seoraj. This latter family has for some generations taken to turning in wood, and its members are called Kharadis as well as Kolis. They do not touch carcasses, probably because they have a profession of their own and are richer; but they call themselves Kolis or Dagis and intermarry on equal terms with the Kolis round them. This illustrates the unsettled state of these low castes, and also the gradual advance of Hindu ideas.

"In Kulu there is not much difference between the Koli, the Dagi, and the Chanal, but they are not admitted to be the same as the Kolis and Chanals of Kangra.

"In Kulu *Bateras* are merely Kolis, that is Dagis, who take out slates. They have taken "to this trade, but are really Kolis. They are found only in Plach, and hence are called Kolis, "which name is more common there than that of Dagi. So Barhais are Kolis or Dagis that use the "axe. Bádhis and Barhais are the same in Kulu, but not in Kangra Proper. A Tarkhan of the "plains would shudder to associate with the Barhai of Kulu, who does not scruple to eat the flesh "of dead animals. Kharadis are Kolis of Seoraj that turn wood, and mix with Kolis and Dagis on "equal terms. They are considered rather more respectable than the common Kolis or Dagis, as "they will not touch the dead. In Kulu Barhai or Bádhi and Kharadi are names applied to differ-"ent trades, not to different castes. The position of Lohars and Chamars is described in paragraph "113 of the Settlement Report (quoted below). Baráras are Kolis that work in the *nargáli* or hill "bamboo. They were once probably all of one caste, and have merely got the names of the pro-"fessions they follow; but Lohars and Chamars can scarcely be called Dagis.

"But Thavis cannot be classed with Kolis and Dagis. They occupy a much higher position. "They are just below the Kanets, who will smoke with them, but not eat with them. They work "both in wood and in stone, as the style of building in Kulu requires that they should do so. It is "only their trade that connects them with Barhais or Kharadis, with whom they will not eat "nor intermarry."

651. Mr. Lyall thus describes the constitution and functions of the menial class in Kulu.

"The Dagis are the impure or Kamin caste. They are also commonly called Kolis, a name "however, which out of Kulu is applied to any Kulu man.[1] In Seoraj they are commonly called "Betus. Those among them who have taken to any particular trade are called by the trade name, "*e. g., barára*, basket-maker; *barhái*, carpenter; *dhogri*, iron-smelter; *pumba*, wool-cleaner; "and these names stick to families long after they have abandoned the trade, as has been the case "with certain families now named Smith and Carpenter, in England. So also Chamars and "Lohars, though they have been classed separately, are probably only Dagis who took to those "trades; but at the present day other Dagis will not eat with the Lohars, and in some parts they "will not eat or intermarry with the Chamars. Most Dagis will eat the flesh of bears, leopards, or "*langur* monkeys. All except the Lohars eat the flesh of cattle who have died a natural death. "They stand in a subordinate position to the Kanets, though they do not hold their land of them. "Certain families of Dagis, Chamars, and Lohars are said to be the Korídárs, *i.e.*, the 'courtyard "people' of certain Kanet families. When a Kanet dies his heirs call the Koridar Dagis through "their *jatái* or headmen; they bring in fuel for the funeral pile and funeral feast, wood for "torches, play the pipes and drums in the funeral procession, and do other services, in return for "which they get food and the *kiria* or funeral perquisites. The dead bodies of cattle are another "perquisite of the Dagis, but they share them with the Chamars; the latter take the skin, and all "divide the flesh. The Dagis carry palanquins when used at marriages. The Lohars and Chamars "also do work in iron and leather for the Kanets, and are paid by certain grain allowances. The "dress of the Dagis does not differ materially from that of the Kanets, except in being generally "coarser in material and scantier in shape. Their mode of life is also much the same."

In Spiti the Lohár would appear to be the only artisan or menial caste, [P. 338] society consisting of the cultivating class, the Lohár, and the Hesi or gipsy minstrel.

652. The Barwala and Batwal (Caste Nos. 49 and 78).—Barwála and Batwál are two words used almost indifferently to express the same thing, the former being more commonly used in the lower hills and the latter in the mountain ranges of Kángra. In Chamba both names are current as synonyms. But I have separated the figures, because the Batwál of Kángra is a true caste while Barwála is little more than the name of an occupation. Both words correspond very closely with the Lahbar or Baláhar of the plains, and denote the village watchman or messenger. In the higher hills this office is almost confined to the Batwáls, while in the lower hills it is performed by men of various low castes who are all included under the generic term of Barwála. These men are also the coolies of the hills, and in fact occupy much the same position there as is held by the Chamárs in the plains, save that they do not tan or work in leather. In Kángra they are also known as Kiráwak or Kirauk, a word which properly means a man whose duty it is to assemble coolies and others for *bigár* or forced labour, and they are also called

[1] But see section 657. The word is *Kola*, not *Koli*.

Satwág or "bearers of burdens." Like most hill menials they often cultivate land, and are employed as ploughmen and field labourers by the Rájpúts and allied races of the hills who are too proud to cultivate with their own hands. They are true village menials, and attend upon village guests, fill pipes, bear torches, and carry the bridegroom's palanquin at weddings and the like, and receive fixed fees for doing so. In the towns they appear to be common servants. They are of the lowest or almost the lowest standing as a caste, apparently hardly if at all above the Dúmna or sweeper of the hills; but the Batwál has perhaps a slightly higher standing than the Barwála. Indeed the name of Barwála is said to be a corruption of *Báharwála* or "outsider," because, like all outcasts, they live in the outskirts of the village. They are returned in considerable numbers for almost all our sub-montane districts and for Kángra, but in the Hill States they would appear to have been included under some other of the menial castes. The term Barwála seems to be current also in Jálandhar, Amritsar, Lahore and Siálkot, as considerable numbers are returned for these districts. In the higher ranges and where they are known as Batwál, they are almost all Hindus; but when they descend to the lower hills or plains and take the name of Barwála they are almost entirely Musalmán, except in Siálkot where a considerable number of them are still Hindus. In fact their difference of religion seems to correspond very largely with the difference in the name; and indeed a portion of the Hindu Barwálas of Síálkot consists of 1,455 persons of that district who returned themselves as Ratál, and whom I classed as Barwála and not as Batwál because they were sub-montane and not montane in their habitat. The Ratáls would seem to be almost if not quite identical with the Barwálas or Batwáls, and are very largely employed as agricultural labourers on the footing of a true village menial. Bráhmans are said to officiate at the weddings of the Batwál; but if so I suspect it must be an outcast class of Bráhmans. The Barwálas claim Rájpút origin, a claim probably suggested if any suggestion be needed, by their clans being called after Rájpút tribes, such as Manhás and Janjúa.

653. The Meg, (Caste No. 57).—The Meg or as he is called in Ráwalpindi Meng, is the Chamár of the tract immediately below the Jammu hills. But he appears to be of a slightly better standing than the Chamár; and this superiority is doubtless owing to the fact that the Meg is a weaver as well as a worker in leather, for we have already seen that weaving stands in the social scale a degree higher than shoe-making.[1] Like the Chamárs of the plains the Megs work as coolies, and like all hill menials they work much in the fields. General Cunningham is inclined to identify them with the Mechioi of Arrian, and has an interesting note on them at page 11 *f*, Volume II of his Archæological Reports, in which he describes them as an inferior caste of cultivators who inhabited the banks of the upper Satluj at the time of Alexander's invasion, and probably gave their name to the town of Makhowál. They seem at present to be almost confined to the upper valleys of the Rávi and Chanáb, and their stronghold is the sub-montane portion of Siálkot lying between these two rivers. They are practically all Hindus.

654. The Dumna (Caste No. 41).—The Dúmna, called also Domra, and even Dúm in Chamba, is the Chúhra of the hills proper, and is also found in

[1] In Bíkáner and Sirsa a man who is pleased with a Chamár calls him Megwál, just as he calls him Dherh if he is angry with him. The Chamárs of the Bágar say they are descended from Meg Rikh, who was created by Nárain.

large numbers in the sub-montane districts of Hushyárpur and Gurdáspur. Like the Chúhra of the plains he is something more than a scavenger; but whereas the Chúhra works chiefly in grass, the Dúmna adds to this occupation the trade of working in bamboo, a material not available to the Chúhra. He makes sieves, winnowing pans, fans, matting, grass rope and string, and generally all the vessels, baskets, screens, furniture, and other articles which are ordinarily made of bamboo. When he confines himself to this sort of work and gives up scavengering, he appears to be called Bhanjra, at any rate in the lower hills, and occasionally Sariál; and I have included 261 Bhanjras and 31 Sariáls in my figures. In the Jálandhar division Bhanjras were not returned separately from Dúmnas. The Dúmna appears hardly ever to become Musalmán or Sikh, and is classed as Hindu, though being an outcast he is not allowed to draw water from wells used by the ordinary Hindu population.

The Dúmna is often called Dúm in other parts of India, as in Chamba; and is regarded by Hindus as the type of uncleanness. Yet he seems once to have enjoyed as a separate aboriginal race some power and importance. Further information regarding him will be found in Sherring (I, 400) and Elliott (I, 84). He is of course quite distinct from the Dúm-Mirási whom I have classed as Mirási.

655. The Barara (Caste No. 137).—The Barára or Barar is the basket-maker and bamboo-worker of the higher hills, though he has spread into the sub-montane districts. He is not a scavenger by occupation, though he is said to worship Lál Beg, the Chúhra deity. He is fond of hunting, which fact, combined with his occupation, would almost seem to point to a gipsy origin. He is also called Nirgálu, because he works in the Nargáli or hill-bamboo. The name is probably that of an occupation rather than of a true caste, and appears to be hardly distinguishable from Bhanjra. In Kúlu the Barára is said to be generally Koli by caste. He is an outcast, like all workers in grass or reeds, and only 66 are returned [P. 339] as Musalmáns.

656. The Sarera (Caste No. 97).—In my tables I found two castes returned, Sarera and Sarára; the former in the Amritsar, Lahore, and Ráwalpindi divisions, and the latter in the Jálandhar division and the Hazára district. It appeared on inquiry that the Hazára people were probably, though not certainly, distinct; while the others were certainly one and the same, and were sometimes called by the one name and sometimes by the other. I therefore entered them as Sarera, reserving Sarára for the Hazára people. The Sareras are returned only from Kángra and its neighbourhood. In Kángra they are for the most part general labourers; and they specially scutch cotton like the Penja or Dhunia of the plains, and are also said to make stone mortars. But they are likewise largely employed in field-labour. They are outcasts of much the same status as Chamárs, and almost all of them are classed as Hindu.

657. The Koli and Dagi (Chanal, Hali and Sepi) (Castes Nos. 66 and 50)[1].—These two words, together with a third name Chanál, are used almost indifferently to describe the lower class of menials of the highest hills. The Koli of the plains has already been described in section 611, and my figures for Koli include him also; but he is easily distinguishable by his locality, the

[1] For the figures for the Kolis of the Native States, see the *end* of Table VIII A in Appendix B.

figures for the Dehli and Hissár divisions and for Ambála referring to him and not to the Koli of the hills. The former is probably nothing more than a Chamár tribe immigrant from Hindústán; the latter, of Kolian origin. The two would appear, from Mr. Anderson's remarks quoted in section 650, to meet in the Siwáliks. General Cunningham believes that the hills of the Panjáb were once occupied by a true Kolian race belonging to the same group as the Kols of Central India and Behar, and that the present Kolis are very probably their representatives. He points out that *dá* the Kolian for water is still used for many of the smaller streams of the Simla hills, and that there is a line of tribes of Kolian origin extending from Jabbalpur at least as far as Allahabad, all of which use many identical words in their vocabularies, and have a common tradition of a hereditary connection with working in iron. The name of Kúlu, however, he identifies with Kulinda, and thinks that it has nothing in common with Kol. Unfortunately Kola is the ordinary name for any inhabitant of Kúlu; and though it is a distinct word from Koli and with a distinct meaning, yet its plural Kole cannot be discriminated from Koli when written in the Persian character; and it is just possible that our figures may include some few persons who are Kole, but not Koli.

The names Koli, Dági, and Chanál seem to be used to denote almost *all* the low castes in the hills. In the median ranges, such as those of Kángra proper, the Koli and Chanál are of higher status than the Dágí, and not very much lower than the Kanet and Ghirath or lowest cultivating castes; and perhaps the Koli may be said to occupy a somewhat superior position to, and the Chanál very much the same position as the Chamár in the plains, while the Dági corresponds more nearly with the Chúhra. In Kúlu the three words seem to be used almost indifferently, and to include not only the lowest castes, but also members of those castes who have adopted the pursuits of respectable artisans. The very interesting quotations from Messrs. Lyall and Anderson in sections 650, 651 give full details on the subject. Even in Kángra the distinction appears doubtful. Mr. Lyall quotes a tradition which assigns a common origin, from the marriage of a demi-god to the daughter of a Kúlu demon, to the Kanets and Dágis of Kúlu, the latter having become separate owing to their ancestor, who married a Tibetan woman, having taken to eating the flesh of the Yák, which, as a sort of ox, is sacred to Hindus; and he thinks that the story may point to a mixed Mughal and Hindu descent for both castes. Again he writes: "The Koli class is pretty numerous in "Rájgiri on the north-east side of parganah Hamírpur; like the Kanet it "belongs to the country to the east of Kángra proper. I believe this class is "treated as outcast by other Hindus in Rájgiri, though not so in Biláspur "and other countries to the east. The class has several times attempted to "get the Katoch Rája to remove the ban, but the negotiations have fallen "through because the bribe offered was not sufficient. Among outcasts the "Chamárs are, as usual, the most numerous." Of parganah Kángra he writes: "The Dágis have been entered as second-class Gaddis, but they "properly belong to a different nationality, and bear the same relation to the "Kanets of Bangáhal that the Sepis, Bádis, and Hális (also classed as second-"class Gaddis) do to the first-class Gaddis." So that it would appear that Dágis are more common in Kángra proper, and Kolis to the east of the valley; and that the latter are outcast while the former claim kinship with the Kanet. It will be observed that, while Chamárs are returned in great numbers from Kángra and the Hill States, Chúhras seem to be included under

Dági or Koli, probably the former. The word Dági is sometimes said to be derived from *dágh*, a stain or blemish; but it is hardly likely that in the hills, of all parts of the Panjáb, a word of Persian origin should be in common use as the name of a caste, and Mr. Anderson's derivation quoted in section 650 is far more probable. At the same time the word is undoubtedly used as a term of opprobrium. Chanál is perhaps the modern form of Chandála, the outcast of the hills, so often mentioned in the Rájatarangini and elsewhere.

658. The Koli and Dági are found in great numbers throughout the hills proper, and in no other part of the Province. Unfortunately the Kolis of the Native States were omitted when Table VIII A was being printed. They will be found at the end of the table for those States, while the total for the Province in the British territory tables is corrected in the *errata*. They are almost without exception classed as Hindu. I have included under the head Dági those returned as Dági, Chanál, Háli or Sepi. The 461 Dágis of the Ambála division returned themselves as Chanál. In the Jálandhar division 12,981 are returned as Dági-Koli, 4,687 as Dági-Chanál, 48 as Dági-Barhái, and 1,188 as Sepi. The Dágis of the Hill States are all returned as Chanál, except 3,228 shown as Dági in Mandi and 550 in Biláspur, and the Hális of Chamba. The Hális are all returned from Chamba, where they number 16,228. Major Marshall, the Superintendent of that State, informs me that Háli is the name given in Chamba to Dági or Chanál; and that the Hális are a low caste, much above the Dúmna and perhaps a little above the Chamár, who do all sorts of menial work and are very largely employed in the fields. They will not intermarry with the Chamár. The Sepi, the same gentleman informs me, is a superior kind of [P. 340 Háli. The word is used in Amritsar and the neighbouring districts for any village menial who assists in agriculture, just as Háli means nothing more than ploughman in the plains. Mr. Lyall classes both Sepis and Hális with Dágis. The main sub-divisions returned by the Kolis are given in the margin. The Dágis show no large divisions. The Hushyárpur Kolis are said to be divided into two sections, Andarla and Báharla, of which the former ranks higher and the latter lower than the Chamár.[1]

Koli divisions.			
1. Barhái	... 4,064	3. Chauhán	... 11,616
2. Basehru	... 5,018	4. Dági	... 3,990

659. The Rehar (Caste No. 176).—The Rehar or Rihára appears to be very closely allied to the Dúmna. He is found in the hills. Like the Dúmna he works in bamboo, but like the Hesi he travels about as a strolling minstrel. He is said to make the trinkets worn by the Gaddi women, and to furnish the music at Gaddi weddings. He is much dreaded as a sorcerer. He is an outcast.

660. The Dosali (Caste No. 178).—The Dosáli is a hill caste of superior standing to the Chamár, who makes the cups and platters of leaves which are

[1] Mr. Anderson notes on this, that in Kúlu Dágis, Kolis, Chamárs, and in short all outcasts, are commonly described by the people as *báhar ke* (outsiders), as opposed to *andar ke* (insiders), which latter term includes Kanets and the better castes. The words simply imply that the former class must remain outside the place where food is cooked and water kept, while the latter may go inside. It is very probable that the terms Andarla and Báharla express the relation in which the respective sections of Kolis stand to each other in this respect; and it may be that the two names are applied to the Chamár and Kolian section respectively, which, as we have seen above, meet on the Hushyárpur and Kángra borders.

used at Hindu weddings. The word is perhaps more the name of an occupation than of a caste, and is derived from *dúsa*, the small piece of straw with which he pins the leaves together; but the Dosáli is said not to marry out of his caste. Probably many of them have been returned as Kolis. They are a very low caste, but not outcast; indeed if they were, articles made by them would hardly be used for eating from.

661. The Hadi (Caste No. 185).—This is also a hill caste, and returned from Kángra only. They would appear to be general labourers, to make bricks, carry earth, vegetables, &c., for hire, and to be something like the Kumhár of the plains. But I have no detailed information regarding them.

662. The Ghai (Caste No. 151).—I am in absolute uncertainty regarding this caste, even as to whether it is a caste at all. It was represented to me as a separate caste called Ghási or Ghái, who are the grass-cutters of the hills. But the derivation sounds suspicious. I can obtain no trustworthy information about the caste, and I never heard of grass-cutting as a hereditary occupation. I am not at all sure that the word is not simply Khas or Khasia, the great branch of the Kanets, and probably the representatives of the ancient Khas who once inhabited Kashmír and the western portion of the lower Himálayas; and that it has not been written with a *g* instead of a *k* by an ignorant enumerator. Mr. Anderson tells me that the word Ghái is used in Kángra for a grass-cutter.

PURBIA MENIALS.

663. The Purbia Menials.—The group for which the figures are given in
P. 338. Abstract No. 107 on the opposite page have little in common in their place of origin, but much as they exist in the Panjáb. They are all immigrants from the North-West Provinces, who have for the most part come into the Panjáb with our troops. Some of them belong to castes which are properly agricultural; but these men have as a rule settled down to menial occupations or taken to service, and they are almost confined to the Panjáb cantonments. They are almost all Hindus. They will not need any lengthy description, for they are essentially foreigners in the Panjáb.

The Kori (Caste No. 99) is a great tribe of Chamárs whose head-quarters are in Oudh and the neighbouring country; and it is probably identical with the Koli of the eastern districts of the plains who have already been described. The Kori Chamár seldom works in leather, rather confining himself to weaving and general labour. In the Panjáb cantonments the latter is his occupation. He is a coolie and grass-cutter, and not unfrequently takes service in the latter capacity or as a groom.

The Kurmi (Caste No. 119) or Kumbhi is a great caste of cultivators very widely distributed over the eastern parts of Hindústán and the Deccan. "A "good caste is the Kunbin. With hoe in hand she weeds the field together "with her husband." But in the cantonments of the Panjáb they are generally occupied, like other Púrbis, in cutting grass, weaving and serving as grooms; and they are even said to keep pigs. They are of course a very low caste; lower far in social standing than our indigenous agricultural castes.

The Jaiswara (Caste No. 127).—Many of the north-western castes include a tribe of this name; more especially the menial and outcast classes, though there are also Jaiswára Rájpúts and Banyas. The name is supposed to be derived from Jais, a large manufacturing town in Oudh. But the Jaiswáras of the Panjáb cantonments probably belong to the Chamár tribe of that name. They are generally found in attendance upon horses, and a considerable proportion of our grooms and grass-cutters are Jaiswáras. They also frequently take service as bearers.

The Pasi (Caste No. 156).—This caste is closely allied with the Khatíks, who indeed are said by some to be nothing more than a Pási tribe. They are said to be the professional watchman and thief of the North-West Provinces, which is not the only part of India where the two occupations go together. It is said that their name is derived from *pása,* a noose; and that their original occupation is that of climbing the toddy palm by means of a noose and making toddy. They are a very low caste, and great keepers of pigs; and in the cantonments of the Province they are often employed in collecting and selling cowdung as fuel.

The Purbi (Caste No. 146).—This word means nothing more than an "east country man," from *púrab,* the east, and is used generically in the Panjáb for all the menial immigrants from the North-West Provinces who compose the group now under discussion.

Abstract No. 107, showing the Purbia Menials. [P. 341]

	PURBIA MENIALS.									
	FIGURES.					PROPORTION PER 1,000 OF TOTAL POPULATION.				
	99	119	127	156	146	99	119	127	156	
	Kori.	Kurmi.	Jaiswára.	Pasi.	Púrbi.	Kori.	Kurmi.	Jaiswára.	Pási.	TOTAL.
Dehli	145	233	...	20	...	...	...	...	...	...
Karnal	817	101	...	221	...	1	...	...	...	1
Ambala	3,404	508	741	356	73	3	1	1	...	5
Simla.	540	112	257	11	...	13	3	6	...	22
Jalandhar	...	486	107	17	117	...	1	...	...	1
Amritsar	127	407	...	...	433	...	...	...	...	...
Gurdáspur	54	1	76	...	111	...	...	...	...	...
Siálkot	...	...	...	99	23	...	...	...	...	...
Lahore	1,462	136	...	198	93	2	...	...	...	2
Gujránwala	42	28	...	9	...	...	...	...	...	...
Firozpur	662	362	...	90	...	1	1	...	...	2
Ráwalpindi	1,475	623	1,174	194	39	2	1	1	...	4
Jehlam	...	345	102	...	35	...	1	...	...	1
Shahpur	2	...	24	...	128	...	...	...	...	...
Multan	578	33	226	...	55	1	...	...	...	1
Derah Ismail Khan ...	49	...	36	8	156	...	...	...	...	...
Derah Ghazi Khan ...	77	31	107	11	60	...	...	...	...	...
Bannu	101	3	17	...	4	...	...	...	...	...
Peshawar	666	3	169	87	10	1	...	...	...	1
British Territory ..	10,522	3,675	3,419	1,349	1,668	1	...	...	...	1
Patiala	71	181	20	29	41	...	...	...	...	...
Nabha	...	40	2	134	10	...	...	...	1	1
Kapurthala	75	23	27	...	55	...	...	...	...	...
Total East. Plains ...	157	285	51	165	109	...	...	...	...	...
Bahawalpur ...	...	...	...	...	250	...	...	...	...	...
Total Hill States ...	60	57	21	128	...	...	...	...	...	...
British Territory ...	10,522	3,675	3,419	1,349	1,668	1	...	...	...	1
Native States ..	217	342	72	193	359	...	...	...	...	...
Province	10,739	4,017	3,491	1,542	2,027	...	...	...	...	...